HEGEL AND THE FREEDOM OF MODERNS

Post-Contemporary Interventions

Series editors

Stanley Fish and Fredric Jameson

HEGEL AND

Domenico Losurdo

THE FREEDOM

Translated from the Italian by Marella and Jon Morris

OF MODERNS

Duke University Press   *Durham and London 2004*

© 2004 Duke University Press

All rights reserved

Typeset in Trump Mediaeval by Keystone

Typesetting, Inc.

Library of Congress Cataloging-in-Publication Data

are on the last printed page of this book.

This book has been published in

collaboration with l'Istituto Italiano

per gli Studi Filosofici.

To the

Istituto Italiano per gli

Studi Filosofici

and to its president,

Gerardo Marotta

CONTENTS

TRANSLATORS' NOTE

Professor Losurdo most often cites texts directly from their original language, occasionally modifying the Italian translations. For this reason, we have translated the majority of the non-English citations directly from the Italian, though at times the standard translations have been used, consulted, or altered.

Several of Hegel's English language translators have appended useful glossaries to the works we consulted: among them *Elements of the Philosophy of Right*. Trans. H. B. Nisbet. Cambridge: Cambridge University Press, 1991; *The Encyclopedia of Logic*. Trans. T. F. Geraets, W. A. Suchting, and H. S. Harris. Indianapolis: Hackett Publishing Company, 1991; and *The Philosophy of History*. Trans. J. Sibree. New York: Dover, 1956. Michael Inwood's *A Hegel Dictionary*. Oxford: Blackwell Publishers, 1992 has also been helpful.

Many of the numerous texts cited by Professor Losurdo are now available online in the original English or in English translation. Two useful websites have proved to be www.constitution.org and www.marxists.org.

Full references can be found in the Bibliography.

Finally, we would like to thank Professor Losurdo for his constant assistance and cooperation, which has been greatly appreciated.

HEGEL SOURCE ABBREVIATIONS

A Anmerkung. (Annotation)

AL Vorlesungsnotizen. (Lesson Notes)

B Briefe von und an Hegel. Ed. J. Hoffmeister and F. Nicolin (Hamburg, 1969–81)

B.Schr. Berliner Schriften. Ed. J. Hoffmeister (Hamburg, 1956)

H.B. Hegel in Berichten seiner Zeitgenossen. Ed. F. Nicolin (Hamburg, 1970)

Mat. Materialen zu Hegels Rechtsphilosophie. Ed. M. Riedel (Frankfurt, 1975)

Ph.G. Vorlesungen über die Philosophie der Weltgeschichte. Ed. G. Lasson (Leipzig, 1930)

Rph.I Die Philosophie des Rechts: Die Mitschriften Wannenmann (Heidelberg 1817–18) and Homeyer (Berlin 1818–19). Ed. K.-H. Ilting (Stuttgart, 1983); and *Vorlesungen über Naturrecht und Staatswissenschaft.* Ed. C. Becker et al. (Hamburg: Hegel-Archiv, 1983)

Rph.III Philosophie des Rechts: Die Vorlesung von 1819–20 in einer Nachschrift. Ed. D. Henrich (Frankfurt: n. p. 1983)

V.G. Die Vernunft in der Geschichte. Ed. J. Hoffmeister (Hamburg, 1955)

V.Rph. Vorlesungen über Rechtsphilosophie. Ed. K.-H. Ilting (Stuttgart-Bad Cannstatt, 1973–74)

W Werke in zwanzig Bänden. Ed. E. Moldenhauer and K. M. Michel (Frankfurt, 1969–79)

z Zusatz. (Addition)

PREFACE TO THE ITALIAN EDITION

The editions of Hegel's works most frequently cited are abbreviated as follows: *W* = *Werke in zwanzig Bänden*, edited by E. Moldenhauer and K. M. Michel (Frankfurt: n. p., 1969–79); *Ph.G.* = *Vorlesungen über die Philosophie der Weltgeschichte*, edited by G. Lasson (Leipzig: n. p., 1930); *V.G.* = *Die Vernunft in der Geschichte*, edited by J. Hoffmeister (Hamburg: n. p., 1955); *B.schr.* = *Berliner Schriften*, edited by J. Hoffmeister (Hamburg: n. p., 1956); *B* = *Briefe von und an Hegel*, edited by J. Hoffmeister and F. Nicolin (Hamburg: n. p., 1969–81); *V.Rph.* = *Vorlesungen über Rechtsphilosophie*, edited by K.-H. Ilting (Stuttgart-Bad Cannstatt: n. p., 1973–74); *Rph.III* = *Philosophie des Rechts: Die Vorlesung von 1819–20 in einer Nachschrift*, edited by D. Henrich (Frankfurt: n. p., 1983). As for the lecture course on the philosophy of right dated 1817–18, there are two editions: one, published by the Hegel-Archiv: *Vorlesungen über Naturrecht und Staatswissenschaft*, edited by C. Becker et al. (Hamburg, 1983); the other is *Die Philosophie des Rechts: Die Mitschriften Wannenmann (Heidelberg 1817–18) und Homeyer (Berlin 1818–19)*, edited by K.-H. Ilting (Stuttgart: n. p., 1983). In these last two works, reference is made directly to the paragraph, preceded by the abbreviation *Rph.I.* This is true also for the *Encyclopedia*, abbreviated as *Enc.*; and for the *Lectures on Philosophy of Right*, abbreviated as *Rph.* The paragraph is occasionally followed by *A* = *Anmerkung* (Annotation), *Z* = *Zusatz* (Addition), *AL* = *Vorlesungsnotizen* (Lesson Notes). When citing Hegel, we have used two additional abbreviations: *H.B.* = *Hegel in Berichten seiner Zeitgenossen*, edited by G. Nicolin (Hamburg: n. p., 1970); and *Mat.* = *Materialen zu Hegels Rechtsphilosophie*, edited by M. Riedel (Frankfurt: n. p., 1975).

Other abbreviations for Fichte, Kant, Marx, Engels, Nietzsche, and Rousseau are indicated throughout.

For Hegel, we have freely consulted and used the following Italian translations: *Lineamenti di filiosofia del diritto.* Trans. F. Messineo (the annotated manuscripts, the lesson notes, are edited by A. Plebe) (Bari: n. p., 1954); *Lineamenti di filosofia del diritto.* Trans. G. Marini (Rome-Bari: n. p., 1987); *Fenomenologia dello spirito.* Trans. E. de Negri (Florence: n. p., 1963); *La scienza della logica.* Trans. A. Moni. Ed. C. Cesa (Rome-Bari: n. p., 1974); *Enciclopedia delle scienze filosofiche in compendio.* Trans. B. Croce (Bari: n. p., 1951); and *Enciclopedia delle scienze filosofiche in compendio.* Vol. 1. *La scienza della logica.* Ed. V. Verra (Turin: n. p., 1981) (this edition includes also the translation of the *Additions* and prefaces to the different editions of the work); *Lezioni sulla filosofia della storia.* Trans. G. Calogero and C. Fatta (Florence: n. p., 1963); *Lezioni sulla storia della filosofia.* Trans. E. Codignola and G. Sanna (Florence: n. p., 1973); *Scritti politici.* Ed. C. Cesa (Turin: n. p., 1974); *La scuola e l'educazione. Discorsi e relazioni (Norimberga 1808–1816).* Trans. L. Sichirollo and A. Burgio (Milan: n. p., 1985); *Le filosofie del diritto. Diritto, proprietà, questione sociale.* Ed. D. Losurdo (Milan: n. p., 1989).

From time to time the translations of Hegel and other authors have been modified without indication. For all of the texts cited, the use of italics has been maintained, eliminated, or modified in order to emphasize various points.

Finally, some clarification of the arrangement and composition of the present work.

The first ten chapters consist of reworked, expanded, and rearranged texts that have appeared in other books, collections, or journals. In particular, chapters I through VI are taken from *Hegel, Marx e la tradizione liberale: Libertà, uguaglianza, Stato,* published by Editori Riuniti in 1988. Chapters VII through X are reworkings of essays previously published in the following:

"Diritto e violenza: Hegel, il Notrecht e la tradizione liberale." *Hermeneutica* 4 (1985): 111–36.

"Zwischen Rousseau und Constant: Hegel und die Freiheit der Modernen." In *Rousseau, die Revolution und der junge Hegel.* Ed. H. F. Fulda and R. P. Horstmann (Stuttgart, Klett-Cotta: Istituto Italiano per gli Studi Filosofici, 1991), 302–30.

"Scuola, Stato e professione in Hegel." In G. W. F. Hegel, *La scuola e l'educazione: Discorsi e relazioni.* Ed. L. Sichirollo and A. Burgio (Milan: Angeli, 1985).

"Moralisches Motiv und Primat der Politik." In K. O. Apel and R. Pozzo, eds. *Zur Rekonstruktion der praktischen Philosophie. Gedenkschrift für Karl-Heinz Ilting* (Stuttgart:-Bad Cannstatt, Frommann-Holzboog: Istituto Italiano per gli Studi Filosofici, 1990). This appeared also, in an expanded version, with the title of "Tension morale et primauté de la politique," *Actuel Marx* 10 (1991).

The three final chapters have never been previously published, even though chapter XIII has borrowed in part from an essay entitled "Libéralisme, conservatisme et philosophie classique allemande (1789–1848)." In *Les trois idéologies*. Ed. E. Balibar and I. Wallerstein (Paris: in press).

I would like to thank the editors and publishers for kindly granting permission to republish the above essays.

ONE
A Liberal, Secret Hegel?

I

Searching for the "Authentic" Hegel

1. Censorship and Self-Censorship

In 1766, Immanuel Kant confessed in a letter: "Indeed I believe, with the firmest conviction and the utmost satisfaction, many things that I will never have the courage to say, but I will never say anything I do not believe." At the time, Kant's native Prussia was ruled by Friedrich II, an interlocutor and at times even a friend of the major representatives of the French Enlightenment, a king who flaunted his tolerance, at least with regard to religion and that which did not pose a threat to the governmental machine. Almost thirty years later, in 1794, the times are much more dramatic: Friedrich II has died, the restlessness caused by the French Revolution even on this side of the Rhine has made Prussian censorship particularly severe, and the authorities have become intolerant even on religious matters. On this occasion, Kant writes another letter to express his feelings and thoughts: yes, authorities can forbid him from "fully revealing his principles," but that is—he declares—"what I have been doing thus far (and I do not regret it in the least)."[1]

We do not have such explicit letters from Hegel. Yet, we do have several meaningful testimonies, elements, and facts. It is after the publication of the "complete edition of his works, especially his lectures" that Hegel has "an enormous impact:" this remark, by a young Friedrich Engels, is not unique.[2] Two years earlier, commenting on the publication of the *Lectures on the Philosophy of Religion*, Johann K. F. Rosenkranz foresees that they will end up reinforcing the "hatred against Hegel's philosophy."[3] While Hegel was still alive, his contemporaries noticed that in the *Lectures* he used a particularly bold and spirited language, and for this reason they went to great lengths to obtain them, even after they had been collected and printed in a volume. Sometimes they would go so far as to contact

Hegel himself, who was very accessible and open about it, and who did not disclaim in any way the paternity of the lectures which his students transcribed and circulated even outside academia and sometimes even outside Germany.[4] Reading one of those transcriptions, we stumble upon a revealing passage: "From France, the Enlightenment moved to Germany, where it gave birth to a new world of ideas. Its principles were interpreted more deeply. Yet, these new notions were not so often distinguished publicly from dogma; rather, sacrifices and distortions were made in order to maintain at least the appearance of the recognition of religion, something which is done, after all, even nowadays" (ph. G., 916–17).

Which author or authors is Hegel referring to in this last statement? Or is it to be interpreted as a confession? One thing is certain: the techniques he describes are those of dissimulation and self-censorship, and the use of these techniques, as Hegel emphasizes, has been ongoing and has lasted through to the present. The above-cited passage is not the only one in which Hegel reveals his full awareness that the objective situation demands a careful and cautious style; even Johann Georg Hamann, he points out, was forced to "hide his satire from the royal authorities" (w, xi, 334).

And yet, resistance to facing this issue is still strong. One of Hegel's most authoritative scholars, Claudio Cesa, does not seem willing to attribute much importance to the problems of censorship and self-censorship: "German intellectuals and academics could express themselves quite freely, within reason, of course."[5] In reality, even one of Hegel's "moderate" disciples mentions, referring to the end of the 1920s and the beginning of the 1930s, his own "first struggle against censorship."[6] In a letter to his publisher, written in 1840 (and thus in circumstances that were undoubtedly less threatening than those in Prussia after the Karlsbad resolutions), Heinrich Heine writes: "As I said to you before, in writing this book I kept in mind your problems with censorship, and I have carried out a very conscientious self-censorship."[7] But why go so far, after all?

Let us compare § 127 in the achroamatic text to that in the printed text of *Philosophy of Right*. In the former we read: "A man who is starving to death has the absolute right to violate the property of another; he is violating the property of another only in a limited fashion. The right of extreme need (*Notrecht*) does not imply violating the right of another as such: the interest is directed exclusively to a little piece of bread; one does not treat another as a person without rights" (v.Rph., iv, 341). In the printed text the figure of the starving man essentially disappears, and there remains only an allusion to the fact that the right of necessity can come "in collision with the rightful property of another," while theft becomes "an injury only to a singular and limited aspect of freedom" (in the printed text Hegel chooses not to mention at all the "absolute right" that the starving man has to this theft). The effort at self-censorship is evident.

More examples could be produced.[8] Here, however, it might be more useful to clarify the methods of censorship by means of a contrast between the text of the essay *Reformbill*, published in the *Preußische Staatszeitung*, and the text of Hegel's manuscript. Thanks to the Hoffmeister edition we are able to examine the variations that have taken place: at least in appearance, the discourse centers exclusively upon England; and yet, unlike the original manuscript, the printed text is characterized by a constant effort to tone down the harshness of the criticism. Thus, the "greed" (*Habsucht*) of the dominant British classes and clergy in their oppression of the Irish people becomes mere "selfishness" (*Eigennutz; B.schr.*, 478). This term is not only milder, but more importantly, it has abandoned its political significance in favor of a tone that would be better suited to a moral lecture. The "aridity" of the principles that preside over England's political and social order becomes mere "shallowness" (*wenig Tiefe; B.schr.*, 484), and the reference to its "most bizarre, most awkward" aspects (*B.schr.*, 463) disappears. In the same context, "absurdity" becomes "anomaly," while the "depravity" (*Verdorbenheit*) that characterizes elections and that involves both the active and passive organs of corruption becomes once again "selfishness" (*B.schr.*, 466). If Hegel denounces the "presumptuousness" that British people have about their freedom, the State Gazette is decidedly more anglophile (something which is worth reflecting upon and which will be discussed later) and opts for the term "pride" (*Stolz*) (*B.schr.*, 482). We can even cite a more titillating example: the manuscript denounces the plague of Church tithes in England, titles which serve to finance the parasitical, dissolute life of a clergy that remains irremovable despite the gravity of the scandals it is often involved in. Even a priest who used to stroll "around the streets and on the bridges of his city with two whores from a public brothel, one on each arm" manages to keep his position and his prebend. The State Gazette merely mentions the fact that the priest was accompanied by "an utterly inappropriate party." Analogously, the "details" pitilessly exposed by Hegel about the odd "relations" of this priest "with his own wife and with one of her lovers, who lived in his house" become the details of the "domestic relations of the man" in question (*B.schr.*, 475).

It is unlikely that these changes were suggested by mere prudishness. At any rate, in other cases the political preoccupation is more evident: the State Gazette completely eliminates the "coarse ignorance of fox hunters and agrarian nobility" denounced in the manuscript (*B.schr.*, 482). It is true that, apparently, the target of the accusation is only England, but the attack could well be applied to other countries, all the more so since the term used to indicate agrarian nobility, *Landjunker*, was actually more reminiscent of Prussia than of England. And here is yet another statement that the State Gazette completely dismisses: "The prejudice according to which a person is automatically endowed with the necessary intelligence to fulfill a position to which he had been appointed to by birth or through wealth is more rooted and unshakable in England than in any other place" (*B.schr.*, 482). England is cited here as the most sensational—though not as the only—example of the prejudice and arrogance of the nobility, vices from which Prussia itself was not exempt, as Hegel and the State censors knew very well.

At this point, however, there emerges a more general problem, which had already been raised by one of Hegel's disciples: the essay *Reformbill*—Arnold Ruge writes in 1841—"is very truthful and instructive with regard to England," but what is not very clear (partly because Hegel writes in the State Gazette, and behaves like a "diplomat") is whether "British feudal wretchedness" is contrasted to Germany's or the "continent's" (and therefore to "the products of the French Revolution").[9] Indeed, the essay *Reformbill* is permeated by a calculated ambiguity. What is certain is that, when the "positive" that dominates England is contrasted to the "general principles" which "generated the codes and political institutions of the continent" (*B.schr.*, 469), one allusion, if not the first allusion, is clearly to France, though the latter remains unmentioned, concealed within the generic category of "continent" (*B.schr.*, 469). Hegel strongly condemns the ideology centered upon the celebration of the positive and that which is historically handed down, the celebration of what rests upon the "wisdom of ancestors" (*Weisheit der Vorfahren*; *B.schr.*, 466–67). The essay *Reformbill* formulates this condemnation with exclusive reference to England, but Hegel could hardly ignore the fact that such ideology was also present and deeply rooted in Germany and Prussia, as is demonstrated by his harsh criticism of Gustav Hugo and Friedrich Karl von Savigny.

About fifteen years later, Friedrich Wilhelm IV himself will contrast the French model, with its "patched-up and negotiated constitutions," to the British model, whose constitution "is the result not of a piece of paper, but of centuries of work, and an inherited wisdom that has no match" (infra, ch. XIII, 2). The *Weisheit der Vorfahren* denounced in the essay *Reformbill* becomes here the *Erbweisheit* (inherited wisdom) celebrated by the King of Prussia. It is true that fifteen years elapse between the two texts. Yet, during the years in which he was still a crown prince shielded from arbitrariness and from the violence of external legislative interventions, Friedrich Wilhelm IV learned to support the idea of historical continuity from Savigny, who on other occasions had been a target of Hegel's attacks, though Hegel himself, in the *Preußische Staatszeitung*, is careful not to refer to Prussia's current historical school of thought or to its ideology and ideologists.

It is well known that the publication of the second part of Hegel's article *Reformbill* was vetoed by an authoritative intervention that came from on high. Even if one accepts the official motivation that attributes the veto to considerations of opportunity on the level of international politics, there still remains the fact that Hegel was not allowed to express himself freely. And even less freedom of expression was allowed to Eduard Gans, who complained about the fact that the obituary written for his dead teacher and published in the *Preußische Staatszeitung* had been so thoroughly "whitewashed with censorship" that it had become unrecognizable (H.B, 502).

One could add, only partially in jest, that if Hegel had ever admitted that Prussian intellectuals were given "considerable freedom" of expression, it would have been regarded as definitive proof of his enslavement to the Restoration. This goes to show how uncertain understanding of Prussia is at the time: its characteristics are redefined over and over and with little coherence, depending upon whether the goal is to condemn or to defend Hegel. What emerges is the need for a more precise and articulated view of the historical period and milieu. At any rate, the presence of censorship is a fact, as Claudio Cesa acknowledges elsewhere: "In 1847, Bruno Bauer wrote a three-volume work about the "struggles among parties" in Germany between 1842 and 1846. In the chapter dedicated to the *Rheinische Zeitung* he amuses himself by showing how, throughout 1842, when the newspaper had been directed first by Moses Hess and then by Karl Marx, no chance was missed to express faith in the good intention of the Prussian government. Bauer was revealing only half of the truth: we know, and he could not ignore the fact that the editors of the newspaper were fighting an exhausting battle against both censorship and the threat of suppression; expressions of faith in the government had the function of counterbalancing unpleasant news, or critical judgments, and the same can be said about most of the political articles written at the time, at least those that were printed within the boundaries of the German confederation."[10]

Therefore, the problem of eluding the watchful eye of the censor was real and present even before 1842, a more urgent situation, when the repressive system was already starting to come undone at the seams. In addition, if one were to take Cesa's statements literally, "the expressions of faith in the government" would constitute a case not so much of self-censorship (the author does not deny his own convictions; rather, he limits himself to formulating them in an obscure and convoluted manner; if anything, he decides against a full expression of his thoughts), but of authentic double-dealing (the author makes statements that do not correspond in the least to his thoughts, but function only to confuse the censors, and in this way smuggle out content that is not so loyal to the powers that be). Needless to say, this double-dealing would force us to face even more difficult problems, since it would not be enough to decode an obscure or cryptic text, but would require one to separate, on the basis of extremely problematic criteria, the authentic from the spurious.

Paradoxically, despite the overt intention to drastically reduce or even eliminate Hegel's "secret" or "different" dimension, Cesa ends up proposing a methodology that is essentially similar to that of Karl-Heinz Ilting. If the latter ultimately considers the printed text of *Philosophy of Right* as inauthentic and spurious, the former considers as ultimately inauthentic many articles in the *Rheinische Zeitung*. Marx, on the contrary, seems to draw a completely different balance of this journalistic experience. "It is a shame—he writes in a letter to Ruge—that one has to put on a servile attitude, even though it is for the sake of freedom, fighting with pins rather than with clubs." Practicing self-censorship is certainly a painful task: one is forced to "adapt, bend, twist oneself, chisel one's own words."[11] Some of these terms are reminiscent of those used by Hegel to indicate the methods of the German Enlightenment, which strove to conceal disagreements with regard to the dominant religion. Particularly instructive are Marx's and Heine's confessions-descriptions, which suggest a precise interpretation. The point is to decode a text which is inevitably cryptic, not to choose between spurious and authentic material. The category to be used is that of "self-censorship" (explicitly indicated by Heine), not that of double-dealing.

In other words, this favorable recognition of the Prussian Government corresponded in part to the views, if not of Marx himself, then of some on the editorial staff of the *Rheinische Zeitung*. After all, in October 1842, Engels praises Prussia as a "bureaucratic, rationalist State that has become almost pagan," a State that had attacked, "between 1807 and 1812, the vestiges of the Middle Ages," and whose legislation had nevertheless remained "under the influence of the Enlightenment." Certainly, as he writes such things from Switzerland, this young revolutionary does not deny the fact that the Prussia he talks about has by now been defeated by the Christian-feudal Prussia of the "Historical School of Law."[12] It might be interesting to compare this text to a similar one, published only a few months earlier in the *Rheinische Zeitung*. The themes are fundamentally the same: "Our past lies buried under the ruins of pre-Jena Prussia"; "we no longer have to drag the ball-and-chain of the Middle Ages that prevents some States from moving on." Up to this point, the recognition of Prussia is no different from what appears in the uncensored text. Criticism also is present in the article published in the *Rheinische Zeitung*. To renounce the heritage of Prussia's antifeudal reforms that followed the Jena defeat, to renounce this heritage in the name of the theories supported by the Historical School of Law *"would be* the most shameful retreat ever carried out," since it *"would repudiate* in an infamous way the most glorious years of Prussian history"; and if this happened *"we would betray* our most sacred heritage, *we would assassinate* our own vital force," etc.[13]

If we were to synthesize all of this by means of a grammatical formula, we could say that self-censorship is indicated by use of the conditional tense, emphasized above. In the text published in Switzerland, Prussian degeneration is considered to have ended ("Reaction in the State began during the last years of the previous monarch").[14] Here, instead, it is considered ongoing. Consequently, the target of the criticism is, on the one hand, the Prussian monarchy as such; and on the other hand, it is the reactionary circles that have already prevailed, though this has not yet been officially recognized. Thus, the change of direction and betrayal, which are denounced and conjugated in the indicative in the text published in Switzerland, are denounced and conjugated in the conditional in the text published in Prussia. But the choice of the conditional, while it is certainly and primarily a means of avoiding censorship, is also influenced by the remaining illusions about the role of Prussia, illusions that were largely present in the Hegelian Left up to the time when Friedrich Wilhelm IV became king, or rather, up to his first governmental actions.[15]

2. Linguistic Self-Censorship and Theoretical Compromise

The real problem is not whether there is any self-censorship in classic German philosophy, but rather its precise configuration and its real content. In his autobiography, Johann K. F. Rosenkranz reports a revealing debate that took place in 1830. During the anniversary of the *Confessio Augustana*, Friedrich E. D. Schleiermacher released a declaration in which he maintained—writes Rosenkranz—"that a clergyman could recite the Creed of a church even if he is not convinced of its truth," since in that case he would act not as an individual, but as one "in charge" of a "community."[16] The split behavior described here is something that should stir the minds of those who still insist that it is violent to attempt to view a text in light of the time when it was written and published, to consider the practices of censorship, the more or less common habit of dissimulation among intellectuals, etc.

In reality, at least with regard to the historical period we are discussing, no text's meaning is either entirely or automatically self-evident. Rosenkranz agrees with Schleiermacher that what is disparagingly defined as the "theology of the letter" must be rejected: the contrast is limited to the reinterpretation of doctrinal content and the "letter," which Schleiermacher seems to identify with the "feeling of dependency," while Rosenkranz seems to identify it with concept and "speculation."[17] For Hegel's disciple, "God who generates Himself as His own son, the tale of paradise, of Prometheus, the image of God as a being who becomes infuriated, who repents, etc., are symbols, allegories, metaphors"; even "Father and Son are representations"; and "whether at the marriage at Cana the guests received more or less wine is completely indifferent and accidental:" "with regard to the tangible side of the representation, not only the image, but also the historical element is to be taken symbolically and allegorically."[18] Despite his radical position, however, Rosenkranz declares himself in perfect agreement with Christianity, and even seems self-righteous, so much so that he paradoxically reproaches the keepers of orthodoxy, or at least Hegel's critics, by accusing them of somehow being miscreants:

> In the religious convictions of our time, it is undeniable that there is a large, almost universal indifference with regard to the doctrinal contents which were once considered essential; even the theologians themselves are indifferent, both the learned ones and those who pass off as the most devout. If one were to urge most of them to say, truthfully, whether they consider faith in the Trinity as absolutely indispensable to eternal bliss, or whether they believe that the absence of faith leads to damnation, the answer would hardly be a surprise. Even eternal bliss and eternal damnation are expressions that people are not allowed to use among respectable society. . . . One will see that, for them, the dogmas have been reduced considerably, they have been decreased.[19]

Are we witnessing a case of "double-dealing"? No, because Rosenkranz, who is set on a moderate, "central" position—which is why we have used him as an example—sincerely flees atheism and the rejection of Christianity. However, one cannot ignore the fact that the categorical claim of perfect conformity to the orthodox "speculative" reinterpretation of Christianity also meets precise pragmatic needs.

The themes we see in Rosenkranz are already present in Hegel; it is indicative that, in his lectures, Hegel expresses himself with a bold language that could never be found in one of his printed texts. For example, in an *Addition* to the *Encyclopedia* where he discusses the biblical passage about original sin, he does not refer to it as "representation," but more simply and more brutally as "myth," and he goes so far as to speak jokingly about the "so-called curse that God is supposed to have cast upon mankind" (§ 24, z). Certainly, therefore, there is an element of "self-censorship" in the printed text, but is it to the point that one might suggest Hegel's "double-dealing"? Hegel himself, in July 1826, writes a letter to a theologian who is not very far from the orthodox position; nevertheless, the letter constitutes a private document, and thus it can hardly be said to have an "amended" language: "I am a Lutheran, and philosophy has fortified me in my Lutheranism" (B, IV b, 61).

On the other hand, Hegel is very careful not to highlight the abyss which separates his Lutheranism from the official, orthodox one. In the case of the philosophy of religion—and this can be said about Hegel as well as about his disciples, like Rosenkranz—self-censorship is not restricted to the external expression of thought, but one could say that it influences the very process of elaboration and development of thought, which is thereby hampered and prevented from reaching extreme conclusions. By being exercised continuously and forcefully, self-censorship has become somehow interiorized. But the two levels presented here must be kept separate: one thing is the "act of writing," the technical strategy that leads one to tone down some expressions that might sound too irritating to the dominant ideology and power;[20] another thing, in the example of Hegel's philosophy of religion, is the development of a vision according to which the substantial rejection of the doctrinal, "representational" content of Christianity results not in the denunciation of that religion, but in the convinced, sincere adhesion to a "speculatively" reinterpreted Christianity.

Linguistic self-censorship is a conscious method that involves only the external formulation of thought; theoretical compromise is, instead, inherent in the development process, and indistinguishable from it. It is true that linguistic self-censorship, too, brings about a compromise with the dominant power and ideology (the toning down, the mitigation, the choice not to emphasize the boldest ideas, all of these objectively constitute a real concession to power, which no longer sees itself confronted by an open or declared opposition), but it is a pragmatic compromise that only pertains to the techniques of thought-expression, not the very theoretical categories and the conceptual apparatus.

Even though it is not easy to determine the line of demarcation, the distinction between the two must always be kept in mind. For this reason we disagree with those who contrast Hegel's problem regarding censorship to the—no matter how legitimate—need to search for an "amended" language intrinsic to the very process of theoretical development.[21] It is not fruitful to contrast these two aspects of the problem.

Certainly, this contrast is favored by the fact that not even Ilting manages to keep the two aspects separated. In fact, after he has distinguished between 1) the "fundamental concept" that seems to result from the lectures and that is truly the authentic one, and 2) the concept pragmatically adapted to the political constellation of the time, Ilting adds that not even the "fundamental concept" . . . is free from concessions," as would seem to emerge from the anticontractual controversy in which Hegel is constantly embroiled. And such "concessions" would be inevitable, given that even Hegel's philosophy is but "his time, learned through his thought."[22] For the moment we shall not introduce the anticontractual controversy, which we will later interpret in a completely different way. For now, we will discuss the most strictly methodological aspect, since we believe it involves a double error.

First of all, the term *Konzessionen* (v.ʀph., 1, 105) seems to confuse and conflate two phenomena which are qualitatively different: on the one hand, the theoretical compromise dealing with the "authenticity" of the paradigm, and on the other, the pragmatic compromise dictated by the immediate considerations of a specific political situation. Secondly, this pragmatic compromise, as we shall see later, is interpreted not as a translation of the "fundamental concept" (*Grundkonzeption*) into a more or less coded, allusive language, but rather as a rejection of the *Grundkonzeption* itself. Consequently, the "concept" that emerges in the printed text would necessarily be different from that of the *Lectures,* and would not correspond to Hegel's authentic thought. What is considered to have a "double authenticity" as a result of being a "non-inessential adjustment to the politics of the Restoration" is one of Hegel's fundamental works: *Philosophy of Right!*[23] If this is a spurious text, why was it written and published? As we have seen, Kant confessed to hiding part of his thought, but he also claimed that he would never say something he did not believe. Did Hegel behave differently? In the letter we mentioned earlier, in which Heine assures his publisher that he has already carried out a scrupulous self-censorship, he also adds: "Rather than have people accuse me of being servile, I would give up writing books altogether." Hegel, on the other hand, would appear to have made the opposite choice by publishing *Philosophy of Right,* though it did not correspond to his ideas, and though it was even marred by conscious "servility." Faced with the accusations brought up by Hegel's liberal critics, sometimes Ilting seems to play the role of a defense attorney, but his defense has actually turned into a most implacable accusation.

Yet, this is not the main point. It may be useful to consider the debate that develops soon after Hegel's death. On the one hand, young Hegelian scholars accuse their teacher of denying his truest, deepest thought because of a pragmatic need to "adjust" to the powers that be. On the other hand, Marx maintains that Hegel is "incoherent *within his very* philosophy."[24] Even if Hegel had actually resorted "to an adjustment, his disciples need to explain, *beginning with his essential and deepest conscience (Bewußtsein),* what *for Hegel himself* has taken the shape of *exoteric conscience.*" The young Hegelian scholars who were attributing certain theses to Hegel's opportunistic double-dealing had personally accepted those same theses, and with no double-dealing at all.[25] Thus, thanks to the category of double-dealing, Hegel ended up embodying two successive moments in his disciples' development, as well as two successive moments of interpretation, which his disciples gave to his philosophy. Let us now apply these notions to the current debate on Hegel: even if certain elements and his explicit confession were to prove that he considered *Philosophy of Right* to be a mere pragmatic adjustment to the powers that be, carried out to avoid repression—even in that case we should look for the deepest motives for this not simply in the cowardice of a private man, but first of all in his philosophy itself.

Yet, we must not misunderstand the meaning of Marx's criticism of the young Hegelian scholars: Marx opposes the thesis of a theoretical compromise to that of a "double-dealing," one dictated by moral cowardice and pragmatic considerations; he does not oppose it to the thesis of self-censorship as such. As we have seen, Marx was intimately familiar with the techniques of self-censorship and could describe them with great precision. The attempts, on the part of a sometimes lazy academic culture, to exorcise the disturbing image of a "secret" and "different" Hegel have obscured the considerable differences that exist between Jacques D'Hondt's approaches and those of Ilting. True, D'Hondt, too, seems to dismiss the printed text: "When a thinker cannot publish everything he thinks, it is necessary to search for his true ideas elsewhere, and not in his publications." In the situation Prussia was going through at the time, Hegel "was forced to express his real thoughts with means other than printed texts."[26] From this point of view, it would appear that, while Ilting likens the printed text to the *Lectures,* D'Hondt likens it to the letters, or to private lectures and "hidden sources."[27] And yet, D'Hondt seems to enunciate a completely different methodological criterion when he observes that "his [Hegel's] friends and bright disciples read between the lines of the published text, supplying it with the oral indications which Hegel gives at the same time."[28] Therefore, while Ilting considers the printed text of *Philosophy of Right* to be fundamentally inauthentic, D'Hondt, instead, anticipates the discovery of the various philosophies of right, and seems to be affirming here its essential unity. According to this approach, one should try and read *Philosophy of Right* alongside Eduard Gans' *Additions* (which we now know were gathered from transcriptions of the lectures), and use the achroamatic text, which is relatively freer and uninhibited, not in order to reject the printed text, but in order to offer a more appropriate reinterpretation of it, by reading "between the lines."

This method of interpretation can already be found in Hegel and his contemporaries. If the printed text of *Philosophy of Right* defines itself in the subtitle as a support for the lectures, in turn the lectures do not contradict the paragraphs of *Philosophy of Right:* indeed, after quoting them word-for-word and often even in their entirety, they proceed to clarify their meaning by using further explanations and examples. Whether the charge of inauthenticity is referred to the lectures, *Philosophy of Right,* or any of the other printed texts, we are nevertheless dealing with a colossal *corpus philosophicum* which, legitimate or not, cannot be left out of consideration when attempting to trace the history of Hegel's thought. Hegel's disciples did not question the authenticity of the *Additions* and the *Lectures.* In the same way, they did not question the authenticity of the printed text. Even after the attack which Rudolf Haym and the national-liberals carry out against the so-called "philosopher of the Restoration," Rosenkranz, Michelet, and Lassalle (who take for granted the authenticity of the *Additions* and the *Lectures*) frantically and forcefully defend the memory and heritage of their teacher. Never do they contemplate the possibility of redeeming him by absolving him of his responsibility for writing and publishing *Philosophy of Right.* D'Hondt argues for and brilliantly applies the methodology of a consistent reading, but he does not remain faithful to it.[29] He declares, in fact: "Hegel proves to be bolder and more energetic in his actions."[30] Here again the text, particularly the printed text, runs the risk of being accused of inauthenticity, and oddly enough, the reason for this is the opposite of Ilting's. According to Ilting, *Philosophy of Right* is inauthentic because it is the product of fear, a fear which the hunt for demagogues has instilled in a fundamentally cowardly man who refuses to come forward and openly express his thought. According to D'Hondt, on the other hand, the printed text and even the achroamatic text are less authentic than Hegel's behavior, that is to say, than his connections with the opposition. Thus, Ilting redeems the philosopher despite the private man's bargaining and open agreement to conform to power, whereas D'Hondt is more willing to redeem the private man than the philosopher.

3. Private Dimension and Philosophical Dimension

The weakness of D'Hondt's position is evident: after all, the object of the debate is primarily Hegel's thought, and the critics who denied the philosophical importance of Hegel's commitment to save some of his disciples from the clutches of the police have thus gained a favorable position.[31] Furthermore, privileging the "boldness" of the private man in comparison to the philosopher contradicts the testimonies of Hegel's contemporaries, and upturns a traditional topos which is significantly present in the criticism of both the "left" and the "right." One of the conservative and reactionary critics, Karl Ernst Schubart, declares that "his [Hegel's] particular side was better than his doctrine, that is, than his universal side" (Mat., I, 264). The "left-wing" disciples proceed in a similar manner, formulating the distinction, later consecrated by Engels, between "method" and "system" (the latter suffers more from the private man's adjustment to the powers that be). In both cases, despite the diverse and even antithetical value judgments, what is considered most subversive with regard to the socio-political order of the time is the theoretical aspect. The research on the various connections between Hegel and the anti-Restoration movement is valuable, but its usefulness will emerge only once it is systematically applied to the texts. Only in this way will it be possible to counter the objections made by critics like Cesa. Cesa observes with methodological cautiousness that "the parallels between different historical situations are always debatable," but in the same breath he compares Hegel's position to Gentile's, who tried to protect even antifascist disciples and students, but who nevertheless could not be considered an "opponent of Fascism."[32] The only acceptable significance of this comparison is the invitation to avoid endowing certain aspects of one's private life with a philosophical or political importance. Paradoxically, this opinion is also shared by Ilting, who reduces the publication of *Philosophy of Right* to a mere episode in Hegel's life (the fear and surrender of a cowardly character before a dangerous, or seemingly dangerous, situation). These two critics, whose ideas are undeniably very different, do not in fact share the same view with regard to what should be considered authentic or spurious in Hegel's philosophy, and yet they agree on keeping Hegel's private and philosophical sides separate.

Although too generic, the invitation to keep the two dimensions separate is undoubtedly sensible. On the one hand, it is absurd today to insist on expunging a text which was published over one hundred and fifty years ago, and whose authenticity was never questioned by Hegel's intimate friends or his contemporaries. Such a text cannot simply be labeled as a mere incident in Hegel's private life. On the other hand, it is quite problematic to deny any connection between the private relationship Hegel had with some disciples who were disliked by those in power, and the overall meaning of a theory which after all inspired and thrilled many disciples whose positions were revolutionary or "subversive." And all the more so since these disciples followed Hegel's example not primarily as a "private" man, but as the author of a philosophical system which they interpreted and adopted as an ideological platform for a political battle promoting opposition and even revolution. Hegel's intervention on behalf of Friedrich Wilhelm Carové, a militant, or rather, a leader of the student movement, the *Burschenschaften*, could in itself constitute an episode linked exclusively to Hegel's private life.[33] Yet, when we see that Carové makes use of his teacher's analyses and keywords, and that he quotes him, even explicitly and repeatedly, not in private conversations, but in public works and speeches, in the midst of the political battle, then it becomes difficult to deny the philosophical and political meanings of Hegel's intervention on Carové's behalf.[34]

The cautious comparison made by Cesa between the philosophy professor in Berlin at the time of the Restoration and the influential minister of the Fascist regime, Gentile, could have meaning if it were possible to demonstrate that Hegel too had written something similar to the *Origins and Doctrine of Fascism*, something along the lines of *Origins and Doctrine of the Restoration* (possibly signed by Metternich, in the same way that the former was signed by Benito Mussolini). Hegel, instead, wrote *Philosophy of Right*, which after all legitimates constitutional monarchy, using a category which, at the time, was far from the prevailing ideology, and actually quite suspect. Cesa's methodological caution aside, the comparison enjoyed a remarkable and utterly undeserved popularity. Such a comparison could have meaning if it were possible to demonstrate that, for example, Gentile's passion when he spoke about the October Revolution was similar to Hegel's passion when he spoke about the French Revolution. In other words, the comparison could have meaning only on one condition: one must leave the texts, as well as the different peculiarities of the two situations, out of consideration.

4. Hegel . . . a Mason?

Searching for the secret, clandestine connections that are supposed to prove Hegel's revolutionary or progressive character well beyond his explicit formulations in the philosophical field, D'Hondt comes across some evidence which would seem to link Hegel to the circles and doctrine of the Freemasons. As in many other cases, this research boasts some useful results and suggestions important to the understanding, for example, of the early "poem" *Eleusis*, the title of which is already a reference to the cult of the Eleusinian mysteries characteristic of the Freemasons.[35] To the names and information meticulously provided by D'Hondt, one could perhaps add, without searching through remote or hidden sources, the explicit title of a public journal which publicly professes loyalty to the Freemasons, and in which Fichte's lectures on the philosophy of Freemasonry are published anonymously.[36] Should we therefore consider Hegel a Mason for all intents and purposes and throughout the development of his thought? It is not our intention to participate in this debate.[37]

It might instead be useful to approach the issue from another perspective: even if we take Hegel's lifelong connection to the Freemasons for granted, we still need to ask ourselves to what extent this can provide a better understanding of his philosophy. Besides Fichte, about whom we have solid evidence, it seems very likely that among the Freemasons were even Schelling, Jacobi, Kotzebue, Schiller, Goethe (just to name a few of Hegel's major contemporaries), that is, authors who, on a cultural and political level, express very different, and sometimes even contrasting, opinions.[38] Thus, the mere fact of belonging to the Freemasons is too vague and generic to provide us with any concrete clarifications on these authors' individual positions. Putting such authors together results in some paradoxical conclusions: D'Hondt, who on another occasion rightly points out that Hegel's condemnation of Kotzebue's murder does not mean that Hegel himself is siding with this "reactionary writer," now describes Hegel's character as liberal and progressive merely because he belonged to the Freemasons, a group which had, among its members, even a "reactionary writer" like Kotzebue.[39] Another example: still on the basis of the fact that they were both Freemasons, we would need to put Hegel and Jacobi on the same level, despite their irreducible contrast on a philosophical plane, and despite Jacobi's good relationship to Fries.[40] Who knows, perhaps if we take this research method to an extreme, we could even come to the conclusion that Fries, too, had connections to the Freemasons, and as a result of that, we could put him side-by-side with his implacable rival, Hegel!

Certainly, the Freemasonry motif serves a polemical function against the old cliché that would label Hegel a philosopher of the Restoration: despite their differences, almost all of the Freemasons—D'Hondt observes— were "reformers"; some in the religious field, some in the political field; not to mention those few "extremists" who were active in both the political and religious fields.[41] Thus, to prove that, even in Berlin, Hegel was a Freemason is to prove that to some extent and manner he was a "reformer." Yet, aside from the extreme vagueness of this claim, in reality the evidence is not convincing because, as D'Hondt himself observes, the Freemasons also inducted Joseph-Marie de Maistre and, in Germany, Karl J. H. Windischmann, who—we wish to point out—had translated de Maistre's work into German, and who still had a good relationship with Hegel, despite the fact that the latter certainly could not share the position expressed in the *Abendstunden zu St. Petersburg* translated by his friend or acquaintance, de Maistre.[42]

In other words, even if it were possible to prove with incontestable arguments that the mature Hegel was affiliated with the Freemasons, this fact would mean very little or nothing at all to us, unless some concrete historical research was added to this hypothetical affirmation. This research would need to shed light upon the ideological and political orientation of the various lodges and currents; to join one of the Masonic lodges meant—as Fichte observes in Zurich—to become an enemy of all the others.[43] Apparently, German Freemasonry did not have that substantially unitary character that seems to emerge from D'Hondt's pages. On the contrary, a historian, Klaus Epstein, wrote that "the role of Freemasonry in the history of German Conservatism was very ambiguous" (there were some currents that were connected "not only in spirit, but also in their praxis to the conservative defenders of German society"). Epstein also spoke of an "involution of 'enlightened' Freemasonry as a result of 'obscurantism.'"[44] Similar claims could be made also with regard to France, where "an aristocratic Freemasonry, which hid in the shadow of the throne," was present and "nearly official." Louis XVI himself was quite probably a Freemason, and at any rate, on the whole Freemasonry was such a varied movement that de Maistre was able to conceive the plan to create, within it, "a secret general staff that would turn Freemasons into a sort of papal army in the service of a universal theocracy."[45]

The problem we have raised seems to be taken into consideration, though only briefly, by D'Hondt when he observes that the mysteriosophistic attraction of Freemasonry could lure those "who came to seek the revelation of some secret: the demon of thaumaturgism, of magic, of alchemy led them into a society made up also of many enemies of charlatanry. Clearly, however, this remains secondary."[46] The reference seems to be to the Rosicrucians, at the center of which were precisely the practices mentioned above. Yet, we are not in the presence of some bizarre individual, but of an organized force which—observes Epstein—plays "an important role in the campaign of the conservatives against the Enlightenment," and, in the religious, political, and social struggles of the time, constitutes the bastion of conservatism.[47] The fact is that D'Hondt seems essentially to consider "secret" a synonym for progressive and, to some extent, for subversive: "People who hide have renounced acceptance from others when they show themselves openly; they are heretics, nonconformists, enemies of the existing order."[48] Things, however, are quite different, or at least much more complex: the conservatives resort to the same weapons used by the enemies of the established order, and they engaged themselves in a sort of "imitation" even with regard to secret societies, which did not remain a monopoly of the reforming, revolutionary movement, as we can see in the example of the Rosicrucians.[49] Even in the most progressive lodges, like the one that received Fichte when the latter was accused of atheism, secrecy is not at all a synonym for deception and opposition to power: in Berlin, Fichte observes, "Freemasons" are anything but suspicious, and their well-known chief is "highly esteemed" by King Friedrich Wilhelm III.[50]

It should be added that Hegel's possible affiliation with Freemasonry does not seem to have left any trace either in his correspondence or even in the debates of the time. No traces can be found in the public debate or in the private discourse that emerges from letters, diaries, or more or less confidential conversations. For example, the Freemasons honor Goethe with poems and other tokens of esteem.[51] And the shadow of Freemasonry still looms over Fichte even after the latter has broken with the organization. In 1806, Friedrich Schlegel, who was well aware of the break which had occurred six years earlier, still relates Fichte's "anti-Christian" position to "Freemasonry."[52] Indeed, to the very end, Fichte is suspected of drawing largely from the "most secret doctrines" of Freemasonry. One who harbors this suspicion besides Schlegel is Franz X. B. von Baader—Varnhagen von Ense writes in 1811, many years after Fichte's connection with Freemasonry has ended.[53] The debate even has a public significance, as Schleiermacher writes that "Freemasonry is always on the tip of [Fichte's] tongue, though he never openly utters the word."[54] According to D'Hondt, Hegel's first connection to Freemasonry supposedly dates back to his stay in Berne. What is certain is that, in 1793, Fichte becomes a member of the Freemasons in Zurich, less than sixty-five miles from Berne, still in the German-speaking part of Switzerland.[55] Yet, the two philosophers do not seem to notice their almost contemporaneous affiliation or membership, despite Hegel's eager interest in Fichte, who was older than him and already famous at the time.[56] Finally, not even during the harsh debate that followed the publication of *Philosophy of Right* was Hegel accused or suspected of being a Freemason, even though such accusations had become quite common, and all the more so since those who had accused Fichte of being a Freemason were the same people who engaged most passionately in the controversy against Hegel.

Clearly, none of this excludes the possibility that Hegel might ultimately have been a Freemason, and not only in Berne, but in Berlin, as well. At any rate, a central question still remains unanswered: how productive can it be, on a historical and interpretative level, to formulate a hypothesis in such generic terms, a hypothesis which sheds no light on Hegel's position (German Freemasonry offered very different options) or on the debate that surrounded that position at the time?

5. Esoteric and Exoteric History

We seem to foresee a danger: that of contrasting a sort of esoteric history to an exoteric one. To give an example, according to official documents, Hegel, Jacobi, and Kotzebue appear to hold different positions. Yet, according to "secret" documents, all three are members of an organization whose internal ramifications and oppositions—that is to say, its history and configuration—remain mysterious. As a result, Freemasonry appears to be an essentially homogeneous phenomenon. Rather than serving exoteric history, esoteric history takes its place (through the discovery of hidden or secret sources and documents), and runs the risk of becoming merely sensational. Rather than a reconstruction of the political and social history of German Freemasonry, where we could possibly place Hegel, this is a sort of game of associations: one name draws another, or a keyword takes us from one name to another, until we stumble upon Hegel's. And yet, our knowledge of the concrete history of Freemasonry and its various ramifications remains quite limited.

Let us go back to *Eleusis*, with particular reference to a line that extols a "tie (*Bund*) sealed by no oath" (B, 1, 38): does not this refute the hypothesis of Hegel's affiliation to Freemasonry? No, since there are Masonic currents which protest against the use of oaths during the initiation ceremony (and indeed, anything can be found in Freemasonry).[57] However, a different cultural line can be followed to explain the one from *Eleusis*. One needs only consider Kant's harsh criticism of oaths in public documents: he considered them to be "instruments to extort truthfulness" and even forms of *"tortura spiritualis."*[58]

Nevertheless, D'Hondt seems to prefer the esoteric history of Masonic gatherings to exoteric history. Besides, contrary to D'Hondt's intentions, the most progressive side of Hegel emerges from exoteric history, not from esoteric history. One needs only think that Kant's position on oaths (a position regarded as a hypocritical and convenient veil used by revolutionary and subversive intellectuals to conceal their ideas and intrigues) is harshly opposed by Christian Friedrich Nicolai, who was personally affiliated with Freemasonry.[59]

An esoteric history stemming from mysterious ties which are kept secret from the outside world is the view proposed by Fichte's anti-Masonic critics, who accused the philosopher of drawing from the "most secret doctrines" of Freemasonry. However, in reconstructing the history of thought, Fichte himself believed that, beside the so-called exoteric approach (based, for example, upon Hume's influence on Kant and upon Kant's influence on Fichte), it was possible to discover an "esoteric tie," mediated and defined by a "secret society."[60] Indeed, according to a thesis which Fichte formulates precisely in his *Vorlesungen über die Freimaurerei*, in history there has always been, alongside "public culture," a "secret" culture, or rather, a "*secret doctrine*" transmitted by means of an "oral tradition."[61] Fichte goes so far as to openly compare "secret and public history."[62]

Hegel's position is radically different: behind the mysteries of Freemasonry there is nothing at all, just like there is nothing outside or beyond the culture and knowledge accessible to everyone (W, XX, 499–500). The esoteric history of Hegel's development which D'Hondt tries to construct, and particularly Hegel's relationship to Freemasonry (and the ample assistance he supposedly received from it), is not consistent with Hegel, who is not by chance involved in a harsh debate against the Masonic fascination with esoteric and mysteriosophistic matter.[63] With regard to this, the *Lectures on the History of Philosophy* make it clear that there is a "depth" which is empty because, despite its promises, it does not lead to anything. "Thought consists, rather, of its manifestation: to be clear, that is its nature, its essence. Manifesting itself is not, so to speak, a State which can or cannot be, and thought does remain as such even if it has not been manifested; the fact of manifesting itself constitutes its very essence" (W, XVIII, 110). These words call to mind the Preface to *Phenomenology of Spirit*: "just as there is an empty expansion, so there is an empty depth . . . , so there is an empty intensity which, acting like a force without expansion, coincides with its superficiality. The power of the Spirit is as large as its expression; its depth is deep to the extent that it dares to expand itself" (W, III, 17–18).

The polemic against the Masonic cult of esotericism is an integral part of Hegel's general battle against the aristocratic, clitist conception of knowledge, in defense of a knowledge which must not be the "esoteric possession of some individuals," but something "exoteric," which possesses the "characteristic of universal *intelligibility*." In other words, a knowledge that "can be conceived by everybody, can be learnt by everybody, and belongs to everybody" (W, III, 19–20). Not by chance, the target of this last criticism is Schelling, who, already in 1795, on the basis of the limits set by "nature itself" against the "communicability" of knowledge, articulates a philosophy "which becomes *esoteric itself*," a philosophy which is accessible only to "those who are worthy of it," protected from the intrusions of "enemies and spies," a philosophy which constitutes a "bond (*Bund*) among free spirits," while for the others it remains an "eternal enigma."[64] The keyword *Bund* reappears during a period when, according to D'Hondt, Schelling had supposedly joined the Freemasons. Indeed, the conclusion to the *Philosophical Letters on Dogmatism and Criticism* (*Philosophische Briefe über Dogmatismus und Kriticismus*) we just mentioned seems to define the philosophy of Freemasonry in all of its ambiguity, since, on the one hand, it supports esotericism, while, on the other, it affirms that it would be a crime "to hide principles which are universally communicable."[65] Yes, there are various levels of knowledge, ranging from the exoteric to the esoteric, and here the hierarchical structure of the lodges seems to emerge. And yet, in his later works, Schelling will only need to radicalize certain motifs which are already present in the conclusion of the *Philosophische Briefe*, in this sort of "philosophy of Freemasonry," in order to come to the conclusion that knowledge is something eternally inaccessible to the common man.

Precisely during his struggle against this aristocratic and tendentially reactionary perspective, Hegel goes so far as to condemn the Masonic mysteriosophy that conditions, in a negative sense, Fichte himself.[66] It might be, as D'Hondt claims, that Hegel's condemnation of esotericism does not exclude his involvement with lodges that criticize such esotericism, but in this case, Freemasonry would reveal itself, once again, as an empty category that can assume the most diverse shapes.[67] And in any case, contrary to D'Hondt's intentions, the most progressive side of Hegel is not the one that emerges from the esotericism that would link him to the mysterious history of Freemasonry. The most progressive side of Hegel stems from his exotericism, from his public and private criticism of the esotericism of a Freemasonry which he attacks with no allusions to various currents, and with no distinctions or differentiations within his critical judgment.

Analogous considerations can be made for the other pieces which form Hegel's secret history as reconstructed by D'Hondt. Let us say this once and for all: there is no lack of new and interesting results, we do not deny that. Hegel reads Constantin-François Volney's *Ruins*, and Volney is an author who certainly does not call to mind the Restoration, but rather, the circles which support the French Revolution and the ideas of 1789. But are we dealing here with a forbidden or concealed reading? In his later works, Schelling cites *Ruins* explicitly,[68] and even Schiller, in January 1798, has no problems suggesting Goethe read Volney—not the same work, granted, but one in which the theme of ruins is still present.[69] Besides, the theme of ruins and the melancholic fascination they radiate is far from possessing an exclusively revolutionary meaning: for example, it is strongly present in François-René Chateaubriand.[70] In reality, as has already been observed, this topos can be found as far back as Cicero.[71] With regard to the more recent history which precedes Volney, it is also present in the works of the English poet Edward Young, and it spreads throughout Europe during the second half of the eighteenth century (in Germany, Friedrich Gottlieb Klopstock, an author whom Hegel knows well, dedicates one of his poems, *An Young*, to Young himself.)[72] Still with regard to Germany, in 1800 Schelling speaks sorrowfully of the "collapse of those great kingdoms which remain alive only in our memories, and whose greatness we can fathom from their *ruins*."[73] Later, Schlegel will speak of the "sad, melancholic impression" which ancient history leaves us with its heap of ruins.[74]

Let us not linger too long on this topic. One thing is for sure: during the years of the Restoration, that is, during the period which can help us most to understand Hegel's *Philosophy of History*, the poetry of ruins has an anything but revolutionary meaning. In 1826, one of Hegel's disciples, Heine, confesses that the "mournful sentiments" inspired by the contemplation of ruins have touched him, too, even though his heart is "to the left, with the liberals." The fascination (or the celebration of fascination) with ruins is felt as contradictory to the "leftist" (in a liberal sense) political commitment. Indeed, Heine goes so far as to claim that the Prussian government has interest in promoting journeys among "Italy's mournful ruins" in order to stimulate and spread "a comfortable, soothing notion of fatality."[75] If in *Philosophy of History* Hegel has truly and irresistibly felt the melancholy charm of ruins, at least from Heine's perspective, and from that of the philosophical-political culture of the time, he would have been (or he would have found himself) in an antithetical position to that of the "left" and the "liberals." This is exactly the opposite of what D'Hondt intends to demonstrate. But once again, in comparison to an esoteric image of Hegel, we find his exoteric criticism more progressive and persuasive. It is the criticism of a position which, by reducing universal history to a heap of ruins, to a "slaughterhouse" (v.G., 80), produces—to use Heine's words—"a mournful indifference" toward political events, and constitutes the most radical refutation of the idea of progress.[76]

6. Philosophical Arguments and Political "Facts"

It is best now to go back to exoteric history. However, if, on the one hand, esoteric history runs the risk of being overshadowed by an excessive emphasis on "hidden sources," on the other hand, it seems to be blatantly ignored by a philology which discusses texts only insofar as they are taken out of their historical context. The research done by D'Hondt (and indirectly by Ilting) has been criticized on the basis that the "facts" he has highlighted (that is, Hegel's relationship to the movement that opposes the

Restoration) are not "philosophical arguments."[77] Here, what is "philosophical" or theoretical is clearly defined by disregarding the "facts" which deal with the historical environment. In reality, however, historiographical research demands that the relationship between the two fields be reestablished, by transcending the weak elements which are present in Ilting's and D'Hondt's fundamental works. The "facts" which they brilliantly highlight must be used to retrace, in Hegel's texts, his political positions. The goal is to place such positions in a precise historical context, even the positions that are expressed most indirectly and implicitly because of self-censorship, or because they are filtered and mediated by the more strictly speculative discourse. For example, when in *Philosophy of History* we encounter an attack against "the will of a sovereign which, being the will of one anointed by God, must be divine and sacred" (*Ph.G.*, 917), it is not difficult to perceive an echo of the events and controversies of the time: upon ascending the throne, Charles X restored the secular tradition of a "sacred anointing" of the king, who was thus divinely invested with power. In so doing, Charles X had also met the demands of the ultra-royalists and personalities like Chateaubriand (infra, ch. II, 2). At this point, it is impossible to ignore the following elements: Hegel's relationship to an opposition figure like Cousin; Cousin's claim that Hegel was "genuinely constitutional and openly favorable to the cause supported in France by Royer-Collard" (*H.B*, 527), Royer-Collard being a leader of the opposition movement; and the enthusiasm which Hegel expresses in his letters about the fact that, as a result of the defeat of the reactionaries, Paris was spreading the "reinvigorating music of liberal energy" (*B*, III, 222). All these can no longer be regarded as merely private "events" bearing no relation to the philosophical sphere. The text of *Philosophy of History*, Hegel's correspondence, and private testimonies all shed light upon each other: what emerges from this is, on the one hand, the political importance of the "philosophical argument," and on the other, the philosophical relevance of Hegel's private relationship to Cousin and, indirectly, to Royer-Collard.

The connection between "facts" and "philosophical arguments" is disregarded not only in Hegel's case, but also in the case of his enemies and critics. It is Fries (*H.B*, 221) and the majority wing of the fraternity (*Burschenschaften*) movement who, during a harsh political battle, first accuse Hegel of serving the dominant power and the politics of the Restoration. This position is later developed by Haym during another harsh political battle, and Haym's position has not been questioned since. There has not even been a discussion of Haym's political role and the political goals he was trying to achieve. We have reached a point where a valuable critic like Löwith has defined Haym as a sort of Marx, though a little more "academic," when Haym himself, in the subtitle to one of his major works, *Die deutsche Nationalversammlung bis zu den Septemberereig-nissen: Ein Bericht aus der Partei des rechten Zentrums*, explicitly declares that he belongs to the "center-right."[78]

The complete lack of information on Haym's role has contributed to the credibility and even irrevocability of his thesis. Yet, his criticism of Hegel goes hand in hand with his condemnation of the French Revolution and the effect that it has on classic German philosophy, a philosophy which Haym accuses of naïveté precisely because of its enthusiastic reaction to the French Revolution.[79] If this fact had been recognized, certainly some doubt would have been raised about the legitimacy of Haym's condemnation of Hegel as a philosopher of the Restoration. The arbitrary association of Haym to Marx has turned the former's judgment (which had grown out of a precise historical period and, not only from a political perspective, but also from a compelling political strategy) into an opinion shared by all the Restoration's various enemies. It has become an *opinio recepta:* an accepted opinion. That which Haym himself defines as a "war cry" motivated by compelling political preoccupations and as a "philosophical and political pamphlet" has acquired the status of indisputable and scientifically incontrovertible truth.[80]

Contrary to Löwith's opinion, Marx's interpretation is in no way similar to Haym's: the young Marx informs Ruge that he is writing "a criticism of Hegel's Natural Law," in relation to the "internal constitution," and he adds: "The core of all this is the struggle against *constitutional monarchy* as a totally contradictory hybrid which eliminates itself."[81] The harshness of this controversy does not prevent Marx from acknowledging that what Hegel supported was neither the Restoration nor the divine right of kings, but constitutional monarchy. Marx recognizes this not in an isolated passage, but throughout his writing, even when his position is radically different from Hegel's.[82] And the reason for this is that Marx's explicit point of departure is the notion that classic German philosophy (which finds its culmination with Hegel) is the only reality in Germany capable of facing modern historical development, so much so that the criticism of the idealism which characterizes Hegel's *Philosophy of Right* is strictly tied to the criticism of the idealism of the State which resulted from the French Revolution.

Many years later, Engels takes up again the criticism of *Philosophy of Right:* "And thus we find, at the end of *Philosophy of Right*, that the absolute idea must be realized in that *representative monarchy* which Friedrich Wilhelm III promised, so tenaciously but in vain, to his subjects." Once again, the praise is implicit in the criticism: not only does Hegel take inspiration from constitutionalism, but he does so despite and in opposition to Prussia's reactionary turn.[83] Engels emphasizes that the

French Revolution is extolled in *Philosophy of History*, and he does so also to criticize the national-liberals who condemn the enthusiasm of classic German philosophy (Hegel included) for the French Revolution, and who at the same dismiss the author of *Philosophy of Right* as some sort of theorist of the politics of the Restoration![84]

Clearly, Marx's and Engels' judgments can easily be rejected, and in any case they should not be generalized; but they can and they must be used to make the various positions more relative. And all the more so since Marx and Engels are not the only ones who are radically different from Haym. In *Vormärz*, Friedrich A. Trendelenburg writes that, if one attacks Hegel's philosophy, one runs the risk of being labeled the "hangman's servant." This, Trendelenburg continues, has been the case "since Hegel's philosophy began to be passed off as an oppressed spirit of freedom (*Freisinn*), and its enemies as hypocrites and servile. That is, since Hegel's philosophy began to be passed off as the one and only light of the time, and its enemies as those who serve an obscurantist government." Therefore, in *Vormärz*, not only for single critics but for a whole cultural and political movement, Hegelian is a synonym for *freisinnig*, that is, "liberal," and anti-Hegelian— or even non-Hegelian—is a synonym for "servile."[85] Well, how can one explain the radical overturning that takes place with Haym, then?

7. An Interpretative "Misunderstanding" or a Real Contradiction?

Modern critics should beware of assuming they are prophets, as if the truth, the authentic meaning of Hegel's philosophy, had remained hidden and inaccessible to everybody for over 150 years, and then had suddenly revealed itself epiphanously to a fortunate and genial critic, a critic who, of course, is always the latest and trendiest one on the list. What comes to mind are the words with which Engels describes the attitude of prophets who announce, by religious inspiration, the coming of a new social order, finally free from the old mistakes: "This is exactly what we needed: one genial man who has now come to recognize the truth. . . . If he had been born five hundred years ago, he would have spared humanity five hundred years of mistakes, struggles, and sufferings."[86] In our case, the time saving made possible by such an utterly new interpretation of Hegel would have been less prominent, though still considerable; but the essential element would remain the same: the prophetic attitude.

We believe that the reading of a text can be accurate to the extent that it is able to account for the history of interpretations; to the extent that it does not dismiss it as a sequel of misunderstandings and mistakes; and in the final analysis, to the extent that it takes into account the reception of a text and the historical importance of the philosopher who compiled it. In other words, a re-reading of Hegel will prove penetrating and stimulating to the extent that it does not contrast —and that it is not forced to contrast—its "authentic" truth to profane history. And yet, we witness a strange phenomenon: those who see Hegel as a liberal also seem to consider Haym's accusations against him as a misunderstanding. On the other hand, even those who agree with Haym's interpretation are forced to consider Marx's and Engels' readings as well as those of the young Hegelian scholars (basically, of the whole school, since the "right," too, usually reads Hegel in more or less liberal and progressive terms) to be the result of a misunderstanding. They must consider even the interpretations given by clerical and religious circles as misunderstandings. These clerical and religious circles, in fact, far from identifying with the supposed theorist of the Restoration, attacked him on a theological and political level even while he was still alive. The misunderstandings denounced by each side are in opposition to one another, and yet both sides make implicit or explicit use of this category to clarify the contrasting history of interpretations.

However, when we are dealing with readings which cannot be traced back to a single critic, but rather, to concrete socio-political movements (as in this case, Haym's national-liberal party on one side, and the Hegelian school and even the protagonists of the workers' movement, Marx, Engels, Lassalle, on the other), then the notion of misunderstanding reveals itself as particularly inaccurate, since it dismisses actual history as "spurious" in favor of the "authenticity" of a single interpretation. And trying to mediate the two opposite interpretations by turning Hegel into a two-faced philosopher who supports both the Restoration and liberalism is just as ineffective. Such an interpretation would only end up combining the problems of the other two. The notion of misunderstanding would still stand strong, and now it would actually apply to both interpretations, which would become equally responsible for simplifying arbitrarily the figure of a philosopher whose complexity and ambiguity they could not grasp. Furthermore, this "conciliatory" reading would still need to explain how a great philosopher can "reconcile" such contradictory aspects. Certainly, gross distortions and falsifications can occur (like those which some Nazi "theorists" have created in contradiction to others, and not only with regard to Hegel), but their emergence and diffusion is linked to substantive extra-academic realities and situations.

Thus, it is not very productive to discuss real or possible "misunderstandings" without taking into account their socio-political history. It is necessary to follow a different track, and to do so we must take heed of a methodological indication which comes from Hegel himself: according to Hegel, a *"sharp* reflection" must be able to "recognize and formulate a contradiction" (*w*, VI, 78). On the contrary, an interpretation which resorts to the notion of misunderstanding, or which tries to come to a generous reconciliation, is guilty of softening the contradiction, or even of erasing it. The clash between opposing interpretations cannot be reduced to the contradiction between the printed text and the achroamatic text, between the public sources and the secret or "hidden" sources, or between an exoteric Hegel and an esoteric Hegel. If one reads Ilting, it would seem at times that the contradiction could be resolved simply by means of the yet unpublished lectures, once their authenticity has been proven. Yet, the transcriptions of the lectures were already largely in circulation among Hegel's contemporaries, and this did not stop the accusations of servilism from spreading. To prove his accusations, Fries also refers to the essay on the Diet (*H.B.* 221), that same essay which Carové, on the contrary, cited as both a stimulus and a guide for the movement which called for Germany's modern political transformation. We are not in the presence of a dispute between different philological schools which make use of contrasting materials and sources, but of a political contrast which feeds off of the same texts.

The same can be said about later developments. Marx and Engels interpret *Philosophy of Right* as an argument for constitutional, or representative, monarchy, without making any reference to the lectures, and citing, rather than the *Additions,* the printed text. On the opposite side, Haym discusses at length the *Addition* to § 280 (we now know that it is an excerpt taken from the 1822–23 lecture course), in which the role of the king is relegated to that of "crossing t's and dotting i's," but this does not prevent Haym from regarding Hegel's philosophy and even the above-mentioned *Addition* as totally incompatible with liberalism.[87] The contradiction which Ilting tries to remove by associating Haym's interpretation with the printed text and the liberal interpretation with the achroamatic text reemerges here quite strongly.

Far from being the result of a misunderstanding, Haym's criticism is the expression of a sharp, irreconcilable contrast which puts Hegel in opposition to the editor of the *Prussian Annals.* And the *Prussian Annals* constituted the organ and point of reference for the national-liberal party which was forming at the time. Even with regard to the history of great interpretations, it is useless to contrast "spurious" and "authentic:" the point is instead to try and grasp the all-political common thread of such history.

Let us read Haym more carefully: Hegel is guilty of constantly harboring "servile and antipatriotic sentiments," of prostituting himself repeatedly to France and Napoleon, and finally, of sharing the antinational tendencies of the Restoration.[88] From Haym's perspective, it is not contradictory to accuse Hegel of supporting an adjustment to the Restoration while at the same time accusing him of praising uncritically the French Revolution and Napoleon. Hegel, who reveals his servile and antipatriotic attitude by admiring Napoleon and the French Revolution, confirms this position in Berlin, when he continues to praise the French political and cultural tradition. In so doing, he sides against the philo-Germanic, anti-French party which was hand-in-glove with Metternich and the Restoration. The latter two are in turn condemned by Haym for humbling Germany's national aspirations: for one, Metternich and the Restoration did not allow Germany to annex the territories (Alsace, Lorraine, etc.) it aspired to, and besides, they smothered the "party" that embodied such aspirations. Haym's criticism remains consistent in accusing Hegel of betraying the nation. Such betrayal emerges first of all in the very theoretical notion of Hegel's philosophy, starting from the notion of "ethicality." According to Haym, this notion bears no connection to German Christian individualism; rather, it is associated with the pathos of the community and collectiveness, which is characteristic of the French revolutionary tradition.

Those who misinterpret Hegel are not the national-liberals (even though, of course, exaggerations abound, along with the insults which usually accompany a political struggle). Those who misinterpret Haym's reading of Hegel are, instead, certain contemporary critics, who uncritically support an attack they do not really understand, since they do not even perceive the issue of nationhood which constitutes its center of gravity. Yes, the attack against Fries, in the Preface to *Philosophy of Right*, allows Haym to critically liken Hegel to Metternich's followers, to the servants of power, and Haym does so by resuming the accusation which Fries and his "party" had already launched against Hegel. Yet, it is the contemporary critics who liken the centrality of the notion of ethicality, the so-called deification of the State, to the Restoration rather than to the French revolutionary tradition. Yes, Haym denounces the fact that, in Hegel, the political community, the *"politeia,"* presents itself as an authentic realization of the divine.[89] However, it was on the basis of the same motif that Schelling had condemned the French revolutionaries for forgetting that "true *politeia* only exists in Heaven."[90] And Haym, who denounces the young Hegel's supposed idolization of the State as a persistent attachment to ancient models, knew very well that the celebration of classical antiquity was associated with Rousseau and the Jacobins rather than with the Restoration.[91] Instead, contemporary critics interpret Haym's attack of Hegel's "idolization of the State" as a sort of defense of the ideas of 1789, when instead these ideas are not only criticized, but considered irreconcilable with the "German-Protestant principle of freedom."[92]

In other words, contemporary critics are the ones who forget that Haym is a national-liberal whose critical target is not only Hegel, but also, for example, Varnhagen von Ense, Heine, Gans, and *Junges Deutschland*. And these are the targets of his criticism not because he suspects them of serving the Restoration, but because of their "French culture" and their fascination "with French liberalism, with Voltaire's and Rousseau's ideas."[93]

Once the true nature of the contradictory oppositions Hegel vs. Haym and Hegel vs. Marx and Engels becomes clear, it is unnecessary to dismiss either interpretation as the result of a misunderstanding. On the contrary, there are several points common to these two opposite interpretations. For example, the admiration which Hegel and his disciples express for the French Revolution and for French culture and political tradition is recognized by both interpretations. Also, Marx highlights the fact that Hegel depicts civil society as *bellum omnium contra omnes*; but what Haym criticizes about Hegel is precisely the fact that the latter refuses to acknowledge the value and inviolability of civil society.[94] In both examples, the contrast is limited to a value judgment, a value judgment which Haym formulates by passing off the theories regarded by Marx as the most advanced, as essentially antiliberal and typical of the Restoration. Historically, Haym's value judgment has prevailed, but only his value judgment, not the concrete elements of his analysis. In fact, in the case of the latter, we sometimes witness an actual overturning. On the one hand, Haym argues the antiliberal nature of Hegel's philosophy on the basis of its connections to the French Revolution and to French political tradition (all permeated by a totalitarian pathos of the political community). On the other hand, some contemporary critics, after uncritically borrowing Haym's value judgment, go on to prove its validity by trying to demonstrate that Hegel had no connection with, or was even hostile to, the ideas of 1789. Hegel, who, according to Haym, could not comprehend modern freedom because he had no connection to the German or German Protestant tradition, is still considered removed from modern freedom, but is now made to belong to a tradition which ultimately leads to Hitler.[95] Of course, there is also a tradition which goes from Haym to Ernst Topitsch, or to Karl Popper and Friedrich August von Hayek, and it is the celebration of liberalism in opposition to "totalitarianism," no matter how defined.

An understanding of the all-political history of Hegel's popularity can be revealing. At this point we can and must return to the text, but not as if we had miraculously been plunged to the very starting point of the history of interpretations.[96] Rather, we must return to it carrying with us the rich and plentiful information that emerges from the reconstruction of the political history of interpretations. As contemporary critics, we must make use of this information to understand the presuppositions of our own readings, to become aware of the cultural and political notions behind the questions we ask Hegel. The political history of interpretations has nothing to do with the "history of effects" (*Wirkungsgeschichte*) so dear to Gadamer's hermeneutics. Yes, he does replace, by way of a truly priceless conciliatory strategy, the notion of a "misunderstanding" with that of a "dialogue" articulated between critics and text in various ways. However, the manner in which he disregards the notion of actual contradiction and the socio-political dimension of the hermeneutic debate is no less radical than the historiography we are criticizing here.[97]

Our study, instead, is based upon a conscious, explicit hypothesis: to ask oneself whether Hegel was a liberal is a circular question which compromises the comprehension of *Philosophy of Right*. It is a circular question because it implies a categorical, yet unconscious position within the political debate which surrounds the history of the interpretations of Hegel, a debate which is no less prominent today than it ever was. Such a position leads to an uncritical acceptance of the self-serving way in which liberal thought traditionally describes itself. Marx and Engels did not search for an esoteric Hegel to contrast to the exoteric one. They did not do so because, right from the start, they were aware that Hegel's thought, despite the limits of the "system" (which can be traced back to "German misery"), went well beyond the positions of those whom Engels, in defending Hegel from Haym's attacks, defines as "petty liberals" (infra, ch. ii, i).

II

The Philosophies of Right:
A Turning Point or Continuity

1. Reason and Actuality

We have insisted upon the need to proceed with a uniform reading of the many versions of *Philosophy of Right* without contrasting the lectures to the printed text, which, despite being indirect and at times cryptic, does not contradict the lectures. But this methodology must nonetheless face up to the radical objection that emerges in the work of Ilting. There are at least two subjects (the relation between reason and actuality in the Preface to *Philosophy of Right*, and the role and power of the sovereign) in which the *Philosophy of Right* differs substantially from the lectures. And, given that this gap would be clearly evident in a comparison between the lectures which were given both before and after the publication of the printed text, only one hypothesis remains to explain the "oddness" of the positions expressed in *Philosophy of Right*: adjustment to the Restoration.[1] We will start by examining the two subjects in question, beginning with the first, the relation between reason and actuality. Is it really true that what is said about rational and actual in *Philosophy of Right* is so radically different from the lectures? Let us start with a synoptic comparison:

1817–18: S 134 A	1818–19: v.Rph. I, 232	Philosophy of Right	1824–25: v.Rph., IV, 654
That which is rational, necessarily occurs (*muß Geschehen*).	Only the rational can occur.	What is rational, that is actual (*Was vernünftig ist, das ist wirklich*).	What is rational is also actual.

For the moment we will consider only the first part of the statement in question. It is clear that the assertion in *Philosophy of Right* is also present in the lectures of 1824–25, and even in the earlier lectures no major differences seem to emerge with respect to *Philosophy of Right*: the rational necessarily occurs, becomes actual, is actual. *Wirklich* has this meaning of movement, and already § 1 of *Philosophy of Right* substitutes *Wirklichkeit* with *Verwirklichung* when it declares that the *Philosophy of Right* is concerned with the "concept of right and its actualization." And even with regard to the second part of the statement, while the differences are perhaps more prominent, they hardly indicate a change of position.

1819–20: *Rph.III*, 51	*Philosophy of Right*	1822–23: *v.Rph.III*, 732	1831: *v.Rph.*, IV, 923
The actual becomes rational.	What is actual, that is rational.	Actuality is nothing irrational (*kein Unvernünftiges*).	What is actual is rational.

Yes, in the lecture course of 1819–20, the rationalization of the actual is more explicitly a process, but this is already somewhat implicit in the term *Wirklichkeit*. And yes, in the lecture course of 1824–25 we have the clarification that "not everything that exists is actual." But it should be noted that as far as *Philosophy of Right* is concerned, in the opening statement (§ 1 A) we find the same distinction between "actuality" (*Wirklichkeit*) and "transitory existence (*Dasein*), external contingency." Not to mention that already in the Preface we find the assertion that "nothing is actual (*wirklich*) except the idea" (*w*, VII, 25). On the other hand, it is understandable that it is primarily after the controversy that Hegel feels the need to specify the meaning of *Wirklichkeit*, contrasting it to empirical immediacy. The distinction is neither new nor instrumental: for one, it is present in *Philosophy of Right*; not only, but all one has to do is glance through, for instance, the *Encyclopedia* of Heidelberg to find, at the beginning of the section dedicated to "actuality," the distinction between *Wirklichkeit* and *Erscheinung*. Notably, from the first edition to the third, the text remains identical, except the numeration (§ 91 becomes § 142).

The distinction in question is formulated not only at the level of general logic, but it is applied even in historical analysis. In his writing on the Diet, the Diet is accused of clinging to "a merely positive platform which, in turn, being positive, no longer has any actuality" (*w*, IV, 536). Here, what is positive is contrasted to *Wirklichkeit*: actuality is not the immediately existent positive. Another example: Rejecting the new constitution, the appointed members of the Diet "declare, yes, that they are a representative body, but of another world, a past era; and they demand that the present transform itself into the past, and actuality transform itself into inactuality" (*w*, IV, 493). Putting into practice claims that are no longer in line with the times means transforming *Wirklichkeit* into *Unwirklichkeit*; to the extent that it no longer corresponds to the profound needs of the time, actuality is downgraded to immediate empirical existence.

It is therefore absurd to try and explain a fundamental Hegelian theoretical principle, throughout its development, as an immediate need for adjustment.[2] Indeed, in the *Phenomenology* one finds not only the problematic, but even the expression which is the cause of so much controversy in *Philosophy of Right*:

Phenomenology of Spirit: *w*, III, 192.	*Philosophy of Right*
That which must be, is, also de facto (*in der Tat*); and that which *must* merely be, without *being*, has no truth. The instinct of reason follows this logic.	What is rational is actual; and what is actual is rational. Every ingenuous consciousness, and philosophy too, follows this conviction.

One might go back to the 1798 essay on Württemberg (later lost), where Hegel decisively rejects the juxtaposition of "that which is and that which should be." In citing this passage, Haym points out that the essay, pervaded with the "pathos of the revolutionary period," attributed the above juxtaposition to the "laziness and the selfishness of the privileged."[3] The liberal or national-liberal Haym condemns the renowned statement from the Preface of *Philosophy of Right* as an expression of the spirit of the Restoration. Yet, when he, as a philologist, is faced with the same problem with regard to one of Hegel's early works, he is forced to put it in relation not with the Restoration, which is yet to come, but with the French Revolution. On the other hand, if Ilting shares the horror of that notorious statement with a large portion of the liberals, it should be recalled that the claim of the rationality of the actual is by no means outside traditional revolutionary thought. The young Marx, who subjects *Philosophy of Right* to scathing criticism, does not even mention the statement. To the contrary, in letters, Marx argues with Hegelian fervor against the "opposition of actual and ideal," against "the total contrast between that which is and that which must be," an opposition which he considers a means of evading the mundane and political world. To the latter, and with obvious reminiscence of the notorious Preface, he counters the notion that one must "seek the idea in actuality itself."[4]

For his part, Lenin cites and highlights in his *Philosophical Notebooks*

Hegel's assertion in *Lectures on the History of Philosophy* that: "What is real [actual] is rational. But one must know, distinguish, exactly what is real; in common life all is real: but there is a difference between the phenomenological world and reality." Then, Lenin notes in the margin: "what is real is rational." And, reading *Lectures on the Philosophy of History*, the great revolutionary writes twice that "reason governs the world." The second time, in the margin, he writes "NB," to underscore the importance of the claim and his complete agreement with it.[5] It is perhaps Lenin himself who can provide the conceptual apparatus most suitable to our understanding of the Hegelian distinction between actuality and mere empirical immediacy: there is a strategic actuality and a tactical actuality; in every historical situation one thing is the main current (for example, putting an end to serfdom at the twilight of feudalism), and another thing is the reactionary current at that time (for example, attempts to revitalize, in all of its antique "splendor," the institution of serfdom at its twilight— or well on its way, and as such "inactual"). The reactionary current is certainly not able to erase strategic actuality from the main current; however, on a tactical level it is nonetheless present and must therefore be appropriately dealt with.

As for Hegel, he does not contrast actuality (*Wirklichkeit*) to nothingness either. The "phenomenal world" (*Erscheinungswelt*) mentioned in the first of the two citations we are considering is not non-being. It is Lenin himself who positively emphasizes, this time commenting upon *Science of Logic*, that in Hegel "semblance" (*Schein*) has its own objectivity. In the *Philosophical Notebooks* we are told that, "semblance is objectivity, because in it one side of the *objective* world is present . . . Not only essence (*Wesen*), but also semblance (*Schein*) is objective."[6] "Semblance" and "appearing" are both actual, but obviously they do not possess the same degree of actuality as *Wesen* and *Wirklichkeit*, and only the latter, by expressing the strategic dimension—the main current—can aspire to the predicate of rationality.

We have mentioned Lenin, but Antonio Gramsci not only states that "rational and actual are one," but adds, importantly, "It seems that without comprehending this relationship one cannot understand the philosophy of praxis," which is Marxism. The reference is to the "Hegelian proposition that 'what is rational is actual, and the actual is rational,' a proposition that will be valid also for the past,"[7] as well as for the present and future.

The enthusiasm of thinkers of the revolutionary tradition is understandable: negativity is not only an activity of the subject, but is first and foremost inherent in objectivity itself. If the negative "appears as the inequality between I and the object, it is also the inequality of substance in contrast to itself. What seems to be produced outside substance, and to be an activity against it, is its true functioning, and this is what makes it essentially a subject" (*w*, III, 39). Socio-political transformations are not the result of a merely subjective project: the "change" (*Veränderung*)—we are told in the *Philosophical Propaedeutic*—"is marked by the disparity between one and itself," that is, by the contradictions objectively present in the actual; it is therefore "the negation of the negative that the something (*Etwas*) has in itself" (*w*, IV, 14). This is how the dynamic of the French Revolution is explained as well: the "negative tendency" assumed by the Enlightenment did nothing but "destroy what was already destroyed in itself" (*w*, XX, 295–96). The assertion of the rationality of the actual is not therefore the rejection of the change, but its anchor to the objective dialect of the actual. Even the lecture course of 1817–18 that Ilting contrasts specifically to the printed text claims that the rational *muß geschehen*: note that Ilting uses *muß*, not *soll*. Once again the change is the result not first and foremost of a moral postulate, but of both an objective dialectic and an objective necessity, no matter how favored and accelerated by human awareness.

Ilting condemns the claim of unity between actual and rational as essentially spurious because the interpretation he gives to that claim is inferior to that of the liberal tradition. Already Engels had noted that it was the "narrow-minded liberals" who cried shame at the claim, when, instead, it best expressed the revolutionary aspect of Hegel's philosophy:

> Actuality, according to Hegel, is in no way an attribute always applied, in every circumstance, to a socially and politically determined state of things. To the contrary. The Roman Republic was actual, but the Roman Empire that replaced it was also. The French monarchy became so inactual in 1789, that is, so lacking in every necessity, so irrational, that it had to be destroyed by the great revolution, of which Hegel always speaks with the utmost enthusiasm. In this case, the revolution was actual, the monarchy was inactual.[8]

And the texts bear Engels out: in its twilight, the Roman Republic lived a feeble existence, it was merely the "shadow" of its former actuality (*ph. G.*, 711). On the eve of what Hegel calls the Christian "revolution," the Roman State "no longer constitutes any actuality" (*Wirklichkeit*); it is merely an "empty semblance" (*leere Erscheinung*).[9] And the French political structure prior to the Revolution was in a state of "collapse" (*Zerrüttung*); it was even, as we have seen, "collapsed in itself" (*w*, XX, 295–97); therefore, it cannot be regarded as actuality.

The celebration of the ideal in comparison to the irremediable opacity of the actual might excite "narrow-minded liberals," but Engels was of another opinion: one of Hegel's greatest merits is to have "viciously derided the philistine enthusiasm, derived from Schiller, for unrealizable ideals."[10] Once again, we are directed to the notorious Preface of *Philosophy of Right*, with which the revolutionary Engels thoroughly identifies. Engels sees in the celebration of unrealizable ideals, in the celebration of the moral subject in contrast to the irremediable opacity of the actual, an escape motif. And, in the final analysis, a conservative instrument.

Of course one might not subscribe to Engels' interpretation, but it is worth noting that it seems to be confirmed by other authors, even those of the opposite political persuasion. The assertion of the rationality of the actual was particularly irritating to those ideologues who preached escape from the vale of tears of the mundane and political world, and to those praisers of times past (*laudatores temporis acti*). Friedrich Stahl, for example, denounces the fact that the Hegelian school, presupposing the presence of reason and the divine in actuality and in history, argues that "the present, the actual must always be the best; thus, the modern world is absolutely better than the medieval one."[11] Did not the notorious Preface aim precisely at those who looked down upon "the *present* as *something vain*"? (*W*, VII, 25).

Even today, many critics emphasize the link between Hegel's notorious statement and the Marxist vision of the objectivity of revolutionary process.[12] But this link is highlighted only for the purpose of denouncing the category of historical necessity as the root cause of every injustice and perversion of morals. In truth, it is already an established part of the liberal tradition. This is true particularly for Tocqueville, for whom "the gradual development of equal conditions" is not only an irreversible historical process, but is something "providential." The language is unequivocally religious. Not by chance does the author of *Democracy in America* declare that he has written his work "under the influence of a sort of religious terror springing up in my soul at the sight of this irresistible revolution." Of course, the current historical process must be controlled, but in it one finds "the sacred nature of the sovereign's will," so, "trying to halt the march of democracy would be like fighting against God Himself."[13]

What distinguishes Tocqueville from Hegel (and Marx) is the unease with which Tocqueville, despite everything, faces the historical process that he knows is unstoppable: the tenderness with which he speaks of the equally unstoppable twilight of the *ancien régime*.[14] Hegel, on the other hand, is in complete agreement with the actual-rational of the historical process that is at the same time the increasingly richer actualization of both freedom and equality. (As we will see, for Hegel progress is marked by the subsumption of every human being, including ex-slaves, in the category of man to the extent that he has inalienable rights.) This historical process is irreversible because men, over time, no longer allow their hard-earned human and moral dignity to be stripped from them: "If the sovereign's mere will were law, and he wanted to introduce slavery, we would know that this would not be acceptable. Everyone knows that a person cannot be a slave. . . . This fact has attained the status of a natural condition (*Natursein*)" (*w*, XVIII, 121–22). The claim of the strategic rationality of the historical process is intimately linked to a philosophy of history that is in some way democratic: progressively, it is humanity in its totality which comes to acknowledge its humanity and its freedom, and to consider this acknowledgment an unalterable fact. The same ingenious individuality itself is such to the extent that it expresses the needs of the time, not when it claims to proceed to create *ex nihilo!*

Tocqueville links historical process to natural process. To demonstrate the "providential" character of the former, in the Introduction to *Democracy in America* he observes: "It is not necessary that God Himself speak in order to discover the sure signs of His will; it is enough to examine the regular steps of nature and the constant tendency of the events. I know, without the Creator telling me, that the heavenly bodies follow the orbits traced by His finger." And this same regularity and inexorability is observable in the field of history with regard to the "gradual development of equal conditions."[15]

Hegel, instead, makes a clear distinction between historical process and natural process, and the category of historical necessity is linked not to nature per se but to "second nature" (*Rph.*, s 4). Second nature is clearly the result of history, and therefore of man's freedom; nevertheless, the result is not revocable by the "will of the sovereign" or any other individuality which believes itself ingenious and wants to shape history and the masses according to its pleasure. The criticism most often leveled at Hegel (and Marx) today is the same criticism made by Stahl and the reactionary writers taking aim not only at Hegel, but at liberal-democratic revolution in its entirety, which is seen as a logical and inevitable consequence of Hegelian philosophy: "If man can fully comprehend the World Spirit, as Hegel claims to comprehend it . . . , why shouldn't man himself have the ability to take the place of the World Spirit?"[16] The Revolution of 1848, which had eliminated in Germany the *ancien régime*, is here seen as firmly linked to Hegel's philosophy of history and to his assertion of the rationality of the actual, of actuality historically formed. For contemporary and reactionary critics of Hegel, to put into discussion the results of the French Revolution (and the other revolutions which follow on its heels) requires the elimination of Hegel's thesis on the rationality of the actual. Therefore, it makes no sense to consider such a thesis, as Ilting does, as a spurious and practical concession to the politics of the Restoration.

2. The Power of the Sovereign

The second theme which would confirm the idea that *Philosophy of Right* is a radical political turning point is that of the power of the sovereign, a theme which is more highly emphasized in the printed text than in the lectures. Above all, the recent discovery of the Heidelberg course on the philosophy of right seems to confirm that, in comparison to the original liberal position, *Philosophy of Right* is the expression of an opportunistic adjustment to the politics of the Restoration and to the situation that emerges after Karlsbad and the "hunt for demagogues." In this way, we would move from a position very close to being liberal ("The king reigns but does not govern") to the justification of a monarchy by divine right.[17]

Rather than examine, once again, parallel passages from the different versions of *Philosophy of Right*, it is worth pausing a moment to consider the true significance of the problem that the critic is called upon to clear up.[18] Specifically, we are faced with not one but two problems which, while certainly connected, are nonetheless different. The first concerns the relative importance of the monarch and the political institutions. Conservative or reactionary thinkers stress the subjective qualities of the sovereign, the moral excellence of his personality, as the best guarantees of the well-being and authentic freedom of the subjects or citizens. It is a view that, steering attention away from political institutions, considers their change irrelevant—or even deceptive—and therefore in the service of the status quo. In this sense, Hegel's early critics accuse him of failing to understand that at the center of Prussian actuality and history is free "personality," not the rigid and dead institutions of constitutional monarchy. Regardless of the claims about the greater or lesser breadth of the sovereign's power, and regardless therefore of the *Addition*, which compares the role of the monarch to crossing the t's and dotting the i's, Hegel's political philosophy is condemned because it represents "the decisive victory of objectivity over subjectivity" (*Mat.*, I, 262).

These reactionary critics were not wrong about Hegel. The privileging of politics and institutions, in comparison to the supposed excellence of the monarch's personality—and thus, to the rhetoric of the monarch's good intentions—is evident throughout the development of Hegel's ideas, and is the centerpiece of his political philosophy. It is clearly present in the printed text of *Philosophy of Right*, where we read: there exists "despotism" when "particular will as such . . . counts as law, or rather, replaces law," even when the "particular will" is that of an excellent monarch (§ 278 A). "It is not enough for the heads of the State to be virtuous"; rather, "another form of rational law is required apart from that of the [individual] *disposition*" (§ 273 A). Later, Schelling, in order to condemn the July Revolution which broke out in support of the *Charte*, contrasts this "most intimate *state of mind*," the "law written on the heart," to the demands for a written constitution.[19] For Hegel, instead, when the life of the State rests upon a privileged personality and comes to depend upon his "permission," it means that the monarchy is not modern and developed, that is, constitutional. On the contrary, it means that it is still feudal, and that within it relationships are founded not upon the "objectivity" of the law, but upon "representation" and "opinion" (§ 273 A), upon the "permission" of specific individuals (§ 278 A). *Belieben, Vorstellung, Meinung:* these negative terms are used by Hegel to characterize the *Persönlichkeit*, the keyword used by the defenders of absolutism who tried to oppose liberal and constitutional demands. In a modern State—we are told in *Philosophy of Right*—tasks are carried out by specific individuals, but these individuals are subordinate to their function and cannot assert their "immediate personalities," their "particular personalities" (§ 277). The despotism of "particular will" is replaced by the "constitutional State" (§ 278 A).

Regardless of the opinions and political options of the time, it is clear that this view is contrary not only to reactionary feudal and romantic ideology, but to the theories of absolute monarchy as well. Once again, Hegel's early critics are well aware of it, and attack him in these terms: "It is the evil one himself who, in recent and even the most recent of times, introduced into the political life of people and States those paper or parchment documents which are called constitutions or law as such. And the philosophers who work to justify this union of statutes and laws as absolute, as that which conforms to the supreme idea, serve only evil" (*Mat.*, I, 263). Hegel's philosophical vision appears identical to the constitutional movement's; indeed, it stands out, in the Germany of the time, as its most coherent theoretical foundation.

Once the preeminent role of institutions is clarified, there is the problem of the relationships between the many spheres and powers of the State. The fact remains that, despite the significant differences between various works and lectures, Hegel places greater emphasis on the role of the sovereign, and this for a very concrete reason, one that has not been adequately addressed by either side in the debate over Hegel's "liberalism:" Hegel is forced to support a constitutional monarchy in a period in which often the courts or the government take a more progressive stance than the representative bodies, or at least the majority of them. So it was in France at the time of the *Chambre introuvable*, dominated as it was by extremist inductees voted into the cult of the *ancien régime*. This was also the case in Württemberg, where the severity of the Diet's opposition to the "poisonous" revolutionary ideas originating in France and to the rather progressive decree of the King of Württemberg was fostered by none other than Metternich. There, the Diet did not hesitate to appeal to the Holy Alliance to intervene in the constitutional conflict and to restore the institutions of the good old days.[20] This was also partly true in Prussia where, at least according to Hegel, there was a danger that the Teutonic opposition might develop into a mass reactionary movement.[21]

If, on the one hand, conforming to the general philosophical current, Hegel was willing to drastically reduce the role of the monarch's personality to the point of reducing him to a sort of figurehead, on the other hand, given the concrete political situation, it was impossible to exclude the sovereign from legislative power. Could one leave legislative power in France in the hands of the *Chambre introuvable*, or in the hands of the extremists in Württemberg, those who in the years following the French Revolution "had neither learned nor forgotten a thing"? (*w*, IV, 507). What sense did it make to drastically reduce the power of the sovereign when, in the concrete situation of the time, the only hope was for an *octroyée* constitution based on the French *Charte*?

That said, the transformation of the monarchy into a constitutional one is one thing, the function of a constitutional monarchy already consolidated is another. Not by chance, reducing the sovereign's role to that of a sort of figurehead is supported by Hegel in the lecture course of 1822–23, in reference to a "developed organization." In the same context he specifies that there may be situations in which "the personality [of the monarch] is the decisive element"; but at the time "no such State has been constructed" (*v.Rph.*, III, 763 and 765). The claims which most radically alter the political-constitutional role of the king usually cite what occurred in England, as in the "reply" to Friedrich Wilhelm III's objection to the theory of the figurehead: "in England . . . a monarch does not have much more to do than issue the final decision, and even in that he is limited" (*v.Rph.*, IV, 677–78).[22] This is also the case with the lectures of 1817–18 (s 133 A). And, however Hegel articulates his hopes for an initiative in favor of a constitutional monarchy in Germany, Prussia, and even France, his view is consistent from Heidelberg to Berlin. As for what is written about the Diet, "no layman's spectacle is more grandiose" than the consitutional reelection of a monarch (*w*, IV, 468). The first lecture course on the philosophy of right declares that in the case of a disjunction between political-constitutional position on the one hand, and the spirit of the people and the times on the other, the inevitable "revolution" "can proceed from either the sovereign or from the people" (*Rph.I*, s 146 A). Once again the lecture course of 1824–25 asserts the necessary political-constitutional reform can come from or be "mediated by the free will of the sovereign" (*v.Rph.*, IV, 697): the first hypothesis to be considered is still that of a revolution or reform that begins from the top-down. In this sense, the role of the sovereign continues to be emphasized without interruption. But the general philosophical view still favors a constitutional monarchy, the orderly and institutional function of which leaves little room for the personality and whims of the monarch. In the Heidelberg course one finds the claim that "in England too the king is this highest point, but by virtue of the constitution he decays to almost nothing" (*Rph.I*, s 133 A). In turn, the printed text also asserts that in an orderly State every "sphere" must be "determined by and dependent upon *the end of the whole*" (s 278 A). The subsequent element of continuity, represented by the preeminence of the whole, and for which the various organs and powers of the State cannot be "autonomous and stable in and of themselves or with regard to the personal will of individuals," (s 278) is clearly evident.

We do not intend to deny the oscillation and diversity of the lecture courses brought to light by Ilting, but, in order to adequately examine and trace Hegel's development in this regard it is necessary to consider many factors: 1) The general philosophical view (essentially a matter of responding to questions about the requirements and procedures of an organically developed and consolidated constitutional monarchy) and the immediately defined political tasks (in this case the question about the steps taken to make Prussia and other German States constitutional monarchies); 2) The necessity to avoid hastily considering certain claims to be in opposition, claims which, with a careful decoding of the printed text (which was subjected to rigorous self-censorship) may after all be harmonious. In this light, one might say that Ilting fails to consider the fact that Hegel must face the powers that be and censorship. In order to demonstrate his theory of the "turn," he begins with a somewhat mechanical confrontation between two reciprocally heterogeneous greats, like the lectures on the one hand, and the printed text on the other; 3) The criticism that, despite all of this, is and must be made should not be attributed solely and exclusively to Hegel's desire and need to "adjust" the text to avoid run-ins with those in power; rather, the text should first and foremost be considered Hegel's genuine appraisal of the new political situation that comes about. In other words, Hegel, faced with the radical complexity of the politics and ideology of the Teutonic "party," must conceal more than ever his hopes for political-constitutional reform from the top-down, and is forced to justify and even call for the repression of a movement which had taken on reactionary connotations.

It is hasty to correlate Hegel's claim about the role of the sovereign to the legislative process of the Restoration, or to a specific decision of the Congress of Vienna.[23] We should not lose sight of the complexity of the situation emerging at the time: Hegel is not fooled by the ostensibly "liberal" catch phrases of the extremists attempting to embellish their reactionary project; given the choice between *Chambre introuvable* and the Crown, there is no doubt that Hegel decisively chooses the latter. Indeed, he hopes the Crown will crush the resistance of the *Chambre introuvable,* and this political stance remains unchanged, from Heidelberg to Berlin. Yet it does not, in a specific and determined situation, imply a position in favor of either absolute monarchy or divine right. No, in the given circumstances, the Crown was not supposed to completely cut off ties linking the present to the legacy of the French Revolution, rather it was to further advance the liberal and constitutional movement.

This complex and contradictory situation is lost upon many of Hegel's contemporary critics, but it was well understood in the context of Hegel's historical concreteness and in the political realism of the ideologues of the Restoration. As far back as 1831, Franz von Baader described the paradoxical aspects of the political climate in this way: "One cannot but help admire the delicate sincerity of our liberals: though they never fail to overlook an opportunity to insinuate that most of the legislative chambers under their control have been issued to them, and that this control could therefore easily be revoked, they nonetheless immediately talk of rebellion should a certain unfavorable class attempt to legally demand its rights."So, Hegel was not the only one to defend the Crown in relation to a nostalgic and contentious nobility, even when the latter had control of the Parliament. In fact, it was the same position taken by "our liberals," at least according to Baader. And as far as Restoration France is concerned, François-René Chateaubriand (who boasts of having been the first to formulate the liberal principle "the King reigns not governs" (*le Roi règne et ne gouverne pas*)) claims that at the time "the liberals themselves were against me."[24] In that specific historical situation, the distinction between progress and reaction was completely different from the way in which today's naïve liberals imagine it. As for Baader, the ideologist of the Restoration concludes: "The revolution (*der Revolutionismus*) can proceed from top to bottom, or from the bottom-up."[25] Those who defended the Crown against the extremists of the nobility and the *Chambre introuvable* were not only considered "liberals" but also "revolutionaries."

It is therefore absurd to consider Hegel's liberalism in comparison to that of someone like Chateaubriand, the voice of extremists and the "*ultraroyalistes* opposed to the King and to the moderate governments inspired by him," that is, the voice of those "in the majority in the *Chambre introuvable* who make it an uncompromising element of the government."[26] If, however, what Ilting claims is true and the Heidelberg lecture course on the philosophy of right places Hegel in a position close to that of Chateaubriand, it would be necessary to conclude that *Philosophy of Right,* by reaffirming the power of the sovereign and by distancing itself from the *ultraroyalistes*, represents not a capitulation to the Restoration but rather a more realistic and more mature elaboration of the facts of the situation and those of the political struggle at hand.[27] It would mean that Hegel, who, in his battle for "freedom" had enlisted the likes of Louis-Gabriel-Ambroise de Bonald and Félicité Robert de Lamennais, and socially, as he points out in his memoirs, "the great families of France," the "feudal nobility," and a "sovereign of the Church" had distanced himself from Chateaubriand.[28] Yes, Chateaubriand defended the legislature (or rather the *Chambre introuvable*), but his defense served to support the demand for the reinstatement of the privileges of the aristocracy, the reinstatement of the "control of education," "the possession of the Registry Office," and "property" to the clergy.[29] His support was for a program aimed "at courageously defending religion against impiety," and therefore against modern ideas.[30] In sum, his defense was a reactionary program in opposition to the Crown and those governments which, according to Chateaubriand, were guilty of having acted "on behalf of revolutionary interests."[31] Chateaubriand not only praises the counter-revolutionaries of Vendée, accusing governments of "cruel ingratitude" in their regard, but, with the ascension of King Charles X to the French throne, he even argues for the reinstitution of the centuries-old ceremony affirming the divine origins of the monarchy's power, the sacred "anointing" of the new king.[32] The very same ceremony that Hegel denounced as a pretext for legitimizing and consecrating the "arbitrariness of sovereigns," absolute monarchy (*Ph. G.*, 917). One can of course consider Chateaubriand more "liberal" than Hegel, or at least more liberal than the Hegel of *Philosophy of Right*. But this would mean that what we really have is an inadequate category for understanding the historical dialectic, a category that is useless in helping us to concretely grasp the distinction between progress and reaction. We will later consider this distinction in depth, but for the moment we should further characterize the "liberalism" of Chateaubriand: it is worth noting that if, on the one hand, he defends the *Chambre introuvable* against the Crown and the government, at the same time he demands that the legislature be protected from the criticism of newspapers and other lowly critics, and even holds the government responsible for the "crimes of the press."[33]

In any case, defending the Crown against the "liberalism" of Chateaubriand are—as Ilting himself points out—liberals such as Pierre Paul Royer-Collard, François Guizot, etc. And, like Hegel, these liberal "doctrinaires" make a distinction between the general philosophical view and immediate political options. Royer-Collard, in clear contrast to the instrumental "liberalism" of the extremists, raises the idea that "it is the King who governs" to a "fundamental and sacred principle." And Guizot, in his memoirs, explains that the most pressing issue of the time was preventing the "right" from taking power. One of today's critics has stressed that for Royer-Collard the crown was a guarantee of "actual freedom."[34] With this expression, we are directed back to Hegel, who, as we will see, insists upon never losing sight of "actual freedom" throughout the development of his ideas, from Heidelberg to Berlin. Two more authors are worth citing in this context. In 1843, Marx credits the *Rheinische Zeitung* for not having perpetually defended the legislature or the estates (*Stände*) against the government, as "crass liberalism" does (which sees "every good on the side of representative bodies and every evil on the side of the government"), and for distinguishing case by case, without wavering, and in specific circumstances, "the general wisdom of the government from the private egoism of the Houses."[35] These passages, which will fail in their attempt to spare the newspaper he edits from censure by the powers that be, have clearly been self-censored, and again bring us back to *Philosophy of Right*. It would be extremely erroneous to overlook the very concrete political and historical situation that Marx's passages beg us to consider while they redirect us back to Hegel.

The other author to consider is quite removed from Hegel (and Marx). Following the July Revolution, Ludwig Börne complains that the legislature, thanks to the electoral laws in force, basically consists of "the rich," who, for obvious reasons, are of "aristocratic dispositions." If "the government, which is more liberal than that of the legislature," should fall, the electoral mechanism would inevitably reproduce the same situation over again. Perhaps, the radical democrat seems to suggest, "the king should proclaim a [new] electoral law." It is just that the French would never tolerate the "use of force," not even in the service of "freedom." And so, "I do not see how the government can support itself or the country outside a *coup d'état*; and a *coup d'état*, even if carried out in the name of freedom, would open up all sorts of possibilities."[36]

Naturally, we have no intention of trying to integrate authors as diverse as these. We merely want to underscore the fact that it is absurd to attempt a comparison between the liberalism of Hegel and that of Chateaubriand without considering the concrete situation. Moreover, it is absurd to link *Philosophy of Right* to the Restoration and, even more absurdly, with the politics born out of the Karlsbad resolutions, given that *Philosophy of Right* express a problematic that not only precedes those *Resolutions*, but returns to the liberal, democratic, and even radically democratic themes in rigorous opposition to the ideology of the Restoration, among whose defenders one might easily include the "liberal" Chateaubriand. The position which favors the power of the sovereign is so scarcely an expression of illiberal adjustment that it completely corresponds to the philosophy of history that emerges, as we will see (infra, ch. V).

It is, of course, still necessary to explain the particular details of Hegel's ideas as they develop, but some elements of continuity are clear, and Ilting himself cannot but help highlight them: the anticontractual argument, for example, and the "monarchical principle" (interpreted by Hegel to mean in an absolute sense).[37] The fact is, the theory of the turn seems to become a volatile topic thanks to the texts that Ilting discovered and to which he called so much attention. When we look at the *Encyclopedia* of the Heidelberg period, s 438, we find the following: the "sovereign" is defined as "the highest ranking person, deliberately and indisputably," of the "government." Not only does the printed text bear this out, but so do Hegel's handwritten notes to this paragraph in the manuscript; they too are clearly headed in the same direction: "The power of the sovereign is indisputable will"; "the power of the sovereign is in and of itself the best thing" (*v.Rph.*, I, 193). In the course of lectures of 1824–25 we read: "The power of the sovereign is the decisive element; the governing power is the executive one, *pouvoir executif.* According to the flawed French view, the power of the sovereign is merely executive, but the executive power is always the decisive power, even with regard to the law. Executive power is gubernatorial power" (*v.Rph.*, IV, 689).

What does this mean? With regard to the power of the sovereign, one of Ilting's disciples, one who cites him repeatedly, counters the argument based upon the first lecture course on the philosophy of right in the *Encyclopedia* of the Heidelberg period. We are told that for the first time Hegel formulates "the separation of royal power from government power," the latter being given more weight in accordance with the doctrine and the praxis of the constitutional monarchy. "It is not by chance that Hegel changes his position after his first meeting with Victor Cousin. That meeting took place during the summer of 1817."[38] Hegel thus turns not once, but twice. Turns which are qualitatively different, being motivated, on the one hand, by the imminent logic and development of his thought, and, on the other hand, by his concern with the logic of philosophical discourse. Moreover, with the second turn, Hegel essentially returns to the position held prior to the first turn, given that the *Encyclopedia* of the Heidelberg period attributes to the sovereign powers that are not significantly different from those assigned the sovereign in the printed text of *Philosophy of Right.* In fact, at this point, in order to bring closure, it would be necessary to hypothesize still a third turn with which Hegel, during the course of his lectures on the philosophy of right in 1822–23 and 1824–25 would retract his significant concessions to the politics of the Restoration. Not only, but he would deny any agreement with either the politics of the Restoration or those of his own printed text, and would return to a position prior to the second turn.[39] In effect, two theoretical turns and one practical turn. A bit much.

What is more, these turns themselves seem to be configured differently each time. The "second turn" must be dated to the Karlsbad period, or should we make it earlier given that the decisive role of the sovereign is already evident in the notes made to the manuscript of the *Encyclopedia* of the Heidelberg period, just after the 1817–18 lecture course on the philosophy of right? It is argued that, as far as the limitation of the power of the sovereign goes, and as far as Hegel's vision of the State and political authority goes, he never attained "the same depth" of his course at Heidelberg.[40] But at this point the opposition between printed text and "authentic" text breaks down, and the main argument becomes the comparison between the philosophy of right of 1817–18, and the other versions of it, to include that of the *Encyclopedia* of Heidelberg which contains Hegel's handwritten notes. Above all, however, it makes no sense to define the *Philosophy of Right* of 1817–18 as the original (and therefore authentic) version; not only is it preceded by the *Encyclopedia* of Heidelberg, but the version of 1817–18 itself stands out among his texts as the most isolated and "inauthentic." Ilting's theory comes to an impasse the moment in which one attempts to develop or expand upon it.

With respect to the theory of Hegel's turns, we will attempt a more "economical" one. If, on the one hand, we accept the preeminence of institutions and their proper function with regard to the "personality" of an absolute monarch (or one not bound by a constitution), and if we accept on the other hand Hegel's sympathetic view of "revolution from the top-down" (the active intervention, if necessary, of the Crown to overcome the resistance of nostalgic and reactionary extremists); if we accept these two binaries, then the proposals vary both in relation to the development of the objective situation as well as with regard to Hegel's exhaustive reflection upon it. We should not forget that when *Philosophy of Right* appears in print, reactionaries are fighting against the revolutionary government in Spain. In France, there is an enormous uprising by extremists after the assassination of Duke Charles-Ferdinand de Berry. In Germany, at least according to Hegel, the Teutonic movement turns anti-Semitic and reactionary. *Philosophy of Right* appears at a moment in which, to borrow the words of the liberal Dominique Dufour de Pradt, "courage no longer means attacking the government, but defending it." It is an observation that Hegel is in agreement with according to a private notation that cannot be considered an "adjustment" (B.schr., 699).

Certainly, by taking this position one risks being branded a servant of power by one's political adversaries, and indeed this happens at Berlin. But already at Heidelberg Hegel realizes that by taking a position against the (at least in his eyes) nostalgic and reactionary Diet, he may be accused of "obsequious stupidity, of allowing himself to be blinded like a slave and be nurtured by secret designs" (w, IV, 469). One who does denounce Hegel as a servant of power is Ludwig Börne who, as we have seen, very clearly sides with the government (as did Hegel, whom he so harshly judges), and even supports a *coup d'état* by the monarchy.[41] It is not because of this that Börne is transformed into a supporter of absolute monarchy. This is of course only an example, but one worth taking note of, especially when one evaluates a philosopher who explicitly argued for the subordination of "formal freedom" to "actual freedom."

As for the 1820 theory that Hegel's turn is an "adjustment," we would like to consider one more point: if this theory were true, it would mean that with the publication of *Philosophy of Right* we would witness a radical repositioning of the main front in the struggle, as well as those involved in it. But this is not the case. As is well known, Heinrich Paulus breaks with Hegel not after the publication of *Philosophy of Right,* but prior to it, after Hegel's writings on the Diet.[42] In his review of *Philosophy of Right,* Paulus considers it scandalous for condemning the elected monarch, but this condemnation is already out of date (мат., I, 63). During the lecture course on the philosophy of right at Heidelberg, pausing to consider the tragic events in Poland, he explicitly criticizes the country's constitutional situation (s 120 A and s 163 A). Not to mention that, even before this, his painful reflection upon Germany's disintegration clearly implies a negative judgment of the elected Emperor. Paulus considers Hegel's support for a constitutional monarchy while condemning an elected one to be contradictory, especially when emphatically supporting—as *Philosophy of Right* does—the role of the sovereign. This is because according to Paulus constitutional monarchy has, historically, come into being from the bottom-up (мат., I 63). Hegel holds the opposite to be true: "The fact that sovereigns are no longer elected" constitutes an important stage "in the movement of history towards a rational constitution, towards constitutional monarchy" (v.Rph., IV, 688). The power of the elective monarchy is a reflection of the power of feudal barons, and by crushing this power the Crown plays a progressive and modern role: this is one of the central theses of Hegel's philosophy of history, and not a unique, untrustworthy or "opportunistic" printed text.

In any case, Hegel anticipates Paulus' criticism and responds to it already at Heidelberg, where he had drawn a continuous line *not* from the French Revolution to the actions of the Diet of Württemberg, but from the French Revolution to the reforms of the sovereign: "If the majority of the French estates and the popular party were responsible for reclaiming the rights of reason, while the government favored privileges, in Württemberg, instead, it was the king who drew up his constitution according to the public right of reason, and the Diet which appointed itself protector of the positive and the privileges" (w, iv, 507).

Similar observations can be made about Hegel's relationship to Fries, who draws a continuous line from the "servility" displayed by Hegel, first with regard to Napoleon, then in response to the constitutional conflict in Württemberg, and finally regarding the crisis brought about by the assassination of August von Kotzebue (H.B., 221).

Even Hegel considers his adversaries to be clearly hostile to the French Revolution, against which the Diet—but even more so, the Teutons—thunder.[43] In the Diet of Württemberg "the members of the nobility . . . denied, even to the point of absurdity, the abdication of the Roman Emperor" (w, iv, 495), a clear demonstration of how rooted in the positive they are. Still, they are not far from the position taken by the Teutonic movement, with its agonizing nostalgia for the ancient glory of imperial Germany.

One might argue that it was the publication of *Philosophy of Right* that triggers the split between Hegel and Nikolaus von Thaden, but Thaden himself clarifies the real reasons for his disagreement with Hegel. Thaden (*Mat.*, I, 76–77) is decisively opposed to the "new campaign" waged against the folklorists (*Volkstümler*), that is, against those who talk of the original and pure German folk wisdom (*Volkstum*). In other words, against those opposed to the Teutonic Order. But Thaden had warned Hegel about this "new campaign" even before the publication of his *Philosophy of Right* (B, II, 224). In this case too, a continuous line emerges.

To consider the debate that emerges from *Philosophy of Right* to be the result of an increase in liberal public opinion is a mistake. Is Gustav Hugo a liberal? Hugo, who justifies slavery and is for this reason attacked in *Philosophy of Right?* (S 3 A) Is Savigny a liberal? Savigny, who was one of the first to challenge the book and its author in his letters (H.B, 230), and the same man who was the head of what Marx called that "German theory of the French *ancien régime*" to which he alleges Hitler and Stahl belong to?[44] The same Savigny who declared the Napoleonic code a "cancer" and who, as minister following Friedrich Wilhelm IV's reactionary turn, became one of the most hated targets of the liberal and constitutional movement? Should he be considered a liberal?[45] The truth is that the makeup of the battle lines is much more complex.

Here too, despite what might seem to be apparent agreement, the difference in approach taken by Ilting and Jacques D'Hondt becomes clear: Ilting manages to reconstruct a "different" Hegel, somehow using the printed text of *Philosophy of Right*, but neglecting to discuss the criticism that the book received in liberal circles for its "adjustment" regarding "absolute monarchy"; D'Hondt reconstructs Hegel as a sort of progressive by contesting that his critics were liberals, and by attempting to demonstrate that for the most part they were reactionaries (a position argued most insistently by Shlomo Avineri).[46] Yet, in this way one takes sides with those who object all too easily, drawing from the likes of Fries and other repressed "demagogues," who triumphantly proclaim that Hegel was not a liberal because: "Only the dire necessity to impose a predetermined thesis rather than an authentic investigation, could make one believe that the architects of the Holy Alliance had persecuted the *Burschenschaft* because it was reactionary."[47] Here, we see a common presupposition made, paradoxically, by Hegel's critics and defenders alike. The battle lines are arbitrarily simplified so that everything is reduced to the opposition between liberal and reactionary, without any notice of the contradictions within not only the revolutionary movement and opponents of the powers that be, but also within these powers themselves. Little or no attention is paid to the complexity of Hegel's position not only with regard to absolute monarchy but, above all, with regard to the question of the German nation, the balance of history, etc. In reality, as we have attempted to demonstrate elsewhere, the publication of *Philosophy of Right* marks the beginning of the clash between two parts of the revolutionary movement which oppose Restoration politics, a clash which had already been delineated years earlier, with Hegel and the "philosophical party" on one side and the "Teutonic party" on the other.[48]

In any case, with regard to the position that attacks *Philosophy of Right* as being sympathetic to the Restoration, a final point: According to Ilting, the lecture courses on the philosophy of right in 1822–23 and 1824–25 mark the end of Hegel's adjustment to the politics of the Restoration and a return to his original and authentic liberal ideas. Yet, despite the fact that Hegel's lessons were well-known, the debate by no means ends. Indeed, Hegel, who has turned "liberal" again, continues to be harshly attacked by his adversaries.

At this point we might conclude by positing a theory which we will later attempt to substantiate: Ilting, with his tireless editing and interpretation, has the merit of demonstrating the profound weakness of the theory of the end of the "liberal" Hegel (in accordance with a tradition that goes, though from time to time with different emphases, from Rudolf Haym to Norberto Bobbio). Ilting is unable to complete his revisionist project because despite the new points that he introduces, he continues to use an uncritical approach which relies upon the categories of the liberal tradition.

TWO

Hegel, Marx, and the Liberal Tradition

III

Contractualism and the Modern State

1. Anticontractualism = Antiliberalism?

Here is an illuminating example that demonstrates that Hegel's "liberal" critics and defenders draw upon the same interpretative categories (deduced by contemporary liberals and arbitrarily and surreptitiously unqualified). For Bobbio, Hegel's rejection of the contractual theory becomes evidence that he situates himself in a conservative position, hostile to liberalism.[1] In turn, Ilting, despite his liberal interpretation of Hegel, views the anticontractual argument as a revision of the philosopher's liberal principles.[2] This is merely a reduction of Bobbio's theory: The tacit and unsupported presupposition that anticontractualism equals antiliberalism remains unchanged. The only variation is that, according to Bobbio, Hegel consciously rejected liberalism, while Ilting considers Hegel's position with regard to contractualism as incoherency or chance weakness. Naturally Bobbio's theory holds up better given that the anticontractual argument characterizes Hegel's work throughout the course of its development. Nevertheless, liberal critics and defenders of Hegel have failed to reconstruct the concrete historical significance, the concrete socio-political contents of the contractualism against which Hegel's argument is directed.

One might begin by asking a question: Did contractual theories that were either conservative or reactionary exist at that time (not to mention the present)? In Hegel's *Encyclopedia* of the Heidelberg period Hegel argues against the view that the "constitution" is "a contract, that is, an arbitrary agreement between different people regarding something *arbitrary* and *accidental*" (§ 440). To this, the manuscript note to the paragraph in question contrasts "superior natural right" to "change of the constitution" or even "revolution" (*v.Rph.*, 1, 197). These were the precise terms of the constitutional conflict of Württemberg: the Diet, in support of the ideology of antiquity, saw the introduction of a new constitution as a violation of the previous constitutional contract stipulated by the sovereign and the nobility. That the anticontractual argument targets feudal and reactionary ideology, the capital concept of the State, is clearly evident in Hegel's text: only within feudalism does the contract between "prince and people, both proprietors and possessors of privileges," make any sense. Above the prince and people, the Emperor is called upon to intervene in the case of any violation or contention regarding the contract in question (w, IV, 504). It is during the Middle Ages that "rights had the nature of private property, upon which one could stipulate a contract" (w. Rph., III, 269).

It is true that the contractual theory experienced a revival, "even recently," following the just argument against the "representation" of monarchy by divine right, a representation alien to reason. And yet the contractual theory continues to make the mistake of wanting to apply the "legal norms of private property" to State relations (w, IV, 504–5). Hegel clearly describes the polemic between the two opposing theories of contract, a polemic that fails to produce unambiguous norms to regulate the conflict: "Nowadays, to change the contract is [claim those nostalgic for antiquity] unilateral will: not right, but violence; that contract has been valid for a very long time. Not so, say those [who would change the constitution in the name of liberal-democratic contractualism]; it is not a contract, but violence: only *now* is it a matter of drawing up a contractual agreement; the venerable era [of existent legal institutions] does not bind us to the old contract." In the first case, the contract is married to the past, and violence is married to the present. In the second, the reverse is true. But now it has become clear that the desired political change is entrusted to a single "contract," one based upon "submission to the majority" (AL, § 75; v.Rph., II, 303–5). The supporters of Burkean contractualism object instead that, in order to be legitimate, a change to the political order presupposes the unanimous consent of the signatories who drew up the contract.

Hegel does not intend, with his anticontractual argument, to dissociate himself in any way from the objectives of constitutional reform. Rather, he wishes to highlight the absolute inadequacy of contractualism as a theoretical platform for a program of politico-constitutional reform. If anything, with a schematic but correct formula, one could say that liberal-democratic contractualism is criticized because it ultimately supports reactionism. In fact, Rousseau-style contractualism makes the mistake of siding with private right, a right dear to the theoreticians of the capital concept of the State: "However different these two points of view may be, they both have transferred the limits? of private property to a totally different and higher sphere of nature." With regard to contractualism, it is unable to effectively contest and eliminate the medieval view, still so slow to die, that holds rights and civic duties to be "the immediate private property of single individuals in opposition to the right of the sovereign or the State" (Rph., § 75 A). The anticontractual argument is hardly a concession to absolutism; indeed, Hegel sees an "enormous revolution" (v.Rph., IV, 253) or "enormous progress" (v.Rph., III, 270) in the transcendence of contractualism and the private conception of the State. The anticontractual argument that Hegel supports is so far from being a concession to the powers that be, or to the spirit of Restoration, that the celebration of the "revolution" is present not only in the lecture courses in 1822–23 and 1824–25, cited above, but also in the private notes pertaining to § 75: "Around it [that is, around the transcendence of the private and contractual conception of the State] revolves the passage from old times to new, the world revolution: not merely the noise in the streets, but the revolution that every State has completed" (v.Rph., II, 303).

The anticontractual argument by no means justifies absolutism or the rejection of individual rights, but a diverse theoretical basis for them: "The obligations of the citizen with regard to the State, like the obligations of the State with regard to the citizen, are not born of a contract," Hegel declares, still commenting upon § 75 (v.Rph., III, 269), which is dedicated to the anticontractual argument. This argument—still taken from the 1822–23 lecture course that we have been citing—is motivated by his celebration of "universal and inalienable goods" which cannot be the objects of a bill of sale or contract (v.Rph., III, 271). In writing on the Diet, Hegel so clearly targets the reactionaries that the argument merges with his questioning of the positive: the Diet "is obstinately fixed to a position which demands an ancient right because it was positive, and ratified by a contract." Old political relationships are considered untouchable because everything is "contractually defined"; the "fundamental law" is sacred and inviolable because it is nothing more than a "fundamental contract" (W, IV, 506 and 510).

In this way the Diet becomes part of the reactionary tradition. Not by chance, in criticizing the legislative will and fury of the French Revolution, Edmund Burke, as translated by Friedrich von Gentz, argues that every politico-constitutional change must be the subject of a "negotiation" (Negotiation in the German translation; compromise in the English original). It must come about by way of a "contract" and not through a unilateral violation of the contract (Vertrag in the German translation;

convention in the English original).[3] From this point of view, the contractual theory, far from being a synonym for reform and change, is synonymous instead with conservation and immobility.

Again, Burke is illuminating with this regard. Is it possible to modify the institutional shape of the State and go from, say, a monarchy to a republic? Yes, we are told by French revolutionaries who cite the will of the people, or at least the majority of them. "And if the majority of another group of people, say the English, want to bring about the same change, they have the same right." Once the view of the revolutionary movement in France (or in England) is configured as such, Burke counters with the following: "Yes, we say, the same right. That is, no one, neither the few nor the many, have the right to act according to their own absolute personal will in matters connected to duty, mandates, commitments and obligations. Once bound to the constitution of a nation, there is no power or force that can alter it without either braking the accord or achieving a consensus among the interested parties. That is the true nature of a *contract*."[4] The idea of the contract and its necessary respect is depicted as the ideological legitimation of the status quo; the "contract" is the seal of the inviolability of the existent socio-political order given that it "binds not only the living, but the living, the dead, and those yet to be born."[5]

We have considered Burke's argument against the French Revolution and the Diet of Württemberg's struggle to defend antiquity. But if we consider Prussia, we see that there too the reactionary opposition to antifeudal reforms during the Stein-Hardenberg era is also articulated in terms of contractualism. "Contracts" (*Contrakte*) can only be dissolved by way of contracts (*Contrakte*), while in the case of any doubt, the present situation, to the extent that it has been the product of centuries of experimentation, is preeminent.[6] To this contractualism that is blindly linked to the positive of an outdated "contract," Hegel contrasts the French Revolution and the "twenty-five years" of turmoil and political and constitutional renewal that follow it (*w*, IV, 506–7).

2. Contractualism and the Doctrine of Natural Law

It would be a serious mistake to interpret Hegel's argument against contractualism as support for unconditional power, against the abuse of which individuals would have no right. The rejection of contractualism is not the rejection of the doctrine of Natural Law per se. To the contrary. Are there inalienable and indefeasible rights? Hegel's response is not only unequivocal, but also solemn: "Those goods, or rather substantive characteristics?, which constitute my own distinct personality and the universal essence of my self-consciousness are therefore inalienable, and my right to them is imprescriptible. They include my personality in general, my universal freedom of will, ethical life, and religion" (*Rph.*, § 66).

A person's freedom is an inalienable and indefeasible right, and no positive legal order can annul it:

> The right to such inalienable things is imprescriptible, for the very act whereby I take possession of my personality and substantive essence and make myself a responsible being with moral and religious values and capable of holding rights removes these characteristics from that very externality which alone made them capable of becoming the possessions of someone else. When their externality is superseded in this way, the determination of time and all other reasons which can be derived from my previous consent or acceptance lose their validity. This return on my part into myself, whereby I make myself existent as Idea, as a person with rights and morality, supersedes the previous relationship and the wrong which I and the other party have done to my concept and reason in treating the infinite existence of the self-consciousness as something external, and in allowing it to be so treated (§ 66 A).

Any contract or positive right that violates the fundamental freedoms of a person is in fact an injustice (*Unrecht*), and therefore the "act . . . whereby I take possession of my personality" becomes the re-establishment of the right. Hegel has in mind first and foremost slavery, but one should not overlook the fact that to this he assimilates not only "serfdom," but also "disqualification from owning property, restrictions on freedom of ownership," and therefore the persistent relationships regarding feudal property as well as religious constraint and the rejection of the freedom of conscience that it entails (§ 66 A). To the extent that he is denied the status of legal subject, the slave has no legal obligations and may immediately retake his freedom, without compensating his master, regardless of the type of title that the latter produces.

The respect for Natural Law is explicit: "the fact that the State has begun to think is the work of the enlightening doctrine of Natural Law" that was able to question the positive laws consecrated in "old parchments" (*Ph. G.*, 917–18). In at least one case, the language of the *Encyclopedia* seems similar to that of the French revolutionaries, specifically when it supports the slave's struggle for the "eternal rights of man" (§ 433 z). Elsewhere Hegel speaks of the "inalienable rights of man" (*W*, I, 190), "eternal rights" (*Ph.G.*, 904), the "eternal rights of reason" (*W*, IV, 496). However, this language is the exception, not the rule. Hegel's criticism of the doctrine of Natural Law is this: a person's freedom, the rights of man, are inalienable, but this does not make them eternal since, rather than a sanctioned original contract, they are the result of a long and tumultuous historical process. The doctrine of Natural Law is criticized, then, because the state of nature to which it claims to refer is a condition without any room for right, except for that of violence. But there is another critical observation which has perhaps received less attention: not only are "natural rights" the product of historical process, but so is the subject of these natural rights. Yes, the very concept of man as man is the result of great historical turmoil: in ancient times, and in the modern colonies, slaves are not placed in the category of men; and as far as Rome goes, even women and children are considered on a par with slaves.[7]

Thus, it is necessary to consider natural rights not in terms of a mythical state of nature, but as nature itself, a characteristic that is unique to man (w, xx, 507). It is true that man is free per se, but he becomes free only after a long and complex historical process. "The fact that today man, as man, is considered the possessor of rights, should be highly valued, because it means that man is something superior to his *status.* For the Israelites, only Jews had rights; for the Greeks, only free Greeks; for the Romans, only Romans; and these had rights only to the extent of their status as Jews, Greeks, or Romans, not as men per se. Now, the source of rights is universal principles, and in this way the world embarked upon a new epoch." (v.Rph., III, 98)

Ilting reads in *Philosophy of Right,* and in Hegel's notorious preface, a concession to the doctrine of natural positivism and the consecration of the status quo, but in reality Hegel's doctrine of Natural Law is by no means in opposition to the theory of the rationality of the actual: "natural rights" are not in conflict with historical actuality; indeed, they are the highest and most mature form of its expression.

3. Liberal Anticontractualism

The claim that anticontractualism and antiliberal conservatism are identical is even more absurd for the fact that, in addition to ignoring the existence of conservative and reactionary contractualism, it overlooks the existence, in Hegel's day, of an anticontractual current that was clearly liberal. Bobbio has the merit of at least addressing the problem that emerges from this fact, a fact which is ignored entirely by Ilting. Yet, even Bobbio, though aware of the issue, essentially dodges it by maintaining that Hegel's rejection of contractualism does not have a "historical" foundation, but a "logico-systemic" one.[8] It seems that we are to consider Hegel's anticontractualism to be antiliberal not only because it declares the hypothesis of the original contract a fiction, but also because it contests the unjust extension of an institution of private right into the realm of public right.

At this point it is worth closely comparing Hegel's anticontractualism with that of one of his contemporaries, Jeremy Bentham, whose status as a liberal thinker is uncontested. In Bentham, the rejection of contractualism also implies a rejection of the doctrine of Natural Law. It is precisely what the French liberal Benjamin Constant criticizes in Bentham.[9] Indeed, commenting upon the French *Declaration of Rights* of 1791, after criticizing its underlying idea of "contract," Bentham continues: "No government, consequently no rights . . . no legal security, no legal liberty." Therefore, to speak of "*natural rights* is simple nonsense: natural and imprescriptible rights, rhetorical nonsense, nonsense upon stilts."[10] In Hegel, on the other hand, the rejection of the contractual theory does not question the existence of inalienable and imprescriptible rights, and this thanks to the distinction made between two meanings of the word "nature." Certainly no rights are based upon nature, which is the reign of generalized violence. Hence, it is deceptive to posit the idea of a "contract" guaranteeing rights that already exist in nature. This notion is true for both Hegel and Bentham, but Hegel isolates a second, different meaning of the term, nature, which comes to signify the substantive and inalienable essence of man.

Arguing against Bentham, who mocks the uninterrupted violation and alienation of rights he nevertheless considers "inalienable," Benjamin Constant states: "Claiming that these rights are inalienable and imprescriptible simply affirms that they must not be renounced. We are speaking of what must be, not what is."[11] This claim could easily have been made by Hegel, but with the qualification that this *must* is not the expression of a need of private conscience, a postulate thoroughly supported by the morality of a single individual, but rather the objective result of an irreversible historical process which can no longer go backwards. Precisely because the actual is rational in its strategic dimension, we know that freedom, non-slavery, has become a "natural condition" against which the "arbitrary will of the sovereign," in the final analysis, would fail (*w*, XVIII, 121–22). Freedom is indeed a natural, inalienable right, but of a historical nature, a "second nature." Freedom and inalienable rights do not precede progress, but are the result of it. The result of man's complex and contradictory struggle to build a world in which he can recognize and actualize himself. And it is in this "second nature" that man gains "awareness of his freedom and rational subjectivity" (*v.G.*, 256–57). The fact that now natural rights invoke not the first but the second nature does not mean that they have lost their inalienability, but the contrary. Only now do they have an actual foundation as opposed to a purely imaginary one.

Only with great difficulty could Hegel have subscribed to Bentham's theory. Bentham opposes his principle of utility to the theory of Natural

Law: "there is no right which ought not to be maintained so long as it is upon the whole advantageous to the society."[12] If Bentham proceeds from the refutation of the contract and the idea of a natural state to the refutation of the doctrine of Natural Law, Hegel instead proceeds to a more effective basis of Natural Law and manages to overcome the difficulties of the traditional theory which are clearly evident even in critiques à la Bentham. From this view, Hegel seems closer to a liberal like Constant than Bentham does. And it should be added that if Bentham's anticontractual argument (and argument against the doctrine of Natural Law) targets the French revolutionaries accused of "anarchic sophism," then Hegel's anticontractual argument (which serves to recast Natural Law) is opposed to the arguments of, above all, the feudal reactionaries.

4. The Celebration of Nature and the Ideology of Reactionism

There is another point to keep in mind. Since the time of Rousseau, the objective socio-political meaning of the return to the natural state has changed significantly: if before it consisted of an element in opposition to the existing order (one is reminded of the famous beginning of the *Social Contract*: "Man is born free, but everywhere he is in chains"), in the years of the Restoration the celebration of this mythical state of nature becomes reactionary, given that, with the French Revolution in mind, it aims at portraying the historical process as a relentless decline from a state of original perfection. As for Hegel, he maintains that, of the natural state, "nothing truer can be said except that *it must be abandoned*" (*Enc.*, § 502 A). Hegel expresses himself similarly with regard to Eden, where man is said to have lived before the original sin, just as in the natural state: "Heaven is a park where only animals can remain, not men" (*Ph. G.*, 728). In both cases the problem is that of "transcending mere nature" (*W*, XIX, 499). The ideology of the Restoration begins to project upon the concept of the state of nature, the notion of an Eden which is prior to original sin and, in the final analysis, prior to historical development. The confrontation with the theory of decline (a theory that condemned the modern world, the world that sprung forth from the Enlightenment and the French Revolution) required a redefinition of Natural Law. The recovery of freedom, in the tradition of Natural Law, goes hand in hand with criticism of the idea of the natural state and the original contract as being a mere step in the shift toward the social state.

In this, as in other cases, the fundamental flaw of any historiography that considers only pure and abstract ideas reveals its shortcomings by failing to recognize that formal continuity can hide radical differences in socio-political content, that is, radical differences in concrete historical meaning. Hegel does not begin his re-reading of the contractual theory, or that of Natural Law, in a vacuum. Indeed, he constantly confronts the problems of his day, and his main concern is not the solitary construction of his system, but first and foremost intervention in the actual debates and struggles of the time.

Why invoke a natural state when, beginning with the French Revolution, nature becomes the backbone of the reactionary argument? These are the years when, in contrast to the idea of equality (*égalité*), the theoretical notion of what will become "social Darwinism" is being developed. The "abstract" claim of legal equality—Burke declares—violates the "natural order of things," the "natural social order." In fact, it is the "most abominable of usurpations" which specifically threatens "nature's prerogative."[13] Already elements even more direct than "social Darwinism" can be traced back to an author whom Hegel harshly criticizes. *Philosophy of Right* strongly rejects Carl Ludwig von Haller's assertion that, by law of nature, "the larger displaces the smaller, the powerful the weak" and it is part of the "eternal and unalterable order . . . that the more powerful rules, must rule and always shall rule." In Haller, the reference to nature is, in Hegel's words, a celebration of the "contingent violence of nature" (§ 258 A).[14] Such ideas were becoming widespread in Germany; twenty years after the publication of *Philosophy of Right*, in fact, one of Hegel's disciples, Johann Rosenkranz, argues against the argument made in one of the most influential reactionary journals, according to which "nature" would confirm that "equality" contradicts "God's system." Taking Hegel's lectures to heart, Rosenkranz replies: "An abstract application of the concepts of nature to practical philosophy can only lead to the right of the most powerful."[15]

Given this new political and cultural framework, it is understandable that the central categories of the doctrine of Natural Law are already in crisis with Kant: if "everything which occurs or can occur is reduced to a mere mechanism of nature"—as we are told in *Perpetual Peace*—then it is clear that "the concept of right is an empty thought."[16] Those who drew upon nature were by now the reactionary theoreticians: awareness of this fact already begins with Kant, and becomes particularly evident with Hegel. Hegel himself, in fact, had witnessed the further developments in the political-ideological struggle against reactionism, and it is precisely during this struggle that Hegel is forced to face the weakness of the conception of history typical of the Natural Law tradition, a conception shared also by some of the protagonists of the French Revolution. Within this conception it was difficult, if not impossible, to formulate an idea of progress that would not consist in a re-establishment of natural rights, as this would have represented a step backwards. What was difficult was to formulate an idea of progress as a development, as the production of a new and higher social condition. "Nature shall reclaim her rights," Saint-Just proclaimed.[17] And the formula he used could easily be shared by a reactionary theoretician in the tradition of Haller, though with an obviously different and contrary meaning of "nature."

Rejecting the sort of *ante litteram* social Darwinism proffered by the reactionary ideologues in opposition to the revolutionary declaration of *égalité*, Hegel develops an idea of progress as the transcendence of immediacy, as history. Given this, society, and not nature, however conceived, "is the only condition in which right is realized" (*Enc.*, § 502 A). It is society, or, more precisely, the State. The State is the transcendence of the natural state, and the violence and oppression that accompanies it: "Only with the recognition that the idea of freedom is true to the extent that it is the State" can slavery be overcome and there be mutual recognition (*Rph.*, § 57 A). This paragraph reappears in one of the final passages from *Philosophy of Right:* the "struggle for recognition," that is, the struggle of the slave to be recognized as having rights, takes place before the "actual beginning of history" (§ 349 A). As long as there is slavery, as long as there is no mutual recognition, there is no actual State; the slaves of classical antiquity were excluded from the State. In practice, between owners and their slaves exists—Rousseau said—a state of war, which for Hegel coincides with the state of nature.

It is important to emphasize that even in the harshest inequalities of civil society, *Philosophy of Right* discerns a remnant of the natural state (§ 200 A). Yet, despite this idea of nature as the space of generalized violence and overall absence of right, and despite the distance with which he positions himself with regard to that doctrine of Natural Law upon which the claim of inalienable rights was based, Hegel neither eliminates nor limits the sphere of the subject's inalienable rights. To the contrary, he expands upon it. In civil society there is a remnant of the natural state evident in the persistent contrast between opulence on the one side, and the most miserable poverty on the other. There is this remnant, in short, because after all is said and done, the impoverished are not recognized as having the "right to life" (infra, ch. VII, 5–6).

Yes, nature is the kingdom of oppression, the dominion of the strongest, as counter-revolutionary literature and the theorists of *ante litteram* "Social Darwinism" argue. But to this, Hegel opposes the "freedom of the spirit" and the "equal dignity and independence" of men and citizens (*w*, XX, 22 7). *Freiheit, gleiche Würde* and *Selbständigkeit*: this seems to be another version of the motto of the French Revolution. But these rights (in addition to a new right that has begun to emerge, that is, the right to life) are said to be inalienable, inseparable from "nature" and from the concept of man to the extent that they are the result of a long period of historical suffering from which there is no turning back. Beginning with Hegel, inalienability does not derive from nature, but rather from history, from the universal history that developed and accumulated an undeniable common legacy for all men, for man as such.

From this point of view, not only can Hegel's criticism of Natural Law not be confused with reactionary criticism, but it is in direct opposition to it.[18] Let's consider more specifically the latter. Does the French Revolution proclaim the rights of man? Well, Burke rejects the concept of man itself: the English demand rights that are their due as Englishmen; but they want to hear nothing of "abstract principles" related to the "rights of man."[19] Joseph-Marie de Maistre's position is even more radical: the "theoretical error that set the French down the wrong path from the very first moment of the Revolution" is the concept of man: "In my life I have seen French, Italians, Russians, etc.; I know very well, thanks to Montesquieu, *that there may be Persians*; but as for man, I hold that I have never met one in my entire life. If he exists, it is without my knowledge."[20] For Hegel, on the other hand, it is precisely this development of the concept of man that marks decisive progress in the history of humanity. If Burke's primary targets in the argument are general principles, Hegel credits the Enlightenment for asserting those principles (*Ph. G.*, 919–20). And even if these principles must be purged of Jacobin "abstractness," they constitute an essential step in the march of freedom. It is nominalism that permits Burke to justify slavery in the colonies, or at least to condemn the notion of the "absolute equality of the human race" along with the "supposed rights of man." To condemn, that is, those who in the name of "abstract [and general] principles" demand the immediate abolition of slavery in accordance with the ideals of the French Revolution. Hegel sees in the persistence of slavery the unacceptable remnant of anthropological nominalism that remains opposed to the universal concept of man developed by universal history with the help of the French Revolution.[21]

If Burke scornfully equates "philosophers" with "republicans" and "Jacobins,"[22] Hegel on the other hand sees in philosophy the universality of reason. And he praises philosophy for developing the universal categories and concepts which develop from it. Burke's contractualism serves to oppose the doctrine of Natural Law. In contrast to the concept of a right to which individuals are entitled as men (and such pathos of Natural Law is present even in Hegel, though with a different theoretical foundation), Burke proposes a concept of right as acquired by specific subjects on the basis of a history, a tradition, a peculiar contract handed down "in the same way that we enjoy and hand down our property and our lives."[23]

Contract, inheritance, property: it is the confusion of private right with public right, the persistence of a capital conception of the State and right. Indeed, Hegel denounces this confusion and persistence, and rejects contractualism in order to recoup and re-establish the doctrine of Natural Law.

5. Hegel and Feudal, Proto-Bourgeois Contractualism

What importance can Hegel's argument against contractualism hold for us today? The issue is raised by Bobbio, who responds: "Today, the State is, more than the actuality of substantive will, the mediator and guarantor of contracts between large organizations, parties, unions, businesses." Hegel's anticontractual argument, in addition to being considered an expression of a dangerous and tendentially totalitarian organicism, is not actual: "When I say contract and negotiation, I mean precisely that institution of private right which Hegel characterized as resulting from the will of two contracting parties, the constitution of a will that is merely common and not universal."[24]

Indeed, to reject Hegel's theoretical and political acquisitions in his battle against reactionary contractualism, to insist on recouping and revisiting the latter, would mean questioning once again the results of the French Revolution and even modern historical development. In Hegel's view, the birth of the modern world is marked by the progressive separation of the realms of public and private right (and, in this sense, it is also marked by the progressive limitation of the application and validity of the institution of the contract).

This is how *Philosophy of Right* describes the way a feudal society operates: at the center of it is a sort of contract between the vassal and the feudal lord according to which one promises fealty, and the other promises protection and security (*Ph.G.*, 785–87). This stage of social development is marked by the lack of an organization of right which would maintain order and administer justice; there are no public offices. In the modern world, the first fundamental limitation in the realm of the contract is this: legal responsibilities and the protections afforded by the law have universal characteristics; they are not the object of an exchange between private parties.

Still, the private view of the State, or some of its characteristics, lingers well after the end of feudalism: "With regard to private right [the English] have remained far behind: property has a major, almost absolute importance. Just consider the majorats, who purchase for their children positions in the clergy and in the military. Even in elections, the electorate sell their votes" (*Ph.G.*, 935). Thus, public offices continue to be the object of a contract, a commercial exchange that is sometimes explicit and open, and sometimes under the table. The second part of Hegel's anticontractual argument targets the corruption of public offices (and of course the reference is to judicial offices). Though liberal authorities such as Montesquieu and Hume had defended this corruption, other authors, for example Voltaire, had condemned it as barbaric well before Hegel.[25]

The restriction upon how contracts may be applied brings us to the third part, the recognition of goods or "substantive characteristics" (the freedom of the person, freedom of conscience) which under no conditions should be subject to commercial exchange. The State must therefore guarantee these substantive characteristics, even against "freely" stipulated contracts. It is interesting to note that Hegel's condemnation of slavery goes hand in hand with his anticontractual argument. A "contract" that sanctions slavery would be "in and of itself null," and the slave would still have "the divine, imprescriptible right" to take back his freedom. Analogous points are made about any "contract" that alienates the individual's freedom of conscience or morality (Rph. III, 78). The contract already displays its limits at the level of private right. Once again, the anticontractual argument is embedded in the pathos of freedom, and in the defense of inalienable rights Hegel is much more radical than the liberal tradition that sometimes (as in the case of Locke) seems to justify slavery in the colonies with "contractual" arguments (infra, ch. XII, 3).

The alienation of such goods or characteristics can also come about indirectly. With the Germans, even murders "were expiated by pecuniary punishments" (Ph. G., 782–83). Yet, "if it is the case that the only punishment to follow the crime is financial compensation, then there is no more right per se. When a sum of money is distributed in compensation for the mutilation or murder of a man, then the man for whom the indemnity is paid is deprived of rights, he is merely an external thing" (v. Rph., IV, 282). Here too it is a question of exchange, a sort of contract in which a sum of money is paid to the victim (or family of the victim) which ensures the impunity and freedom of the offender.

At this point it is worth considering the problem in more general terms. There is a major difference between the contractualism recognized (and indirectly praised) by Bobbio as characteristic of the modern State and modern freedom, and the contractualism denounced by Hegel. Consider the fact that the parties of the pact, the *pactum subjectionis* which is characteristic of a feudal or proto-bourgeois contractualism, are barons or landowners on the one side, and the sovereign and the government on the other. The latter, far from acting as a mediator which Bobbio attributes to the modern State, is explicitly understood to be the agent, a body bound by original contract to act as the speaker, executor, and "board of directors" for the barons or landowners with whom the pact was made. This fact is made clear by the classics of liberalism: "The poor—we are told in what is almost the manifesto of liberalism, *De la liberté des anciens comparée à celle des modernes*—take care of their business on their own; the rich hire professionals." As for the government: "Yet, unless they are foolish, the rich who have hired professionals rigorously and closely examine their work to make sure they are doing their duty." Constant is close to a view of political power that, with the exception of the judgment of value, is not far from what is to be found in Marx, a view which sees the government, even when legitimized by the parliament, as a mere board of directors serving the bourgeoisie. Constant declares outright that wealth is, and must be, the arbiter of political power, for the very essence of modern freedom resides in the government's undisputed and indisputable dependency on landowners: "Credit did not have the same influence among the ancients; their governments were stronger than individuals, while in our time individuals are stronger than the political powers. Wealth is a power that is becoming more and more available, more readily applicable to all interests, and consequently more concrete and better obeyed."[26] John Locke had already declared that "the preservation of property," that is, existing and legitimate property relations, legitimate to the extent that they are natural, is "the end of government, and that for which men enter into society."[27] Therefore, if the government does not respect the contract which ties it to landowners and which in fact makes it an agent of their interests and will, then the other signatories are released from their contractual obligation, and regain their freedom.

This blackmail is also openly stated. For Constant, those without property are excluded from the original contract. If those without property were admitted to the "representative assemblies" then "the wisest laws" would become "suspect and therefore [be] disobeyed," while a monopoly of landowners in the representative assemblies "would have earned the popular consensus [that is, of landowners who identify with the contract's signatories] even for a somewhat flawed government."[28] At the base of the unquestionable right or fact that landowners may disobey when the threat of legislative intervention regarding property becomes even a vague possibility is once again the contractual theory. In fact, "political institutions are nothing but contracts," and "the nature of contracts is to establish fixed conditions," which evidently fail to consider, or rather exclude, those without property from even partial or limited participation in the "representative assemblies."[29] In this case, it is the original contract itself which authorizes the landowning signatories to disobey any unilateral modification or violation. In the final analysis, any political intervention in the realm of private property is to be considered illegal, even a change of the make up of the legislative assembly, since it could pave the way for overbearing intervention. Indeed, since "the necessary goal of those without property is to attain it, they will attempt to attain it by any means that they are given." And political rights too, "in the hands of the majority, would undoubtedly lead to an invasion of property."[30] Even when mediated by political bodies, the intervention of those without property in the realm of property is forever an act of violence, an "invasion:" in both cases it is considered an impermissible violation in an untouchable realm that is "contractually" guaranteed. To confirm all of this it may be worth remembering the debate that develops as the French Revolution becomes progressively more radical: after the very first interventions with regard to bourgeois property, the moderates protest that the "social contract" has been violated, and thus declare that landowners are free to act as they please.[31]

6. Contractualism and the Modern State

Proto-bourgeois contractualism legitimizes the landowners' political monopoly and consecrates the relegation of political powers to the role of defending property interests. But if this is true, proto-bourgeois contractualism has little or nothing in common with contemporary "contractualism" (as exemplified by Bobbio), within which the State tries to pass itself off as the mediator between the various classes, that is, between diverse and contending social subjects. The extent to which this attempt is successful is debatable, but it nonetheless presupposes that the State, at least minimally, transcends these diverse and opposing interests. From this point of view, at least with regard to its stated ambitions, the modern bourgeois State is much closer to Hegel's theory than to proto-bourgeois contractualism. Or better, feudal or proto-bourgeois contractualism continues to reveal itself in acts of force (or in the threat of such acts) by the privileged classes against changes to the right to property or to the relationships between property and production. In short, they are reactions to changes considered despotic or illiberal.

Yes, contemporary parliamentary democracy is sewn together by negotiations and collective bargaining, but one should not confuse two very heterogeneous definitions of contract. Examining the contradictions between North and South which will eventually lead to the American Civil War, Tocqueville provides an enlightening example of "contractualism" in the contemporary world. The future secessionists define their position on Union laws which they consider unacceptable in this way: "The constitution is a contract between sovereign states. So, every time that a contract is made between parties who do not recognize a common mediator, each party holds the right to judge for itself the extent of its obligations."[32] Therefore, the "contract" implies that each party has a veto. In this sense, the law is null and void to the extent that, even after its proclamation, it requires the approval of parties who have the right to determine its conformity to the said contract. Thus, the contracting parties are, when all is said and done, sovereign, or at least claim substantive sovereignty: just as it was in the Middle Ages, just as appears in the classic proto-liberal texts, and just as it appeared in the United States at the time of the South's secession. Hegel argues against this contractualism, as does Tocqueville, who observes with dismay the collapse of the Union's powers caused by the Southern contractual-secessionists.

Yet, Bobbio speaks of modern contractualism in the sense that the State, before intervening legislatively, attempts to take into consideration the interests of the various parties involved, pressuring them to negotiate. In essence, it takes on an active role as mediator. Once a law has been issued, however, it does not depend upon the systematic approval of the parties involved. The major distinction of this second type of contractualism emerges in Bobbio's text: the State is "the guarantor and arbiter of the negotiations" between diverse political and social subjects. Thus, more than just one of the parties negotiating, the State is the guarantor *super partes* of agreements between parties. And there is more. With regard to how the "contract" should work at the political-parliamentary level, Bobbio writes: "A party which does not have enough votes to send representatives to parliament is not authorized to take part in the negotiations and the social contract, and so it has no contractual power."[33] The State is not only guarantor *super partes*, but it determines from time to time which parties will be allowed to negotiate.

It should also be added that no argument against this second type of contractualism is present in Hegel; in fact, Hegel requires that the various corporations, associations and local communities be directly represented in the Lower House in order to express their actual interests so as to allow the government to proceed to an authentic and efficient mediation (*Rph.*, s 308). Is the extension of the realm of negotiation and mediation proof of the falsity of Hegel's anticontractual argument? Today's democratic-parliamentary State is not, and can no longer be, a mere gathering of vigilantes on the private property theorized by proto-liberals; the State is not the same "night-watchman" of the landowners' goods that is condemned by the Hegelian scholar, Ferdinand Lassalle.[34] This sort of contractualism fell into crisis the moment that, following bitter and complex struggles, the property-less imposed upon the State a series of additional duties that directly intervened in the socio-economic realm and were therefore considered by property-owners to be an illicit extension of the State's influence beyond defined contractual limits. It is out of this situation that the need for constant, rigorous mediation between social parties is born.

For Hegel, the universal is actualized precisely in the work of mediation. The State is an ethical community to the extent that it is concerned not only with the security of property, but also, as we will see, with guaranteeing the maintenance of individual "well-being," the "right to work," and even the "right to life." The State is ethical to the extent that it recognizes the inalienable rights of every citizen, rights which are indisputable and removed from the realm of contracts. With Hegel, inalienable rights tend to take on a material content. The condition of the poor is likened to that of the "slave," and it demands public intervention which will concretely guarantee the inalienable right to freedom. Such an intervention necessarily implies a restriction on the market and on freedom of contract. Every time the State has prohibited or regulated the use of child-labor (an intervention that Hegel openly urges) by reducing the number of hours of work, etc., the most reactionary capitalists have always cried out that it violated the freedom of the contract: just consider, in the pages of *Das Kapital,* the history of the struggle to limit the work-day to ten hours. As for Prussia, in Hegel's day, or even immediately after his death, employers vehemently condemned "Hegelians" and "socialists" who, lacking the "practical liberal spirit," are guilty of appealing to the State for "artificial" interventions which would limit the use of women and children in the factories and "organize labor."[35]

In this defense of "freedom" of contract, employers are often supported by the absolute monarchy. In 1832, voices rose in protest against the hated *Trucksystem* by which extremely exploited workers were paid not with money, but with goods produced by the factory in which they worked. Friedrich Wilhelm III silenced those voices, arguing that the State did not have the right to intervene in a "relationship of private right" and arbitrarily crush or limit "civil liberty."[36] An absolute monarch who decisively intervenes on behalf of liberal employers so as to defend the freedom of contract from the dangerous advances of the State: now this is a paradox for modern liberals whose condemnation of nationalization is so far removed from history that they forget that even Adam Smith considered State intervention with regard to the abominable *Trucksystem* "completely just and equitable," while Friedrich Wilhelm III thoroughly favored the inviolability of the contract.[37] Had he known, the King might have cited Locke, who finds nothing to object to in a specific contract, apparently freely drawn-up, according to which "the clothier, not having ready money to pay [his workman], furnishes [him] with the necessaries of life, and so trucks commodities for work, which, such as they are, good or bad, the workman must take at his master's rate, or sit still and starve."[38]

Bobbio finds additional evidence of the expanding role of the contract in the solemn, periodic renewal of collective bargaining contracts, often drawn up after a bitter and prolonged struggle. But it is necessary to understand just what exactly is new here. Obviously, not the contract as an institution; instead, what is new is its collective character. It presupposes the existence of organized unions, which for a whole historical era had been forbidden under the pretext that they violated the individual's freedom to sell his labor on the market; they violated, that is, the individual's autonomy with regard to the contract. This was particularly intolerable to employers when strikers would attempt to block "scabs" from working, thereby negating or restricting the labor force from free bargaining. Thus, there is no continuous line between old and new contractualism, despite Bobbio's attempt to defend the idea by dismissing the Hegelian-Marxist tradition of statism as organicistic and totalitarian. Unions have long been persecuted not in the name of State "organicism," but in the name of liberal individualism.[39]

The truth is that collective agreements have a history that Bobbio would like to eliminate: first of all, Marx and the socialist workers' movement, but even to a certain extent Hegel, who supports the "guilds," ascribing to them functions not very different from those of the emerging union movement. In any case, Hegel's argument is clearly in opposition to that of the supporters of liberal individualism who consider trade unions to be a violation of the "so-called natural right" of individuals to make use of their labor (Rph., § 254), that is, to contract the sale of it without any outside interference, merely making use of their freedom. This is a period in which, according to Marx, the ideologues of capital like Bentham deny the very real oppression and exploitation inflicted upon the working classes. Instead, they make reference to the freedom of the contract negotiated between individual workers and individual employers.[40] Authors for whom misery was understood and felt to be a social issue did not dwell on the sacred and inviolable nature of the contract. And today, the contracts between individuals which were praised by proto-liberal theorists no longer exist: contractual "freedom" is limited by government legislation on one side, and by workers' unions on the other (in addition to the associations of employers, which have always existed). This is the reality of contemporary contractualism; and it could not be understood without Hegel and his anticontractual polemic, without tracing the path that leads from Hegel to Marx.

IV

Conservative or Liberal? A False Dilemma

1. Bobbio's Dilemma

We have discussed the issue of contractualism, but we now need to consider the question more broadly: Is Hegel liberal or not? The question implies that Hegel may be a philosopher of the Restoration, or at least a conservative.

At this point, any answer is incorrect, because the formulation of the question is already invalid. To this end, it may be helpful to follow Bobbio's lead: "Hegel is not a reactionary, but neither is he—when he writes *Philosophy of Right*—a liberal: he is plainly and simply a conservative, to the extent that he favors the State more than the individual, authority more than freedom, the omnipotence of law more than the irresistibility of individual rights; moreover, he favors the cohesion of the whole over the independence of its parts, and obedience over resistance, the top of the pyramid (the monarch) over the base (the people)."[1]

Here, Bobbio very clearly and concisely outlines many of the objections leveled at Hegel by modern liberals, and it is worth noting that this conceptual framework is often not even questioned by those determined to demonstrate liberal elements in the philosopher. Generally, the debate consists of a continuous series of juxtaposed citations, and in the midst of this exchange what is most essential is lost from view: Hegel is subjected to questions which he himself had already considered poor and misleading due to their imprecision and formal abstractness. An excellent example of this is the opposition provided by Bobbio in demonstration of Hegel's "conservatism:" Authority or freedom? Bobbio is searching for a definitive answer to an impossible alternative in Hegel, but Hegel himself had already made a distinction between formal freedom and actual freedom (about which more will be said below). Hegel had already specified that the term "freedom" may also provide an ideological cover for the pursuit of "private interests," interests that are myopic and regressive. Obviously, Hegel's approach may be considered unacceptable, but it cannot simply be ignored so that we may impose upon him a question that he himself had already considered poorly formulated.

In order to comprehend just how much more sophisticated Hegel's approach is in comparison to Bobbio's, it is worth examining in detail the dilemmas and alternatives that are obstinately listed by the latter, assessing first and foremost their general historical-political validity before considering the responses that emerge from Hegel's text.

2. Authority and Freedom

Hegel should be considered conservative rather than liberal because he "favors . . . authority more than freedom."

This abstract statement completely ignores any historical-political context, and presents the dilemma as a sort of tautology. This tautology ends up surreptitiously assuming an apologetic value, since it judges liberalism exclusively on the basis of its inherent conscience, that is, on the basis of the excellent intentions which its representatives claim to have. Liberalism is freedom's will; therefore, to oppose liberalism or to be suspicious of it necessarily implies being either an enemy of freedom, or a timid supporter of it. At best, Hegel may be considered a conservative. Naturally, in terms of the polemic between Hegel and his critics we know no more than before, except that liberalism, or laissez-faire, has come to be considered, without any proof whatsoever, to be the latest fashion in political wisdom, the supreme court before which the authoritarian "statism" of yesterday and today is called on to justify itself.

The reading suggested by Bobbio and liberal historiographers is inadequate and useless for helping us to understand the great debates that accompany the development of modern thought. In France, as is well-known, Voltaire fiercely opposes reactionary parliaments, and in the clash between these parliaments and absolute monarchy he decisively sides with the latter, which at least is expected to suppress the "shameful venality of judicial offices" and the most hated characteristics of aristocratic privilege.[2] Montesquieu, instead, defends not only the corruption of these offices, but also the aristocratic parliaments, one of the intermediate bodies essential to preventing despotism and limiting central power.[3] Should we now conclude that Montesquieu is a liberal and Voltaire a conservative or illiberal? Certainly, this is the model more or less suggested by Tocqueville, who vehemently criticizes Voltaire. Voltaire is condemned as an example of ignorance (on the part of the French as well as the representatives of the Enlightenment) of the spirit of freedom. From Tocqueville's argument emerges the key to another reading, one much more persuasive: Voltaire's position against that institution of the *ancien régime*, the parliaments, is an expression of the ruinous egalitarian and antiaristocratic tendency that characterizes French politics, which is inclined, throughout its development (from absolute monarchy to the rise of socialism), to sacrifice freedom for the sake of equality.[4] Even in this dubious opposition one can catch a glimpse of the real socio-political significance of the contradiction which places Montesquieu against Voltaire: what is at play is one's attitude to the aristocracy. Not by chance, praise for the role of the parliaments is present in Henri de Boulainvilliers, who certainly could be—and sometimes is—considered a "liberal," even a forerunner of parliamentarianism, for his opposition to absolute monarchy and the antifeudal role it plays.[5] But with regard to Boulainvilliers, that champion of the aristocracy's privileges who defends the superiority of the victorious noble "race" in contrast to the defeated and cowardly plebeian "race:" Has he really made a greater contribution to the true cause of freedom than that made by the implacable enemy of aristocratic parliaments (and the corruption of public offices), the champion of freedom of conscience and the struggle against intolerance? Is it possible to understand the genesis of the modern individual and modern individual freedom without considering Voltaire's contribution as well as his struggle against the aristocratic privileges which Boulainvilliers (and Montesquieu) defend *even* against absolute monarchy?

For now, let us return to the author who concerns us more directly. Was freedom less important to Hegel than to his (more or less) liberal critics and opponents? We will begin by examining some specific questions. "Civil society has the right and the duty to oblige parents to send their children to school"; it is both just and necessary that there be "laws according to which, at a certain age, children must be sent to school" (*v.Rph.*, IV, 602–3). The argument in favor of compulsory education certainly questioned one of the traditional "freedoms" of parents. From this moment on parents are subjected to state and social regulation, when previously there had been none. On the other hand, even Bobbio would perhaps agree that this discussion would also have to include the actual freedom of children, who are now entitled to the "right" of an education, as explicitly highlighted by Hegel. And compulsory education immediately calls to mind child labor in the factories, and the incipient State intervention aimed at regulating or prohibiting it. An intervention supported by Hegel: "small children are forced to work," but "the State is responsible for protecting children"

(*Rph.i,* § 85 A). This government intervention provoked outrage in entrepreneurs who, more than ever, extolled the "practical spirit of liberals" as opposed to "Hegelian and socialist theories."

Certainly, one could say that Wilhelm von Humboldt, a firm supporter of "State limits" even in the area of education, and the great capitalist David Hansemann, a relentless enemy of statism with regard to education, are more liberal or laissez-faire than Hegel, who is decidedly opposed to the "free will" of parents and, given his position on child labor, to the free will of capitalists as well. In this sense, Benjamin Constant is also more "liberal" than Hegel. Indeed, while Constant is convinced that "public education is healthy, especially in free countries," he is nonetheless resolutely opposed to compulsory education, or, to use his words, to every form of "restriction" which would violate the "rights of individuals," including "those of fathers over their children." True, poverty is what drives families to remove their children from school and send them precociously off to work, and yet it is necessary to refrain from coercion, and wait for this poverty to disappear; while Constant objects to the introduction of compulsory education, he does not even consider the possibility of state intervention against the scourge that is child labor.[6] So there is no problem with calling this "liberalism," but it should be added that this sort of "liberalism" is also evident in the work of ideologues of the Restoration, though in much more exalted terms to be sure. Among them, Friedrich von Gentz, during the course of his polemic against the French Revolution, argues against plans in which "children [from a certain age onward] would be wrenched from the parents" and sent off to school. This, without considering that such an oppressive measure would be useless anyway given the fact that the impoverished classes could not afford to not have their children work. Even for Gentz, political intervention in this realm is unthinkable.[7]

Hegel appears to be less liberal, less laissez-faire, than Humboldt, Hansemann, and Constant (not to mention Gentz), but can one translate this claim into another, according to which Hegel, unlike Humboldt, Hansemann, and Constant, favors "authority" over "freedom"? It makes no logical sense to equate the two claims: the latter claim is easily overturned given that Hegel favored, unlike his liberal critics, less "authority" for parents and capitalists. Among the "rights of individuals" Constant includes "those of fathers over their children." Kant, closer to the liberal tradition than Hegel, goes so far as to argue for a "right of parents over their children as part of their own house," the right of parents to recover their fugitive children "as though they were things," or as though they were "pets who have run away."[8] Hegel condemns Kant for reducing children to "things" and argues that Kant is tainted by the remains of a tradition according to which, in ancient Rome, children were considered the slaves of the *paterfamilias* (*Rph.I*, § 85 A). Instead, the child, given that "he must be a member of civil society, has rights and claims within it, just like those he had within the family" (*v.Rph.*, III, 700). But concrete recognition of these rights demands intervention or public regulation. By declaring his support for compulsory education as well as for the prohibition or limitation of child labor, Hegel might be considered illiberal. Yet, contrary to what Bobbio maintains, illiberal cannot be considered to be synonymous with conservative. Indeed, history has proven Hegel right to the extent that mature liberalism, or at least that which is most similar to what we have today, has itself supported compulsory education: "The State . . . is bound to maintain a vigilant control over the exercise of any power which it allows him [each individual] to possess over others." John Stuart Mill, of whom we are speaking, constantly refers to Humboldt, but the truth is that his approach calls to mind Hegel, as is evident even in the controversy about the "mistaken notion of freedom" held by parents who oppose compulsory education, "notions" which call to mind the "formal freedom" criticized by Hegel.[9]

In sum, if today someone were to apply the catchwords of liberals like Humboldt, Hansemann, and Constant in order to defend a parent's "freedom" not to send their children to school, or to defend the "freedom" of capitalists to put children of a very tender age to work in their factories, that person would be considered the most despicable of reactionaries. This condemnation would probably even be shared by Bobbio, though he would have to rely upon a statist's approach of the sort that he rejects in Hegel.

In his consideration of the themes of "freedom" and "authority," the liberal John Stuart Mill encourages us to keep in mind not only the relationships between individuals and the State, but also those among individuals themselves. Thus, before condemning Hegel in the name of liberalism, and before praising Hegel's liberal critics, we should also consider the fact that Locke recognizes the absolute power—a power not limited by the State in any way—of plantation owners in the West Indies and slave owners in Carolina (infra, ch. XII, 3). Alternatively, he calls upon the employer to exercise a sort of parental authority over servants, who in fact belong to the family and are thus subject to the "normal discipline" in force therein.[10]

However, even if we ignore the relationships between social classes (in which case the "freedom" or "authority" of one may conflict with the "freedom" or "authority" of others), even if we consider only the relationship between the individual and the State, ignoring social context and concrete political aspects, there is no reason to consider the liberalism's self-description to be a series of obvious statements. C. B. Macpherson, a renowned scholar, has written that "there was no question in Locke's mind of treating the unemployed as fellow free members of the political community. There was equally no doubt that they were *fully subject to the State.*"[11] And, indeed, with regard to those "idle vagabonds," Locke calls for firm military discipline, which in extreme cases may even mean the death penalty (infra, ch. XII, 3).

It is not our intention to enter into the debate about Locke, even though the text referred to is sufficiently clear. The objection could be made that quite a few years separate Locke from Hegel, and that it therefore makes no sense to mechanically compare the two. But it is precisely the validity of this objection that casts doubt upon Bobbio's approach (and not only Bobbio's), an approach which attempts to measure, independent of concrete socio-political aspects, the degree of "freedom" and "authority" present in different authors. On the other hand, it might be interesting to compare Hegel with his liberal critics in Germany. Hegel insists upon the state or public aspect of the solution to the social question, and yet, faced with relentless overproduction and the uselessness of its "remedies," he advises allowing for begging (§ 245 A). The position of his liberal critics is quite the opposite: in their opinion, in order to avert "the source" of every attack against the right to property, beggars and those who cannot support themselves should be confined to "work-houses" for an indefinite period, subjected to harsh and even ruthless discipline. It is worth noting that the confinement could be determined by the magistracy, or might even be "an autonomous measure taken by police authorities." Not only is Hegel's position less "authoritarian" and more respectful of individual freedom than that of his liberal critics, but it should be added that those same liberal critics do not consider the repression of the unemployed and beggars to be contradictory to their efforts to limit the actions of the State: precisely because the State is not responsible for resolving matters of a supposedly social nature, and because every individual is considered responsible for himself, regardless of class; it makes sense for the State to repel "the source" of any violent attack on the right to property by idle and debauched individuals who are by nature unfit for work or an orderly life.[12] Police repression is the result of a "Minimal State" and of the emphasis on the central role of the individual.

It is a dynamic evident even in the work of today's neo-liberal theorists. Take, for example, Robert Nozick: even amidst gross inequality, as long as proprietors can show a "valid title" for their possessions, even the most desperate hunger remains a private matter between those that suffer from it and any possible benefactors who are moved, by moral or religious scruples, to show pity upon them. It is not to be considered a social issue. Not only this, but a State that takes legislative action in an attempt to mitigate the worst inequalities is no longer "minimal," but rather unjust and tyrannical.[13] Bobbio himself holds that the "Minimal State" can be quite strong.[14]

Actually, in this case, it is very strong given that it views (and it cannot fail to view) protests against poverty and inequality to be mere questions of public order. This becomes even clearer in the work of a neo-liberal like Hayek: the only purpose of political institutions is to "preserve public order and the law"; it is absurd to speak of "social justice" (that is, to consider specific socio-economic relationships to be unjust), whereas instead "the administrative justice of the courts is extremely important."[15] And justice is nothing more than the defense of property because—Hayek tells us, citing Locke—"where there is no property there is no injustice."[16]

Minimal State is not synonymous with weak State: this is the case according to both liberal thought and reactionary thought. Schelling is among those philosophers who most insist on limiting the State, considering it nothing more than a "means" for guaranteeing the "individual" space so that he may pursue loftier, more noble endeavors.[17] But this does not prevent Schelling from calling for strong-arm tactics and even "dictatorship" when it is necessary to repress the Revolution of 1848. Nor does it prevent him from welcoming the *coup d'état* of Louis Napoleon in France.[18] Similar points could be made about Schopenhauer, who, as far as the State is concerned, is no more emphatic than Schelling, and even makes cutting remarks against Hegel's philistine "apotheosis" of the State (infra, ch. XI, 2, 3, and 5); nonetheless, he cannot conceal his pleasure at having contributed to the suppression of a revolution among whose instigators were more than just a few Hegelians.[19] And in the very same period in which socialist statism preaches "as little State as possible,"[20] Nietzsche calls for struggle against "that international hydra" (the bloody repression of the Paris Commune had just taken place) and clearly believes in crushing the (socialist and statist!) Working Men's Association.[21]

In short, the theory of the Minimal State, in complete disregard of political community, the community of *citoyens*, ends up taking repression and organized violence to an extreme in order to maintain existing property relationships. And this is why Marx so harshly criticizes Hegel for having ignored and concealed this fact by idealizing the State. What is certain is that, for both Marx and Hegel, the theorists of the Minimal State who celebrate the "free" expansion of a civil society beyond any and all political interventions are those who are claiming that the State be simply the strong-arm of the privileged classes.

3. State and Individual

According to Bobbio, Hegel must be considered a "conservative" rather than a "liberal" because he "favors the State more than the individual."

Yes, according to Hegel's philosophy of history, the individual's subordination to a judicial organization is essential to the formation of the modern State: for ancient Germans there was no proper "State"; "the isolated individual (*Individuum*) was for them the main thing." But in no way does this apparent centrality of the individual coincide with the defense and guarantee of actual rights; in fact, since there is no objectively defined judicial organization, even in the case of a horrible crime, "if an individual is at fault, he is not to be punished by the State, but rather must settle with the victim" by paying an indemnity. The end result is that in reality, for the Germans, "an individual has no value" (*Ph. G.*, 783–84). The centrality of the individual becomes its opposite: if the formation of the modern State means subjecting the individual to an objective legal mandate, at the same time it affirms and defends the individual's actual value: a crime which consists in the death or grave injury of an individual can no longer be expiated by means of an exchange of money, nor by an agreement between individuals.

But in Bobbio's model, antistatism seems synonymous with liberalism. In reality, the argument against statism is widespread among the ideologues of the Restoration, those who, like Baader, see in the "pantheism of the State" remnants of the revolutionary and Napoleonic era. We can even define these ideologues as "liberals," as they often defined themselves. (Didn't F. R. de Lamennais, in 1831, declare Pope Gregory VII to be the "great patriarch of European liberalism" for having opposed—even if only in the name of theocracy—oppression, unlawful appropriation, and the expansion of political power?)[22] At this point it becomes quite clear just how empty the category of "liberalism" is once it is removed from concrete socio-political aspects and historical context. Today's liberal critics of Hegel would find themselves hard-pressed to state definitively whether or not they are "liberals" in the completely vague and imprecise sense of the word. Before deciding, they would surely feel the need to make distinctions and clarifications, and end up ultimately confirming, involuntarily but objectively, the superiority of Hegel's approach, especially his close attention to the concrete historical realization of "freedom" and "liberalism."Likewise, it is necessary to have a clear understanding of "statism." It is true that the liberal tradition tends to minimize the role of the State, to a certain extent it even tends to negate it completely, relegating it to the status of an institution of private right, like a joint stock company. This is the direction in which Locke is headed, according to the common interpretation,[23] and the comparison is explicit in Burke: "In this partnership all men have equal rights, but not to equal things. He that has but five shillings in the partnership has as good a right to it as he that has five hundred pounds has to his larger proportion. But he has not a right to an equal dividend in the product of the joint stock."[24] The idea of the State as a joint stock company is shared by liberals, conservatives, and even reactionaries. It is found in the work of Justus Möser, who, inspired by liberal, mercantile England, and the East India Company, explicitly states that serfdom is perfectly normal. The serf is a man just like any other, except that he is without stock and has neither the advantages nor the responsibilities of a full citizen.[25]

In a State that is like a joint stock company the responsibilities of the shareholders are strictly limited, and there is no room for the discussion of social issues. That is, there is no problem with the side-by-side existence of dire poverty and shameless wealth; the distribution of dividends is equitable. Too bad for those who failed to invest or did not invest enough. With respect to this model, Hegel's vision of the State is much broader. The State has positive responsibilities (though perhaps not well-defined) in the social sphere, including the responsibility for guaranteeing everyone the "right to life." Does this ambitious vision entail the transfiguration and consecration of the intangibility of political authority? Is the "Minimal State" synonymous with a critical view of the State and authority? Hardly, and Bobbio's mistake is to again presuppose, when speaking about Hegel, the equivalence of propositions with completely different meanings. Hegel notes critically that in England political power continues to remain firmly "in the hands of that class" which is tied to the "current system of property" (B.schr., 480). Given the increasing importance of "currency trading" and "banks," States find themselves "dependent upon this currency trade, which is in and of itself independent" (v.Rph., IV, 520–21). The State acts as a vehicle for the accumulation of private wealth: "Wealth is accumulated by factory owners. When one works solely for the State, the accumulation of wealth becomes all the more significant thanks to the business affairs of suppliers and industrial entrepreneurs" (Rph.III, 193–94). Requiring the State to intervene in socio-economic matters (with the goal of creating an ethical community) does not in any way entail a sacred transfiguration of the existent State. On the contrary, this requirement leads one to conclude that, when the class struggle and inequality become too bitter and too rigid, as they did between the patricians and the plebeians in ancient Rome, then the State becomes an "abstraction" and actuality is defined solely by "antitheses" (*rph. III*, 288).

Similar considerations can be made for an author who is removed from the liberal tradition. Rousseau, who takes social issues to heart, calls for the imposition of high taxes on wealth and luxuries, and for an expansion of the role of political power, an expansion that Montesquieu would have found intolerable given that he already considered the imposition of property taxes to be akin to despotism (infra, ch. VIII, 5). At the same time, Rousseau does not hesitate to declare that "public authority" is completely controlled by the "rich."[26] On the one hand, considering poverty to be a social issue calls for decisive public intervention, without being hindered by the right to property; on the other hand, it leads one to condemn the subordination of political power to property. This is true, though in different ways, for Rousseau as well as for Hegel (and Marx). The opposite is true in the liberal tradition. The State should be "minimal" because it must not interfere with existing property relations, yet, with regard to the rest, political authority is never questioned. Even when Constant reveals the State's organic dependency upon wealth, he does not do so to denounce it, but rather to confirm its correct functioning as a joint stock company, within which the government is a sort of managing director who works on behalf of shareholders.

Thus, as far as the relationship between political power and wealth goes, Rousseau, Hegel, and Marx are much more critical of the State than members of the liberal tradition. From this point of view, the accusation that Hegel is a "statist" can easily be overturned.

It is the destiny of abstract categories to come to mean different things. The line from Rousseau to Hegel to Marx can be described and condemned as an expression of "statism" or "organicism."[27] And certainly the pathos of the community of *citoyens* is absent from the liberal tradition. How could it be otherwise when Constant equates the propertyless to foreign residents without political rights?[28] Organicism and the pathos of community cannot coexist because in reality there is no community; landowners and the propertyless cannot even be placed in a single category, as citizens.

Let us consider another of Constant's metaphors for defining the propertyless: those who are forced to work in order to live can be compared to "youngsters" who are "eternally dependent."[29] Similarly, we already mentioned that Locke situates the servant in the owner's family, subject to the authority of the *paterfamilias*. From this perspective it is the liberal tradition that is organicistic, and the reversal of positions is easy to understand: the refusal to include citizens with and without property within a single community explains why the latter must necessarily obey rules, about which they have no say, by resorting to the image of the family. That is, a reality much more organicistic than the political community.[30]

Statism and organicism are clearly the opposite of individualism. It is an opposition that surreptitiously equates individualism with freedom, while casually eliminating any reference to the harsh repression of workers' "coalitions" (which were guilty of violating the employment contracts between "individuals"). Even individualism can be brutal; indeed, in its name one did not hesitate to imprison workers stubbornly and organically tied to the emerging unions. In any case, individualism suffers no better fate than previous categories. There is at least one moment in which the sides seem to switch in the sense that it is Hegel who accuses the liberals of losing sight of the individual, or of wanting to sacrifice him to universalism. It is liberalism or laissez-faire which takes the "undisturbed security of persons and property" to an extreme. In this way, it aims for the universal of the correct functioning of the legal system, yet loses sight of the "welfare of individuals," of "particular welfare" (Rph., s 230). "It is now a matter of having the individual considered, as a person, in his uniqueness as well" (Rph.III, 188). Laissez-faire theoreticians are opposed to political intervention in the economic sphere. They argue that, if left alone, the economy finds a point of equilibrium on its own, overcoming momentary crises and disturbances. Hegel's response is the following: "We are told that, in general, equilibrium is always re-established; that is correct. But here we are dealing with the particular no less than with the general; the issue must therefore be resolved not only in general, but it is the individuals in their uniqueness that constitute an end and have rights" (v.Rph., III, 699). Adam Smith contrasts "the statesman who should attempt to direct private people" to the "invisible hand" of providence that ends up eventually producing harmony.[31] It may be that the claim in *Philosophy of Right*, that "God does not provide [solely] for men in general; He provides for single individuals as well," is an answer to this vision. Moreover: "The aim is the particular individual as such; it is necessary to provide for single individuals, and no one should trust a principle according to which 'things will adjust, they will take care of themselves'" (v.Rph., III, 699).

As we can see, in this case it is Hegel who insists upon the centrality of the individual, in contrast to the liberal tradition. To understand this paradox one must keep in mind that according to the liberal school of thought the individual is the proprietor who is opposed to political intervention in his inviolable private sphere. Hegel, on the other hand, has in mind the plebeian, or potential plebeian, who calls for political intervention in the economic sphere in order to guarantee his sustenance. For the former, what is defended is the uniqueness of the bourgeoisie, or of the nobility and the bourgeoisie; for the latter, it is the uniqueness of the plebeian, or potential plebeian. And the abstract universal attacked by the former is the State, the political force that could become an instrument of the propertyless; by the latter, it is the law of the market that sanctions existing property relations.

That Hegel's argument against what we might call the "anti-individualistic" aspect of liberalism is grounded in actuality can be confirmed by the position of, for example, Hayek. If, on the one hand, Hayek relentlessly criticizes statism, that oppressor of individuals' (proprietors') freedom, on the other, he considers pleas for social justice by the disadvantaged as expressions of an unjust "revolt" against "abstract requirements," a "tribal" revolt against the "Western world." The latter is characterized by the gradual emergence of a universal application of rules of just conduct," rules to which the impoverished have no right to object.[32]

Instead, Hegel openly states that he begins, in the development of his system, with the "freedom of individuals" (v.Rph., IV, 617). Once again, equating liberalism with the affirmation of the individual's centrality means taking as a point of departure the self-serving characterization of that political movement. We have seen how the two parts can be easily overturned. Pierre-Joseph Proudhon provides an ironic and paradoxical, though significant, example of this. It is the liberals who argue that T. R. Malthus' theory should become a sort of State doctrine, that it should be taught as an incontrovertible truth that everyone must be aware of, from childhood on. It is the liberal school that proposes this indoctrination. "[The liberal school of thought] which in every circumstance and in every place preaches *let be, let go*, and which criticizes socialists for replacing Natural Law with their own convictions; that school, which protests against any sort of State intervention, and which demands freedom left and right, nothing less than freedom, does not hesitate when one speaks of the fruitfulness of marriage to yell at the couple: Halt! What demon calls you!"[33] Proudhon makes this claim the same year that Mill's *On Liberty* was published. Mill, who rigorously denounces "the great evil of adding unnecessarily to its [the State's] power," does not hesitate to then go on and say: "the laws which, in many countries of the continent, forbid marriage unless the parties can show that they have means of supporting a family, do not exceed the legitimate powers of the State"; they "are not objectionable as violations of liberty."[34] Proudhon was right to point out that, in the contrast between liberalism and its critics, a switch in positions had taken place with regard to the individual's laissez-faire.

To give another example, in 1835, when faced with a flood of impoverished masses, Tocqueville can propose nothing better to prevent it than police measures, gravely detrimental to the individual's freedom (or, that of poor individuals): "Is there a way to prevent the rapid displacement of population, so that men do not leave the land and move into industry before the latter can easily respond to their needs?"[35]

4. The Right to Resistance

According to Bobbio, Hegel should be considered a "conservative" rather than a "liberal" for the simple fact that "he favors . . . the omnipotence of law more than the irresistibility of individual rights . . . the cohesion of the whole over its independent parts, and obedience over resistance." Bobbio bases Hegel's alleged conservatism upon the latter's rejection of the right to resistance.[36] Yet, an analogous rejection can be found in an author who contributed significantly to the ideological preparation of the French Revolution: that is, Voltaire.[37] Or, should we prefer to limit ourselves to Germany, Kant too rejects the right to resistance. On the other hand, the counter-revolutionaries, beginning with Burke and Gentz, do not hesitate to affirm it.[38] And the list could go on and on, as is always the case when dealing with generic categories that are thoroughly removed from historical concreteness. Even in Hitler one finds the claim that in extreme cases "the rebellion of every single member" of the "people" becomes "not only a right, but an obligation."[39]

As for Hegel, he is well aware of the historical and political ambiguity of the right to resistance: yes, the "right of insurrection" had been "consecrated by some of the numerous constitutions created in France in the last decade," but something similar was also the point of departure of the feudal reactionism and particularism responsible for the fact that Germany was no longer a State (w, 1, 521): "Resistance against the supreme royal authority is called freedom, and it is hailed as legitimate and noble, because it has before it the idea of self-will" (ph. G., 860). Reference to the right of feudal reactionaries to resist was not merely a historical fact. One of the most vehement ideologues of the Restoration, Haller, calls upon the Spanish people to resist and revolt against the "usurpation" represented by the constitution born of the Spanish Revolution, a constitution which was sanctioned, at least in appearance, by the approval and loyalty oath of the king himself.[40] Notably, *Philosophy of Right* criticizes Haller, who, to justify his rejection of positive laws and legislation—muddled wastepaper he considered superfluous and destructive, demanded not only respect for Natural Law, but also *"resistance* to injustice" (note to § 258 A).

If Hegel's criticism of the right to resistance targets primarily feudal reactionism, Bentham criticizes the French revolutionaries for the fact that

their *declaration of rights* aims only "to excite and keep up a spirit of resistance to all laws—a spirit of insurrection against all governments."[41]
Bentham's rejection of the right to resistance, with the French Revolution
in mind, in no way prevents us from considering him a liberal, of course.
Once again, the judgment about Hegel's "conservatism" is not even based
upon the unconditional liberal tradition as a whole, but rather upon one
particular thread.

To return to Hegel, even independent of the concrete historical-
political reactionary aspects which often characterize the right to resistance, it remains to be seen just what could counter Hegel's more
strictly theoretical arguments. If the right to resistance is considered inherent to the concrete historical process, then this leaves no doubt: the
superior right of the World Spirit with respect to the State is a given fact,
and it is based upon this view that Hegel does not condemn the great
revolutions as criminal acts, but instead justifies and celebrates them. Of
course, to particularism, free will, and noble and feudal oppression, Hegel
contrasts the objectivity and the superiority of State order, but State order
is to be considered inviolable and sacrosanct from a legal point of view,
not a historical-universal one. The historically-existent "positive" may
take the shape of "violence," and as a result the "thought" that criticizes it
tends to become "violent" itself (*Ph. G.*, 924): this is how the French Revolution, or others for that matter, is explained and legitimized; but it is a
legitimacy that cannot derive from a legal norm, but rather from concrete
conditions and a concrete historical analysis. It is a legitimacy that, after
all is said and done, can only be claimed and verified *post factum*.

If instead, the right to resistance is to be considered a constitutional
mechanism that legally permits, in certain circumstances, disobedience
of authority, it is clear then that we are dealing with something imaginary.
In the case of conflict or bitter clashes, the possible but in practice nonex-
istent ability to coerce, that is the "potential force" (*mögliche Gewalt*) of
the right to resistance, represents the only opposition to "actual force"
(*wirkliche Gewalt*), the actual violence of authority and its effective ability to coerce. So, one can resort to "insurrection," but it certainly is not a
right to which the law will guarantee a tranquil and undisturbed exercise
(*W, II, 474–75*). From a legal point of view, that which cannot be exercised
without grave risk is not a right; a right to resistance can be found not in
the legal order, but only in the "World Spirit," in history.

Here, Hegel is not as removed from Locke and other classical liberal
European thinkers as it might seem; or rather, the difference revolves
around very different aspects than the ones usually referred to. Yes, Locke
follows the right to resistance to its logical conclusion, to that of armed
insurrection, well beyond simple passive disobedience: "he therefore who

may resist, must be allowed to strike." But, for precisely this reason, resorting to resistance brings about a "state of war" between ruled and rulers, or rather ex-rulers. Thus, we have a return to the state of Natural Law, where there is no place for positive legal norms or for the legally-definable right to resistance: "Where there is no judge on earth, the appeal lies to God in Heaven." The call is for arms, but he who resorts to arms will have to answer on "the great day, to the supreme judge of all men."[42] Divine judgment in Hegel becomes the judgment of history, but it is clear in both cases that the right to resistance cannot appeal to an ordinary court of men, as with rights sanctioned by law; instead, it can only appeal to the good Lord in Heaven or the World Spirit.

It should be added that within the liberal tradition itself the magnitude of the right to resistance is progressively reduced. If for Locke the right to resistance included or might have included bearing arms, in Constant this is no longer true: "It is a positive, general duty not to carry out a law on those occasions when it seems unjust. And this should be done without reservation. This act should not bring about subversion, revolution, or disorder." Not only is armed resistance no longer mentioned, but the right to resistance has inadvertently become a "duty," that is, it has gone from the legal sphere to a moral one. And Constant is well aware of the difficulties that hinder an actual exercise of the right to resistance: "How can one limit power if not by way of power?" One can appeal to public opinion, once the public has been sufficiently enlightened.[43] But the question remains: how does one transform this moral force into actual power? Or, to use Hegel's terminology, how does one transform a potential force (*mögliche Gewalt*) into a real one (*wirkliche Gewalt*)? And how does one bring about this transformation while avoiding, as Constant would like to, "subversion," "revolution," and "disorder"?

On the other hand, the rejection of the right to resistance is not unusual in the German liberal tradition, and this on the basis of arguments that call to mind Hegel's. Consider, for example, F. C. Dahlmann's critical reflections on the ephorate: to function, "power (*Gewalt*) called upon to protect must want to be stronger than governing power."[44] In the final analysis, actual power, the organization of operative forces actually present, makes decisions. This is just a re-elaboration of Hegel's contrast between *wirkliche Gewalt* and *mögliche Gewalt*, a contrast with which Hegel criticized Fichte's idea of the ephorate. If anything, it is worth noting that whereas in Hegel the rejection of the right to resistance does not mean denying the right of the World Spirit to go beyond the existing legal order and even to completely unhinge it, Dahlmann is much more cautious on this point. While Hegel, in connection to the right of the World Spirit, can defend and even celebrate the French Revolution as well as other rebellious movements that mark the birth and development of the modern world, Dahlmann is more concerned with condemning and preventing possible proletarian subversions rather than justifying past bourgeois revolutions: one must therefore avoid positions that might cause the "inferior classes" to doubt that "the right of our possession" is "sacred."[45]

Still, as for the right to resistance in and of itself, Dahlmann's theories are close to Hegel's: "Within the actual State order violent resistance cannot be legally sanctioned. . . . The constitutional right to armed resistance rested upon the right of the nobility to participate in power; it constituted a part of it, and with it, it disappeared. . . . As long as privileged classes held a portion of power they swore allegiance only with reservation; they built fortresses, denounced obedience, and they chose the most complaisant lord."[46] As with Hegel, so too in Dahlmann the right to resistance is considered an integral part of the feudal world. Only prior to the creation of the modern State was the feudatory able to counter the "actual" power of the sovereign with a power not merely "possible" in the modern world, but itself "actual" and recognized in law.

Therefore, the liberal proclamation of the right to resistance is not a demand for a law which sanctions a risky and problematic right; rather, it is fundamentally a declaration of principles about the limits of political power. This fact is particularly clear in Constant's text: "freedom" must be vigorously defended not only against governments that have yet to abandon their despotic inclinations, but above all against "the masses who demand the right of the majority to enslave the minority." Instead, "as far as industry goes, everything that allows for the free exercise of industrial competition is individual, and could not be legitimately subjected to the power of society."[47] A political power that interferes in the free development of industry and property relations would be committing an "illegitimate" act, and would therefore rightly provoke "resistance" from the citizens (owners) whose freedom (and property) was affected.

That political power has precise and insuperable limits is clear also in Hegel, as is evident in his argument in favor of inalienable rights, those of individual freedom, of conscience, etc. Yet, while "the limit must remain sacred, and political power is not to interfere in the private life of citizens"; it is also an incontestable right of the State to ensure the education of all children (and intrude upon, when necessary, the will of the parents), to intervene with regard to schooling, medicine, etc. In short, political power has the right to interfere in those spheres which are "most directly related to the goals of the State" (*w*, IV, 372). For example, the State has the right to intervene in the economic realm, in order to try to reduce social costs: thus, in certain circumstances "the right to property . . . can and must be violated" (*v.Rph.*, IV, 157). In Hegel, we do not find a declared position on the insurmountable limits of political power over property, that is, over the absolute inviolability of property rights (a position which liberal tradition calls the "right to resistance"). However, this fact should not be interpreted as Hegel's illiberal "conservatism"; on the contrary, it reveals the greater influence which *social* conservative interests exert upon liberal authors whose origins are already tied to the proprietary class.

It should also be added that a declared position on the limits of political power in no way impedes even the most progressive liberals from calling for the use of force under certain circumstances to maintain order. To some extent the Revolution in June 1848 in Paris had the declared right to resistance based upon the Jacobin constitution of 1793 behind it, but obviously that did not hinder Tocqueville from recommending that whoever was caught "in a defensive position" be shot.[48]

5. The Right of Extreme Need and Individual Rights

Bobbio equates the dichotomy obedience to law—irresistibility of individual rights to another dichotomy, obedience—resistance (that is, acceptance or rejection of the right to resistance). However, this correspondence is not as obvious as it might appear. Hegel, who decisively rejects the right to resistance, does not hesitate on the other hand to solemnly declare that "a man who is starving has the absolute right to violate another person's property" (infra, ch. VII, 2).

What we are dealing with, clearly, is the legitimation of the *Notrecht*, which is not to be confused with the *ius resistentiae*. Nor is it the traditional *ius necessitatis* that refers to exceptional circumstances generally caused by natural disasters (for example, the casuistic and rudimentary conundrum of the two shipwrecked survivors who grab onto a plank that can support only one of the two). No, in Hegel *Notrecht* refers to conflicts, concrete clashes brought on by existing social relationships. *Notrecht* becomes the right of extreme need, that of those who risk starving to death. Not only do they have the right to steal the bread that will keep them alive, but the "absolute right" to transgress the right of property, that legal norm which condemns theft.

It might be useful to consider the liberal school of thought on this issue. There does not seem to be any social justification for the violation of the right of property in Locke. Hegel's assistant, Leopold von Henning, interpreted *Notrecht* as "the right to keep oneself alive" (v.Rph., III, 400). Instead, Locke speaks of the "right to preservation," but only to explain and justify the genesis of private property: "men, being once born, have a right to their preservation, and consequently to eat and drink, and such other things as nature affords for their subsistence."[49] Even if we suppose that this right still has meaning in the social realm, it can only be proffered in relation to nature, not society, and only in order to justify the fact that nothing remains without an owner.

Explicit opposition to *Notrecht* is instead found in the writings of one of the most authoritative representatives of German liberalism, and his position merits all the more attention given that he is extremely critical of Hegel. It is already significant that Carl von Rotteck discusses the "so-called *Notrecht*." But what is more, the example that we have already seen in Hegel returns: Are those who risk "death by starvation" allowed to steal the bread that would ensure their survival? The response is decidedly negative: under no circumstance can there be "a right to commit a wrongdoing" (*Recht, Unrecht zu tun*). Not even in the traditional *casus necessitatis* can extenuation or non-punishability be considered, even if the situation thwarted the ability to think clearly. The absolute right to property must be respected at all costs, even the life of a human being. Imagine a "fugitive" who, in a desperate attempt to escape his pursuer, "runs into a fence that is not his and that blocks his passage, or who steals a horse from the pasture to flee more quickly." What does one do in that case? One can assume the proprietor's consent, but if it turns out that "he responds negatively," then in that case the individual is to be considered guilty, even in light of what we recognize to be extenuating circumstances or a temporary inability to think clearly. In no case does one have the "right" to violate the property of others.[50]

With respect to his liberal critic, Hegel's view is much less rigid on the inviolability of the law. In Bobbio's words, "the irresistibility of the individual right" to life certainly questions "the omnipotence of the law." But in reality Bobbio's thesis would be erroneous even if it were overturned. Given the merely formal nature of the two terms being compared, it could lead to contrasting results: for the liberal school of thought the right of a proprietor's undisturbed enjoyment of his property is undoubtedly "irresistible," so much so that "resistance" is justified against political powers that intend to transgress its inviolable limits. In Hegel (and even more so in the proto-socialist movement) what is "irresistible" is the subjective right of the starving man who, to ensure his life, calls upon the State to intervene in the existent property relations. Or, in extreme cases, is even authorized to violate the right to property in order to procure the bread that will keep him from starving.

Locke, who affirms the right to resistance, is silent on *Notrecht*; the opposite is true of Hegel: the line of demarcation between obedience to the law and the irresistibility of individual rights is even more tortuous than what emerges in Bobbio's text. There is, however, a logical thread. On the one hand, making the right of property absolute leaves Locke no room to legitimize the right of extreme need; on the other hand, it requires a justification of the right to resistance against a political power that intends to claim transcendence with respect to mandated property-owners: "The reason why men enter into society is the preservation of their property," and it is for this reason that they institute laws.[51] It is clear that the "people" (in reality, the proprietary promoters and custodians of the contract) have the right to institute "a new legislative, when their legislators have acted contrary to their trust, by invading their property."[52] In this sense, the right to resistance is the right to defend property against possible "usurpations" by the State. Significantly, political usurpation is compared to banditry: "That subjects or foreigners, attempting by force on the properties of any people, may be resisted with force, is agreed on all hands," and the same is true for rulers.[53]

Yet, recognition of the right to resistance is so little a recognition of a bottom-up initiative that, as far as the relationship between the people and the legislature, Locke not only denies the people any right to resistance, but even the right to abolish or modify, in structure or function, the Parliament: "When the society hath placed the legislative in any assembly of men, to continue in them and their successors, with direction and authority for providing such successors, the legislative can never revert to the people whilst that government lasts; because having provided a legislative with power to continue for ever, they have given up their political power to the legislative, and cannot resume it."[54] The individual right of the proprietor, with all of its "irresistibility," can question "the omnipotence of the law" in certain circumstances, but only in order to sacrifice it on behalf of that supreme "omnipotence:" existent property relations. Not only can they not be violated by the starving or by the State, but they cannot even be weakened by any reform that would challenge the existence or efficiency of the political bulwark of property, that is, the legislature.

Hegel, instead, is so convinced of the "irresistibility" of the individual right of the starving that he does not hesitate to claim, even if in the context of the Roman struggle between patricians and plebeians, that, regarding the problem of procuring "sustenance," "right as such" is only an "abstraction." Actually, in this context, *Philosophy of History* even speaks of the "useless question of right" (*Ph. G.*, 698). What is clear is that Hegel repeatedly discusses, and tries to support in opposition to the existing legal and social order, the "right to work," the "right to life" (*Rph. I*, s 118 A), that is, individual rights, and "material rights" (*B.schr.* 488), as he defines them. Such rights are ignored by the liberal tradition.

Up until now we have, for the sake of convenience, discussed the liberal tradition without further description. Yet, it is clear that for a school of thought opposed to the doctrine of Natural Law, it becomes difficult to speak of "irresistible" individual rights. In fact, Bentham, after denying the existence of natural or inalienable rights, adds—as we have already seen above—that "there is no right which not ought to be maintained so long as it is upon the whole advantageous to the society." So much for irresistibility!

6. Formal and Substantive Freedom

In essence, according to Bobbio, Hegel is "conservative" rather than "liberal" because he "favors . . . the top of the pyramid (the monarchy) over the base (the people)."

In reality, as we will see, far from being fetishistically attached to the top of the pyramid, Hegel celebrates the revolutions that mark the birth and development of the modern world. Yet, at the same time he is aware that the consensus of the people, "common" people, can in certain circumstances stir up decidedly reactionary movements as well. Hence, the insistence upon distinguishing between "formal freedom" and "substantive freedom."

Formal freedom is that moment of subjective consensus, and in this sense it has no negative meaning in Hegel, rather, it constitutes an essential moment for the modern world, for modern freedom: "formal freedom is the development and establishment of laws" (Ph. G., 927). In England, "formal freedom, in the discourse of State affairs, takes place to the highest degree"; this is not a negative judgment, because what Hegel appreciates about England is precisely its "Parliament open to the people, the practice of public meetings by all classes, the freedom of press." However, these were merely conditions that favored the establishment of "the French principles of freedom and equality" (Ph. G., 934). Formal freedom is the necessary precondition for establishing "objective or actual freedom." To this sphere belong the freedom of property and the freedom of the individual. And with this, the lack of freedom inherent in feudal bondage ceases, along with all of the norms which derive from it, the tithes, the canons. "The freedom to work, that is, man's freedom to use his force as he wishes, and the free access to all State offices, also make up actual freedom" (Ph. G., 927). Therefore, formal freedom and substantive freedom are not contradictory terms in and of themselves: "Freedom has two aspects. One concerns the content of the freedom, its objectivity, the thing itself. The other concerns the form of the freedom in which the subject recognizes himself to be active, because the requirement of freedom is that the subject feels himself fulfilled and performs his duty, it being in his own interest that the thing is achieved" (*Ph. G.*, 926).

Formal freedom should be the vehicle of actual freedom. When this happens, we have the free will of freedom, and this means the support and conscious consensus that enables socio-political institutions to achieve objective freedom. But in a concrete historical-political situation formal freedom may clash with actual freedom. In fact, "actual freedom . . . does not lie with sentiment, because sentiment also allows for the continued existence of slavery and serfdom; instead, it lies with thought and the self-consciousness that man has of his own spiritual essence" (*Ph. G.* 927). The arbitrariness of emotions, practices, and traditions could deprive actual freedom of consensus; formal freedom may negate actual freedom and attach itself to institutions that deny freedom. A particularly clamorous example, according to Hegel, is Poland: the continuous discussions of the Diet are certainly a moment of formal freedom, but in this specific case, it is utilized in order to perpetuate the power of barons and the practice of serfdom. It perpetuates non-freedom. A similar clash, though less bitter and more limited in nature, occurs in England. Formal freedom is un-disputed, and yet very little progress has been made since medieval feu-dalism: "the English constitution has remained basically the same since the era of feudalism, and it is based almost exclusively upon antique privileges." In theory, England's liberal tradition should have made the transition to "freedom and equality," or actual freedom, easier. But for a series of historical reasons (national pride, etc.) the opposite occurred. It is not by chance that England led all of the anti-French coalitions (*Ph. G.*, 934). Furthermore, the aristocracy that stripped the Crown of "formal freedom" now uses it to prevent antifeudal reforms, to block the estab-lishment of "objective freedom" and "rational right" (*Enc.*, § 544 A).

It is possible that the reforms needed to challenge feudalism and bring about the actual freedom of individuals and property (the latter being freed from its feudal chains) come from the top. But this transition to actual freedom does not correspond with formal freedom, or does so late, and only partially. This is the case in Germany, and even more so in Prussia beginning with the reforms of the Stein-Hardenberg era. With these reforms objective freedom begins to seep through (and is the ori-gin, according to Engels, of the bourgeois revolution in Prussia and Ger-many).[55] But it does not occur at the same rate as formal freedom: Frie-drich Wilhelm III does not keep his promises to reform the constitution. Yet, Hegel continues to hope that formal freedom will catch up with substantive freedom thanks to reforms from the top, even if they are instigated from the bottom by the opinion of intellectuals and "enlight-ened" officials, those enlightened by the spread of "philosophy."

It is interesting to note that the liberal tradition also makes a distinc-tion between formal freedom and substantive freedom, but the meaning is different and contrary to what we have just seen. Consider Montesquieu: "There are always those in a State whose prominence is distinguished by birth, wealth, and honor: if they were mixed in with the rest of the people and had nothing but the same voice, then common freedom would be their slavery, and they would have no reason to defend it since the major-ity of the resolutions would be against them."[56] These considerations are developed by Montesquieu in a chapter on England's constitution, where he emphasizes the positive role that the aristocracy has played in the country. It is because of feudal privilege that Hegel considers English freedom to be formal: it ignores the universality of principles, and in the final analysis, therefore, it ignores equality. For Tocqueville the opposite is true: it is egalitarian leveling that risks crushing freedom. Formal free-dom and substantive freedom are constantly defined in radically antithet-ical ways, but undoubtedly the distinction is made by both of the schools of thought that we have considered.

7. Interpretative Categories and Ideological Presuppositions

At this point it might be useful to take a look at the categories used by some of the protagonists in the political debate of that period, categories needed to evaluate the historical dilemma explicitly proposed by Bobbio, but also implicit in the views of theorists whose opinions appear to be quite dif-ferent from his own. Liberal or conservative? Chateaubriand, against whose "liberalism" Ilting measures Hegel, considers himself "conser-vative," indeed, he is the editor of a journal that is titled, clearly enough, *Le Conservateur*.[57] In this light, it remains to be seen whether the distance between *Philosophy of Right* and *Le Conservateur* represents the distance between liberalism or and conservatism.

Contrary to the liberal, does the conservative "favor the State more than the individual, authority more than freedom," etc.? For Chateau-briand, the struggle is between the *"parti royaliste"* and the *"parti minis-teriel,"* and it is the latter that identifies with liberalism. The *"parti royal-iste,"* however, with Chateaubriand at the helm, insists upon limits on the Crown and the executive branch, in order to take the process of Resto-ration as far as it will go. In Germany, Stahl writes: "Hegel excessively favors rule from the top, rather than free development from the bottom and from within. His theory is neither *ultramonarchical* nor *ultraliberal*, but *ultragubernatorial*."[58] For Chateaubriand as well as for Stahl, to be "ministerial" or "ultragubernatorial" does not mean supporting absolute monarchy or, even less, supporting feudal reactionism. In the meantime, the political situation has changed: the liberal party, in its struggle against the nostalgic extremists of the *ancien régime*, no longer needs the support of the Crown and the bureaucratic governmental apparatus (which in Prussia, after 1840, are strongly influenced by the Junkers). So, according to Stahl, three parties emerge, but the fact remains that being "ministerial" or "ultra-gubernatorial" is not the same as being reactionary or conservative.

This is the case with regard to the political debate. If we look at the social question, things become more complex. If in Hegel the term liberal oscillates back and forth, going from positive to negative, in Saint-Simon the term has a constantly negative meaning: in fact, "liberals" are contrasted with "industrialists," and groups that are primarily manufacturers.[59] And Saint-Simon who contrasts the principle of *"organisation"* to laissez-faire, *laissez-aller,* is likened by Constant to de Maistre and Lamennais.[60] On the other hand, as has been noted, Constant repeatedly accuses Rousseau of having armed "despotism" with his *Social Contract.*[61] For Constant, on the one side is liberalism, and on the other are absolutism and despotism, where the Rousseau-Jacobin tradition merges with that of the newly-born socialist movement. This schema definitively triumphs after the 1848 Revolution. For Tocqueville, Jacobinism (with its economic policy of intervention with regard to private property) and "modern socialism" are nothing more than a return to the themes of "monarchial despotism," themes found throughout Enlightenment culture, and not only in the work of utopians like Morelly, but also in that of "economists" who have themselves been duped by the nefarious myth of the "omnipotence of the State."[62] From this moment on anything that cannot be categorized as strictly "liberal" is considered synonymous with despotism, and follows a continuous line from Louis XIV to Louis Blanc. This schema triumphs, after 1848, even in Germany, and is found in Rudolf Haym, the author who accuses Hegel of having formulated a "statist" theory that is incompatible with modern freedom. Clearly, we have stumbled once again upon the same accusation and the same line of demarcation between freedom and despotism.

Even today, Ralf Dahrendorf not only considers the Hegelian Lassalle's theory of the State as the guardian of private property to be "illiberal" and indifferent to poverty and social issues, but beginning with Lassalle he thinks the entire German (and not only German) workers' movement is "fundamentally illiberal."[63]

It is easy to see why Hegel is placed beside such different authors and movements: Tocqueville sees France, saturated by Enlightenment culture and on its way to revolution, as nurturing a profound "passion for equality," but not for "freedom." This France is driven by the ideal of a society "with no other aristocracy than that of public servants, a unique and omnipotent administration, the guide of the State and the guardian of privacy."[64] How can one not think of the pathos with which Hegel celebrates bureaucracy as a "universal class"? Another characteristic of the "despotic" school of thought (this, according to Tocqueville, but also Haym and other German national-liberals) is the demand that poverty be remedied from above, by way of State intervention: by, for example, guaranteeing the "right to work."[65] But this is precisely Hegel's tendency: he argues for a decidedly interventionist State and, as we have noted, even goes so far as to proclaim the "right to life" (through labor). This model (supplied by Constant, Tocqueville, Haym) responded to the immediate needs of political struggle by proffering the bourgeois liberal as the only true interpreter of the cause for freedom and progress, and by categorizing all other political forces as absolutist and reactionary, is the very same propagandistic model that, in the final analysis, presupposes a false dilemma (liberal or conservative?) and continues to dominate the debate about Hegel even today.

Likewise, it is not difficult to trace the political and ideological genesis of Bobbio's model: to favor the "top of the pyramid (the monarchy)" or the "base (the people)"? It was Stahl (whose politics we already know) who provided the alternatives formulated by Bobbio. In fact, after criticizing Hegel for being "extremely governmental," the socially and politically conservative (and to a certain extent reactionary) Stahl denounces Hegel's serious error as follows: "All things must be worked out through the objectively mandated power, that is, the government, and people consciously and therefore freely accept this. But the opposite cannot happen, that is, work cannot be initiated by the most intimate impulses of individuals, associations, people, corporations, and the government cannot limit itself to directing, sanctioning or moderating, and corporations cannot stop and correct the government."[66] Stahl speaks of the "people," but what he really means is "corporations," which are aristocratic and bourgeois lobbies. Instead, Hegel is well aware that the appeal to the "people" can from time to time mean different things: "will of the people is a grand word," but it can be "used lightly" and even "profaned" (w, IV, 528).

In the end, it is because of his historical concreteness, his attention to socio-political aspects, that Hegel is criticized by Bobbio. Yet, during the Restoration, even the advocates of bourgeois liberalism more often than not very clearly reveal themselves, if not in their general view of history then at least politically, to be opposed to *extremists* who would limit the Crown's powers. At this moment at least, the liberal bourgeoisie shows itself to be thoroughly aware of the class division among the "people," and for this reason it refuses to be instrumentally and temporarily branded as "liberal" by the feudal aristocracy. It is only after the latter has been defeated that bourgeois liberals formulate the dichotomy in the same terms as Bobbio, attempting to relegate the politically defeated class to that of the "people," and contrasting the social demands of the proletariat by reducing the political struggle of the time to a struggle between freedom and absolutism, initiatives from the bottom and initiatives from the top (the dreaded political intervention in the realm of property), the individual and the State.

Why not substitute, then, the conservative-liberal dichotomy with right-left? To the "center left" (*centre gauche*), where Royer-Collard is to be found, Chateaubriand contrasts the "independent right" (*côté droit indépendant*) and thus he seems to equate the "government party" (*parti ministeriel*) with the left and the "royalist party" (*parti royaliste*) with the right.[67] Based upon these criteria, and given his support of the "*parti ministeriel,*" Hegel should be situated on the left or center-left. After all, we have already seen Cousin link Hegel to Royer-Collard. Yet, it is not so much a question of substituting one criterion for another. Rather, both need to be contextualized; it is necessary to take into account the ideological presuppositions that are embedded in the criteria, and focus upon the concrete social and political context of these positions, as well as of Hegel's overall philosophical view.

V

Hegel and the Liberal Tradition:
Two Opposing Interpretations of History

1. Hegel and Revolutions

At this point, rather than continuing to ask ourselves whether Hegel is a liberal or a conservative, it would be better to make a direct comparison with the liberal tradition, beginning with the analysis of the historical process which created the modern world. We shall see that, even when Hegel is radically removed from this tradition, his position can hardly be called conservative or reactionary.

First of all, Hegel's antagonistic position with regard to the culture of the Restoration is quite clear, and we can use as our point of departure his judgment of the French Revolution. We are not referring so much to the famous page that *Philosophy of History* devotes to the "gorgeous dawn" and to the "noble emotion" produced by the Revolution (*Ph. G.*, 926). We are referring above all to the note made in Berlin, where Hegel mocks the Restoration cliché that this great historical event was a punishment inflicted by God to expiate the sins of mankind. In this case, Hegel comments bitingly, the "sins" would date back to a time before the outbreak of the Revolution, and they would seem to take us back to the good old days of absolutism and feudalism; in conclusion, these are "presumptuous claims, hardly forgivable even if uttered by a Capuchin friar who tries to use them to embellish his ignorance"; claims that are completely unaware of the "peculiar principles that characterize the essence of the Revolution and confer on it the almost inestimable power it has over people's souls" (*B.schr.*, 697–98). In his defense of the French Revolution, Hegel is able to switch between a lyrical tone and an almost Voltairean sarcasm, directed mainly against the bigoted reactionaries.

Going back in time, it may be interesting to examine Hegel's position on other revolutions. Let us start with the American Revolution: "the tax which the British Parliament had imposed on the tea imported into America was in itself very small, but what caused the Revolution was the feeling, shared by the citizens, that the loss of that sum, no matter how insignificant, would go hand in hand with the loss of their most important right" (w, I, 258). This early position is quite significant, and Hegel defends it again, in almost identical terms, in his 1824–25 lecture course on the philosophy of right (v.Rph., IV, 616). He establishes a connection between the American Revolution and the French Revolution: "In the American war, what triumphed was the idea of liberty. The principle of the universality of principles became stronger among the French people, and it produced the Revolution" (ph.G., 919–20). Not only does Hegel acknowledge the American settlers' right to revolution and independence, but he warmly extols their struggle, the struggle of a people with no experienced military force, and supported merely by enthusiasm, against a regular army: "During the war of liberation, the militia groups of the free North American State proved themselves just as worthy as the Dutch under Philip II" (ph.G., 198).

While Hegel explicitly condemns England with regard to the American Revolution, he celebrates it when England itself becomes the protagonist of a revolution: "In England, the wars of religion were at the same time constitutional struggles. In order to achieve religious freedom, a political change was necessary as well. The struggle was aimed against the kings, as the latter secretly leaned towards Catholicism, in which they found a confirmation of absolute will." Thus, the English Revolution was aimed "against the assertion of absolute power, according to which kings were to be held accountable for their actions merely before God (that is, before their confessor)"; during this Revolution, too, a radicalization and "fanaticization" process takes place, but Cromwell showed that he well "knew what it meant to govern" (ph.G., 896–97). As for the values that animated the Glorious Revolution, they are by now to be considered a heritage of humanity, as can be seen from this passage from *Lectures on the History of Philosophy:* "What Locke achieved in other fields such as education, tolerance, natural or public law in general is not our concern here; rather, it belongs to general culture" (w, xx, 221).

Proceeding further back in the history of revolutions, we find the Dutch insurrection against Philip II, but we have already discussed Hegel's comparison between this uprising and the American Revolution. Hegel praises the Netherlands as the country which "set the first example of general tolerance in Europe, and provided a shelter for free-thought for many individuals" (w, xx, 159). For Hegel, the Dutch "insurrection represented not only a liberation from the yoke of religion, but at the same time a political liberation from the oppression of foreign occupation." In other words, the struggle aimed at achieving freedom of conscience as well as political freedom and national independence: "The Netherlands fought heroically against its oppressors. The working class, the corporations, and the shooting clubs organized militia groups, and with their heroic valor they defeated the Spanish infantry, which was quite renowned at the time. Just like the Swiss peasants stood up against the knights, here the industrial cities stood up against the regular troops" (Ph. G., 896). One revolution calls to mind another. The Dutch Revolution was first compared to the American Revolution; now it is compared to the struggle for the Swiss cantons to free themselves of the Habsburg oppression: "The peasants, armed with clubs and scythes, won the struggle against a nobility armed with cuirasses, spears, and swords, and trained chivalrously in tournaments" (Ph. G., 863).

Not only does Hegel analyze and celebrate the Reformation as a revolution, but he provides a balanced judgment even of the Peasants War: "The peasants rose in mass to shake off the oppression that weighed upon them. But the world was not yet ripe for a political transformation, as a consequence of the Church's reformation" (Ph. G., 884). Hegel interprets the coming of Christianity itself as a revolution, or rather, as a "full revolution" which (most importantly) did not occur "within the inner man" (in interiore homine), though it demolished "the whole structure" of the "state life" and "social reality" of the time, the conditions of which had become quite intolerable. Hegel also compares the Christian revolution to the French Revolution—the cross is the "cockade" (Kokarde) that accompanies the struggle to overthrow a decrepit, intolerable order—to justify, once and for all, an event which the ideologues of the Restoration insisted on condemning and demonizing in the name of religion and Christianity.[1]

With regard to antiquity, Hegel praises the slave rebellions: slavery existed in the "free states" of ancient times; "during the Roman Empire, bloody wars broke out, in the course of which slaves attempted to free themselves and to achieve acknowledgment of their eternal rights as men" (Enc., § 433 z). And even with regard to the great struggle within the ancient Roman world, the struggle between patricians and plebeians, Hegel is definitely against the established powers and the existing social order: the Gracchus family held "for themselves the higher justification of the World Spirit" (Ph. G., 708). This statement is all the more significant given that, in Hegel's time, the Gracchus family was synonymous with "de facto equality," "agricultural law," and even socialism and communism.[2] As for the first centuries of the republic, Hegel still justifies or celebrates plebeian insurrection: "The harshness of the patricians, their creditors, who were to be paid in the form of slave labor, forced the plebeians to revolt. Many times they rebelled and left the cities. Sometimes they refused to serve in the military." Far from justifying the sacredness of the established order as such, Hegel wonders how "the Senate was able to resist for so long against a majority frustrated by oppression and exhausted by war." He ascribes this to the respect that, despite everything, the plebeians felt "toward the legal order and the *sacra*" (ph.G., 695). It was a respect fostered by the interests of the dominant class, a respect Hegel does not share; on the contrary, he reveals its ideological, mystifying function. Every achievement of the plebeians, obtained through struggle and insurrection, was labeled by the patricians "as an impiety, a violation of the divine. Where did the patricians acquire the right to overthrow kings and to seize those rights, which they now passed off as sacred?" (ph.G., 697). The patricians, who had set themselves up as the sacred custodians of the established order, did not hesitate to violate it for the sake of their interests. And yet, the plebeians who had been reduced to slavery because of their debts were entitled, like all slaves, to "man's eternal rights" to freedom.

In short, every revolution in the history of humanity was supported and celebrated by Hegel, despite his reputation as an incorrigible defender of the established order. A possible objection might be the following: What was Hegel's position on the revolution he personally witnessed in his adult life? The reference is of course to the July Revolution, but it is worth starting out by spending a few words on another revolution, or rather, on a series of revolutions which so far have not been particularly examined by critics. I refer to the first revolutionary wave which occurs after the Restoration, and which tests the political system of the Holy Alliance. This revolutionary wave had reached Europe after leaving Latin America shaken by the Spanish colonies' struggle for independence. The *Lectures on the Philosophy of History* comment favorably on the "recent efforts for the constitution of autonomous States" that had taken place in Latin America. In addition, Hegel's indirect support for the colonies' right to revolution emerges from his blunt description of colonial domination: the Spaniards took possession of Latin America "to dominate and grow richer, both through political offices and through oppression. As the motherland upon which they depended was far away, their will could expand widely and freely, and thanks to their strength, ability, and self-confidence, they largely prevailed over the natives. Everything that is noble and magnanimous in their character the Spanish did not carry to America" (v.G., 201, 205).

At the same time as the uprising in the colonies, the Revolution broke out in Spain. Hegel transcribed excerpts from a French writer explicitly committed to the defense of the Spanish Revolution (b.schr., 698–99), and Hegel's support for the latter also emerges, though indirectly, in *Philoso-*

phy of Right, in the harsh criticism of the Inquisition which had just been abolished by the new revolutionary government, but which was still defended by authors such as de Maistre and Haller, and by Spanish reactionary groups.[3]

Finally, the July Revolution. Yet, even in this case Hegel's initial reservations mostly concerned the Belgian insurrection, which appeared to be a Vendée-like reactionism, and which was therefore shunned to a far greater degree by the likes of Heine, despite the latter's strong democratic commitment. The initial fear, widely spread and not at all unjustified, was that international complications and a new war with France risked provoking anti-French elements implacably hostile to France's enlightened, revolutionary political tradition.[4] Once these reservations and fears were overcome, Hegel accepted with conviction the results of a revolution which had put an end to the "farce" of the Restoration (*Ph. G.*, 932), and which, by driving out the Bourbons for the second time, had proved itself able to fulfill an inexorable historical need (*Ph. G.*, 712). His judgment is unequivocally positive. By sanctioning "the principle of worldly freedom," the July Revolution turned France into an essentially Protestant—and thus politically modern—country (*W*, XVI, 243). The July Revolution marked the irreparable twilight of absolute monarchy and divine right: "nowadays . . . we no longer hold as valid that which rests merely upon authority; laws must be legitimized by means of concept" (*V. Rph.*, IV, 923–24).

2. Revolutions from the Bottom-Up or from the Top-Down

There are not only revolutions from the bottom-up; there are also revolutions from the top-down: "Revolutions proceed either from the sovereign or from the people. Thus, Cardinal Richelieu oppressed the great and raised the universal above them. That was despotism, but abolishing the vassals' privileges was the right thing to do" (*Rph. I*, § 146 A). Hegel uttered this statement during his philosophy of right lecture course in Heidelberg; hence, even before he arrived in Berlin, Hegel was a "monarchical philosopher," in the sense that, according to his analysis, in the contradiction between the sovereign on one side and the "people" and representative bodies on the other, progress could also be achieved by the sovereign. This position remains unchanged throughout his philosophical thought. It is within this framework that we can place his denunciation of elective monarchy, found in *Philosophy of Right* (§ 281 A). Already in Hegel's time, this denunciation stirred angry reactions, and even today it is regarded with perplexity and perhaps embarrassment by those critics who are determined to portray a liberal image of Hegel (infra, ch. XII, 6). Yet, that denunciation has a rigorous philosophical, historical, and political justification. The reference is first of all to Poland, with regard to which *Philosophy of History* contains an enlightening analysis: "Freedom in Poland was but the freedom of barons against the monarch, a freedom for the sake of which the whole nation was submitted to absolute slavery. Consequently, the people shared the kings' interest in fighting the barons, and in fact it was by crushing the barons that they regained their freedom throughout the country. When we speak of freedom, we must always consider whether what we are dealing with are in fact private interests" (*Ph. G.*, 902). Poland was an elective monarchy, and it was precisely this fact that weakened the power of the crown against a rebellious nobility. Hegel's position could, and perhaps still can, generate shocked responses in liberal circles, but it meets the approval of Lenin, who sees in it the "seeds of historical materialism" thanks to the dutiful attention Hegel pays to "class relations."[5]

Hegel speaks of "despotism" with regard to Richelieu, but abolishing feudal privileges, as we have seen, "was the right thing to do." Yes, "despotism" and "despotic" can take on an essentially positive connotation: it was precisely by the "Natural Law of the Enlightenment" that the privileges of feudal tradition were first questioned and abolished, and the value of the universal was asserted; "from the starting point of these principles, on the one hand, private rights were despotically violated, but, on the other, universal goals of the State were achieved against the positive" (*Ph. G.*, 918). This use of the language is a real scandal for the liberal tradition, all the more so since it is the term "liberal" itself that sometimes appears to bear a negative connotation. An analogous use of the language can be found in the young Marx: we have already seen how he distances himself from the "vulgar liberalism" that sees "the representative bodies (*Stände*) as always good, and the government as always evil" (supra, ch. II, n. 35); on the other hand, the *Communist Manifesto* calls for "*despotic* inroads on the rights of property, and on the conditions of bourgeois production."[6]

The similarities we have observed in these two authors with regard to a certain use of the language can be easily grasped if we keep in mind how both are well aware of the various socio-political meanings that, from time to time, the terms "liberal" and "despotic" can assume. During the Restoration period, one of its ideologues, Franz X. B. von Baader, denounced the State's demand for the unilateral abolition of the nobility's traditional privileges and tax exemptions as utterly "illiberal."[7] In this sense, then, Hegel and Marx were clearly "illiberal," and "illiberal" was obviously synonymous with "despotic," except that the "despotism" referred to by Hegel was targeted against the "private rights" and privileges of feudal tradition, whereas Marx's "despotism" in the *Communist Manifesto* was targeted not only against feudal property, but also and above all against bourgeois property and right to property generally.

The positive connotation that the term "despotism" sometimes takes on can be explained by the fact that Hegel celebrates revolutions from the bottom-up as well as revolutions from the top-down. We have already seen his remarks on Richelieu. He comments in similar terms on the "enormous revolution" which Friedrich II participated in, and which led to the "disappearance of the definition of private property with regard to the State" (*v.Rph.*, IV, 253). The difference between revolution and counter-revolution, or between progress and reactionism, and even between freedom and oppression does not at all coincide with the difference between initiative from above and from below: enlightened absolutism and the French Revolution are two steps in the same revolutionary process that led to the destruction of feudalism and the birth of the modern State; therefore, they represent two steps in the progression toward freedom. With this observation, Hegel certainly moves away from the liberal tradition, but even more so from the theorists of the Restoration. The subversive role of feudalism historically carried out by "despotism" is pointed out with clarity by Carl L. von Haller, in the course of a controversy closely followed and harshly criticized by Hegel (*B.schr.*, 680). This ideologue of the Counter-Revolution insists nostalgically on rejecting not only the French Revolution, but also the modern world as a whole, and thus enlightened absolutism. Yes, for this theorist of the property State, even the public aspect of justice, which puts an end to or limits the will of feudal aristocracy, is to be considered "unseemly violence, oppression of freedom, and despotism" (*Rph.* § 219 A). If, on the one hand, Hegel celebrates revolutions from above and from below, on the other, the theorists of the Restoration condemn them both: "Revolution"—cautions Baader— "can proceed both from the top-down and from bottom-up" (supra, ch. II, n. 25). And Joseph Görres, who embraces the Restoration after repudiating his early Jacobin enthusiasm, thunders against "this eternal revolution of despotism from above and this despotism of revolutionary ideas from below."[8]

Besides, it would be incorrect to believe that Hegel limits himself to overturning the perceptions of "despotism." The latter certainly had the merit of shaking, violently and for the first time, the feudal structure, yet this was but the first step in the march toward freedom. It would be superfluous to name all the circles in which despotism was denounced, and not only Eastern despotism, which was constantly equated with a lack of freedom and the barbaric oppression carried out by the will of the monarch's unpredictable individuality (*Ph.G.*, 759–60). Even the despotism of absolute monarchy that accompanies the dawn of the modern world, which no longer stands for the complete absence of the rule of law, but rather represents the first self-assertion of the law to the detriment of the barons' will, even this despotism is far from carrying out a merely positive function. At most, it can achieve the "equality of private individuals:" thus, as the ancient Roman world declined, by means of the imperial power "a large number of slaves were liberated"; but such equality is not everything, on the contrary, it actually represents a very small achievement, since the "equality" introduced by "despotism" was only "abstract [equality], it was that of private law" (*Ph.G.*, 692 and 716). The fact that slavery and then, in the modern world, serfdom were eliminated is certainly quite significant, but we still lack consensus and subjective freedom, free and conscious participation in public affairs, and "that cannot be neglected," since without "subjective freedom" we are only dealing with the "power relations of despotism" (*V.Rph.*, IV, 253–54).

The march towards freedom must necessarily take as its starting point the acquisition of the results of the French Revolution and the acknowledgment of the rights of man and citizen—and therefore the acknowledgment of an inviolable individual freedom, but antifeudal despotism, too, represents an important step in this march. And while this comment shocked the liberals, it was instead essentially accepted by Marx and Engels, who saw absolute monarchy as a power that could serve as an intermediary between the bourgeoisie and the nobility, and therefore limit the excessive power of the barons. In other words, it was an essential element in the formation of the modern State.[9]

3. Revolution According to the Liberal Tradition

We have seen that, for Hegel, Richelieu's work represents a revolution from the top-down, since it halts and crushes the excessive power of feudal barons. Montesquieu's position is quite different: "Even if this man had not had despotism in his heart, he would have had it in his mind."[10] It is important to notice that both Montesquieu and Hegel speak of "despotism" with regard to Richelieu. Yet, the former sides with the aristocracy's liberal resistance against absolute monarchy, whereas the latter sides with the anti-feudal "despotism" of the central power. Montesquieu's position is essentially shared by his admirer Benjamin Constant, as emerges from his denunciation of Louis XIV's commitment "to destroy the authority of the parliament, the clergy, and all of the intermediate bodies," to dismantle, that is, all of the various centers of power of the feudal aristocracy.[11] Montesquieu and Constant's position is shared also by Madame de Staël, who sees Richelieu and absolute monarchy unjustly destroying the freedom that France had enjoyed since time immemorial.[12]

Hegel, however, moves away from the liberal tradition not only because he celebrates revolutions from above and revolutionary "despotism," but also because he celebrates revolutions from below. This observation might sound paradoxical, but the facts speak for themselves. Let us read this statement by Montesquieu: "Equality in London is also the equality of gentlemen, and in this sense it differs from equality in the Netherlands, which is the freedom of scoundrels." To Montesquieu, the Dutch Revolution celebrated by Hegel smacked of plebeianism; one only needs to think of the role played by the Beggars (*Gueux*) and of the battle cry "Long live the Beggars!" (*Vivent les gueux!*) that accompanied and promoted it. And Montesquieu in turn celebrates England for the same reasons that Hegel used to accuse it: the predominance of the "gentlemen" of the aristocracy.

At this point, even their different attitudes to the English revolutionary tradition become clear. The admiration shared by Montesquieu and the liberals is directed solely toward the Glorious Revolution which is extolled as fundamentally peaceful and painless. Hegel, instead, though he obviously moves away from the "leveling" thinkers and the most radical currents, still praises Cromwell because he "knew what it meant to govern" (*Ph. G.*, 897). As for Montesquieu, he speaks instead of King Charles I's execution as the beginning of a long series of "misfortunes"[13] that witnessed "the English nobility . . . buried with Charles I beneath the rubble of his throne."[14] In the eyes of this liberal theorist, the failure of the first English Revolution actually has an exemplary pedagogic value: "During the previous century, it was quite a sight to see the helpless efforts of the English to establish democracy in their country. . . . In the end, after many changes, clashes, and confusion, it was necessary to find peace again under the very same government that had been banned."[15]

In turn, Locke criticizes Filmer-style absolutism precisely because it was susceptible of justifying obedience even to Cromwell.[16] And after 1789, in France, Hume rose to the role of "prophet of the Counter-Revolution" with his grim portrayal of the English Civil War.[17] The representation provided by Hume re-emerges in de Maistre, who does not hesitate to subscribe to it in the last chapter of his *Considerations on France*, thus denouncing the repetition, during the French Revolution, of the same crimes that had been committed in England. More in general, it should be noted how "in English historiography, even that of the Whigs" during the seventeenth century, the celebration of the Glorious Revolution is constantly used in contrast with the harsh judgment given the first revolution.[18] Madame de Staël, who sees the English Civil War as "soiled" by the execution of Charles I, compares Cromwell to Robespierre, calling him "envious and evil."[19] As for Constant, he seems to speak of "inhumanity" and "raving" as the only characteristics of "civil wars" in England. Constant's portrayal of Cromwell as the "usurper"[20] puts this liberal theorist side by side with an author like Burke,[21] and in any case, Constant resorts to a kind of liberal legitimism that is completely absent in Hegel's philosophy of history.

Even with regard to the French Revolution, Hegel is far more progressive, or at least he proves to be much bolder than the liberal political press of his time: he does criticize the Jacobin Terror, even sternly at times, but he never demonizes it or reduces it to a mere orgy of blood. One need only compare this to the grim portraits of 1793 painted by Madame de Staël and Benjamin Constant.[22] Tocqueville speaks of the Montagnards as "renowned villains" who should be remembered only for their "bloody madness."[23] Hegel, on the other hand, though his judgment of this period is essentially negative, does acknowledge the work of Robespierre, and, in his philosophy of right lecture course at Heidelberg, he goes so far as to claim that Robespierre "carried out universally admired *facta*" (*Rph.I*, § 133 A). The Jacobin leader was not the savage beast referred to by the political press of the Restoration as well as by the liberal political press; certainly, virtue, which he took "very seriously" (*Ph.G.*, 930), did turn into something terrible, it became terror, and yet, "the fact that man grasped these principles has a very profound significance" (*v.Rph.*, IV, 657). On this point, Hegel's distance from the German liberal thought, at least that of post-1848, is all the more visible. Haym, who insists on calling Hegel the theorist of the Restoration, denounces not only, together with Jacobin Terror, the dramatic and tormented period of the French Revolution and "the terror and horrors of that horrible movement," but also the ideas of 1789 as a whole: "Those that grew out of the French Revolution were not the most noble and right political ideas."[24] This is not at all an isolated case, since at the time Haym was the editor of the *Prussian Annals*, the organ of the German liberal or national-liberal party.

Madame de Staël condemns not only Jacobinism, but the wrongful shift from a political revolution to a social revolution, from the ideal of freedom to that of equality, and this shift took place already on October 5 and 6, 1789, when the Parisian people, tormented by famine and exasperated by Louis XVI's refusal to sanction the decree that would abolish feudal rights, marched on the Palace of Versailles.[25] One could actually say that, for Madame de Staël, the highest moment of the French Revolution was the so-called "aristocratic" or "nobiliary" revolution, that is, the agitation of the parliaments (*Parlements*) (not representative organs, but judicial and administrative bodies) in defense of their privileges and their ancient prerogatives.[26] This agitation preceded the storming of the Bastille and the intervention of the masses that wiped out everything that was perceived to be an instrument of the aristocracy. The aristocratic nature of parliaments is recognized by Madame de Staël, who nevertheless writes: "in a great country, no revolution can succeed, except when it is initiated by the aristocracy. . . . At the time, a sincere, disinterested enthusiasm animated all French people; there was a public spirit."[27] The opposed material interests had not yet emerged: it was only later that the Revolution became violent and plebeian. For Hegel, instead, the violent character the Revolution took on can be explained by the fact that "the court, the clergy, the nobility, the parliament would not yield their privileges, neither by force, nor in the name of the right subsisting in and for itself" (*Ph.G.*, 925–26). No sympathy is expressed for the aristocratic-liberal opposition.

Some sympathy can perhaps still be perceived in Tocqueville: "In the first phase of the Revolution, when the war had not yet been declared between the classes, the language of the nobility is quite similar to that of the other classes, except that it goes further and takes on a higher tone. Their opposition bears some republican traits. They share the same ideas, the same passion that kindles the proudest hearts, and the souls that are most used to gazing directly and closely at human greatness." It is a moment when "a single visible passion, a common passion" dominates, the passion for freedom, not the passion for equality that was to cause the bloody "war between the classes."[28]

As for Hegel, he justifies the French Revolution as having been caused also by the "greed" and the "wealth" of the dominant class, and by its insistence on continuing to "plunder government funds and the people's hard work" (*w*, xx, 296–97). *Philosophy of History* portrays and celebrates the French Revolution first as a social revolution: "The hard, terrible weight on the people's shoulders, and the difficulty for the government to provide the court with the means to sustain its opulence and dissipation were *the first reason for the discontent*." The italics are mine, and they serve to emphasize the fact that, while, according to the liberal tradition, the agitation and social pressure of the underprivileged masses were the reason for the degeneration of the French Revolution once it had forgotten its true task as a system of liberty (*constitutio libertatis*), according to Hegel, those agitations and social pressures were a fundamental cause of, and justification for, the French Revolution, as well as the birth of the new spirit of freedom.[29] It was due to the social indignation of the starving masses that "the new spirit became active; the oppression (*der Druck*, the material burden which, as we have seen, was an intolerable weight on the people) pushed people to investigate the matter. What was discovered was that the sums extorted from people's hard work were not used for the sake of the State, but squandered in the most insane manner. It was at that point that "the whole system of the State revealed itself as unjust" (ph. G., 925).

The different positions with regard to the French Revolution are also reflected in the different attitudes toward Rousseau and other philosophers who had contributed to its ideological preparation. Constant accuses first of all Gabriel B. de Mably of paving the way for Robespierre, spreading the principle according to which "property is evil; if you cannot destroy it, at least weaken its power in every possible way." But also Rousseau was to blame for inspiring, with "his tirades against wealth and even against property," the most terrible phase of the French Revolution, that is, the social agitation of the underprivileged masses and the Jacobin politics of intervention in the economic and private sphere.[30] This kind of criticism is completely absent in Hegel who, on the contrary, places Rousseau among "those spirits who profoundly speculated and felt" the tragedy of poverty (infra, ch. VIII, 3). Rousseau's solution certainly does not satisfy Hegel, but he nevertheless praises him for having felt and conceptually framed poverty as a social issue: hence "the tirades against wealth and even against property" that Constant and the liberal tradition criticized in Rousseau.

We can conclude on this point. With regard to the world revolutionary process that destroys the *ancien régime,* German and other European thinkers can be divided into three ideological groups: 1) those reactionaries, like Friedrich Schlegel, who during the Restoration, wholly condemn the "epidemic disease that contaminates the people" and drags them into a ruinous revolutionary process;[31] 2) those who, following Burke's example, attempt to discredit the French Revolution by comparing it unfavorably to other, less radical, revolutions (this is what, for example, Friedrich von Gentz does in Germany when he condemns the French Revolution as a "total revolution");[32] or those who redeem the French Revolution to the extent that they ignore the struggle for equality and the social upheaval that were absent in other revolutions (Madame de Staël, Benjamin Constant, etc.). This second position still prevails, in various forms and shades, in liberal thought;[33] and finally 3) the position held by Hegel and classic German philosophy, which regards as generally positive the global revolutionary process that marks the end of the *ancien régime.*[34]

4. Patricians and Plebeians

In the light of these considerations, a scheme that would distinguish liberals on one side and conservative-reactionaries on the other, as if such classification were the only possible one, becomes completely useless. And it remains useless no matter how one presents it: we can regard Hegel as a conservative or a reactionary, but then it remains to be explained why he celebrates revolutions; we can "absolve" him as a liberal, but then the gap that separates him from the "classic" liberal tradition with regard to the theoretical devices he employs, as well as with regard to the historical and political judgments he expresses, still remains unclear. We can therefore try to choose a different interpretative key. We can try and use, rather than the pair of opposite concepts liberal-conservative, the pair aristocratic-plebeian, or tendentially plebeian. We can start to test the practicability of this interpretative key by directly comparing the reading of Roman history given, on the one hand, by Montesquieu and, on the other, by Hegel. Let us examine the passage from the monarchy to the republic. The two authors agree on the fact that the violence perpetrated upon Lucretia and her death were merely the incident, not the real cause, that triggered the political upheaval in question.[35] They also essentially agree on the aristocratic character of the passage from the monarchy to the republic. As for the rest, however, their value judgments are opposite. A clue to this opposition is their judgment of Tarquin the Proud, Rome's last king. Montesquieu writes: "Tarquin seized the throne without being elected by either the Senate or the people . . . ; he exterminated most of the senators; he no longer consulted those who were left, nor called them to be present at his deliberations. His power increased, as did the most hateful aspect of that power itself; he usurped the power of the people, created laws without them and against them. He was going to become the sole possessor of all three powers, but the people suddenly remembered that they were the legislators, and Tarquin ceased to be."[36] Hegel writes: "The last king, Tarquin the Proud, did not consult the Senate very often with regard to affairs of state, and did not find a replacement when a member of the Senate died; in short, he seemed eager to gradually rid himself of this institution. Under this last king, Rome achieved great prosperity" (Ph. G., 691). Montesquieu attributes the expulsion of the kings to the "people" (populus), but Hegel answers, or could have answered: "Populus, at the time, only referred to the patricians" (Ph. G., 690).

With the republic, the clash between patricians and plebeians became fiercer. Hegel writes: "Another privilege of the patricians was the administration of justice, which made the plebeians all the more dependent, since there were no precise written laws. The problem was solved by appointing a committee of ten members, the Decemvirs, whose function it was to draw up a code of laws. Thus, the Law of the Twelve Tables was written. From then on, the patron-and-client system became less and less widespread" (Ph. G., 695). Montesquieu writes: "In the heated dispute between patricians and plebeians, the latter asked for the promulgation of fixed laws, so that judgments would no longer depend on a fickle will or on an arbitrary power . . . . The Decemvirs were appointed to draw up this code of laws. The decision was to entrust them with considerable power, since they were to draw up laws that would apply to sides that were practically irreconcilable. . . . As a result, ten men from the whole republic were given all of the legislative power, all of the executive power, and all of the judicial power. Rome was subjected to a tyranny just as cruel as Tarquin's. When Tarquin carried out his oppression, Rome was indignant over the power he usurped; when the Decemvirs carried out their oppression, Rome was shocked at the sight of the power with which it had entrusted them."[37] The "tyranny of the Decemvirs" was an obstacle that needed to be removed in order for the greatness of Rome to develop; under the Decemvirs, "the State seemed to have lost the soul which animated it."[38]

As for the tribunes of the people, Montesquieu writes: "due to a malady eternal in man, the plebeians, who had obtained tribunes to defend themselves, used them for attacking. Little by little they removed the prerogatives of the patricians—which caused continual conflict. The people were supported, or rather, incited by their tribunes."[39] We have already seen, instead, Hegel's celebration of the Gracchi's noblemindedness; independent of his judgment on individual historical figures, Hegel saw in the institution of the tribunes of the people an important victory, not only for the plebeians, but also for the cause of freedom as a whole. In *Philosophy of History* he adds: "the number of tribunes was first limited to two; later they became ten, which was to the detriment of the plebeians, since the Senate only needed to win one of them over to its cause in order to invalidate, with merely one opponent, the decisions made by the rest of them" (*Ph. G.*, 696). Even Montesquieu acknowledges that "the opposition of one tribune to another" was one of the weapons used by the Senate, but on the whole, the description he gives of the struggle carried out by this institution against plebeian insurrection leaves no doubt as to which side Montesquieu felt more sympathy for: "The Senate defended itself by means of its wisdom, its justice, and the love of country it inspired; by its benefactions and a wise use of the republic's treasury; by the respect the people had for the glory of the leading families and the virtue of illustrious men."[40]

Montesquieu also expresses admiration for Sulla's defense of the prerogative of the senatorial aristocracy. In the light of the historical events that were to follow, both the struggle and its extreme harshness certainly appear useless. And yet, Montesquieu leaves no doubt as to the political and social significance of his position: "the people, vexed by the laws and the strictness of the Senate, always aimed at overthrowing them both." And the Senate was not able to stop "the people, in their blind desire for freedom," from handing themselves over "to Marius's hands, or to the hands of the first tyrant who would give them some hope for independence." The severity of the dictatorship imposed by Sulla in favor of the senatorial aristocracy made "people pay for the insults Sulla himself had perpetrated against the nobility."[41] Montesquieu's identification with Sulla (who nevertheless deserves some praise for having "restored freedom" in Rome)[42] is certainly not absolute, but one could say, paraphrasing Marx, that the former criticizes the latter especially for the plebeian methods with which he fought the enemies of the senatorial aristocracy (by using the army, distributing the lands confiscated from the most influential figures of the rival party among his soldiers, etc.).[43] Hegel's position is completely opposite: "Sulla returned then to Rome, he was victorious against the people's party led by Marius and Cinna, he occupied the city and ordered a systematic slaughter of important Roman figures: forty senators and sixteen-hundred knights (*equites*) were sacrificed to his ambition and his lust for power" (*Ph. G.*, 707). There is no doubt: if Montesquieu's position in favor of the senatorial aristocracy is quite manifest, no less manifest is Hegel's position in favor of the "people's party." Later we will examine their opposite judgments on Julius Caesar. For now we will just observe the fact that, for Montesquieu, Julius Caesar merely skillfully continued the work begun by Marius, the leader of the people's party defeated by Sulla who now had a chance to take their revenge. And in any case, on the one hand, we have the "party of freedom," on the other, "the assaults of an enraged and blind mob."[44]

It is necessary to draw a conclusion: concerning the great class struggles throughout Roman history, the positions chosen by Montesquieu and Hegel are consistently opposed: the former sides with the senatorial aristocracy, which in his eyes embodies the cause of freedom and the struggle against tyranny; the latter sides with the "party of the people," with the plebeians, and with the institutions that in some way protect them.

We will now continue to examine the collapse of Roman monarchy, in order to grasp all of its general implications. While the passage from the monarchy to the republic represents no progress for freedom, Hegel repeatedly speaks of "progress of freedom" and "extension of freedom" in reference to the "lawful demands" that the plebeians succeed in making in their struggle against the patricians and the aristocratic republic, in reference to the "intervention to the detriment of the patricians' rights" (*Ph. G.*, 696–97). The tortuous march toward freedom seems to coincide with the ups and downs of the plebeian class. A point of regression is the overthrow of the monarchy that counterbalanced the arrogance of the aristocracy, whereas an instance of progress toward freedom is the acceptance, after a harsh struggle, of the plebeians' demands, not only the political ones (the institution of the tribuneship of the people, the access to public offices, etc.), but also the economic and material ones (such as the forgiveness, at least partial, of debts). This represents an achievement of certain goals which, at least in appearance, does not change the institutional structure and the sphere of formal freedom, but nevertheless brings about an extension of actual freedom. And the political goals that are gradually achieved must not be evaluated in the abstract: the institution of the tribunes of the people (*tribuni plebis*) constitutes an "extension" of freedom, but the decision to increase their number from two to ten constitutes a moment of regression, since it favors the maneuvers of the aristocracy against the plebeians. Once again, the plebeians are the real subjects of the march toward freedom, beyond all institutional transformations.

In this lucid perspective on ancient history more general implications are embedded, and it is Hegel himself who points them out: both then and now, the question is not to choose in the abstract between monarchy and republic, nor between the power of the sovereign and the power of the *Stände*, the more or less representative bodies, government and opposition, the recognized authorities and freedom. The question is to determine, for every single case, the concrete political and social contents. In Sparta and Rome, the republic coincided with the freedom of the patricians, in the same way as in the modern world the struggle against the central monarchical power was often led in the name of that enchanting ideal, freedom, though in reality it was the freedom of the barons: "With the development of the internal life of the State, the patricians witnessed a reduction in the power of their position, and, as would frequently happen even in the European history of the Middle Ages, the kings often sought support among the people against them" (*ph. G.*, 691).

Hegel constantly draws comparisons between ancient Rome and England (*ph. G.*, 693 and 695): his position against the patricians is at the same time a position against the barons. But even in Montesquieu we read: "Just as Henry VII, king of England, increased the power of the Commons in order to degrade the Lords, so Servius Tullius, before him, extended the privileges of the people in order to reduce the Senate."[45] It is the same comparison drawn by Hegel, except that Montesquieu's position is in favor of the patricians and the feudal barons who opposed the reforms made by the Crown.

5. Monarchy and Republic

The historical concreteness revealed by Hegel differentiates him not only from the liberal tradition, but also from the Rousseauian-Jacobin tradition; the reading of ancient history provided by the latter, in fact, is often inferior and in any case similar to that of the liberal tradition. We will limit ourselves to a few examples: at the time of Louis XVI's execution and of the wave of criticism and execration stirred by it, in an attempt to defend or justify the French "regicides" a German democrat drew a comparison, though with some distinctions, between the execution of Louis XVI and that of Charles I of England, and also between the former and that of "Agis of Sparta."[46] For his part, Rousseau had already painted a grim portrait of King Agis, who in reality had been put to death by the aristocracy for his attempt to introduce some democratic reforms. According to Rousseau, Sparta's most glorious era dated back to the beginning of the republic, after the collapse of the monarchy.[47] In Hegel, instead, we read: "Cleomenes and Agis [are] the most beautiful figures we can find in history" because they attempted to overthrow "a terrible aristocracy" (Rph. I, § 133 A). Hegel's historical sense does not fail to notice the fact that the collapse of the monarchy in Sparta brought about no extension of actual freedom.

The same considerations can be made for the collapse of the monarchy in Rome. When Rousseau celebrates the "venerable images of ancient times," he refers to the ancient republics: "Rome and Sparta brought human glory to its highest peak. . . . Both of them were republics, first they were governed by kings, then they became free States."[48] Robespierre, too, constantly extols a republican France modeled after the republics of Sparta and Rome, and he even compares the overthrow of the monarchy in France and Rome: "Was Tarquin ever summoned before a court?"[49] Still following Rousseau's example, the end of the monarchy is compared to a revolution.[50] Hegel's judgment is quite different: "The plebeians gained nothing from the expulsion of the kings. In the civil community, the latter had at least raised the status of the plebeians before the patricians, and prevented the patricians from crushing them." And in fact, "the patricians were responsible for overthrowing the kings," due to their discontent for the reforms made by the kings in favor of the plebeians (Ph. G., 693 and 690–91). Republic is not synonymous with actual freedom: the ancient republics in Sparta and Rome were the result of counter-revolutions. Let us examine the collapse of the Roman Republic: for Montesquieu, Julius Caesar acted in the name of an "evil cause," and therefore his victories were "shameful,"[51] whereas Brutus, "covered with blood and glory," showed "people the dagger and freedom."[52] Constant speaks of Julius Caesar's "ruinous career" in opposition to Brutus' love of freedom.[53] Paradoxically, however, this is also the judgment given by the Jacobins: for Robespierre, Caesar was a tyrant committed to "crush and betray the people" for the sake of his "wicked ambition."[54] And in order to show the necessity to judge and condemn Louis XVI without bothering too much with legal niceties, Louis A. L. Saint-Just uses the example of Brutus: "then a tyrant was slain in the midst of the Senate" in the name of "the liberty of Rome."[55] Once again, the influence of Rousseau is evident: Caesar represents the crucial point used to demonstrate that "the chains of Rome" were forged "in her armies." Besides, Caesar who, pleading for Catiline, trampled on the precepts of "civil religion" and "tried to establish the dogma that the soul is mortal," spoke as a "bad citizen," as Cato and Cicero observed.[56] This last theme was used by Robespierre in the speech with which he championed national holidays and the cult of the Supreme Being: "observe the profound art with which Caesar, defending Catiline's accomplices before the Roman Senate, began a digression against the dogma of the soul's immortality; he held those ideas perfectly suitable to extinguish, in the judges' hearts, the energy of virtue; he saw the cause of the crime strictly tied to that of atheism. Cicero, on the contrary, called upon the sword of the laws and the thunderbolt of the gods against traitors."[57]

A few decades later, Tocqueville provides a reading of ancient history that is not very different from the one given by the very same Jacobin leaders he had labeled as "villains:" the collapse of the Roman Republic is viewed as a shift "from freedom to despotism."[58] Yet, when the Jacobins condemn such despotism, they have the *ancien régime* in mind, whereas Tocqueville has in mind the revolutionary, egalitarian dictatorship that, he maintains, resulted directly in the Bonapartist regime.

If in the Rousseauian-Jacobin tradition on one side and in the liberal tradition on the other, Julius Caesar is equally portrayed as the oppressor of republican freedom and Cicero and Brutus as its most extreme defenders, Hegel's position is completely different. In the struggle against Caesar, the Senate, far from representing the "universal," represented the "particular," that is, the interests of the aristocracy: "Pompey and all those who supported him raised the flag of their *dignitas*, their *auctoritas*, *their* particular power as if it were the flag that represented the power of the republic." Instead, it was just a semblance, or rather, a mystification; it was actually Caesar who, though by means of "violence," defeated "particularity" and asserted the value of "the universal" (*Ph. G.*, 711–12).

6. The Repression of the Aristocracy and
the March Toward Freedom

If for Madame de Staël "aristocracy is better" than absolute monarchy,[59] for Hegel "the aristocratic order is the worst" (*Ph. G.*, 698). Hegel's distance from the liberal tradition and from Montesquieu (the theorist, according to Marx, of "aristocratic-constitutional monarchy") is evident.[60] If there is any connection, it's with Rousseau, who maintained that "aristocracy is the worst among sovereign powers," it is within this context that we should consider the strongly negative judgment of England given by Hegel in opposition to Montesquieu's.[61] The fact is that England's historical development is quite different from France's, which constitutes Hegel's model: in France, political freedom and the equal rights of the *citoyens*, sanctioned by the Revolution, came about only after absolute monarchy had largely crushed the excessive power and privileges of the nobility, thus carrying out a leveling and somehow emancipating function. In England, on the contrary, freedom—or rather, the various types of freedom—affirmed itself as a result of the struggle of the aristocracy against the Crown. Hegel makes a precise comparison between the developments of the two countries: "What is particularly relevant is the fact that the King of France declared that, within the Crown's dominions, the serfs were allowed to free themselves and redeem their land for a low price." While in France the existence of a strong central power made such results possible and ensured a condition of "public peace" by dealing a heavy blow to feudal "anarchy," in England the barons forced King John to sign the *Magna Carta*, the foundation of freedom in England; in other words, the foundation of the privileges of the nobility" (*Ph. G.*, 865–66).

About the *Magna Carta*, which constituted the reference point of the liberal tradition, Hegel's judgment is constantly negative: "England's barons extorted the *Magna Carta* from the king; yet, the citizens gained nothing by it, and their condition remained unchanged" (*Ph. G.*, 902). English legislation—he declares in the essay *Reformbill*—"is completely founded upon particular rights, freedoms, and privileges that kings and parliaments conferred, sold, gave out (freely or not) in particular circumstances: the *Magna Carta*, the *Bill of Rights* . . . were concessions extorted by force, gracious gifts, *pacta*, etc., and constitutional rights never moved on from the private form they originally had" (*B.schr.*, 468–69). The same position can be found in Edmund Burke, though with an opposite value judgment: "You will observe that from *Magna Carta* to the *Declaration of Rights* it has been the uniform policy of our constitution to claim and assert our liberties as an entailed inheritance derived to us from our forefathers, and to be transmitted to our posterity."[62] This is precisely the private form denounced by Hegel, whose value judgment is shared by the revolutionaries who opposed Burke. Thus, for example, Thomas Paine speaks disparagingly of the "*Magna Carta*, as it was called," and then adds: "The act, called the Bill of Rights, comes here into view. What is it, but a bargain, which the parts of the government made with each other to divide powers, profits, and privileges?"[63]

For Hegel, the common thread of modern history and the progress toward freedom is the "process of submission to aristocracy" (Ph.G., 902). And the reading of modern history does not revolve, as certain liberal schemes would have it, around the opposition between royal power and the freedom of the individual, an opposition that in this way would conceal the real political and social subjects involved in the struggle. With greater realism and historical sense, Hegel speaks not only of the Crown, but of the aristocracy (the barons and the nobility), on the one hand, and of the "people" (who practically coincide with the Third Estate), on the other, and of the antagonism between these two classes. The contradiction is not so much between freedom and authority, since there is also a "freedom of the barons" (*Freiheit der Barone*) that entails the "absolute servitude" (*absolute Knechtschaft*) of the "nation" (a term which calls to mind the community of the *citoyens* celebrated by the French Revolution) and obstructs the "liberation of the serfs" (*Befreiung der Hörigen*; Ph.G., 902–3). In other words, the "freedom of the barons" perpetuates a condition that for Hegel is substantially analogous to slavery (Rph., § 66 A). "Freedom" (*Freiheit*) and servitude-slavery (*Knechtschaft*) do not exclude each other as they do in the liberal tradition; they are not the antithetical terms of a logical contradiction according to which they cannot be present simultaneously in the same situation. Here, on the contrary, they are both present; their political and social subjects are contrasting, but connected by a relationship of contradiction. This relationship of contradiction, however, is not logical, but real and objective. Proof of this is the following statement: "people . . . everywhere freed themselves (*befreit*) thanks to the repression (*Unterdrückung*) of barons" (Ph.G., 902). Here is a pair of concepts bearing a similar meaning to the ones we previously examined: *Befreiung-Unterdrückung*, except that now the relationship has been overturned, and the people's emancipation (including that of the ex-serfs) goes hand in hand with the repression of the aristocracy, or at least with the repression of its privileges. But the aristocracy, as we have already seen, perceives the loss of the privilege which, for example, made it the exclusive administrator of justice, as "an unseemly violence, oppression of freedom (*Unterdrückung der Freiheit*), and despotism" (Rph., § 219 A). We are before a sharp contradiction and a harsh struggle between two political and social subjects, and the people had to side with the Crown in order to achieve their goals of freedom, and to make it possible for "the private rights of the nobility" to be damaged (Ph.G., 902): "With the support of the people, the kings overpowered injustice; but when the people sought the support of barons, or when the latter maintained their freedom against the kings, all positive rights, or rather, positive injustices, remained unchanged" (*positive Rechte oder Unrechte*; Ph.G., 903). In this passage, Hegel's violent anti-feudal passion is quite evident: he speaks of aristocracy not only as a "caste," but a *Kaste der Ungerechtigkeit*, whose *Rechte*, celebrated as "positive" by the reactionary ideologues and sometimes looked upon respectfully, for the same reason, by a certain liberal tradition, are in reality *Unrechte*, illegal or unjust, and have no reason to exist.

In order to eliminate all of this, Hegel does not hesitate to call for revolution from the top-down, or at least a strengthening of the Crown's powers. Is this a proof of Hegel's "conservativeness"? In reality, Madame de Staël's celebration of freedom in France before the advent of absolute monarchy is but a classic theme of the aristocratic political press, and in France such celebration was opposed by personalities who had held democratic-radical positions during the Revolution.[64] Above all, it may be useful to examine the lucid, impartial analysis that emerges from an excellent passage by Tocqueville: "Nations that turn toward democracy habitually begin to increase the attributions of royal power. The sovereign inspires less jealousy and fear than the nobility. . . . English aristocracy made an extraordinary move: it led the democratic classes of society to believe that their common enemy was the sovereign, and in this way it became the representative of those classes, instead of their main adversary."[65] Here the main contradiction is not between authority and freedom, as it is for Bobbio and essentially also for Ilting, but between the aristocracy and the people, exactly as it is for Hegel; and appealing to royal power to subdue the aristocracy is not synonymous with conservatism (as it is for Bobbio, Ilting, and all those who participated in the antihistorical process aimed at condemning or absolving Hegel in the name of categories, prejudices, and current liberalism). Rather, it is synonymous with democracy, people's democracy.

7. Anglophobia and Anglophilia

The most sensational example of a victory of the barons' freedom over the central, royal power as well as over the actual freedom of the "people" is the case of Poland. Yet, a rather similar example is represented by England, and Hegel unequivocally speaks up in favor of strengthening the royal power: "People everywhere owe their liberation (*Befreiung*) from aristocratic oppression (*Unterdrückung*) to the king. In England, such oppression still exists because the king's power is irrelevant" (*Ph.G.*, 693). The term "anglophobia" has sometimes been used in reference to Hegel, who is definitely not an anglophile, but to liken the difference between anglophobiacs and anglophiles to the difference between liberals and reactionaries or conservatives would be a serious misrepresentation.[66]

Even before the French Revolution broke out, Rousseau had used harsh words in reference to England: a liberal author like Montesquieu welcomed a limitation of the Crown's powers carried out by a feudal aristocracy with the sole objective of defending its own privileges, an aristocracy that constituted a characteristic of English political and constitutional history.[67] On the contrary, a democratic author like Rousseau decisively rejected it.

It was especially after the French Revolution broke out that England began to be denounced by critics: Hegel shares his "anglophobia" with several authors of the democratic and even revolutionary tradition, whereas not a few reactionary theorists appear among the most fervent anglophiles. A polemical celebration of the English model against the French one is in fact one of the most recurring and beloved themes of the conservative and reactionary political press, beginning with Burke and his followers.[68] Let us not forget that, until the Revolution of 1848, both the admirers and critics of England, though with opposite value judgments, regarded it as the country that had led the coalitions against revolutionary and Napoleonic France; the country—Engels points out after the February Revolution—where the Bourbons who had been driven out of the throne ran for shelter, and to where it was only logical that a "crypto-Bourbon" like Louis Philippe would run.[69]

On the other hand, the categories of anglophilia and anglophobia cannot be used correctly without making some internal distinctions: Kant clearly sympathized with Adam Smith and the classic political economy, he extolled the Glorious Revolution and admired Milton, the poet and singer of the English Civil War. Yet, at the same time he distanced himself sharply from England during the American war of independence, and especially during the counter-revolutionary crusade against the new France. He considered the England of those years as the bulwark of "slavery and barbarism" and labeled its Prime Minister, William Pitt, an "enemy of mankind."[70] So, should Kant be considered an anglophile or an anglophobe? If these categories are regarded in their ahistorical abstractness, they become completely useless: we must keep in mind that for the representatives of reactionary anglophilia, the celebration of England as a whole did not exclude the denunciation of certain specific aspects that were important to English tradition as well as to its cultural and political life. They therefore denounced not only the radicalism of the English Civil War, but also, for example, its political economy, which they rightly considered a subverter of the feudal order and the good old times. On the opposite side, instead, following Kant's tradition, Hegel (but also Marx and Engels) condemned and disparaged the English model, yet they still celebrated or at least held a largely positive opinion of the English Civil War and the Glorious Revolution and of the classic political economy

(*Rph.*, § 189 A), and they even admired and respected the freedom and liveliness of English parliamentary debates (*v.Rph.*, IV, 707–8).

8. Hegel, England, and Liberal Tradition

Before 1848, even the authors who were most directly tied to the liberal tradition revealed a critical tendency toward England. One example is the following statement by Carl von Rotteck: "With regard to the constitutional science of the State, the French are on top of everyone else. On the theoretical level, if not on the practical one, they are directly emulated by the Germans. The English, instead, have lagged sensibly behind, due to their extreme attachment to historical right." In order to fully grasp the bitterness of this judgment on England, we should keep in mind Rotteck's denunciation of historical right: "The origin of historical rights is largely, or most largely, illegal. They are born out of the *ignorance of right*, the *contempt of right*, or *blind chance*, and are enforced by *violence*."[71]

Is the criticism of England an exclusive characteristic of the German cultural and political tradition? If we look outside Germany during the period between 1789 and 1848, we find that, for Madame de Staël, for example, England constitutes "the most beautiful monument of justice and moral greatness."[72] We shall see later what it is exactly about England that draws so much admiration. However, let us now examine a liberal critic who is more sensitive to the needs of democracy: for Tocqueville, at least until 1848, England is synonymous with "aristocratic society" dominated by "great lords,"[73] and this aristocratic society sometimes appears to be on the verge of revolution.[74] This kind of criticism is not very different from Hegel's, and at times even Benjamin Constant, despite his close ties to Madame de Staël, expresses a rather negative judgment of England: "Essentially, England is but a vast, opulent, and vigorous aristocracy. Boundless properties held together by the same pair of hands; colossal riches concentrated among the same people; a numerous, faithful clientele that revolves around each large property-owner, whom they endow with political rights that the constitution had apparently granted them only so that they would give them up; and finally, as a result of this combination, a national delegation made up in part of government workers, and in part of representatives elected by the aristocracy; such has been so far the organization of England."

To this picture, which from the constitutional and liberal points of view is already quite grim, we should add the tragedy of mass poverty, a poverty that is perhaps even worse than on the continent and which the dominant power and the property-owners treat with more brutality: mass lay-offs not only in the factories, but also on the domestic level at the expense of the ex-clients, carried out by an aristocracy so unscrupulous that, according to Constant, it runs the risk of bringing discredit upon itself, or even digging its own grave. Thus, when the crisis struck, "in London alone ten to twenty thousand servants were reduced to poverty almost in the same day," and the whole city was crowded with "long lines of peasants" and "groups of craftsmen" desperately looking for food and alms. Naturally, the safety of private property suffered from it: there were robberies and, as a result of the bitter poverty and hunger, even "partial lootings, poorly organized." Those responsible for these crimes were punished with "sentences no less severe than the ones they would have received if they had committed political assassinations" (in other words, they were often sentenced to death as if they had organized an insurrection). But the disproportionate severity of the sentences was not the only thing: there was also "the horrible expedient of sending spies to stir ignorant individuals to revolt, in order to denounce them later. . . . These wretched informers lured those who had the misfortune of listening to them, and probably they also accused those whom they had not been able to corrupt." Is it so surprising, then, that some strata of the population revealed "a certain insurrectional exaltation"? "England's internal situation" was "far more alarming than the continent could imagine."[75]

Hegel, too, briefly criticizes the practice, carried out in England by the police and the dominant classes, of resorting to agents who stir people to revolt, and denounces the "abyss of rottenness" created by such practice (*Rph.I*, § 119 A). Hegel also condemns the "draconian" severity which demands that "every thief in England be hanged," creating an absurd equivalence between life and property (*v.Rph.*, III, 304), between two "qualitatively different" crimes such as murder and theft (*Rph.I*, § 45 A). In addition, Hegel isolates and condemns the class origins of this "draconian" severity: the peasants who are guilty of hunting illegally are sentenced to "the harshest and most disproportionate punishments" because "those who made those laws and who are now sitting in the courts as magistrates and jurors" are the aristocrats, the members of the social class which has secured the monopoly of the right to hunt (*B.schr.*, 479–81). The anglophobe Hegel is set on a more liberal position than liberal England herself.

However, if we exclude their critical positions on the cruel repression of the people, Hegel and Constant remain quite different. The former does not limit himself to denouncing the harshness and close-mindedness of the English aristocracy, but seems to be questioning its dominant role as such. He strongly condemns the "formal" character of English freedom, in the sense that, in practice, the aristocracy dominates public life and has the exclusive use of those political rights that, in theory, also belong to a much larger number of citizens.[76]

In the case of England, too, Hegel hopes that a revolution from the top-down will prevent a revolution from the bottom-up, even though his hope progressively fades . . . It is precisely this hope that a revolution from the top-down will bring about a reform that differentiates Hegel most sharply from the liberal tradition. Despite his realistic and blunt portrayal of England under the domination of the aristocracy, Constant continues to place his hopes on this very same social class. In his view, the English aristocracy cannot be equated to the French feudal nobility of the *ancien régime:* the former shared their "need for freedom" with the "people"; in France, instead, "the large property-owners . . . always tried to share the power rather than to limit it: they preferred privileges over rights, and favors over guarantees."[77] Hegel, instead, does not identify any substantial differences between the feudal nobility in the two countries: in both cases, the feudal nobility aspired to defend and extend its *libertates,* the freedoms (and privileges) of the barons. Constant's fear is that the English aristocracy, hanging on too tightly and too blindly to its particular interests, might end up like the French aristocracy. With its unscrupulous mass lay-offs of servants and clients, with the renunciation of its national duties, "the English aristocracy did unto itself what royal power had done in other countries to the aristocracy."[78] This much is clear: Hegel is not so soft on the aristocracy, and, to the extent that this social class continues to dominate England, he is decisively more "anglophobic" than Constant.

9. Equality and Freedom

As a final demonstration of Hegel's "anglophobia," Bobbio cites this passage: "In England, right is set up in the worst possible manner: it exists only for the rich, not for the poor" (*Ph. G.*, 906). Several years later, examining the institution of bail in America, Tocqueville observes that it works "to the disadvantage of the poor and to the advantage of the rich," for whom "all of the punishments sanctioned by the law are reduced to mere fines." Is there anything more "aristocratic than such a legislation"? And how can one explain its presence in America? "The explanation—Tocqueville observes— must be sought in England: the laws I talked about are English laws."[79]

Hegel's tone is perhaps more plebeian, and it reminds us of Engels: in England, "the practice of favoring the rich is explicitly acknowledged even by the law"; even the "*Habeas corpus,* that is, the right for any defendant (except those charged with high treason) to remain free until the trial upon payment of a bail, this much-celebrated right is itself a privilege of the rich. The poor cannot provide any warranty, and must therefore go to jail."[80] Doesn't the liberal tradition confirm, to some extent, this view expressed by Hegel and Engels? We have seen how Montesquieu extolled the English "gentlemen" as opposed to the Dutch "scoundrels." After the French Revolution "degenerated" from "political" to "social"—according to the liberal political press—the English "gentlemen" came to be contrasted to the French "mob." Madame de Staël observes that the "vulgar classes" that defiled France and its Revolution were never of any consequence in England, where the "empire" of "property" remains uncontested.[81] We have seen, instead, how Constant expresses some doubts and reservations, but on one point his admiration does not falter: England is "the country where the rights of each person are most guaranteed," as well as the country where "social differences are most respected." As a proof of this last statement, Constant cites an episode that would seem to confirm Hegel's anti-aristocratic anglophobia: "On seeing me arrive on foot, people at an inn treated me in an utterly unacceptable manner. In England, only beggars and the worst kind of robbers, the so-called *Footpads*, travel in such fashion. . . . I put on such airs and complained to such extent that the following morning I succeeded in having them treat me like a *gentleman* and pay as such."[82] Hume, too, had recognized this as an obvious fact: "A traveller is always admitted into company, and meets with civility, in proportion as his train and equipage speak him a man of great or moderate fortune."[83] In 1840, in his criticism of England, Tocqueville quotes and subscribes to the following observation made by an American: "The English treat their servants with such haughtiness and absolutism that it cannot but shock us. On the contrary, the French sometimes treat them with such familiarity, or behave towards them with such courteousness that we cannot conceive of it. It almost seems like they are afraid of giving orders. Neither one of these attitudes—of superiority or inferiority—is suitable."[84]

The rigid "class differences" which Hume and Constant admire so much in England appear instead excessive both to Tocqueville and Hegel. Their arguments are rather similar: Tocqueville explains that England lacks "general ideas" because inequality is so sharp and insurmountable that "there are as many different humanities as there are social classes."[85] For Hegel, the haughty attitude towards servants, in vogue in a still feudal Prussia, represents an "abstract" form of thought, since it leaves man's concreteness out of consideration and instead it classifies him according to a single "abstract" quality, that of wealth or of social class. With reference to post-revolutionary France, Hegel contrasts this attitude to the cordial, even friendly relationships that link a servant to his master (*w*, II, 580). Between the two "extremes" of England and France, Tocqueville instead chooses a middle way, that of America.

One could therefore say that, contrary to the liberal tradition, Hegel emphasizes equality over freedom. We purposely used a conditional tense here because we believe that the alternative that has been reproposed even recently is formulated incorrectly: according to it, in the case of a contrast between freedom and equality, priority should necessarily be given to the first term.[86] Even before Marx, Hegel had the merit of justifying the existence of inalienable "material rights" (*B.schr.*, 488): he highlighted the fact that, if pushed to a certain level, inequality annihilates even freedom itself, concrete freedom. A situation of extreme need "attacks the whole scope of the realization of freedom" (*v.Rph.*, IV, 342), it results in a "total lack of rights" (*Rph.*, § 127).

Nevertheless, the liberal tradition has often contrasted freedom to equality. Thus, after 1848, Tocqueville, fearing the specter of socialism, writes that "the English Revolution was carried out exclusively in the name of freedom, whereas the French Revolution was carried out exclusively in the name of equality."[87] Tocqueville's criticism extends itself to the culture of the Enlightenment that prepared the ground for the outbreak of the French Revolution. Tocqueville sees its pathos of the State as an element in common with socialism, and indicates, as its fundamental flaw, the fact that a firm "passion for equality" was paired up with a rather "uncertain" "love of freedom."[88] Obsessed by the specter of socialism, Tocqueville affirms that "those who seek in freedom something other than freedom itself are made to serve." A possible answer to Tocqueville's position would be the very same observation that he had made several years earlier when faced with England's spectacle of terrible mass poverty and the most clashing inequality: "Here the slave, there the master, there the wealth of some, here the poverty of the greater number."[89] In this passage, extreme inequality is synonymous with an essential mass slavery, and thus the *pathos* of freedom makes no sense without the *pathos* of equality.

The opposition between freedom and equality sometimes presents itself as an opposition between safety and inequality. This is the case with Jeremy Bentham: "When safety and equality are in conflict with each other, there should be no hesitation: equality must be given up."[90] Like Tocqueville, Bentham criticizes the pathos of equality that characterizes the French Revolution (infra, ch. XII, 3). Hegel, instead, not only reveals a clear preference for the French political tradition, but he declares that the freedom-safety of property and the individual sphere is incomplete without the "guarantee of subsistence" (and such guarantee is more related to the value of equality than to that of freedom, or rather, it tends to guarantee the basic conditions for equality in absence of which freedom becomes merely abstract and formal).

Hegel's passion for equality sometimes seems to give him the illusion that, with regard to the new industrial lobbies (to "modern feudalism," using an expression coined by one of Hegel's disciples),[91] the Crown might play a similar role to the one it historically played by crushing the excessive power of the feudal nobility. Until the very end, Hegel expresses his disapproval of the "weakness of royal power" in England, that is, of the absence of a "force" that might stand up to the "enormous wealth of private citizens" (B.schr., 480 and 473). Should we then see a connection with respect to the idea of a "people's monarchy, social and revolutionary," argued for a few decades later, though only briefly, by the Hegelian thinker Ferdinand Lassalle in his correspondence with Bismarck?[92] The issue at stake is much more legitimate than the one expressed by the false dichotomy of liberalism vs. conservatism. And yet, one should not lose sight of the radical difference in the historical situation, nor of Hegel's *pathos* of the doctrine of Natural Law.[93] It is precisely this pathos that leads him to regard individual freedom as an absolute value; the same pathos that, ever since the Jena period, leads him to indicate, as the inalienable presupposition of modern freedom, "the awareness of individuality as an absolute, an absolute being-in-itself."[94] And this lesson is somehow present also in Marx's *Critique of the Gotha Programme*, where Marx harshly criticizes Lassalle for his support of an "alliance with the absolutist, feudal adversaries against the bourgeoisie."[95] All further progress presupposed instead the realization of the bourgeoisie's revolutionary program, and thus the acknowledgment of the individual's "absolute being-in-itself." It is precisely this acknowledgment that Lassalle perhaps lacks, though he was right when he observed: "The rights that liberalism demands . . . are never meant for the individual as such, but always for an individual in a particular situation, an individual who pays certain taxes, an individual who owns capital, etc."[96] As for the emphasis he puts on the particular limit of a certain conception of the individual, Lassalle is instead a worthy disciple of Hegel, for whom it is precisely the construction of the universal concept of man (or individual) that defines the progress of freedom, progress as such. Another new aspect is that, in Hegel even more than in Marx, the *pathos* of the doctrine of Natural Law in the sense we have already explained (nature has now become "second nature") somehow begins to refer to "material rights." If these "material rights" are disregarded, then the acknowledgment of the category of man (and individual) in every human being becomes purely formal. At this point, the issue of the guarantee of freedom becomes much more complex, and can no longer be reduced to a definition of the limits of political power. Political power is instead called to be present and active in the economic and social fields.

VI

The Intellectual, Property, and the Social Question

1. Theoretical Categories and Immediate Political Options

Given that he is neither a conservative-reactionary nor a liberal, should Hegel be considered a revolutionary? Once again, before venturing a response we would do well to consider the ambiguities inherent in the formulation of the question itself. In this case, it might be useful to take as our point of departure Ilting's argument against Joachim Ritter: to speak of Hegel's philosophy as a "philosophy of the Revolution" is a "grotesque mistake"; it is clear that Hegel opts for political reform and gradual change. Of course, the inability of institutions to rise to the "spirit of the time" may make violent clashes inevitable, but this admission is not the propaganda of a revolutionary program, rather, it is evidence of the necessary and beneficial nature of reform.[1] On this point, there can be no doubt: Hegel's opting for reform is definitive not only on a political level, but on an emotional level as well. After the July Revolution, Hegel openly declares himself to be sick of the incessant upheavals that have characterized his times (Ph. G., 932). Even before Berlin, in *Phenomenology of Spirit*, a work characterized by a patient faith in political change, Hegel emphasizes his distance from "revolutionary" cries (W, III, 47).

As long as we consider immediate political options, there can be no doubt. But is this all that we should consider? Arguing against Hegel's claim that political-constitutional change should take place slowly and gradually, Marx observes that "the category of *gradual* transition is, first of all, historically false; and secondly, it explains nothing."[2] The young Marx has no doubt about Hegel's support for gradual reform: but this is only part of the problem. The other is that criticism of this position is developed not only based upon Hegel's thought, but seems to be literally drawn from his text. In the *Encyclopedia* we read: "Gradual change is the last superficial resort able to bring calm and duration to things" (§ 258 z). If *Philosophy of*

Right, at least when it expounds a concrete political program for the Germany of the time, is dominated by the category of gradualism (which elicits the criticism of Marx), *The Encyclopedia of Logic* is dominated by a qualitative leap, and for this reason elicits the enthusiasm of Lenin.[3]

It is clear: we are dealing with two different schemas, ones that Engels attempted to distinguish as "method" and "system." As we saw in chapter I, the deceptiveness of the schemas is recognized to some extent even by reactionary critics. Naturally, this distinction does not outline two completely separate schemas, but has itself the same methodological category. We can say that the "method" reflects the historical experience of the French Revolution and the great upheaval of the time, and also reflects the profound need for a theoretical struggle in opposition to the conservative and reactionary ideology. The "system" refers to immediate political choices.[4] For example, support for gradualism, before becoming one of the catchwords of liberal moderation, was part of the lexicon of conservatives and reactionaries: in the name of "wise gradualism," the Junkers' spokesmen opposed what they considered the reckless reforms which demolished the feudal structure in Prussia after the Jena defeat.[5]

Later, the struggle against codification is carried out with equal vigor by Friedrich Karl von Savigny, to mark the celebration of history as an uninterrupted process, the "indissoluble organic relationship of generations and epochs, between which there can only be evolution, not an absolute end or absolute beginning." Savigny argues against those reformers who would like to "cut every historical link and begin a completely new life."[6] Later still, a Restoration ideologue like Baader directs his opposition to the demands of the liberal and constitutional movement by distinguishing between *Evolutionismus* and *Revolutionismus.* He supports the former, that is, the category of gradualism, and condemns the latter, that qualitative leap and revolutionary break.[7]

Both authors surely have Burke's theory in mind. Burke is the first to contrast the revolutionary upheaval in France to the tranquil course of "nature," or that union of nature and history which is inheritance. Inheritance "furnishes a sure principle of conservation and a sure principle of transmission, without at all excluding a principle of improvement."[8] It needs to be added, however, that if these are the beginnings, then as an ideological tool employed against the Revolution, the category of gradualism is developed above all in Germany. It is Germany that must confront the political and ideological reality of the new France, and it must do so with a past marked by, on the one hand, an antiquated socio-political framework, and on the other, a rich cultural and philosophical tradition. One could say that if France experienced the most radical developments and socio-political conflicts, as Marx and Engels claim, then it was in

Germany that the ideological battle was most profoundly theorized. This is true for reactionary theorists as well as for those who struggle against them, and the greatest moment of this struggle against reactionism is represented by Hegel. Not only is Hegel, as we have seen above, politically aware of the conservative significance of his celebration of gradualism, but the category is even vigorously refuted on a theoretical level. Are, as we saw with Burke, revolution and progressive reform contrasted to the painless gradualism of changes in nature? It is not true—he firmly objects in *The Encyclopedia*—that nature does not make leaps, because the category of the qualitative leap is the necessary condition for understanding natural processes.

The confutation comes at another, more advanced level as well: the course of history is assimilated with the course of nature, so now what do the exponents of reactionary Romanticism do? Well, *Philosophy of History* contrasts organic-natural development with historical development: the first "takes place in a direct, unopposed, unhindered manner" (*auf unmittelbare, gegensatzlose, ungehinderte Weise*), while instead the "Spirit is at war with itself." If organic-natural development is the "simple, peaceful growth," historical development is "a stern, reluctant working against itself" that entails "a severe and mighty conflict with itself" (v.G., 151–52). In other words, one cannot understand the historical process and ignore the category of "contradiction" (v.G., 157) and qualitative leap. As far as the latter is concerned, even if it is not unique to the historical world, it is there that it fully reveals itself because only in the historical world can change be complete, beyond any return and any circularity (v.G., 153). Indeed, in the historical world quantitative definition is clearly less important than in the natural world (*Enc.* § 99 z).

The necessary struggle against feudal reactionism results in some important theories that go well beyond Hegel's historical framework and its immediate options and political proposals, theories that will be regarded with suspicion by the liberal school, especially after 1848, and the categories of contradiction and qualitative leap will be no exception.

Yet, the aspects being investigated here are of a more general nature. Consider Hegel's argument against immediate knowledge. The celebration of sentiment is the conservative or reactionary response to the enlightened, revolutionary pathos of reason. Hegel's rebuttal to even this celebration is both theoretical and political: immediate knowledge is susceptible to subsuming and legitimizing any content, even the most contemptible and immoral (*Enc.*, § 72); and not only, but immediate knowledge destroys the community of concepts which is the necessary precondition for political community. The political value of Hegel's argument against knowledge that is understood as immediate, and therefore

126   Hegel, Marx, and the Liberal Tradition

privileged, is evident: during the Restoration, Catholicism is denounced by Hegel as a basic ideological tool of reactionism, precisely because it seeks to justify and fix the division between the initiated and the uninitiated. On the other hand, the great merit of the French Enlightenment is considered to be the fact that it politically suppressed the uninitiated class (*w*, xx, 287). Therefore, with the celebration of immediate knowledge, which (according to the *Phenomenology*) reduces knowledge itself to an "esoteric possession of a few individuals," there re-emerges a class of uninitiated people without access to science and political life.

Even here we are in the presence of a motif that, born of the struggle against reactionary ideology, is considered suspicious by the liberal bourgeoisie that has become the dominant class, and is thus busy defending its privileges and its privileged "peculiarity" against the objections, this time, of the proletarian class. In fact, Haym considers Hegel's view of knowledge and dialectics to be "crude" and "shoddy:" "What up until now only the scientist appeared capable of comprehending, suddenly seems approachable to anyone, if they study the new logic. Like the *Novum Organum*, this logic claims to be the universal standard, an instrument, accessible to all, of a more keen scientific knowledge, *ut ingenii viribus et excellentiae non multum reliquatur.*"[9]

In his polemic against the celebration of immediate knowledge, Hegel highlights the theoretical superiority of the philosophical and rational "concept" as opposed to religious "representation." Religion's desire to represent a privileged instrument of knowledge is reduced even more because its content is not considered to be different from that of philosophy, though it lacks the cognitive dignity of philosophy. It is for this reason that Haym criticizes Hegel. According to Haym, Hegel only "appears to preserve that which is specifically religious, while in reality he reduces it to a shadow." Hegel, Haym continues, failed to understand that religion is something "incommensurable" with respect to reason, and tried in vain to imprison "living sentiment within the rigid confines of the intellect."[10] In particular, Haym values Jacobi for celebrating the powers of sentiment, faith, and imagination, while claiming instead that Hegel makes the mistake of presenting himself as the continuator of the Enlightenment, the founder of a new and even more barren rationalism, and always for the same reason: the desire to expand reason and make it an "instrument of universal truth."[11] At a time when the pathos of the community, so dear to the revolutionary and Jacobin tradition, might serve to contest the political and economic domination of the bourgeoisie, Haym again dismantles Hegel's community of concept erected to oppose reactionary ideology. On the one hand, rejection of Hegel's reinterpretation of religion re-establishes the privileged knowledge of "forces of the mind and excellency"; on the other hand, it protects the religious beliefs of the "multitude" from rationalist criticism, beliefs which should be shown respect and "tolerance," even when they are "miraculous, mythical, [or] superstitious" in nature.[12]

Once again "method" and "system" need to be distinguished from each other. Despite Hegel's repeated assurances, and even despite his claim to be the true theorist of orthodoxy, the fact remains that Hegel's "method" is trusted neither by Haym nor by the liberal bourgeoisie after 1848, in the same way that it was not trusted by political and clerical reactionaries in Hegel's own day. Before 1848, Hegel had been accused of being an atheist; Haym now accuses him of "secularizing religion under the dominion of philosophy."[13] In other words, Hegel's philosophy of religion, in its very foundation (thus, in its "method"), is considered by Haym to be pervaded by the Enlightenment and revolutionary pathos of reason. It is excessively secular given that the uniqueness of religious sentiment is sacrificed to universal reason, that community of the concept that, as the French Revolution (condemned by Haym) had taught, was the necessary precondition to reclaiming community by the *citoyens*.

2. The Individual and Institutions

There is another important theoretical motif in Hegel that calls to mind the revolutionary school of thought: his alleged emphasis on the objectivity of the ethical and political institutions—an emphasis which, strangely enough, was generally considered conservative (or worse). In reality, one of Hegel's most relentless critics, Wilhelm von Humboldt, goes much further: "Individualism by nature is not revolutionary."[14] Individualism had saved Wilhelm von Humboldt from the German enthusiasm for the French Revolution, a Revolution that, not by chance, demanded radical change not "within the inner man" (*in interiore homine*), but rather in objective political institutions. That is, by a forceful transformation of the configuration and organization of social life.

Yes, Haym was right: Humboldt defends the centrality of the individual against the revolutionary absolutization of "political institutions" (*Einrichtungen der Regierungen*) and the demand for their radical transformation through "political revolutions" (*Staatsrevolutionen*).[15] It is this idea which is responsible, from the very beginning, for the struggle against or distance from the French Revolution in Germany, a revolution which, as Schiller says, spreads the illusion of "regeneration in the realm of politics," beginning with the "constitution" and political institutions, rather than by way of the individual's way of thinking and feeling.[16] Indeed, "the good of the people," Gentz argues, "is not strictly linked to any form of government," to any form of "State constitution."[17] This philosophical orientation is the exact opposite of that which accompanies the preparation and outbreak of the French Revolution. For Rousseau, "it is certain that all people become, in the long run, what the government makes them."[18] And Kant, defending the French Revolution, says: "What is important is not a good government, but rather a good form of governing";[19] attention—he says in *Perpetual Peace*, arguing against the counter-revolutionary Mallet du Pan—must be paid not to the quality of the individuals who govern, but to the "form of governing," to the "political constitution." In fact, history has demonstrated that even excellent monarchs have bloody tyrants as successors.[20] Hegel's remarks are no different: "That a people have been fated to have a noble monarch is certainly to be considered a great fortune. Yet, in a great State even this has little importance: its strength lies in its reason" (*Ph. G.*, 937).

Contrary to that liberal theorist lauded by Haym for his individualism, that is, contrary to Wilhelm von Humboldt, Hegel expresses enthusiasm (and continues to do so, even in his later years) for the French Revolution. It is not by chance that emphasis on the objectivity of the ethical and political institutions characterizes Hegel's work throughout its development: "If there must be a change," an early writing underscores, "then something must be changed," and thus his attention to the "structure of the State," and to the "institutions, constitutions, laws" (*Einrichtungen, Verfassungen, Gesetze; W, I*, 269–70). Up until the very end Hegel underscores the fact that real change presupposes intervention with regard to "laws and situations" (*Gesetze und Verhältnisse*), not a recourse to "moral means" or to "associations of single individuals," but rather a "modification of institutions" (*B.schr.*, 466 and 479). The ideological struggle and consequent change of conscience are certainly of great importance, but only to the extent that they stimulate a "change in the laws and institutions of political life" (*ad corrigendas leges et instituta civilia*), to the extent that they cut into the "laws" and "institutions of the political community" (*instituta civitatis*) (*B.schr.*, 42 and 52). Not even the individual's freedom can be guaranteed without intervention with regard to the objective shape of institutions.

Instead, theories opposed to revolution and the constitutional movement attempt to steer attention away from political institutions and relations, and redirect it to the inner dimensions of conscience. We mentioned Schelling in the second chapter. He is not the only one. One thinks of Baader, who contrasts the "self-liberation" that each and every individual is called upon to first achieve within himself, to the "exterior freedom," guaranteed by laws and institutions, that can proceed concomitantly with an "inner non-freedom."[21] To August Wilhelm Rehberg, who opposes the abolition of serfdom by arguing that "the freedom of the serf, of the slave, is found only in the spirit," Hegel responds by claiming that "the Spirit, to the extent that it is only Spirit, is an empty representation; it has to have actuality, existence; it has to be objective" (v.Rph., IV, 196). For Schelling, Baader, and Rehberg, the only significant change occurs *in interiore homine*, in the moral improvement of the individual; everything else is exteriority. By affirming the centrality of the "exterior" or objective configuration of laws and institutions, once again Hegel draws on the legacy of the school of thought that paved the way for, and defended, the French Revolution. Kant, though attentive to the demands of morality, writes: "a good constitution is not to be expected from morality, but, conversely, a good moral condition of a people is to be expected only under a good constitution."[22] And before Kant, Rousseau asserted that "vices belong not so much to man, as to the man poorly governed."[23]

To contrast the change of political institutions with a change of conscience or an individual's internal change, whether he be subject or sovereign, means contrasting change to stasis. Hegel was aware of this: "something (*etwas*) must be changed." Even more aware was Marx: "The demand that [people] should change their conscience will bring about another demand: that they interpret what exists in a different way, that they recognize it by way of a different interpretation," and this is the greatest conservatism.[24] Yet, even when political change is contrasted not merely with individual conscience, but with the substitution of one individual for another, the result is not very different. As the young Hegelian, Karl Marx, notes: "the objective flaws of an institution are attributed to individuals, so as to suggest, despite no real improvement, the semblance of improvement."[25] The problem loses its objective dimension, and attention is directed away from the thing and onto the person: "When scrutinizing the situation of the State, one is easily tempted to overlook *the objective nature of relations* and explain everything as the *will* of acting individuals." Instead, a correct political analysis demands that "relations" (*Verhältnisse*, a term that immediately calls to mind Hegel) be distinguished "there, where at first only people seemed to act."[26]

For having relegated the king to the dotting of i's and crossing of t's, and for having devalued the individual, even at the level of the monarch, Hegel is considered by Haym to be irremediably opposed to the fundamental inspiration of modern liberalism. Yet, once again an inconsistency emerges in the alternative between liberal and conservative, because Haym holds individualism to be the best defense not against conservatism, but rather against "revolution." It is true, on the other hand, that Haym, the author of *Hegel and His Time*, denounces Hegel as a theorist of the absolute, but this brings us back to that liberal topos that attempts to categorize anything that is not considered part of the liberal tradition, as absolutism.

3. Institutions and the Social Question

Of course, liberal individualism does not take the same shape as that irreducibly personal individualism justified by reactionaries. At least in its revolutionary phase, it is forced to demand laws and institutions that guarantee the freedom of the individual, but with regard to mass poverty, it tends to transform the social question into a problem exclusively or primarily about individuals. In this way, poverty is not considered in light of the objective configuration of legal and social relations, but becomes a question of the ability, the habits, and the spiritual state of the impoverished individual. For Hegel, this is absurd: "All individuals, the collective is something other than just single individuals themselves" (Rph. III, 154). To this, one might add a young Engels's observation ten years later, according to which "socialism" rests "upon the principle that single individuals cannot be held liable" at the political level.[27] The objectivity of the social question cannot emerge until attention has shifted from the individual to socio-political.

Once more a comparison to the liberal school of thought on the matter might be useful: to begin, let us consider one of Hegel's contemporaries. W. von Humboldt decisively rejects the notion that the State should be positively concerned with the welfare of its citizens; the State only has the negative duty to guarantee the security, and thus the autonomy, of the private sphere: "The happiness to which man is destined is nothing more than what he achieves on his own."[28] Contrary to popular belief, it is this liberal view that equates wealth with individual merit, attributing to the individual complete responsibility for his failures, that gives rise to the ideological sanctification of the status quo—if not with regard to political institutions, then at least with regard to social and property relations. Precisely because it challenges this sort of pre-established harmony between merit and social position, Hegel underscores the positive tasks to be carried out by the political community in order to eliminate or reduce poverty. According to the liberal laissez-faire tradition, the purpose of right and social life is "the undisturbed security (Sicherheit) of persons and property." This is not questioned in Philosophy of Right, though it is paralleled, significantly and polemically, by discussion about the guarantee and security of "the livelihood and welfare (Wohl) of individuals—i.e. particular welfare (Wohl)" (Rph., § 230). That "happiness" (Glück) which according to Humboldt is contingent solely upon individual initiative and responsibility now takes on a more material and objective configuration, one less personal. That is, after having become *Wohl*, "welfare" is tied not to an indefinable feeling, but above all to its security; *Wohl* is not only an "essential characteristic" (*v.Rph.*, III, 689–90) at the level of social life, but demands to be "treated as a right" (*Rph.*, § 230).

By this point, Hegel considers poverty to be a social issue, one that cannot be simply attributed to the putative laziness of the poor, or other similar characteristics. Hegel's distance from Locke is notable on this point, since for Locke, the individual can always turn to nature in order to ensure his personal survival. In fact, "though the race of men have now spread themselves to all the corners of the world," there still exists land ready to give up its fruit in some "vacant places of America" and elsewhere: "I have heard it affirmed, that in Spain itself a man may be permitted to plough, sow and reap, without being disturbed, upon land he has no other title to, but only his making use of it. But, on the contrary, the inhabitants think themselves beholden to him, who, by his industry on neglected, and consequently waste land, has increased the stock of corn, which they wanted."[29] So the individual has only himself to blame for his poverty. Hegel seems to answer Locke when he states that "nature is fertile, but limited, very limited," and that, in a developed society there are no more lands without owners and so "it no longer has anything to do with external nature" (*v.Rph.*, IV, 494). If, for Locke, poverty has nothing to do with the socio-political order, the opposite is true for Hegel: it makes no sense to claim a right with regard to nature; indeed, "social conditions are determined by society, by men; poverty is caused by the immediate injustice perpetrated against one or another class." In a developed, civil society, man no longer has nature as a yardstick, and poverty can no longer be attributed to natural "misfortune" or natural disaster (*v.Rph.*, IV, 609). Again, Hegel's superiority, or greater modernity, becomes evident when compared to the liberal tradition. We have already mentioned Locke, but for Bentham, "with respect to poverty, it is not the work of the laws . . . [it] is precisely the man in a state of nature."[30] While, in his polemic against the doctrine of Natural Law, Bentham mocks claims to rights in the social sphere that are based upon nature, in the citation above, nature is evoked in order to relieve society of the responsibility of poverty. And even Tocqueville considers it dangerous to allow the "multitudes" to believe that "human suffering is the work of laws and not providence."[31] In this case, providence is another word for nature, a sphere outside political institutions and social relations, which are declared innocent.

At this point, let us reconsider the criticism by German liberals, already in the *Vormärz* period, of Hegel's theory of the centrality of political institutions: he makes the mistake of wanting to remedy mass poverty, not by appealing to "love," or to the "voluntary will, thus meritorious" will of the individual, but by calling upon a State which is unable to "love," or relying upon legal norms that are likely to wither away the "generosity" of the rich. Even outside Germany, Tocqueville's position is not much different; in fact, he vehemently opposes the proclamation, in 1848, of the right to work (infra, ch. x, 5) which Hegel placidly justifies together with the "right to life" (Rph.I, § 118 A) and the right of the individual to "demand his well-being" (v.Rph., IV, 604). It would be superfluous to dwell upon the mediocrity and inconsistency of the concrete political program that is essentially based upon this position: it is a matter of the disproportion, already highlighted, between "method" and "system." What is important is that, if for Tocqueville the impoverished individual can appeal only to charity, private or public as it may be, for Hegel the individual has an explicit "right" that directly corresponds to "the responsibility of a civil society" (v.Rph., IV, 604).

The rejection of the social issue is even more radical in contemporary neo-liberal writings, which, not by chance, again lead to Nietzsche. Hayek never tires of arguing that it is absurd to speak of "social" justice or injustice when the state of things is not the "result of [someone's] conscious will." When things have not been "deliberately produced by men, they have neither intelligence, nor virtue, nor justice, nor any other human value."[32] Nietzsche, in turn, argues against those who speak of "gross injustices" in the social order; he accuses them of having "imagined responsibilities and forms of will that in no way exist. It is not right to speak of injustice when the preliminary conditions for justice and injustice are not present."[33] For Nietzsche, social protest, far from deriving from objective conditions and real "injustice," is the product of *ressentiment*, that is, the rancor which life's failures harbor against better or more fortunate individuals. Similarly, for Hayek, what fuels the demand for "social justice" are "sentiments" that are anything but lofty: "the contempt for persons who are better off than us, or simply jealousy" and "rapacious instincts."[34] The objectivity of the social issue is reduced to individual responsibility and even the psychological makeup of individuals who suffer from poverty.

4. Labor and *Otium*

Constant refuses to give the propertyless political rights because they lack the "leisure needed to acquire culture and proper judgment."[35] The continuity with respect to the conservative and reactionary school of thought is quite clear. In his later period, Schelling refers to Aristotle, declaring his agreement that every rule, "from the moment it is born," entails a distinction between ruler and ruled, and he agrees that "the primary function of the State is to guarantee *otium* to the best."[36] The distinction between ruler and ruled coincides with the distinction of those entitled to *otium* and those who are confined to a life of toil and hardship. For Nietzsche, *otium* is so very important to the development of culture and civilization in general that he does not hesitate to justify the slavery of those who must labor to produce material goods. The line of continuity is quite clear. Constant permits himself an unrequested excuse (*excusatio non petita*): manual laborers, forced to work day and night, and limited to "eternal dependence" because they lack *otium*, are not "slaves," but "children."[37] Burke does not seem to have such scruples: it is natural that the most humble occupations are "servile," and that he who is employed in such an occupation be compared to an *instrumentum vocale*.[38] The Whig or liberal Briton Burke does not cite the learned Varro, who defines the term, but Nietzsche knows classical antiquity too well not to know that an *instrumentum vocale* is nothing other than a slave.[39]

This notion of *otium* as a necessary condition for freedom is absent in Hegel: hardly by chance a renowned chapter in the *Phenomenology* demonstrates the superiority, even the cultural superiority, of the labor of slaves in contrast to the *otium* of their masters. Even with regard to the contemporary laborer, proprietors who know the comfort of wealth and *otium* cannot claim superiority. Wealth and property are hardly considered synonymous with civic integrity and political maturity, as they are in the liberal tradition. In fact, there is a course of lectures on the philosophy of right in which the master and servant dialectic, which we know from the *Phenomenology*, seems to be applied to the new capitalist relations: it is the slave, ancient or modern, who represents progress and even substantive culture (infra, ch. VII, 7).

Is similar praise for labor found in the liberal tradition? One must not confuse rather diverse problems. By labor, one may mean man's relationship to nature, man's increasing dominion over nature, in which case the theme is indeed present in the work of authors such as Locke and Smith, who philosophize in the most highly developed capitalist country while the Industrial Revolution takes shape. On the other hand, if in the realm of labor we emphasize man's relationship to man, then it becomes clear that what we have are two completely different positions. Only in Hegel do we see, on both a productive and cultural level, the celebration of the superiority of the servant's labor over the master's sterile leisure. This is certainly not the case in Smith. In the *Wealth of Nations*, he contrasts the wage laborer who, because of the monotony of labor, "generally becomes as stupid and ignorant as it is possible for a human creature to become," a person unable to take part "in any rational conversation" or of "conceiving any generous" sentiment, to those who have "a good deal of leisure, during which they may perfect themselves in every branch either of useful or ornamental knowledge."[40] The liberal school is certainly able to grasp the alienating nature of wage labor, but not the formative and emancipatory aspects of productive activity, which does not slip by Hegel (and Marx). A clamorous confirmation of this fact is provided by Locke, who, though rendering a factual situation, provides an almost animal-like description of the wage laborer who generally lives "from hand to mouth," and thus is forced to struggle for "bare subsistence," never having "time or opportunity to raise their thoughts above that."[41] In this case too, *otium* is the necessary precondition for culture and even true human existence. Intellectual life is not possible for "the greatest part of mankind, who are given up to labor, and enslaved to the necessity of their mean condition, whose lives are worn out only in the provisions for living." These men are "laid out to still the croaking of their own bellies, or the cries of their children. It is not to be expected that a man who drudges on all his life in a laborious trade should be more knowing in the variety of things done in the world than a park horse, who is driven constantly forwards and backwards in a narrow lane and dirty road, only to market, should be skilled in the geography of the country." Not only is all of this fact, but it is also immutable: "So that a great part of mankind are, by the natural and unalterable state of things in this world, and the constitution of human affairs, unavoidably given over to invincible ignorance of those proofs on which others build, and which are necessary to establish those opinions." Locke does not hesitate to claim that "there is a greater distance between some men and others in this respect than between some men and some beasts." It is true that this is a classic theme present in Montaigne as well, but it is noteworthy that Locke, in order to clarify this distinction between some men and others, cites "Westminster Hall" and the "Exchange," on the one hand, and "alms-houses" and "Bedlam" on the other.[42] This is not an isolated argument in Locke, but a recurrent theme: "The difference is exceedingly great between some men and some animals: but if we will compare the understanding and abilities of some men and some brutes, we shall find so little difference, that it will be hard to say that that of the man is either clearer or larger."[43]

Ignorance, or rather the lack of full possession of one's faculties, is directly linked to the condition of labor, and it is so radical that at a certain point a theological problem emerges: To what extent can a laborer be considered responsible for his own eternal salvation or condemnation? Locke responds (is forced to respond, so as to not compromise the universality of the Christian Word and the concept of imputability on a theological and legal level), that "no man is so wholly taken up with the attendance on the means of living, as to have no spare time at all to think of his soul, and inform himself in matters of religion."[44] But for the most part, laborers continue to be thought of as minors or, as Constant says, "children."

Of course, to prevent *otium* from becoming dissolute living, Locke suggests that the "gentleman" not only familiarize himself with books, but also engage in some physical activity: gardening, husbandry, carpentry, wood turning.[45] Yet, he immediately makes it clear that "these I propose not as the chief end of his labor, but as temptations to it; diversion from his other more serious thoughts and employments by useful and healthy manual exercise." For the "gentleman" physical labor means "delight" or "recreation."[46] So, manual labor as such, wage labor, appears in Locke as either the opposite of a way of life that permits the exercise of reason, or part of the book-keeping that the "gentleman" must take care of in order to run his affairs wisely, keeping track, among his various expenses, of those that bring about "debauchery, idleness, and quarrels amongst his servants."[47]

This is very different from Hegel's thought! It is true that, for Hegel, the division of labor in the factories deadens the intellectual faculties. Nevertheless, Hegel values the formative discipline of labor since it allows one to acquire a "qualification" (*Geschicklichkeit*) that has an objective value, it is *allgemeingültig* (*Rph.*, § 197). Furthermore, Hegel cites the "worker" (*Arbeiter*) as an example of the development of "culture," contrasting him to the "incompetent" who has not experienced the tough, yet highly instructive and formative discipline of labor, and who therefore is not able to develop himself and become his own master: "The incompetent (*der Ungeschickte*) always produces something different from what he wants because he is not in charge of his own actions. . . . The competent worker (*der geschickteste Arbeiter*) is the one who produces something exactly as it should be, and [who] finds no obstacles as he operates subjectively with a goal in mind" (*v.Rph.*, III, 608). Traditionally, *otium* serves as a symbol of culture since it does not involve the risk of becoming tied to a restricted activity that would limit and suffocate one's intellectual potential. For Hegel, however, if it is true that the extreme division of labor causes an enervation of the intellectual faculties, it is also true that precision and an education to precision have a positive value even from an intellectual point of view. Quoting Goethe, Hegel affirms: "Those who want something great, says the poet, must know how to limit themselves." If they do not, then they condemn themselves to empty wishes and helplessness: "An active life, effectiveness, and character require, as their essential condition, concentration on a specific point" (*W*, IV, 365). This is what a "worker" does; if he wants to achieve concrete and universally valid results, he is called upon to *"limit one's activity"* according to a precise finality (*Rph.*, § 197).

From the *Phenomenology of Spirit* we learn that labor achieves "true independence," whereas the "independent conscience" of a lord who has no need to labor turns into its opposite (*W, III, 152*). With a radical reversal of traditional positions, freedom is conceived here as the result of a productive process, and not in opposition to the need to work and produce.

It is true, after the Revolution of 1848 and the workers' June insurrection in France, even the liberal tradition seems to reconsider its positions. In particular, François Guizot's celebration of labor is filled with the most exalted expressions, and yet, in spite of this, it cannot conceal its instrumental and essentially hypocritical character. Yes, now "the glory of modern civilization consists in having grasped and revealed the moral value and social importance of labor, of having restored it to the esteem and rank it deserves." However, the labor Guizot refers to here is not a paid, menial labor; rather, it "is everywhere in this world"; it is a category that coincides with the infinite "variety of human tasks and missions," and it ultimately includes even those social classes which, before the social issue and the workers' movement threateningly emerged, had not hesitated to exalt their own *otium* and uncontaminated purity in contrast to manual labor. By celebrating this type of labor, Guizot explicitly aims at changing the meaning of "the word labor" so that it no longer represents a "war cry" against the privileged classes. Indeed, the attempt here is to twist "the word labor" to make it serve the opposite purpose: the targets of criticism having become the "scarcely intelligent, lazy, dissolute" workers.[48] The implicit or explicit targets of criticism are the revolutionary workers who, instead of going to work, devote themselves to political vagrancy. On the eve of the workers' insurrection in June, 1848, Tocqueville stares fearfully and even contemptuously at the "dreadful idlers" who have surrounded the Assembly.[49] *Oisif:* the term had already been used by Claude Henri Saint-Simon to denounce the parasitical classes who lived off other people's work, and now it is used to label the revolutionary workers and the "demagogues" as a whole.[50] In contrast, Guizot celebrates the "father of a family,"[51] or the farmer, whose common sense counters, for Tocqueville, the inexperience and "philosophical presumptuousness" of revolutionary intellectuals.[52] The meaning that the term "labor" had in classic German philosophy, which used it to exalt intellectuals over property-owners, has now been completely overturned. Despite all of the changes that have made it obsolete and dangerous to celebrate *otium*, that leisure so dear, for example, to Constant (as it might worsen the workers' resentment and the class conflict), and despite Tocqueville's journey to America where he experienced a society dominated by the ethics of productivity, not even the most advanced representatives of the liberal tradition choose to consider the claim made by Hegel: the claim of the formative effectiveness, even on an intellectual level, of the labor performed by craftsmen or factory workers.

Significantly, in Germany, where the social conflict is less acute than in France and where the resort to a hypocritical celebration of labor like Guizot's is less compelling, Schopenhauer and Nietzsche will continue to consider *otium* a necessary condition for the authentic development of intellectual faculties, and will therefore condemn those intellectuals (and Hegel first of all) contaminated, in their very theories, by the mechanism of labor and professional activity.

5. Intellectuals and Property-Owners

In excluding the propertyless from electoral rights, Constant wonders whether there is any such thing as "intellectual property" that derives not from the possession of goods and capital, but from the very practice of a profession, first of all the liberal profession. His answer is negative, but the motivation is even more important than his answer: "Liberal professions demand, perhaps more than all other professions, to be accompanied by property, in order for their influence not to be ruinous during political discussions. Such professions, no matter how recommendable they might be from various points of view, cannot always claim to have, among their advantages, that common sense of measure necessary to make decisions for the positive interests of mankind." All this is confirmed by the experience of the French Revolution and the extremist, negative influence exerted upon it by intellectuals. The common habit of these intellectuals was to "scorn conclusions drawn from facts and to despise the real, sensible world, to reason like fanatics on social conditions." Intellectuals who do not own any property have the tendency to elaborate, to insist on applying "chimerical theories," and in this they are also pushed by their "discontent toward a society in which they feel ill-adjusted."[53]

With this penetrating analysis of the subversive potential of intellectuals who are socially and materially cut-off from property-owners, Constant clarifies the fundamental reasons for the abyss that separates him from classic German philosophy. Classic German philosophy, in fact, cannot be understood without recognizing the decisive role of those intellectuals who would support themselves exclusively by means of their profession, and who therefore lack organic ties to the dominant social systems (and in this sense lack concreteness). Those same intellectuals are denounced by Constant in his preoccupation over the fate of property. Kant's high esteem for these "abstract" intellectuals emerges from his harsh polemic against those (the proponents of conservatism and reactionism) who insist on considering theory irrelevant on a practical level and who, in "attacking the *scholar*," the elaborator of theories, "would have him locked in a school . . . like a pedant who is perfectly useless in practice and who merely constitutes a burden on their consummate wisdom."[54] By defending theory, Kant defends at the same time those "metaphysicians" (abstract intellectuals according to Constant and Burke) who, in their "passionate hope to improve the world," are willing to do "the impossible."[55] The celebration of the role of the intellectual culminates with Fichte's exalted vision: the intellectual is the "teacher" and "educator of mankind." He looks "not only at the present, but also towards the future"; he does not let himself be trapped in the status quo, but constantly strives to keep a prospect for progress open. In this sense, one could even say, using an expression from the New Testament, that the intellectual is "the salt of the earth."[56]

In Hegel, this pathos undergoes significant changes. The celebration of the intellectual continues to emerge from the celebration of philosophy as a theory that accompanies and promotes the march toward progress and freedom. Kant had ironically remarked that the denunciation of "metaphysics" as the "cause of political revolutions" could be perceived as a "wicked calumny" or as an "undeserved honor."[57] Hegel agrees with the claim that "the Revolution found its first impulse in philosophy" to which it is indebted for the "immense discovery" of "freedom" (*Ph. G.*, 924). On the other hand, Hegel criticizes the role played in France, in the National Assembly and in the process of radicalization of the Revolution, by "imposters, lawyers, intemperate monks" and various charlatans, that is, intellectuals with no political competence or experience (*Rph. I*, § 150 A). The role of the intellectual-philosopher has now been reduced: in France, too, "philosophers" expressed the rightful demand for serious reforms, they formulated "general thought," an "abstract idea" of the necessary changes, but they certainly could not indicate "how these changes should be carried out" (*W*, xx, 296–97). In comparison to Kant and Fichte, politics here enjoys a much larger autonomy: the intellectual is not "the salt of the earth," and the politician is not a mere executor. And yet, if Constant (and also Burke) contrasts the "abstract" intellectual to the property-owner, Hegel contrasts the intellectual to—or places him side by side with—the "officer." As in Kant and Fichte, the intellectual remains the privileged interpreter or mediator of universality, except that now, as a civil servant, he has acquired professional qualification, political maturity, and sense of the State.

It is important to remark that this new figure continues nevertheless to embody the polemic against feudal or bourgeois property-owners. Contrary to what happens in England, in Germany the "ruling spheres of administration and politics" are occupied exclusively by those who have been exposed to "theoretical studies" and have received a "university education," not the property-owners as such, no matter how noble or rich. Thus, the intellectual who has achieved his status by means of his own merits celebrates his superiority over the property-owner, even though his theoretical education is not sufficient, and—this is a new aspect in comparison to Kant and Fichte—"he needs to have experience of practical problems, too" (B.schr., 482). Certainly, Constant has also England in mind when he opposes the socially ruinous political improvisations of intellectuals to the wisdom and reliability of the property-owners, who should therefore be entrusted with the monopoly of political representation. Hegel, instead, harshly criticizes the owners of this monopoly in England, and denounces "the crass ignorance of these foxhunters and country lords." Still referring to England, but probably also to Germany, Hegel condemns the "prejudice" according to which, "birth and wealth," and not the "intelligence" of the candidate, are the only requirements for an official position (B.schr., 482). Once again, the protest of the intellectual against the feudal and bourgeois property-owner becomes manifest.

Certainly, intellectual-philosophers have lost their anarchist rebelliousness. They are not "plastic individualities" with a way of life already recognizable from the outside, they are not "monks" living in isolated, contemptuous opposition to the surrounding world and to common humanity. On the contrary, they are part of a specific "social class" with various ties to civil society and the State (W, XX, 71–73). More precisely, intellectual-philosophers have now become civil servants who read or write the "cabinet orders" of the World Spirit, and who "receive a salary for collaborating in writing them." And yet, this has not stopped their rebellion against power and property. Hegel's answer to those who consider philosophy to be a combination of "verbal abstractions" (it is the position already denounced by Kant in particular reference to Burke) is that, in reality, philosophy is made up of "facts of the World Spirit." And he adds, with both power and property-owners in mind, that intellectual-philosophers are the privileged interpreters of the universal because they are not driven by "particular interests" such as "power" or "wealth" (W, XIX, 489).

If in the liberal tradition it is the lack of property that casts a shadow of suspicion over intellectuals who are forced to earn their own living, the opposite is true in classic German philosophy. Significantly enough, while reiterating his idea of knowledge as a community of reason to which everyone participates or can participate, Kant observes that those who support the (aristocratic) idea of a solitary and privileged enlightenment are usually "those who live on a private income, in an opulent or mediocre manner, in contrast to those who are forced to earn their own living." "In short, they feel they belong to a class of their own since they believe they should not work." As a result, they feel they own the right to speak and philosophize "with the tone of a master who is exempted from the trouble of proving the ownership of his possessions (*beati possidentes*)."[58] To *otium* corresponds the exemption from that "trouble of the concept" (*w*, III, 56), which for Hegel is the very presupposition of knowledge. For Hegel, Kant, and classic German philosophy as a whole, labor intervenes in the definition of authentic intellectual activity. Not by chance, Nietzsche will later speak of Kant and Hegel as the "laborers of philosophy!"[59]

From this debate there emerges a sort of class analysis of the various and opposed intellectual classes which will later be used by Marx. For this very reason, Marx cannot share the *pathos* of the intellectual per se who, especially in Fichte, rises to become a solitary prophet of the universal. And yet there is an element in common with classic German philosophy: far from being the only guarantee of a serenely impartial judgment, property and *otium* can be "suspected" of conditioning, surreptitiously and ideologically, theory, far more than need and labor do.

6. Property and Political Representation

While Constant excludes even intellectuals from political representation, the position held by classic German philosophy is quite different. At the same time that Kant defends the attribution of political rights on the basis of census, of property, he strongly affirms that culture, too, constitutes a form of property.[60] And this is not even restricted to great intellectuals: a mere "teacher," too, must have political rights.[61] A polemic against the political monopoly of property-owners can also be found in Hegel. The criterion of census must be made valid only for the House of Lords, not for the House of Commons: that would be a useless and unacceptable "repetition." Even if the census requirements are set at a very modest level, the main point remains the same (*v.Rph.*, IV, 719). Therefore, Hegel condemns "the rigidity of the French Chamber of Deputies, whose only membership criterion to qualify for participation is set around two hundred francs, with or without additional cents," thus excluding experienced civil servants and even doctors and lawyers "who do not pay taxes of that amount" (*B.schr.*, 494). The "learned ones," instead, as Napoleon understood very well, are a fundamental element in political representation (*B.schr.*, 486). For Constant, only property-owners can guarantee "the love for order, justice, and preservation."[62] Hegel, on the other hand, remarks: "It is commonly said that property-owners are those most directly concerned with the preservation of order, right, and the law, but there can also be other guarantees" (Rph. III, 268). Hegel's proposals (the rejection or the strong reservations about direct elections) are rather weak and naïve on a political level, as they clearly suffer the influence of German "misery," that is, of Germany's historical delay in comparison to France and England. Nevertheless, Hegel decisively rejects the property-owners' monopoly over political representation.

The concept of "German misery" has sometimes been questioned in light of the "extraordinary cultural level" of Germany at the time and its close and fruitful relationship to European culture.[63] Yet, this is not the main issue. The problem is precisely the gap between an extraordinary cultural development and a political, social backwardness. Nevertheless, it is Hegel himself who contrasts "the great States, e.g. France, or even more so, England," to the various States into which Germany was divided, where "the extension of territory and wealth are more limited, and society is less articulated," and where intellectuals are "forced to seek a platform for their economic and social existence in a government office" (W, IV, 473–74). This would explain why the boldness of more general theoretical elaborations is hardly matched by the modesty of the political proposals, the backwardness of which, however, should not be exaggerated: if Constant is strongly in favor of direct elections, though strictly based on census, in 1835, in reference to America itself, Tocqueville supports second-grade elections as "the only means to make the use of political freedom accessible to all classes of people" (infra, ch. XII, 5).[64]

7. Intellectuals and Craftsmen

We have observed how Hegel transforms the figure of the intellectual. However, even after this intellectual-philosopher has become a civil servant with a regular salary, he continues to be regarded and feared as politically unreliable, dangerous, and socially rebellious. In 1821, Freiherr vom Stein, who had been a key figure during the period of reforms after the Battle of Jena but had subsequently retreated to a conservative position, thunders against "a caste of scribblers," with "no property of their own," who would go so far as destroy "ancient rights that have been handed down for centuries."[65]

On closer scrutiny, the criticism expressed against German intellectuals at the time is not very different from the criticism expressed against the French revolutionary intellectuals, whom Burke defines as "beggars of the pen" (gueux plumées).[66] With their forced "obscurity" and their exclusion from public life, the intellectuals who had participated in the French

Revolution and its ideological preparation ended up being associated with the "poor."[67] Something analogous takes place with regard to the great intellectuals of classic German philosophy. Together with the intellectuals, Constant also denies electoral rights to "the craftsmen gathered together in the cities," since they would be at the mercy of the subversives (what Constant has obviously in mind is the role that the Parisian craftsmen played during the French Revolution).[68] For Kant, instead, political rights must be granted not only to intellectuals, but also to "craftsmen."[69] This type of solidarity between intellectuals and craftsmen ends up emerging in Hegel, as well, as can be observed by comparing him to Constant. In the *Principles of Politics* we read: "During our Revolution, it is true that property-owners as well as the propertyless contributed to issue absurd, dishonest laws. But the fact is, property-owners feared the propertyless who had been invested with power, and sought forgiveness for what they owned. . . . The errors and crimes committed by property-owners were the consequences of the influence exerted by the propertyless."[70] Thus, the property-owners' monopoly over political representation must be total, with no access whatsoever to anyone else. For Hegel, on the other hand, the Lower House should provide an expression for all the various interests, all the articulations of civil society, the "trade guilds, local communities, and all types of corporations" (*Rph.*, § 308). Indeed, in the Heidelberg lecture we read that Deputies of the Lower House must be elected "by the citizens . . . with no exclusion, regardless of census" (*Rph.I*, § 153). This kind of observation would not be found so easily in the liberal tradition of the time. It is true that, during the same Heidelberg lecture and with no particular consistency, Hegel ends up excluding from electoral rights "day-laborers" and servants, but only because they do not belong to a "trade guild" (*Rph.I*, § 153 A). Therefore, a *Gewerbsmann*, a tradesman or permanent worker who belongs to a corporation—as opposed, Hegel remarks in *Philosophy of Right*, to a "day-laborer" (*Rph.*, § 252 A)—has the right to participate in elections.

This kind of solidarity between intellectuals and craftsmen emerges even more from theoretical categories than from political standpoints. Intellectual activity is no longer subsumed in the category of *otium*, but in that of labor: the expressions used are in fact those of "intellectual labor" (*v.Rph.*, III, 256), or "intellectual production," that is, "spiritual" (*Rph.*, § 68 *AL*; *v.Rph.*, II, 281), and the intellectual, the writer, or the philosopher, has now become a "spiritual producer" (*Rph.*, § 69 A), and even an "individual who produces" (*Rph.*, § 68 A). Significantly enough, Hegel discusses both manual and intellectual labor in the same paragraph of *Philosophy of Right*: "I can *alienate individual* products of *my particular physical and mental skills* and active capabilities to someone else . . ."

(§ 67). Only in the following paragraph does Hegel deal with the "pecu-liarities of *spiritual* production" (§ 68). To the category of "producers" (which includes intellectuals, craftsmen, and even skilled workers under the hegemony of intellectuals-officials), Hegel sometimes seems to con-trast the category of "mere consumers," those who produce nothing and who can therefore be compared to "hornets," to parasites (*v.Rph.*, IV, 499).

We have observed how Constant rejects the very concept of "intellec-tual property." Kant, on the other hand, dedicates a whole essay to the de-fense of copyrights, the "authors' ownership of their own thoughts."[71] This theme is also discussed in depth by Hegel: "industry" and "com-merce" are well protected from "robberies," whereas, at least in Germany, the protection of "spiritual property" is quite lacking (*Rph.*, § 69 A). Here emerges the discontent with wealth and large properties, and this discon-tent is extended also to publishers: "A publisher's interest is for the most part different from that of a writer" (*v.Rph.*, III, 259). True, publishers must be protected against unauthorized reproductions, "but so too writers from publishers, who can make enormous profits, while writers cannot. Schiller often found himself in dire poverty, and died in poverty, but ac-cording to booksellers' calculations, his publisher made a profit of 300,000 thalers from the latest edition of his works. In France, perhaps Schiller would have owned a million francs. Equity requires sharing" (*v.Rph.*, IV, 235–36). Sometimes, this intellectual property seems to proudly proclaim its superiority over the others. The result of hard work and personal merit, only intellectual property reveals itself "indestructible" despite the disor-der caused by politics and war" (infra, ch. IX, 5).

Furthermore, the concept of intellectual property sometimes seems to stretch beyond the actual intellectual classes: the "best property" is the one that derives from man's "taking possession" of himself, his skills, his abilities, and his strength by means of education and culture (*v.Rph.*, IV, 211). In this sense, the craftsman and even the skilled worker who edu-cates their own labor force participate in that "property" that is to be considered the "best." Of course, Hegel emphasizes intellectuals, and yet, even here the solidarity or potential solidarity with craftsmen can be detected.

At this point we can make a further consideration on Hegel's concep-tion of the right to property, which obviously continues to be completely out of the question. Yet, when in *Philosophy of Right* Hegel argues for the "inalienable" right to property, he does not do so to affirm the invio-lability of private property and to fight off the intrusiveness of political power; on the contrary, he does so to condemn the exclusion of serfs from the right to ownership in a full sense, and he even compares such exclu-sion to slavery (*Rph.*, § 66 A). Property, or the right to property, is defended with particular passion from the point of view of intellectuals, craftsmen, and even serfs.

8. A Banausic, Plebeian Hegel?

A philosopher who had already established a link between Hegel's philo-sophical thought and his social standing was Arthur Schopenhauer. His de-nunciation was actually aimed at classic German philosophy as a whole: "True philosophy requires independence," it requires people "to support themselves and have no masters."[72] The social classes that need to work to earn their own living are not in a position to express authentic philosophy and culture, whose inescapable presupposition is the *schole.* In this way, Schopenhauer (as will later Nietzsche) radicalizes a motif largely present also in the liberal tradition (infra, ch. VIII, 8). The liberal tradition, in fact, excludes the propertyless from political rights by using the same argument with which Schopenhauer excludes them from authentic culture. We can therefore understand Schopenhauer's condemnation of classic German philosophy, which in his opinion lacks an independent material basis and is thus prone to confusing culture with a work aimed at "earning a living for oneself and one's own family."[73] Worse even, most of the time philoso-phers holding a university position began their career as "private tutors." In this way, from a young age, the habit of dependence, the habit of enslav-ing philosophy to pragmatic goals (or goals which are in any case alien to pure theory) have become for them "second nature."[74]

Apparently, Schopenhauer proceeds to a sort of class analysis. A central point emerges: the protagonists of classic German philosophy, from Kant to Hegel, have gone through an apprenticeship that must have been quite hard and humiliating for intellectuals at the time, since an author of the *Sturm und Drang,* in a novel entitled, indeed, *The Tutor,* denounces the humiliations inflicted upon intellectuals-tutors by their aristocratic em-ployers.[75] Fichte himself explicitly refers to these "humiliations" in a text that seems filled with bitterness and perhaps even resentment: a tutor would want to perform his educational task well, but he is "forcibly pre-vented" from doing so. The text is a letter addressed to Kant,[76] who in turn went through this experience, and who, not by chance, examines the conflict between "parents and tutors," that is—quoting the terms he uses in his essay *On Pedagogy*—between the "precepts of the teacher" and the "whims of the parents."[77] Such conflict can be solved only by fully re-affirming the authority of tutors in the educational field. In general, pub-lic education is to be preferred to private education since the former is consonant with "forming a citizen's character," whereas the latter per-petuates and sometimes magnifies "family flaws" even further (including, presumably, the caste-like arrogance of aristocrats). But if aristocratic parents insist on resorting to private education and to the help of a tutor, they must give up their educational authority in favor of the latter.

Of course, in practice things went very differently. Kant's and Fichte's experience was the same as Hegel's. The letters that this "children's tutor" (*gouverneur des enfants*) sends from Berne express the difficulty of reconciling work and study.[78] The beginning of a poem addressed to Hölderlin is particularly significant: Hegel craves the night to come, because, when he is finally free from his daily occupations, the night brings "freedom" and leisure (*Muße*) (B, I, 38). *Otium* reappears once again, that *otium* which the liberal tradition, Schopenhauer and, later, Nietzsche, regard as the necessary requirement for culture. Here, however, *otium* is confined to the night at the end of a hard day's work, and it does not call to mind a comfortable material independence, but rather, a hard struggle for survival.

In contrast to classic liberalism, classic German philosophy develops within a radically different framework: the social standing of its protagonists is decisively more "plebeian." These intellectuals are not organically tied to the social classes that dominate, economically or politically, the existing society; on the contrary, their relationships with these classes are quite antagonistic and tense. To give just a few examples: in England, Locke develops his philosophical thought and at the same time secures some profitable financial opportunities.[79] Obviously, we must be very cautious lest we establish a mechanical relationship between social standing and philosophical elaboration, and yet a relationship clearly emerges. One thing is certain: if the major representatives of classic German philosophy went through the humiliation of working as tutors, this work is regarded by Locke only within the realm of the advice given to a "gentleman" on the best way to invest his money: certainly, a "well-bred" tutor is expensive, at the "ordinary rates" it is difficult to find one who is truly up to his task.[80] But it is a fruitful investment: a "young gentleman" should not be sent to a public school; he should instead receive a private education.[81] Rather than doing without a tutor, it would be preferable to give up one of the many "useless servants."[82] If Fichte and Hegel make reference to the problems and humiliations of tutors, Constant tells about one of his tutors (among the many who were hired and fired by his father as he became increasingly "disgusted"), who was "the butt of jokes and a general laughing stock."[83] Before Constant, Locke had discussed the difficulties that a gentleman had to face before finding a person worthy of occupying the position of tutor, given that the intellectuals who possess the necessary qualities "will hardly be got to undertake such a charge."[84]

This reluctance is understandable since, in the final analysis, a tutor is a servant: in this sense, Schopenhauer was right in denouncing the "servile" character or origin of classic German philosophy.[85] If Locke's private correspondence and notes are filled with considerations and calculations on the most profitable investments, the image that emerges from classic German philosophy is quite different. In Königsberg, Fichte writes in his diary: "I have calculated that, starting from today, I can survive for fourteen more days."[86] Calculations and confessions are not always so dramatic, but certainly now the problem of survival is no longer a philosophical issue, but it acquires a direct existential relevance that conditions the very writing of philosophy. Hegel is forced to speed up the publication of *Science of Logic:* the fact is—he confesses—that "I need money to survive." At the time, he did not occupy a position at the university, and was therefore in financial straits (B, I, 393). Schopenhauer sees Hegel's philosophy as perfectly congenial to the "referendaries," those who wished to earn a living by finding a position as "civil servants."[87] With the acute sensitivity that he partly owes to his position as a well-off *rentier,* Schopenhauer perceives the extraordinary novelty that classic German philosophy already represents from a social standpoint. Despite profound differences on a political and ideological level, Schopenhauer's criticism calls to mind Tocqueville's criticism of the French representatives of the Enlightenment: their ideal is a society in which "all positions are obtained by means of literary contests," a society whose only "aristocracy [are] the scholars."[88]

Not by chance, Schopenhauer compares the philosophical triumph enjoyed by Hegel and his school to the dreadful coming to power of the "more abject class," the "scum of society." The target of this denunciation is not only classic German philosophy; it is aimed at all of the "starving scholars who earn their living by means of a false, deceitful literature."[89] We are facing a general barbarization of intellectual life which is no longer synonymous with disinterested *otium;* intellectual life has now become a job, and wears the mark of plebeian baseness. It is a denunciation that will later be voiced, sorrowfully, by Nietzsche, and inspired this time not by the safety of a comfortable bourgeois position, but by the tormenting nostalgia for the *schole* of classical antiquity and the impossible wish to undo the standardization of the modern world. For Nietzsche, too, the vulgarization of the intellectual, as shown by the confusion between "culture," on the one hand, and "usefulness," "profit," and therefore profession, on the other, finds one of its most significant expressions in Hegel, whose "influence" is credited with "*extending* culture in order to have the largest possible number of intelligent clerks" (infra, ch. IX, 7).

What re-emerges here is the figure of the civil servant, the intellectual who, instead of identifying culture with *schole,* identifies it with labor. Hegel becomes the symbol of the banausic, plebeian intellectual, and

indeed, in one of his letters, he did not hesitate to claim that his "occupation," his "bread and water," was the study and teaching of philosophy
(B, I, 419).

9. The Social Question and Industrial Society

Sensitivity to the social question is not enough to define Hegel's importance. With regard to Germany, Fichte reveals an even deeper sensitivity:
for him, poverty is an absolutely intolerable scandal, so much so that
only a State that has completely defeated poverty can be classified as
"rational."[90] However, Fichte's plebeian radicalism is also the result of an
extremely humble social condition; sometimes, his radicalism takes on
regressive tones and seems to question industrial civilization, the boundless expansion of expenditure and exchange that characterizes the modern
world. The condemnation of the "tyranny of the dominant classes op-
pressing the lower classes" goes hand in hand with the condemnation of
"luxury," "dissoluteness" and "dissipation," the "wealthy traders' arrogance," the "art of seduction," "gluttony," and even the condemnation of
"our corrupt times" as a whole.[91]

Certainly, Hegel's portrayal of civil society with its "spectacle of dissipation, poverty, and the physical and ethical corruptions that come with
them" (Rph., § 185) is no less crude than Fichte's. However, Hegel's lucid
description never reveals nostalgia, it never takes on the shape of a moral
condemnation: modern civil society represents a great progress because it
brings about "the autonomous development of particularity" (§ 185 A).
Therefore, the desire to retrieve the "simple traditions of primitive populations" and the lost "natural simplicity" ultimately reveals itself as
impotent and regressive. Despite its idyllic appearance produced by nostalgia, in fact, "natural simplicity" is merely "passive selflessness or a
barbarism of knowledge and volition" (§ 187 A).

Hegel realizes that this nostalgic (or tendentially nostalgic) criticism of
civil society can very well express, as happens with Rousseau, a sympathetic solidarity with the suffering of the masses (v.Rph., IV, 477). And yet,
the solution of a problem that is felt so deeply cannot be found by going
backwards, beyond the Christian-bourgeois discovery of autonomy, particularity, and the infinity of the subject.

Not by chance, Rousseau and Fichte are indeed very passionate about
the social question, but especially from the starting point of the peasants'
world. In proclaiming that peasants need to be protected "against the risk
of poverty," Rousseau denounces the fact that "industries and arts that
produce luxury goods [are] favored at the expense of useful and arduous
jobs; agriculture is sacrificed for the sake of commerce." It would seem

that the main contradiction is between city and countryside: "the richer the city the poorer the country. The product of the taxes passes from the hands of the Prince or his financial officers into those of artists and traders; and the husbandman, who receives only the smallest part of it, is at length exhausted by paying always the same, and receiving constantly less."[92]

For Fichte, the first victims of the "oppression" carried out by the "dominant classes" are "those who till the soil."[93] In the course of a correspondence, after agreeing with the thesis that ascribes the cause of the "collapse"—that is, of the French Revolution—to the "enormous privilege given to factories at the expense of agriculture," Fichte adds: "Of all the means that contribute to humanity's physical support and growth (which in turn serve spiritual culture), agriculture is the main one, and all other branches must be *subordinated to it*."[94] The condemnation of luxury sometimes seems to entail a condemnation of "commerce" and "factories."[95]

In order to better understand Hegel's position in comparison to Rousseau's and Fichte's, we can cite a passage from Adam Smith:

> In every civilised society, in every society where the distinction of ranks has once been completely established, there have always been two different schemas or systems of morality current at the same time; of which the one may be called the strict or austere; the other the liberal, or, if you will, the loose system. The former is generally admired and revered by the common people: the latter is commonly more esteemed and adopted by what are called people of fashion. . . . In the liberal or loose system, luxury, wanton and even disorderly mirth, the pursuit of pleasure to some degree of intemperance, the breach of chastity, at least in one of the two sexes, etc., provided they are not accompanied with gross indecency, and do not lead to falsehood or injustice, are generally treated with a good deal of indulgence, and are easily either excused or pardoned altogether. In the austere system, on the contrary, those excesses are regarded with the utmost abhorrence and detestation. The vices of levity are always ruinous to the common people, and a single week's thoughtlessness and dissipation is often sufficient to undo a poor laborer for ever, and to drive him through despair upon committing the most enormous crimes.[96]

Smith has the merit of highlighting the connection between "liberal" morality and wealth, between "austere" morality and the plebeian condition. Hegel's sensitivity to the social question lacks those plebeian characteristics that appear in Rousseau and Fichte; but the other side of the coin is Hegel's distance from the "austere" celebration of the sobriety and simplicity of the peasants' pre-industrial world. Hegel compares Rousseau to Diogenes, and so does Voltaire (infra, ch. VIII, 2), the author of *Le Mondain* and the representative of that "liberal" morality which Smith considers typical of property-owners.[97] But unlike Hegel, Voltaire has no sympathy for the Rousseau who gives voice to the suffering and poverty of the masses. On the contrary, he labels Rousseau's *Discourse on the Origins and Foundations of Inequality* as "the philosophy of a beggar (*gueux*) who wishes that the rich be robbed by the poor."[98] Voltaire only questions aristocratic privilege, and at any rate, his praise of the worldly man seems to erase or ignore the political and social dimensions of poverty. As for Hegel, he is immune to bucolic nostalgia, and decisively affirms that it is in the cities and among the urban classes that "the consciousness of freedom manifests itself most strongly" (*Rph.III*, 166), whereas peasants "are the most inclined to submissiveness" (*v.Rph.*, III, 629–30; cf. also *v.Rph.*, IV, 505–6). However, Hegel's unrestricted acceptance of advanced industrial society never turns into a romanticized account of it. The fact that poverty continues to exist alongside opulence is a "remnant of the state of nature," which in turn is synonymous, as Hegel constantly emphasizes, with a condition of generalized violence (infra, ch. VII, 10).

Leaving aside the political implications that arise from this, implications which Hegel himself does not seem to fully grasp, we are nevertheless well beyond the liberal tradition which views "nature" as the place where the seal of the eternal and historically determined socio-economic relationships can be found. In nature, the liberal tradition seeks the comfortable guarantee that—and here we are citing Marx, although with him the criticism of such ideology reaches an epistemologically new level—"there has been history, but there is no longer any."[99]

THREE

Legitimacy and Contradictions of Modernity

VII

Right, Violence, and *Notrecht*

1. War and the Right to Property: Hegel and Locke

The argument against the absolutization of the right to property characterizes the whole of Hegel's thought. Even after the difference between ancient and modern ethics—and thus the role played by the inviolability of the private sphere within modern man's freedom—has become unquestionable, Hegel still emphasizes the subordination of private property to the political community. This subordination reveals itself most powerfully in time of war: it would be absurd to insist on maintaining that private property is inviolable when, in order to defend all and to safeguard national independence, the State demands that citizens risk their very existence (*Rph.*, § 324 A). Clearly, the value of life is higher than that of property.

Subordinating the value of property to that of life is by no means an obvious operation. We only need to examine Locke's considerations on war. In order to demonstrate that political powers should under no circumstances be permitted to "take to themselves the whole, or any part of the subjects' property, without their own consent," Locke proffers the "common practice of martial discipline" by way of example: "the preservation of the army, and in it of the whole commonwealth, requires an absolute obedience to the command of every superior officer, and it is justly death to disobey or dispute the most dangerous or unreasonable of them; but yet we see, that neither the sergeant, that could command a soldier to march up to the mouth of a cannon, or stand in a breach, where he is almost sure to perish, can command that soldier to give him one penny of his money; nor the general, that can condemn him to death for deserting his post, or for not obeying the most desperate orders, can yet, with all his absolute power of life and death, dispose of one farthing of that soldier's estate, or seize one jot of his goods; whom yet he can command any thing, and hang for the least disobedience."[1] An individual's property is more inviolable than his own life.

It would seem that for Locke and the liberal school, the most intolerable violence is that which is carried out against private property. On the contrary, the obligation imposed upon citizen-soldiers to sacrifice their lives without resistance in time of war is not regarded by Locke as a kind of violence. On this point, Locke goes even further than Hobbes himself, who, in his rejection of the right to resistance, formulates an important exception: "Covenants not to defend a man's own body are void. Upon this ground a man that is commanded as a soldier to fight against the enemy, though his sovereign have right enough to punish his refusal with death, may nevertheless in many cases refuse, without injustice." Besides, in the case of men who are not professional soldiers and who therefore did not choose military life freely, except for some exceptional circumstances in which the very existence of the State is at stake, "there is allowance to be made for natural timorousness." Therefore, "when armies fight, there is on one side, or both, a running away; yet when they do it not out of treachery, but fear, they are not esteemed to do it unjustly, but dishonourably. For the same reason, to avoid battle is not injustice, but cowardice."[2] To condemn a nonprofessional soldier to sacrifice his own life in battle constitutes for Hobbes an inexcusable violence, against which resistance—at least passive resistance—is justifiable. For Locke, instead, such an obligation is perfectly legitimate, and any breach of it would be wrong and violent. Political power takes on the shape of tyranny and therefore violence when it violates private property, and in that case it is lawful to resist it. In this way, the citizen, or rather, the individual, takes possession once again of the power it owned in the state of nature, a power that allows him "to use such means, for the preserving of his own property, as he thinks good, and nature allows him."[3] The sphere of lawfulness is the sphere of the respect of private property, whereas violence is defined first of all as the violation of private property, of its absoluteness.

Hegel's position is diametrically opposed to Locke's. As we have seen, in analyzing the consequences of war on the right to property, Hegel uses Locke's example, but completely reverses its meaning. The principle according to which life constitutes a decisively higher value than property is valid not only in time of war. In the case of extreme need, Hegel holds that it is lawful to injure "a singular and limited existence of freedom" such as property, if the only alternative is "an infinite injury to existence with total loss of rights" (Rph., § 127).

2. From the *Ius Necessitatis* to the Right of Extreme Need

Let us now turn from the printed text of *Philosophy of Right* to the *Lectures*, which convey a more intense passion and boldness with regard to the theme in question: "A man who is starving has the absolute right to violate another person's property, since he is violating property only in a limited fashion: the right of necessity requires him not to violate another person's right as such: he is only interested in a piece of bread, he is not treating the other person as an individual without rights. Abstract intellect is prone to consider any legal violation as absolute, but a starving man only violates the particular, he does not violate right per se." When motivated by hunger, by the necessity to preserve life, the violation of the right to property does not stand for arbitrariness and violence, but for the affirmation of a superior right. Indeed, on one side is "this limited property," on the other, "the life of a man" who, in his desperate hunger, is suffering "a complete violation of his existence"; on one side, then, what is at stake is something finite and limited, on the other it is "an infinite." In the latter case, "the right as a whole is violated by the violation of the actuality of right." If Locke considers questioning the sphere of private property in its absoluteness and inviolability as an expression of arbitrariness and violence, Hegel sees arbitrariness and violence precisely in the absolutization of private property, the imposition of an unlawful abstraction from man's concrete needs and from the duties of solidarity with the political community. The one who negates the other as a legal subject and who therefore acts violently is not the starving man who hopes to save his life by means of a limited violation of the right to property, but the property-owner who would sacrifice a man's life on the altar of a stubborn inviolability of the right to property. If the property-owner embodies the abstract legal fury, the starving man struggling to survive embodies reason in its historical and political concreteness.

Hegel defends the reason and reasons of the starving man with a passion that cannot go unnoticed: the absolutization of the right to property holds "something revolting for every man, and this is based on the fact that man loses all of his rights the moment in which it is affirmed that he should respect limited right" (*v.rph.*, IV, 341–42). It is extraordinary to hear this theorist of the objectivity of institutions declare: "if a man who is struggling to survive steals a piece of bread, he undoubtedly violates "a man's property"; "his action is unjust (*unrechtlich*), but it would be wrong (*unrecht*) to consider it an ordinary theft. Yes, man has the right to this unjust action" (*v.rph.*, III, 400 and 402).

Before moving any further in our examination of Hegel's thought, we would do well to consider some of the philosophers who preceded him, in order to fully grasp the fundamental innovations introduced into the traditional doctrine of *ius necessitatis*. *Notrecht* had already been discussed by Kant and Fichte, though within a completely different conceptual framework. Two people are drowning as a result of a shipwreck—Fichte writes, using an example formerly used by Kant.[4] They are hanging on to the "renowned, miraculous plank we remember from our school days," which, however, can only support and save one of them; on the basis of which legal norm can we then settle the inevitable controversy between these two possible candidates for death? For Kant, the drowning man who saves his own life at the expense of the other can be considered "guilty" but at the same time "not-punishable" (in cases like these, the threat of a sanction does not act as a deterrent). But—Fichte observes—we can talk about "positive right" when the possibility of "coexistence of more free beings" can be presupposed; and this possibility is explicitly excluded from this example. In their struggle for life and death, the two drowning men are practically thrown back into their state of nature by this exceptional situation. We can therefore define "the right of necessity (*Notrecht*) as the right to consider oneself completely exempted from any legislation."[5] This solution has the merit of eliminating an endless and pointless series of cases from the appropriate legal debate; nevertheless, for Fichte, too, *Notrecht* continues to be part of this series, except that this *Notrecht* does not represent an actual right.

Fichte's example and solution reappear in Hegel: "If they are both in danger of death and only one of them can hang on to the plank, then the condition is non-legal, and the decision pertains to a subjective sensation; we are no longer dealing with right or wrong, but only with abnegation" (*Rph.I*, § 63 A). However, Hegel uses this example only to express his irritation about this series of cases: such examples can be rattled off at will, imagination can be unbridled and make up borderline cases; but this game can only give pleasure and energy to "trivial reflections" that bring up the usual example of the "plank" in order to dodge more serious and dramatic problems, real problems (*Rph.*, § 137 AL; *v.Rph.*, II, 485). Rather than chasing imaginary conflicting duties in abnormal and fictitious situations, it is better to keep in mind that the contrast between opulence, on the one hand, and extreme poverty, on the other, "is not a merely casuistic conflict, but an antithesis that is always and necessarily present and clashing especially in a developed society" (*v.Rph.*, III, 398).

We have seen instead the polemic raised against *Notrecht* by Rotteck, one of Hegel's liberal critics (supra, ch. IV, 5). Rotteck's position on the inviolability of legal regulation is much less rigid when compared to many representatives of liberalism. What is particularly important is the fact that this inviolability is qualified from the starting point of the anal ysis of existing contradictions and social relations. We have reached the heart of the problem. For Kant and Fichte, *Notrecht* is only related to exceptional situations; the *Not* stemmed from a natural catastrophe and from an accidental event that could not question the existing legal system. Hegel's position is quite different: the *Not* that causes the *Notrecht* is a social issue that does not refer to an extraordinary situation during which, under accidental and unusual circumstances, the protagonists are briefly cast back into a state of nature. On the contrary, the *Not* refers to an everyday experience that takes place on the basis of existing socio-legal relations. Indeed, in civil society, "as wealth is accumulated, the other extreme also arises: poverty, indigence, and destitution." "In civil society, the poor do not have to struggle with a mere natural calamity (*Naturnot*); the nature that the poor are forced to face is not a mere being, but my will" (*Rph.III*, 194–95). This means that the poor, unlike the drowning men in the example, are not faced with the violence of a natural catastrophe and an unusual situation of struggle produced by nature, but with a violation that is produced by the socio-political order itself: "The poor are faced with arbitrariness, with human contingency, and in the final analysis, the fact that they are forced into this contrast by arbitrariness is revolting. Self-consciousness appears to be pushed to an extreme point where it is left with no right at all, where freedom does not exist" (*ibid.*).

3. The Contradictions of Modern Economic Development

We have seen (supra, ch. vi, 3) that, in complete opposition to Locke, Hegel regards mass poverty as a social issue that calls to question not the responsibility of the individual, but the responsibility of the socio-political order. English liberals told stories about untilled lands in America and even in Europe, lands that were only waiting for the energetic, laborious intervention of a poor individual who would then be rewarded with their richness. Hegel, on the other hand, remarks that, within a developed civil society, "taking immediate possession of something is no longer possible" given that "everything already belongs to another" (*v.Rph.*, IV, 497), and "every tree, every animal no longer belongs to nature, but to an owner" (*v.Rph.*, IV, 494). A material that is properly natural can be molded with hard work, but here we are confronted "with a matter which offers infinite resistance, i.e. with external means whose particular character is that they are the property of free will and are therefore absolutely unyielding" (*Rph.*, § 195). It is very common to observe how "an *unutterable* multitude is carrying the heavy load of unhappiness. The unhappiness of many could be eliminated with very small means that, however, are the free property of others. We can therefore see the struggle of poverty and, right next to it, the means that could put an end to it; but between the two is an insurmountable abyss" (v.Rph., III, 398). This abyss is political and social, not natural, and the "infinite resistance" is not offered by nature as such, but by property and its owners.

We are not only confronted with a social issue, but a social issue that becomes particularly serious in modern industrial society. This awareness represents a further step away from that apologetic vision of economic development on the basis of which Locke had thought it suitable to claim that "a king of a large and fruitful territory there [in Native America], feeds, lodges, and is clad worse than a day-labourer in England."[6] This vision could be found even earlier with Bernard de Mandeville, who believed that "the very poor liv'd better than the rich before," and even better than the powerful individuals in ancient or still primitive societies, who had none of those "great many comforts of life that are now enjoy'd by the meanest and most humble wretches."[7] Analogous terms can be found also in the works of another representative of the liberal tradition, Adam Smith, who claims that an "industrious and frugal" European farmer lives much better than "many an African king"[8] or the "chief of a savage nation in North America."[9] For Hegel, instead, it makes no sense to place the poor, in modern industrial society, at a higher level of welfare than the rich of earlier times or of societies with an inferior economic development. This economic development is not representative of a uniform and painless progress; on the contrary, it creates new needs that it cannot satisfy: "the condition of poverty leaves man with these needs, these multiple needs of civil society, and at the same time it deprives him of the support of nature: everything is already owned by others, people cannot fish, hunt, or pick fruit" (v.Rph., IV, 605).

A rejection of this justification of economic development can also be found in Sieyès, who, in one of his fragments, explicitly criticizes Smith on this point.[10] Sieyès does not hesitate to write that, in the modern world, "the working classes (laborieuses) of advanced societies . . . are crushed by the needs of a whole society," a society that is "a million times greedier and more consumerist than it ever was in ancient times." In conclusion, "these men, overpowered and corrupted by excessive toil, by the uncertainty of remuneration, by cruel dependency and the infinite series of new sorrows, these men are the weakest, they have more needs, more urgent ones. You, instead," Sieyès presses in his polemic against Smith, "celebrate the quality of their subsistence, a subsistence they achieve by living a kind of life you would not accept to live even if you were offered a throne."[11] Yet, on the flip side of this negative view is Sieyès' claim that this condition is absolutely irreparable: "we are forced to regard most men as working machines" whose "happiness" is forever precluded by the modern organization of society, an organization founded upon "consumption" and "production," as a result of which all European States are turning into "large factories."[12] For Sieyès it is inevitable, and in this sense even right, that masses of people sacrifice themselves to the needs of this gigantic factory that is now the modern world. His apparently negative view has become a sort of "indirect apology" that reveals all of the contradictions and sorrows of modern economic development, but only to affirm their absolute insurmountability.[13] In this sense, even the French tribune of the Third Estate ends up denying the reality of the social question, since no political transformation will ever be able to improve the condition of those (the majority of the population) who are destined to serve as "working machines" with no right to happiness.

Partly analogous considerations can be made with regard to Tocqueville, who is well aware that economic development is not a painless process, that it produces new, unsatisfied needs[14] and an increased insecurity in the "industrial class" which is exposed to the risks of the economic cycle and thus to "sudden and irremediable evils."[15] He is aware that economic development even exposes the more unfortunate ones to the danger of starvation, a danger that was unknown in earlier times when, despite general poverty, the land offered "anyone" the bare minimum to survive.[16] Economic development seems to go hand in hand and "continuously" with the increasing number of those who are forced to resort to the assistance and charity of others in order to avoid starvation.[17] And yet, this brutally realistic portrayal is marred, especially in the 1835 text we are examining, by two ideological elements. The first element is Tocqueville's insistence on claiming that the social costs of modernity are "inevitable evils"[18] and the results of the "immutable laws that govern the growth of organized societies."[19] The second element is the nostalgia that sometimes emerges in Tocqueville's text when he describes the *ancien régime*, premodern society: in it, the fate of servants "was less deserving of pity than that of the common people of our era," if for no other reason than the former had been accustomed to their condition and "enjoyed a kind of vegetative happiness. It is as difficult for the very civilized man to understand its charm as it is to deny its existence."[20] Other times, it sounds as if this *bonheur végétatif* is applied to the present, as seems to emerge from Tocqueville's affirmation that, when the higher classes of society make an effort to alleviate the misery of the poor, they are often moved to do so by an "imagination [that] exaggerates in their eyes the suffering caused by privation," a privation which the poor are instead well accustomed to.[21]

Moving now from France back to England, we can observe that an "indirect apology" like the one examined in Sieyès is also present in Thomas Malthus. Locke affirmed that there are still lands to till and that they readily offer themselves to the exertions of the poor, who can become their owners: there is still "land enough in the world to suffice double the inhabitants."[22] When *Philosophy of Right* is published, instead, in Germany what prevails is Malthus' thesis that the earth is overpopulated.[23] However, though the starting point is the opposite, the conclusion is the same: there is no social question, and if poverty were for Locke the result of a lack of initiative on the part of individuals who were not able to take advantage of nature's fertility and generosity, for Malthus it is the result of improvidence and sexual intemperance that makes individuals blind to the reality of an ungenerous, harsh nature. In both cases, poverty does not call into question the political and social order, and the reference to nature is ideological.

Hegel is a lucid critic of this ideology: "The general property of society is, for the individual, inorganic nature, which must present itself to him so that he can take possession of it; in fact, the earth is completely occupied, and thus the individual is referred back to civil society" (Rph. I, § 118 A). Since referring back to civil society is inevitable, poverty now appears as a social question, a "wrongdoing perpetrated against one class or another," using Hegel's words once again. We have translated *Unrecht* in the text we are discussing as "wrongdoing," but we could translate it even more literally as "violation of right." The conception of poverty as a social question makes the separation between legality and illegality and between right and violence less clear, since this separation no longer coincides automatically, as Locke would have it, with the difference between defense and violation of the right to property.

4. *Notrecht* and Self-Defense: Locke, Fichte, and Hegel

In order to explain the concrete meaning of *Notrecht* as articulated by Hegel, his assistant Leopold von Henning speaks of "right to self-preservation" (*Recht der Selbsterhaltung; v.Rph.*, III, 400). At this point it is clear that, with Hegel and his school, the traditional *ius necessitatis* has turned into something different: *Notrecht* is now the right of extreme need, the right of the poor struggling to survive. Once again, we can see the contrast between Hegel and part of the liberal tradition. Rotteck denies the existence of *Notrecht*, as well as the existence of an "absolute right to self-preservation" (*absolutes Recht der Selbsterhaltung*), whereas Locke's "right to survival" only aims at justifying the genesis of private property and, ultimately, the existing relations of property (supra, ch. IV, 5).[24] For Hegel, instead, the "right of extreme need" consciously aims at qualifying the right to property, though Hegel obviously acknowledges its legitimacy.

According to Locke, no social situation can justify the violation of the right to property, and any theft represents a declaration of war on the victim of it, a declaration that makes it lawful, if not necessary, to respond in kind. It is lawful to kill one who "sets on me to rob me but of my horse or coat,"[25] and "this makes it lawful for a man to kill a thief, who has not in the least hurt him, nor declared any [aggressive] design upon his life."[26] Indeed, self-defense is one of the examples that Locke uses to demonstrate the absolute inviolability of private property, which in this case, too, reveals itself as more inviolable than life itself: "For though I may kill a thief that sets on me in the highway, yet I may not (which seems less) take away his money, and let him go: this would be robbery on my side."[27]

In contrast to the liberal tradition, Fichte, too, believes in the subordinate role of the right to private property. Since in "rational States" there should be no "poor people,"[28] an individual in need (*Notleidender*) should be considered entitled to "an absolute coercive right to assistance" and can lawfully claim as much of another's property as is necessary for his survival.[29] It remains to be seen, however, whether Fichte remains consistently loyal to this position. He likens "self-defense" to *Notrecht*, which for him is the traditional *ius necessitatis:* they are two forms of "self-defense" (*Selbstverteidigung*) in a situation in which the State cannot intervene, and justice cannot be regularly enforced. Fichte insists passionately on this theme: "Everyone has the absolute right not to let others seize one's things by force," even if this should cost the "attacker" his own life. In the *Foundations of Natural Right*, he does not hesitate to refer to Roman Law and the "Law of the Twelve Tables, [which] authorized the victim of a theft to kill the thief who was defending himself. And the thief had every right to defend himself if the stolen goods were not labeled, that is, their ownership could not be proved."[30] In 1812, in his *Doctrine of Right*, Fichte goes so far as to criticize "a certain laxity on the part of the legislation" with regard to assailants, and the fact that "compassion for criminals [is] often greater than compassion for honest men."[31] The emphasis with which the right to self-defense is presented seems here to result in absolutization of the right to property. According to Fichte, it is not fair "to ask: what is money in comparison to life? If anything, this is an evaluation based on goodness, not on right."[32]

Hegel does not seem interested in discussing the right to self-defense. Instead, he makes an accurate distinction between violence against a person and violence against property: "Because I feel, contact with or violence to my body touches me immediately as *actual* and *present*. This constitutes the difference between personal injury and infringement of my external property; for in the latter, my will does not have this immediate presence and actuality" (RPh., § 48 A). Certainly, property, too, is an expression of a person's will, but it needs to be ascertained whether what was harmed was the person's "entire extension," as happens in the most serious crimes, that is, "in murder, slavery, religious coercion, etc." (Rph., § 96). Crimes against property do not belong to this sphere, and therefore they cannot be punished with death: "If theft is punished with death, the nature of what the thief violated is quite different from the means with which he is punished" (v.Rph., IV, 293). By the same token, it is outrageous that a murderer, or one who has committed a serious crime against a person, can get off by paying a mere fine: "If a serious crime is punished with a simple fine, then right as such no longer exists. When a sum can be paid for the mutilation or the killing of a man, then the man for whom the sum is being paid has no rights, he is simply an external thing" (v.Rph., IV, 282).

The most serious crimes are not those committed against property, but those which, in one way or another, turn man into a mere object, beginning with slavery and serfdom, both of which are regarded as examples of an unacceptable "alienation of personality" (Rph., § 66 A). Next to slavery and serfdom, Hegel also cites "mutilation." This is not an *exemplum fictum:* corporal punishment against serfs or ex-serfs continued to be carried out for a long time in Prussia. Even after the antifeudal reforms of 1807, the State permitted property-owners to educate ex-serfs with whippings, though the use of sticks was prohibited, or at least discouraged, in order to avoid "excesses." Even after the July Revolution, in some sections of the State apparatus, "the continuation of the right to corporal punishment [was considered] perfectly rational."[33]

Hegel explicitly criticizes those who affirm that "pure freedom cannot be attacked by any external force, so if I order someone to be beaten, that does not damage his freedom" (Rph.I, § 29 A). He also criticizes those who "make the following distinction: if a man is beaten one hundred times, only his body is harmed, not his spirit, and his soul remains free," since "the freedom of a serf, of a slave, is supposed to have its seat in his spirit" (v.Rph., IV, 196). According to Hegel, instead, whereas an attack against property does not necessarily harm a person's entire extension, an attack against the body affects much more than a person's physical being: "It is only because I am alive as a free entity within my body that this living existence may not be misused as a beast of burden ... Violence done to *my body* by others is violence done to me" (Rph., § 48 A). This is why a person who is responsible for a "mutilation" cannot get off by paying a mere fine. If this occurred—and in Prussia there were indeed cases in which those who had exceeded their authority, acknowledged by the law, to inflict corporal punishment, were ordered to pay a mere fine—it would mean that the victim has been reduced to a thing, just like a serf or slave. Hegel's qualitative distinction between thing-property on one side, and body-man on the other, is not shared by Locke, who places the "servant," though rigorously distinguishing him from the "slave," into the master's family, and regards the master himself as a *paterfamilias* with a (limited) right to inflict corporal punishment on his servant.[34]

With regard to the denunciation of violence, Locke concentrates primarily on the attack against property carried out by the lower classes, whereas Hegel insists especially on the crimes that cause an "alienation of personality" and, given the conditions and social relations of his time, he focuses particularly on the crimes committed by the dominant classes. One proof of this is that, unlike Locke, Hegel acknowledges a starving man's right to violate private property.

5. "Negative Judgment," "Negatively Infinite Judgment," and "Rebellion"

How does the right of extreme need manifest itself? "The poor feel excluded from everything, mocked by everyone, and an inner rebellion (*innere Empörung*) necessarily ensues." "Once this point has been reached—a point when the existence of freedom becomes completely accidental—an inner rebellion becomes necessary" (Rph.III, 195). Apparently, *Notrecht* does not go beyond an inner rebellion, consummated in the intimacy of consciousness. Yet, in the same context Hegel remarks that the poor "are conscious of themselves as infinite, free beings; hence their demand that external existence, too, correspond to this consciousness" (*ibid.*). On the other hand, we have seen how a starving man cannot only perform a wrong action, but he has an "absolute right" to do it. Hegel does hasten to explain that "only the extreme need of a present situation, in its absoluteness, authorizes a wrong action" (*v.Rph.*, III, 403). However, he also expresses the awareness that in a developed civil society, "extreme need no longer has this temporary character" (Rph.III, 196). On the contrary, the analysis of civil society leads to a precise result: the *Not* becomes progressively more urgent as wealth is amassed on the opposite side: "Wealth and poverty increase simultaneously" (Rph.III, 193).

Is this an indirect, implicit formulation of a sort of right to revolution, the revolution of the poor? This is the thesis suggested by Dieter Henrich in a published course of lectures: "Throughout Hegel's works, this is the only place in which he not only regards revolution as a fact and a historical necessity, but he posits a right to it from the starting point of a systematic analysis of a current institution."[35] In reality, similar or even more radical expressions can be found in other courses of lectures as well. Besides Hegel's claim that a starving man has the "absolute right" to commit a wrong action, we can also read: "This feeling, this rebellion, is inherent in extreme need. This right must be attributed to man in the rebellion caused by extreme need" (*v.rph.*, III, 402). If property is an "abstraction" in relation to the State, it is even more so in relation to the "World Spirit." Regardless of how "elevated" and "sacred" the "right to property" might be, it is always "quite subordinate, it can and must be violated." And if it can be "violated" by the State, it can be violated even more so by the "World Spirit:" "Even the constitutional law is not supreme: above the constitutional law is the right of the World Spirit: this right is unlimited, sacred, the most sacred" (*v.rph.*, IV, 157).

As examples of "individuals" who had "for themselves the higher justification of the World Spirit" and who essentially questioned the dominant property relations though they were later forced to submit to the ruling "rapacious nobility," Hegel cites the Gracchi, extolling their noblemindedness (*ph. G.*, 708 and 706). On the other hand, according to Hegel, in a "state of violence" there is room for the "right of heroes" (*rph.*, § 93 A), for a "higher right of the idea" (*v.rph.*, III, 296). Indeed, a social condition that condemns masses of people to a "total lack of rights" undoubtedly represents a form of violence.

The conviction that this condition represents a form of violence clearly emerges in Hegel's text. There is a well-known distinction between "civil controversy" as an example of "negative judgment" ("only this particular right" is denied here, not "right as such" or the "legal capacity of a specific person"), and criminal law considered as the sphere of application of "negatively infinite judgment" (crime per se denies even the universal, it denies right as such, a victim's "legal capacity").[36] In one of his lectures, Hegel affirms that those who live in extreme poverty suffer an "infinite judgment of crime" (*rph.*, III, 196).[37] Reducing a mass of people to a condition of extreme need is equal to denying them "legal capacity" as a whole, and here the comparison with crime becomes clearer. A starving man who violates property expresses a negative judgment on the property-owner, a negative judgment that does not violate the property-owner's legal capacity. Property relations that hopelessly condemn a starving man, on the other hand, pronounce a negatively infinite judgment on him; they do not deprive him of a specific, limited right, but of the totality of rights. They essentially inflict the same violence upon him that a criminal could.

Another comparison, more succinct but no less significant, emerges from Hegel's text: a "negatively infinite judgment" is expressed on a living organism by "death," whereas a simple "negative judgment" is expressed by an illness that only denies or hinders a "specific vital function" (*Enc.*, § 173 z). Given the situation of extreme poverty, the "right to life" of an entire social class is not hindered or denied by "single moments" or "particular moments" like the mere onset of an "illness" (Rph. I, § 118 A). The social class that suffers extreme poverty is indirectly compared to an organism whose life itself, its "right to life" rather than its single vital functions in specific moments, has been damaged. "Death" is to "illness" as "crime" is to "civil controversy:" the "negatively infinite judgment" crushes not only "legal capacity," but the very life of the social class that has fallen into extreme poverty. Starting from the fact that, in time of war, the State sacrifices the "right to life," Hegel refutes the thesis of the inviolability of property (since the latter cannot possibly be put on a higher level than the right to life) (v.Rph., IV, 157). Now, however, we see that sacrificing the "right to life" for the sake of property relations is a perfectly normal social practice.

The violence inherent in the absolutization of private property is so blatant that at times Hegel seems to consider Notrecht not only legal, but even somehow rightful. Going back to the example of the starving man who avoids death by stealing a piece of bread, we read: "We have here two kinds of wrongdoing (Unrecht), and the problem is to determine which of the two is greater. What is less important represents a wrongdoing in comparison to what is more important." To reject the sacrifice of life to property means to oppose the occurrence of an even greater wrongdoing, violation of right (Unrecht). To maintain rigorously (streng) the predominance of "rigorous right (strenges Recht) over extreme need means to support Unrecht, the violation of right, or at least a greater violation of right" (v.Rph., III, 403 and 405). Henning's comment is even more explicit: though Notrecht violates the right to property, in reality it represents a "re-establishment of right" (v.Rph., III, 401). The re-establishment of right, therefore, occurs when a starving man is forced in the struggle for survival to become a thief: there could be no greater separation between this position and the position defended by Locke and the liberal tradition!

Notrecht also represents the re-establishment of equality; not the "equality of external goods," which for Hegel is "something false," but legal equality. It is absolutely necessary to recognize that a starving man in danger of death has the right to do a wrong deed: "This is what equality consists of: another person must not hold an advantaged position over my existence; before it, the other person's right disappears" (Rph., I, § 63 A). A property-owner cannot arrogate to himself the power of life or death over a starving man, since this would undermine the very principle of legal equality. At times, Hegel's criticism of the formal character of legal equality reveals many points in common with the criticism that will later be formulated by Marx: "Everyone has the right to life, and this right cannot be merely limited to defense [from external assaults]; a person has not only a negative right, but also a positive right. . . . The fact that man has the right to life implies that he has a positive, full right; the actuality of freedom must be essential" (Rph.I, § 118 A). Another point in common with Marx is the criticism of "formal right." Hegel consistently regards it as an unavoidable element, though the right to life cannot be denied in the name of "formal right" (Rph., § 127 AL; v.Rph., II, 459), and one cannot "hide behind formal right" in order to fight off the demands of a starving man (Rph., § 126 AL; v.Rph., II, 457).

6. *Notrecht, Ancien Régime,* and Modernity

Notrecht is founded precisely on the right to life. And from the right to life, at least during a phase of the evolution of his thought, Hegel deduces the right to work. Given that "the right to life is an absolutely essential element for man, and that civil society must provide this essential element" (Rph.I, § 118 A), "anyone who is unemployed has the right to demand work" (Rph.III, 192). Significantly enough, Hegel already speaks in favor of the right to work a few decades before the Revolution of 1848.

A more general consideration can be made with regard to this point. The debate on the right to life (that is, essentially, *Notrecht*) accompanies the whole course of the French Revolution. The right to life is already criticized before 1789 by Condorcet, who draws a polemical analogy between the "right to life" (*droit de vivre*) and the "right to plunder" a property-owner.[38] A few weeks after the storming of the Bastille, the right to life is argued for by an author influenced by Rousseau,[39] then it is celebrated by Marat, Robespierre, and Babeuf.[40] The right to life is also the target of criticism and derision in the Thermidorian circles, to which Constant belongs.[41] In England, Malthus' criticism of the French Revolution is first of all a criticism of the right to life, that is, a "*droit de subsister*" that is considered incompatible with the "principle of population:" "Neither before nor after the institution of social laws, could an unlimited number subsist."[42]

Those who continue to defend the right to life in England are the representatives of radical populism,[43] while in Germany the "right to existence" (*Selbsterhaltung*) is supported by an author like Fichte, who is still faithful to the most radical phase of the French Revolution.[44] The justification of the right to life is a *leitmotiv* that characterizes the heirs of the Jacobin-Babeuvian tradition and the forerunners of socialism. Thus, for example, Blanqui declares in 1832 before his judges: "I am accused of telling thirty million French people, proletarians like me, that they have a right to life."[45] During the same year, another French representative of the same political tradition declares that "the most important rights of man are those of self-preservation and freedom."[46] In this sense, the reflection on the French Revolution that can be found in Hegel includes even its most radical moments, and its heritage emerges in socialism.[47]

It is true that, after the Revolution of 1848, Tocqueville sees something that resembles "socialism" already in the Code of Friedrich II, according to which it is the responsibility of "the State to provide food, work, and a salary to all those who cannot support themselves."[48] However, this claim is part of Tocqueville's attempt to establish a connection between the *ancien régime*, Jacobinism, and socialism, with the ultimate goal of denouncing the latter two. Besides, the affirmation of this possible connection is hardly reconcilable with the alarm sounded against the mortal danger that socialism supposedly represented for the whole of "European civilization." Socialism, in fact, would threaten "not only political institutions, but also civil institutions, social institutions, old society as we know it."[49] Here socialism is portrayed as something new, something terribly new, to the point that it is likened to a "new race" devoured by an "illness" and "a new, unknown virus."[50] But the main point is different: Tocqueville is obsessed by the specter of socialism. He condemns any state intervention in the economy as the expression of a conservative, reactionary mentality, a mentality that suffocates the sense of initiative and individual responsibility, a mentality that is essentially infected with nostalgia for the paternalism of premodern absolute regimes. For Tocqueville it is easy to object that Montesquieu had already asserted that the State "must guarantee a sure existence, nourishment, decent clothing, and a healthy lifestyle to every citizen."[51] Would this be enough reason to include even the author of *Spirit of Laws* into the lineage so dear to post-1848 liberalism?

Against the insistence on replacing "individual foresight and wisdom with the State's foresight and wisdom," Tocqueville declares that "nothing authorizes the State to interfere with industry."[52] The source is a renowned speech delivered September 12, 1848, in which Tocqueville urges the Constituent Assembly to fight off the demand for the "right to work," a demand that had already been suppressed by violence during the June days. Tocqueville's laissez-faire goes so far as to regard the "twelve hour day" (*le travail de douze heures*) law a "socialist doctrine," which he consequently proceeds to condemn.[53] Analogously, he rejects any legislative measure that aims at alleviating the poverty of the "lower classes" by limiting renting costs as an expression of socialism and despotism.[54] In the light of subsequent historical experience, it is difficult to consider this position particularly "modern." And it is just as difficult to classify as modern a position that is largely present, though with substantial ideological differences, in the liberal tradition and in Tocqueville's thought. According to this position, the causes of poverty lie in individual merit, fortune, and chance, the natural and even providential order of things, rather than the economic and social relations or political institutions. Why does Tocqueville maintain that the Revolution of 1848 should be condemned, as early as February, as essentially socialist and antibourgeois (and antiliberal)?[55] He does so because he sees it as being strongly influenced by "economic and political theories" that insist on spreading the conviction "that human poverty is caused by laws and not by providence, and that it could be eliminated just by changing the social order."[56] Precisely because he denies the social question, Tocqueville is forced to give credit to Malthus' theory.[57]

Premodern elements can indeed be detected in the above-mentioned citation by Montesquieu, which not by chance is contained in a chapter of the *Spirit of Laws* dedicated to hospices (*Des hôpitaux*). The help and assistance of the State are linked to an institution that shows very little respect for the demands of modern freedom. It is an institution which, despite several transformations, continues throughout the nineteenth century in liberal Europe. One needs only think of the work-houses, actual penitentiaries, that, from 1834, become the only form of "relief" to the poor of England. Once they entered into these work-houses, the poor "ceased to be citizens in any true sense of the word" since they forfeited the "civil right of personal liberty."[58] Tocqueville seems to have no objections to this institution. He does recognize that it is very similar to a prison, but as soon as he writes his memorandum on pauperism in 1835, right after the law in question is approved, he expresses no reservations about the antiliberal, despotic administration of work-houses, despite the wide and various protests raised against them in England.[59] On the contrary, Tocqueville is on very good terms with Nassau Senior, one of the authors of the 1834 law.[60] Hegel's argument is quite different: for one, Hegel uses the terms "work-house" (*Arbeitshaus*) and "penitentiary" as synonyms (*Zuchthaus; v.Rph.*, IV, 341 and Rph., § 126 AL; *v.Rph.*, II, 457), and he seems to have precisely that institution in mind when he declares that "people" must not "be tamed with disciplinary measures," since by doing so, "the citizens' fundamental rights would be humiliated" (Rph. III, 197).

We can conclude by observing that Hegel's justification of the right to life and *Notrecht* is based upon his analysis of the contradictions of emerging capitalist society. And as an example of a capitalist society, Hegel examines England and the effects of the French Revolution, thus looking not back at the past, but toward a future he still cannot glimpse.

7. The Starving Man and the Slave

Significantly, Hegel draws an analogy between the situation of a starving man and that of a slave: "A slave has no duties, because he has no rights. Absolute right consists in having rights. Man feels that, if his rights are not recognized, he is not obliged to recognize his own duties either" (*Rph.III*, 127).[61] Furthermore, Hegel observes that poor people have "no rights or duties" (*v.Rph.*, I, 322). The condition of a starving man is that of a "total lack of rights," and this very condition gives him the right not to respect the existing legal system, and to perform a wrong action such as violating the right to property: "Since individual freedom does not exist, the acknowledgment of general freedom disappears as well" (*Rph.III*, 195). The condition of extreme poverty is compared to a "crime" because of the "negatively infinite judgment" pronounced against the starving man. The same can be said about slavery, which configures the "negatively infinite judgment" in its totality, an "infinity" perfectly suitable to its concept (*Rph.*, § 96), so much so that it can be defined as "absolute crime" (*Rph.I*, § 45 A).

To describe the situation of a slave or starving man, Hegel uses very similar expressions: "A slave has the absolute right to break free" (*v.Rph.*, III, 251). Analogously, "a starving man has the absolute right to violate another person's property" (*v.Rph.*, IV, 341). To uphold the right to property over desperate hunger would be the *höchstes Unrecht*, the worst wrongdoing or illegality (*v.Rph.*, III, 403). The awareness of illegality or "absolute wrongdoing" (*absolutes Unrecht*) against a slave must be the starting point in any debate on slavery (*Rph.*, § 57 A). In describing the different condition of slaves and freemen, Hegel remarks: "If a person feels that his right over a single thing has been violated, that is not enough reason for him to believe that he no longer has any duties. The difference between quantitative and qualitative must be kept in mind" (*Rph.III*, 127). Only a slave is not obliged to respect the existing legal system. Hegel notes the same qualitative difference in a comparison between the situation of a starving man whose entire legal capacity is at stake, and one who, though his right to property has been violated by a starving man, still continues to be a free legal subject.

In at least one case, the similarity between a starving man and a slave becomes explicit: "A rich person considers everything venal in itself, because he regards himself as the power of the particularity of self-consciousness. Wealth can therefore lead to the same derision and shamelessness experienced by the poor. A master's attitude toward a slave is the same as that of the slave himself." Not only is a starving man compared to a slave and a rich man to a slaveowner, but the wrongdoing of a starving slave counterbalances the wrongdoing of a satiated master. This dialectic of master and servant is reminiscent of the *Phenomenology*, except that here it is applied to new capitalist relationships: "A master recognizes himself as power, just like a slave recognizes himself as the realization of freedom, of the idea. To the extent that a master recognizes himself as the owner of a slave's freedom, the essence of attitude has disappeared" (*Rph.III*, 196). The progress of history is clearly represented here by the starving slave.

A few years later, Eduard Gans makes an explicit comparison between the situation of the wage laborers of his time and that of slaves: "Isn't it slavery to exploit a man like an animal, even though he is free to starve to death?"[62] We have already seen how Hegel compares a starving man to a slave: a line of continuity leads to Marx's condemnation of "hired slavery"; not by chance, the young Marx had attended the lectures given by Gans, the publisher of *Philosophy of Right!* The comparison is also present in other cultural circles of the time: a year before *Philosophy of Right* was published, a renowned representative of the Historical School of Law writes that, at least with regard to sustenance, the situation of the poor is worse than that of slaves. Rather than to denounce the intolerability of pauperism, however, this condemnation is meant to praise the "security" that slaves purportedly had, and to demonstrate the legitimacy of slavery. According to the young Marx, Gustav Hugo—he is the renowned representative we are discussing—"thinks the *false flowers* have been plucked from the chains in order to wear real chains without any flowers."[63]

What is left is the widespread association of desperate poverty with slavery, a recurring association in Hegel's works, though not in the sense meant by Hugo. To prove that a slave is at least free from the preoccupation of providing material sustenance for himself, Hugo cites Abbot Galiani: "Every being that renounces or loses its liberty, abandons and at the same time is freed from the responsibility of feeding itself." With regard to this, Hegel writes the following note: "Slaves and serfs have a safe sustenance . . . see Gagliani" (*Rph.*, § 46 *AL*; *v.Rph.*, II, 219). The target of this polemic is clearly Hugo, and Galiani's name is misspelled. And, interestingly enough, Hegel's criticism targets the very same paragraph of Hugo's works that will later be attacked by Marx.[64]

Using an extreme case as his starting point, Hegel ends up questioning existing social relations as a whole. The starving man, the point of departure of Hegel's justification of *Notrecht*, is not the only one who has no rights. Things are not much better for the "poor" man either: "Because of the costs related to the formal administration of justice, it is impossible for him to defend his right by resorting to formal justice, and by appearing in court" (*Rph.I*, § 118 A).

8. *Ius Necessitatis, Ius Resistentiae, Notrecht*

The number of reasons that would seem to justify what Dieter Henrich calls the "poor people's right to rebellion" is quite astonishing. It is important to notice, however, that with regard to the Luddites' uprisings that occur during this period, Hegel's position is negative. In his *Lectures* he provides an extraordinarily objective description of the destruction of machines carried out by "workers, especially factory workers," who "become easily angry" since they are "losing their sustenance because of the machines" (*V.Rph.*, IV, 503; *V.Rph.*, III, 613). Yet, in a note written in Berlin, he speaks of the "excesses" of the "English people," who are responsible for the destruction of "steam engines" (*B.schr.*, 782). Of course, Hegel's position on Luddism can be explained by the fact that Luddism does not grasp the potentially liberating significance of machines. Not by chance, Hegel remarks that "the universal must favor the introduction of new machines, but at the same time it must seek to support those who are left without sustenance" (*Rph.I*, § 120 A). Hegel's position is not characterized by the argument for or the questioning of an alleged right to revolution or resistance (a right that is contradictory in itself), but by the analysis of objective contradictions which, in the absence of timely reforms, make the outbreak of a revolution inevitable. And this revolution can only be justified *post factum*, from the point of view of the World Spirit (supra, ch. IV, 4).

The argument for the right of necessity does not coincide with a call for revolution or resistance against authority; rather it is an appeal not to absolutize the right to property: "What is important belongs to the ethical, universal life; and the issues concerning these antitheses of welfare and right, including the right of necessity, only refer to a very limited range of cases" (*Rph.*, § 126 *AL*; *V.Rph.*, II, 459). Hegel's *Notrecht* is neither the *ius necessitatis* nor the *ius resistentiae* of tradition (two categories that Heinrich does not seem to distinguish); rather, Hegel's *Notrecht* aims at revealing the explosive potential caused by the social question, and at condemning the unreconciled, violent traits that continue to exist in the existing social relations. Hegel's hope is that an intervention from the political power will succeed in bringing about a reconciliation. On the one hand, the justification of *Notrecht* constitutes a criticism of the generalized criminalization of workers, whose uprisings were condemned at the time as attacks against private property and often likened to ordinary criminality. On the other hand, Hegel's argument intends to demonstrate, first of all, the "abstract" character of private property, and to emphasize the conflicts that such property is inevitably met with. Hegel was already familiar with Adam Smith's observations: "In order to bring the point to a speedy decision, they [the workers] have always recourse to the loudest clamour, and sometimes to the most shocking violence and outrage. They are desperate, and act with the folly and extravagance of desperate men, who must either starve, or frighten their masters into an immediate compliance with their demands." Smith describes, with cold lucidity, the "ruin" that awaits these "desperate" people, inexorably attacked by the police and by civil magistrates.[65] One of the rights of these desperate people who are destined to starve to death is now acknowledged; it is not the right to revolution, yet, despite the vagueness of its content, this right still manages to demonstrate the "abstract" character of private property, and to highlight the conflicts that such property is inevitably met with.

9. The Conflicts of Right with Moral Intention and Extreme Need

Hegel concentrates particularly on two conflicts: one between *Recht* ("right") and *Wohl* ("welfare"), and the other between *Recht* and *Not* ("extreme need"). The first conflict is clearly settled in favor of right, which represents substantiality and universality. "Welfare" represents "particularity," since, in contrast to the legal system, it only expresses the moral demand of an individual. "Welfare" belongs to "chance, to the arbitrariness of a particular decision" (*Rph.*, § 125 *AL; V.Rph.*, II, 455). Such "particularity" cannot be imposed "in contrast" to right. Even when it represents an "intention to promote my welfare and that of others," it cannot in any way "justify an *action which is wrong*" (*Rph.*, § 126). The contrast between "right" and "extreme need," instead, is quite different, since the latter can justify a "wrong action." The "life" that the "right of necessity" is called upon to defend "has a true right against formal right; in other words, it represents an absolute moment." This contrast is very different from the previous one, which regarded will, though disguised beneath the noblest intention, as opposed to the objectivity and concreteness of the legal system. What criticizes right is now "personality," but a personality in its "actual aspect," and therefore something "determined in and of itself," not a mere "opinion" (*Rph.*, § Al; *V.Rph.*, II, 459 and 461). Indeed, at this point, the contrast is between "welfare" (*Wohl*)—which in reality is the subjective moral intention to achieve such welfare—and "extreme need" (*Not*): "Welfare is an abstract term; welfare is not in one thing. Life, on the other hand, exists in a circumstance, in a moment." "Extreme need is a sacred term, if it is authentic: it is the whole of a situation; extreme need is a whole, it is life and family" (*Rph.*, § 127 *AL; V. Rph*, II, 461).

In order to understand Hegel's position on these two categories (*Wohl* and *Not*), it is not enough to refer back to the overall inspiration of his philosophical thought. History also must be taken into consideration. In Hegel's time, two different social classes with contrasting points of view are engaged in criticizing the absolutization of the right to private property. At times, this criticism is motivated by feudal reminiscences and nostalgia: an author like Adam Müller does not hesitate to condemn the concept of "unconditional private property," a concept that would undo any relationships founded "upon faith and belief" (auf Treu und Glauben). In a way, even in a reactionary critic like Müller we can find the contrast—in Hegel's terms—between right and welfare (or private moral intention toward welfare). According to Müller, once "unconditional private property" and the "one-sidedness of ownership" characteristic of Roman Law have been sanctioned, all "reciprocal obligations" are nullified, and so is every obligation on the part of the property-owner with regard to his employees' "sickness, accidents, and old age." To affirm the "absolute private property" of a land means to refuse to provide a poor individual with "life's basic needs." Müller cites the New Testament: "If a son shall ask bread of any of you that is a father, will he give him a stone?" This is what the abolition of feudalism and the consequent rejection of "theological foundations" in politics and economics have led to: "Children are given stones instead of bread."[66] The triumph of Roman Law and its cold objectivity require a sacrifice from the actual person. The poverty of the rising capitalist society is evoked only in contrast to the celebration of the good old times.

On the contrary, Hegel's criticism of the absolutization of private right never questions the outcome of bourgeois development; rather it presupposes such an outcome: "The specification of property represents enormous progress that is often not appreciated the way it should be" (v.Rph., IV, 223). If someone imitated St. Crispin in the modern world and attempted to solve the problem of poverty by stealing leather to make shoes for the poor, he would end up, and rightly so, in a penitentiary. Hegel uses this example in discussing the "conflict" between "right" and "welfare," where the latter coincides with the attempt by private conscience to set itself up as a judge of other people's welfare, thus yielding to the arbitrariness of a solitary moral or religious inspiration (Rph., § 126 AL; v.Rph., II, 457).

Against the absolutization of the right to private property typical of the bourgeois world, Müller proposes the Christian precept "love thy neighbor."[67] But this "commandment"—Hegel had already remarked in the Phenomenology—is only "the relationship of an individual with another," and therefore a "relationship of sensation." For this precept to make sense, it is necessary to move beyond mere sensation, so as to determine correctly the good or the "welfare" (Wohl) to which "loving thy neighbor" presumably leads. In the *Phenomenology*, the *Wohl* that moral intentions and religious conscience intend to celebrate as opposed to the cold objectivity of secular and political institutions ends up cutting a very poor figure. In order to rise above the level of "unreasonable love" which, Hegel observes ironically, can sometimes be more harmful than "hate" itself, it is necessary to transcend the individual's immediate knowledge and reach the level of political community, the level of the State: "The richest and most important expression of intelligent and essential good behavior is the intelligent, universal action of the State." If, in the name of "love thy neighbor," a person performed an action based upon his individual knowledge and attempted to counter the "universal" and "right," he would rightly end up being restrained (one only needs to think of St. Crispin's example). "Acting for the welfare of another" (*Handeln . . . zum Wohl anderer*)—an expression used in *Philosophy of Right* and recommended by the precept "love thy neighbor"—remains vulnerable to chance, it has no "universal content"; this and other similar precepts "do not move beyond the level of recommendations, they have no actuality; they are not laws, but mere commandments" (*w*, III, 314–15).

The "welfare" (*Wohl*) preached and celebrated by an abstractly moral intention is unable to realize itself as "law" within a legal system. In the celebration, widespread among Hegel's contemporaries, of the precept "love thy neighbor," and of moral intention as opposed to political institutions, Hegel recognizes an instrument of feudal ideology. Hence his criticism of "those who consider laws as something evil and profane, and who accept the precepts of Natural Law as the true order of life, thanks to faith and belief (*durch Glauben und Vertrauen*), while they consider the existing legal order corrupt, unjust." Certainly, the content of a law can be "irrational and therefore unjust," it can be characterized by "chance" and "arbitrariness" (*Enc.*, § 529 A), but those who appeal to moral intentions actually deny not a specific content, but the very form of universality, and on a legal and political level they represent the positions of immediate knowledge. They refer to religion in order to affirm that "the righteous do not need any laws" (*Rph.*, § 137 AL; *v.Rph.*, II, 489), and thus to eliminate ethics as such.

The criticism of abstract right by "extreme need" is quite different. Here, a specific content is questioned in the name of the demand to participate in the community, a demand raised by a social class that so far has been left out. What is demanded is a richer, more concrete universality, laws and institutions able to limit even more the level of "irrationality" and "arbitrariness" present in institutions that are all the more concrete when they are able to intervene in the "abstract" sphere of the right to property.

This is why Hegel, who consistently condemns the category of "welfare" (*Wohl*) whenever it is contrasted to the objectivity of the legal system, later justifies it on the level of a "system of needs"; on the level of morality, the contrast between "welfare" and "right" is carried out by "private people against other private people," and thus it becomes clear how "right is the essential quality" (*v.Rph.*, III, 400). On the level of a system of needs, instead, the category of welfare is an "essential quality" (*v.Rph.*, III, 689–90), since it demands that "the livelihood and welfare of individuals should be *secured*—i.e. that *particular welfare* should be *treated as a right* and duly *actualized*" (*Rph.*, § 230). The category of welfare is accepted only to the extent to which it coincides with the demand fulfilled by the right of necessity: the demand that right be given concreteness within ethical and political universality. Discussing the conflict between right and moral intention-welfare, Hegel cites an emblematic anecdote: a minister is caught red-handed and justifies himself by saying: "My Lord, one must live," to which Richelieu answers: "I do not see the necessity." Hegel concludes with the following remark: "Life is not necessary in comparison to the higher value of freedom." "Moral intentions," even if they were St. Crispin's, are worth nothing before the need that freedom be given universal and objective existence as right (*v.Rph.*, III, 398–99). On the other hand, Hegel justifies *Notrecht* with the need to preserve life as an actuality of right, as the concrete possibility for a starving man to exist as a legal subject.

Once again, the answer to the inadequacy of the legal system is not a celebration of a lawless individuality or a narcissistic retreat into an intimacy that takes pride in what it considers its moral excellence. On the contrary, the answer to such inadequacy is the effort to build a better legal system. In the last paragraph we cited from *Philosophy of Right*, Hegel declares that right is "actual" to the extent that it realizes the "tranquil safety (*Sicherheit*) of person and property," as well as the "security (*Sicherung*) of an individual's sustenance and welfare." The demand for *Sicherheit*, characteristic of the liberal tradition, is counterbalanced here by that of *Sicherung*, which is placed side by side with it.

It is interesting to notice that the theme of conflict between right and extreme need can also be traced in the culture of the time. Hugo describes men who "are forced to die" though the "necessary things for life's sustenance" are right in front of them, but belong to others. In this case, too, "an individual's exclusive right" is countered by the hopeless misery of a poor man who, unlike a slave, does not have the "good fortune" of being fed by his master. But this is not enough reason to violate the positive and sacred right of private property in the name of an animalistic appetite![68] If anything, it is an excuse to discuss the advantages of slavery. Hugo, whose position is the complete opposite of Adam Müller's, refers to Roman Law to emphasize the absoluteness of the right to property, including the possession of slaves.

As for Hegel, while, on the one hand, he rejects nostalgia for the feudal world that has been swept away by what Müller calls the "French-Roman Revolution," on the other hand, he criticizes the absolutization of private property carried out by Roman Law.[69] Fichte himself refers to Roman Law to justify the property-owner's right to defend his own possession even at the expense of the thief's life, and so does Hugo to legitimize slaveholding as one of the possible forms of private property. In *Philosophy of Right*, instead, Hegel denounces "the abominable law which, after a specified interval had elapsed, gave the creditor the right to kill the debtor or to sell him into slavery" (§ 3 A).[70] To the Law of the Twelve Tables, Hegel contrasts *Notrecht*, which creates the benefit of competence, "*beneficium competentiae*, whereby a debtor is permitted to retain his tools, agricultural implements, clothes, and in general as much of his resources—i.e. of the property of his creditors—as is deemed necessary to support him, even in his accustomed station in society" (*Rph.*, § 127 A). *Notrecht* excludes first of all the legitimation of slavery—let us not forget that this debate is not limited to ancient times, but slavery's tragic developments last at least until the American Civil War; indeed, they last even longer, as becomes clear from Nietzsche's position in this regard.[71] Hugo writes that "insolvency as the genesis of bondage is at least as fair (*billig*) as the right to kill a debtor."[72] Hegel, however, declares that *Notrecht* is to be understood "not in equity (*Billigkeit*) but as a right" (*Rph.*, § 127). At any rate, no "just title" can justify slavery (*Rph.I*, § 29 A). This qualification of the right to property does not call to mind a moral intention, but an objective legal norm, and it goes well beyond the condemnation of slavery as such: "If a man goes bankrupt, his whole property becomes the property of his creditors." And yet, not everything is taken from him; he can still support himself and his family; what "is violated [is] the creditors' right" (*v.Rph.*, IV, 342).

This does not occur thanks to *Billigkeit*, a magnanimous concession, but thanks to an actual right. Kant had defined *Billigkeit* as a "right without coercion," that derives exclusively from a "tribunal of conscience." Let us imagine a "servant" who gets paid with money that has lost value since the contract was drawn up: in that case, the re-evaluation of the salary is not demanded by an actual right, but only by *Billigkeit*, which is only "a silent divinity, and as such it can be ignored."[73] Later, Rotteck defines *Billigkeit* as something between "right" and "love," and he uses the following example: "Love requires me to give alms. *Billigkeit* can demand that the beneficiary of these alms returns what he has received if in the meantime the giver has fallen into poverty." From this point of view, *Billigkeit* represents a moral obligation that concerns everyone, without class distinction. If, for Kant, the poor could appeal to the *Billigkeit* of the higher classes, now they can only appeal to *Liebe*, that is, to an act of generosity that bears no relation to any legal obligation: "Love requires kindness to the poor, especially toward debtors who have become poor by accident," that is, through no fault of their own.[74] Hugo maintained that insolvent debtors could easily be turned into slaves without violating either right or *Billigkeit;* Kant believed that debtors could perhaps count on their creditors' *Billigkeit*, while Rotteck believed that they could count only on their "love." Hegel, on the other hand, claimed that insolvent debtors were, by virtue of an actual right, still entitled to keep the necessary means to perform their jobs and ensure their survival.

The fact that the legislation of modern States explicitly includes this *beneficium competentiae* means that the legislation itself has been forced to recognize the non-absolute character of the right to property. Thus, "necessity brings about a dialectic moment" (*Rph.1*, § 64 A) that still has a long way to go before concluding its task. The printed text of *Philosophy of Right* cites *beneficium competentiae* as an example of how the right to property is subordinate to necessity. In his lectures, however, Hegel goes well beyond that, and explicitly affirms that an individual may perform a wrong action, for example steal a piece of bread to avoid starvation.

10. An Unsolved Problem

We have seen how Hegel, during a specific phase of the development of his thought, argues for the right to work. However, a closer analysis of the crisis caused by overproduction leads him to conclude that the increase in production inevitably brings about an increase in unsold and unsellable stock, and causes a new wave of layoffs: "The principle of civil society is characterized by the following notion: the one who is needed is the one who makes money. Let's say, for example, that there are 200 workers more than is needed: these 200 will necessarily lose their jobs, while 12,000 more workers are hired. If those 200 were given a job, then 200 of the other 12,000 would lose it, since only a specific number of workers is needed, and if those who were unemployed were given a job, then those who were already working would lose it" (*v.Rph.*, III, 703–4). In the 1822–23 lecture course we have cited, it is clear that Hegel has lost faith in the belief that civil-bourgeois society will be able to guarantee the right to work. The nature of the crisis has destroyed many illusions: the various remedies have proved to be short-lived. In London, the capital of a country that, more than any other, can boast exports and "colonization," *Not* is "enormous" (*übermässig; v.Rph.*, IV, 494–95). And we must not forget that *Not* "embraces the whole sphere of the realization of freedom" (*v.Rph.*, IV, 342). Without the right to work, the right to life disappears as well; the very same right to life that Hegel defended through *Notrecht*.

"Freedom cannot (*darf*) succumb to an individual's particular right" (*v.Rph.*, I, 286); in other words, freedom cannot be sacrificed for the sake of the right to property. But it is precisely this sacrifice that defines the actuality of civil-bourgeois society. Through *Notrecht*, Hegel justifies the subordinate position of the right to property to the right to life, but the reality of civil-bourgeois society proceeds in the opposite direction. What can be done, then? "The important question of how poverty can be remedied is one which troubles and torments modern societies especially" (*Rph.*, § 244 Z; cf. *v.Rph.*, IV, 609). The question that torments modern societies is the same question that torments Hegel. The fact is, that in civil society, there are always "remnants of the state of nature" (*Rph.*, § 200 A), that is, remnants of violence. In analyzing the state of nature as a condition of generalized violence where oppression and slavery reign, and where reciprocal recognition is completely absent, Hegel repeatedly affirms that "one should flee the state of nature" (*exeundum est ex statu naturae*) (*v.Rph.*, IV, 209). Is this true also for the remnants of the state of nature that Hegel observes in civil society? Certainly, the State, the political community, is called upon to act so that these remnants can be overcome. However, things become complicated since the violence embedded in specific property and economic-social relations is not the only violence; there is also political violence, the violence that, directly or indirectly, aims at maintaining or prolonging the status quo, those "remnants of the state of nature" present in civil society. It is very difficult for the "poor" to gain acknowledgment of their rights due to the "costs" of the administration of justice, and there are also political obstacles. Hegel accuses the historic school of right and Hugo (both of whom justified slavery) of conceiving right and the administration of justice in a way that makes citizens become not only "profane" but, above all, "serfs on a legal level" (*Rechtsleibeigene; Rph.*, § 3 AL; *v.Rph.*, II, 99). As a result, a privileged class exercises a sort of "lordship" (*Herrenrecht*) over the "serfs," that is, over what the citizenry has been reduced to (*Rph. III*, 186).

While exploring the developments of the social question, Hegel sometimes seems to doubt whether the State (at least the State of his time) will really be able to overcome class conflict and thus eliminate the remnants of the state of nature from civil society: the influence of "currency exchange" and "banks" in political life is increasing and, "since States need money for their interests, they depend on a currency exchange that is in itself independent" (*v.Rph.*, IV, 520–21). There are many links between capital and the state apparatus: "Wealth is accumulated by factory owners, and if one works exclusively for the State, the accumulation of wealth becomes even more significant because of the business of industrial suppliers and entrepreneurs" (*Rph.III*, 193–94). Despite the reforms, power in England remains "in the hands of that social class" tied to the "current system of property" (*B.schr.*, 480). Hegel goes so far as to declare that, when social conflict is particularly harsh (as in the conflict between the patricians and plebeians in ancient Rome), the State becomes a mere "abstraction," while actuality seems to be defined by a "contradiction" (*Gegensatz*) "merely solved in the theory of the State" (*Rph.III*, 288). In what way, then, can the State eliminate the remnants of the state of nature and violence in civil society, in the property relations, and in the absolutization of the right to property? Hegel's celebration of the State is born out of, and in support of, the antifeudal struggle, the struggle against the particularism, the privileges, the oppression, and the violence that typifies feudalism; its goal is to build a community of *citoyens*, since "only within the State is freedom fully realized." This celebration, however, is haunted by the reality of oppression, the "negatively infinite judgment," the violence perpetrated by economic and social relations against a class excluded from that reciprocal "recognition" that serves as the basis for the community of *citoyens*.

VIII

"Agora" and *"Schole"*: Rousseau, Hegel,
and the Liberal Tradition

1. The Image of Ancient Times in France and Germany

"In the beginning, it was Montesquieu who was quoted and discussed; in the end, it was only Rousseau:" this is how Tocqueville describes the ideological and political parable of the French Revolution.[1] Conversely, in liberal, post-Thermidorian writings, the condemnation of Jacobinism is accompanied by a critique of Rousseau. This is particularly the case with Constant, who repeatedly likens Rousseau to Gabriel Bonnot de Mably, and then goes on to accuse them both of sacrificing individual autonomy and modern freedom for the sake of their admiration of the ancient *polis.*

More precisely, Constant believes that Mably was fascinated not only by Greek and Roman antiquity, but even more so "by the Egyptians, because, he said, everything in their society was regulated by law, even pastimes and needs: everything and everybody bowed before the power of the legislator."[2] Constant brands the persistent Jacobin tendencies and the rising Jacobin-socialist movement as "the new apologists of Egypt."[3] In *Philosophy of Right,* Hegel contrasts to the extremist positions of laissez-faire and *laissez-aller,* "the opposite extreme," that is, "public arrangements to provide for and determine the work of everyone." To do so, he, too, uses the example of the "building of the pyramids in ancient times, and other enormous works in Egypt and Asia which were undertaken for public ends, and in which the work of the individual was not mediated by his particular arbitrary will and particular interest" (Rph., § 236 A).

From Rosenkranz we learn that, already in Berne, Hegel read very attentively "the writings of Benjamin Constant, whom he never ceased to follow, even during the last years of his life."[4] Undoubtedly, after his first attempts, Hegel tried to be a theorist of the modern world and modern freedom, which is founded upon the recognition of an individual's dignity and autonomy. At any rate, nothing is more distant from Hegel than the position held by Rousseau who, in a sarcastic polemic against the "admirers of modern history," contrasts the misery of his time with the "venerable images of ancient times" and with "Rome and Sparta, [which] brought human glory to its highest peak."[5] A reader of Rousseau, Saint-Juste, goes so far as to exclaim: "After the Romans, the world has been empty."[6]

A break with this position was all the more necessary since, in Germany, the cult of ancient times soon changes its meaning, from a critique of the *ancien régime*, to an escape from the modern world, thus assuming a conservative political significance. Schelling, for example, mourns "the twilight of the most noble humanity that ever flourished,"[7] or the "most beautiful flowering of humanity";[8] however, his mournful lamentation aims at condemning the modern world and the "so-called civil liberties" (*bürgerliche Freiheit*) which Schelling despises as the basest and "murkiest mixture of slavery and freedom."[9]

A certain discrepancy between the ideological development in France and Germany can already be detected before 1800. On one side of the Rhine, the Jacobins seek inspiration in the *polis* in order to build a community of *citoyens* upon the rubble of the *ancien régime*. On the other side of the Rhine, however, the neo-classicism of Wilhelm von Humboldt in 1793 sees Greece as the place where servile work always produced the comprehensive development of free individuals, individuals no longer forced into the "one-sided exercise of mind and body."[10] If in France the reference to ancient times is a celebration of *agora*, in Germany it is a celebration of a *schole* that has unfortunately been lost in the modern world, a world whose ruinous downfall is repeatedly lamented.

2. Cynics, Monks, Quakers, Anabaptists, and *Sansculottes*

Hegel, on the contrary, firmly upholds the legitimacy of the modern world and its superiority over ancient times (infra, ch. xi, 1). Indeed, to understand and justify the modern world also means to refuse to look back to a mythical "simplicity of customs." Once this simplicity is abandoned—Hegel observes in a fragment written in Berne, a fragment where he seems to be countering Rousseau's position—"it . . . irremediably disappears" (*w*, 1, 56–57). Later, in the Heidelberg lecture course on the philosophy of right, Hegel likens Rousseau to Diogenes and the cynics on the basis of his search for "simplicity" and his condemnation of the "increase in needs and pleasures" (*Rph. i*, § 90 A). This association can already be observed in a letter written by Voltaire to Jean-Baptiste d'Alembert during a debate on theatre, which Rousseau (and the lower classes in Geneva) rejected as an expression of dissoluteness and an immoral yielding to idleness and luxury.[11] From this comparison, Hegel draws the following conclusion: "In the same way as there cannot be a people made up of Quakers, there cannot be a people made up of cynics" (*Rph.* I, § 90 A). In other words, with his rejection of luxury and his celebration of a mythical simplicity of manners, Rousseau makes the community of *citoyens* impossible to realize. Already in his early fragments, Hegel cites the Quakers and the Jesuits as examples of sects that cannot take their "relationship to the State" seriously (*w*, I, 444). In *Philosophy of Right*, they are put on the same level as the "Anabaptists," with whom they share the will to act only as "active members of civil society," as "private persons" (*Rph.*, note to § 270; *w*, VII, 421), that is, as bourgeois and not as *citoyens*. From this point of view, Hegel's criticism is the exact opposite of that of Constant, who denounces the Rousseauian and Jacobin tradition because it absorbs the private sphere of the State.

Still, in the Heidelberg lecture course on the philosophy of right, Hegel likens Rousseau to Jesus. This comparison, however, is not new. It comes, not from Voltaire, but from the debates that began during the French Revolution. In his polemic against the restriction of political rights based on census, Camille Desmoulins had observed that such restriction ended up excluding, from the ranks of active citizens, Rousseau, Corneille, Mably, and . . . Jesus Christ, who were consequently thrown among the "proletarians" and the "scoundrels."[12] Later, the figure of Jesus is stylized to resemble a *sansculotte ante litteram*. Hegel seems to have this motif in mind when, in a handwritten note to the 1821 lecture course on the philosophy of religion, he observes that primitive Christianity, with its "negative" polemic "against the existing order," is "so to speak, *sansculottesque*."[13] However, Hegel's association has now acquired a negative meaning: the celebration of poverty and the condemnation of wealth can only provide a basis for the organization of a sect. In *Lectures on the History of Philosophy* we read that "the ideal of a perfect human being" can find its realization "in monks, Quakers, or other pious people of that kind," and yet "a whole bunch of these melancholy creatures cannot form a people, just like fleas or parasitic plants cannot exist by themselves, but only on an organic body" (*w*, XIX, 109).

The various texts we have cited reveal a resemblance between Quakers, Anabaptists, *sansculottes*, Christian monks, cynics, and ascetics of different persuasions. What these various movements have in common is their withdrawal into the spirit of their sect, and their incapacity to form a society. With regard once again to the debate about luxury and superfluous needs in the 1819–20 course on the philosophy of right, we read: "Certainly, one can get rid of these needs for moral or economic reasons (for example, nowadays in England, a certain class of men abstains from drinking beer and the like). However, in all these attempts to end certain behaviors is the illusion that this can be attained through the will of every individual. But the community of *all* individuals is something other than the individuals themselves. Universality implies the presence of a moment of necessity" (*Rph.III*, 154). A sectarian attitude cannot transform society. Rousseau had criticized Christianity for being unable to serve as the religion of a community of *citoyens*, and the young Hegel had accepted this criticism. Now it is Rousseau himself who is likened to the figure of Jesus, and against whom a similar criticism is made: in the modern world, the condemnation of luxury and the increase in needs can produce a sect of bourgeois, private people who can be more or less virtuous; however, it cannot produce that "life in and for the universal" that, in the maturity of his thought, Hegel will continue to compare favorably to Christian monastic communities (*W, XIX*, 109).

3. Rousseau, the "Poor People's Grudge," and Jacobinism

At any rate, the fact that Hegel unequivocally sides with the modern world does not mean that he agrees with the historical evaluation given by Constant. The latter criticizes Rousseau's "tirades against wealth and even against property" (supra, ch. v, 3), a motif already present in Voltaire. Of Rousseau's *Discourse on Inequality*, Voltaire makes the following comment: "Here is the philosophy of a beggar who wishes that the rich be robbed by the poor" (supra, ch. vi, 9). Constant's accusation spreads in Germany, where one of Hegel's contemporaries and critics, Gustav Hugo, follows Constant's pattern and includes Rousseau (alongside Mably) among the "enemies of private property."[14] This type of criticism becomes popular in conservative, reactionary culture as well: Taine will later condemn Rousseau's "grudge (*rancune*) typical of the poor,"[15] and Nietzsche, who declares he attended Taine's "school,"[16] will denounce Rousseau as the "grudging man" (*Ranküne-Mensch*) who has the nerve to accuse "the dominant classes [of being] the cause of his misery" (*Miserabilität*).[17] He will also call him the man of "*ressentiment*,"[18] "this first modern man, an idealist and a scoundrel at the same time" who, precisely because of his "idealism and scoundrelism," embodies the ruinous leveling tendency of modernity, a tendency that gave rise to the French Revolution and the socialist movement.[19] In this sense, "underneath every socialist tremor or earthquake, Rousseau's man is always stirring, like old Typhon under the Etna."[20]

This is not only a harsh argument, but even a sort of *ad hominem* attack, and not only by Nietzsche. After describing the contamination (similar to the "strange disease that can generally be found in poor areas") that spreads throughout revolutionary France, "intoxicated by the nasty liquor of the *Social Contract*,"[21] Taine denounces the "alteration in the mental balance" suffered by the Jacobins,[22] fanatic admirers of Rousseau. Similar terms are used today by Jacob Leib Talmon, who believes he can identify a "paranoid streak" in Rousseau, Robespierre, Saint-Just, and Babeuf.[23] The only difference between Nietzsche, Taine, and Talmon is the greater awareness that the above-cited authors have of the social and antidemocratic significance of their attacks.

None of this type of criticism, which develops out of the Thermidor and targets Rousseau in order to denounce the popular Jacobin tendencies of the Revolution, is present in Hegel. On the contrary, Hegel includes Rousseau "among the spirits who deeply felt and reflected upon" the tragedy of poverty (*tiefdenkende und tieffühlende Geister*). We will now refer again to an excerpt from the 1824–25 lectures (supra, ch. v, 3) in order to grasp all of its implications. Here, Hegel expresses particular admiration for Rousseau: "Especially in *Rousseau* and in some other authors we can find the dramatic description of the misery caused by the unfulfillment of needs. These men were profoundly affected by the misery of their time and of their people; they deeply recognized and passionately described the ethical ruin caused by such misery, the rebellion (*Empörung*) of men against their poverty, against the contradiction (*Widerspruch*) between what they could demand and the condition they found themselves in, the exasperation, the sarcasm regarding their situation, and the personal bitterness and the resentment it produced" (*v.Rph.*, IV, 477). Of course, Hegel cannot imagine any solution to the social question since the development of the modern industrial world. And yet, he still praises Rousseau, who observed people living in poverty in a rather opulent society, for highlighting the "contradiction between what they could demand and the condition in which they found themselves," and for the *Empörung*, his rebellious attitude to this contradiction.

The terms mentioned here are the same ones that Hegel uses elsewhere to justify *Notrecht*, the right of extreme need: "struggle" (*Kampf*) and "contradiction" (*Widerspruch*) exist between "poverty and, right next to it, the means to eliminate such poverty" (*v.Rph.*, III, 398). Hegel's lectures on the philosophy of right insist on repeating that this situation represents "something repulsive (*ein Empörendes*) to everyone" (*v.Rph.*, IV, 342), something that could cause a rightful "rebellion" (*Empörung*) (*v.Rph.*, III, 402). In arguing for *Notrecht*, Hegel perceives a connection with Rousseau: the latter, too, maintains that a human being with no means to support himself is essentially prey to the "absolute authority" of the rich, and is therefore forced to a "boundless obedience"; in other words—this time citing Hegel—he would find himself "totally without rights" (Rph., § 127).[24]

In his justification of Notrecht and the right to life, Hegel somehow draws nearer to radical populism. At the outbreak of the French Revolution and increasingly throughout its course, the representatives of radical populism, who were sometimes inspired by Rousseau's thought, proclaimed that the right to life is the first among human rights, thereby questioning existing property relations (supra, ch. VII, 6). From this point of view, György Lukács' theory according to which, throughout his evolution, Hegel "was hostile to Jacobin populism," should be reconsidered.[25] Political positions and theoretical categories are two different things. If Condorcet, engaged in a polemic against the "right to life" (droit de vivre), maintains that no condition of poverty or "need" gives a poor human being "the right to steal" or to violate property, a property that must be respected "even to the point of superstition," Hegel believes instead that "a starving human being" has not only the right, "but the absolute right to violate another person's property" (v.Rph., IV, 341).[26] Furthermore, the very same right to life (das Recht zu leben or das Recht des Lebens) that the Thermidorians mock is explicitly justified by Hegel in the Heidelberg lectures on the philosophy of right (Rph. I, § 118 A).

A further point can be made: liberals à la Constant attack Rousseau in order to purge the French Revolution of any plebeian trace and to preserve freedom from the contamination of any social or material demand. For Tocqueville, the shift in the French Revolution from Montesquieu to Rousseau reveals a shift from pure and shared enthusiasm for freedom to the baseness and barbarity of "class war" (guerre des classes).[27] It is not difficult to understand why Rousseau is considered an accomplice of this class war. Did he not somehow justify it a priori when he condemned societies in which "the privileged few gorge themselves with luxuries, while the starving multitude lacks the bare necessities"?[28] We have already seen (supra, ch. V, 3) how Hegel does not hesitate to extol the French Revolution as a social revolution. On the one hand, is "greed" (Habsucht) and the "dissipation of riches" carried out by a social class determined to "plunder government funds and to exploit people's hard work"; on the other, is "public poverty" and "the hard, terrible burden" that weighs on the people (W, XX, 296–97 and Ph.G., 925). If we keep in mind that both texts cited here mention "people's hard work," and that in the first of the two, people's hard work is contrasted to the parasitic life of "loafers" (Müßigganger), we conclude that the French Revolution is justified in terms reminiscent of Rousseau's language, terms that Constant and liberal historiography consider unacceptable. And this conclusion provides further proof against Lukács' position: plebeian motifs are indeed present in Hegel. The lesson that Hegel draws from the French Revolution is that the legitimization and "conciliation" of large property requires heavy taxation and a redistribution of wealth (infra, ch. VIII, 5).

4. Politics and Economics in Rousseau and Hegel

At this point, a theoretical consideration becomes necessary: the affirmation of the right of extreme need or the "right to life" constitutes for Hegel the starting point for an overall redefinition of the relationship between politics and economy. As a result, new categories emerge, categories that are fundamentally unknown in the liberal tradition and that necessarily find Rousseau as their antecedent in the history of philosophy. Hegel speaks of "material rights" (*materielle Rechte*) (B.schr., 488) and also argues for, next to the "negative right," a "positive right" with a substantive content: "Everyone has the right to live (*das Recht zu leben*), and this right must not merely reside in protection [from violent aggression]; one has not only this negative right, but also a positive right. The actuality of freedom is the goal of civil society. The fact that a human being has the right to live implies that he has a positive, fulfilled right; the actuality of freedom must be essential . . . The right to life (*das Recht des Lebens*) is absolutely essential to a human being" (*Rph.I, § 118 A*).

For Rousseau, too, "social security" or the "security of individuals," the autonomy and inviolability of the private sphere, is essential; and this corresponds to what Hegel calls "negative right."[29] Yet, this is only one important and unavoidable aspect of right. It is not enough to "protect" (*protéger*) the citizens, "it is also necessary to consider their subsistence." Of course, this does not mean that the political power must "fill the larders of individuals," but that they need to be given the means to support themselves by labor.[30] For his part, starting from the categories of "material right" and "positive right," Hegel develops a criticism of merely formal equality. One only needs to think of the argument with which Hegel, during his Heidelberg lecture course, justifies *Notrecht*, the right of a starving man to commit an illegal act and violate the private property of another: "This is what equality consists of: another individual must not hold a privileged position over my existence" (*Rph.I, § 63 A*). Where the distribution of wealth is extremely polarized, the affirmation of the absolute inviolability of private property essentially bestows upon a property-owner the power of life or death over a starving human being. This means denying equality not only within the sphere where legitimate inequality occurs, that is, "the sphere of the particular, of the accidental," of "external goods," but also within an "essential sphere" that puts at stake "life" and "right" as such, as well as the very dignity of a human being (*Rph.1*, § 63 A).

Hegel criticizes merely formal equality in another way as well, that is, by observing that a poor human being cannot count on actual protection by the law: "because of the costs related to the formal administration of justice, it is impossible for him to defend his right by resorting to formal justice, and by appearing in court" (*Rph.1*, § 118 A). Especially in England, the home of liberalism, "only the rich can afford resorting to court . . . because of the exorbitant costs demanded by the Byzantine legal system" (*B.schr.*, 473).

A criticism of merely formal equality is also present in Rousseau. In the conclusion of the first book of the *Social Contract*, he observes: "Under bad governments, this equality is only apparent and illusory: it serves only to keep the pauper in his poverty and the rich human being in the position he has usurped."[31]

On another point, however, the positions held by the two philosophers begin to diverge: "The distinction between necessities and superfluities," so clear and fundamental in Rousseau, becomes more problematic in Hegel: there is no distinct "line of demarcation between natural and imaginary needs, no border where the former end and luxuries begin" (*v.Rph.*, IV, 493).[32] If anything, the border is historical, not set permanently by nature. Rousseau condemns luxury because it affects consumption and the sphere of distribution. Hegel, on the other hand, emphasizes the fact that "it is not so much the consumers, but the producers, who multiply needs" in order to provide an outlet for productive forces that are constantly expanding (*v.Rph.*, IV, 493). In an advanced industrial society, a moralistic approach that would denounce individuals based on the fact that their consumption goes beyond natural needs no longer makes sense.

Even a vital minimum cannot be determined once and for all: "this necessary minimum (*Minimum der Nothwendigkeit*) . . . varies considerably among the different populations" (*v.Rph.*, IV, 608). Consumer goods that used to be considered superfluous can later form part of the definition of "vital minimum." It should be noted, however, that in emphasizing the historical character of his definition, Hegel not only moves away from Rousseau, but also from the justification of economic development typical of the liberal tradition, on the basis of which Locke claims that a "day-labourer" in the England of his time enjoys a higher lifestyle than the "king of a large and fruitful territory [in Native America]." Far from guaranteeing well-being and steady improvement in material needs and lifestyle to everyone, modern economic development has created new needs, new privations, and a burden of actual suffering (supra, ch. VII, 3): at any rate, in modern civil society, opulence and luxury go hand in hand with poverty (*Rph.*, § 185).

In rejecting the justification of economic development advanced by a large part of the liberal tradition, Hegel draws on Rousseau's legacy: he refuses to turn a blind eye to the internal contradictions of industrial society. However, this awareness does not lead him to embrace a solution that would promote a withdrawal from such a society. On the contrary, Hegel rejects the "complaints about luxury," which he considers "empty, merely moralistic claims," (*Rph.III*, 161) and criticizes "those who maintain that industry and luxury are superfluous, and who would give them up because of the poverty connected to them" (*v.Rph.*, IV, 505). A negative assessment of Rousseau is evident here. Precisely because he rejects any withdrawal from modern civil society and from the "right of particularity" (*v.Rph.*, IV, 505)—an inalienable conquest of modern world, as Constant had showed—, Hegel defines the idea of overcoming the "inequality of resources" "a dull chimera" (*Rph.I*, § 102 A).

Certainly, Rousseau did not believe in material equality either, and yet, from Hegel's point of view, he is still to blame for not acknowledging fully an integral part of modern freedom, the right to particularity and even to luxury: "To protest against civil society because it damages natural [equality] is an inane complaint" (*v.Rph.*, III, 620). Hegel, who, on the one hand, regards Rousseau as one of the "spirits who deeply felt and reflected," on the other hand, seems to accuse him of abandoning himself to inane complaints.

At least in one case, the separation between Rousseau and Hegel is sharply evident. In the conclusion of the first book of the *Social Contract* we read: "Instead of destroying natural inequality, the fundamental compact substitutes, for such physical inequality as nature may have set up between men, an equality that is moral and legitimate, and that men, who may be unequal in strength or intelligence, become every one equal by convention and legal right."[33] In § 200 A of *Philosophy of Right*, on the other hand, we read: "The Spirit's objective *right of particularity*, which is contained within the Idea, does not cancel out the inequality of human beings in civil society—an inequality decreed by nature, which is the element of inequality—but in fact produces it out of the Spirit itself and raises it to an inequality of skills, resources, and even of intellectual and moral education. To oppose this right with a demand for *equality* is characteristic of empty understanding." And yet, the disagreement between the two philosophers is only apparent: the "moral and legitimate equality" argued for by Rousseau is "according to right"; and at the same time, the legitimate inequality justified by Hegel is certainly not inequality before the law.

Furthermore, both Rousseau and Hegel maintain that legal equality, in order to be actual, cannot be completely removed from life's material relationships. Hegel, too, believes that if material inequality is pushed to an extreme, it ends up eliminating legal equality and freedom, to the point that a starving human being experiences a "total lack of rights." Of course, for Hegel, speaking of "natural equality" (*égalité naturelle*) makes no sense; indeed, the extreme inequalities that can develop in civil society are to be considered "the remnants of the state of nature" (*Rph.*, § A). And yet, despite his radically different position on the relationship between nature and society, Rousseau, too, believes that society has the task of overcoming the "physical inequality" that nature distributes among men. And he also adds, in the endnote we have cited, that bad political institutions can impede the realization of "moral and legitimate equality," thus perpetuating natural inequality. Using an expression from *Philosophy of Right*, we can say that these institutions create a more or less significant "residue of the state of nature."

5. The Social Question and Taxation

There is a discrepancy in Hegel between the implacable lucidity with which he describes the disparities and contradictions of modern industrial society and the ordinariness of the solutions he proposes. The instrument he perhaps suggests most often in the course of his evolution is the levying of taxes. For his part, Rousseau had already proposed a taxation system that would "prevent extreme inequality of fortunes," and thanks to which "the poor are eased, and the burdens thrown on the rich."[34] Though in his *Discourse on Political Economy* cited here, Rousseau speaks of a "proportional" or "truly proportional" criterion, it is clear that, in reality, he means a progressive tax scale.[35]

(The technical term of "progressive tax" (*impôt progressif*) distinguished from the "flat tax" (*impôt proportionnel*) will emerge in France only during the Revolution, as we gather from a speech delivered by Condorcet on June 1, 1793: already in the opening remarks, Condorcet feels the need to define and distinguish the two types of taxation.)[36] As for Hegel, in Jena he writes: "The inequality of wealth can be tolerated if heavy taxation is applied on the wealth itself; this helps to dissipate envy as well as the fear of need and the fear of expropriation."[37] In his *System of Ethical Life*, he calls on the "government" to contrast the polarization of "great wealth" and "deepest poverty," and to "work hard, by increasing taxation on high incomes, against this inequality and general destruction." He also defines the levying of taxes as an "appropriation" that "overrides" "an individual's [previous] possession."[38] And in the *Constitution of Germany* he remarks that "the taxes that it [the State] must demand are a transcendence (*ein Aufheben*) of the right to property" (*w*, 1, 538). Clearly, *Aufhebung* does not consist of simple abolition. And yet, there is no doubt that Hegel, too, justifies the levying of taxes as a means of redistributing wealth.

Should we suspect a direct influence of Rousseau on Hegel? At this point, a general reflection is necessary. Any discourse concerning the influence of one philosopher on another inevitably calls to mind a merely individual relationship between two authors, a relationship that does not occur in a concrete historical framework, but in an academic, politically sterile space. This approach is not only questionable and limited, but it becomes completely meaningless when applied to an intensely political author like Hegel. From the very beginning, Hegel's connection with Rousseau is mediated by the lively debate that takes place around the link between Rousseau's philosophy and the French Revolution. Not by chance, a young Hegel examines "sansculottism in France" in conjunction with the typically Rousseauian thesis of the danger that "the disproportionate wealth of a few citizens" represents to a free constitution (*w*, 1, 439). Therefore, we cannot separate Hegel's thought from the debate on taxation that accompanies the course of the French Revolution. And it is within the same debate that Rousseau's ideas are brought forth, even before the Revolution assumes a radical tone, in order to demand a taxation system capable of reducing inequality and redistributing wealth.[39] Condorcet's speech of June 1, 1793, is dedicated, already in its title, to the analysis of " *impôt progressif*," a central element in the political debate.

The *impôt progressif* becomes the target of post-Thermidorian France: it is regarded as synonymous with "agrarian law," and as such, it is perceived as an attack against the right to property.[40] François Boissy d'Anglas declares that non-property-owners must be excluded from political rights, lest they "establish, or demand the establishment of, ruinous taxes."[41] This is also Constant's position: indeed, he maintains that the measures that require tax exemptions and special treatment for the poor end up unjustly penalizing "affluence" and treating "poverty as if it were a privilege. A privileged caste is created in the country."[42] It is an odd position, if for no other reason than it emerges during a time in which, according to various testimonies, the joint effect of famine and inflation is reducing "the lowest social class to the most miserable condition," plagued by "unprecedented evils,"[43] and to the "starvation" that constitutes the starting point for Hegel's legitimation of *Notrecht*.[44] And yet, Constant's thinking has its own logic: if for Hegel and Rousseau, the levying of taxes is an instrument meant to decrease material inequality and to bring about legal equality, for Constant, instead, legal equality is violated and crushed by the progressive levying of taxes (and this is what Hayek continues to maintain even in our own times).[45]

In contrast to what Lukács affirms, Hegel's position remains clearly separated from post-Thermidorian political writings. With regard to the issue of taxes, Hegel's early works are clearly influenced by the historical experience of the French Revolution, and by the overturning of property relations that occurred during that time. In the Jena writings on the philosophy of Spirit, after proposing "heavy taxation" even as a means to decrease the fear that property-owning classes have of "expropriation," Hegel continues: "Aristocrats, who pay no taxes, run a terrible risk: that of losing their wealth by force, because such wealth has no conciliation through sacrifice."[46] In other words, the fiscal privileges enjoyed by the French nobility have accelerated its downfall; "conciliation" and social stability can only be guaranteed by imposing high taxes on the wealthiest classes. In the *System of Ethical Life*, after defining taxation as "the transcendence" of property, Hegel adds that such *Aufheben* "must take the shape of formal universality and justice."[47] Even with regard to tax issues, Hegel clearly prefers reforms from the top-down rather than the violent expropriations that occurred during the French Revolution.

Hegel's distance from the post-Thermidorian political writings that criticize Rousseau also represents the distance between Hegel and Rousseau, on the one hand, and the liberal tradition, on the other. According to Montesquieu, "a poll tax is more natural to slavery; a duty on merchandise is more natural to liberty, because it has not so direct a relation to the person."[48] In his criticism of the French Revolution, Bentham, too, condemns direct taxes as fundamentally repressive, and expresses a strong preference for indirect taxes that apply to goods freely chosen by the consumer, and that can therefore be defined as "voluntary."[49] For the liberal tradition, even before the progressive tax, it is the income tax that constitutes an attack on freedom. In 1835, Tocqueville condemns "legal charity" (that is, assistance to the poor carried out using the means that the State obtains by taxing wealth), affirming that "the rich who are deprived, without consultation, of part of their surplus by the law, see in the poor but greedy strangers who have been summoned by the legislators to share their goods."[50] In this sense, any redistribution of income carried out by the law which "in guaranteeing the rich the enjoyment of their goods, protects at the same time the poor from excessive misery by demanding from the former a portion of their surplus so as to grant what is necessary to the latter," is to be considered unacceptable or impossible.[51] And all the more unacceptable, on a moral and political level, are the laws that favor the poor: these laws would, in fact, in the long run, end up turning the "proletarians" into the actual beneficiaries of the land, and the "owners" into "their bailiffs."[52] Furthermore, those laws constitute one of the main causes of the evermore frightening increase in poverty in England: "the rich cannot make use of the poor as they would if such a large portion of their income did not end up being swallowed by the State."[53]

Perhaps one should speak of "possessive individualism" in this regard, rather than of the liberal tradition.[54] Indeed, though at first it might sound paradoxical, in the fiscal and social field even Hobbes is a theoretician of the minimal State. The purpose he ascribes to it is exclusively public, and taxation is carried out only in view of that: "Customes, and Tributes, are nothing else but their reward who watch in Armes for us, that the labours and endeavours of single men (*industria singulorum*) may not be molested by the incursion of enemies."[55] Clearly, Hobbes, too, believes that only the taxes on goods guarantee an equal treatment of citizens before the revenue service: "For what reason is there that he which laboureth much and, sparing the fruits of his labour, consumeth little should be more charged than he that, living idly, getteth little and spendeth all he gets; seeing the one hath no more protection from the Commonwealth than the other?"[56] Hobbes' objection could have been raised by Constant, as well, but instead it seems to find an answer in Rousseau, according to whom the "advantage" which the protection of the "social confederacy" guarantees to the rich human being's "immense possessions" is largely superior to the advantage enjoyed by a poor human being.[57]

Despite some shifts of position (more apparent than real), Rousseau supports a fiscal instrument that would mitigate inequality, and certainly cannot look favorably upon the celebration of indirect taxes on goods;[58] thus, he explicitly criticizes Montesquieu and his thesis of a strict connection between direct taxes and despotism.[59] Perhaps, a veiled criticism can also be found in Hegel: "Audits and investigations are carried out by the police especially with regard to the direct taxes required by the State; in order to avoid frauds, several audits and frequent reports are needed. In England, personal freedom is well guaranteed, and yet, England is the country with the highest taxes. There are taxes on everything: on windows, shops, salaries, beer, bread, dogs, horses; therefore, many audits are necessary, the most thorough and painful investigations, that even entail raids on private homes" (v.Rph., IV, 593). The example of England, a country so dear to the liberals, means to show that there is no contradiction between freedom on the one hand, and direct taxes and an elaborate tax system on the other, even despite the rigorous audits imposed by that system.

On the issue of taxes, during his mature years Hegel settles on a more moderate position than the one he held in his youth. One of the reasons for this shift is that, starting from the experience of Poor Laws in England, Hegel becomes more skeptical about the actual capacity of the State of his time to solve the social question.[60] Moreover, the distinction between "superfluous" and "necessary" upon which Rousseau developed his theory on taxation is in disarray. However, Hegel's main position does not change: in Berlin, too, he continues to believe that, though the "right to property" is "high" and "sacred," it still remains something "quite subordinate" that "can and must be violated. The State requires taxes; it requires everyone to yield something of their own property. The State takes some of the citizens' property" (v.Rph., IV, 157). In Jena as well as in Berlin, Hegel continues to consider taxes as somehow "transcending" private property. Significantly, one of Hegel's disciples, the young Engels, writes: "For the principle of taxation is, after all, a purely communist one . . . For either private property is sacrosanct, in which case there is no such thing as national property and the State has no right to levy taxes, or the State has this right, in which case private property is not sacrosanct, national property stands above private property, and the State is the true owner."[61] For Hegel and Engels, taxes represent a potential transcendence of private property, even though now Hegel's *Aufhebung* seems to have lost its complexity and ambiguity and to have taken on the shape of mere abolition.

6. State, Contract, and Joint-Stock Company

According to Hegel, the State as an ethical and political community transcends private property. Precisely for this reason, he cannot accept contractualism, and all the more so since the latter often ends up taking on a conservative or reactionary political significance. Even before the end of the French Revolution, some right-wing thinkers attempted to co-opt Rousseau to denounce the current political and social changes as violations of the social contract.[62]

This issue is clarified and developed by Burke (supra, ch. III, 1). Not by chance, Burke contrasts the ruinous course of the French Revolution to the English political tradition. Burke emphasizes how this tradition was always respectful of the contract that binds the various social orders and State institutions, and even in 1688–89, it limited itself to rejecting the Stuarts' arbitrary initiatives, without trying to reconstruct the country's constitutional, political, and social order. In this light, it is not difficult to understand Condorcet's attack on the view, widespread in England at the time, that the Glorious Revolution was a legitimate response to the Stuarts' violation of the "original contract" with the nation. According to Condorcet, this is not only a cunning deceit, but a deceit that plays a fundamentally conservative role: invoking this debatable historical event, in fact, can only inhibit the will to a radical renovation and contradict the principles of reason. The idea of "original contract" could only assert itself "during a time in which authority established what should instead have been established by reason, a time in which facts and examples replaced principles, and rights were founded on titles rather than on nature" and reason.[63] In this contractualism, Condorcet detects a sort of positivism of "facts" that cannot but thwart the revolutionary process.

Conservative or reactionary contractualism spreads throughout Europe, and perhaps especially in Germany. According to Gentz, a "total revolution" like the French one constitutes "a violent breach of the social contract" (gesellschaftlicher Contrakt).[64] A modification of existing social relations can only occur with everyone's consent: "To breach, on one's own authority, a social contract is, according to the most common concept, an illegal and invalid act."[65] Thus, the anticontractualist polemic does not have an antiliberal, conservative significance as is commonly believed. On the contrary, in Prussia, those who defend the contract and the necessary respect for the contract are the aristocratic reactionaries, who oppose antifeudal reforms and who hold on stubbornly to the "spirit of old Europe."[66] The conservative or reactionary use of contractualism assumes the most diverse forms. According to Justus Möser, the "original contract" is signed by landowners, or by the first "conquerors," who are joined only later by the others, the signers of a "second social contract" that sanctions their inferior position.[67] Elsewhere, he assimilates the social contract to the founding agreement of a joint-stock company that sanctions the inequality of its partners on the basis of the various capitals they have invested.[68] Möser is a particularly interesting author, not only because, as Hegel observes, he confuses private and public right, but also because, even before the French Revolution, he juxtaposes the idea of contract to a human being's general principles and rights. The "philosophical theories" of radical Enlightenment, on the other hand, attempt to "bury all original contracts, all privileges and freedoms," and French revolutionaries, together with their followers, replace the concept of "shareholder" with that of "human being."[69] In so doing, they arbitrarily equalize the positions of the various members of society, to the point where even a serf, as "human being," can claim rights to which he is not entitled, rights that are not mentioned in any "particular contract."[70]

In this light, it is easier to understand Hegel's criticism of Rousseau on the basis that the latter, in order to explain the genesis of the State, compares it to an institution of private right. According to Hegel, there is a contradiction between Rousseau's ambition to build a community of citoyens and his use of social contract theory. The culture of the time, in fact, often uses the theory of the contract to represent the State in a strongly anti-egalitarian manner, that is, as a private joint-stock company. This metaphor or conceptual model is not only present in Burke or Möser (supra, ch. iv, 3), but also in Sieyès, who maintains that "the true shareholders of the great social enterprise" are "the true active citizens, the true members of the association."[71] The others, the non-owners who have not invested any capital, cannot participate in the management of the joint-stock company, and therefore can only be passive citizens.

In *Vormärz*, one of Hegel's liberal critics, Rotteck, moves away from the most reactionary interpretations of the theory of the State as a joint-stock company, interpretations that end up denying the very equality of civil rights (as happens with Möser, who views serfs as mere individuals with no shares). However, Rotteck grants "some truth" to this theory, mainly because of its anti-egalitarian implications with regard to the ascription of political rights. Comparing the State to "a private joint-stock company" has the advantage of consecrating the absolute inviolability of "all private rights that have been legally acquired"; in other words, all those rights which, "thanks to a title of private right that has been consistently acknowledged as valid, have come to belong to the private sphere of the one who has acquired them."[72] These words call to mind Robert Nozick, who, even today, somehow continues to subscribe to the theory of the State as a joint-stock company.[73]

All this serves to highlight the progressive nature of Hegel's anticontractualism. Hegel is well aware that Rousseau's contractualism is quite different from conservative or reactionary contractualism. The category of contract is inclined to assume the most diverse political and social meanings. For this reason, and also because it is a category that derives from private right, it is utterly inadequate for an understanding of the State as political community.

7. Christianity, Human Rights, and the Community of *Citoyens*

Not only in his early years, but well into his maturity, Hegel continued to admire the rich political life that characterized the Greek and Roman world: the "true" ethicality is still the "ancient" one (v.G., 115). Certainly, this ethicality has not yet discovered the infinity of being-for-itself: it must be adapted to the conditions of the modern world, it must be able to respect and subsume the individual and the particular, the concrete differences of civil society. And yet, on the occasion of the third centenary of the Augsburg Confession, Hegel extols the Greeks and the Romans as "immortal examples" of patriotic virtue, of active and committed participation in political life. At the same time, he criticizes the fathers of the

Church (and the Catholic Church) because they consider all of these as "sumptuous vices" and because they encourage a withdrawal from the world and from political institutions (B.schr., 44).

In Hegel's early period, we can find some elements which were heavily influenced by Rousseau, as well as some differences. Rousseau writes: "Christianity as a religion is entirely spiritual, occupied solely with heavenly things (choses); the country of the Christian is not of this world."[74] The young Hegel writes: "Our religion strives to educate its followers as citizens of Heaven, who always look up to the skies and who have consequently become alien to human emotions" (W, 1, 42). What kind of interest could Christians have—Rousseau observes—in matters that occur in a "vale of misery" or, as Hegel calls it, a "vale of tears" (Jammertal; W, 1, 81)?[75] Precisely because it is an ideology of escape from the world, Rousseau continues, "Christianity only preaches servitude and obedience" and it "supports tyranny."[76] For the young Hegel, too, Christianity is a religion that invites its followers to seek a "reward in Heaven" to make up for the loss of political freedom (W, 1, 211), a religion that "has never opposed despotism" (W, 1, 46); on the contrary, it has always been its accomplice (B, 1, 24). For this reason, Hegel contrasts Christianity to "Greek and Roman religion," which he sees as a "religion for free peoples," one that stimulated a loyalty to the political community (W, 1, 204–5).

Rousseau's influence is once again mediated by the debate on the French Revolution. Therefore, when we read that Christianity never opposed the "slave trade" (W, 1, 46), and that in fact it continues to be an accomplice to the "current slave trade" (W, 1, 59), what comes to mind is not only the relation, emphasized by Rousseau, between Christianity and despotism, but also the debate that develops later about the abolition of slavery in the French colonies, an abolition that had been brought about thanks to the Jacobin Convention. The very same Convention was the target of a crusade led by a counter-revolutionary coalition which had, among its goals, that of protecting the Christian religion.[77]

During Hegel's mature years, his position on the historical role of Christianity and on its contribution to the progress of freedom changes dramatically. The profound political significance of this change can be examined by comparing two passages. One dates back to the Berne period:

> "In Rome there were no men, only Romans" (W, 1, 50). The other, written in Berlin, is a text we already know: "The fact that today, a human being as such can be considered a holder of rights, is to be regarded as a great achievement, since being a human being comes to signify something greater than his mere *status*. For the Israelites, only the Jews had rights, for the Greeks, only free Greeks, for the

Romans, only the Romans, and they only had rights as Jews, Greeks, and Romans, not as men per se. Now, instead, universal principles constitute the new source of right, and a new era has dawned for the world" (v.Rph., III, 98).

The defining moment and the greatness of the modern world lies in the elaboration of the concept of man, and in the proclamation of human rights. These rights cannot be envisioned without the waning of the ancient community and ethicality, and without the advent of Christianity. The latter, in fact, had the merit of affirming "the freedom of personality" (Rph., § 62 A), that is, "the freedom of a human being as a person," not according to a particular configuration, as in ancient times, but in his universality (v.Rph., III, 234).

The contrast with the early period and with Rousseau clearly emerges here, though Rousseau had already discussed the issues which are later developed by Hegel. In the final analysis, the question at issue is the relationship between the rights of man (droits de l'homme) and the rights of citizens (droits du citoyen). Rousseau, too, sees a connection between Christianity and "sound ideas on natural right and on a common brotherhood among mankind."[78] However, Rousseau's position is uncertain: precisely because of its universal spirit, which "embraces mankind as a whole," the Christian religion cannot "produce either republicans or warriors, but only Christians and men."[79] This type of universalism does not encourage a concrete political community to participate in public life; on the contrary, it seems to belittle and discourage that community, and it ultimately ends up being part of the escapist ideology which Christianity is accused of supporting. Christianity constructs the image of man, but it destroys the image of citoyen. Rousseau, who feels strongly for the pathos of human beings, finds himself caught up in a deep conflict.[80] Christianity does posit a "divine natural right" that should supposedly be effective in countering tyranny; however, it falls short of its task without the active participation of the citoyen in political life. Rousseau seeks a solution to the contrast between "the religion of a man, and that of the citizen"[81] in the "profession of a purely civil faith," which should guarantee the "unalterable (invariable) limit" of the private sphere of freedom, while at the same time should teach "the sanctity of the social contract and laws."[82] Hegel, instead, who witnesses the historical failure of Robespierre's attempt to introduce a new religion, seeks a solution in a profoundly reinterpreted Protestantism, which he opposes to Catholicism. At any rate, it is useless to feel nostalgia for the ancient polis, because it is now clear that if the autonomous sphere of subjectivity and human rights is not acknowledged—a sphere that first emerged with Christianity—then ethicality and the most solid community of *citoyens* are destined to crumble (*Rph.* § 185). And yet, the preoccupation expressed by Rousseau has not completely disappeared: not by chance, in *Philosophy of Right*, after emphasizing the "infinite importance" of the fact that now "a man counts as such because he is a man," Hegel hastens to add that this should not be interpreted as a "cosmopolitanism" in opposition "to the concrete life of the State" (*Rph.*, § 209 A). The legitimation of human rights must not bring about a devaluation of the figure of the *citoyen;* with his conscious participation in the political community, in fact, the *citoyen* is the only one who can embody those human rights.

The denunciation of Christianity as an escapist ideology, a theme developed by Rousseau, is present not only in Hegel's early writings, but in his later ones as well. In the latter, however, the criticism of Christianity turns into a criticism of Catholicism. According to Hegel, Catholicism "establishes a religious ideal" beyond the physical world, thus extolling "the abstraction of the spirit over tangible reality. A fundamental resolution to escape, to renounce actuality and the struggle, thus emerges. The substantive, genuine foundation is contrasted to something that should be more elevated." However, by destroying the figure of the *citoyen*, Catholicism also ends up rejecting or impeding the concrete realization of human rights. By belittling or disparaging what belongs to the world and to politics, Catholicism ultimately fails to acknowledge "any absolute right in the realm of actual ethicality"; it even requires "man to denounce every freedom" (which, in the final analysis, is the same as regarding man as "having no rights").[83] With reference to Christianity, a young Hegel had written: "Religion and politics have always gotten along fabulously: the former has taught what despotism wanted" (*B*, I, 24). This accusation has survived, except that now its target is Catholicism, not a Protestantism which has instead been reinterpreted as the religion of freedom, to the extent to which it reconciles man with the actuality of the world and politics.

Still, the contrast with the liberal tradition remains clear. Even for the mature Hegel, "actual religion and actual religious feeling only stem from ethicality, conscious ethicality, which is aware of the free universality of its concrete essence . . . ; outside the ethical Spirit, searching for actual religion and religious feeling is vain" (*Enc.*, § 552 A; *w*, x, 354–55). Religion cannot limit itself to being the consecration of the bourgeois' private sphere. Hegel's philosophy of religion insists on the pathos of the political community and the figure of the *citoyen*, and for this reason it is criticized by Rudolf Haym. According to Haym, Hegel is guilty of belittling "pious spirituality" (*fromme Innerlichkeit*)[84] and of sacrificing it for the sake of ethicality: "The true essence of God is the essence of man," Ludwig Feuerbach affirms. "The true essence of God," Hegel affirms, "is the essence of an accomplished *politeia.*"[85]

8. The Liberal Tradition and Criticism of Rousseau and Hegel

Significantly, the very same criticism voiced by Constant and the liberal tradition against Rousseau is aimed, in the *Vormärz*, at Hegel by Rotteck (who, not by chance, is called "the Constant of Baden") and by the *Staats-Lexikon* he edits with Carl Welcker. While Constant criticizes the Rousseauian and Jacobin tradition for not moving on from the freedom of ancient times, the *Staats-Lexicon* criticizes Hegel for celebrating an ethicality and a State that evoke ancient times and even paganism. This is also the position held by Haym, an implacable critic of Rousseau who also attacks Hegel's "whole" system for being "configured according to the model of the great ancient systems" and for being "permeated by the ancient vision and temperament."[86] The political motivations of the criticism of Rousseau and Hegel might even appear at odds, but they are not. First of all, according to Constant, "the two extremes" of "despotism" and "demagoguery" converge; indeed, "they meet."[87] Not by chance, Mably's political ideal, consistently likened to Rousseau's, somehow represents "a joint constitution of Constantinople and Robespierre," that is, it contains at the same time some elements of Jacobinism and Asian despotism.[88] In turn, the *Staats-Lexicon* accuses Hegel and his antiquity-inspired model of providing weapons to both the "destructive and the conservative parties,"[89] and of encouraging "every *revolutionary aspiration* and violent action" aimed at overturning the status quo.[90] As for Haym, he condemns Hegel as a theorist of the Restoration, but at the same time, paradoxically, he attacks him for the enthusiasm he expressed, in his early years, for the French Revolution,[91] and for having later regarded and admired Napoleon "not as one man, but as an entire nation."[92] After all, Haym is on good terms with Rhenish businessman David Hansemann, who, in his criticism, likens "Hegelians to socialists" (supra, ch. III, 6, and infra, ch. X, 5).

In the name of the same political and social preoccupations, the same liberal circles accuse Rousseau and Hegel. Are these accusations justified? There's no doubt: Rousseau's celebration of *agora*, which plays an important role in the French Revolution, is ultimately, though indirectly, present in Hegel as well. Constant, too, draws inspiration from ancient times, in his celebration of *schole* and *otium*. Why should political rights be the prerogative of property-owners? Why are they the only ones who can enjoy "leisure," that is, the necessary *otium* that can help foster mature political judgment?[93] What is it that, according to Wilhelm von Humboldt, made it possible to have a multifaceted, harmonious, and solid education in Greece? It was leisure (*Muße*), that is, once again, the *schole* and the *otium* enjoyed by Greek freemen. Political neo-classicism continues to influence liberal theorists of modern freedom.

Furthermore, when Constant compares any wage laborer to an eternal child who is unable to express an autonomous will, someone who needs guidance from property-owners, it is not difficult to glimpse, behind this position, the tradition of the Aristotelian *familia*.[94] And when Constant likens wage laborers to strangers in order to justify their denial of political rights, what emerges once again is the shadow of Aristotle, according to whom the metics, *metoikoi*, shared residency with the citizens, but not their political rights. Rousseau anticipates and criticizes these antiquity-inspired traits of liberalism à la Constant when he observes that, in a well-organized State, no one should feel like a "stranger."[95] The metaphor according to which entire social classes (not even just wage laborers) are to be considered a mass of strangers—like the metics—irremediably contradicts the ideal of the community of *citoyens* supported by Rousseau and Hegel. The whole Aristotelian tradition falls into crisis with Rousseau and Hegel, if nothing else because of the fact that one of its central elements disappears: the celebration of *otium* as opposed to labor.

9. Defense of the Individual and Criticism of Liberalism

According to the liberal tradition, it is precisely due to Rousseau's and Hegel's enthusiasm for ancient freedom that they sacrifice the individual for an excessively powerful State. In reality, Rousseau argues that the social contract runs the risk of becoming null and void "if in the State a single citizen who might have been saved were allowed to perish, or if one were wrongfully confined in prison, or if in one case an obviously unjust sentence were given"[96] He also affirms solemnly that "the pretext of the public good is always the most dangerous scourge of the people."[97] While Claude-Adrien Helvétius maintains that, "for the sake of public good (*salut*), everything becomes legitimate, and even virtuous," Rousseau claims that "public good (*salut*) amounts to nothing if not everyone can enjoy security."[98] Rousseau's pathos of the individual's unique and irreplaceable value seems to make the representatives of the liberal tradition quite uneasy: they either choose to avoid this issue, in order to attack Rousseau more easily, calling him the prophet of "democratic State idolatry"[99] or "totalitarian democracy."[100] Or they regard Rousseau's position as a sort of early polemic against the Jacobins and the Committee of Public Safety.[101] This interpretation, however, cannot be supported historically, since the French Constitution of 1793 seems to be inspired precisely by Rousseau when it affirms (art. xxxiv) that "when a single one of its members is oppressed, the whole social body is oppressed." Another follower of this tradition is Saint-Just who maintains: "Happiness is a new notion in Europe. Let Europe learn that, on French territory, you refuse to have so much as a single unhappy or oppressed individual";[102] "do not bear to have so much as a single unhappy or poor individual in your State."[103]

To insist on drawing a direct link between the Terror, the dictatorship of the Committee of Public Safety, and Rousseau's philosophy, disregarding the concrete historical context, makes no sense. True, on the one hand, Rousseau vehemently emphasizes the irreplaceable value of the individual to the point of affirming, in a letter, that "the blood of a single man bears greater value than the freedom of the whole human species";[104] while, on the other hand, he does not hesitate to justify dictatorship, though of a temporary kind, if exceptional circumstances demand it in order to safeguard the "existence of the country" and "public security."[105] However, this does not differ from the liberal tradition. Montesquieu points out that "a habit of the freest peoples that have ever lived on earth" has been that of "drawing, for a moment, a veil over freedom, just like they cover the statues of the gods." This used to be an ancient practice, but in exceptional circumstances, even the most freedom-loving modern States, like England, can resort to it.[106] As for Constant who, during the Restoration, accuses Rousseau of providing a justification for the Jacobin dictatorship, it should be noted that, during the Terror, he expresses his hopes for some "rest under a dictatorship" (a dictatorship clearly different from the one that was in power at the time), while he then proceeds to regard favorably, even enthusiastically, the fall of the Republic and the *coup d'état* of Napoleon Bonaparte. Constant initially welcomes the latter as the necessary antidote to persistent plebeian and revolutionary uprisings.[107] Several decades later, John Stuart Mill declares in turn that "the assumption of absolute power in the form of a temporary dictatorship" is fully legitimate in cases of "extreme emergency," that is, of "diseases of the body politic which could not be cured by less violent means."[108]

While the liberal tradition has created the myth that the value of the individual is only respected by liberals, while in fact the pathos of the individual and the inviolable uniqueness of his rights is equally respected by Rousseau and his followers. The difference between the two traditions is that the latter's defense of the individual's rights has an unequivocally plebeian tone. The starting points of his polemic are a keen awareness of the social question, and a sympathetic identification with the masses: the main goal is that of "protecting the poor against the tyranny of the rich."[109]

Certainly, Rousseau employs an organicist metaphor according to which society can be viewed "as an organized, living body, resembling man's." Yet, aside from the fact that Rousseau himself makes it clear that it is a "very common, and in some respects inaccurate, comparison," it is particularly interesting to examine the political significance of such a metaphor: the pain felt by a part, by any member of the body, is inevitably felt by the rest of the organism.[110] In other words, the organicist metaphor serves to highlight the value of each individual to the whole society. Thus, the "body of the nation" must "provide for the security of the least of its members with as much care as for that of all the rest"; the safety of so much as a single citizen is the "common cause," just like the safety of the State.[111] The organicist metaphor does not stand here for the subordinate value of the individual, as though he could be sacrificed, with no great loss, for the sake of the whole; on the contrary, it stands for the absolute value that each individual, even the poorest one, must represent to all the other members of society and for society as a whole: "So little is it the case that any one person ought to perish for all, that all have pledged their lives and properties for the defense of each."[112]

Undoubtedly, Rousseau could not have shared Adam Smith's position, according to which safeguarding "the peace and order of society is of more importance than even the relief of the miserable";[113] nor could he have shared the position held by Mandeville, who maintained that, "to make the society happy . . . , it is requisite that great Numbers of them should be Ignorant as well as Poor."[114] It makes no sense to juxtapose Rousseau, as organicist and holist, and the fathers of the liberal tradition, regarded as individualists for all intents and purposes.

Analogous points can be made with regard to Hegel. He criticizes the theorists of laissez-faire because they sacrifice the raison d'être of the concrete individual, the "welfare of the single," the "particular welfare," for the sake of an abstract universal, no matter whether this universal is represented by the "security" of property and the legal system, or by the laws of the market and the requirements of economic development. In any case, this universal ends up sacrificing "individuals as particularities," when instead, according to Hegel, they constitute an "end" in themselves and hold "rights" (*v.rph.*, III, 699; supra, ch. III, 3). This criticism is also aimed at Constant and the other representatives of liberalism and laissez-faire. The latter extol the prodigious effects that laissez-faire has on the economy. True, Hegel objects, "commerce" does develop in this way, but this does not automatically guarantee the "subsistence of the family" and the "safety" of individuals. On the contrary, "individuals come and go, at any moment new ones reach the height of their fortune and are then chased away by others." Yes, "some make large profits, while six times as many others are ruined." In other words, economic liberalism sacrifices individuals in the name of the "abstract of trade and commerce" which, Hegel continues, cannot be considered an autonomous "end" and be valued over the subsistence of families and actual individuals of flesh and blood (*v.Rph.*, IV, 626). The theorists of laissez-faire defend the thesis that the crisis of entire economic sectors "has nothing at all to do with the State," since, "even if some individuals are ruined, this would help to make the whole flourish," to which Hegel objects that every single individual "has the right to live" (*Rph.I*, § 118 A).

During the polemic against those who, in the name of laissez-faire, refuse every legislative regulation of factory work, Marx seems to draw on Hegel's legacy. Marx, in fact, compares the "blind power of the law of supply and demand that constitutes the political economy" of the bourgeoisie, and the "mysterious ritual of Moloch's religion," that demands "infanticide," and that, in modern times, shows "particular preference for poor people's children."[115]

Going back to Rousseau and Hegel, they are attacked by the liberal tradition because they establish a relationship between politics and economics, between freedom and actual living conditions, because they argue, more or less clearly, what Hegel defines as "positive right," or "material right." It remains to be added that, whereas Rousseau's new and richer conception of right remains loyal to an ideal of society prior to the modern industrial world, Hegel's conception takes, as its starting point, the problems and contradictions of this world from which there is no turning back.

IX

School, Division of Labor, and
Modern Man's Freedom

1. School, State, and the French Revolution

How many books have been written on the following question: Is Hegel a liberal or not? The debate on this issue is still quite lively; indeed, it is surprisingly intense. Beyond all the different positions, a common idea seems to unite the participants in this debate: liberalism is tacitly, surreptitiously hailed as the latest trend in political wisdom, as if the only possible alternative to it were enslavement to absolutism and despotism. In order to provide further proof of the superficiality of this proposal, it might be useful to continue to examine Hegel's position on pedagogy and education, as well as the debate that developed around these issues at the time (supra, ch. IV, 2).

Certainly, a much more liberal figure than Hegel is Wilhelm von Humboldt, who constantly calls for reducing the role of the State to a minimum. Humboldt emphasizes the "limits" of the State's sphere of influence, and therefore considers "public education, imposed or directed by the State," suspicious and worrisome.[1] At the time, in France, drastic changes were taking place even in the field of education: soon, the National Convention would sanction the principle of free and compulsory elementary education. And in developing his criticism, Humboldt clearly has France in mind, a France devastated by a "violent volcanic eruption."[2] "Education" does not fall within the "jurisdiction" of the State, which exceeds its "authority." Hegel's position is the complete opposite of Humboldt's: society is a "universal family," and has not only the "right," but also the "duty" to intervene in the field of education. Hegel's position echoes the principle of compulsory education that was established during the French Revolution, a principle that was furiously attacked by the theorists of the Restoration. While Hegel expresses this position in general terms in the printed text of *Philosophy of Right* (§ 239), his formulations in the *Lectures* are clear and unequivocal: "Civil society has the right and duty to make parents to send their children to school; consequently, people resent this obligation and often affirm that they are responsible for their children, and that no one can give them orders. On the other hand, children have the right to be educated to live in civil society, and if parents neglect this right, civil society must intervene. This is why we have laws stating that, from a certain age on, children must be sent to school" (*v.Rph.*, IV, 602–3).

Hegel glimpses a contradiction in the liberal position. In all modern States, the community has the right to act as "guardian" of a family unit if the *paterfamilias* or the parents fail to fulfill their obligations and are unable to guarantee their own subsistence and security, and that of their children (*Rph.*, § 240). How, then, can the problems of upbringing and schooling still be considered the exclusive prerogative of the family? In order to carry out the principle of the universality of education, it is necessary to resort to "institutions of public education." Already in Nuremberg, Hegel observes:

> The various shortcomings of the school system, related to the views of parents about regular attendance, will not improve by themselves as long as schools remain private institutions. The history of most state institutions begins precisely with the fact that people took care of a generally felt need by resorting to private individuals and organizations, and to occasional donations. This happened, and still happens here and there, in the case of help for the poor, medical assistance, and even, in many aspects, in the case of religious service and the administration of justice. However, when the life of the community in general becomes more multifaceted and the civic progress becomes more complex, the laxity and limitations of these separate institutions becomes more and more evident (*w*, IV, 371–72).

Hegel's political vision and philosophy of history are very far from, and are in fact opposed to, the liberal tradition. Hegel's answer to Humboldt, who had tirelessly emphasized the "limits" of the State's jurisdiction, even in the field of education, is the following: "Political power cannot invade the sphere of the citizens' private life; that sphere is and must remain sacred, in the same way that the government is obliged to take care of issues that have a closer relation to the purpose of the State, and to regulate them according to a specific plan" (*w*, IV, 372).

On the other hand, Hegel's positions are also irreconcilably opposed to those of the theorists of the Restoration. Humboldt's "liberal" criticism does move away from royal absolutism, but it targets mainly the French theorists who make the role of "political institutions" (*Einrichtungen der Regierung*) absolute, and who have great expectations of revolutions, or *Staatsrevolutionen*, as Humboldt labels them.[3] At the same time, Hegel vehemently defends, in *Philosophy of Right*, the active function of the State even in the field of education. And this occurs during a period in which a theorist of the Restoration, Carl Ludwig von Haller, denounces the plan for public education recently approved by the Spanish Revolution as an "arbitrary imposition," and even as an attempt to rob citizens of their very "soul."[4]

After all, the progressive political significance of Hegel's discourse on education and culture is quite evident: "In Germany, in order to be admitted into administrative or political office (both in the general and particular sectors), even those who are born of noble families, who are rich, own property, etc., are required to have devoted themselves to theoretical studies; they must have a university education" (B.schr., 482). In his renowned inaugural lecture in Berlin, Hegel extols the fact that, in Prussia, culture plays an important role even within the "life of the State" (B.schr., 4). Perhaps the figure that Hegel has in mind is Friedrich II, who, in 1770, had appointed a committee in charge of examining candidates for ministerial positions, thus questioning the traditional monopoly that the aristocracy had over public offices.[5] We must not forget, on the other hand, that the *Declaration of the Rights of Man and Citizen* produced by the French Revolution also sanctioned the eligibility of all citizens to hold public offices on the basis of their "capacity." In Hegel's eyes, Prussia had accomplished, at least in part, this principle. And such a principle is diametrically opposed to the aristocratic principle according to which, "one who, by birth and wealth, is entitled to a public office, receives with it the intelligence he needs in order to carry out his task" (B.schr., 482).[6] A few years later, expressing the position held also by Hegel and his disciples, Rosenkranz will observe: aristocratic "will" is kept in check by the "examination" required to gain access to public offices.[7] And the examination takes us back to the issue of schooling.

2. Compulsory Education and Freedom of Conscience

We have examined the antifeudal criticism in Hegel's discourse on schooling. Other targets are clericalism and Catholicism. The latter is characterized by the hierarchical principle of the separation between clergymen (as the sole repositories of truth) and laymen. This principle had been challenged by the Protestant Reformation, as well as by the growth of public education. These are two fundamental steps of a single process: in Protestantism there is no laity, and thus, dogmas and hierarchy are replaced by "universities and schools" (B, II, 89), "educational establishments accessible to everyone" (*allgemeine Unterrichtsanstalten*), the "general cultural development of the community" (*Gesamtbildung der Gemeine*), the "cultural and intellectual education of everyone" (B, II., 141), and "universal awareness and culture" (B, II, 89).[8] With the rise of Protestantism, the priest is replaced by the teacher, the "instructor" (*Lehrer*; w, IV, 68). Hegel contrasts the figure of the aristocrat who claims the monopoly of public offices by virtue of his noble birth to the "official" (*Beamte*) who has been trained at school and university, and who has taken the public service examination. In the same way, Hegel contrasts the figure of the priest as the privileged repository of truth, with an ability inaccessible to "laymen," to the teacher, who conveys a knowledge which everyone can and must, in various degrees, share.

Hegel, therefore, who was also the headmaster of a high school, feels the need to emphasize the importance of improving elementary schools, *Volksschulen*, by strengthening their public nature (w, IV, 316 and 317). Schools cannot be abandoned to the will and contingency of private initiatives, because they represent an "ethical condition," a decisive passage for every individual, "an essential moment in the development of the whole ethical character" (w, IV, 348), a sort of fundamental step in the "progress from the family to civil society" (*Enc.*, § 396 Z; w, X, 82–83). Schooling seems to be represented here as the condition for the full development of ethicality. The pathos of ethicality, which plays such an important part in Hegel's philosophy, is also present in his discourse on education. Despite his past experience as a private tutor, Hegel never forgets to emphasize the superiority of public education over "private education." Public schools, in fact, can better meet the needs of that regulation "according to a specific plan" that is fundamental to a socially important field like that of education. In addition, public education can guarantee better cultural preparation (w, IV, 400).

Inevitably, at this point the polemic against the Catholic Church develops even on the issue of education policy. It might be useful now to refer back to Carl Haller, who had vehemently denounced the programs that aimed at introducing compulsory schooling: Haller, a reactionary theorist, also condemns the plan to introduce "a brief overview of civil obligations" into the school curriculum, and calls it an expression of Jacobinism. He denounces the criticism voiced in progressive circles of the "ecclesiastic exception" as an integral part of a horrifying revolutionary plan.[9] The reactionary, clerical denunciation targets some central points of Hegel's discourse on education. On the first point: doesn't Hegel, the headmaster of the Nuremberg High School, declare that school must prepare students for "public life" (*öffentliches Leben*) and guarantee "everyone an education as citizens" (*allgemeine Bürgerbildung; w,* IV, 352 and 316)? School must not only form "good private people," but also and above all, "good citizens" (*Rph. I,* § 86 A). And, with reference to the second point: school, as general education, represents an essential instrument that can help transcend that distinction between clergymen and laymen, the initiated and the uninitiated, that Hegel constantly condemns.

Haller expresses this position right after the outbreak of the Spanish Revolution; and when the Revolution ends, Hegel speaks even more harshly against the clergy, which insists on usurping jurisdictions, like that of education, that belong first of all to the State. His Heidelberg lectures on the philosophy of right do not contain any of the *excursus* on the relationship between Church and State that appears in the note and footnotes to § 270 of *Philosophy of Right.* We must instead use, as a starting point, the course of lectures from the fall semester 1819–20 (the date on the *Nachschrift* is June 25, 1820; on January 1 of the same year, the revolt led by Colonel Riego had broken out; on March 7, Ferdinand VII had been forced to swear loyalty to the constitution, while in Spain, the reactionary uprisings were spreading against the blasphemous demands of a government guilty of threatening the "freedom" and privileges held by the Church even in the field of education). Hegel declares: "To the extent that it must have teachers, property, etc., religion falls under the jurisdiction of the State, and here is where government regulation intervenes"; issues pertaining to school and to teaching (*das Lehrgeschäft*) cannot evade the control and competence of the State (*Rph. III,* 220–21).

State control, however, also ends up extended to the contents of religious teaching. On this issue, the printed text of *Philosophy of Right* contains some very harsh comments. Considering the period in which it appears, the printed text clearly echoes the events taking place in Spain, and Hegel's bitter condemnation of the counter-revolutionary uprisings. These uprisings were aided by the massive influence that the reactionary clergy continued to exert thanks to the positions of power it occupied in the past, or still occupied, in the sphere of education. *Philosophy of Right* harshly rejects "the claim according to which, with regard to *teaching,* the State should not only leave the Church free to do as it pleases, but that it should even bear infinite respect for its teachings, regardless of their content, due to the fact that this power belongs exclusively to the Church, as the sole educational authority."

Undoubtedly, Hegel's position is not very liberal; indeed, it is not liberal at all. Hegel's polemic against liberalism is explicit: clerical demands are based on an image of the State that reduces it to a mere instrument in the defense of "property" and the private sphere; liberalism seems to share with clericalism a notion of the State as "laical," in the sense of profane, as opposed to what is ethical and spiritual (*Rph.*, § 270). In this way, the clerical demand to monopolize the field of education is endorsed *de facto*. Thus, the State as a whole comes to be considered "laical" in comparison to the Church and its clergy, and with no legitimate right to intervene in a spiritual sphere like education, a sphere concerned with the problem of salvation.

But in the meantime, Hegel objects, this view of the Church's role in religious education does not have a merely personal, private meaning: specific "principles constitute at the same time the basis for action" (*Rph.III*, 222). By appealing to freedom of conscience and opinion, the Church wants to spread, with impunity, "bad principles" that come to form "a general existence (*Dasein*) that erodes actuality" (*Wirklichkeit*). In other words, they represent not mere subjective opinions, but a solid, articulated organization, or rather, a sort of counter-power to the State. Not only that, but the Church wants to direct, against the State, the same "educational institutions of the State" itself (*Lehrveranstaltungen des Staates*) by subjecting them to its ideological control (*Rph*, § 270). The proof that Hegel had in mind here the uprisings in Spain is provided by his reference to the problems in education policy, as well as by his reference to the other themes that constituted a matter of controversy in Spain (marriage laws, the Church's demand for tax exemption and exemption from ordinary jurisdiction for the clergy). Besides, Hegel adds, referring back to § 234 of *Philosophy of Right*, it is not possible to determine, rigidly and *a priori*, what can and must be subjected to the control of political power. One must also consider "every situation, case by case, and in light of the dangers of that specific time." Again, we can note a reference to the events in Spain, an echo of the Counter-Revolution under the banner of the Holy Faith (*Santa Fede*). Significantly enough, the reference to the section in question ended up appearing later in *Vorlesungen*, when the intervention of the Holy Alliance had already "normalized" the situation in Spain, and the idea of the "danger of specific moments" no longer had any meaning, even though the lesson that had emerged from those events remained quite effective).

The powerful demand for an active role of the State in education, as well as in the determination and control of the content taught, certainly does not call to mind the liberal tradition. Yet, at a certain point, the positions seem to reverse. Hegel's celebration of the State ends up affirming the need for a separation between Church and State. Contrary to those who see the unity of the two as the "supreme ideal," Hegel emphasizes the need for a phase of "difference." "In Eastern despotism, that unity that is so often craved for does indeed exist," but where it does, not only is there no freedom, but "there is no State, either" (*Rph.*, § 270 A). Not by chance, from the point of view of clerical reactionaries, "the State is considered a sort of usurpation of the Church" (*Rph.III*, 223). Against the clerical rejection of the independence and autonomous dignity of the community and political institutions, the 1819–20 course on the philosophy of right maintains instead that "insomuch as the State constituted itself as State, it separated from the Church, so that various confessions now coexist in it. The rational affirmed itself in the State only when the latter separated from the Church" (*Rph.III*, 225). Here, Hegel is the one defending freedom of conscience and thought, and thus revealing the best side of liberalism: according to Hegel, it is necessary to destroy the position that would dismiss the State as a merely "laical" and profane sphere compared to the spiritual, religious sphere of the Church, in order to uphold the secularity of the State in the field of education as well.

Only Protestantism was able to comprehend the ethical dignity of civil society, the State, and worldly matters in general. With regard to school, "it was first in Protestant countries that universities developed the way they are now, independent of the Church" (*Rph.III*, 224). Hegel's admiration for Dutch universities, after all, is well-known: Holland was the first country to give Europe "an example of general tolerance" (*W*, XX, 159), and where Hegel, at a certain point, even considered looking for a "tranquil refuge" to flee, so he writes to his wife, from "priests" and their persecutions (*B*, III, 202). Academic freedom is also the result of the struggle led by the State against clerical pressure. And Hegel's position against the 1827 Netherlands Concordat and "clericalism" (*Pfaffengeist; B*, III, 106 and 199–200) must also be regarded in light of all this.[10]

At this point, it might be useful to take a step back. When Holland was absorbed into the Great Nation led by Napoleon, Hegel laments the fact that the free and glorious Dutch universities, now reorganized according to the model of "French institutions," have become totally subordinate to the "goals of the State" (*B*, I, 329). It becomes clear that Hegel's celebration of the State is not an end in itself, but a weapon in the struggle against the clerical reaction.

3. School, State, Church, and Family

To fight clerical reaction also means to fight the pressure of parents and families influenced by such reaction: "With regard to education, parents usually believe they are completely free to do anything they want. The main opposition to public education comes from parents; they are the ones who slander and scream against teachers and public institutions: the will and the discretionary power of parents are opposed to these general institutions. And yet, society has the right to proceed according to the views dictated by its experience, and to oblige parents to have their children be taught everything that has been deemed necessary for their introduction into civil society" (v.Rph., III, 701).

The Church's demand to maintain control over schooling and education lurks behind the family's choice, behind their freedom of choice. Family ideology constitutes the strength of clerical demands. In order to refute them, Hegel uses analogous terms. In the same way that the Church represents a moment of "faith" and "sensation" compared to the moment of rationality and science represented by the State and by the political community (Rph., § A), so "the life in the family, which precedes life in school, constitutes a personal relationship, a relationship of sensation, love, natural faith and trust." School is the first institution to value the objectivity of the "thing," objective "capacity" and "usefulness," the "sense of universal being and acting" in a "community independent of subjectivity" (W, IV, 349). School is the first to educate children to "universal precepts" (Enc., § 396 Z; W, X, 82). Whereas, in the family, children have a value "immediately," at school they have a value for their "merit" (Rph.I, § 86 A).

In Nuremberg, Hegel personally experienced the pressure that came from families and religious circles. In a letter to Friedrich Niethammer, Hegel the philosopher reveals his frustration at having to teach religion, or rather, at being forced to stuff his students' heads with religious revelations, feeding them through a "funnel."[11] Analogously, Hegel the high school headmaster is forced to defend himself from the "many moralistic arguments" (W, IV, 346) made by parents who insist that school should give a wider, more rigorous moral education, to which Hegel answers: "*Formal culture*, too, is necessary for ethical deeds, since such deeds reveal a capacity to comprehend the case and the circumstances, to distinguish clearly, among them, the ethical precepts themselves, and to use them appropriately. Just this capacity is formed through scientific teaching, since the latter provides a training in relationships, and represents a continuous passage from singular to universal points of view, as well as from the universal to the singular" (W, IV, 348).

Hegel's criticism indirectly targets the vagueness and inconsistency of moral and religious precepts. In *Phenomenology of Spirit*, he makes some ironic comments about the commandment "love thy neighbor." Such love "aims at removing a certain evil from a person, replacing it with a certain good. With regard to this, it is necessary to distinguish what the evil in that person is, what the good is that should appropriately replace such evil, and what, in general, the happiness of that person is: in other words, I must love this person *intelligently*, since an unintelligent love might harm him even more than hate itself" (W, III, 314). Hegel makes similar points in Nuremberg in response to the moral speeches made by parents and in religious circles, speeches that are all the more passionate and grandiloquent as they are unable to produce, or illuminate, a concrete ethical deed. Aside from everything else, Hegel will observe a few years later, that some parents who get carried away by a sacred moral and religious zeal end up "nauseating their children with religious commandments" (*Rph.i,* § 86 A). At any rate, not even in school should philosophy be reduced to a mere "uplifting" instrument (*B,* II, 101).

Along the same line, we can place Hegel's criticism of the "old, stale complaints" so widespread among the elderly, who maintain that "the young people who are growing up now are much more reckless than they were in their youth" (*w,* IV, 336). For this reason, schools are the first to be accused, despite the fact that these youths "are the children of those same parents, [despite the fact that] they are the children of this time" (*w,* IV, 351–52). In reality, the wish is to "keep education separate from the *Zeitgeist*" (*w,* XVIII, 271), that is, from the Spirit that promotes and accompanies the march of freedom. And yet, "everyone is a product of his own time, and only the ones who follow closely the spirit of their own time can be great in their time" (*Rph.i,* § 86 A). To the moralistic fervor of parents and above all to the religious circles, Hegel contrasts the distinction between the ancient and modern world, applying it to education. An integral part of modern freedom is the acknowledgment of a private sphere, and this is the case also for the young people who attend school: "The discipline and moral action of the school cannot encompass a student's entire sphere of existence" (*w,* IV, 345). This is no longer Sparta, the "spirit of the tradition of our time" has profoundly changed, and surveillance of morality as well as punishment of transgressions no longer constitute a "public issue." They no longer concern the school, but rather, the family (*w,* IV, 334).

In considering the relationship between Church and State, Hegel points out that religious precepts cannot be raised to the level of legal precepts, since that would threaten "the right of inwardness:" "a moral government is despotic" (*v.Rph.,* III, 735). But wasn't it a despotic moral government that the Church tried to impose on the school through the incessant moral speeches uttered by the very same parents it influenced? Once again, the sides are reversed. Hegel, who tirelessly emphasizes the role of the State even in the field of education, and who openly denounces the *Liberalität* typical of clerical reactionaries, ends up expressing the best part of the liberal tradition.[12] The celebration of public schools (and indirectly, of ethicality and the State) goes hand in hand with the acknowledgment of modern man's freedom, even for the young people who attend those schools. Conversely, the denunciation of statism has turned into a refusal to acknowledge the students' private sphere, so that the very same public schools that had been accused of intrusiveness are now accused of not controlling sufficiently the individuals who are entrusted to them.

4. The Rights of Children

The inconsistency of the position criticized by Hegel has become clear. It remains to be added that, from Hegel's point of view, there is a dangerous closeness or continuity between the liberal positions and those of the theorists of the Restoration: both, in fact, are characterized by the belief that upbringing and schooling belong exclusively to the private sphere. In fact, doesn't the intrusion of political power violate the sacred rights of the family, its sacred intimacy? But children, too—and this is Hegel's exceptionally modern answer to this—have rights of their own; in no case can they be considered "things" (Sachen), the exclusive property of their parents (Rph., § 175). This statement is anything but obvious. We have seen how Kant argued for a "right of parents over their children as part of their own house," the right of parents to recover their fugitive children "as though they were things" (Sachen), or rather, as "pets who have run away" (supra, ch. IV, 2). Even though he never used such extreme analogies, Fichte himself affirmed that, with regard to children's upbringing, "parents are their children's judges."[13] Hegel openly criticizes Kant about the above-mentioned passage, but he probably also has Fichte in mind when he writes that parents can never be "judges" of their children, because a judge is a "universal figure" (Rph.1, § 85 A).

At any rate, on this and other occasions, Hegel emphasizes the need to do away with Roman Law, or with its remnants, which considered children their parents' slaves. Children, in fact, have rights: "If children are to become members of a civil society, they have rights and claims with regard to society itself, just as they had them within the family. Civil society must protect its members, it must defend their rights" (v.Rph., III, 700). What kind of rights are referred to here? It is true that education is not "such a rigorous right that it can be claimed in this form" (v.Rph., IV, 457), that is, by appealing to a court. As Fichte writes, "a child has no coercive right (Zwangsrecht) to an education."[14] And yet, in the compendium that Tutorial Fellow (Repetent) von Henning writes on his teacher's philosophy, we find reference to an "absolute right" (v.Rph., III, 550) that goes beyond positively sanctioned laws.

This right was called into question by the practice of introducing children quite early, after a rather limited attendance of school, into the family business. This practice was common among small businessmen and craftsmen, as is also evident in Friedrich Schleiermacher's account of his times: referring to this issue, Schleiermacher speaks of a "conflict between work and education."[15] And Hegel seems to have this phenomenon in mind when he declares that "children have the right to be brought up and supported at the expense of the family" (*Rph.*, § 174). Children can therefore demand an education worthy of their family's means. Fichte believed that "children have no part in property, they have no property of their own," whereas Hegel not only speaks of "family property," but he also adds: "Children are part of the family, and therefore they have the right to demand [some] of the family property for their needs and education. If their parents should refuse to do this for their children, the State must intervene to affirm and enforce this right" (*Rph.I*, § 85 A).[16]

Philosophy of Right and related lectures also refer to another practice, that of child labor in factories or in other workplaces outside the family: "The right of the parents to their children's *services*, as services, is based on and limited to the common concern of caring for the family in general" (*Rph.* § 174). In other words, "children's services to their parents are limited to the fact that children in the family must not be idle" (*v.Rph.*, III, 549). Even the services within the family must be in keeping with the "family relationship" (*Rph.III*, 143), they must not represent an actual employer-employee relationship; therefore, "they must not hinder education" (*Rph.I*, § 85 A), and they must allow children enough time for education and attendance of classes. The reference to child labor in factories and in other workplaces is explicit: "Parents must not endeavor to exploit their children's work; therefore, the State must protect children. In England, six year-old children are used to sweep narrow chimneys; in England's industrial cities, young children are forced to work, and only Sundays are devoted to giving them an education. The State has the absolute duty to make sure that children receive an education" (*Rph.I*, § 85 A).

The child's right to an education is not only challenged by feudal ideology, but also by the reality of the capitalist factories rising in Prussia. Here, too, debate develops on this issue, and State intervention aimed at prohibiting or regulating child labor in factories is rejected on the basis of liberal arguments.[17] Indeed, soon after Hegel's death, "the liberals' practical spirit" is contrasted to the "theories devised by Hegelians and Socialists alike," both of them clearly infected with statism (supra, ch. III, 6).

We can now return to Wilhelm von Humboldt and examine what happens to the liberal tradition. Humboldt strongly rejects State intervention to guarantee citizens' welfare. On the contrary, the State has only the negative task of providing security and autonomy to the private sphere: "The happiness to which man is destined is only that which gives him his strength," his capacity. Precisely because he questions this sort of pre-established harmony between merit and an individual's social standing (supra, ch. VI, 3), Hegel ends up reflecting on the role that schools and education play, not only in an individual's cultural development, but also society's. Individual nature and merit cannot be used to explain the poverty suffered by a social class, a poverty which questions the political and social organization as a whole, including the education system. Individuals "have no actual right with regard to nature. On the contrary, in social conditions, when one depends on society, or on other people, poverty immediately takes on the shape of an injustice committed against a particular social class" (v.Rph., IV, 609). Individuals, then, "have the right to claim their own subsistence," and to this right corresponds a "duty on the part of civil society" (v.Rph., IV, 604).

But how can civil society fulfill this duty without an appropriate school policy, without intervening in the sphere of education? Here, the question of education ends up revealing itself indissolubly tied to the social question: "Anyone who is unemployed has the right to demand that work be provided for them. . . . Individuals must first of all acquire the capacity (Geschicklichkeit) to fulfill their needs by owning part of the common wealth. Hence, civil society must be authorized to make sure that parents provide children with an adequate education" (Rph. III, 192–93).

With no education, one is condemned to poverty: "Poor are the ones who own no capital or skill" (Geschicklichkeit; Rph. I, § 118 A). Hegel goes so far as to see, in the school system and in the limited access to education, an instrument that reproduces class differences: "The poor cannot hand down any skill, any education to their children" (keine Geschicklichkeit, keine Kenntnisse; v.Rph., IV, 606). Furthermore, if the acquired Geschicklichkeit is limited, it will not be enough to dodge the blows of a crisis and to save one from a life of poverty. As a result, we have workers who "perhaps had an unskilled job in a factory that went bankrupt, and their limited skill prevents them from being able to take on a different activity" (ibid.). Following the ruin of a branch of industry that used to be flourishing, workers are forced to look for another job, but it is not easy; an appropriate "skill" is necessary (Geschicklichkeit; v.Rph., IV, 625). A lack of education or an adequate level of schooling seals the fate of the poor. Not by chance, among the duties of a guild, there is, according to the statutes of the trade unions that were forming at the time, the duty of providing its members with education and training (Erziehung; v.Rph., III, 710).[18]

5. School, Stability, and Social Mobility

For Hegel, school represents an instrument of social promotion: by attending high school, students coming from poor families can "rise above their condition," or they can at least "develop talents" that are usually stifled by poverty (*w*, IV, 340). However, for the lower classes, a scholastic career depends on charity. As the headmaster of the Nuremberg High School, Hegel emphasizes the high moral value of such charity, but Hegel the philosopher considers it synonymous with contingency (infra, ch. x, 2): doesn't *Philosophy of Right* compare charity to the "burning [of] lamps before the images of saints" (§ 242 A)? The persistence of this contingency hinders severely that process of social mobility which, according to Hegel, would be favored by a more open education system. Hegel's pathos of education is clearly aimed at the feudal tradition, and at times it even seems to claim that culture and education, earned with great difficulty by the middle or lower-middle classes, are superior to property as such. At this time, Europe is torn apart by the wars of the Napoleonic era and by their inevitable devastation: "Receiving a good education has never been more important than it is in our time, when every external possession, no matter how honestly and legitimately acquired, must be considered so often as precarious, when the safest things have become doubtful. The personal treasure that parents hand down to their children by means of a good upbringing and the use of school institutions are, instead, indestructible, and they preserve their value in all circumstances. It is the best and most secure good that parents can acquire and hand down to their children" (*w*, IV, 366).

Hegel's pathos of education is met by a relentless political and social resistance. We have seen how Haller condemns the spreading of education as a subtle, subversive attempt to rob citizens of their very "soul." However, the preoccupation expressed by these political social circles is even more concrete. In 1836, a record of the most reactionary Prussian nobility paints a grim portrait of the serious threats constituted by the spreading of education: traditionally, children had learned their trade simply by observing and imitating their parents, tending to geese and pigs, and learning to love "God's nature, the animals, the birds, the fields, and the tasks of agriculture." With school, children "almost always turn their minds away from their work, they start speculating over a better, more comfortable position, and for the most part they end up going astray." All the more so since almost all school books have a "demagogic" inspiration, loaded as they are with ringing expressions like "freedom and equality." Clearly, then, no aristocrat would want to hire as his "servant" a child who has attended school.[19]

Similar preoccupations eventually emerged even within the liberal tradition. As we shall see in the next paragraph, Wilhelm von Humboldt clearly conveys the sense of uneasiness caused by the fact that the spreading of education drives "many laborious hands" away from the work they traditionally performed. The same point has been made earlier in more drastic terms by Mandeville, who maintained that "the welfare and felicity . . . of every State and kingdom require that the knowledge of the working poor should be confin'd within the verge of their occupations, and never extended (as to things visible) beyond what relates to their calling. The more a shepherd, a plowman or any other peasant knows of the world, and the things that are foreign to his labour or employment, the less fit he'll be to go through the fatigues and hardships of it with cheerfulness and content."[20] The spreading of education can only be detrimental to society. In England there are already too many people who are educated or knowledgeable,[21] and this endangers the perpetuation of the current division of labor: "going to school in comparison to working is idleness, and the longer boys continue in this easy sort of life, the more unfit they'll be when they are grown up for manual labour, both as to strength and inclination."[22] "Social stability" demands that the "laboring poor" remain "ignorant to all that is not directly related to their job." The spreading of education among common people can only stimulate a pretentious, ambitious attitude, thus causing an increase in the cost of the labor force: "people of the humblest condition come to know too many things to be useful to us."[23] Education undermines the ascetic sense and the serene acceptance of one's current condition and destiny of hard work: "knowledge both enlarges and multiplies our desires, and the fewer things a man wishes for, the more easily his necessities may be supply'd."[24]

Mass ignorance is not only the precondition for the division of labor (and civilization as such), but also for law enforcement. Mass ignorance is proverbially considered, and rightly so, "the mother of devotion, and certainly we will never find a more widespread innocence and honesty than we can find among poor dumb contryfolks."[25] Thus, it is absolutely "requisite that great numbers of them should be ignorant as well as poor."[26] A complete, unconditional obedience also requires cultural inequality: "No creatures submit contentedly to their equals, and should a horse know as much as a man, I should not desire to be his rider."[27] Finally, the "laboring," "ignorant" poor contribute to social stability: they represent, in fact, the prerequisite for the country's military strength, since "they are the never-failing Nursery of Fleets and Armies." It is necessary to keep a great mass of people in poverty and ignorance in order to have laborers willing to perform "dirty slavish Work," and in order to make soldiers submit to, what Locke calls, their superiors' "absolute power of life and death."[28] This condition of total subordination calls to mind, once again, the condition of slaves (supra, ch. VII, I).

Certainly, quite some time elapses between Mandeville and Hegel. However, even in nineteenth century liberal England, there are still some who consider it "wiser for the country's government and religion to let the lower classes remain in that state of ignorance where they were originally placed by nature itself," or who denounce Sunday schools and charitable institutions as "schools of Jacobin rebellion."[29] In 1857, Bishop Samuel Wilberforce still preaches that excessive education makes "everyone unfit to follow the plough." Acquired knowledge makes not only plowmen and farmers, but also servants, "more ambitious:" they are no longer used to obeying orders, and end up abandoning their occupations.[30]

Clearly, within the liberal tradition it is possible to find very different positions from Mandeville's. Smith, for example, believes in the necessity to spread, on the largest scale, "the most essential parts of education, to read, write, and account." He claims that, "for a very small expense the public can facilitate, can encourage, and can even impose upon almost the whole body of the people the necessity of acquiring those most essential parts of education." The "children of the common people" must not be taught notions that lie beyond their world and that are useless to their future jobs, but rather, the "elementary parts of geometry and mechanics," that can be applied to any "common trade."[31] In this sense, unlike what Mandeville believed, educating the lower classes can be useful to society and valuable to the division of labor.

By educating the lower classes, Smith observes in *The Wealth of Nations*,

> The state . . . derives no inconsiderable advantage from their instruction. The more they are instructed the less liable they are to the delusions of enthusiasm and superstition, which, among ignorant nations, frequently occasion the most dreadful disorders. An instructed and intelligent people, besides, are always more decent and orderly than an ignorant and stupid one. They feel themselves, each individually, more respectable and more likely to obtain the respect of their lawful superiors, and they are therefore more disposed to respect those superiors. They are more disposed to examine, and more capable of seeing through, the interested complaints of faction and sedition, and they are, upon that account, less apt to be misled into any wanton or unnecessary opposition to the measures of government.[32]

Thus, spreading education can ensure political and social stability, and to strengthen the influence of the ruling classes over the lower ones. Without any education, in fact, the latter would be essentially hostile to any advice from the former. Smith probably has in mind the experience of the English Civil War and the influence that the radical factions had over the masses. Education is therefore considered an antidote to political and social extremism.

Education also performs another important function. Without an education, a poor worker, and especially a factory worker, lives in a state of torpor that is harmful even from a military point of view: "Of the great and extensive interests of his country he is altogether incapable of judging, and unless very particular pains have been taken to render him otherwise, he is equally incapable of defending his country in war."[33] In this sense, ignorance and cowardice are one and the same. "But a coward, a man incapable either of defending or of revenging himself, evidently wants one of the most essential parts of the character of a man. He is as much mutilated and deformed in his mind as another is in his body, who is either deprived of some of its most essential members, or has lost the use of them. He is evidently the more wretched and miserable of the two." At this point, State intervention is necessary:

> Even though the martial spirit of the people were of no use towards the defence of the society, yet to prevent that sort of mental mutilation, deformity, and wretchedness, which cowardice necessarily involves in it, from spreading themselves through the great body of the people, would still deserve the most serious attention of government, in the same manner as it would deserve its most serious attention to prevent a leprosy or any other loathsome and offensive disease, though neither mortal nor dangerous, from spreading itself among them, though perhaps no other public good might result from such attention besides the prevention of so great a public evil.[34]

All in all, Mandeville's and Smith's positions are not very different: their conclusions are antithetical, but the political and social preoccupations that determine them are the same: while Mandeville believes that political and social stability can only be achieved by keeping the masses ignorant, Smith believes that social stability can be attained by providing the lower classes with some education. In the meantime, the Industrial Revolution has progressed, and the labor force it demands has changed from Mandeville's times. However, the issue of schooling and education still depends on society's need for economic, political, and military stability, and in this context, even a liberal like Smith gives wide responsibilities to the powers-that-be. In order to increase internal cohesion, strengthen the productive and military potential, and remove the spectacle of gross degradation, the State has the authority to enforce school attendance, even though schools are not all public (and State support only partial).[35] At any rate, the compulsory or semi-compulsory attendance supported by Smith does not derive from an acknowledgment of children's rights, nor from the aspiration to social promotion on the part of the underprivileged, as in Hegel. Once again (supra, chs. IV, 3 and VIII, 9), the interpretation that promotes the liberal tradition as a judge of the holism attributed to Hegel reveals its inconsistency.

6. Professions and the Division of Labor

What is the goal of education according to Hegel? The answer is clear: while it prepares one for public life, school also provides professional training: whoever goes to school becomes a member of the political community, as well as a member of civil society, a *citoyen* and a bourgeois. Since we have already discussed the education of the *citoyen*, we shall now examine that of the bourgeois. To educate a pupil for membership of civil society means to provide him with the instruments that will allow him to practice a profession. This applies not only to elementary schools, accessible even to the poorest classes which have no other future than a life of hard work after very few years of study, but also to high schools, which serve as the "nurseries of State servants." In a rather mediated manner, high school education, too, serves to provide a "future professional competence" (*w*, IV, 362–63), and so does university education, which gives "further training in a specific profession" (*w*, IV, 365). If school must prepare students for membership in a civil society, it is important to remember that in school, one is valued and recognized "on the basis of one's own capacity and usefulness" (*w*, IV, 349). And civil servants, too, are evaluated according to their "usefulness to the State" and "state service" (*w*, IV, 380).

Once again, Hegel's position may be contrasted to the liberal tradition expressed by Wilhelm von Humboldt. Humboldt links the progressive reduction of the sphere of freedom in the modern bureaucratic State to the progressive increase in the number of "civil servants." Consequently, "minds that could perhaps be intelligent are turned away from thinking;" thus, the very profession of a civil servant is considered incompatible with the act of thinking. True education must not be directed exclusively toward the forms and concrete structure of society (*bürgerliche Formen*), that is, toward the civil society or the society of the State to which man is expected to contribute. The main fault of public education-instruction (*öffentliche Erziehung*) is precisely that it gives man a determined *bürgerliche Form*, making him lose the sense of the whole. But this whole is beyond the division of labor that characterizes the modern world, and it cannot be reached by the masses. Not by chance, with the bureaucratization of the modern State, not only are "excellent minds . . . turned away from thinking," but, Humboldt adds significantly, "many laboring hands that could be useful in various ways are turned away from actual work."[36] These laboring, uncultured hands are the requirement for the subsistence of a superior culture unburdened by the preoccupation of work.

According to Hegel, entrance into civil society can represent, for young people, the moment of separation from their aspirations to the whole. To

practice a "specific profession" bears a much "more exclusive" significance than it did in ancient times, and thus, the "life of the whole in a
larger sense" comes to be ignored (*w*, IV, 365). Even intellectuals, "academics" who should be more likely to have a vision of the whole, constitute a sort of peculiar class; their lives, too, are characterized by the
"customary relationships within their class" (*w*, XX, 73).

The division of labor affects intellectual work, as well: in the modern
world, particular "classes and ways of life have formed" (*w*, XX, 72). It is
necessary to face this irreversible historical process, and to grasp its progressive aspect. Hegel cites Goethe to emphasize the fact that determinacy is the condition for authentic greatness, and therefore to reclaim
cultural dignity not only for the intellectual profession, but also for manual labor (supra, ch. VI, 4). Even within a limited sphere, "it is essential to
remain faithful to one's goal" (*w*, XX, 73).

For these reasons, Hegel encourages young people not to despise concrete work in society, and not to regard a specific profession as something
irremediably banal. On the one hand, Schleiermacher and other Romantics contrast the beauty and the quest for ideals and knowledge of a student's life to the banality and philistinism of a specific profession which
requires him to abandon his studies and his youth.[37] On the other hand,
Hegel not only defends one's specific profession from the accusation of
philistinism, but he also adds a consideration inspired by common sense
(at least from the point of view of his adversaries): a youth cannot have his
family support him forever; indeed, he should "start taking care of his own
subsistence, and become active for others, too. Culture alone does not
make him a mature, complete man" (*Enc.*, § 396 Z; *w*, X, 85). Again, the
anti-aristocratic motif of Hegel's discourse on education and culture becomes evident: man does not make himself complete by turning away
from work and from a specific profession; on the contrary, culture must
shape a profession.

Young people tend to regard the loss of the ideal quest which comes
with a profession as a fall into the particular. Instead, in order to avoid the
feeling of helplessness, they need to give concreteness to their own ideals
by realizing that "if they must act, they must proceed to the *particular*."
Again, true greatness does not consist in abandoning oneself to reveries
that try to avoid contamination by concrete daily life, but in being able to
meet and confront actuality: "Because they are drawn toward ideals,
young people seem more concerned with nobler and more disinterested
sentiments than adults, who are instead preoccupied with particular and
concrete interests. We must not forget, however, that adults are no longer
slaves to their particular impulses and subjective views. They are no
longer preoccupied by their personal development; on the contrary, they

embody the reason of actuality, and are active in the world." It is necessary to reconcile oneself to the world, avoiding the temptation to withdraw narcissistically into a supposed inner perfection. Actuality is not to be despised, precisely because it is not "something dead or absolutely motionless"; rather, it should be compared to "life's process." Therefore, young people must be able to take leave of the "visionary spirit," lest they fall prey to immobility. To abandon "the hope for improvement," in fact, represents just another way of being "bored and irritated by the world's condition," and in any case it is not a sign of maturity, but of growing older (Enc., § 396 Z; w, x, 83–84). The concreteness of professional life also has a positive influence on one's political views, which become more mature and realistic, seemingly less demanding than were the ideals of youth, but more capable of acting concretely if need be. Young people need to be educated to the concreteness of professional commitment as well as to the concreteness of political commitment.

7. Division of Labor and the Banality of Modernity: Schelling, Schopenhauer, and Nietzsche

It may be useful now to compare Hegel's position with Schelling's later works. According to Schelling, young people must resolutely avoid "baseness, regardless of the form under which it might be disguised." While Hegel is mainly concerned with concreteness, Schelling is concerned with purity: "Let youthful dreams remain dreams—they are not meaningless, if, in the life to come, they contribute to making one impervious to all that is base." Safely away "from baseness" (vom Gemeinen), "noble (edel) youths" can experience "joy openly, with neither worries nor cares," and at the same time they can face the "seriousness" of metaphysical questions. This is the only "seriousness" suitable for them. In contrast to Hegel and his school, Schelling maintains: "Those who try to burden young people with the worries and cares of the world, the government , and the State, are not doing them a favor. Young people should first of all acquire the strength to hold the sentiments and convictions able to guide them. Therefore, to use young people for the sake of so-called demonstrations in favor of freedom of thought and academic freedom is merely an abuse dictated by hidden intentions, or an authentic foolishness." On the one hand, youthful carelessness, on the other, the effort "to achieve convictions and enlightenment on supreme issues"; such is, for Schelling, the essence of university life: there is no room for political commitment or for the preoccupations concerning a future profession: both are two forms of "baseness."[38]

For Hegel, the shift from being a student to being a professional is also the condition for reaching concrete freedom. We must follow the example of those peoples whose youths "come of age only when they no longer let a so-called paternal guardianship deny them control of their own material and spiritual interests" (*Enc.*, § 396 Z; *w*, x, 85). The problem of recovering a vision of the whole certainly exists, but it will not be solved by rejecting a profession. The bourgeois, the member of civil society who is subject to the division of labor, must not lose his dimension as *citoyen*. From this point of view, studying classical antiquity becomes indispensable, because it shows the "close relationship between public and private life." And, once school is over and one has become a member of civil society, that person, in the midst of the "fragmentation of actual life," can still think about classical antiquity. However, the goal of such reminiscence should be to return, with renewed freshness and energy, to life's "determinacy," and not to languish in the impotence of "nostalgia" and "visionary" escape (*w*, IV, 366).

This last statement seems to constitute an early criticism of a position that will later find its highest expression in Schopenhauer and Nietzsche. The profession which Hegel encourages young people to embrace now becomes all that is banausic, all that the lowest classes can and must be condemned to, as they are unable to overcome their congenital narrow-mindedness. On the contrary, according to a certain ancient model, the noble spirits who really want to participate in culture, and not lose sight of the whole, must keep away from it. The division of labor can be transcended by restricting work to laborers or slaves. At this point, the main target of criticism becomes Hegel, as the representative of those philosophers who made philosophy their profession: first they went through a rigorous training as "private tutors," and then they became "speculators of teaching," following the motto: "live first, then philosophize" (*Primum vivere, deinde philosophari*). They always lacked the "independence" and detachment from material cares that are the conditions, as Schopenhauer declares, citing and commenting on Theognis (who will become so important for Nietzsche), of "authentic philosophical activity," and even of authentic culture.[39] And what about Hegel's theory that school and culture must educate young people to live within civil society and the State? According to Schopenhauer, Hegel's flaw, or rather, his crime, especially in *Philosophy of Right*, consists first of all in inoculating young people with "the most shallow, philistine, vulgar vision of the world, extinguishing every "impulse toward something new," and giving excessive importance to "material interests, including political interests."[40]

If for Hegel the celebration of the figure of the *citoyen* ends up investing the bourgeois with some of the ancient ethicality and sense of whole, Schopenhauer and Nietzsche confine the *citoyen*, together with the bourgeois, to the sphere of the banausic. In contrast to this, the *schole* that is necessary to attain authentic culture acquires an immaculate purity which in fact was unknown even in ancient times. Therefore, it is not difficult to understand how the education to political life within the State, an education that Hegel promoted, now becomes an expression of philistinism, a will to create an arrangement similar to that of the "bees in a beehive." Hegel's philosophy, then, is only good for "referendaries," people who wish to earn their living by working in the civil service.[41]

Nietzsche subsequently criticizes those who confuse "culture" with "usefulness" and "profit" and, in the final analysis, with one's profession. Nietzsche links "Hegel's influence" not only to the "*spreading* of culture aimed at gathering the largest possible number of intelligent clerks," but even to "communism," the presupposition of which is "general culture."[42] This half-culture, which has been spread among the people, is neither pure nor authentic, as it is contaminated with material and professional preoccupations and interests. Elsewhere, we have mentioned the long history behind the accusation of philistinism which has been aimed at Hegel; now philistine becomes a synonym for banausic and plebeian.[43]

Going back to the long-pondered question: Is Hegel a liberal? He certainly is, with regard to his position on education and culture. Despite the differences, Wilhelm von Humboldt is closer to Schopenhauer and Nietzsche than he is to Hegel; Hegel, the headmaster of the high school who calls for an improvement of elementary schools and who justifies compulsory education; Hegel, the philosopher who denounces child labor in factories; Hegel, the professor who insists on ties between culture and profession, and who does not hesitate, in his letters, to claim that studying and teaching philosophy was his "occupation," his "bread and water" (B, I, 419). Ultimately, in comparison to this issue, another issue, the one indirectly suggested by Schopenhauer and Nietzsche, appears less abstract and, despite its polemic vehemence, more lucid: Is Hegel banausic and plebeian? This question cannot be solved by substituting one schema for another (thus restructuring the history of philosophy on the basis of a distinction between banausic plebeians and non-banausic non-plebeians rather than on the basis of a distinction between liberals and nonliberals). Both of these schemas need to be qualified in order to emphasize the need to understand Hegel, not on the basis of general categories whose complex, contradictory history is not even discussed, but instead by means of a concrete analysis of the problems and struggles of Hegel's time. And among these problems and struggles, those of education and schooling must also be included. On these issues, Hegel takes positions that are perhaps not "liberal," but that are certainly among the most progressive of his time; indeed, they are so modern that, thanks to the growing amount of material that is now available thanks to the *Vorlesungen*, they never cease to astonish.

X

Moral Tension and the Primacy of Politics

1. Modern World and the Waning of Moral Heroes

Søren Kierkegaard maintains that Hegel's thought lacks morals, and his well-known accusation has often been repeated by philosophers; but is it justified?[1] Hegel stresses the fact that the modern world is characterized by the centrality of political institutions, and by the objectiveness of legal regulations: hence, there is no room for heroes. And saints, the heroes of morals, seem to share the same fate. St. Crispin, who used to steal leather to make shoes for the needy, would now end up in a "work-house" or a "penitentiary." Anyone who, in the Middle Ages, was viewed as a moral hero, is, in the modern world, subject to the full force of the law and treated as a thief. Hegel does not show any compassion for St. Crispin's fate. Certainly, St. Crispin was a pious man, but "in a well-ordered State" it is only fair that he should suffer legal punishment (*v.Rph.*, IV, 341 and *Rph.*, § 126 AL; *v.Rph.*, II, 457); "in fact, what is rightful (*das Rechtliche*) to the extent that it represents the existence of freedom is an essential precept in contrast to moral intention" (*v.Rph.*, III, 399).

The modern world is the world of "rectitude" (*Rechtschaffenheit*), and "rectitude" is defined by the respect for laws. The shift from heroes—including moral heroes—to citizens who form part of a well-ordered State is also the shift from poetry to prose, from the poetry of the individual inspired by one's personality and moral conscience, to the prose of a behavior established for everyone by the law: "But while the order based on the law has developed more fully in its mundane form and has become predominant, the adventurous autonomy of chivalrous individuals is now out of place" (*w*, XIII, 257). The time when the moral heroism of privileged individuals compensated for the absence of objective and orderly political institutions is now over. The end of the aesthetic period brings about a reduction in the role of morals.[2] In the *Aesthetics*, we read: "The reflective development of our modern life requires us, in relation to both will and judgment, to establish some general points of view and, consequently, to adjust the particular, so that universal forms, laws, duties, principles, can serve as determining motives, and become what essentially guides us" (*w*, XIII, 24–25). The motivation that Hegel uses here and elsewhere to account for the lost centrality of art in the modern world is also valid for moral intention.

2. Inconclusiveness and Narcissism in Moral-Religious Precepts

Hegel makes a coherent criticism of the internal structure of moral-religious precepts. One example is the commandment, "love thy neighbor." Firstly, if by "neighbor" we mean all people, an essential contradiction emerges, since love indicates a particular intensity of feeling. When, instead, we attempt to direct this love toward everyone, it becomes the "opposite of what love is."[3] And even if we leave this essential contradiction out of consideration, the commandment, "love thy neighbor" is doubly contingent. First, the fulfillment of this commandment is entrusted to the good will of the individual. "It is directed toward individuals in relationship to other individuals, a relationship that is *understood as being of an individual to another individual*, or as a relationship of sensation" (*Empfindung*). In other words, the fundamental inadequacy of moral commandments is that they "remain *duties*, they have no *actuality*"; they "are not *laws*, but mere *commandments*."

The contingency of moral commandments also reveals itself in another way. Even if we accept an individual's good will, another problem arises: for the fulfillment of a commandment to be meaningful, the individual needs to know what the neighbor's "welfare" (*Wohl*) is: "in other words, I must love this person *intelligently*, since an unintelligent love might harm him even more than hate itself." In such a case, the act of "doing good" prompted by the commandment, "love thy neighbor," "immediately dissolves and turns into an evil" (*Übel*). Moral commandments work on the level of immediate knowledge, and the shift from the contingency of sensation to the universality of knowledge represents the passage from moral commandments to the law, to the objectivity of legal regulations: "the act of doing good in an intelligent manner is represented, in its richest and most important form, by the intelligent, universal action of the State," of the political community (*w*, III, 314–15). The conquest, not only of the "actuality," but also of the "universality" of the good can only occur on the level of ethicality, of politics. Essentially, Hegel overturns the traditionally established relationship between morality and politics, making the latter the most suitable means of representing actual, fulfilled universality. Or rather, "morality" expresses only the "most immediate universality" (*nächste Allgemeinheit*) (*v.Rph.*, IV, 338), still affected by the particularity of the subject, of the "moral individual" (*moralisches Individuum*) who proclaims the excellence of his own intentions, but who still is not subject to objective, universal regulation (*Rph.III*, 188). We are not yet in the presence of the "universal in-and-of-itself" with an objective formulation; this universal is only fulfilled on an ethical level (*v.Rph.*, III, 396). Once laws prevail in a well-ordered State, it is illegitimate to violate such universality, not even out of "love for another," that is, not even in the name of the commandment, "love thy neighbor" (*W*, III, 315).

This commandment can sometimes assume an apparently more concrete shape and require one to renounce one's own possessions in order to give them to others. But, Hegel objects, "giving one's own possessions to the poor is a hypothetical imperative, since, in that case, there would be no more poor people left" (*Rph.I*, § 90 A). Such is the third fundamental criticism that Hegel directs at moral commandments. Not only are they affected by a dual contingency and by an overall inconclusiveness; they represent the very cause of this inconclusiveness, since the following is the presupposition of the celebration of their unconditional, eternal nature: "If poverty must continue to exist so that the duty of helping the poor can be fulfilled, then, by letting poverty continue to exist, that duty is not being fulfilled" (*W*, II, 466). One of Hegel's disciples provides an effective commentary on this excerpt from the Jena text on natural right: "The ethical precept orders: 'Help the poor.' Yet, the actual help would consist in freeing them from their poverty, but when there is no more poverty, there are no more poor people, and no more duty to help them. And if, for the sake of charity, we let these poor people continue to be poor, then, by letting poverty continue to exist, the duty [to actually help the poor, by freeing them from their poverty] is not being . . . fulfilled."[4]

The internal dynamics of this moralistic, narcissistic tendency that aims at perpetuating moral-religious commandments is analyzed with logical rigor and psychological insight in *Science of Logic*: actuality is contrasted to an ideal; apparently, what is required is the necessary fulfillment of the ideal, but in fact, the nonfulfillment of the ideal is presupposed, since this nonfulfillment constitutes the unspoken presupposition of the permanent validity of the moral commandment and of the permanent excellence of the subject's acclaimed moral intention (*W*, V, 164). This position is "untrue" (*unwahr*) (*W*, V, 145), it tirelessly professes high ideals and goals, but it does not take them seriously.[5] In other words, in order not to be narcissistic, moral commandments must aim at transcend-

ing themselves ethically. If taken seriously, the commandment that requires one to help the poor must aim at creating an ethical order where
poverty, and therefore also the commandment that requires one to help
the poor, has been concretely eliminated. In a passage from his 1824–25
lecture course on the philosophy of right, Hegel claims that, "helping the
poor" belongs to the "moral sphere," but within an ethical order this
moral sphere "becomes more and more limited. The act of giving alms
takes place much more often in conditions of underdevelopment than in
ones of development (*v.rph.*, IV, 527).

3. Modern World and the Restriction of the Moral Sphere

In this sense, the development of the modern world brings about a gradual
replacement of the moral sphere by the sphere of ethicality. This process
can be observed at various levels. Legally-sanctioned contracts replace
commitments based on one's word of honor. This causes some to fall prey
to nostalgia and to protest against the "formality" of a legal obligation,
which leaves no room for spontaneity and for the free respect of a purely
moral obligation. To these protests, Hegel answers: "Both forms must be
observed: one must respect a merely verbal contract as well as a formal
one, but one cannot be asked to always be content with a mere word of
honor" (*v.rph.*, III, 660). The moral obligation to respect a merely verbal
contract remains valid, just like the renowned deposit in Kant's *Critique
of Practical Reason*. Nevertheless, with the development of society, legal
"formality" tends to replace one's word of honor, and the nostalgic protests against this development that restricts, or seems to restrict, the
moral sphere are not only unjustified, but they ultimately reveal a disproportionate attachment to one's particularity, narcissistically enjoyed as
moral. And these protests are all the more unjustified for the fact that
morality continues to influence the development of the legal system: "for
moral peoples," and "in our times, when morality has taken solid roots,"
there is no need to resort to excessive, draconian punishments (*v.rph.*, IV,
280). Once the respect of norms has become a common habit, one can
resort to lighter or more balanced punishments, since no contaminating
effect of the crime needs to be feared. Morals influence legal norms, which
continue to represent the rules of behavior for the citizens of a well-
ordered State.

Yet, the extension of the ethical world seems to face insurmountable
obstacles. One needs only think of the problem, still unsolved despite
migration and colonization, of the poverty suffered by large masses of
people.[6] Well, "this is a situation in which, notwithstanding all public
institutions, *morality* finds plenty to do" (*rph.*, § 242). Where political

institutions fail or reveal themselves to be lacking, where ethicality cannot fulfill itself concretely, this is where only morality can prevail. The appeal to a moral conscience emerges once again in modern society, and again it plays a fundamental part in a situation (that of the harsh inequality and poverty of civil society) in which the "remnants of the state of nature" continue to reveal themselves (Rph., § 200 A).

Poverty must be relieved through charity. As the headmaster of a high school, Hegel warmly thanks the citizens of Nuremberg for their "charity" and "donations" to "needy students." Not only does he thank and praise "noble philanthropists," but he also emphasizes the effectiveness of their deeds: "In this way, those who were born of destitute parents have been offered the possibility to rise above their condition or, while remaining in that condition, to develop talents that poverty would have extinguished or led astray!" (W, IV, 340–41, *passim*).

Only three years earlier, in *Phenomenology of Spirit*, Hegel had criticized what we have defined as the dual contingency of the commandment, "love thy neighbor." Should we then come to the conclusion that, with regard to charity, due to the practical demands of his position, Hegel the headmaster of a high school and public official expresses himself—or is forced to express himself—in a less strict manner than Hegel the philosopher of politics and history? We need to remember what Hegel had already pointed out in *Phenomenology of Spirit*: "individual charity, this 'doing good' that is sensation, only has the value of a wholly personal act, of an accidental and temporary emergency assistance (*Nothilfe*)." Thus, even though it is right and proper to offer this assistance, it certainly does not solve the problem, and the ones who do offer it have no reason to brag. In comparison to an effective functioning of ethical and political institutions—once they have been suitably transformed—"the actions of an individual appear so irrelevant that they are hardly worth mentioning" (W, III, 315).

In Nuremberg, too, Hegel (as philosopher of history) continues to emphasize the tendency of modern world development to remove services that are essential to social life from the domain of "private will." This applies to schools (supra, ch. IX, 1), but also to "medical assistance" and to "assistance to the poor." In this case, too, what needs to be carried out is a "regulation according to a plan." This regulation should respect the "sacred" limit of the private sphere of freedom, but it should not leave the fulfillment of needs that affect man's dignity and his actual freedom to chance and to a potential morailty. Essentially, it should not leave it to the arbitrary power of more fortunate individuals.

Hegel strongly insists on the idea of the dual contingency of charity in *Philosophy of Right*. It is a contingency that concerns "this help, both in itself and in its effects." For this reason, "society endeavours to make [this help] less necessary by identifying the universal aspects of want and taking steps to remedy them" (Rph., § 242). Political institutions need to be improved so that they can properly confront the problem of poverty. What needs to be reduced is the sphere in which an individual's accidental help intervenes, in the final analysis, "the situation in which . . . morality finds plenty to do" (ibid.).

True, so far the expansion of the ethical world has faced insurmountable obstacles, but the goal remains a society within which moral commandments, or at least the commandment that requires one to help the poor, are superfluous. The persistence of charity, the fact that we are still forced to resort to a chance remedy, all of this underscores the dramatic problems that the modern world has yet to solve. Hegel's criticism is directed once again at those who would stretch to the limit, or even perpetuate, this sphere of contingency, in order to extol the presumed excellence of one's moral inwardness: "Charity still retains enough scope for action, and it is mistaken if it seeks to restrict the alleviation of want to the *particularity* of emotion and the *contingency* of its own disposition and knowledge, or if it feels injured and offended by universal rulings and precepts of an *obligatory* kind. On the contrary, public conditions should be regarded as all the more perfect the less there is left for the individual to do by himself in the light of his own particular opinion (as compared to what is arranged in a universal manner)" (Rph., § 242 A). In other words, the development and the improvement of ethical institutions reduce the sphere within which one is forced to appeal to an individual's moral sense.

4. Hegel and Kant

It may be useful at this point to compare Hegel and Kant. At first glance, the contrast between the two seems evident. In *Conflict of the Faculties*, Kant describes mankind's "progress toward improvement" in the following terms: "There will be a little more charity. . . , more reliability in the respect for promises."[7] On the contrary, according to Hegel, historical progress is marked by two main steps: 1) legal formality replaces a type of commitment that rests merely on one's given word; and 2) charity becomes unnecessary. However, the author of *Foundations of the Metaphysics of Morals* makes an interesting observation about a rich individual's "giving to charity" (*Wohltun*): "This can hardly be considered the praiseworthy fulfillment of an obligation . . . The pleasure that this person affords himself in such a way, without making any sacrifice, is a way for him to indulge in moral sentiments."[8] The hypocrisy of a good moral conscience is precisely what Hegel tirelessly criticizes.

Kant goes even further: what is the point for a feudal lord to give alms to his "hereditary serf" (Erbuntertan), a man "whose freedom he has taken away"? The scope of the conclusion that Kant reaches in *Foundations of the Metaphysics of Morals* seems to go beyond the institution of "hereditary serfdom" (Erbuntertänigkeit): "Being able to give alms, which is dependent upon one's fortune, is mainly the result of certain individuals being favored by the injustice of the government. The government introduces an inequality of welfare that makes charity indispensable. Under these conditions, does the assistance that the rich may give to the poor really deserve the name of charity, that charity that some individuals brag so much about?"[9] Here, Kant's position seems to approach Hegel's. Yes, charity continues to be "every man's obligation"; it is a moral commandment, but a commandment that makes sense only in an unjust political situation that must be overcome.[10] Therefore, Kant poses a crucial question: "Wouldn't it be better for the welfare of the world as a whole, if man's morality were reduced to legal obligations (Rechtspflichten) to be fulfilled with the utmost conscientiousness?"

This question also addresses Hegel's position: an appeal to moral conscience is made superfluous or secondary by the objectivity of ethical institutions. Kant himself recognizes that "man's happiness" would not suffer from such objectivity. And yet, he adds in *Foundations of the Metaphysics of Morals*, "a great moral ornament of the world, that is, philanthropy (Menschenliebe)" would be eliminated, and without this ornament, we could no longer picture "the world as a beautiful moral totality in its fulfilled perfection."[11] The "moral ornament" does not impress Hegel in the least; in fact, Hegel regards such an ornament (Zierde) as a sign of ethical imperfection.

5. Hegel, Schleiermacher, and the Liberal Tradition

There is a much greater difference between Hegel and Schleiermacher. The latter, in fact, wishes that the assistance to the poor would cease to be "the business of the *secular* government in its various branches," and that it would go back to being "a thing of the *religious* community." He defends his position in these terms: "The fact that an individual's good will is hindered by an external law is already quite negative as it is." Morality founded upon spontaneity has been replaced by an impersonal legal obligation, and "civic (bürgerlich) life has been able to *swallow up religious* life away from us."[12] In the hopes that progress toward the modern world can be reversed, Schleiermacher makes the following wish: "May the *assistance to the poor* be conceived in Christian love," and may "*care for the needy*" be restored to the hands "which originally held it, in the bosom of Christianity."[13]

Schleiermacher's speech celebrating "Christian charity" was published in Berlin, together with his other *Speeches on Domestic Christian Economy*, in 1820. It is possible, therefore, that Hegel might have had Schleiermacher himself as his target, when in *Philosophy of Right* he criticizes the "wrong position" that would have the fate of the poor depend exclusively on the warm "charitable" feelings. The fact remains that Schleiermacher's position was shared by many at the time, not only on a cultural level, but on a political level as well. A few years later, the liberal Rotteck, after denying that the poor should have the right to an assistance from the State, adds that the absence of a legal obligation on the part of the political power does not harm the poor; on the contrary, it stimulates the generosity and charity of the rich: "That which is done because of a legal obligation is usually done with less zeal than if it stemmed from a voluntary, and therefore commendable, decision, which would find its reward in a noble self-conscience." Making charity and help for the poor a legal obligation can only dry up the moral source from which they originate.[14]

Hegel's criticism appears to be an attempt to ridicule the position held by his liberal critic: "Prescriptions are often seen negatively; one example is constituted by the taxes for the poor, with regard to which everyone would want the contribution to be entrusted to one's own charity. But in this way, the individual puts himself in an unjust position towards the law. The most intelligent laws are the ones that prescribe what people already do spontaneously; this is the authentic, true meaning of the laws, laws that prescribe what man's intellect, his reason, already does. The law, then, only serves to regulate the quantity." And in answer to those who complain about the fact that legal obligation suffocates the spontaneity of their moral sentiments, Hegel points out that nothing prevents them from doing, with the utmost naturalness, what the law justly prescribes: "men who do not steal do not do so because it is forbidden, but because they spontaneously do not do it" (*v.Rph.*, IV, 603). The moral norm continues to exist, but now it is expressed as a legal norm.

This is precisely the point which Hegel's reactionary and liberal critics focused on at the time: in Hegel's system, Friedrich Stahl remarks, there is no room for "charity" (*Carität*), that is, the "charity" that takes place "only between one person and another."[15] As for the liberal businessman Hansemann, he criticizes the attempt to provide legal regulation of the factory work performed by women and children, and he considers the

"Hegelians and socialists" who support this attempt (supra, ch. III, 6) to be guilty of trying to replace "love" with the State.[16]

With regard to this, Hegel responds: "Usually, men prefer to retain discretion over how they will assist others rather than let the State help the poor according to general rules." However, Hegel continues, "individual help must be reduced to a minimum, because it can be more damaging than helpful" (*Rph. I*, § 107 A). The objection that, in his Heidelberg course on the philosophy of right, Hegel makes against laissez-faire opposition to State intervention in the social sphere is the same objection that *Phenomenology of Spirit* makes against the Christian commandment "love thy neighbor." Of course, individuals do not want to renounce their freedom to act as they think fit, but, Hegel objects, "free will intervenes even where the individual regards this interference from the State as rational, and in that case, by following this injunction, the individual can perform a beneficial function" (*wohltätig sein; ibid.*). The "charity" (*Wohltätigkeit*) celebrated by Schleiermacher becomes here a civic commitment to a political solution to the social question. And the shift from moral commandments to legal norms is an essential moment in the secularization of the modern world.

The position held by Schleiermacher and Rotteck continued to manifest itself for a long time within the liberal tradition, even outside Germany. In 1835, Tocqueville declares that, rather than "public charity" or "legal charity," he strongly prefers "individual alms," that is, the "private virtue" that has been raised to the rank of "divine virtue" since the birth of Christianity.[17] The reason is simple: "Individual alms establish precious links between the rich and the poor," links of a moral nature. In contrast, "legal charity . . . does not eliminate the act of giving alms, but it divests it of its morality." Moreover, legal charity arouses the indignation of the rich, who see the levying of taxes by the State as a poorly-disguised way of plundering their property.[18] Faced with the threat of the socialist movement and by the specter of "servile wars," during the Revolution of 1848, Tocqueville partially modifies (is forced to modify) his position:[19] he now acknowledges the presence of "duties of the State towards the poor," but he still includes these duties in the category of "philanthropy,"[20] that is, charity, though now he calls it "public charity" or "Christian charity applied to politics."[21] The poor are still not regarded as having rights per se, because their poverty continues to be considered part of the natural and immutable order of things, or due to individual improvidence. Political or social institutions are never deemed responsible for it.

Upon closer scrutiny, there are no relevant differences between the more recent text and the one written thirteen years earlier, in which

Tocqueville recognized the usefulness, and even the necessity, of "public charity," but only for the benefit of children, elderly people, invalids who are physically unable to work, or, in extraordinary and temporary circumstances, such as unforeseen and unforeseeable "public calamities that sometimes fall from God's hands and come to announce His wrath to the nations."[22] The 1835 text concedes that, "by regulating the assistance, an association of charitable people could increase the effectiveness and scope of individual charity."[23] As for the 1848 text, it does make some concessions (prompted by the need to confront the threatening demand, by workers, for the right to work), yet it does not seem to give the State a different or larger role coordinating individual charity prompted by personal Christian conscience. The proof is that, during these years, Tocqueville continues to condemn any legislative regulation of factory work or rents as an expression of intolerable socialist despotism (supra, ch. VII, 6).

If we move from France to England, we find that Herbert Spencer compares the so-called "State charity" (that is, laws in favor of the poor) to the "State Church" so dear to royal absolutism. And, just as the old dissenter used to fight for the respect of the spontaneity of authentic religious sentiment, so the new "dissenter, with regard to laws for the poor, continues to claim that charity will always be all the more widespread and beneficial to the extent that it remains voluntary." Just as the old dissenter denied any authority the right to lay down laws regarding his religious conscience, the new "dissenter, with regard to institutionalized charity, objects that no one has the right to interfere between him and the *practice* of his religion." The new dissenter objects indignantly to "state interference in the practice of one of the most important precepts of the New Testament," that of charity. Thus, to replace "moral obligation" with a legal norm is for Spencer an illiberal, oppressive move that ends up, for the most part, drying up the "generous sentiments" that alone can provide effective assistance to the poor.[24] Here, the celebration of morality is at the same time an expression of conservatism and narcissism: maintaining mass poverty is necessary for the rich to enjoy their good moral conscience, without having to make any real sacrifice. Hegel's pathos of ethicality represents an early criticism of this ideology: "The more one speaks of Spirit, the more one usually lacks it. Spirit consists in this: that which is merely inside becomes something objective" (*Rph. III*, 188). Hegel's remarks about the Spirit are clearly also valid for morality.

6. Hegel, Burke, and Neo-Aristotelian Conservatism

The replacement of the moral sphere by the ethical sphere, however, does not represent the return to conventional morals which Apel and Habermas denounce in contemporary neo-Aristotelianism.[25] And yet, this de-nunciation does not question the validity of Gadamer's and Ritter's inter-pretation of Hegel's thought. It is precisely this interpretation that we intend to question. Hegel sharply criticizes the conservative motif of the "wisdom of ancestors" and "customary rights" (*Gewohnheitsrechte*): "Custom (*Gewohnheit*) as such is nothing but contingency; man can be-come accustomed to bearing the worst things, he can become accustomed to being a slave, a serf" (*v.Rph.*, IV, 534). Joachim Ritter, who reinter-prets Hegel in neo-Aristotelian terms, recognizes that, for Aristotle, "laws based on habit are more important, and deal with more important matters, than written laws."[26] For Hegel, instead, without a written text, law loses its "universality"; in this way, freedom is threatened or denied (*Rph.*, §§ 211, 215). Not by chance, *Philosophy of History* celebrates the plebeians' struggle in ancient Rome to obtain "written laws:" the absence of such laws, in fact, consecrated the "privilege of patricians" in the "administra-tion of justice" (thus making plebeians "all the more dependent" on the patricians) (*Ph.G.*, 695). Quite significantly, Hegel accuses Hugo and his Historical School of Law of wanting to reduce, with their polemic against legal codification, "the rest of men" to "status of serfs" (*Rph.*, § 3 *AL*; *v.Rph.*, II, 99). In contrast, Hegel applauds the *Charte*, which instead Schelling belittles or despises as a "written letter," and therefore "ephemeral and perishable," a trifle in comparison to the "most intimate disposition of the soul" and the "law written in one's heart."[27]

According to Hegel, the essential flaw of Greek ethicality consists in the fact that it is "only habit and custom, and therefore it still represents a particularity within existence" (*Ph.G.*, 611). This is not a negligible limita-tion. Where habit is dominant, there is no universality, or at least, the "universality of thought is more obscure" (*Rph.*, § 211 A; *W*, VII, 362). Hence, Greek ethicality is tainted by slavery: "In order not to have slav-ery, what is necessary first of all . . . is to have the notion that man as such is free. But in order to have that, man needs to be considered as universal, regardless of the particularity that sees him as citizen of one State or another. Neither Socrates, nor Plato, nor Aristotle regarded abstract, uni-versal man as free" (*Ph.G.*, 611).

Hegel's ethicality contains the pathos of reason, of universality: "Rea-son must be the dominant element, and that is the case in a developed State" (*Rph.*, § 3 *AL*; *v.Rph.*, II, 89). Hegel accuses moral-religious com-mandments of being ultimately tied to immediate knowledge, and this is even truer of habit and custom: these, too, can encompass the worst ele-ments. Hegel's ethicality presupposes the results of the doctrine of Natu-ral Law, the awareness that there are inalienable rights that belong to man as man, not only to the free citizen of a certain *polis* or State. Certainly, these inalienable rights cease to be a mere moral demand to the extent to which they are fulfilled within the ethical institutions of a State; and yet, they do not necessarily lose their intrinsic universality.

On the opposite side of Hegel is Edmund Burke, an author who is influenced by the "practical politics of ancient times" and Aristotle and who criticizes the French Revolution, every "abstract principle," and every "general principle."[28] Aristotle's lesson seems to have taken root in the land of Common Law and "English liberty" so despised by Hegel because of its superstitious cult of customs (the "wisdom of ancestors:" B.schr., 467–68; cf. also Rph., § 3 AL; v.Rph., II, 99) and its lack of universality.[29] Burke contrasts the "abstract principles concerning 'man's rights,'" to the "rights of the English regarded as a heritage handed down to them by their ancestors."[30] For Hegel, instead, the development of the "abstract" category, of the universal concept of man, not only represents enormous progress, but it is ultimately the *leitmotiv* of history as the development and extension of freedom. And it is precisely man—not man in the state of nature, but man historically constructed by colossal struggles—who claims those inalienable rights that by now are his "second nature" (supra, ch. III, 2–4). On the one hand, Burke rejects the "abstract principles" of the rights of man for that "practical wisdom" that is, in England, the heir of the "practical politicks" of ancient times.[31] On the other hand, Hegel denounces the so-called "practical sense, which aims at profit, subsistence, wealth," as the obstacle that prevents the "English nation" from eliminating "ancient privileges" and from replacing them with a "general principle" (B.schr., 487–88). While Burke's condemnation of the general principles of the French Revolution (which he contrasts to the English one) is also made in the name of Aristotle, Hegel criticizes "English freedom" in a manner similar to his criticism of Greek morality.

A more general point can be made. In Burke's and Hegel's time, Aristotelianism was the official ideology of conservatism: the abstractness of revolutionary principles was contrasted to the concreteness of *eudaimonia*, a dreamy happiness savored in the rut of tradition and away from revolution. Not by chance, one of the main reactionary publications of the time was called *Eudäimonia.*[32] Classic German philosophy is aware of the political significance of this debate. On the basis of "happiness" (*Glückseligkeit*), Kant objects that "no universally valid principle can be established for the laws."[33] Precisely because it can subsume any content, "happiness" can be sought even in the shadow of a "despotic government."[34] For Hegel, too, any allusion to "happiness" (*Glückseligkeit*) is an allusion to "subjective sentiment and consent" (*Enc.*, § 479). In *Lectures on the History of Philosophy*, after translating Aristotle's *eudaimonia* as *Glückseligkeit*, Hegel continues: "We see [that the Greeks] regard happiness as the most desirable end, as man's ultimate goal; and up to Kant's philosophy, the foundation of morals, as eudemonism, is the goal of achieving happiness" (w, XVIII, 186). Clearly, Hegel shares Kant's criticism of eudemonism, and in fact, *Philosophy of Right* does not begin from the concept of happiness, but from that of will, giving Kant credit for defining will in its "infinite autonomy" (§ 135 A). For this reason, the revolution that takes place in political form in France "settles and expresses itself in the form of thought" in Kant's philosophy (w, XX, 314).

7. Hegel, Aristotle, and the Rejection of Solipsistic Escape

Hannah Arendt maintains that a central characteristic of ancient (and Aristotelian) thought is the view that economics is a "prepolitical phenomenon" that only concerns "private domestic organization." In other words, "according to ancient thought, the expression 'political economy' is an oxymoron."[35] In light of Arendt's position, Hegel's philosophy is diametrically opposed to ancient thought, and not only because it extols "political economy" (*Staatsökonomie*) (Rph., § 189 A), but also because it establishes a close relationship between economics and politics. A starving man at risk of death is already in a situation of "total lack of rights" (Rph., § 127) and therefore of slavery (Rph. III, 196). In other words, it is not possible to create a space of actual freedom by leaving economics out of consideration. From this perspective, Hegel is less drawn towards antiquity than is the liberal tradition he criticizes for consigning economics to the sphere of political irrelevance, the sphere within which any cure for poverty can only come from private acts of charity and morality.[36] In classical antiquity, a thoughtless attachment to habit and to a historically-determined community makes it impossible to achieve a universality of thought, and thus, a universal definition of man (within which slavery cannot be subsumed) (Rph., § 2 AL; v.Rph., II, 85). This definition has been made possible since Christianity, but in the modern world it runs the risk of being undone by a situation that prevents a starving man from being subsumed within the category of man.

The universal concept of man, a concept that entails the affirmation of the right to freedom for every individual ("not a slave, not a serf, but a free man"), is the result of a difficult and complex process of historical development. This concept is essentially a "modern" achievement (Rph., § 105 AL; v.Rph., II, 389).[37] However, this conquest must not remain confined to moral subjectivity; it must translate itself into ethical and political institutions: within the State, "man is recognized and treated as a rational, *free* being, as a person" on the basis of "universal" (*allgemein*) and "universally valid" (*allgemeingültig*; Enc., § 432 z) laws. This process is still ongoing. The pathos of universality ("universality constitutes the character of reason," *v.Rph.*, I, 238) is what separates Hegel from Aristotelianism and ties him to the French Revolution.[38] This pathos is already present in Kant, although, at least in the writings that precede the outbreak of the Revolution, it mainly relates to the moral community.[39] In Hegel, on the other hand, this universality is explicitly embodied in a political community.

In conclusion, when applied to Hegel, neo-Aristotelianism essentially consists in the affirmation of the primacy of politics and in the rejection of a comforting escape from the mundane and the political into a merely solipsistic sphere. It consists in the ambition to create an earthly polis as a place where men can find fulfillment and reciprocal recognition. However, all of this does not bring to mind an academic event, but a philosophical and political vision that prepares and accompanies the outbreak of the French Revolution. Schelling accuses the French revolutionaries in Stuttgart of attempting to create, on the earth, that "true *politeia*" that instead can only exist "in Heaven."[40] And Friedrich Stahl, who considers himself a disciple of Schelling, accuses Hegel of pointing to the State—that is, to an earthly political community—as "the solution to the contradictions" that strain human existence, of "placing the coveted universal redemption not in the afterworld, but in this world, thus returning it to the present" (in *v.Rph.*, I, 575–76). In this light, it is not difficult to understand Stahl's celebration of "charity" motivated by a personal religious or moral sentiment, compared to the objectivity of Hegel's ethicality.

On the other hand, the young Marx, who was Hegel's disciple, refers back to Aristotle's lesson in order to denounce the "unpolitical" existence into which Prussia and Germany forced their subjects.[41] In this sense, the reference to Aristotle is nothing but another justification of the community of *citoyens*.

8. The French Revolution and the Celebration of Ethicality

Conservative neo-Aristotelians see themselves tied to Hegel. In reality, their influence is Burke, the implacable enemy of the French Revolution, which is instead indissolubly linked to Hegel's pathos of ethicality and political community. The celebration of politics over personal morality constitutes an essential phase in the ideological preparation for the French Revolution. We can see this theme in Rousseau, who is well aware that "everything is radically dependent on politics," so that "vices belong not so much to man, as to poorly-governed man."[42]

Claude-Adrien Helvétius expresses himself in similar terms. After seeing "the various vices of nations as the necessary consequence of the various forms of government," Helvétius points out that "legislation" is the decisive turning point. For this reason, morality is ultimately "but a frivolous science if it is not subsumed by politics and legislation."[43] According to Rousseau, "those who insist on treating politics and morality separately will never understand anything about either of them."[44] In turn, a philosopher of the Enlightenment, Paul d'Holbach, maintains that morality can be effective if it joins politics, and to express this necessary "unity between Morality and Politics," d'Holbach coins, based upon a Greek derivation, the term *"ethocratie,"* a neologism somehow reminiscent of Hegel's *Sittlichkeit.*[45] The cultural climate that precedes the outbreak of the French Revolution finds what might be its clearest expression in Abbé de Saint-Pierre, who, referring to himself in the third person in his autobiography, writes: "He realized that most of happiness and unhappiness derived from good and bad laws . . . This reflection, that often occurred to his spirit, persuaded him that the most important science for man was not morality, but politics, or the science of government. And he realized that one wise law could make many more people happy than one hundred moral treatises could. Thus, in order to become more useful to society, he abandoned the study of morals and took on the study of politics."[46] On the eve of the Revolution, the center of attention becomes the objective configuration of political institutions.

It becomes clear why Hegel insists on the fact that, in order to find a remedy against the widespread poverty in Ireland, it is not enough to resort to the "moral means of protests, exhortations, associations among individuals." First of all, it is necessary to carry out a "change of institutions," "laws and relationships" (*B.schr.,* 466 and 479). Appeals to morality make little sense or are hardly relevant, since we are not dealing with "the blame of one individual or another." Stress must be placed on a "change in the general situation" (*Änderung des allgemeinen Zustands; Rph.,* § 57 *AL; v.Rph.,* II, 243), and therefore, on political transformation.

The French Revolution, with the hopes it stirs, brings about a shift of priorities in Kant, as well. In *Foundations of the Metaphysics of Morals,* Kant claimed that "nothing unconditionally good can be conceived except for *good will,*" which must be recognized and appreciated regardless of its "capacity to achieve the goals it sets for itself."[47] After 1789, Kant's statements seem to argue for the centrality of politics, even with respect to morality, which cannot "be expected to produce a good State constitution." On the contrary, "it is above all from a good State constitution that one can expect a good moral education of its people."[48] By relying on morality alone, "nothing will be achieved" (*ist nichts auszurichten*).[49]

Certainly, Kant has never been the philosopher of an exemplary or politically-harmless morality. "Good will" must not be confused with inert indulgence in velleities: in order to be genuine, in fact, it must "resort to all means that are in our power."[50] The fact that Kant's morality is built on the category of universality already reveals precise political implications capable of questioning the existing political order (infra, ch. XIII, 1). Not by chance, Kant had already stated several years before the French Revolution that "people always speak of virtue, but in order to be virtuous, it is necessary first of all to eliminate injustice. . . . Every virtue is impossible without this decision."[51] And yet, in defending the French Revolution, Kant is undoubtedly forced to criticize the classic argument of conservative ideology, an argument that aims at belittling the importance of the objective transformation of political institutions compared to the moral change "within the inner man" (in interiore homine). Conservative ideology contrasts the "good will" of the monarch to the political definition, claimed by the Revolutionary and constitutional movement, of his "legal duties."[52] This ideology also denies the possibility of a "republican constitution" based on the fact that its functioning would require a people to possess great moral qualities, and even to be made up of "angels." Kant's answer to this is quite significant: a "morally good man," "moral inwardness" (das Innere der Moralität) is not a necessary requirement for a good "State constitution"; on the contrary, "as hard as it may sound, the problem of setting up a state can be solved even by a nation of devils (so long as they possess understanding)."[53] On the one hand, conservative ideology tends to shift its focus from the political sphere to the sphere of moral inwardness (of the monarch or his subjects), in order to deny the need for and usefulness of political-institutional change. On the other hand, in order to defend the French Revolution and justify the need for a "republican constitution," Kant cannot but emphasize politics and go so far as to argue for the primacy of politics.

When Rosenkranz later affirms that "we no longer live with Kant in the century of the philosopher-king (roi-philosophe), but with Hegel in the century of politics," he is certainly right.[54] Not by chance, in fact, Hegel cites Napoleon who, during a conversation with Goethe, claimed that "ancient fate has been replaced by politics" (W, XII, 339). However, Rosenkranz is perhaps guilty of concentrating too much on Kant's writings prior to the outbreak of the French Revolution. As for Kant's later works, we can instead notice a certain agreement with Hegel. Perpetual Peace emphasizes the political irrelevance of a single monarch's moral qualities: an excellent emperor like Marcus Aurelius was followed by an unworthy one like Commodus. This would not have happened had there been a just "constitution" (Staatsverfassung), a constitution which, on a political level, is more relevant than the moral qualities of an individual monarch.[55] Hegel uses the same example:

Yes, Marcus Aurelius behaved, even in his private life, as a noble and honest man. And still, this emperor-philosopher was not able to change the conditions of the Roman Empire, and nothing prevented his successor, whose temperament was quite different, from causing as much harm as his will and evilness could contrive. Well above all this is the inner principle of the Spirit, of rational will, which manages to come about so that a public life governed by reason, and a condition founded on right and organization, can start to exist . . . This creates a system of ethical relationships; the duties (*Pflichten*) that emerge are part of a system; every precept has its own place, each one is subordinate to the other, and the superior one dominates all others. Therefore, moral conscience (*Gewissen*) . . . is bound, and objective relationships that we call duties remain valid not only on a legal level, but also in moral conscience as solid conclusions (*w*, XIX, 294–95).

9. Morality, Ethicality, and Modern Freedom

This does not mean that morality has been dethroned: moral subjectivity is an integral part of the "right to subjective freedom," which in turn is an integral and irreplaceable part of modern ethicality. In this sense, "morality" and "moral conscience" constitute the "principle of civil society"; they are "moments of political constitution" (*Rph.*, § 124 A). Morality is not being disparaged. On the contrary, Hegel's opinion of morality is so high that, in *Philosophy of Right*, he compares the "alienation of intelligent rationality, morality, ethicality, and religion" to slavery (*Rph.*, § 66 A).

Precisely for this reason, the diverse ways in which Hegel comes to perceive morality become clearer. Morality is no longer an assemblage of eternal values, but it has a history that coincides with the history of modern freedom itself. Not by chance, the principle of "infinite subjectivity and freedom of self conscience emerges for the first time with Socrates, who should therefore not be considered a "teacher of morality" (*moralischer Lehrer*), as if morality were something eternal, but as the "*inventor* of morality" (*w*, XII, 329). Not only are the contents of moral conscience a historical achievement, but so too is the image of moral conscience: "The Greeks had no moral conscience" (*Gewissen*) in the sense that their society identified with the existing laws and customs. As a result, the "reflection" and "separation of inwardness" that constitute moral conscience did not occur (*v.G.*, 263). Together with "morality" and "moral conscience," another historical achievement is "the moral man" (*der moralische Mensch*; *w*, XII, 329), that is, the man who is able to transcend objectivity through the self-reflection and inwardness of his own conscience.

The invention of "morality," "moral conscience" and the "moral man" is at the same time the invention of freedom. This invention has a double meaning: in a strong, modern sense of the term, freedom implies an overcoming of the immediate identification of subjectivity with political objectivity. Subjectivity now acquires an autonomous space of moral reflection that introduces an element of tension and uncertainty to the relationship to objectivity. In this sense, the Greeks who did not know moral conscience (*Gewissen*) did not know freedom either (*v.g.*, 263); freedom as self-reflection was unknown even to free men. Yet, another point should be made: in order for a more rigorously defined morality to develop as a discourse addressed, at least potentially, to all mankind, it is necessary to acknowledge, in every human being, the dignity of a moral subject, capable of self-reflection and entitled to freedom. In ancient times, slaves were regarded as instruments of labor, and therefore they were not included in the category of man. This made the establishment of moral universality impossible. From this point of view, Socrates was not so much the "inventor" *tout court* of morality. Rather, he merely constituted a step, though a step of great importance, in the realization of morality, a process no less laborious and complex than the historical realization of the universal concept of man.

The discovery of moral subjectivity, human dignity, and man's freedom can no longer be forgotten. From the perspective of this historical achievement, one can say that India—where castes are naturalistically established, where no dignity is conferred on lower caste individuals and on women, who are forced to throw themselves on the pyre to follow their dead husbands—lacks "the moral element (*das Moralische*) that resides in the respect for human life" (*w*, xii, 188). Yet, for this very reason, India also lacks "ethicality and human dignity" (*w*, xii, 185). Modern ethicality now requires the legally-sanctioned acknowledgment of moral subjectivity as a citizen's essential right. Precisely because this acknowledgment regards every man as a moral subject and has as its object a right to be enjoyed not only within the intimacy of one's conscience, but also in a concrete public space, some general laws are necessary. In the course of his daily activities, the individual-citizen cannot absolutize his contingent moral intentions, but he must behave according to objective laws that have somehow incorporated the moral element.

Of course, some situations of sharp conflict can occur: these are "epochs when what is recognized as right and good (*das Gute*) in practice and custom is unable to satisfy the better will (*den besseren Willen*). When the existing world of freedom has become unfaithful to the better will, this will must seek to recover in ideal inwardness alone that harmony which it has lost in actuality" (*rph.*, § 138 A). In other words, as in Socrates' time, what could occur is a "break with actuality" on the part of moral subjectivity, a subjectivity that ends up acting, directly or objectively, in a "Revolutionary" direction (w, XII, 329). Thus, deprived of a conscious support of moral subjectivity, the existing ethicality is reduced to "empty appearance" (as happens with the Roman State on the eve of what Hegel defines as the Christian "Revolution"), that is to say, ethicality turns into its opposite: to the "self-consciousness" of French Enlightenment, the political situation of the time, the *ancien régime*, appears as "an alien essence"; we are on the eve of a revolution that develops also as a result of the "rebellion against the lack of ethicality" (*Unsittlichkeit*; w, XX, 291 and 296).[56]

The break or separation from political actuality caused by the fact that moral subjectivity no longer recognizes itself in the existing ethicality is legitimate only to the extent that it constitutes a transitory phase. In other words, it must represent a stimulus to create a richer ethical and political order. On the contrary, Hegel accuses the "perennial obligation" (*perennierendes Sollen*), which the "merely moral point of view" indulges (*Rph.*, § 135 A), of being guilty not only of political ineffectiveness, but also of moral insincerity. In these moments of crisis, the tragic figure of a hero can become relevant again. However, a hero is not relevant only to the extent to which he expresses, at his own risk, an objective need of his time and of the men of his time, but also to the extent to which he can satisfy this need, creating a new, richer ethicality that in turn makes the figure of the hero superfluous. In this sense, Hegel could have exclaimed with Brecht, "Blessed are the peoples who need no heroes," even though the heroes' actions, in tragic situations of crisis, can reveal themselves to be necessary and beneficial. And Hegel could have easily shared Brecht's aspiration to create an objective order that would make "toilsome virtues" superfluous, even though, once again, practicing these virtues can become necessary and even commendable in tragic moments of crisis and in turning points.[57] However, the break or separation from political reality continues to be legitimate only to the extent that it constitutes a transitory phase: it must represent a stimulus to create a richer ethical and political order.

10. Hegel's Ethical Model and Contemporary Actuality

The centrality of ethical institutions in Hegel's thought does not signify the untranscendibility of positive law. We have already examined Hegel's theorization of *Notrecht*, and it is easy to glimpse a moral motivation behind his criticism of the legal system, and in his denunciation of the "extreme wrong" or wrongdoing (*höchstes Unrecht*) perpetrated on the hungry (*v.Rph.*, III, 403). The moral pathos is just as evident in his condemnation of the "abstract intellectual's" demand to sacrifice the hungry for the sake of respecting the right to property and formal right as such; a demand that Hegel considers "revolting to every man" (v.Rph., IV, 341–42). And yet, one must move beyond that point, the point of a merely moral protest and casuistic discussions of cases in which a violation of the right to property might be lawful or tolerated. We know that what is "important belongs to the ethical, universal life," and that "man's great interests, his true relationships, belong to the sphere of ethicality. His moral interests and relationships are only elements" (Abschnitzel; Rph., § AL; v.Rph., II, 459).

Once again, Hegel's position remains opposed to the tradition that descends from Stahl, through Schleiermacher, to liberals like Rotteck, Hansemann, and Spencer. This tradition condemns any objective, ethical solution (in the Hegelian sense of the term) as a humiliating and depersonalizing coercion, and contrasts it to a "solution" based on the individual's free will and moral conscience. If in progressive industrial countries the social question has for the most part lost its earlier dramatic character (though there are signs of a possible reversion), this has happened because the position held by the liberal tradition has been questioned. Thus, Hegel and the others who criticized such positions were historically right. Even Popper is forced to acknowledge this fact. Popper never ceases to denounce the "statism" of this presumed enemy of the "open society," but then he describes the progress that had taken place in the Western world during the last decades in these terms: in Vienna there was a "terrible poverty . . . , an enormous number of unemployed people, and no form of unemployment or sickness compensation—*only private organizations* to help the homeless and orphans . . . *But the State did not participate in them directly.*" It was therefore state intervention that led "the Western hemisphere" so close "to Paradise."[58] The portrait given by Popper is certainly a little too idyllic. Moreover, it attributes the merit of the current semi-heavenly conditions to State intervention only, and passes over the pressures coming from civil society as well as the harsh social struggles that required the intervention of political power in the economy. In so doing, this portrait runs the risk of paving the way for a much more fanatic "statism" than the one for which Hegel is criticized.

At any rate, the desperate want and the risk of starvation which Hegel discusses in *Philosophy of Right* are present today, especially outside progressive industrial societies. It remains to be seen whether the ethical model can be usefully applied to Third World countries, by intervening, first of all, in the objectivity of the international economic order, regarding the terms of trade, etc. Of course, this issue is completely new compared to Hegel's text and its time, and yet it is very compatible with the essence of Hegel's philosophy. One of his statements, however, is quite striking and worth reflecting upon: "The welfare (*Wohl*) of everyone is an empty expression. . . . How can I promote the welfare of the Chinese, of those who live in the Kamchatka peninsula? The Holy Scriptures are more rational than this when they affirm: love thy neighbor as thyself, that is, love the people with whom you already have or with whom you can establish a relationship. To say *everyone* is empty pomposity that only serves to puff up the idea" (*v.Rph.*, IV, 338). Should we then say that Hegel's philosophy is not able to "universalize the love for one's neighbor in the direction of the love for those who are further away"?[59] This would be a hasty conclusion. First of all, we must not forget that today the world is much more united and interdependent than it was over one hundred and fifty years ago. It is especially important not to lose sight of the concrete target of Hegel's criticism. This target is certainly not the universal concept of man. On the contrary, according to Hegel's philosophy, the establishment of this concept constitutes historical progress.[60] Not by chance, Hegel sees the "greatness of the business class" (*Handelsstand*) reflected in its "cosmopolitan" character (*v.Rph.*, IV, 520). Yes, "through commerce the representation of man's universality springs forth, and the particularity of nations, of their customs and culture, disappears. What remains is the universal concept that all strangers are men" (*Rph. III*, 200). The real target of this polemic is once again the "welfare" (of neighbors or of those who are further away) claimed by a moral intention that locks itself up in a self-sufficient and self-satisfied narcissism. In reality, Hegel's explicit target is the "edifying" discourse that does not even consider the problem of giving an ethical and political concreteness to the moral demands it expresses. Hegel's polemic targets the reduction of morality to a "private" and "politically helpless" intention, something that Apel also criticizes.[61] Hegel also attacks the "edifying" discourse from a moral standpoint: this discourse is internally inconsistent and characterized by "particularity," despite the noble sentiments it displays.

Once again, the search for a concrete universality takes us back to politics. The theorist of the primacy of politics and ethicality is well aware of the problem, or rather, of the moral torment caused by the interconnection of opulence and want that characterizes the modern industrial world (supra, ch. VII, 10). Despite the colossal changes that have taken place since then, Hegel's position still remains valid. According to Hegel, the seriousness and sincerity of this moral torment can be measured by the effort made to create a new ethical situation within which the appeal to the good will and to the moral conscience of an individual (or even of a whole class of wealthy individuals or rulers of wealthy countries) becomes superfluous or plays a secondary role.

XI

Legitimacy of the Modern and Rationality
of the Actual

1. The "*Querelle des Anciens, des Modernes*,"
. . . and of the Ancient Germans

Looking back to ancient Greece, Schelling mourns "the waning of the most noble humanity that ever flourished" (supra, ch. VIII, 1). The nostalgia for the *Antike* and the sense of uneasiness about modern developments is strongly rooted in the German culture of the time. Here is where Kant's polemic takes shape: Kant criticizes the "silly folly" of attributing to the ancient, "for the sake of ancient times per se, a greater talent and good will than the modern," as if the world were continuously decaying from its original perfection. Thus, he criticizes the folly of "despising everything that is new compared to what is ancient."[1] Later, in the *Logik*, Kant denounces what he defines as the "prejudice in favor of ancient times" which despises the present and insists on "chasing the intellect back to the years of its infancy."[2]

During this period, a sort of renewed *querelle des anciens et des modernes* develops in Germany: Kant himself cites Bernard le Bovier de Fontenelle. Hegel, too, supports modernity explicitly. Already at Berne, he repeatedly refers to the "progress of reason" (*w*, 1, 56), and attributes to "philosophy" (that is, to the *philosophes*) and to the "most humble light of our time" (the diffusion of the Enlightenment) the merit of having "improved our morals" and of having overcome or questioned "intolerance" and superstition (*w*, 1, 45–46). The elaboration of a theory of history as progress implies a justification of the modern world. In Berlin, Hegel writes: "That which the Spirit has conquered during our time is not to be belittled as something trivial. We must certainly pay respect to ancient times and to their necessary contribution as one of the rings of a sacred chain. But that is only *one* ring. The present is the highest thing" (*w*, xx,

456). And in a letter to Victor Cousin he writes: "Should we consider the modern inferior to the ancient? In many respects, undoubtedly. But as far as depth and width of principles, we are on the whole on a higher level" (B, III, 223). Thanks to its capacity to penetrate the depth of "inwardness" and objective conscience, the "modern Spirit" must be considered superior to the "ancient Spirit" (Enc., § 396 Z; W, X, 82). Hegel tirelessly insists on extolling the "greatness of our time" (W, XX, 329) and the "Spirit of modern times" (W, XX, 518), and on the ineluctability and irreversibility of the "point of view of our time" (v.Rph., IV, 923 and 924).

On German soil especially, the condemnation of the modern world comes not only from those who feel nostalgia for ancient times, but also from those who feel nostalgia for the German Middle Ages. From the time of the resistance to French expansionism and the Napoleonic wars, the German Middle Ages underwent an exalted transformation. With soft and attractive colors, these enthusiasts of medieval times had painted the lost simplicity of customs that characterized the ancient Germans, their scorn for material comfort, their patriarchal, religious concept of life, their sense of honor, the rich personal relationship between individuals, the chivalry, the crusades, that whole world that had been tragically swept away by the advent of a dreary, arid, mechanical modernity; selfish, vulgarly utilitarian and banausic, a modernity which in the final analysis had destroyed the most profound values.[3] Heine's comment about August Wilhelm Schlegel can be applied to very large sectors of the culture of the time: in his eyes, "that which is modern existence" appears as "banal," or rather, as "a vacuous grin."[4]

2. Rejection of Modernity, Cult of Heroes, and Anti-Hegelian Polemic

In contrast, Hegel's affirmation of the actuality of the rational and the rationality of the actual is the final philosophical legitimation of the present. Not by chance, the Preface to *Philosophy of Right* harshly criticizes those who despise and belittle "the present as something vain" (W, VII, 25). This does not remain unnoticed by Hegel's contemporaries, and in fact we have seen how Stahl criticizes Hegel and his school because the latter use the presence of reason in universal history as a starting point, and view the superiority of modernity over the Middle Ages as something obvious (supra, ch. II, 1). Even leaving aside the conservative Stahl, we also see that in other authors, the condemnation of modernity often goes hand in hand with a harsh criticism of Hegel's theory of the unity of rational and actual, and particularly against Hegel's affirmation of the rationality of the actual.

Schopenhauer's position, one that heavily influenced the young Nietzsche, is that Hegel's philosophy of history and the State expresses "the dreariest philistinism" by sanctioning the legitimacy of modernity and the present time (*Jetztzeit*).[5] For Nietzsche, in fact, to accept the theory of the rationality of the actual is equal to "bending one's back and bowing one's head before the 'power of history.'" In this sense, it is equal to letting oneself go to the "naked admiration of success" and to the "idolatry of *faits accomplis*."[6] According to the young Nietzsche, who is beginning to radically question the legitimacy of modernity, the theory of the rationality of the actual cannot but appear as the apotheosis of philistinism. Why should the historical process that goes from Christianity to the French Revolution and that led to the rebellion of the slaves be considered irreversible? "Why should a couple of millennia (or, in other words, thirty-four consecutive human lives, each calculated as sixty years long)" make us resign to the waning of the splendid culture of ancient Greece, a culture founded upon the open acknowledgment of slavery and servile labor for the majority of people?[7]

To acknowledge and legitimize a presumed "power of history" is the same as bowing, "in a Chinese-like, mechanical fashion . . . , to every power, be it a government, a public opinion, or a numerical majority."[8] The relationship between the furious polemic against Hegel's *Philosophy of History* and the antimodern, antidemocratic pathos emerges here in all its clarity. The expression used by Nietzsche, *chinesehaft*, is particularly significant: in the following years, the Chinese will become, in Nietzsche's eyes, the symbol of the humble, helpful, and servile workers who are so useful to their masters. So much so that, according to Nietzsche, if it is not possible to import such human material from far-away Asia, then it will be necessary to transform European workers into a "Chinese-like work force" (*Arbeiter-Chinesenthum*).[9] It is clear: bowing to the "power of history" is for servants, not for masters. The theory of the rationality of the actual and of historical progress represents the very same cult of numerical majority that is expressed in democracy and in the rising presence and pressure of the masses. These masses, who are already expressing their numerical power politics, manage to obtain a precious and unacceptable recognition also on the level of the philosophy of history, thanks to a perspective which, by proclaiming the rationality of the actual, excludes *a priori* any attempt to retreat from the achievements of the modern world. On the one hand, Hegel condemns and derides what he sees as a quixotic attempt to reintroduce slavery into Europe (supra, ch. ɪɪ, ɪ). On the other hand, for Nietzsche the institution of slavery is still valid, and a more or less long historical period can prove nothing against it. And while for Hegel the theory of the rationality of the actual is strictly linked to his affirmation of the legitimacy of modernity and its superiority over ancient times, for Nietzsche anti-Hegelian criticism goes hand in hand with an implacable denunciation of modernity and the present (*Jetztzeit*).[10]

To the "apologists of history,"[11] Nietzsche contrasts the "metaphysics of genius," and he disdainfully rejects any vision of history that "democratizes the rights of the genius."[12] Already at the end of the eighteenth century, within the early German conservatism, the theme of the "genius" had emerged in opposition to the "despotism" of "mediocrity," sanctioned by the predominance, in the modern word, of "general" leveling rules (infra, ch. xiii, 1). And the French Revolution had been accused by the conservative and reactionary political press of harboring hatred for "genius" and of being "disrespectful toward great [historical] figures."[13] Even after the 1848 Revolution, Engels argues against Thomas Carlyle mocking the ideology that tries to transform the dominant class into one that "participates in the genius," while justifying the condition of the oppressed class by presenting it as "excluded from the genius."[14] In *Untimely Meditations* (*Unzeitgemäße Betrachtungen*), Nietzsche highlights yet another democratic aspect of Hegel's philosophy of history by contrasting it to the "metaphysics of the genius." Hegel's well-known remark is not meant to negate the primacy of the rational over the actual, and thus the human subject's planning and transforming action.[15] However, this action no longer has anything to do with the creation *ex nihilo* of new values and ideals, but it has turned into an apparently more modest and prosaic task: it must first of all be able to grasp and express the negativity and the contradictions present in objectivity. Clearly, from this perspective there is no room for the "metaphysics of the genius," and the great historical figures themselves "*seem* to draw exclusively from themselves," they "*seem*" to be carrying out a task that is merely "their own." In reality, according to Hegel, they reveal themselves to be genuinely great to the extent to which they can unearth "the truth of their time and their world" (*w*, xii, 46). One can understand, therefore, why Nietzsche denounces Hegelian thought as the triumph of "philistine reason" (*Philister-Vernunft*).[16]

One of the targets of Hegel's theory of the unity of the rational and the actual is the moral duty (*Sollen*) extolled by Kant's and Fichte's philosophy. In Fichte especially, *Sollen* is embodied in the figure of a sort of intellectual-demiurge, who rises above the common conscience and becomes "the salt of the earth" (supra, ch. vi, 5). Carlyle gives this image of the intellectual a "heroic" interpretation:

> To the mass of men no such Divine Idea is recognizable in the world; they live merely, says Fichte, among the superficialities, practicalities and shows of the world, not dreaming that there is anything

divine under them. But the Man of Letters is sent hither specially that he may discern for himself, and make manifest to us, this same Divine Idea: in every new generation it will manifest itself in a new dialect, and he is there for the purpose of doing that. Such is Fichte's phraseology, with which we need not quarrel. It is his way of naming what I here, by other words, am striving to imperfectly to name . . . Fichte calls the Man of Letters, therefore, a Prophet, or as he prefers to phrase it, a Priest, continually unfolding the God-like to men: Men of Letters are a perpetual Priesthood . . . In the true Literary Man there is thus ever, acknowledged or not by the world, a sacredness: he is the light of the world; the world's Priest,—guiding it, like a sacred Pillar of Fire, in its dark pilgrimage through the waste of Time.[17]

Certainly, Carlyle lacks the progressive socio-political contents that characterize Fichte's pathos of the intellectual (the contrast of the intellectual to the property-owner and the criticism of the socio-political order). What remains in Carlyle is only the cult of the "priest" and the "hero" in opposition to the heathen, vulgar masses. And yet, this cult of heroes developed from the starting point of the pathos exalted by *Sollen.* Hegel recognizes and criticizes the aristocratic and elitist implications inherent in *Sollen,* and, even in the Preface to *Philosophy of Right,* he emphasizes the necessity for philosophers to understand the reasons of common or "ingenuous" conscience (*w,* vii, 25).

3. Kant, Kleist, Schopenhauer, and Nietzsche

It is therefore easy to understand why Hegel becomes the main target of the criticism of the modern world; a world that Kant himself had defended. However, Kant's thought is somehow used by the young Nietzsche in his antimodern polemic. To the standardized mediocrity of the present, Nietzsche, the theorist of untimeliness (*Inaktualität*), contrasts not only the "metaphysics of the genius," but also the "morals," that require people to swim "against the tide of history."[18] This statement may sound paradoxical coming from an author whose philosophy is becoming synonymous with immoralism. Yet, its meaning is clear: it is in fact directed against a political vision or a perspective on the philosophy of history which forgets that, when faced with the rare geniuses, very few "have the right to live (*Recht zu leben*)." Therefore, such vision or perspective would legitimize philosophically the democratic elimination of the "rights of the genius" that has occurred in the modern world. On the contrary, according to the young Nietzsche, the fact "that the majority live while those few [geniuses] no longer survive is but a brutal truth, an irreparable foolishness, a clumsy 'this is the case' ('es is einmal so') in opposition to the moral imperative 'it should not be the case' ('es sollte nicht so sein'). Yes, in opposition to morals!"[19] Nietzsche's language is surprisingly Kantian. The rhetoric of Sollen, of moral duty, is summoned here to found an aristocratic vision of history and politics, to provide them once again with that cult of genius that Hegel had rejected. Appealing both to the "metaphysics of the genius" and to its corollary, the rhetoric of Sollen, the young Nietzsche denies the mass of mediocrities, already on the level of the philosophy of history, the very same right to life which Hegel had ended up affirming even on a strictly political level.

We should point out the fact that Kant's morals are based on the pathos of universality and therefore, in the final analysis, of an essential equality among men (infra, ch. XIII, 1). Therefore, they have nothing to do with morals turned into an instrument to legitimize the "rights of the genius." Nietzsche himself realizes this very soon: as his philosophical thought develops, he denounces the democratic, leveling implications of any universalist morals, and he thus includes the author of Critique of Practical Reason among the despised "laborers of philosophy" (supra, ch. VI, 5). However, the fact remains that, when pushed to the limit, the dichotomy of "is" and "ought" encourages flight from political reality, and prevents one from finding one's place in the modern world. The modern world is in fact condemned by large sections of the culture and political press as arid and irreparably dead to the demands of the Spirit (and morals).

We can now better understand why Hegel deems Kant's philosophy guilty of encouraging, or at least of not being able to prevent, an escape from mundane and political actuality, and therefore from modernity. We can reach the same conclusion if we move from pure to practical reason and examine the dialectics that develop starting with the dualism between appearance and actuality rather than that between "is" and "ought." We can start from two letters written by Heinrich von Kleist, who describes his own reaction to the reading of Critique of Pure Reason as such: "Ever since the conviction that no truth can be found down here [on earth] has occurred to me, I have stopped reading books altogether. I have wandered lazily around my room, I have been sitting by the window, I have gone outside, while a profound restlessness has led me into small and large cafés; I have gone to theaters and concerts to find some relaxation, I have even done something foolish just to dull my senses . . . ; and yet, the only thought that has stirred my soul in the midst of that outward tumult and burning anguish is always the same: your spirit, your highest goal, has collapsed."[20] In another letter, Kleist writes: "I seem to be a victim of folly, one of the many that weigh on the conscience of Kantian philosophy. This society repels me, and yet I cannot break free from its ties. The thought that on this earth we can know nothing, absolutely nothing about truth . . . , this thought has shaken the sanctuary of my soul. My only goal, my highest goal, has collapsed, and I am left with nothing."[21]

Of course, here, too, Kant cannot be charged for the interpretation that the tragic Romantic poet gives to his thought. Yet, it is quite significant that the young Nietzsche turns a "Kantian" Kleist into one of the great interpreters of the principle of untimeliness (*Inaktualität*) and one of the protagonists in the struggle against modernity. On the level of pure reason, appearance plays the same role that "is" plays on the level of practical reason: both represent the banausic sphere which perfectly fits the common, standardized conscience that has prevailed in the modern world. On the one hand, in affirming the unity of the actual and the rational, Hegel intended to warn against the "hypochondria" of those who "are not able to overcome their aversion to actuality" and who, all caught up in their "sadness for the collapse of their ideals," become "tedious and peevish about the condition of the world" (*Enc.*, § 396; *w*, x, 84–85). On the other hand, the young Nietzsche sees that the noble souls who refuse to adapt to a mediocre, philistine actuality feel enveloped "in a cloud of melancholy," which is a sign of their greatness.[22] For this reason, the inclusion of Kleist in the empyrean of "those who do not feel citizens of their own time" goes hand in hand with the criticism of Hegel's theory according to which everyone is "a child of his own time" (*w*, vii, 26).[23] To this, Nietzsche adds: "Even though every great man is usually considered an authentic child of his own time . . . , the struggle fought by such a great figure *against* his own time is only apparently a senseless, destructive struggle against oneself. Precisely, it is only apparently so, since in this struggle he is fighting against what prevents him from being great."[24]

In addition to Kleist's "Kantianism," the passionate theorist of untimeliness (*Inaktualität*) attributes to Schopenhauer the merit of engaging in an exemplary battle to keep away or to expel any trace of "actuality" from himself. "Ever since his youth, he [Schopenhauer] resisted against that false, vain and unworthy mother, his era, and, almost expelling it from himself, he cleansed and healed his own being, and found himself in the health and purity that suited him."[25] This merit is attributed first of all to the author of *The World as Will and Representation*, who, even before Nietzsche, had radicalized Kant's distinction between truth and appearance and turned it into a weapon in the struggle against the philistinism of a modernity banally content with appearance.

According to Schopenhauer, the most notable and therefore most despicable representative of this banausic modernity is once again Hegel who, with his philosophy of history and the importance he attributed to history, "mistakes appearance for essence." Hegel's philosophy has no longer anything to do with idealism, but it is merely "shallow realism."[26] It is typical of "philosophers and worshipers of history to be unilateral realists, and therefore optimists and eudaemonists," and to forget that "constitutions and legislations," that is, "steam engines and the telegraph," all that constitutes the pride of modernity, are merely an event that belongs to the realm of appearance and that can never bring about any change or actual improvement for mankind.[27] With its philosophy of history and its celebration of political and economic modernity, Hegel's school of thought encourages an attachment to the present and to "material interests, including the political ones," and it stifles any "enthusiasm for something noble."[28] In this manner, young people become corrupted and poisoned since, under the influence of Hegel's pernicious and plebeian philosophy, they end up embracing "the most shallow, philistine, vulgar attitude, and they abandon the noble, elevated thoughts that used to energize their closest ancestors."[29] In short, we are in the presence of a perspective on the world and life that, at best, works on the level of the most banal, common conscience of the man-in-the-street and on the level of his daily life (*Alltagskopf*), in irreparable opposition to the genius which, even before Nietzsche, Schopenhauer had contrasted to the philistinism and standardization of the modern world.[30]

Hegel's notorious remark is directed against those who consider the ethical-political world as "*gottverlassen*" (*w*, VII, 16), that is, forsaken by God and therefore incapable of embodying authentic spiritual values. But if, rather than by God, the ethical-political world is regarded as abandoned by moral duty (*Sollen*), by practical or theoretical truth, and is in fact the irreparable antithesis of it, the result is quite similar: it is difficult to recognize oneself and to feel comfortable in the modern world, and the effort to solve the problems that the modern world poses appears equally vain.

4. Modernity and the Uneasiness of the Liberal Tradition

Hegel's remark, however, is not welcomed by the liberal tradition either, at least to the extent to which it faces the developments of the modern world with uneasiness, obsessiveness, and at times even with anguish. Burke clearly expresses a nostalgic idolization of the good old times, of the era of "ancient chivalry" to which, as a result of the French Revolution, the era "of sophisters, economists, and calculators has succeeded," so that "the glory of Europe is extinguished forever."[31] The uprisings in France make the *deprecatio temporum* that characterizes Burke so sharp and tormented that he does not hesitate to define his own time as the "most unenlightened age, the least qualified for legislation that perhaps has been since the first formation of civil society."[32]

The menacing advance of mediocrity in the modern world is a recurring theme in the liberal tradition. We find it also in Wilhelm von Humboldt, who claims that, as the government sphere becomes wider, "excellent minds are turned away from thinking," and are instead compelled to follow a mechanical routine, while the influence of the growing bureaucratization negatively affects the "energy of action" and the citizens' "moral character."[33] Over half a century later, John Stuart Mill remarks that "the general tendency of things throughout the world is to render mediocrity the ascendant power among mankind. In ancient history, in the Middle Ages, and in a diminishing degree through the long transition from feudality to the present time, the individual was a power in himself, and if he had either great talents or a high social position, he was a considerable power. At present individuals are lost in the crowd. In politics it is almost a triviality to say that public opinion now rules the world. The only power deserving the name is that of the masses, and of governments which make themselves the organ of the tendencies and instincts of masses."[34] Clearly, given these presuppositions, an author like Mill could never have shared the theory of the rationality of the actual. On the one hand, Mill cites Wilhelm von Humboldt to denounce the process of continuous "assimilation" that characterizes the modern world (which, by destroying the "freedom, and variety of situations," prevents the development of a strong, original individuality).[35] On the other hand, Mill found that familiarity with Hegel tended to "deprave one's intellect."[36]

To the rampant wave of leveling, Mill contrasts a perspective on history that bears some similarities to Carlyle's. Mill regards Carlyle positively or even enthusiastically, and he credits himself with having immediately celebrated, even before the "commonplace critics," Carlyle's "epic poem" on, or rather against, the French Revolution, as "one of those productions of genius which are above all rules, and are a law to themselves."[37] Despite the differences, Mill's position bears some similarities even to Nietzsche's "metaphysics of genius." Nietzsche, however, despises not only Mill—whose cult of heroes he sees as marred by moralism, that is, by a tendency that calls to mind the very rabble (*profanum vulgus*) that it tries to fight—but also and above all utilitarianism and its representatives.[38] In them, Nietzsche detects the banausic stench of hideous modernity,[39] and he condemns their persistent attachment to the "soft, cowardly concept of 'man,'" to a category that irreparably contradicts an aristocratic vision of life.[40]

Yet, Mill too is committed to fighting the standardization of the modern world. In fact, he claims: "The initiation of all wise and noble things, comes and must come from individuals; generally at first from some one individual. The honour and glory of the average man is that he is capable of following that initiative." True, Mill defends himself from the possible accusation of supporting a "cult of heroes," but he still provides a version of it, though a milder and less threatening one, a version that excludes the right to violence and limits itself to claiming, for the "strong man of genius," the "freedom to point out the way" to the masses.[41]

Mill's relationship to Tocqueville is well known; the former credits the latter with exposing the ruinous leveling process that was occurring in his country: according to Mill, Tocqueville shows "how much more the Frenchmen of the present day resemble one another, than did those even of the last generation." But, Mill adds, "the same remark might be made of Englishmen in a far greater degree."[42]

Tocqueville's uneasiness at the developments of the modern world characterizes his thought as a whole: the process that is occurring is simultaneously a leveling and degrading one; mediocrity and exclusive attachment to material pleasure are becoming the main feature of the time. With the advent of democracy, less and less room is devoted to the "splendor," "glory," and even "strength" of a nation.[43] America is an example of this: "His passions, his wants, his education, and everything about him seem to unite in drawing the native of the United States earthward; his religion alone bids him turn, from time to time, a transient and distracted glance to Heaven."[44] Distressing questions emerge from the vision of a country that Tocqueville, on the other hand, indicates as an alternative model to the radical, Jacobin democracy: "Why is it that, when civilization expands, outstanding individuals decrease? Why, when knowledge becomes accessible to everyone, do intellectual talents become rarer? Why, when there are no lower classes, are there no longer upper classes either? Why, when the intelligence of the government reaches the masses, do the great geniuses that should lead society disappear? America faces us with these problems. Who will be able to solve them?"[45]

Like Mill and Nietzsche, Tocqueville also seeks a way out of the mediocrity of the present in the cult of, or nostalgia for, genius—genius which nevertheless seems doomed to extinction in the increasingly standardized world of modernity. "We live in a time and in a democratic society where individuals, even the greatest ones, count for very little."[46] This has become the fate of all countries: "England has become sterile, it has stopped producing great men, just like us."[47] Satisfying our "hunger . . . for greatness" is impossible "in the century we live in," and so Tocqueville turns to ancient times—hence a further similarity to Nietzsche—and the reading of Plutarch.[48] Yet, there remains an uneasiness about the "levelled society" (société nivelée) and the prevailing mediocrity, in comparison to which even war can constitute an antidote.[49] This emerges in a letter written by Tocqueville to a close friend during the international crisis of

1840. In it, Tocqueville confesses: "You know how I welcome great events and how fed up I am with our mediocre democratic and bourgeois soup."[50] Incidentally, for Nietzsche, too, "if we renounce the war, we renounce life on a large scale" and we remain inextricably prisoners to the mediocrity and banality of modernity.[51]

Once the great ideal passions that had characterized the Great Revolution vanish after 1830, Tocqueville sees a "universal shrinking process." The description of Louis Philippe offered by Tocqueville is the portrait of a whole era: "He loved neither literature nor the arts, but he loved industry with a passion. His conversation . . . afforded one the delight that can be found in the pleasures of intelligence, once delicate and lofty sentiments have been eliminated. His intelligence was notable, but it was limited and hindered by a spirit that did not nourish any elevated or profound sentiments. He was enlightened, refined, flexible and resolute; he was interested exclusively in profit."[52] As this passage has showed, Tocqueville, like Nietzsche, regards utilitarianism as the antithesis of the criticism of modernity, a criticism which Mill himself seems to share. Tocqueville laments the fact that the only "dominant passion" of "human activity" is that of "industry."[53] Thus, he nostalgically looks back at the period before the July Revolution, when "material possessions" were not the only preoccupation, when there were not "merely interests, but beliefs."[54] Tocqueville's decision to set the beginning of cultural decline on a specific date calls to mind Jacob Burckhardt, who claims that the world starts to become "more vulgar" after 1830.[55] Burckhardt, the great Hellenist and passionate scholar of classical antiquity was also Nietzsche's "highly-esteemed friend,"[56] and Nietzsche himself declares in turn that he studied at Tocqueville's "school."[57]

5. Philistinism, Statism, and Modern Standardization

Tocqueville regards uneasiness toward the present as a trifle in comparison to the anguish and disgust caused by a frightening future, by the mortal danger of socialism: "the first trait that characterizes all systems that bear the name of socialism is a vigorous, continuous, unrestrained appeal to man's material passions."[58] This tendency seems to aim at hardening and eradicating, once and for all, all "disinterested sentiments," that is, "great sentiments" like the "love of one's country," "the honor of one's country," "virtue," "generosity," and "glory."[59] These sentiments are destined to disappear in the future socio-political order to which the socialists aspire, in their "society of bees and beavers" constituted "more by wise animals than by free and civilized men."[60]

The terms "bees" and "beehive" had already been used by Schopehauer,[61] while Nietzsche prefers to speak of "the ants' riff-raff" (*Ameisen-Kribbelkram*) to indicate the dreaded, hateful "mob hodge-podge" (*Pöbel-Mischmasch*).[62] And just as Tocqueville laments "universal shrinking," in the same way, despite all other differences, the author of *Thus Spoke Zarathustra* denounces the fact that "the earth has become small" and "the time is coming when man will no longer give birth to a star."[63]

A mediocre, satisfied existence within a standardized political community defines the petty mental horizon of the "bees," "beavers," and "ants" of modernity. In Nietzsche's words, "all-too-many are born: for the superfluous the State was invented," that is, for the "all-too-many," those whom the author of *Untimely Meditations* had already denied the "right to life."[64] Throughout Nietzsche's early years into those of his maturity, this criticism of Hegel's philosophy remains constant. Nietzsche indirectly cites Hegel in *Thus Spoke Zarathustra:* not by chance, he has the "new idol" (the State) utter the following: "On earth there is nothing greater than I: the ordering finger of God am I."[65] Analogously, even before Nietzsche, Schopenhauer had drawn a connection between the "beehive," the philistine attachment to the actual and its presumed rationality, "the Hegelian apotheosis of the State," the hedonistic conception of life ('*Gaudeamus igitur!*'), and "communism."[66] The reasoning behind this connection is clear: by making the actual and the State the sphere of rationality, Hegel's philosophy makes any solipsistic escape, any escape from the mundane and the political, impossible, and it opens the door for a conception which Schopenhauer regards as grossly hedonistic, one incapable of keeping the social demands of the underprivileged masses at bay. Tocqueville, too, sees a relation between socialism and the appeal to "man's material passions." Significantly enough, it is on the basis of this relation that he condemns Hegel's philosophy. Tocqueville accuses Hegel of "having originated all the anti-Christian and antispiritualistic schools that have tried to corrupt Germany, and also the socialist school that favored the 1848 disorders," or, more succinctly, he defines Hegelian philosophy as "sensualist and socialist."[67] The conception of the world that Schopenhauer condemns as "realism" or "materialism" and Tocqueville as "sensualism" is denounced by Nietzsche as the ideal of "petty pleasures," that is, the "happiness of the majority," always in connection to the "mob hodge-podge" and the "ants' riff-raff," or the "bees" and "beavers" that constitute the common nightmare of authors otherwise so different.

These differences are not limited to the sphere of political options. For example, while Schopenhauer likens "material interests" to political interests, Tocqueville laments the fact that great ideas have been replaced by a political life that now only revolves around petty social and class interests. Indeed, Louis Philippe, whom he presents as a symbol of the "universal shrinking," is *"incredulous* in matters of religion, like eighteenth century men were, and skeptical in matters of politics, like nineteenth century men are."[68] Yet, these authors share an uneasiness about the development of modernity, and express it in a polemic against Hegelian philosophy or the theory of the rationality of the actual, despite the fact that in some cases they are only indirectly familiar with this philosophy and this theory.

It should also be noted that, in Germany, the earliest liberal critics accuse Hegel's philosophy of favoring a materialistic, hedonistic vision of life. This is how the *Staats-Lexicon* objects to the notorious remark contained in the Preface to *Philosophy of Right:* "Let us use our own time as an example: as is well known, aside from some undeniably good tendencies, the spirit of our time suffers mainly from a one-sided predilection for so-called *material interests.* Must philosophy therefore be content with accepting this bad side of our *Zeitgeist* as *rational,* or shouldn't it, rather, fight it insofar as it can?"[69]

The unity of the rational and the actual seems to do more than merely justify modernity: it seems to justify even the terrible seeds of the future that it apparently contains. It entails, or runs the risk of entailing, even the legitimation of what, following Schelling's influence, is denounced as the "clumsy scandal of Saint-Simonism," that is, a movement that must be condemned as profoundly materialistic and socially subversive.[70] This is why many notable representatives of European liberalism associate Hegel's theory, even when they know it only indirectly, with the threat of socialism. We have observed this in Tocqueville, but the same can be said about Camillo Benso di Cavour, whom Tocqueville had met in Nassau Senior's house.[71] Writing towards the end of 1845, Cavour, a liberal Piedmontese statesman, remarks that socialism comes mainly from "learned Germany." True, Cavour does not mention any names; nevertheless, his questioning of the "metaphysical system of absolute identity," a system characterized by "fatalism," confusion between "fact and right," and therefore by the tendency to justify all that occurs," inevitably calls to mind Hegel. Cavour continues as follows: if "all that occurs is what was meant to occur; and if true wisdom explains everything and dominates everything" and ends up "absolving and justifying everything," then there is no room to condemn, on a moral level, even communism since communism considers fate and historical necessity as its own justifications. This is "why today we see so many communists coming out of German universities, where this dangerous philosophy is professed."[72]

We have seen how Tocqueville condemns Hegel's philosophy as "sensualist and socialist," but in the same letter he accuses Hegel of having been "the protégé of governments, since the political consequences of his doctrine established that all events were respectable and legitimate, and that they deserved obedience for the very fact that they had produced themselves." The editor of the volume in which this letter is contained defines Tocqueville's critical position as "rather curious:" Tocqueville, in fact, seems to criticize Hegel from both the left and the right.[73] This observation is correct, but it is valid in a more general sense. This constant factor has been completely ignored by critics: when Hegel is accused of complying with the socio-political order, which he invariably legitimizes, the actual target is, despite the differences, the threat of socialism. This is the case with Cavour, who points out the fact that German philosophy's legitimation of *faits accomplis* implicitly justifies socialism. And this was the case already with the liberal journal *Staats-Lexicon*, which maintained that the unity of the rational and the actual also legitimated the materialistic ideologies of the present, which in turn were connected to socialism.

This tendency manifests itself even more clearly in authors like Schopenhauer and Nietzsche. We have seen how the former accuses Hegel of articulating a hedonistic conception of life, one dangerously close to that of communism. However, this does not prevent Schopenhauer from commenting scornfully on Hegel's "obsequiousness,"[74] and on his being a "governmental creature" ready to submit philosophy to "State ends."[75] And neither does it prevent him from expressing his agreement with Haym's denunciation of Hegel's "moral wretchedness," that is, his incurable servility.[76] As for Nietzsche, if, on the one hand, he condemns Hegel's theory of the rationality of the actual as an instrument to legitimize success and *faits accomplis*, on the other hand, he somehow relates "communism" to "Hegel's influence" (supra, ch. IX, 7). These remarks are not as contradictory as they appear: a precise logic connects them, and this is revealed in the pages written by Nietzsche, the most radical and brilliant theorist of untimeliness (*Inaktualität*). To affirm the rationality of the actual does indeed correspond to bowing before *faits accomplis*, but *faits accomplis* are those of the "power of history."[77] In this way, modernity is legitimized, and it is legitimized as a process that is somehow still open and laden with further dangers. Hegel's philosophy calls to mind communism and its "culture that conforms to the times" (*zeitgemäße Bildung*) and to modernity, a culture at the service of "usefulness" and "profit." This vision of the world is considered highly suspicious by the liberal journal *Staats-Lexikon* and the liberal thinker Tocqueville, and denounced as banausic and plebeian by Nietzsche. The latter develops his analysis even further, establishing a relationship between the expansion of the state apparatus, increasing bureaucratization, and the success of Hegelian philosophy, a philosophy committed to promoting "the *expansion* of culture in order to have the highest possible number of intelligent clerks," and to the spreading of "general culture," the culture of the masses, which is the presupposition of "communism."[78]

All of this sheds new light on the accusation of "servility" directed against Hegel from the perspective that downright rejects or is more or less uneasy about modernity. According to Schopenhauer, Hegel's philosophy of history and the State expresses "the most shallow philistinism" and even the "apotheosis of philistinism." The reason for this position is certainly the fact that Hegel's philosophy sanctions the legitimacy of modernity and *Jetztzeit*, but also the fact that it sees, in an utterly modern way, "man's position within the State," within the mundane and political community (where individuals come to be squeezed together like bees in a beehive).[79] Hegel's philosophy leads to an "apotheosis of the State," the State that constitutes the premise for "communism," since it is a concentrated expression of modern standardization.[80] In Nietzsche's words, the State is "antithetical" to "genius,"[81] therefore it is only where the State "ends" that one can glimpse "the rainbow and the bridges of the superman (*Übermensch*)."[82]

The accusation of philistinism and servility directed against Hegel is a corollary of general anguish and uneasiness about modernity. It is a corollary of the specter of a beehive State or ant nest which, despite different shadings and intensities, troubles large sectors of contemporary culture.

6. The Rationality of the Actual and the Difficult Balance between Legitimation and Criticism of Modernity

With his notorious remark, Hegel intends neither to deny the primacy of the rational over the actual (which, to the contrary, he explicitly affirms), nor to conceal the conflicts and contradictions of modernity. Hegel is in fact fully aware of these conflicts and contradictions, whereas such awareness is largely absent among the liberals themselves. Despite the contradictions, however, mundane, political actuality is not irremediably impervious to the ideal: on the contrary, it can embody the ideal; in fact the validity and excellence of the latter can be measured by its capacity to share the actual in its own image. At this point, alongside the general uneasiness about modernity, there emerges another reason that explains the liberals' difficulty to accept Hegel's remark. The liberals refuse to regard mass poverty as a social question that does not derive from a natural calamity or from individual irresponsibility, one that questions specific institutions and social relationships. For Hegel, a solution to this issue can be delegated to charity and private morality only on a temporary basis and only in the case of emergency. Whenever the poor are forced to appeal to the moral duty (*Sollen*) of a hypothetical benefactor, the political situation is imperfect, and the actual not yet fully rational. On the contrary, the representatives of the liberal tradition delegate help for the poor to a charity pricked by moral conscience, maintaining that no sociopolitical transformation can institutionalize moral duty (*Sollen*). In other words, they regard moral duty as being in permanent conflict with actuality. For Hegel, instead, the affirmation of the unity of the rational and the actual signifies that, when authentic, moral duty can be institutionalized, and thus rendered almost unnecessary (supra, ch. x, 2–3 and 9).

It is therefore understandable why the theory of the unity of the actual and the rational, which both the reactionaries and the liberals reject, is instead welcomed favorably by the revolutionaries. The political effectiveness that arises from Hegel's remark has been illustrated quite clearly by a representative of the *Junges Deutschland*, Alexander Jung: "The other world that had so far been inaccessible to the Spirit . . . has now become *this* world, a total presence." We can now look with hope toward mundane, political actuality, which is no longer irremediably impervious to reason and the ideal and is therefore no longer abandoned in favor of religious inwardness or a merely solipsistic, consoling morality: "from a distance, nothing is more debilitating than the mere discontent with earth, with time."[83] This is not only Jung's position, but also the young Hegelians', and Marx and Engels's.[84] Far from justifying the Restoration, the affirmation of the unity of the rational and the actual powerfully stimulates the opposition movement during the German *Vormärz*, and is an integral part of the ideological preparation for 1848. This is not only the case in Germany, but also in Italy, where Bertrando Spaventa actively participates in the revolutionary movement, supported also by the idea that "philosophy, a reflection of natural conscience, must be in agreement with experience. What is actual is rational and vice versa."[85]

It is interesting to notice that, even after the failure of the Revolution, far from favoring resignation, Hegel's theory encourages resistance against the triumphant reactionism. Here is what Ferdinand Lassalle writes to his mother from prison: "Either Germany will really go back, once and for all, to the night of the old conditions, and in that case every science will become a lie, every philosophy a mere game of the Spirit, Hegel a madman escaped from the mental hospital, and there will be no more thoughts in the causality of history; or revolution will soon celebrate a new and decisive triumph. The second case is infinitely more likely to happen."[86] Given the strong, strategic meaning which Hegel and his disciples attribute to the term "actuality," its identification with the rational entails reducing the reactionary success to mere empirical existence, to actuality in a merely strategic sense (supra, ch. ii, 1).

Something analogous can be seen in the case of Italy, with Silvio Spaventa, who is incarcerated as a result of the Counter-Revolution and the Bourbons' repression. Spaventa observes: "A providence that sets, as a goal for the world, a perfection that is never meant to be achieved, has no goal at all. Its goal is something that is never meant to be. Therefore, it is not providence. In order for it to be providence, the reason of the world must not only be an *obligation*, but an actual *being*. Otherwise, it is not providence."[87] Not only does the rejection of the moral duty-actuality dichotomy inhibit resignation, it also completely delegitimizes solipsistic escape.

It is in this sense that, after the failure of the 1848 Revolution, Marx repeatedly and forcefully utilizes Hegel's lesson. He draws from both the Preface to *Philosophy of Right* (though he does not cite it explicitly), and from the *Phenomenology*, which he re-reads meticulously, in particular the passages that, through a variety of themes and an ever-new and increased richness of arguments, criticize *Sollen*. This *Sollen* delights itself in its own inner purity and excellence, which it narcissistically enjoys in opposition to the baseness and dullness of actuality and the world's progress. Hegel's philosophy had contributed to the ideological preparation of the 1848 uprisings, functioning as an exciting "algebra of the revolution," to use Aleksandr Herzen's famous expression.[88] Even after the reactionary triumph, the theory of the unity of the rational and the actual blocks the comfortable way out that would lead to "hypochondria" and "melancholy." Instead, it stimulates the revolutionaries to make an active self-criticism and calls on them to interpret their defeat as proof not of the irremediable misery of the actual, but of the theoretical and practical insufficiency of their projects and ideals. The latter must therefore be thought over in depth, so that their excellence in the concrete process of transformation of actuality can be proved.

This is how Marx interprets the lesson of a philosopher whom, at this moment, he regards also as a role model. Therefore, Marx, still a pugnacious revolutionary, writes the following about Arnold Ruge, who has become discouraged and self-pitying: he "was not able to understand Hegel's philosophy," especially the *Phenomenology*, which "always remained for him a book of seven seals." Yet, according to Marx, Ruge "accomplished in himself" a fundamental category: he personified, "with surprising faithfulness, the 'honest conscience,'" and acted like those who, when faced with difficult situations and the failure of certain ideals, first of all reconfirm their "inner sincerity" and assume the "halo of honest intentions," "just as Hegel prophesized in 1806."[89]

Marx reinterprets another figure of the *Phenomenology* in a similar way: that of the "noble conscience" which necessarily turns into its opposite:

indeed, "according to its nature, the noble conscience must in any case find delight in itself" and brag about itself; but then "we see that this conscience is not concerned with that which is most sublime, but with that which is most ordinary, that is, itself."[90] Private conscience, which insists on contrasting the excellence of its inner *Sollen* to the dullness of actuality, always ends up making a terrible impression, not only on a political level, by demonstrating its impotence, but also on a more strictly moral level, by revealing itself as soft, narcissistic, and essentially hypocritical.

Only a decade later—in the meantime Marx has died—Engels continues to draw inspiration, in his political action, from Hegel's criticism of the "beautiful soul:" this soul is incapable of transforming the actual; before the harshness of the actual it withdraws in horror, and to make up for it, it is always ready to pity itself for being "misunderstood" and ignored by the world.[91]

Of course, Hegel's theory of the unity of the rational and the actual has shared the philosophical tradition inaugurated by Marx only to the extent to which the difficult balance between the legitimation of modernity and its critical evaluation, a balance that characterizes Marx and that Marx himself inherited from Hegel, has survived. Once this balance gives out for a series of complex historical reasons, the theory of the unity of the rational and the actual faces a crisis as well. This is what happens, with particular clarity, to the Frankfurt school. In 1932, on the eve of the seizure of power by the Nazis, Horkheimer takes as his starting point the presupposition that "the Spirit can recognize itself neither in nature nor in history," and sees in the second part of Hegel's remark (that which affirms the rationality of the actual) only a "metaphysical transfiguration" of the socio-political order.[92] Certainly, it would have been difficult to keep up that theory at a moment in which the world had come to be, in Horkheimer's words, under "the totalitarian dominion of evil."[93] In turn, Adorno, this time looking also at actual socialism, criticizes "Hegel's mendacious justification of the socio-political order, against which the Hegelian Left had rebelled."[94] Adorno's last remark is incorrect on a historical level, but it can nevertheless be explained by the collapse of the balance between legitimation and criticism of modernity, a balance that supported Hegel's theory and Marx's program.

FOUR

The Western World, Liberalism, and the
Interpretation of Hegel's Thought

XII

The Second Thirty Years War and the "Philosophical
Crusade" against Germany

1. Germans, "Goths," "Huns," and "Vandals"

Toward the end of World War I, an English liberal, Leonard T. Hobhouse, dedicates one of his books to his son, an Air Force lieutenant. In this book, a refutation of the Metaphysical Theory of the State, Hobhouse, who is still in shock because of a bombing carried out by German airplanes over London, denounces Hegel's "false and wicked doctrine" as the ultimate cause, or the starting point, of this tragic event. He continues: "To combat this doctrine effectively is to take such part in the fight as the physical disabilities of middle age allow. . . . With that work began the most penetrating and subtle of all the intellectual influences which have sapped the rational humanitarianism of the eighteenth and nineteenth centuries, and in the Hegelian theory of the God-State all that I had witnessed lay implicit. You may meet his Gothas in mid-air, and may the full power of a just cause be with you. I must be content with more pedestrian methods. . . . At any rate you will bear with you the sense that we are together as of old, in that in our different ways we are both fighters in one great cause."[1]

Over a quarter of a century later, toward the end of World War II, Hayek comments on the catastrophe that had struck Europe and the whole world: "For over two hundred years, English ideas had spread eastward. The kingdom of freedom, which had already been established in England, seemed destined to spread all over the world. However, around 1870, the predominance of these ideas had perhaps reached its maximum expansion. From that moment on, the retreat began, and a different kind of idea (not really a new kind, but rather, an old one) began to advance from the East. England lost its intellectual leadership in the socio-political field, and became an importer of ideas. During the following sixty years, Germany constituted the center from which the ideas that were destined to govern the world in the twentieth century spread eastward and westward."[2] In the history of the interpretation of Hegel's thought, a striking connection emerges from Hobhouse's pugnacious dedication, a connection which continues even today. In the Royal Air Force, Hobhouse's son was fighting, on a military level, the same barbarians whom his father was trying to crush on a philosophical level, that is, the Goths, or, in Boutroux's words, "the descendants of Huns and Vandals."[3]

This conflict is perceived by both sides in essentially religious terms. If in Germany Sombart speaks of a "war" of opposing "creeds,"[4] Boutroux speaks of "a sort of philosophical crusade, in which two opposing conceptions of good and evil and of the human destiny are involved."[5] As for Hobhouse, he describes it as a clash that breaks out in the name of a more or less secularized religion: "Europe has undergone its martyrdom, millions in the service of false gods, other millions in resisting them."[6] Under these conditions, the ideological (or theoretical) debate is but a harsher continuation of the military conflict. We can therefore understand why Hobhouse calls upon his fellow countrymen and the Entente forces not to lose sight of the "original sin which established this worship in Germany," a sin of which Hegel forms an integral part.[7]

2. The Great Western Purge

To speak of a clash of religions is also to speak of a clash of opposing cultures, between civilization and barbarism. According to Hayek, already since Bismarck, Germany had started to adopt a position antagonistic to "Western civilization."[8] And it is still in the name of Western civilization, a synonym for "open society," that Popper also condemns Hegel.[9] It is interesting to notice how, even today, the pathos of the Western world continues to influence negatively the judgment made by various authors about Germany's cultural tradition, its classical philosophy, and particularly about Hegel. Habermas sees Hegel's limitation in his being "extraneous to the Western Spirit."[10] Hella Mandt, a renowned Kantian scholar, goes so far as to claim that not only Kant's and Hegel's political thought, but the whole "bourgeois culture in Germany" is "in stark contradiction to Western thought."[11] The war of religion goes on. Popper regards the synthesis of "individualism" and "altruism," which he celebrates as "the basis of our Western civilization," as a product of the "central doctrine of Christianity."[12] Even earlier, Boutroux had claimed that Germany had not yet completely "converted to the doctrine of the God of love and kindness."[13]

Oddly enough, however, not much thought has been given to defining precisely what the Western world means. Yet, it would be a task worth undertaking, since this category is anything but unambiguous. Obviously, this is not the place to retrace the history of the manifold meanings of this expression. It shall suffice to remember that, in the mid-nineteenth century, according to Edgar Quinet, the Western world included also Russia, one of the "Wise Men," together with England and France, called upon to carry the light of civilization and Christianity to the Orient, through colonization.[14] A few years later, Francis Lieber (an American author also worth mentioning here because he was on good terms with Tocqueville and who, in more recent times, was praised by Hayek in spite of his German origins) extols the expansive vitality of "Western history." Immediately after, he points out that what he means by "Western history" is the history of the "whole portion . . . of humanity," that is, the "race" that dwells on this side of the Caucasus.[15] Lieber's category of Western world is slightly less vast than Quinet's, but definitely larger than that of the authors we mentioned earlier. Essentially, these authors use this category to identify the Western enemies of Germany during the two World Wars, and of the USSR during the Cold War.

Nevertheless, this drastic and hardly justified restriction does not manage to confer the necessary clarity and unambiguousness on the category of Western world. In order to see how it is used in a heavily ideological sense, we only need note that Popper speaks, without distinction, of "Western world," and "Western hemisphere," as that which comprises those "vast areas of our planet" that by now live "in a sort of garden of Eden," in a condition that is the closest possible "to Paradise" (supra, ch. x, 10). In a similar way, Hannah Arendt writes that "human life has been stricken by poverty since time immemorial, and mankind continues to labor under this curse in all countries outside the Western Hemisphere."[16] At this point, the confusion is extreme. The genesis of the category mentioned here calls to mind American president Monroe, who, in formulating the famous doctrine that bears his name, denies the European powers right to intervene in America, that is, in "this continent" and in "this hemisphere."[17] According to this statement, the Western world does not include Europe, though it does include the Latin American countries despite their tragic conditions of poverty. From this point of view, Popper's and Arendt's claims sound completely absurd, since they use, perhaps carelessly, the expression "Western hemisphere" as a synonym for a political and military alliance, that is, NATO, whose organization is quite different. But in this case, from the Western hemisphere or Western world we should exclude the GDR, which was very active at the time when the two authors made their claim. They include, instead, Turkey, which, out of strategic reasons rather than economic or social ones, was generously made part of that exclusive club that Popper defines as "a sort of garden of

Eden." In short, from time to time the Western world is variously defined in racial, geographic, geo-political, military, or cultural terms, but its concrete extension is never discussed. What remains clear and immutable is merely its function as an ideological interdict, one called upon to condemn and exclude from a communion with Civilization all those who, from time to time and always arbitrarily, are considered alien or hostile to the Western world.

This emerges particularly in Hayek, who proceeds to give a further turn of the screw, banishing from the authentic Western world not only Germany, but also that which he condemns as the " 'French' tradition." What is left, therefore, is the Anglo-Saxon tradition, though Hayek forces it, too, to undergo a strict selection, excluding from it the "enthusiasts for the French Revolution" in England and in America, for example William Godwin, Joseph Priestley, Richard Price, Thomas Paine, and Thomas Jefferson himself, at least the Jefferson who had been fatally contaminated by his "stay in France."[18]

As for Popper, from "Western civilization" or from the Western "open society" he excludes not only Hegel and Marx, but also Plato and Aristotle, all of whom he labels "totalitarians." Another victim of this purging rigor is, to mention a "minor" author, poor Karl Mannheim, who had moved to London to escape Nazism, and who could in no way be suspected of sympathizing with the Soviet Union. Yet, because of Mannheim's rejection of laissez-faire and his insistence upon planning, Hayek includes him, together with Hegel and Marx, among the disastrous Eastern imports,[19] and Popper condemns him as a supporter of a "collectivist and holistic" theory, as well as of a theory of " 'freedom' " . . . which he derives from Hegel."[20]

One might imagine that some agreement would exist at least between these two purgers of the Western world, who are connected to each other in many ways. Yet, it is not so. On the one hand, Hayek constantly praises Burke, whom he defines as "the great seer," and whom he considers one of the fathers of Western civilization.[21] On the other hand, Popper's position on Burke is much more reserved or even downright critical: indeed, Popper points out the influence that the great enemy of the French Revolution bears on Hegel and German Romanticism,[22] and he compares Burke's dangerous influence to that of a notably "totalitarian" philosopher like Aristotle.[23] The contrast between Hayek and Popper is also visible in their perspectives on the French Revolution. Following Burke's lead, Hayek expresses extreme diffidence or even overt hostility towards the French Revolution, which he deems guilty of destroying the intermediate societies between the individual and the State.[24] On the contrary, Popper looks favorably upon the French Revolution, and warmly praises the "ideas of 1789."[25] And this is not all. According to Popper, the synthesis of "individualism" and "altruism," which he celebrates as "the basis of our Western civilization," is a product of the "central doctrine of Christianity." Hayek, on the other hand, views Christianity with suspicion, as becomes clear from the fact that "a large section of the clergy of all Christian denominations" has borrowed the aspiration to "social justice" from socialism: the ruinous motto "social justice," therefore, has become "the distinguishing attribute of a good man, and the recognized sign of the possession of a moral conscience." Unfortunately, "there can be no doubt that moral and religious beliefs can destroy a civilization." "Sometimes saintly figures whose unselfishness is beyond question may become great dangers to the values which the same people regard as unshakable."[26] These words remind us of Nietzsche, even though Hayek, the patriarch of neo-liberalism, seems to lack Nietzsche's intellectual courage and therefore cannot openly proclaim his horror of Christianity. In short, even Hayek and Popper perceive the Western world in two different ways. They both agree that it is synonymous with "individualism"; yet, for Hayek, that which develops out of the French Revolution is only a "false individualism," one alien and even in irreconcilable opposition to the authentic Western world, from which Hayek seems to exclude not only the French Revolution, but also Christianity.[27] Popper, instead, credits Christianity with ultimately inspiring the "ideas of 1789."[28]

The category of Western world is extremely vague and ambiguous, and lends itself to a continuous, endless reinterpretation. Hobhouse uses fiery words against the Goths, and yet he supports a liberalism that, according to Hayek, smacks terribly of socialism, that is, a doctrine which, in all of its various forms, falls among the disastrous Eastern imports.[29] Habermas, too, indulges in the pathos of the Western world, but in Hayek's eyes, he is guilty of normative and constructivist arrogance with regard to the social order, and therefore he reveals himself a typical intellectual of "French and German thought."[30] In other words, Habermas, too, is alien to the authentic Western world, which for Hayek is the Anglo-Saxon one.

It is precisely because of the easy game of reinterpretation that the category of Western world functions as a deadly weapon, one that implacably expels, from the authentic Western world, those elements that from time to time are considered undesirable, a category that makes it possible to indict Germany's cultural and philosophical tradition as a whole. The representatives of this tradition are absolved or condemned depending upon whether or not they are considered worthy of becoming part of the empyrean of the authentic Western world. The punishment can vary over time, but the crime is always the same: the point is always to decide if and to what extent a certain author is guilty of the crime which Habermas defines as being "extraneous to the Western Spirit." During World War I, in the course of his "philosophical crusade" against Germany, Boutroux does not even spare Kant, whom he resolutely includes among the other representatives of the barbarism pouring in from the East.[31] Decades later, Hella Mandt condemns Kant for being "in stark contradiction to Western thought." When, on the other hand, Ralf Dahrendorf claims that Kant "discovered and developed the British tradition for Germany, or rather, for Prussia," it is clear that Kant's redemption is complete, since the philosopher has now become, for all intents and purposes, a citizen of the Western world, and moreover, of the most authentic Western world, the Anglo-Saxon one.[32] Already in 1919, Joseph Schumpeter tried to redeem Kant on the basis of the "British influences" that he seemed to recognize in the thought of the theorist of perpetual peace.[33] Kant is thereby arbitrarily included in the Anglo-Saxon tradition, and becomes the victim of a sort of posthumous *Anschluß*. And this despite the fact that, particularly during the time when he wrote *Perpetual Peace,* Kant had violently criticized the country that led the anti-French and antirevolutionary coalition, and Kant did not hesitate to call the British Prime Minister, William Pitt, "an enemy of mankind."[34] In spite of himself, Kant becomes an honorary citizen of that which Dahrendorf defines as "the blessed island, though not utterly perfect," that is, Great Britain.[35] And this redemption takes place even though Kant considered Great Britain "the most depraved of all nations," a nation which—as proven by its implacable hatred for the new republican France—regarded "other countries and peoples" as mere "appendices" or "instruments" for its will to power.[36]

3. The Transformation of the Liberal Western World

In every war of religion, the elements of demonization, self-justification and hagiography are strictly tied. The irrevocable condemnation of the Orient and Germany's cultural tradition goes hand in hand with the transformation of the liberal tradition, particularly the Anglo-Saxon one. Although we commend the Anglo-Saxon tradition for its struggle against royal absolutism, in the previous chapters we have also discussed its essential limitations. These limitations consist not only of a clear-cut separation between politics and economy and a merely formal definition of freedom, but also in the most beloved *leitmotiv* of the Anglo-Saxon tradition: negative freedom, which is tirelessly extolled as freedom *tout court,* but which fails to be conceived in truly universal terms.

In light of this, Locke's serene justification of slavery in the colonies is perfectly understandable: Locke sees nothing wrong with the "plantation owners of the West Indies" who possess slaves and horses thanks to the rights they acquired through a regular deed of sale (contractualism can serve here to justify even the institution of slavery).[37] In another text, the great theorist of the limitation of governmental power expresses his wish that the constitution of a British colony in America would sanction the principle according to which "every freeman of Carolina shall have absolute power and authority over his negro slaves, of what opinion or religion soever."[38] Thus, in *Two Treatises of Government*, one of the classic texts of liberalism, we read: there are men who are "by the right of nature subjected to the absolute dominion and arbitrary power of their masters."[39]

Or perhaps, these cannot be properly called men, since in *The Whole History of Navigation from its Original to this Time*, in reference to trade with African colonies, Locke writes: "All the commodities brought from thence, are gold-dust, ivory, and slaves." Together with other "commodities," black slaves form an integral and essential part of the political economy of liberal England at the time. They are the object of a "remarkable trade," one which provides "great help to all of the American plantations,"[40] and which Locke follows with particular interest, since he himself invested some of his money in it.[41] Remarkably, one of the most relevant actions taken in the field of international politics by the liberal England that grew out of the Glorious Revolution was the acquisition, through the Treaty of Utrecht, of the *Asiento*, that is, the right to sell slaves in Spanish America—a right hitherto monopolized by Spanish companies.

The liberal tradition's reluctance to include every human being within the category of man, its unwillingness to conceive of man in his universality, and its anthropological nominalism, do not manifest themselves merely in relation to the black slaves imported from Africa. If Locke includes slaves within the category of "goods," a century later Edmund Burke includes laborers or hired workers within the category of "speaking tool" (*instrumentum vocale*) (supra, ch. VI, 4). Among Burke's adversaries is Emmanuel Sieyès, though his position does not appear any different from Burke's, since he too speaks of "most men as labor machines," or as "human instruments of production," or even as "two-footed tools."[42]

Once again, the liberal tradition reveals its essential limitations even with regard to negative freedom. Slaves are not the only ones who are denied negative freedom: so are the poor and "vagabonds," who are locked up together in "houses of correction" or "work-houses," a totalitarian institution against which Locke raises no objection. On the contrary, he would like its discipline to become even harsher: "That whoever shall counterfeit a pass [and leaves without permission] shall lose his ears for the forgery the first time that he is found guilty thereof, and the second time that he shall be transported to the plantations, as in case of felony," and therefore be practically reduced to a slave. But there is an even simpler solution, at least for those unlucky enough to be caught begging outside their parishes or near a seaport: they should be forced to serve in his majesty's ships. And they shall "be punished as deserters [that is, through capital punishment] if they go on shore without leave, or, when sent on shore, if they either go further or stay longer than they have leave."[43]

The institution of work-houses has its nucleus in England. In discussing the classic country of liberalism, the young Engels gives some shocking details: "The 'paupers' wear the house uniform and are subject to the principal's authority with no protection at all"; in order to prevent " 'morally degenerate' parents" from influencing their children, families are separated: the man is sent to one wing, the woman to another, the children to a third one." Families are split, but as for the rest, up to twelve or even sixteen people are crammed in a single room, and everyone, even children and elderly people, and women especially, are subjected to all kinds of violence. In short, inmates of work-houses are defined and treated as "disgusting and horrible objects, whose place is outside the law and the human community."[44] If the portrayal offered by Engels seems too emotionally-charged, we can examine the more detached analysis given by Thomas Marshall, a twentieth-century liberal scholar. Even Marshall recognizes the fact that, once the poor entered the work-houses, they "ceased to be citizens in any genuine meaning of the word," since they lost the "civil right to their personal freedom" (supra, ch. VII, 6).

Even when they manage to avoid the work-houses, the lower classes still witness a dramatic decrease and mutilation of their negative freedom. Hayek insists on praising Mandeville as the one who held that "arbitrary exertion of government power" should be "minimized."[45] In reality, Mandeville, the notable representative of early English liberalism and supporter of boldly secular ethics, still demands that attendance of Sunday service in church and religious indoctrination become "compulsory for the poor and the illiterate," and that in any case, on Sundays, "no access to any kind of entertainment should be allowed . . . outside of church."[46]

Sieyès goes so far as to propose the institution of indentured servitude for the poor: "The lowest class, made up of people whose arms are their only possession, might need indentured servitude in order to escape the slavery of need." Fans of the most authentic representative of the Western world, the Anglo-Saxon tradition, might immediately object that Sieyès is not part of this tradition; so much so that, according to Talmon, Sieyès made some arguments in support of "totalitarian democracy."[47] The fact is that, in proposing the introduction of indentured servitude (*esclavage de la loi*), Sieyès makes explicit reference to the Anglo-Saxon model: "I want to sell my time and services of any kind (I will not say my life) for one year, two years, etc., as they do in British America."[48] The reference is to so-called indentured servants, or in other words, to "semi-slaves," at least for the duration of their "contract" (a contract which, through various excuses, their masters often prolonged arbitrarily). These "semi-slaves" were in fact sold and purchased in a regular market, advertised even by the local press, and if they escaped or left their workplace without permission, they were hunted down.[49] In so doing, Sieyès points out, the "Americans" succeeded brilliantly in "importing all kinds of laborers they needed," using a "method" that continued to arouse suspicion in France.[50]

Thus, when we read that from the very beginning liberalism was synonymous with freedom for everyone, and when we read Talmon claim that liberalism always abhorred "coercion" and violence, we immediately realize that the field of historiography has long been abandoned and that we have entered the clouds of hagiography.[51] The same thing happens when we read Bobbio maintain that "the declarations of the rights of man" are "included in the constitution of the liberal States" and that "the idea that man as such has rights by nature" comes originally from Locke.[52] Or when we read Dahrendorf declare that the idea of "citizenship" for all men developed (though only minimally, as "equality before the law") after the Glorious Revolution.[53] In all of these cases we realize that the perspective is that of an imaginary historical space, a space from which macroscopic realities like slavery, work-houses, and the actual labor relations have been expunged. Even the ideology that prevailed for so long in liberal England has disappeared from this perspective, an ideology that supported such a harsh treatment not only of black slaves, but also of the "new industrial proletariat," "which has no modern parallel except in the behavior of the less reputable of white colonists towards colored labor."[54]

After hastily associating the liberal tradition with the rights of man, Dahrendorf affirms that he shares "the underlying beliefs of that great Whig," Burke, as if these fundamental ideas did not include, first of all, a categorical rejection of the discourse on the rights of man.[55] Burke, in fact, condemns the discourse on the rights of man as a subversive theory that would pave the way for political and social demands on the part of a "hairdresser" or a "tallow-chandler," "to say nothing of a number of other more servile employment," the demands of a "swinish multitude," or at least of people whose "sordid mercenary occupations" themselves imply "a mean contracted view of things."[56] The recurring identification of the rights of man and the British liberal tradition becomes all the more absurd when we consider that even a radical-liberal like Bentham rejects the demand for equality (*égalité*) in the French Revolution's theorization of the rights of man. And he does so by means of arguments that are very similar to Burke's, that is, from the belief that a similar discourse might stir the arrogance or anarchic disobedience of "apprentices" and lower classes in general: "All men are born equal in rights. The rights of the heir of the most indigent family equal to the rights of the heir of the most wealthy? In what case is this true?" And how can the necessary "subjection of the apprentice to the master" be explained?[57]

Finally, the identification of the liberal tradition with the rights of man is as false even with regard to America, and this is due not only to the presence of slavery there (which took the harshest form of "chattel slavery"), a presence which lasts until the Civil War, while semi-slavish employment and a sort of "debt slavery" last well after 1865. The identification turns out to be false also because of a more or less explicit criticism expressed by Alexander Hamilton: Hamilton successfully opposes the inclusion, in the United States Constitution, of a *Bill of Rights*, which he considers suitable only for a "moral treatise." Not by chance, two of the most implacable denouncers of the French Revolution (and the rights of man) exert a remarkable influence on the American political tradition: Edmund Burke and Friedrich von Gentz. The latter was translated immediately, in 1800, by John Quincy Adams, who was to become the sixth president of the United States.[58]

4. An Imaginary Western World, an Imaginary Germany

The construction of an imaginary Western world entails a parallel construction, by antithesis, of an imaginary Germany. The permanent and eternal characteristics of the latter are obtained by mere contrast to the former's values. Hence, Germany's entire cultural and political tradition is doomed by a sort of original sin that constantly leads it to negate the autonomous value of the individual, and the individual himself is destined to be swallowed up by a greedy statism. In addition to this, the Western world has set itself up as the keeper of moral values and the principle that maintains the superiority of right over might. As a result, Germany is portrayed as prey to the cult of force and violence throughout its history, to the legitimation of *faits accomplis* for the sake of which the autonomy and dignity of ethics is sacrificed. A particularly sensational proof of this is Hegel's affirmation of the unity of the rational and the actual.

European history is therefore split into the history of two opposing cultural traditions which bear no relationship to each other, or a very superficial relationship at most. The stereotypical image of the liberal Western world is contrasted to the equally stereotypical image of its enemies. We have discussed this issue elsewhere.[59] It shall suffice here to cite Friedrich Meinecke's astonished remarks during World War I: "The French boast about their individualism and their guarantees of their personal freedom from the State, and regard us as mere instruments serving the will of the government." "I feel like I am in a bad dream," adds Meinecke, who cannot understand the radical change that the images of Germany and France have undergone since Fichte's times. For Fichte, Meinecke observes, "the Latin or foreign—as he calls it—art of the government strives with strict consequentiality to achieve a machine-State. It treats all of the components of the machine as homogenous material and reveals an impulse towards an increasingly monarchical constitution. The German art of the State, instead, educates man and the future citizen to an autonomous ethical personality. In the Western world there is uniformity and enslavement; here there is freedom, autonomy, and an original quality."[60]

When Meinecke writes this, a radical change has taken place since the Napoleonic era, at least with regard to the relationship between Germany and France. During the Napoleonic period, in *Address to the German People,* Fichte tried to stir resistance against the French occupation, and to strengthen the conscience of Germany's national and cultural identity. He had done so by contrasting the "authentically German art of the State" (*echte deutsche Staatskunst*) to the "social machines," which he considered foreign, reminiscent, that is, of Napoleonic and imperial France. Within these "social machines," the individual was ultimately reduced to one of the many, uniform and interchangeable "cogs" (*Räder*) in an impersonal "machine," the movement of which was determined and regulated from without and from above.[61] Therefore, Meinecke's astonishment is fully justified. After all, he is the lucid witness of an extraordinary event: during World War I, France seems to be using, against Prussia (and Germany), the very same ideology which had placed France itself in the dock during the Wars of Liberation (*Befreiungskriege*).

And yet, the stereotypes that developed in Germany during the Napoleonic era continue to exist there even during the two World Wars. Therefore, for Georg Simmel, "individualism" is "totally inseparable from German essence,"[62] whereas in France, writes Max Scheler, the "congenital habit and superstitious faith in an absolute, omnipotent State" is quite common.[63] Almost two decades later, Carl Petersen, an ideologist of the Third Reich or at least close to Nazism, harshly criticizes the "Western fanatics of the State" (*westliche Staatsfanatiker*).[64]

We can reach the same conclusions by examining the second fundamental stereotype. This stereotype targets Hegel's affirmation of the unity of the rational and the actual, and contrasts the Western respect for ethical principles to a Teutonic cult of force. In reality, the barbaric use of force does not prevent Rainer Rosenberg from singing the praises of "moral duty," to the "categorical imperative," and man's moral side."[65] In this case, too, an exalted cult of moral duty (*Sollen*) may serve to delegitimize modernity (supra, ch. xi, 3). Understandably, then, to Nazism (and Fascism), Hegel's theory of the rationality of the actual is an eyesore, and so is his philosophy of history, which sanctions the irreversibility of the historical process and views its results as representative of the progressive extension of freedom to everyone. Referring to Nietzsche, Alfred Baeumler explicitly criticizes the notorious *Preface* to *Philosophy of Right*: Baeumler maintains that Hegel's theory (according to which we are children of our time and philosophy itself is but the conceptual understanding of one's time) was warmly welcomed by the "learned German bourgeoisie," which found in it the consecration of its philistine ideal of life.[66] Analogously, Franz Böhm thunders against "a century that has become completely historicist." His target is, once again, Hegel, to whom he opposes Rudolf Haym, whose monograph-length reprimand has the honor of being mentioned "among the texts written on Hegel which are particularly topical today."[67] Hegel's philosophy of history is also implicitly attacked by Rosenberg, who expresses his complete revulsion for "materialistic historicism."[68] Once again, a movement that is the expression of a categorical imperative coming from the depths of the German soul, a movement committed to a "heroic" struggle to erase centuries of modern "degeneration," cannot help but regard Hegel's theory of the rationality of the actual as synonymous with philistinism and materialism. It is on the basis of this logic that, after World War ii, an ideologist like Julius Evola claims that the "historicist dogma 'World history is the tribunal that judges the world' (*Weltgeschichte ist Weltgericht*) . . . is warmly embraced by men who have no backbone."[69]

First Bergman and then Popper find it appropriate to contrast Hegel—the presumed worshiper of *faits accomplis*—to Schopenhauer.[70] Yet, if they had read Hitler's *Table Talk*, they would have been disappointed to notice that the Führer of the Third Reich himself fully agreed with the opposition they proposed. Hitler, in fact, credited Schopenhauer with "pulverizing Hegel's pragmatism." The "pragmatism" mentioned here is precisely the "historicism" or "materialistic historicism" denounced by Rosenberg and the other ideologists we have cited. The three terms are all synonyms meant to condemn Hegel's philosophy of history as philistine and antiheroic, a philosophy of history which Schopenhauer had already attacked, thus earning Hitler's admiration. And not only did Hitler proudly affirm that he had carried, during World War I, Schopenhauer's complete works,"[71] but he also loved to quote, during his table conversations, "entire passages" written by Bergson's and Popper's beloved philosopher.[72]

At this point, a more general consideration should be made. To try and contrast German reactionism and Nazism on the basis of an exalted pathos of the Western world is another major mistake. In reality, in Nazism and in the Third Reich, the criticism of the West as an enemy of Germany is strictly tied to a boundless celebration of the Western world, of which Germany sees itself as a bulwark and as an authentic interpreter. When Hayek passionately praises the "Western man" from ancient Greece on,[73] he is unaware that he is using an expression and a motif that had already been largely present in the culture of the Third Reich.[74]

5. Hegel Faces the Western Tribunal

It is before a liberal Western world transformed by fantasy or ideology that the imagined German culture is called upon to defend itself. This type of trial reminds us of Kafka: both the judge and the defendant, in fact, do not correspond to reality. Their positive or negative characteristics have been manipulated and transformed by ideology, and they have come to resemble ghosts. Authors are absolved or condemned to the extent to which they can demonstrate their ideal membership of the Western world. In this sense, we have seen how Schumpeter and Dahrendorf fully absolved Kant for his so-called "British" citizenship. However, there are some who see in Kant an anticipation of the "Hegelian concept of the sovereignty of the State," and who therefore condemn him for being antithetical to "the liberal or egalitarian-democratic theory" of the Western world.[75] The latter is made to undergo such a blinding transformation that every internal conflict and even every difference between democracy and liberalism is erased, to the point that liberalism itself is considered synonymous with egalitarianism!

Hegel's situation is far more difficult than Kant's. Hegel's pathos of the State is prone to rendering him a "typical" representative of that imaginary Germany which is regarded as eternally statist. But there are also other reasons why he occupies an absolutely privileged position among the ruinous German imports meticulously enumerated by Hayek.[76] Hegel is branded as alien to the Western world and tied to the despotic and illiberal (if not even barbaric) Orient for two reasons. First of all, he is one of the Goths denounced by Hobhouse. And second, he exerted, through Marx, an extraordinary influence on the East, tying his own fortune with those of Leninism and Bolshevism. With this accusation, Hayek is drawing on a motif that had widely spread throughout European culture after the October Revolution. According to authors as different as Bernstein and Weber, or Mondolfo in Italy, the cause of the October Revolution is to be found in Hegel's dialectics and philosophy, which for the most part they equate with the cult of success and force.[77]

The fact remains, however, that the charges against Hegel derive directly from the transfiguration of the Western world. If the liberal Anglo-Saxon tradition is synonymous with freedom for all, if England is the promised land, then Hegel's critique of English liberalism raises suspicions to say the least. Hegel's "anglophobia" is condemned, for example by Bobbio, as synonymous with an illiberal, authoritarian conservatism that is "typically" German (supra, ch. v, 7). In addition to the previous considerations regarding Europe's historical situation—a situation in which Hegel's stern criticism of England develops—we should add that in England, the reform movement harshly denounces the Common Law and the cult of customary law. Bentham's language is much more spiteful than Hegel's in condemning the "all-embracing imposture" of British legal and cultural tradition, which paves the way for all sorts of "falsehood and deceit,"[78] and which, by entrusting a few chosen ones with the interpretation of the law, damages particularly the poor and "unlearned citizen."[79] As for John Stuart Mill, he credits Bentham with dealing a "death blow" to the "monster" (once again, British legal and cultural tradition), by proving "that the cult of British law was a degrading idolatry which, instead of portraying the perfection of reason, constituted a disgrace for human intellect."[80]

Bentham's outright rejection of the *Declaration of the Rights of Man* and the concept of man makes him a very different thinker from Hegel, but his "anglophobia" is certainly no less virulent than Hegel's. Yet, the imaginary and elusive Western tribunal unhesitatingly disregards all of this. Instead, it immediately interprets this "anglophobia" as synonymous with that statism that the ideology of the Entente and Germany's Western enemies identify as the deepest essence of German spirit. Is there any more eloquent proof of this charge than Hegel's anticontractual polemic? As a result, this argument is incessantly reiterated by various political presses up to the present. Once again, scruples and historical methods are sacrificed for the sake of ideology. After all, in England, even Bentham's reformism had harshly criticized that very same contractualist theory, denouncing it as an ideology aimed at preserving the status quo and at concealing the violence of the dominant classes. This ideology, so popular among Whig aristocrats, was the product of the Glorious Revolution, and its goal was to legitimize existing socio-political relationships by presenting them as the result of a "contract" and an "agreement" among the people.[81] In the ideology of the "original contract" that starts with Locke and finds its official consecration with William Blackstone, the privileged classes—Bentham observes—are united as in a choir that, indicating the existing configuration of society, tirelessly sings: "Let it endure forever!" (*Esto perpetua*).[82] And it is against this ideology of the contract, against this "chimera" that is in reality a mixture of violence and fraud, that Bentham proudly claims to have "declared war."[83]

As for the other charges, it is easy to demonstrate that they derive from the transformation of the liberal Western world, that is, from the political tradition of the countries situated to the west of Germany. As is well known, Hegel explicitly supports a second-degree electoral system, and this, too, is considered proof of his traditionalism. What is forgotten, however, is the fact that Tocqueville defends this very same system (as "the only way to make political freedom available to all people regardless of their class") in a work that is regarded as a classic of democracy. In so doing, Tocqueville goes against his own aristocratic distaste for that mass of "obscure figures" ("provincial lawyers, merchants, or even men who belong to the lower classes") who, through a direct election that gives a "vulgar appearance" to the whole assembly, gain access to the American House of Representatives.[84] It should be added that, in his private correspondence, Tocqueville shows an even harsher attitude towards direct elections than appears from his public position. This is what seems to emerge from a letter written at the end of 1835, in which Tocqueville indicates "multi-degree elections" (it is therefore possible to go beyond the second degree) as the only "remedy against the excesses of democracy." To this he adds that, given the prevailing ideological climate, it is necessary to use "great discretion" in presenting this theory, and in fact Tocqueville himself discusses it very cautiously in public, even softening its edges a little.[85] Another point that is not often discussed is that, well after Hegel's death, representation in England "was nowise regarded as a means of expressing individual right or forwarding individual interests. It was communities, and not individuals, who were represented."[86] It might be possible that, in supporting the second-degree electoral system, Hegel had England in mind; after all, England was at the basis of his support of a hereditary House of Lords, or the institution of a majorat (*v.Rph.*, III, 810). If anything, it should be added that Hegel finds the extension of that institution in England unacceptable, and in fact he harshly condemns "majorats, by means of which one can buy positions in the military and in the Church for one's youngest sons" (*Ph. G.*, 935). As for Hegel's argument for second-degree elections, it does not have the class-based meaning that it has in Tocqueville: in other words, it does not aim at purging the representative bodies of those elements Tocqueville regards as "vulgar." On the contrary, its goal is to question, in the only way that Hegel deems possible, the property-owners' political monopoly (supra, ch. VI, 6).

Clearly, then, the elimination of actual historical facts from the image of England and the liberal Western world of the time is a necessary condition for them to serve as a tribunal.

6. Ilting and the Liberal Rehabilitation of Hegel

Considering how influential the condemnation of Hegel in the name of the liberal Western world has been and continues to be, it is not surprising to find that attempts to rehabilitate him have not questioned the conceptual framework of the verdict that declares him guilty. This is the case with Karl-Heinz Ilting, who interprets Hegel's anticontractualist polemic or his affirmation of the unity of the rational and the actual according to the stereotypes we have already seen. These stereotypes also affect the interpretation of Hegel's view on elective monarchy. After examining the situation in Poland, a country ruled at the time by feudal barons whose only interest was to safeguard serfdom, Hegel condemns elective monarchy, and Ilting has no doubts: this position favors the "monarchic principle" and, in the final analysis, the ideology of the Restoration.[87] And yet, in Smith's *Lectures on Jurisprudence,* he could have read that "serfdom" continued to exist "in Bohemia, Hungary, and these countries where the sovereign is elective and consequently never could have great authority."[88] In that case, too, Ilting does not really move away from the conventional interpretation: far from analyzing the actual historical meaning of a political institution that even a classic liberal thinker like Mill regards with suspicion, this interpretative method merely observes the discrepancy between the demands of a strong central power on the one hand, and England's history and the stereotypical image of the Western world on the other. Therefore, Hegel's condemnation of elective monarchy based on the history of Poland and the excessive power held by the feudal barons, a power which the Restoration tried in vain to support, all of this becomes its opposite: the irrefutable proof that Hegel supported or at least accommodated Metternich's policies.

On the other hand, as an opening to the essay dedicated to the reinterpretation of Hegel's thought, Ilting feels the need to make some fundamental concessions to the stereotypes we have encountered: "Hegel's deification of the State is justly criticized . . . In his classical interpretation of the modern State, Hegel first of all postulated that peoples or nations are almost historical-universal individuals to which man belongs unconditionally in his historical existence. The possibilities of exploiting Hegel's republican ideal of a State for the purpose of creating a wretched nationalistic ideology are countless."[89] This last claim in particular is clearly influenced by the ideological climate of the Second Thirty Years War, according to which Hegel's "statism" is seriously implicated in the development of German imperialism and the triumph of German reactionism.

This accusation can be countered in various ways. On a strictly hermeneutical level, we could point out that beyond objective Spirit is absolute Spirit. Besides, within the realm of objective Spirit, the legal and sociopolitical organization of historically existing States can always be questioned by the World Spirit. And the right of the World Spirit is definitely superior to that of the "right of the State," which is far from being "the supreme thing" (AL, IV, 157). In addition to this, still on a hermeneutical level, Hegel unequivocally acknowledges the rights of man as inviolable, and these place drastic limitations on the expansion of political power.

Alternatively, the accusation could be countered on a historical level. Hegel's pathos of the State and the political community develops during the controversy about the ideology of the Restoration. This ideology justifies royal absolutism and eliminates any possibility for a constitutional transformation of the State. It does so by defaming political institutions, which it considers irrelevant compared to both the issue of moral and religious inwardness and to a personal relationship, unhindered by political and legal rules, between a king and his subjects.[90] Furthermore, Nazism is hardly characterized by a statist ideology: on the contrary, at times the Nazis even thundered against the "Western fanatics of the State."

However, in the passage we are discussing, Ilting takes neither of these two arguments into account. Instead, he makes allowances for the fact that Hegel moved away from the author of the Social Contract: "Contrary to Rousseau's radical democracy, Hegel's State must therefore not be [considered] totalitarian."[91] Clearly, with regard to Rousseau, Ilting agrees with Jacob Talmon (and liberal historiography), who includes him among the fathers of "totalitarian democracy." And by agreeing with Talmon's position, Ilting ends up joining the apologists of the liberal tradition. This emerges particularly in a passage in which Ilting, using Macpherson's concept of "possessive individualism" as a starting point, continues as follows:

> He [Macpherson] showed that this concept constitutes the essence of the liberal theory of civil society that we find expressed in a similar way, though with different degrees of faithfulness and conceptual precision, in Hobbes and Locke, as well as in Kant and Hegel. However, it would be dangerous to argue from this that modern rational right represents merely the ideology of the property-owning class. And this interpretation would not do justice to the demands of this theory of right. Besides, there is no reason why the doctrine that sees all men as having equal rights to freedom must be restricted to the

ideology of a specific social class that emerged under specific historical conditions."[92]

Certainly, Ilting is correct when he argues that the liberal theory of the necessary limitation of State power transcends its socio-historical genesis. However, when he attributes the argument for the right to freedom for "all men" to Locke, he is clearly in agreement with the usual transformation of the liberal tradition. This agreement emerges from other details, as well. Ilting believes that the printed text of *Philosophy of Right* "no longer contains a positive view on the French Revolution" and, on this basis, he attempts to prove Hegel's temporary agreement with the Restoration.[93] It would be easy to argue that *Philosophy of Right* contains a solemn acknowledgment of the existence of "inalienable" and "imprescriptible" rights (*Rph.*, § 66) to which a human being is entitled as a "universal person" and "a human being ... as a human being" (*Rph.*, § 209). In other words, it would be easy to argue that in the printed text of *Philosophy of Right* Hegel continues to speak passionately of that *Declaration of the Rights of Man* which is instead attacked by the political press that criticizes the French Revolution. Yet, the main point is different. Even if Hegel had condemned the French Revolution, that would be proof of his antiliberalism only if the image of the liberal political press of the time were distorted, by attributing to it a univocal adherence to the ideas of 1789, which is instead very far from the historical reality. Indeed, not only Burke, but also Bentham harshly condemn that *Declaration of the Rights of Man* which Hegel instead hails in the printed text of *Philosophy of Right*.

Going back now to the passage in which Ilting places both Hegel and Locke under the banner of "possessive individualism:" in reality, this association is wholly Ilting's, because Macpherson's book never mentions the author of *Philosophy of Right*. Is it possible to speak of "possessive individualism" with regard to a philosopher who never ceases to maintain that, no matter how "elevated" and "sacred" the "right to property" might be, it always remains something "very subordinate," something that "can and must be violated" (*v.Rph.*, IV, 157)? Isn't it also because he emphasizes the role of the State in the levying of taxes and, somehow, in the redistribution of income, that Hegel is condemned a statist by the liberal tradition? He was the first—Hayek points out—to argue that "positive" freedom that constitutes the bugbear of all supporters of neo-liberalism. The latter denounce it as the theoretical basis for that "social democracy" they easily equate with "totalitarian democracy" (infra, ch. XIII, 8). Hayek's coherence is beyond question. Ilting, instead, on the one hand, places Hegel, along with Locke, under the banner of "possessive individualism."

On the other hand, though he tries to limit its scope, he is influenced by the accusation of statism or state worship which part of the liberal tradition addresses against Hegel based on the fact that he violated Locke's beloved principle of the absolute inviolability of private property.

By placing Hegel under the banner of "possessive individualism," Ilting ends up taking back the compliment he paid Hegel for attempting to overcome "the weaknesses of liberalism" and the "overt deficiencies of the liberal concept of the State."[94] Undoubtedly, a sort of taboo is at work here: Ilting hesitates, or rather, fails to maintain Hegel's superiority over Locke as the theorist of modern man's freedom. The reason for this is that, from the very beginning, Ilting accepts or is forced to accept the position (which had became popular during the Second Thirty Years War) that sees Hegel as the one called upon to defend himself before a liberal Western tribunal transformed by fantasy and ideology. By drawing Hegel as close as possible to Locke, Ilting tries to secure for him that certificate of British citizenship that Schumpeter and Dahrendorf had already issued Kant, a certificate that is the only guarantee of fair treatment from the judges.

After borrowing, from Talmon and Hayek, the contrast between Rousseau as a father of totalitarianism and Locke as an authentic interpreter of the cause of freedom and the struggle against statism, Ilting faces some problem in his defense of Hegel. The latter, in fact, on the basis of a rich historical experience, developed a belief in the legitimacy and irrevocability of modernity and an awareness of the right of particularity that are simply not present in Rousseau's thought (supra, ch. VIII, 1). And yet, as Ilting himself recognizes, "since his early youth [Hegel] is peculiarly close" to Rousseau. In *Philosophy of Right*, Hegel does move away from Rousseau, but according to Ilting, this change of position might be the result of "political considerations."[95] Thus, once the hasty rejection of Rousseau expressed by Talmon and Hayek has been accepted (whether or not voluntarily), it is difficult to dispel suspicions that, Hegel, too, might be close to totalitarianism. Besides, Ilting emphasizes the differences between Hegel and the totalitarian Rousseau by making a paradoxical reference to the printed text of *Philosophy of Right*, despite the fact that its authenticity is doubtful. Indeed, the passion with which Hegel discusses Rousseau in his courses on the philosophy of right is nowhere to be found among the liberals, whose position does not differ very much from the fierce attack that the conservatives and reactionaries launch against the plebeian author of the *Social Contract* and the *Discourses on Inequality* (supra, ch. VIII, 3).

The fact is that Ilting resorts to categories borrowed indiscriminately from the liberal tradition or even from the political writings of the neo-liberal tradition: the trial ends with Rousseau being resolutely condemned for statism and state worship, and Hegel escaping with a semi-acquittal, while the British liberal tradition remains in any case immune from prosecution. However, in the same text by Macpherson to which he refers in his analysis of "possessive individualism," Ilting could have read that the categories of statism and state worship are quite ambiguous, as is the nature *sui generis* of Locke's individualism and antistatism: Locke, in fact, was firmly convinced that the unemployed and vagabonds should be "totally subject to the State" (supra, ch. IV, 2)—and in this respect, Locke reveals himself to be much more of a statist than not only Hegel, but also Rousseau. In conclusion, Macpherson is able to demystify the distorted image of the liberal tradition, an image which, instead, Ilting succumbs to, and which constitutes the basis for all of the charges against the author of *Philosophy of Right*.

7. Lukács and the Burden of National Stereotypes

Considering the period during which Lukács developed his interpretation of Hegel's thought, he is hardly likely to have fully overcome the stereotypes that emerged during the two World Wars. Undoubtedly, he has many merits, first of all that of rejecting the theory of the continuous line (that supposedly connects Martin Luther to Hitler, or at least, Hegel to Hitler), a theory that would weigh like a curse upon German history. Lukács brilliantly showed how classic German philosophy developed from the starting point of the relation to the Industrial Revolution in England and the political revolution in France. Lukács resolutely discards the interpretation given by Stalin and Zhdanov, according to which Hegel embodies the theoretical expression of the struggle led by Prussian and German reactionaries against the French Revolution,[96] which by the way is a theory shared by Popper.[97]

Lukács, however, goes even further and rejects the materialist, economic interpretation which sees Germany's economic and political underdevelopment in Kant's and Hegel's time mirrored by ideological backwardness. This is the position held by Karl Kautsky, who maintains that "the theoretical revolution in England and France was the result of a growing need by the bourgeoisie for an economic and political revolution. . . . The theoretical revolution in Germany was the product of imported ideas," ideas which, in the process of being imported, become impoverished and diluted.[98] Lukács, on the other hand, insists on what he defines as an "unequal development in the field of ideology," on the basis of which eighteenth and nineteenth century Germany, despite its socio-political underdevelopment compared to the advanced capitalist countries, nevertheless produces an innovative philosophy that looks toward the future:[99] "It was precisely the fact that [in Germany] the foundations and consequences of certain theoretical and literary questions were not immediately clear that gave the spirit, the concepts, and the representations a wide margin of freedom that seemed practically limitless: at the time, this freedom remained unknown to the more developed Western societies."[100] This result is confirmed also by Norbert Elias' research; although his starting point and methodology are different, Elias observes that "Germany's bourgeois intelligentsia, nonpolitical but spiritually more radical" than those in France and England, "forges, at least in spirit, in the daily dream of its books, concepts that are completely different from the models of the higher social classes."[101]

Germany's relative underdevelopment made the process with which the bourgeoisie absorbed the intelligentsia lengthier and more difficult, and this explains the greater boldness and critical drive of the intelligentsia itself. The radicalism of Hegelian intellectuals has been emphasized by Marx in his discussion of the German *Vormärz*: "The bourgeoisie was still too weak to adopt concrete measures, and was forced to drag along the theoretical army, led by Hegel's disciples, against the religion, the ideas, and the politics of the old world. Never before had philosophical criticism been so bold, so powerful, and so popular as it was during the first eight years of Friedrich Wilhelm IV's rule. . . . During this period, philosophy owed its power exclusively to the practical weakness of the bourgeoisie; since the bourgeois were not able to strike down the aged institutions, they had to yield to the bold idealists who launched their attack in the field of thought."[102]

Yet, even Lukács ends up showing signs of the stereotypical thinking we have discussed; thinking which emerges from a small but significant change he makes to Engels' distinction between "method" and "system." Engels maintains that, in Hegel, "a method of thought that is revolutionary from top to bottom" (*durch und durch*) corresponds to a "system" that possesses an intrinsic "conservative aspect," or one that in the very least leads to "very modest political conclusions."[103] As for Lukács, he calls this a "reactionary system."[104] This represents a drastic and wholly unjustifiable turn in Lukács' interpretation of Hegel. Even though Engels insists on sharply differentiating "method" and "system," he never considers the latter (that is, Hegel's political options and positions) wholly conservative, so much so that he emphasized "the outbursts of revolutionary indignation in his [Hegel's] works." Furthermore, what Engels means by the "very modest political conclusions" which the "system" leads to is the "representative monarchy" that Friedrich Wilhelm promises "his subjects," but which is never delivered. In other words, Hegel's conclusions are definitely inferior, more modest than the conclusions that the most radical revolutionaries drew from the "method," but are nevertheless progressive, to the point that Engels regards them as suitable "to the lower middle-class conditions of Germany at the time."[105] For Lukács, on the other hand, not only does the "system" lose its progressive or moderately progressive elements, but it becomes entirely "reactionary." Apparently, then, at least with regard to its concrete political suggestions, Hegel's philosophy would come to be an expression of the reaction to the French Revolution, which is what Stalin, Zhdanov and, on the other side of the barricade, Popper, maintain. In this way, Lukács ends up contradicting the basic approach of his own interpretation of classic German philosophy.

How can this turn be explained? It might perhaps be helpful to read from a letter Lukács writes to Anna Seghers, in which he affirms that "Germany's democratic tradition is less great and less glorious than France's or England's traditions."[106] Of course, this claim must be examined within its own historical period, that is, during the barbarism of the Third Reich and on the eve of the outbreak of World War II started by Hitler's Germany. Still, it is necessary to address the following question: Why should the British political and cultural tradition be considered richer with revolutionary turmoil than the German tradition? During the French Revolution, Condorcet made a passionate appeal to the Germans, asking them, out of loyalty to their glorious revolutionary past (the Reformation that had led to the antifeudal revolution of the Peasants War), to join the cause of the new France against the enemies of the Revolution, who were by now led by England.[107] And in those years, England was regarded by progressive public opinion as the country of conservatism or reactionism: even before becoming the leader of the anti-French coalition, England had been the target of the American Revolution, thus revealing itself as the main enemy of the uprisings that were changing the face of the world and that were stirring great enthusiasm within German culture.

Later, in 1827 (when Germany was still under the Restoration's thumb), Heine continued to have no doubts about which country symbolized the superstitious cult of the established order: "No social uprising occurred in Great Britain." The latter, in fact, cannot claim to have had either "religious Reform" carried through to the end as Germany did, or "political Reform," an actual political revolution, as France did.[108] Later events seemed to fully confirm Heine's claim in the eyes of progressive or revolutionary opinion: together with czarist Russia, England is the only country in Europe not to have been even touched by the great revolutionary wave of 1848, and for this very reason Engels refers to it as "that indestructible counter-revolutionary rock in the sea" of the uprisings stirring all around it.[109]

Except for their opposing judgment on the issue, German conservatives do not have a different position on England, which they constantly view as the country of order and ordered progress, immune to the uprisings that are devastating France and the Continent, including Germany. And Haym, as we are about to see, considers Germany's fault and misfortune to be the result of the lack of a figure like Burke, a figure able to make Germany immune to the revolutionary germs coming especially from the other side of the Rhine.

Today, as far as Germany is concerned, to the Peasants War and the 1848 Revolution, we could at least add the 1918 Revolution, which overthrew the Hohenzollern dynasty and made Germany among the countries that were most receptive to the October Revolution. Lukács' position expressed in his letter to Anna Seghers is clearly influenced by the period in which the letter was written and it explains the difficulties which Lukács encountered in breaking from the cultural and national stereotypes that had developed during the Second Thirty Years War.

XIII

Liberalism, Conservatism, the French Revolution,
and Classic German Philosophy

1. *Allgemeinheit* and *Égalité*

A final elimination of the stereotypes that have spread since 1914 is necessary for outlining a more balanced assessment of the liberal tradition, especially the Anglo-Saxon one, on the one hand, and classic German philosophy, particularly Hegel's, on the other. In addition, it is necessary for gaining a uniform understanding of Europe's cultural history. No country welcomed the outbreak of the French Revolution more enthusiastically than Germany, and the reason for this was not merely geographic proximity. If, from the very beginning, Kant finds himself in agreement with some of the fundamental concepts coming from France, it is because his philosophy contains certain revolutionary motifs that criticize the *ancien régime.*

Let us examine, for example, Kant's *Foundations of the Metaphysics of Morals.* Behavior is only moral when it is endowed with the "form" of "universality" (*Allgemeinheit*) and is carried out "on the basis of principles that can be valid at the same time as universal (*allgemein*) laws."[1] Universality (*Allgemeinheit*): this is one of Kant's fundamental categories, one that is all but innocent on a political level. According to Kant, "strict universality" (*strenge Allgemeinheit*) is what we are dealing with, both in the spheres of science and morality, and "strict universality" as such excludes *a priori* "any exception."[2] The antifeudal pathos of a rule that tolerates neither exceptions nor privileges is immediately noticeable. Already in 1772, in the very title of his work, one of the most brilliant conservative theorists, Justus Möser, criticized "the tendency toward universal (*allgemein*) rules and laws" that "despotically" opposed "all privileges and freedom."[3] Karl Mannheim rightly observes that this rejection of the category of universality is characteristic of "corporate (*ständisch*) thought."[4] Therefore, the debate for or against the *ancien régime,* and for or against the French Revolution, revolves around a central category of Kant's and Hegel's thought.

According to Hegel, the march of revolution is precisely the march of universality. After affirming itself in the American Revolution, "the principle of the universality of principles grew stronger among the French people and caused the Revolution" (*Ph. G.,* 919–20). Significantly, Tocqueville writes the following: "great general ideas . . . announce that a total subversion of the existing order is approaching."[5] Hegel's and Tocqueville's positions are perhaps different, but they both agree that universality is revolution. In particular, Hegel establishes a correspondence between equality (*égalité*) and universality when he speaks of a "principle of universality and equality" (*Allgemeinheit und Gleichheit; W,* II, 491).

In *The Holy Family,* Marx defines equality (*égalité*) as "the French expression for the unity of human essence, for man's consciousness of his species-being (*Gattungswesen*) and his attitude towards his species-being."[6] This definition can be valid for the category of universality, as well. And the "universal man (*maximus homo*)" is extolled by Kant, according to whom, whenever one man is forced into slavery, the whole of humanity suffers an intolerable violation.[7] For this reason, "any agreement to enslavement is null and invalid"; even if it has been freely accepted by the servant, the latter does not have the right to enter a relationship that violates "his own humanity in relation to the human species as a whole" (*Geschlecht*).[8] This theme of humanity as species-being has, even before the French Revolution, specific political implications such as the condemnation of serfdom, an institution within which a servant "is a thing not a person" (*est res non persona*), and thus "degrading to humanity."[9]

German conservative circles are distrustful or even openly hostile to the category of universality, which they suspect has egalitarian implications. Möser believes this category is synonymous with "uniformity" (*Einförmigkeit*), and therefore he contrasts it to the category of "difference" (*Verschiedenheit*), or "multiplicity" (*Mannigfaltigkeit*). Freedom can only exist in the respect of the "diversity of rights" and in the multiplicity and richness of nature. General rules are instead synonymous with "despotism" that suffocates "genius" to the advantage of "mediocrity."[10] Already before 1789, in reference to the Enlightenment, Möser had somehow established an opposition between freedom and equality.

After the French Revolution, in light of Burke's lesson (which will be discussed later), Adam Müller expresses this difference more explicitly: "If freedom is but the general aspiration of the most diverse natures to growth and life, there is no greater contradiction than the one which, under the pretext of introducing freedom, at the same time crushes all particularity (*Eigentümlichkeit*), that is, the diversity of all these na-tures." Given that freedom "expresses itself through the affirmation" of "peculiarity" (*Eigenheit*), any general rule that, in the name of equality, tramples upon man's original and unalterable diversity, is necessarily des-potic.[11] Later, in *The German Ideology*, Marx observes that "it is precisely the reactionaries, especially the Historical School and the Romanticists, who . . . reduce true freedom to peculiarity (*Eigenheit*), for instance, to the peculiarity of the Tyrolean peasants, and in general, to the peculiar (*eigen-tümlich*) characters of individuals, and also of localities, provinces, and estates (*Stände*), so that a German, even if he is not free, finds compensa-tion for all indisputably peculiar (*Eigenheit*) sufferings," to the point that he feels utterly content with his "shabby peculiarity and his peculiar shabbiness" (*lumpige Eigenheit und eigne Lumperei*).[12] Thus, Marx em-phasizes the link between the cult of particularity or peculiarity and what Mannheim will later define as "corporate thought." Not by chance, Marx contrasts Kant's philosophy, a philosophy committed to giving moral and political significance to the category of universality, to the Historical School of Law, and calls the former as "the *German theory* of the French Revolution."[13]

2. The English Origins of German Conservatism

Outside of classic German philosophy, we encounter a paradox. In the development of German conservatism, a decisive role is played by Ed-mund Burke, a thinker highly esteemed by Hayek. Burke's critique of the French Revolution, *Reflections on the Revolution in France*, is imme-diately translated by Friedrich von Gentz—who then becomes Metter-nich's counselor—, and becomes quite popular. Novalis praises it as a book that stands out among all the others of its kind because it is "a revolution-ary book against the Revolution."[14] *Reflections on the Revolution in France* has a profound influence on key figures of conservatism or reac-tionism: August Rehberg, Ernst Brandes—a good friend of Burke and of his son, Richard—and others.[15] "The great Englishman [*sic*], Burke," also con-stitutes the starting point for the new counter-revolutionary "school of politics" inaugurated by Friedrich Schlegel in Germany during the Resto-ration.[16] And even before Schlegel, Adam Müller had spoken enthusi-astically of Burke: "the most important era in the history of the German science of the State was the one that marked the introduction of Edmund Burke in Germany. Burke is the greatest statesman, the most profound, the most powerful, the most human, and the most warlike of all times and peoples." He is the embodiment "of German feeling." And Müller adds: "I say this with pride: he belongs more to us than to the English."[17]

While Burke contrasts "French liberty" to "English liberty,"[18] German conservatism contrasts "French liberty" to both "English liberty" and "German liberty," since, from this moment on, German conservatism regards "German liberty" as based on the model of "English liberty."[19] The English political tradition is praised first of all for its cult of peculiarity: "In Great Britain," Müller observes, "it is particularly clear that every law, every class, every national institution, every interest, every occupation has its peculiar freedom, and each moral person, as well as each human individual, aspires to claim his own peculiar characteristics."[20] Kant had vehemently supported the category of "universality without exceptions." Now, in contrast, Adam Müller celebrates England as the country which has the greatest respect for "peculiarity" (*Eigenheit*) and "particularity" (*Eigentümlichkeit*), even the peculiarity that derives from the power to depart from the rules.[21] On the basis of this, and still following Burke's lead, Müller criticizes the French Revolution which, in its declaration of rights, attributed freedom to a being "deprived . . . of all its particularity, to something abstract, to a concept of "man."

From Burke and the "English liberty" he renovates, German conservatives also derive the cult of a gradual, organic historical development, unhindered by arbitrary external intervention. Schlegel credits Burke with reassessing the value of that which "is historical and divinely positive," and with unmasking the "empty theories" and "revolutionary errors" that turn the State into a leveling and oppressive "legislative machine." These theories and errors promote merely "mechanical" relationships everywhere, and therefore trample upon all that is "personal," "living," and "organic."[22] Schelling will later condemn the *Charte* that issued from the July Revolution of 1830, contrasting the cold, dead objectivity of legal and constitutional rules to the living "personality" of the monarch and the relationship between the monarch and his subjects.[23] In this case, too, Burke's influence seems evident,[24] as is Friedrich Stahl's, who was one of Schelling's disciples and a key figure in German conservatism.[25]

Furthermore, in 1847, Friedrich Wilhelm IV will oppose the drafting of a constitution and the creation a national parliament with the following argument: to call for representation, not by social class but by ideological and political parties or movements, is utterly "un-German" (*undeutsch*), just as it is alien to Prussian and German traditions to seek happiness by means of artificial rules, that is, by means of "drafted and granted constitutions" (*gemachte und gegebene Konstitutionen*). To the French model, Friedrich Wilhelm IV contrasts the English model, inviting his subjects never to lose sight of and respect for "the example of that happy country whose constitution (*Verfassung*) is the result, not of a piece of paper, but of centuries of incomparable hereditary wisdom."[26]

The condemnation of the cold impersonality of the constitutional mechanism goes hand in hand with the denunciation of modernity. Burke
had already expressed some nostalgia for the era of ancient knights, who
were most unfortunately ousted by more prosaic "sophisters," "economists," and "calculators" (supra, ch. XI, 4). A few years later, Friedrich
Schlegel denounces the banality of present times, in which politics and
life are "mechanical and founded upon charts and statistics."[27] The political world that emerges out of the French Revolution, the modern world as
a whole, starts to be perceived as mechanical. And "mechanical" is a
recurring term used by Burke, an implacable enemy of "mechanical philosophy," which he considered the cause of the catastrophe that had occurred in France and that threatened to spread throughout Europe.[28]

The history of *Kulturkritik* in Germany cannot be properly understood
without taking into account Burke's great influence, and this is also the
case for *Gemeinschaft*, a key category of this tradition. The term is Gentz's
translation of the *partnership* articulated and celebrated by Burke. In his
criticism of the French Revolution, Burke insists on the fact that society is
indeed a "contract," but an utterly peculiar type of contract, which cannot
be altered and violated by radical legislative innovations and interventions. These innovations and interventions might in fact question *partnership*, a community "not only between those who are living, but between
those who are living, those who are dead, and those who are to be born."
This *partnership* links "the lower to the higher natures, connecting the
visible and invisible world, according to a fixed compact sanctioned by the
inviolable oath which binds all physical and all moral natures, each in their
appointed place."[29] Without a doubt, this is the same *Gemeinschaft* hailed
by the theorist of antimodern *Kulturkritik*. Indeed, the definition provided
by Adam Müller (a friend of Gentz's, Burke's translator, with whom he
corresponds) is quite similar to Burke's. In his criticism of the vulgar
interpretation given by French revolutionaries to the "idea of contract,"
Müller maintains that "people" are not "a bundle (*Bündel*) of ephemeral
beings with a head, two hands, and two feet," who happen to be together
during a fleeting moment in history. Rather, they are a "beautiful, immortal community," "the sublime community (*erhabene Gemeinschaft*) of a
long series of past generations, living and future, united through life and
death by great, intimate ties."[30] Müller gives credit to Burke for discovering
what he defines as a "spiritual India," the idea that the "social contract"
involves not only the living, but also "past and future generations." According to this idea, society is to be considered an "alliance" that includes not only the "contemporaries" (*Zeitgenossen*), but also the *Raum-
genossen*, those who are tied to each other by a shared space, those who are
born, in the course of time, on the same native soil.[31]

The pathos of *Gemeinschaft* subsequently spreads throughout German culture. Yet, its first theorization and celebration occurs in England: it is a type of association founded upon a "relation in blood" that unites and blends, indissolubly, "our state, our hearths, our sepulchres, and our altars."[32] This community, surrounded by a sacred aura, Burke continues, has nothing to do with the society reduced to a base platform for the experiments and innovative restlessness of French revolutionaries. Not by chance, Burke extols the ties of tradition as well as the "wisdom of our ancestors," which makes us consider socio-political institutions and the community we live in as something "consecrated" that inspires "awe," and as an organic body, in which our fathers and ancestors continue to live.[33] We must therefore view with "horror" those hasty revolutionaries or reformers, "who are prompt rashly to hack that aged parent in pieces and put him into the kettle of magicians, in hopes that by their poisonous weeds and wild incantations they may regenerate the paternal constitution and renovate their father's life." Burke expresses the first coherent and well-articulated celebration of organicism and the first condemnation of individualism: it is necessary to prevent hasty changes and ruinous doctrines from making the community "crumble away, be disconnected into the dust and powder of individuality, and at length dispersed to all the winds of Heaven."[34] Müller, too, criticizes the philosophers' crazy goal of turning the State into an object for "their experiments."[35]

In connection to the theme we are discussing, Joseph Görres' example is particularly interesting. During his early Jacobinism, Görres mocks Burke and his spite for the "swinish multitude." He actually associates this spite with the British practice of purchasing, from German principalities, cannon fodder recruited from the "swinish multitude," and of using it first in the American Revolution and then against the French Revolution.[36] Later, during the Napoleonic era, Görres becomes anti-Jacobin and makes explicit reference to Burke.[37] Especially during the Restoration, Görres converts to Burke's beloved themes, which he also assimilates from reading Adam Müller. Thus, Görres, too, starts to criticize hasty innovations and innovators who forget that "man—blessed be his kind nature—is tied to the past of his existence by deep roots." Görres thunders particularly against the "universal concepts" (*allgemeine Begriffe*) that presided over the ruinous revolutionary uprisings,[38] a point that was already Burke's *bête noire*.

Burke has a clear influence upon the Historical School of Law, thanks to his celebration, as Heine polemically observes, of "historical-English liberty" as opposed to "French liberty [which was] universally human," and also thanks to his superstitious cult of the "anatomy of history."[39] When, in 1799, Novalis describes the struggle that was taking place in Europe between revolution and counter-revolution, he sees the former as partly characterized by "the taste for all that is new and youthful," the "carefree contact among all citizens," and the "pride for universally valid principles for all humans" (*menschliche Allgemeingültigkeit*), and the latter by "the veneration for the past, the attachment to historical forms" (*geschichtliche Verfassung*), the love for the monuments of ancestors and the ancient glorious nation" (*Staatsfamilie*).[40] The "historical form" of a specific community with a rich history is put in contrast to general principles: thus, one of Burke's favorite themes presides over the genesis of the Historical School of Law in Germany. Later, Friedrich Savigny will praise Sir Walter Scott for his "loving attitude" toward history and "historical objects."[41] Savigny, too, will contrast "purely rational" concepts that aim for "universality" to "historical sense" and "history," which have the "sacred" task of restraining the ruinous current of the Enlightenment and the French Revolution.[42]

3. A Selective Anglophilia

Of course, the celebration of British cultural and political tradition by German conservatives is rather selective. For Friedrich Schlegel, "the true greatness and inner strength of Great Britain" resides in all its surviving feudal characteristics, not "in that celebrated constitution whose profound limitations and inner transience will perhaps soon emerge from historical experience."[43] Adam Müller is certainly not fond of political economy with its "false presupposition of universal marketability."[44] On the contrary, Müller foresees ruinous consequences following from Smith's principle of the "liberation from all limitations on trade and the sale of land." However, he adds that if "that great man and incomparable scholar" had experienced "the great school of our time," if he had lived through the tragic but fruitful experience of the ruinous uprisings of the Revolution, "he would have been the first to condemn the revolutionary, leveling tendency of his work; he would have become a divine apostate, like Burke."[45]

One last consideration is necessary. The ideological motif that celebrates historical tradition and spontaneous organic development, and condemns at the same time general "abstract principles" and the "arbitrary" pretext to enforce them by means of political intervention, this motif leads to very different results in the two countries. In England it ensures the rise of a bourgeoisie whose evolution is well on its way, despite the fact that such evolution was achieved through a policy of compromise with the feudal aristocracy. In Germany, on the other hand, where the Industrial Revolution is still to come, this motif hinders the development of the bourgeoisie and runs the risk of perpetuating the conditions of feudal backwardness.

4. Tracing the Origins of Social Darwinism and Fascist Ideology

The influence of Britain's famous enmity to the French Revolution stretches into even the darkest recesses of German conservative and reactionary thought. Burke's ideas, in fact, affected Ludwig von Haller: the very title, or subtitle, of Haller's main work, *Restauration der Staats-Wissenschaft, oder Theorie des natürlich-geselligen Zustands der Chimäre des künstlich-bürgerlichen entgegengesetzt* (*Restoration of Statecraft, or the Theory of the Natural Social State as Opposed to the Chimaera of the Artificial Bourgeois State*), presents some themes that will later characterize social Darwinism.[46] Indeed, the extreme currents of conservatism or reactionism in Germany go so far as to radicalize Burke's thought. According to Burke, the ideal of *égalité*, the "abstract" demand for legal equality, violates "the natural order of things," the "natural course of things," and stains itself with the "worst of usurpations," that which tramples upon the "prerogatives of nature," or the "method of nature."[47] In Gentz's translation, the "method of nature" becomes the "divine method of nature" (*göttliche Methodik der Natur*).[48] And according to Haller, the fact that "the larger displaces the smaller, the powerful the weak," and that "the more powerful rules, must rule, and always shall rule" (supra, ch. III, 4) is a law of nature and part of the *"divine, eternal, immutable order"* (*ewige, unabänderliche Ordnung Gottes*).

Of course, the German autochthonal tradition behind this sort of forerunner of social Darwinism must also be taken into consideration. In particular, an author who plays a fundamental role in Haller's thought, Justus Möser, suggests stopping smallpox vaccinations, which violate "Natural Law" by keeping alive people who are later destined to die of starvation, and by making the world "overcrowded," something particularly ruinous for female and urban populations (since peasants can always be "taken to a battlefield to be mown down by guns").[49]

Möser has many points in common with Burke:[50] well before the French Revolution, he made reference to the *"Liberty* and *Property* of the British,"[51] that is, to Burke's England, which he highly admired. Perhaps Haller was influenced by both Möser and Burke. Not by chance, in celebrating "racial struggle," one of the main figures of "social Darwinism," Ludwig Gumplowicz, cites Haller.[52]

Burke's influence continues to influence even the darkest recesses of German conservative and reactionary thought well into the twentieth century. This is quite understandable: as England struggled against revolutionary France and at the same time possible internal uprisings, Burke provided the first criticism of the Revolution. He perfected the weapon and the theoretical arsenal that would later be used in other countries in their counter-revolutionary struggles. In Germany, in particular, the first implacable critic of the French Revolution ends up enjoying a sort of honorary German citizenship, as we have seen from Adam Müller's remarks. However, during World War I, Werner Sombart considers Burke "anti-British" for being perfectly congenial to Germany in its fight against the "ideas of 1789."[53] Awarding this sort of honorary citizenship to Burke becomes even easier thanks to that brotherhood or community of the "Germanic peoples" which Adam Müller himself had written about.[54] True, this brotherhood or community shatters during World War I, and yet Sombart and Spengler continue to feel very close to the author of *Reflections on the Revolution in France.* The influence of this work continues to be quite strong in Germany during the twentieth century, especially among the most reactionary cultural and political currents.[55] The link between the two terms, *partnership* and *Gemeinschaft,* and thus Germany's indebtedness to England, is emphasized in 1944 by a certain Eugen Lerch. After identifying Burke as the source of these terms, Lerch draws a connection that leads up to the "community of the front" (*Frontgemeinschaft*) of World War I and "National Socialism."[56] Undoubtedly, even during the Third Reich, the author who had the merit of having been the first to denounce the politically and socially subversive character of the French Revolution and the justification of the rights of man continues to enjoy a sort of honorary German citizenship.

Although we have examined the case of Germany more in depth, Burke's conservative influence goes well beyond England and Germany; in fact, Burke "was the role model for all 'reactionaries' " and he "inspired the reactionary ideologists of the late nineteenth century and early twentieth century, like Taine and Barrès."[57] To be more precise, Burke's influence is not at all limited to the early twentieth century. Particularly significant is the reference to the defender of French nationalism, whose presence in Fascist ideology is felt even in Vichy:[58] indeed, in Barrès' rejection of the rights of man and the universal concept of man, as well as his cult of ancestry, Burke's presence is explicit.[59] Some allusion has occasionally been made to the "French origins of Fascism," but it is important to remember that, in tracing the origins of totalitarianism and also discussing Fascism and Nazism, Hannah Arendt uses, as her point of departure, the very first inexorable critic of the rights of man, Edmund Burke.[60] One is tempted to wonder whether and to what extent Burke might have influenced the development of anti-Semitism and conspiracy theory. These ideological motifs certainly have a long history, especially in Germany; yet, they might have found an ally in a text that had become a sort of Bible of counter-revolution, a text that made accusations against, on the one hand, Jewish financiers, and, on the other, "the actual plan for the destruction of religion" devised by encyclopedists and *philosophes*. Thus, with regard to Fascism and Nazism, it is more correct to speak of a long gestation process on a European and international level.[61]

5. Beyond National Stereotypes

At this point, the stereotypical opposition between "Western" tradition on the one hand, and Germany's cultural and philosophical tradition on the other, becomes untenable and even ridiculous. What emerges instead from a concrete historical analysis is that the crucial influence of the "Western world" represented by England cannot be left out when examining the *leitmotivs* of German conservatism. This is true even for the worst aspects of this conservatism, which eventually had tragic consequences, and even for those aspects that, according to current stereotypes, are considered to be typically German. On the opposite side, it is important to remember that the cultural and political legacy of the French Revolution (the rights of man and all that is regarded today as typically Western) penetrates into German culture only to the extent to which the latter is able to resist Burke's influence. In other words, it depends on Germany's ability to counter that Anglo-Saxon tradition which, according to certain contemporary thinkers, represents a sort of tribunal called upon to question German cultural history as a whole, including classic German philosophy.

It is from this starting point that Ralf Dahrendorf insists on condemning Hegel as antithetical to the liberal Anglo-Saxon tradition, and as a Prussian philosopher responsible for the "apotheosis of the Prussian State."[62] However, Dahrendorf, who is indiscriminately enthusiastic about England, his adoptive country, ignores the fact that his celebration of the "blessed island, though not utterly perfect" has a precedent not only in the words of Adam Müller (the Romantic conservative and organicist who speaks of a "happy" or blessed island), but also in those of the more well-known Friedrich Wilhelm IV. The latter was in fact a passionate admirer of "that happy country," and no less Prussian than Hegel, if only for the fact that he was the King of Prussia! Moreover, Friedrich Wilhelm IV extols England as a country without that "piece of paper," that "constitution" which was being demanded at the very same time by the disciples of the philosopher whom Dahrendorf criticizes so vehemently, that is, Hegel.

6. Burke and the History of European Liberalism

Burke plays a fundamental role in the development of conservatism (particularly German), and at the same time in the history of European liberalism. As Marcuse remarks, liberalism evolves during the polemic against the French Revolution.[63] The same is true for Burke, Hayek's revered author, and, though in a different way, for the representatives of French liberalism, whose terror of popular demands during the revolutionary uprisings has already been discussed.[64] In her account of these uprisings, Madame de Staël is clearly influenced by Burke and by the "indignation" he expresses from the very beginning "against the crimes that were already committed in France and against the false political systems that were adopted there."[65]

As for Constant, it is true that, for a while (during what have been called his "apprenticeship years"[66] or his years as a "dandy" (*muscadin*),[67] he defends the moderate stabilization of the Revolution and the politics of the Directory as the only way to fend off the Jacobin threat, thus moving away from Burke and his struggle against France.[68] However, Constant later becomes a passionate admirer of August Wilhelm Rehberg, a German author who has many points in common with Burke, and with whom Constant was personally acquainted.[69] In particular, Constant praises Rehberg's theory according to which "every generation inherits from its ancestors a treasure of moral riches, an invisible, precious treasure that, in turn, it hands down to its descendants." Therefore, this treasure should not be dissipated by hasty legislative innovations, and even less so by radical revolutionary uprisings.[70] On closer scrutiny, this theory is borrowed from Burke, "one of the most excellent writers," to whom Rehberg makes explicit reference.[71] Constant himself seems to be aware of this affinity, since he credits Rehberg with being "one of the foreigners who, from the very beginning, better foresaw our mistakes."[72] In commenting upon Rehberg's passage on the treasure handed down from one generation to the next, Constant makes a sort of confession: "I admit it, I have a great admiration for the past; and every day, as experience teaches me and reflection enlightens me, this admiration grows stronger." Indeed, this remark-confession is directly influenced by Burke.

With regard to Burke, Constant's position is essentially similar to that of Madame de Staël. If, on the one hand, she overtly praises Burke, on the other, in contrast to those who look nostalgically back to the *ancien régime,* she observes: "The representatives of the aristocratic party who, on the continent, now refer to Burke as an enemy of the Revolution, perhaps ignore the fact that, in page after page, he reproaches the French for not conforming to the principles of the British constitution."[73] The point is to make sure that Burke does not become the symbol for absolute or feudal reactionism in France and Europe, but so far as the rest goes, in the struggle against Jacobinism and even against democracy, it can be very useful for the liberals to draw from the author of *Reflections on the Revolution in France.*

Constant accuses the Jacobins and the representatives of plebeian radicalism of being "vandals and Goths," "anarchists and atheists" belonging to a "loathsome race," the "eradication" of which is the only thing worth hoping for.[74] This criticism cannot but call to mind a similar one expressed by Burke, who condemns the leaders of the new France as "savages," "barbaric atheists and assassins" whose "fierceness, arrogance, rebellious spirit, and habit of defying every human and divine law" has made them "wild savages."[75] If Burke speaks of the National Assembly by calling it a "cave of cannibals" (*caverne d'anthropophages*),[76] Constant limits himself to defining only the Jacobins as "cannibals" (*anthropophagi*).[77]

Finally, Burke's influence can be found after 1848 in Tocqueville, particularly in his research for, and text of, *L'Ancien Régime et la Révolution.* At this point, over half a century after the Revolution, the political circumstances have changed radically, not only in France, but internationally. Thus, Tocqueville can no longer share Burke's illusion that the situation can be brought back to the way it was before the revolutionary storm that changed the face of France and Europe. Nor can Tocqueville share Burke's belief that it might be possible to isolate a virus, when instead the events showed that such a virus spread "throughout the civil world."[78] Hence, Tocqueville criticizes Burke for failing to grasp "the general character, the universality, and the ultimate range of the Revolution."[79] Moreover, Tocqueville maintains that royal absolutism leads to Jacobinism and socialism, and so views with suspicion any political transformation of the *ancien régime*. This would explain his criticism of Burke: according to Tocqueville, Burke paints an excessively "flattering" portrait of the "ancient French constitution,"[80] and he fails to understand that the germs of a despotic disease that spreads, like a plague, throughout the French political tradition, were already present in "the monarchy he misses."[81] However, in his denunciation of the "philosophical presumption" and lack of "practical wisdom" of French revolutionaries, Tocqueville is in complete agreement with Burke.[82] And when Tocqueville condemns the "illness" and the "new, unknown virus," what immediately comes to mind is the denunciation of the "intoxication" which Burke ascribes to the French revolutionary intellectuals;[83] a denunciation that Burke expresses in *Remarks on the Policy of the Allies with Respect to France,* a text well-known and cited by Tocqueville.[84]

Moving now from France to Germany, we notice how the liberal current hostile to Hegel extols Justus Möser, who had not a few points in common with Burke, as a "profound expert and dear friend of genuine German liberty."[85] And Burke is also strongly present in post-1848 German liberalism. One example is Rudolf Haym, who, using the enthusiasm stirred by the French Revolution as his point of departure, summarizes the ruinous fall of German culture as follows: "In Germany there was no Burke."[86] And the national-liberal Heinrich von Treitschke defends Rehberg, who admired Burke and was in turn admired by Constant, against what he defines as Fichte's "coarse" polemic.[87]

A general consideration is now appropriate: it is the whole European post-1848 liberalism that, by celebrating and distorting the British political tradition with an anti-Jacobin and antiproletarian goal, returns to Burke. For example, after 1848, François Guizot contrasts the catastrophic revolutionary wave in France to the Glorious Revolution of 1688. Guizot regards this Revolution as effective and victorious: by avoiding any corruption, any "disorder" (égarement), the Glorious Revolution was "carried out by respectable men," by "men of order and government, not by revolutionaries," and "not through popular revolt, but through organized political parties . . . , parties of lawful politics, not of conspiracy and insurrection," parties which did not aim at "overturning the status quo," or at "changing the foundations of society and the fate of humanity."[88] These are clearly Burke's arguments: a revolution is lawful to the extent to which it respects the status quo and is led by men of order; in other words, to the extent to which it is not a revolution. Therefore, in total agreement with Burke, Guizot regards the uprisings in Louis XVI's France as unlawful from the start, well before their Jacobin radicalization.

7. Burke's School of Thought and Classic German Philosophy

If European liberalism has many points in common with counter-revolutionary political writings and is heavily influenced by it, classic German philosophy is characterized by a strong critical opposition to those very same writings. Rudolf Haym is well aware of this fact, and contrasts Burke to the development of German idealism. Except for an obvious difference in judgment, this contrast is historically flawless. Kant attacks Burke by means of a harsh, though indirect, criticism. We have already examined Kant's proud defense of the role of theory in the process of political transformation (supra, ch. VI, 5). It is interesting to note that Kant expresses this defense in the course of a criticism, the target of which is unstated and yet unequivocal: Edmund Burke. In spitefully rejecting the attempt to apply the "clumsy subtlety of . . . metaphysics" to the political world, Burke writes: "Let them be their [the philosophers'] amusement in their schools: *Illa se jactet in aula—Aeolus, et clauso ventorum carcere regnet.* But let them not break prison to burst like a Levanter to sweep the earth with their hurricane and to break up the fountains of the great deep to overwhelm us."[89] With his essay, *On the Maxim (Über den Gemeinspruch)*, Kant aims at countering those who bash the intellectual and "would lock him up in a school *('illa se iactet in aula!')*" like a pedant who lacks common sense and that can only cause trouble.[90] The contrast between the role of intellectuals mirrors the contrast between the role of theory and general concepts. Burke rejects theory and concepts, regarding them—and rightly so—as the theoretical bases for the *Declaration of the Rights of Man*. On the contrary, Kant extols them, and for this very reason he shares the ideals of the French Revolution and the *Declaration of the Rights of Man*.

What emerges here is the arbitrariness of the choice to give Kant unsolicited and unwanted British citizenship for the sole purpose of incorporating him into a tradition that he criticizes vehemently. The arbitrariness of this incorporation is particularly evident with Dahrendorf. In appropriating Kant for England, Dahrendorf overtly expresses his intention to make Kant join the country and the "world of Locke and Burke and Mill," as if Kant had never engaged in a harsh polemic against the author of *Reflections on the Revolution in France!*[91]

If Kant criticizes Burke only indirectly, he is quite explicit in his criticism of Mallet du Pan, a political writer who had left France and who was active in the polemic against the French Revolution.[92] Mallet du Pan was translated and made known to the public by the same translator who had introduced Burke's works into Germany,[93] and Burke himself quotes him favorably.[94] Kant is also explicit in his criticism of Möser, an author praised by the liberal Carl Welcker, but whom Kant condemns as "aristocratic and a defender of hereditary nobility," and as a representative of the counter-revolutionary current which, by belittling the role of theory, aims at dismissing the general principles of freedom and equality that originated from the French Revolution.[95] Finally, with regard to Rehberg, Burke's German emulator, on the one hand, he is praised by the liberal Constant, on the other he is the target of Fichte's passionate defense of the French Revolution, the very same defense that Treitschke deprecates.[96]

After moving to Switzerland, Mallet du Pan settles in Berne and comes into contact with the Bernese oligarchy which, a few years later, becomes the target of young Hegel's criticism (*w,* I, 255–67). As for Hegel, while in Berne he takes up the task of copying excerpts of Georg Forster, who could be considered Burke's main antagonist in Germany.[97] Against Burke, Forster maintains that "the slandered Declaration of the Rights of Man" alone would be enough to erect a "venerable monument" to the Assembly that proclaimed it.[98] And well after his early years, Hegel develops a philosophy of history according to which the march of progress is determined by the establishment of the universal concept of man. Such a philosophy of history is therefore in direct contrast to Burke's denunciation of the abstractness of the category of man and the rights of man, both of which originated in the French Revolution.

As we have seen, the conservative circles in Germany make reference to "German liberty" and, after 1789, they draw from Burke's distinction between "English liberty" on the one hand, and the false, ruinous "French liberty," on the other. It is in this context that Welcker praises Möser by calling him a "dear friend of genuine German liberty." For Forster, on the other hand, despite its tricky appearance, "German liberty" is but "the demon of feudal serfdom."[99] The criticism of the "legend of German liberty" (w, I, 453) is a constant theme in Hegel; a theme reprised in his polemic against the "haughtiness of British liberty" which, with its feudal remnants, has much in common with the "German imperial constitution of the past" (B.schr., 466). The association between "English liberty" and "German liberty" (deutsche Freiheit), an association so popular in Burke's German school, reappears here from the opposite perspective.

It is also important to keep in mind the harsh controversy in which Hegel is involved against the representatives of reactionary Romanticism and admirers of Burke, whose Germanophile positions are for the most part the result of an irreducible hostility to France and against the ideals of the Revolution.[100] Friedrich Schlegel repeatedly expresses his admiration for the "great Englishman, Burke," and at the same time accuses Hegel of indulging in a sort of "philosophical satanism."[101]

The polemic against Burke and his school reveals once again the close relationship between classic German philosophy and the French Revolution. Condorcet, too, criticizes Burke, whom he defines as a "famous rhetorician," certainly endowed with an extraordinary magniloquence, but in the final analysis, an "enthusiast . . . of tyranny."[102] Condorcet's remark is quite similar to the one expressed by one of Hegel's disciples, Heinrich Heine, who maintained that Burke "possessed only one rhetorical talent," a talent he used to serve a cause that was the opposite of that of freedom."[103]

8. Hegel and the Legacy of the French Revolution

Once the national stereotypes have been dismantled and the foundations have been laid for a reconstruction of the cultural and political history of European countries (with their manifold combinations and reciprocal influences); once the fences erected by the ideology of war during the two

World Wars have been torn down, it becomes clear that dragging classic German philosophy before the tribunal of the liberal tradition makes no sense at all. Regardless of whether the verdict is an absolution or a partial or total condemnation, this trial always loses sight of an essential point: it is with Kant, Fichte, and Hegel, that the French Revolution finds its theoretical expression. The liberal authors of the time, on the other hand, develop their thought for the most part during the controversy and the struggle against the French Revolution. And if, as we believe, the political and ideal legacy that stems from the French Revolution constitutes the foundation *par excellence* of modern freedom, in order to gain a thorough understanding of this freedom it is necessary to draw from classic German philosophy rather than from its contemporary liberal tradition.

With regard to Hegel, the legacy of the French Revolution (examined throughout its development) emerges in two fundamental points: 1) the affirmation of the universal concept of man and the interpretation of history as a progressive and difficult realization of that concept; 2) the relationship between politics and economics, a relationship according to which material poverty taken to an extreme results in a "total lack of rights" for the starving individual. These two points are closely connected, since denying a starving man his rights is equal to denying him an actual subsumption under the universal category of man. In this sense, though Hegel's philosophy of history fully legitimizes modernity, it does not regard the emancipation process that has started within it as complete, or at least it suggests the idea that it is not yet complete.

At this point, the problem raised by Lukács can be faced in a different and more appropriate manner. According to Lukács, Hegel was always alien and hostile to the plebeian phase of the French Revolution. We have already emphasized the need, in this case too, to draw a distinction (though not a contrast) between political options and fundamental theoretical categories (supra, ch. VI, 1). Hegel examines the whole development of the French Revolution in great depth, and even though he never identifies with the Jacobin and plebeian positions (certainly not during his adulthood), he fully grasps the way in which the process of radicalizing the French Revolution questions the relationship between politics and economics, a relationship established by the liberal tradition. The theory that sees classic German philosophy as the theoretical equivalent of the French Revolution—a theory that was first formulated by Hegel himself—must therefore be understood in all of its breadth. Indeed, far from exhausting itself in its bourgeois results, during its tortuous development the French Revolution ends up questioning its class assumptions, as Marx and Engels point out in some of their most successful phases.[104]

Essentially, we are dealing with the disorder (*égarement*) condemned by

Guizot (nowadays François Furet would call it "chaotic change" (*dé-rapage*)). Hegel does not withdraw in horror from this plebeian disorder (*égarement*), unlike Guizot, who ends up embracing Burke's theory and rejecting the French Revolution altogether. Hegel's position is quite different: even when he criticizes or condemns the process of radicalization in France, he refuses to dismiss it as a mere anomaly or morbid paroxysm. Above all, he refuses to use these terms to indicate the masses' participation in the Revolution, as emerges from his eloquent, heartfelt depiction of the intolerable oppression perpetrated by a parasitic, corrupt aristocracy at the expense of the masses (supra, chs. v, 3, and viii, 3). In order to explain the revolutionary uprisings, Hegel does not resort to the categories of ideological illness, "intoxication," or "virus," that is to say, the categories used by Burke and Tocqueville. On the contrary, he expresses an understanding and sympathy for the socio-political subject of disorder (*égarement*) that are completely absent in Tocqueville and, before him, in Burke.

This also emerges on the level of theoretical categories. When Hayek ascribes the "distinction between 'positive' and 'negative' liberty," as well as the argument for "positive" liberty, to Hegel, that is, to the philosopher he despises, he ends up unwittingly bestowing the highest recognition upon him.[105] Certainly, the father of neo-liberalism is only revealing part of the truth. He does not mention the fact that Hegel shows the highest respect for the inviolability of the private sphere, for what is called today "negative liberty," and defined by Hegel as "negative right." On the other hand, next to all of this, Hegel also argues for "positive right," "material rights," and the "right to life" (supra, chs. v, 9, vii, 6, and viii, 4).

The legacy of the great debates that developed throughout the French Revolution, even during its most dramatic phases, is quite evident. The Revolution ended up questioning its own class assumptions, since in order to defend itself from the attack of the foreign and domestic Counter-Revolution, it was forced to appeal to the masses, whose support constituted the only hope for survival. Clearly, then, the position of the whole Hegelian school of thought concerning the later developments of the French Revolution is quite different from that of the liberal tradition. We have discussed Guizot's position after 1848, and we have examined Tocqueville's condemnation of the 1848 Revolution, which he denounces as socialist from its very beginning, that is, from February. Alongside this tradition we can place Hayek, who, as we have seen, regards Hegel's "distinction between 'positive' and 'negative' liberty" as the theoretical foundation for " 'social' or totalitarian democracy." After the initial Jacobin wave of enthusiasm, this " 'social' or totalitarian democracy" establishes itself in Europe with the 1848 Revolution and during the second half of the nineteenth century.[106]

If we now move to the opposite side, we can notice the profound impact that Hegel's school of thought had on the ideological preparation for 1848 in Germany. It has been affirmed, and rightly so, that in the *Vormärz*, "the ideological training of the revolutionary democrats was closely connected to the evolution of the 'young' Hegelians."[107] In the Frankfurt National Assembly that was formed after the Revolution, the left is represented by the "Hegelians," who, in the critical portrayal given by Heinrich Laube, a member of the *Junges Deutschland,* are pervaded by the spirit of the system and by an "abstract" and "heartless" (*herzlos*) logical rigor.[108] Hegel's disciples are described as the Jacobins of the period. And in 1858, the mediocre French author of a short story set in Germany during the Revolution defines the victims of violent repression who are ultimately shot and killed as the "*hegéliens.*"[109] Quite significantly, Hegelianism plays an important role in the ideological preparation for the 1848 Revolution in Italy, and it provides a deep source of inspiration for the radicalism of the Spaventa brothers, a radicalism that occasionally borders on socialism.[110]

In light of this main picture, it becomes clear how most of the resistance to the conservative and neo-liberal turn of European liberalism after 1848 seems influenced by Hegelian philosophy. This is the case in Italy, where, in a period when liberal political writers (including Tocqueville) insist on contrasting freedom to equality at the expense of the latter, the Hegelian Silvio Spaventa claims that "without the legal limit constituted by the fundamental equality of human nature, freedom can easily turn into slavery." He adds that, rightfully, or at least understandably, the "multitudes" are not merely content "with being equal before the law; they want to enjoy life's goods, which in the past centuries could only be enjoyed by very few individuals."[111] However, the Spaventa brothers are not an isolated case in Europe. In England, Thomas Hill Green is attacked by Hayek for drawing the category of "positive liberty" from Hegel.[112] Indeed, Green's justification of a "positive liberty" develops precisely during a polemic against his contemporary supporters of laissez-faire.[113] The latter condemned the state regulation of work hours in the factories and the regulation of female and child labor, all in the name of the "freedom of contract," a freedom they interpreted exclusively as the non-interference of the political power in the private sphere. Green is well aware of this ideological campaign, which will later involve Herbert Spencer, Lord Acton, Henry Maine, etc.: "The most urgent political issues of our time are issues the solution of which does not necessarily interfere with the freedom of contract, but it will certainly be hampered in the sacred name of individual freedom."[114] Echoing the pathos of universality that characterizes Hegel and classic German philosophy as a whole, and in contrast to the representatives of laissez-faire or the neo-liberalism of his time, Green maintains that "no contract is valid in which human beings are treated, with or without their consent, as goods." Hence, any form of slavery is regarded as unlawful, and the State has the right to prohibit any work relationships that might constitute a hazard for the worker's health or dignity; in other words, any relationships that represent an attack on "public freedom."[115]

In Germany, Ferdinand Lassalle criticizes the position according to which the only function of the State is that of "protecting the personal freedom and property of the individual," thereby reducing the State to a mere "night-watchman." This position, which identifies the State with the "mere civil society of selfish interests" (and here Hegel's influence is evident), is unfortunately "popular not only with the liberals, but even with many would-be democrats."[116] Interestingly, even leaving Lassalle, Marx, and Engels aside, Hegel's philosophy stimulates socialist tendencies in Germany after the early 1840s. This is the case with the entrepreneur Gustav Mevissen, according to whom, as has been observed, "Hegelianism was . . . like an introduction to socialism," "a socialism that strove to apply exclusively Hegel's formula: The State is an embodiment of right."[117]

The history of Hegel's legacy is intertwined with the history of the French Revolution and the debate on its own legacy, a debate that continues even today. Following the model of the French Revolution, Marx calls for a new and radical investigation of the political institutions that emerged from the first Revolution. The goal is to complete the emancipation process that developed with modernity, and therefore to solve the problems and contradictions, as highlighted by Hegel, in the modern political and industrial society. Other disciples, instead, believe that the social question can and should be solved by perfecting and developing, in an ethical sense, the State that was born out of the French Revolution. At any rate, both positions express the need to move beyond the merely political and legal phase of emancipation, and to place, as Hegel would put it, "positive right" alongside "negative right." Certainly, one can agree with Hayek that the legitimation of "positive" right or liberty is a catastrophe and that it is necessary to reject at least a century of history (starting from the 1848 Revolution or even earlier) in order for the Western world to regain its "authenticity." However, the fact remains that Hegel and the categories he formulated through his historical and theoretical evaluation of the French Revolution continue to be strongly present in the contemporary political debate.

9. The Conflicts of Freedom

There is one more interesting point. Hegel did not limit himself to distinguishing between "negative right" and "positive right," between "formal freedom" and "actual freedom." Although he declared himself in favor of synthesis, he emphasized the possibility or the risk, on the level of historical actuality, that a conflict might arise among these various aspects of right and freedom (supra, ch. IV, 6). Smith had already remarked that, particularly in a "free country" and under a "free government," it is especially difficult or even impossible for slaves to obtain emancipation or even only an improvement of their conditions or relief from their oppression.[118] This can happen more easily in a "despotic government," a government with no ties to the representative organs that are largely controlled by the slave owners.[119] What Smith has in mind are the British colonies in America, which were already based for the most part on self-government, but in which Locke himself wanted to see established, on a constitutional level, the principle that every "free man" must possess "absolute power and authority" "over his Negro slaves." Smith makes an analogous point about serfdom, this time referring to those Eastern European countries in which the weakness of the central power makes it impossible for the monarch to force the feudal nobility to emancipate the serfs (supra, ch. XII, 6).

The awareness of possible conflicts between freedoms, an awareness barely noticeable in Smith and then lost in the later liberal tradition, strongly re-emerges with Hegel. However, Hegel uses this as his point of departure to question the tranquil certainties expressed by Smith, who continues nonetheless to use the terms "free" and "despotic" to indicate, respectively, a government that sanctions slavery or serfdom, and a government that instead confronts the resistance of representative bodies dominated by the privileged classes and abolishes both slavery and serfdom. Although Hegel clearly moves away from Jacobinism, he is keenly aware of possible conflicts between freedoms, and therefore he refuses to subscribe to the superficial demonization of Jacobinism promoted by the liberal tradition. If, on the one hand, Jacobinism imposes a strict dictatorship, on the other hand it abolishes the feudal relationships of property and labor, and it ends up ordering the emancipation of slaves in the colonies. In this way, it acknowledges the results of the Slave Rebellion in Haiti led by a black Jacobin, Toussaint Louverture, and it finally includes the ex-slaves within the universal concept of man, entitled to inalienable and indefeasible rights.

In this sense, Hegel makes the border that separates freedom from oppression more problematic and uncertain. Thus, it is easy to understand the obsessive attempt, particularly on the part of the representatives of neo-liberalism, to confine this great interpreter of freedom (both positive and negative) to the history of totalitarianism, or at best, to the history of totalitarian democracy. Others, though they do not share in the zeal with which the representatives of neo-liberalism carry out their purification of the Western world, still feel nostalgia for their lost certainties and uneasiness about the fact that, from Hegel on, the discourse on freedom has become more complex and problematic. Nevertheless, it is important to remember that the only alternative to this complexity and uncertainty is a merely banal ideological history of the socio-political conflicts that, since the French Revolution, have been troubling the contemporary world.

NOTES

I. Searching for the "Authentic" Hegel

1 I. Kant, "Letter to Moses Mendelssohn, 8 April 1766," *Gesammelte Schriften,* (=*KGS*), vol. 10, 69, and "Letter to Johann Erich Biester, 18 May 1794," *KGS,* vol. 11, 501.

2 F. Engels, "Schelling und die Offenbarung," in Karl Marx and Friedrich Engels, *Werke* (=*MEW*), vol. 2, 175.

3 K. Rosenkranz, *Kritische Erläuterungen des Hegelschen Systems,* 218.

4 D. Losurdo, "Introduzione," in G. W. F. Hegel, *Le filosofie del diritto.*

5 C. Cesa, *Hegel filosofo politico,* 90.

6 K. Rosenkranz, *Von Magdeburg bis Königsberg,* 432.

7 "Letter to H. J. Campe, 18 April 1840," in H. Heine, *Sämtliche Schriften,* vol. 755.

8 See D. Losurdo, "Introduzione."

9 A. Ruge, "Über das Verhältnis von Philosophie, Politik und Religion," in *Sämtliche Werke,* vol. 4, 265–66.

10 C. Cesa, *Studi sulla sinistra hegeliana,* 337.

11 "Letter to A. Ruge, 25 January 1843," *MEW,* vol. 27, 415.

12 F. Engels, "Friedrich Wilhelm IV, König von Preußen," *MEW,* vol. 1, 447–50.

13 F. Engels [von Henning], "Rheinische Zeitung," 24 May 1842, *MEW,* vol. 2, 253–54.

14 F. Engels, "Friedrich Wilhelm IV," 446.

15 See D. Losurdo, *Hegel und das deutsche Erbe. Philosophie und nationale Frage zwischen Revolution und Restauration* (Cologne: Istituto Italiano per gli Studi Filosofici, 1989). This is a collection and translation—essentially, a second edition—of two previous works: *La politica culturale di Hegel a Berlino: Illuminismo, rivoluzione e tradizione nazionale* (Urbino: n.p., 1981), and *Hegel, questione nazionale, Restaurazione: Presupposti e sviluppi di una battaglia politica* (Urbino: n.p., 1983). One last part, ch. 6, § 4 of *La catastrofe della Germania e l'immagine di Hegel,* Milan: n.p., 1987 is also included.

16 K. Rosenkranz, *Von Magdeburg bis Königsberg,* 438.

17 K. Rosenkranz, *Kritische Erläuterungen,* 217.

18 Ibid., 229–32ff., 271.

19 Ibid., 223.

20 The expression is L. Strauss.' See L. Strauss, *Persecution and the Art of Writing*. Strauss' research concentrates on Spinoza and his contemporaries.

21 H. Ottmann, "Hegels Rechtsphilosophie und das Problem der Akkomodation," 242–43.

22 K.-H. Ilting, *Hegel diverso*. The central essay is an Italian translation of *Die "Rechtsphilosophie" von 1829 und Hegels Vorlesungen über Rechtsphilosophie. Einleitung* to *v.rph.*, 1, 119.

23 K.-H. Ilting, *Hegel diverso*, 116, 127ff. According to one of Ilting's disciples, the "original version of *Philosophy of Right*" has been "distorted." P. Becchi, *Contributi ad uno studio della filosofia del diritto di Hegel*, 175.

24 K. Marx, *Zur Kritik des Hegelschen Staatsrechts*, MEW, vol. 1, 300.

25 K. Marx,. *Anmerkungen zur Doktordissertation*, MEW, vol. 1, 326.

26 J. D'Hondt, *Hegel en son temps*.

27 J. D'Hondt, *Hegel secret*.

28 J. D'Hondt, *Hegel en son temps*.

29 See, in particular, D'Hondt's article, "Théorie et pratique politique chez Hegel: le problème de la censure," *Hegels Philosophie des Rechts*, D. Henrich and R. P. Horstmann, 151–84.

30 J. D'Hondt, *Hegel en son temps*. But even in the above-mentioned article, one finds: "Hegel's contemporaries ignored many aspects of his life. We are now able to discern the difference between what he says and what he does." J. D'Hondt, *Théorie et pratique politique*, 179. This view can also be inferred from the title of the article.

31 C. Cesa, *Hegel filosofo politico*, 91.

32 Ibid., 91.

33 J. D'Hondt, *Hegel en son temps*.

34 In order to emphasize the need for substantial political change so that Germany can keep up with the "spirit of the time," Carové refers explicitly to *Phenomenology* and to Hegel's writing on the Diet. See F. W. Carové, *Entwurf einer Burschenschafts-Ordnung und Versuch einer Begründung derselben*, viii.

35 J. D'Hondt, *Hegel secret*, 257–62.

36 J. G. Fichte, *Eleusinen des 19. Jahrhunderts oder Resultate vereinigter Denker über Philosophie und Geschichte der Freimaurerei*. Fichte's text was not included in the book edited by his son, and was recently republished as *Vorlesungen über die Freimaurerei* in J. G. Fichte, *Ausgewählte politische Schriften*, ed. Z. Batscha and R. Saage, 171–216. For Fichte's tormented relationship to Freemasonry, see S. Caramella's introduction to the Italian edition of *Philosophie der Freimaurerei, Filosofia della massoneria*. D'Hondt also insists on the Masonic meaning of a keyword, *Bund* (the "tie" or "alliance" between Hegel and Hölderlin celebrated in the poem), and this too is a fairly reliable reading. We shall soon see how the term is used by Goethe in an unequivocally Masonic context.

37 For a particularly significant contribution see C. Cesa, *Hegel filosofo politico*, 98–103.

38 J. D'Hondt, *Hegel secret*, passim, especially, 294–341.

39 J. D'Hondt, *Hegel en son temps*.

40 This can also be seen from their correspondence: H.B. 87, 118.

41 J. D'Hondt, *Hegel secret*, 337.

42 K. Rosenkranz, *Hegels Leben*, Darmstadt: n. p., 1963, 277. In the Italian translation

(*Vita di Hegel*, ed. R. Bodei), the translator refers to de Maistre's work as *Abendstunden*, but when Rosenkranz speaks of *Abendstunden*, he clearly refers to *Abendstunden zu St. Petersburg*. J. D'Hondt, *Hegel secret*, 300.

43 "Letter to T. von Schön, September 30, 1792," J. G. Fichte, *Briefwechsel* (Hildesheim: n. p., 1967), vol. 1, 258.

44 K. Epstein, *The Genesis of German Conservatism*.

45 D. Mornet, *Les origines intellectuelles de la révolution française*, 364–65, 386. In England, Edmund Burke was a Mason—see J. Rogalla von Biberstein, *Die These von der Verschwörung*, 117—and hostile to Hegel's position.

46 J. D'Hondt, *Hegel secret*, 336.

47 K. Epstein, *The Genesis*.

48 J. D'Hondt, *Hegel secret*, 337.

49 K. Epstein, *The Genesis*.

50 "Letter to his wife, 28 October 1799," J. G. Fichte, *Briefwechsel*, vol. 2, 184. Already in Zürich, Fichte observes that the Masons can supply "fruitful ties," though he adds that he would like to adhere to a Freemasonry with a "superior vision." J. G. Fichte, *Briefwechsel*, vol. 1, 258.

51 Goethe mentions this in a letter dated 9 August 1830. See *Goethes Briefe*, ed. R. Mandelkow, vol. 4, 389. In gratitude for the respect his friends and fellow Masons show him, Goethe writes a poem, enclosed in the above-cited letter, which celebrates an eternally strong "bond" (*Bund*). This would seem to confirm D'Hondt's theory about the meaning of the term *Bund*, and about Goethe being a Mason.

52 "Letter to Schleiermacher, 25 July 1806," in J. G. Fichte, *Fichte in vertraulichen Briefen seiner Zeitgenossen*, 218. For Fichte's "Letter to F. Schlegel, 16 August 1800" ("The Masons have so bored and repulsed me that I have completely withdrawn from them"), see J. G. Fichte, *Briefwechsel*, vol. 2, 251.

53 Varnhagen von Ense, 1811, see J. G. Fichte, *Fichte in vertraulichen Briefen*, 244.

54 F. E. D. Schleiermacher, "Grundlinien einer Kritik der bisherigen Sittenlehre," *Werke*, ed. O. Braun and J. Bauer, vol. 1, 184.

55 This emerges from Fichte's correspondence. See "Letters to T. von Schön, 30 September 1792 and 20 September 1793," J. G. Fichte, *Briefwechsel*, vol. 1, 257–58, 301.

56 Far from seeing Fichte as a "brother," Hegel at this time (1795) accuses him of promoting a theological and obscurantist utilization of Kant's thought with his *Attempt at a Critique of All Revelation*.

57 J. D'Hondt, *Hegel secret*, 247–53.

58 I. Kant, "Über das Misslingen aller philosophischen Versuche in der Theodizee," KGS, vol. 8, 268.

59 J. Ch. F. Nicolai, *Neun Gespräche zwischen Christian Wolff und einem Kantianer über Kants metaphysische Anfangsgründe der Rechtslehre und Tugendlehre*, 123. On Nicolai's ties to the Masons, see K. Epstein, *The Genesis*.

60 This is according to the testimony of Varnhagen von Ense: J. G. Fichte, *Fichte in vertraulichen Briefen*, 244.

61 J. G. Fichte, *Vorlesungen über die Freimaurerei*, 209, 213.

62 This is evident in the correspondence with Fessler. See Fichte's letter of 28 May 1800, and the observations and arguments of the two "brothers," J. G. Fichte, *Briefwechsel*, vol. 2, 226–35, especially 234.

63 See J. D'Hondt, *Hegel secret*, 341.

64 F. W. J. Schelling, "Philosophische Briefe über Dogmatismus und Kriticismus," *Sämmtliche Werke*, vol. 1, 341.

65 Ibid., vol. 1, 341.

66 It seems that Fichte is most revolutionary when he hesitates to abide by Masonic ideals because he feels repelled by "symbols and antiques," and by "masks" behind which may lurk "societies" that pursue "particular goals." See "Letter to T. von Schön, 30 September 1792," J. G. Fichte, *Briefwechsel*, vol. 1, 258. This is a Fichte who, still in the *Beitrag*, and driven by his enthusiasm for the French Revolution, argues against the elitism which strives to keep exoteric truth and esoteric truth apart. See "Beitrag zur Berichtigung der Urteile des Publikums über die französische Revolution," *Fichtes Werke* (=*FW*), vol. 6, 76–78. This is not the Fichte who, influenced by the Masons, justifies the distinction he previously rejected for clearly progressive political reasons.

67 J. D'Hondt, *Hegel secret*, 333–34.

68 F. W. J. Schelling, "Philosophie der Mythologie, Vol. 1," *Sämmtliche Werke*, vol. 11, 76.

69 F. Schiller, *Voyage en Syrie et en Egypte pendant les années 1782–85*. See the "Letter from Schiller to Goethe, 26 January 1798," E. Staiger, ed., *Der Briefwechsel zwischen Schiller und Goethe*, 554–55.

70 F. R. de Chateaubriand, *Itinéraire de Paris à Jérusalem*, part 1.

71 C. Cesa, *Hegel filosofo politico*, 97.

72 E. Young, *The Complaint, or Night Thoughts on Life, Death and Immortality*, VI, verses 176–242. As for the English poet's success in Italy and Europe, as well as for the general theme being discussed here, see R. Ceserani-L. de Federicis, *Il materiale e l'immaginario*, vol. 6.

73 F. W. J. Schelling, "System des transzendentalen Idealismus," *Sämmtliche Werke*, vol. 3, 604.

74 F. Schlegel, "Philosophie der Geschichte," *Kritische Friedrich-Schlegel-Ausgabe*, ed. E. Behler, pt. 1, vol. 9, 339.

75 H. Heine, "Verschiedenartige Geschichtsauffassung," *Sämtliche Schriften*, vol. 3, 21–22.

76 Ibid., vol. 3, 23.

77 H. Ottmann, *Individuum und Gemeinschaft bei Hegel*, vol. 1, 273.

78 R. Haym, *Die deutsche Nationalversammlung bis zu den Septemberereignissen*. For Karl Löwith's view, see his *Von Hegel zu Nietzsche*. Incidentally, the gross confusion between "right" and "left" dominates the anthology which Löwith dedicates to the "Hegelian Left." The decision to include a figure like Kierkegaard, regardless of the theoretical motivation, is in itself odd. (Kierkegaard had studied in Berlin with Schelling, who in his later period was fighting against the "demon seed of Hegelian pantheism.") In addition, the lengthy citations from Bruno Bauer's *Russland und das Germanenthum*, which dates from 1853, when Bauer was clearly no longer left-wing or Hegelian, are equally strange. Bauer is so distant from his ex-teacher that he even considers him "lacking creative power" and goes so far as to support the Austrian government's oppression of a professor who, even after the Revolution of 1848 failed, was so bold as to remain allied to a system like Hegel's, which Bauer considered the "confused product of a poetic fantasy." B. Bauer, "Russland und das Germanenthum," *La sinistra hegeliana*, ed. K. Löwith, 227, 268. The

last judgment calls to mind Rudolf Haym and, in fact, in these later years, Bruno Bauer is no more Hegelian than the author of *Hegel und seine Zeit.*

On this point, one might also examine H. Lübbe, the editor of *Die Hegelsche Rechte*, who, drawing on Löwith, sees Haym's anti-Hegelianism as "merely a repetition and synthesis of the left's argument against Hegel." H. Lübbe, *Politische Philosophie in Deutschland*, 41. As for the authors who are listed as "right-wing," it is true that they are the product of a long tradition that emerges immediately following Hegel's death, but the problematic aspects of this tradition are not thoroughly considered. For example, Michelet, categorized as "right-wing" because of his presumed "atheism," is considered by Karl Rosenkranz not only to be a leftist, but at the furthest point on the left! See K. Rosenkranz, "Über Schelling und Hegel: Ein Sendschreiben an Pierre Leroux," *Neue Studien*, vol. 4, 214–15. See also K. Rosenkranz, *Hegel als deutscher Nationalphilosoph*, 312. Towards the end of the nineteenth century Michelet is viewed as left-wing. See L. Noack, "Hegel," *Philosophiegeschichtliches Lexicon*. After all, Michelet considers himself to be on the left as he calls upon the "center" to join the left against the right: C. L. Michelet, *Geschichte der letzten Systeme der Philosophie in Deutschland*, reprinted in J. E. Erdmann, *Grundriss der Geschichte der Philosophie*, 654. A more general issue is the absurdity of including authors whose positions are liberal and progressive in the category "right-wing." For this reason Cesa, in his edition of the anthology in question, prefers the category "liberals"—*Gli hegeliani liberali*. Yet this by itself does not solve the problem. One must still distinguish between "liberal" and "left-wing." For instance, according to what criteria would Heine be considered left-wing as opposed to liberal? One indication of the persistent uncertainty surrounding this problem is the total silence about Lassalle, who is ignored in both anthologies. On the one hand, Lassalle calls to mind Michelet (with whom he has a friendly relationship and with whom he collaborates in the publication, well after 1848, of the "orthodox" Hegelian *Der Gedanke*). Today, Michelet would normally be classified as "right-wing" or "liberal." On the other hand, Lassalle calls to mind the history of the workers' movement, and its criticism, from the left, of liberalism. In conclusion, a political history of the Hegelian school is still needed, and this lacuna, with its resultant, persistent uncertainty and confusion about the true political location of the protagonists in the nineteenth century debate on Hegel, continues to adversely affect the interpretation of Hegel's thought.

79 R. Haym, *Hegel und seine Zeit*, 32, 34.
80 Haym's was a "cry for war against speculation" and certainly in favor of "liberalism," but it was also, above all, a cry in favor of "national politics." R. Haym, *Aus meinem Leben: Erinnerungen*, 257–58.
81 "Letter, 5 March 1842," *MEW*, vol. 27, 397.
82 For example, in "Zur Kritik des Hegelschen Staatsrechts," Marx writes: "Hegel supported a modern monarchy that is constitutional, not patriarchal" (*MEW*, vol. 1, 299). Hegel has correctly claimed that the "essence of the modern State" was born of the French Revolution, though he then errs in wanting to make the Revolution absolute (*MEW*, vol. 1, 266). The dismissal of Hegel's thought by Della Volpe and his school is fundamentally flawed because they specifically ignore the fact that Marx limits his criticism to Hegel's position as the leading representative of bourgeois thought and development.

83 F. Engels, "Ludwig Feuerbach und der Ausgang der Klassischen deutschen Philosophie," *MEW*, vol. 21, 269.

84 F. Engels, "Die Entwicklung des Sozialismus von der Utopie zur Wissenschaft," *MEW*, vol. 19, 187, 189. Among the national-liberals targeted by Engels is Treitschke, who collaborates on the "Preußische Jahrbücher," the journal edited by Haym, and who later succeeds him.

85 A. Trendelenburg, *Die logische Frage: Zwei Streitschriften*, 32–33.

86 F. Engels, *Die Entwicklung*, 191–92.

87 R. Haym, *Hegel und seine Zeit*, 382.

88 Ibid., 259–60.

89 Ibid., 164–66.

90 F. W. J. Schelling, "Stuttgarter Privatvorlesungen," *Sämmtliche Werke*, vol. 7, 461–62.

91 R. Haym, *Hegel und seine Zeit*, 160–61, 164–66.

92 Ibid., 262.

93 R. Haym, "Varnhagen von Ense," in *Zur deutschen Philosophie und Literatur*, ed. E. Howald, 143–44, 152–54.

94 "Letter from Marx to Engels, 18 June 1862," *MEW*, vol. 30, 249. See also R. Haym, *Hegel und seine Zeit*, 389–90.

95 See E. Topitsch, "Kritik der Hegel-Apologeten," "In critica degli apologeti di Hegel," *Il pensiero politico di Hegel: Guida storica e critica*, ed. C. Cesa, 171–91.

96 Arguing against certain recurring and somewhat ill-considered slogans, Marino has rightly observed that "to try and explain Hegel today by drawing upon Hegel would be both a desperate and useless task. Too many philosophical experiences condition us; too many images pass before our interpretative eyes. Still, if we perhaps risk confusion, on the other hand, to renounce such richness would really and truly amount to historiographic suicide." L. Marino, "Hegel e le origini del diritto borghese," *Rivista di filosofia* 1 (April 1985): 167.

97 See H. G. Gadamer, *Wahrheit und Methode*, 3rd ed., 359–60. The idealistic nature of Gadamer's hermeneutics has already been addressed in J. Habermas, *Zur Logik der Sozialwissenschaften: Materialien*, 289–90. For a particularly vigorous Marxist analysis of Gadamer's idealism, see H. J. Sandkühler, *Praxis und Geschichtsbewußtstein*, 62ff.

II. The Philosophies of Right: A Turning Point or Continuity

1 This theory is already present in *Hegel diverso*, and, according to Ilting, it is confirmed by the recent discovery of the 1817–18 and 1819–20 lecture courses; cf. K.-H. Ilting, *Zur Genese der hegelschen "Rechtsphilosophie,"* 161–202, nn. 3–4.

2 This has been confirmed by the recent discovery of a manuscript that was most likely the transcript of the 1821–22 lecture course on the philosophy of right (the only missing one), and in which the following quote appears, without any significant differences from *Philosophy of Right:* "The rational is actual and the actual is rational" (*Das Vernünftige ist wirklich und das Wirkliche ist vernünftig*). On this course, for which Hansgeorg Hoppe is preparing a critical edition, see Paolo Becchi, "Hegelsche Vorlesungsnachschriften und noch kein Ende?," *Materiali per una storia della cultura giuridica* 16.1 (1986) 251–61.

3 R. Haym, *Hegel und seine Zeit*, 66–67.

4 A letter to his father dated 10 November 1837, *MEW*, vol. 1, 4–8. The rationality of the actual is extolled by Marx not only in prose, but also in verse, though perhaps mediocre verse. "Kant and Fichte wandered gladly among the clouds: / looking up there for a far-away place. / Instead I only want to grasp with dexterity / what I have found on the street!" Karl Marx, *Scritti politici giovanili*, 490.

5 V. I. Lenin, "Philosophical Notebooks," *Collected Works*, vol. 38, 283, 309–10. The important passages are from 1914–15. For his citations of Hegel, see V. I. Lenin, *Collected Works*, vol. 12, 40 and vol. 19, 110–11.

6 V. I. Lenin, *Philosophical Notebooks*, 98.

7 Antonio Gramsci, *Quaderni del carcere*, 1417.

8 F. Engels, *Ludwig Feuerbach*, 266.

9 G. W. F. Hegel, *Religionsphilosophie: Die Vorlesung von 1821*, vol. 1, 641.

10 F. Engels, *Ludwig Feuerbach*, 281.

11 F. J. Stahl, *Die Philosophie des Rechts*, 5th ed., vol. 2.1, 52n.

12 With particular clarity, *Die Konflikte unserer Zeit und das Erfordernis einer ethisch-politischen Grundorientierung*, ed. K. O. Apel et al., 285.

13 A. de Tocqueville, "De la démocratie en Amérique," *Oeuvres complètes*, vol. 1.1, 4–5.

14 "In those days you could find injustice and misery in society, but no spiritual degradation." Ibid., 6. Sainte-Beuve very acutely compares Tocqueville to Virgil's *Aeneas* whose reason draws him towards democratic Rome, but who is full of nostalgia for the Dido of the *ancien régime*. See C. A. Sainte-Beuve, *Causeries du lundi*, vol. 15, 69. After all, Tocqueville himself confesses that "For democratic institutions I have an intellectual liking (*un goût de tête*), but I am aristocratic by instinct. I fear and loathe the masses" (a note written around November 1841, in A. de Tocqueville, *Oeuvres complètes*, vol. 3.2, 87).

15 A. de Tocqueville, "De la démocratie en Amérique," vol. 1, 489.

16 F. J. Stahl, *Die Philosophie des Rechts*, vol. 1, 489.

17 In his edition of the printed text of *Philosophy of Right*, Ilting uses the following subtitle for § 279: "The irreducibility of the monarch's power: Monarchy by divine right" (*V.RPH.*, II, 741).

18 In addition to Ilting's works, see in particular H. Ottmann,: *Hegels Rechtsphilosophie*, P. Becchi, *Contributi ad uno studio della filosofia del diritto di Hegel*, 161–90, and P. Becchi, "Im Schatten der Entscheidung," 231–45.

19 F. J. W. Schelling, "Schlußwort zur öffentlichen Sitzung der Akademie der Wissenschaften in München," *Sämmtliche Werke*, vol. 9, 423–24. See also infra ch. 10, n. 27.

20 See C. Cesa, *Hegel filosofo politico*, 143. Hegel condemns the fact that "the Diet appealed to the guarantee of power . . . in Vienna" and contrasts this to the dignified and respectful attitude of a defeated France to her own independence (*W*, IV, 580–81).

21 In Berlin, Hegel transcribes some passages of the French writer de Pradt who defends the Spanish Revolution and condemns those who, in the name of tradition, would like to return to the days of "the Golden Bull, of Charles V, of Widukind." Hegel comments that this is "the belief of Teutonic (*altdeutsch*) demagogues"(*B.schr.*, 699). The Teutons are essentially the same as the reactionaries. See D. Losurdo, *Hegel und das deutsche Erbe*, 7, 11–13 (in Italian, *Hegel, questione nazionale, Restaurazione*, ch. 5, 11–13).

22   See K.-H. Ilting, *Hegel diverso*, 40.

23   Ibid., 121. See also, P. Becchi, *Contributi ad uno studio della filosofia del diritto di Hegel*, 164–65.

24   F. R. Chateaubriand, *Mémoires d'outre-tombe*, vol. 2, 448, 464.

25   F. X. von Baader, "Über das Revolutionieren des positiven Rechtsbestandes," *Sämtliche Werke*, vol. 6, 61–62.

26   This is according to G. Verucci, "La Restaurazione," *Storia delle idee politiche, economiche e sociali*, 902–3.

27   K.-H. Ilting, *Zur Genese der hegelschen "Rechtsphilosophie,"* 191.

28   F. R. de Chateaubriand, *Mémoires d'outre-tombe*, vol. 2, 459.

29   G. Verucci, *La Restaurazione*, 903–4.

30   F. R. de Chateaubriand, *Mémoires d'outre-tombe*, vol. 2, 513.

31   F. R. de Chateaubriand, "De la monarchie selon la Charte," *Mélanges politiques et littéraires*, 247. See also G. Verucci, *La Restaurazione*, 903.

32   F. R. de Chateaubriand, "De la Vendée," *Mélanges politiques et littéraires*, 143, 152–53.

33   F. R. de Chateaubriand, "De la monarchie selon la Charte," 237.

34   K.-H. Ilting, *Zur Genese der hegelschen "Rechtsphilosophie,"* 190–91. The citations are from Ilting. It is true that Constant takes a different position from Royer-Collard and Guizot in this debate, but this only confirms the complex nature of the situation. The general principles of liberal political theory were unfit to answer the immediate political needs, hence the diverse and contrasting responses of the liberal movement's supporters.

35   Karl Marx, "Randglossen zu den Anklagen des Ministerialereskripts," *MEW*, vol. 1, 424.

36   L. Börne, "Letters 24 and 35," "Briefe aus Paris (1832–34), *Sämtliche Schriften*, vol. 3, 113, 189.

37   K.-H. Ilting, *Hegel diverso*, 119–22.

38   P. Becchi, *Contributi ad uno studio della filosofia del diritto di Hegel*, 176.

39   With *Philosophy of Right*, "Hegel clearly places himself in agreement with Metternich's Restoration politics." P. Becchi, "Im Schatten der Entscheidung," 233.

40   Ibid., 239.

41   L. Börne, "Briefe aus Paris," Letter 33, 170.

42   See *B*, II, 148–49, 175–76, and Hoffmeister's note.

43   For example, one member of the Diet speaks of the French revolutionaries as a "dangerous cult of innovators who have caused much misfortune in the world." See *Scritti politici* di *Hegel*, C. Cesa, ed., 189n.

44   K. Marx, "Das philosophische Manifest der historischen Rechtsschule," *MEW*, vol. 1, 81, 85.

45   After the Silesian weavers' revolt in 1844, Varnhagen attacks "the ignoble minister, Savigny" who had distinguished himself by his merciless repression, and all this because "those villains will not quietly starve to death; rather, they disturb the Excellencies and annoy the king." L. Kroneberg and R. Schloesser, *Weber-Revolte 1844*, 283.

46   See J. D'Hondt, *Hegel en son temps*, 95–128, and S. Avineri, *Hegel's Theory of the Modern State* for criticism of Avineri, who sees Fries and his followers as reactionaries and proto-fascists. See D. Losurdo "Fichte, la resistenza antinapoleonica e la filosofia classica tedesca," *Studi Storici* 1–2 (1983): 189–216.

47   S. Hook, "Hegel Rehabilitated," *Hegel's Political Philosophy*, ed. Walter Kaufmann,
     94. When citing this passage, Ilting raises only one objection: by making *Philosophy
     of Right* an expression of Restoration politics, Hook fails to consider the lecture
     courses on the philosophy of right before and after the printed text. K.-H. Ilting,
     Hegel diverso, 114.
48   D. Losurdo, *Hegel und das deutsche Erbe*, ch. 7 (in Italian, *Hegel, questione na-
     zionale, Restaurazione*, ch. 5).

III. Contractualism and the Modern State

1   Norberto Bobbio, *Studi hegeliani*, xvii, 95–97, 108–13.
2   K.-H. Ilting, *Hegel diverso*, 119.
3   E. Burke, "Reflections on the Revolution in France," *The Works of the Right Hon-
    ourable Edmund Burke*, vol. 5, 82, 121.
4   E. Burke, "Appeal from the New to the Old Whigs," *The Works*, vol. 6, 201.
5   E. Burke, "Reflections on the Revolution in France," 184.
6   "Memorandum from F. A. L. von der Marwitz to Hardenberg, 11 February 1811," in
    Adam Müllers Lebenszeugnisse, ed. J. Baxa, vol. 1, 616.
7   In Rome, women "were slaves." This problem still exists in Africa (*v.Rph.*, IV, 446).
    Hegel expresses a similar view on the relation between fathers and sons.
8   N. Bobbio, *Studi hegeliani*, 95.
9   Benjamin Constant, "De M. Dunoyer et de quelques-uns de ses ouvrages," *Mélanges
    de littérature et de politique*, vol. 1, 97.
10 Jeremy Bentham, "Anarchical Fallacies: A Critical Examination of the Declaration
    of Rights," *The Works*, ed. J. Bowring, vol. 2, 501.
11 B. Constant, "De M. Dunoyer et de quelques-uns de ses ouvrages," 100.
12 J. Bentham, *Anarchical Fallacies*, 501.
13 E. Burke, *Reflections on the Revolution in France*, 104.
14 It is due to these theories that Haller is quoted approvingly by Prussian reaction-
    aries. See W. Scheel, *Das 'Berliner Politisches Wochenblatt' und die politische und
    soziale Revolution in Frankreich und England*. Social Darwinism is also influenced
    by Haller (infra, ch. XIII, 4).
15 This is the argument against 'Berliner Politisches Wochenblatt.' K. Rosenkranz,
    Königsberger Skizzen, vol. 2, 170, 174.
16 Immanuel Kant, "Zum ewigen Frieden," *KGS*, vol. 8, 372.
17 "Discourse at the Convention of 24 April 1793," L. A. L. de Saint-Just, *Oeuvres
    complètes*, ed. M. Duval, 423.
18 Bobbio also puts Hegel next to Burke. N. Bobbio, *Il contratto sociale oggi*, 23.
19 E. Burke, *Reflections on the Revolution in France*, 76.
20 Joseph-Marie de Maistre, "Considérations sur la France," *Oeuvres complètes*, vol. 1,
    74.
21 E. Burke, "Remarks on the Policy of the Allies with Respect to France," *The Works*,
    vol. 7, 129; "Letter to the Right Honourable Henry Dundas," *The Works*, vol. 9, 281.
    See also K. R. Popper, *The Open Society and its Enemies*, vol. 1, 33–34, 216, and vol.
    2, 290. Popper's claim that acceptance of "methodological nominalism" is a neces-
    sary condition for an open and liberal society is arbitrarily "holistic." More than just
    a weapon in the struggle against the doctrine of Natural Law and the French Revolu-

tion, nominalism will become the banner of blatant and brutal theorists of racism, such as Gumplowicz and Chamberlain (cf. G. Lukács, *Die Zerstörung der Vernunft*; D. Losurdo, *Hegel und das deutsche Erbe*, ch. 14, 24; or "La catastrofe della Germania e l'immagine di Hegel," chs. 3, 7), and the banner of Nazism which scorns the very category of "humanity."

22　E. Burke, "Preface to the Address of M. Brissot to His Constituents," *The Works*, vol. 7, 298.

23　E. Burke, *Reflections on the Revolution in France*, 76–79.

24　N. Bobbio, *Studi hegeliani*, 113.

25　Voltaire, A. B. C., first conversation. For Montesquieu, on the other hand, the venality of public offices serves a positive, antidespotic function. Montesquieu, *De l'esprit des lois*, 1748, V, 19. Hume also subscribes to this position in a letter dated 10 April 1749. Montesquieu, *Oeuvres complètes*, ed. A. Masson, vol. 3, 1218–19.

26　B. Constant, "De la liberté des anciens comparée à celle modernes," *De la liberté chez les modernes. Écrits politiques*, ed. M. Gauchet, 511–12.

27　John Locke, *Two Treatises of Government*, II, § 138.

28　B. Constant, "Principes de politique," *Oeuvres*, ed. A. Roulin, 1148.

29　B. Constant, "Des réactions politiques," *Écrits et discours politiques*, ed. O. Pozzo di Borgo, 74.

30　B. Constant, *Principes de politique*, 1147–48.

31　On the opposite side, Marat declares that the notion of social contract "gestures to federalism" and, essentially, aims at dissolving the Republic. See B.-J. Bonchez and P.-C. Roux, *Histoire parlementaire de la Révolution française*, vol. 26, 433.

32　A. de Tocqueville, "De la démocratie en Amérique," vol. 1, 408.

33　N. Bobbio, *Il contratto sociale oggi*, 25, 39–40.

34　Ferdinand Lassalle, "Das Arbeiterprogramm," *Gesammelte Reden und Schriften*, ed. E. Bernstein, vol. 2, 195–96.

35　This is according to the great Rhenish liberal-capitalist, David Hansemann. J. Droz, *Le libéralisme rhénan, 1815–1848*, 242–43.

36　Jürgen Kuczynski, *Die Geschichte der Lage der Arbeiter unter dem Kapitalismus*, vol. 1, 271.

37　Adam Smith, *An Inquiry into the Nature and Causes of the Wealth of Nations*, 3rd ed., bk. 1, ch. 10, part 2. We are citing the reprinted Glasgow edition, vol. 1 (Indianapolis: n.p., 1981), 157–58.

38　J. Locke, "Some Considerations of the Consequences of Lowering the Interest and Raising the Value of Money," *Works*, vol. 5, 24–25.

39　The *Le Chapelier* law of 1791 prohibited worker coalitions against "alleged common interests" in the name of individual "freedom of contract." J. Jaurès, *Storia socialista della rivoluzione francese*, vol. 2, 249–50.

40　Karl Marx, *Das Kapital*, vol. 1, bk. 1, ch. 4, 3, *MEW*, vol. 23, 189–90.

IV. Conservative or Liberal? A False Dilemma

1　N. Bobbio, *Studi hegeliani*, 189–90.

2　Voltaire, "L'équivoque," *Oeuvres complètes de Voltaire*, vol. 7, 423.

3　Montesquieu, *De l'esprit des lois*, 4.

4 A. de Tocqueville, "L'Ancien Régime et la Révolution," *Oeuvres complètes*, vol. 2, 213–17.

5 S. Rotta, "Il pensiero francese da Bayle a Montesquieu," *Storia delle idee politiche, economiche e sociali*, vol. 4, 202.

6 B. Constant, "De la juridiction du gouvernement sur l'éducation," *Mélanges de littérature et de politique*, vol. 2, 8–9.

7 F. Gentz, "Über die National-Erziehung in Frankreich," *Ausgewählte Schriften*, ed. W. Weick, vol. 2, 182n., 185–86.

8 I. Kant, "Metaphysik der Sitten. Rechtslehre," *KGS*, vol. 6, §§ 29, 281–82.

9 J. S. Mill, "On Liberty," *Utilitarianism, Liberty, Representative Government*, ed. H. B. Acton, 159–60, 163.

10 J. Locke, *Two Treatises of Government*, II, § 85. "A freeman makes himself a servant." This is how Locke depicts the status of house servants and wage laborers. Hegel's formulation of labor relations is much more modern and "liberal." The reader is referred to the introductory note to ch. 3 of G. W. F. Hegel, *Le filosofie del diritto*, ed. D. Losurdo, 105–16.

11 C. B. Macpherson, *The Political Theory of Possessive Individualism: Hobbes to Locke*, 223.

12 Such are the terms used in the *Vormärz* by the liberal *Staats-Lexikon*, edited by C. von Rotteck and C. Welcker. See D. Losurdo, *Tra Hegel e Bismarck*, 144–48.

13 R. Nozick, *Anarchy, State and Utopia*.

14 N. Bobbio, *Il futuro della democrazia*, 122.

15 F. A. Hayek, *Law, Legislation and Liberty*.

16 Ibid., vol. 3, 194.

17 F. W. J. Schelling, *Philosophie der Mythologie*, 541ff.

18 Schelling says, according to the testimony of Melchior Meyr (diary entry, 3 March 1848) that the February Revolution was the result of "Louis Philippe's weakness. By letting Guizot fall, he surrendered, and the soldiers lost their faith!" *Schelling im Spiegel seiner Zeitgenossen*, ed. X. Tilliette, 452. A letter dated Christmas, 1848, calls upon Austria, Prussia, and Bavaria to finally establish the "indispensable dictatorship." See "König Maximilian II von Bayern und Schelling," *Briefwechsel*, ed. L. Troste and F. Leist, 169. On his support for Louis Bonaparte's *coup d'état*, ibid., 209, 242.

19 "Letter to J. Frauenstädt, 2 March 1849," *Der Briefwechsel Arthur Schopenhauers*, ed. C. Gebhardt, vol. 1, 638.

20 F. Nietzsche, *Menschliches, Allzumenschliches*.

21 "Letter to C. von Gersdorff, 21 June 1871," F. Nietzsche, *Briefwechsel. Kritische Gesamtausgabe*, ed. G. Colli and M. Montinari, vol. 2, 203–4. The motto "Écr[asez] l'Int[ernationale]" is found in Hans von Bülow's encouraging and laudatory letter to Nietzsche dated 29 August 1873. F. Nietzsche, *Briefwechsel*, vol. 2, 288.

22 On the antistatist polemic and the "liberal" catchwords of Restoration theorists in Germany see D. Losurdo, *Hegel und das deutsche Erbe*, 8–9. For the Lamennais citation, see "De la position l'Église en France," *L'Avenir 1830–31*, ed. G. Verucci, 230.

23 H. J. Laski, *The Rise of European Liberalism*; R. H. Tawney, *Religion and the Rise of Capitalism*.

24 E. Burke, *Reflections on the Revolution in France*, 121.

25 J. Möser, "Der Bauerhof als eine Aktie betrachtet," *Sämmtliche Werke*, ed. B. R. Abeken and J. W. J. von Voigts, vol. 3, 291ff. See also infra, ch. VIII, 6.

26 On Rousseau, see "Discours sur l'économie politique," *Oeuvres complètes* (=OC), ed. B. Gagnebin and M. Raymond, vol. 3, 271. For Montesquieu, see *De l'esprit des lois*, 14.

27 See L. Colletti, "L'equivoco di Lukács," *Mondo Operaio* (Jan. 1986): 99–103.

28 B. Constant, *Principes de politique*, 1145–47.

29 Ibid., 1145–47.

30 This dialectic, though altered, is found in the subsequent history of liberalism. In Mill, workers have achieved the same political rights as other citizens, and yet, as far as "those backward states of society . . . the race itself may be considered in its nonage." J. S. Mill, *On Liberty*, 73. The image of the family abandoned to the metropolis reappears in the relationship between metropolis and colonies. In this case, liberal "organicism" does not disappear but is instead shifted.

31 A. Smith, *An Inquiry into the Nature and the Causes of the Wealth of Nations*, bk. 4, ch. 2, 456.

32 F. A. von Hayek, *Law, Legislation and Liberty*.

33 P. J. Proudhon, *De la justice dans la révolution et dans l'église*, vol. 1, 511.

34 J. S. Mill, *On Liberty*, 165, 163.

35 A. de Tocqueville, "Mémoire sur le paupérisme," *Mémoires de la Société Royale Académique de Cherbourg*, 343. English translation: A. de Tocqueville. *Memoir on Pauperism*, trans., Seymour Drescher, Chicago: Ivan R. Dee, 1997, 71.

36 This is the same charge that Henrich seems to level at Hegel (*Rph. III*, 24). See also the pertinent observations in P. Becchi, *Contributi ad uno studio della filosofia del diritto di Hegel*, 186–89.

37 While it is "abominable theologians" who justify the right to rebellion against sovereigns deemed heretics, it is Voltaire who demands that these theologians are condemned as "lese majesties." "Traité sur la tolérance," "Abus de l'intolérance," *Oeuvres complètes de Voltaire*, vol. 30, 118–19.

38 See D. Losurdo, *Autocensura e compromesso nel pensiero politico di Kant*.

39 G. Lukács, *Schicksalswende. Beiträge zu einer neuen deutschen Ideologie*, 57.

40 L. von Haller, *Analisi della costituzione delle Cortès di Spagna, opera del Signor Carlo Luigi di Haller*, 137–38. In Kant, the right to resistance is rejected with Vandea in mind. Even in France, the right to resistance, initially used to justify the Revolution, quickly becomes a weapon of the reactionaries. See D. Losurdo, *Autocensura e compromesso*, ch. 1. See also: infra chs. VII, VIII.

41 J. Bentham, *Anarchical Fallacies*, 501.

42 J. Locke, *Two Treatises of Government*, II, §§ 21, 235, 241.

43 B. Constant, *Principes de politique*, 1110–11.

44 F. C. Dahlmann, *Die Politik*, 177.

45 F. C. Dahlmann, "Zur Verständigung," *Kleine Schriften und Reden*, 258.

46 F. C. Dahlmann, *Die Politik*, 177–78.

47 B. Constant, "Préface," *Mélanges de littérature et de politique*, vol. 1, vi.

48 A. de Tocqueville, "Souvenirs," *Oeuvres complètes*, vol. 12, 176. Despite tormenting doubts about France's possible intervention, Tocqueville, as Minister of Foreign Affairs, takes a similar position to the revolutionaries of the Roman Republic: troops are called upon to "terrorize the demagogic Party." "Letter to F. de Corcelle, 18 July 1849," in A. de Tocqueville, *Oeuvres complètes*, vol. 15, 323.

49 J. Locke, *Two Treatises of Government*, II, § 25.

50 C. von Rotteck, *Lehrbuch des Vernunftrechts und der Staatswissenschaften*, vol. 1, 154–57.

51 J. Locke, *Two Treatises of Government*, II, § 222.

52 Ibid., vol. 2, § 226.

53 Ibid., vol. 2, §§ 228, 231.

54 Ibid., vol. 2, § 243.

55 F. Engels, "Vorbemerkung zu 'Der deutsche Bauernkrieg,' " *MEW*, vol. 7, 539.

56 Montesquieu, *De l'esprit des lois*, 6.

57 F. R. de Chateaubriand, *Mémoires d'outre-tombe*, vol. 2, 459ff. In fact, it has been noted that Chateaubriand (whose journal puffs the "ideas of the political-ecclesiastic Restoration") is the first to assign to the term "conservative" its present-day meaning. K. Mannheim, "Das Konservative Denken," *Wissenssoziologie. Auswahl aus dem Werk*, ed. K. H. Wolff, 417–18.

58 F. J. Stahl, *Die Philosophie des Rechts*, vol. 1, 475.

59 C. H. de Saint-Simon, "Catéchisme des industriels," *Oeuvres*, ed. Enfantin, vol. 8, 178ff. Volume 8 is in volume 4 in the edition published by Anthropos, Paris: 1966.

60 B. Constant, "De M. Dunoyer et de quelques-uns de ses ouvrages," 107–8.

61 B. Constant, "De la liberté des anciens comparée à celle des modernes," 503.

62 A. de Tocqueville, *L'Ancien Régime et la Révolution*, 214, 233.

63 R. Dahrendorf, *Gesellschaft und Demokratie in Deutschland*.

64 A. de Tocqueville, *L'Ancien Régime et la Révolution*, 214–16.

65 Ibid., 214.

66 F. J. Stahl, *Die Philosophie des Rechts*, vol. 1, 475.

67 F. R. de Chateaubriand, *Mémoires d'outre-tombe*, vol. 2, 512–13.

V. Hegel and the Liberal Tradition: Two Opposing Interpretations of History

1 G. W. F. Hegel, *Religionsphilosophie*, ed. K.-H. Ilting, vol. 1, 641.

2 According to V. Cuoco, this is the case in Italy. V. Cuoco, *Saggio storico sulla rivoluzione napoletana del 1799*, 2nd ed., 100. In Germany, F. Gentz warns against the "agrarian laws" in "Über die Moralität in den Staatsrevolutionen," *Ausgewählte Schriften*, vol. 2, 41. It is worth adding that the image of the Gracchi is particularly dear to Babeuf, who loved to sign his name Gracchus Babeuf.

3 D. Losurdo, *Hegel und das deutsche Erbe*, ch. 2, 5.

4 Ibid., ch. 5 (=*Hegel, questione nazionale, Restaurazione*, ch. 3).

5 V. I. Lenin, *Philosophical Notebooks*, 313–14.

6 K. Marx and F. Engels, "Manifest der Kommunistischen Partei," *MEW*, vol. 4, 481. On the history of the positive meaning of the concept of despotism, see A. Burgio's observations in C. Beccaria, *Dei delitti e delle pene* (Milan, 1991), 149–51.

7 F. X. von Baader, "Identität des Despotismus und des Revolutionismus, Socialphilosophische Aphorismen aus verschiedenen Zeitblättern," *Sämtliche Werke*, vol. 5, 291.

8 J. Görres, "Kotzebue und was ihn gemordet," *Gesammelte Schriften*, ed. W. Schellberg, vol. 13, 490.

9 F. Engels, "Der Ursprung der Familie, des Privateigentums und des Staats," ch. 9, *MEW*, vol. 21, 152–73. However, there are numerous other places in Marx and Engels' work where the same idea is expressed.

10 Montesquieu, *De l'esprit des lois*, vol. 5, 10.

11 B. Constant, "De l'esprit de conquête et de l'usurpation dans leurs rapports avec la civilisation européenne," *Oeuvres*, 1078.

12 A. L. G. Necker de Staël, *Considérations sur la Révolution française*, ed. J. Godechot, 85–86.

13 Montesquieu, "De la politique," *Oeuvres complètes*, ed. R. Caillois, vol. 1, 113.

14 Montesquieu, "Mes pensées," *Oeuvres complètes*, vol. 1, 1152, n. 631. Not even the following reference to the *Glorious Revolution* is without ambiguity: "How many private citizens have we seen, during the course of the recent turmoil in England, lose their lives or goods!" ("Mes pensées," *Oeuvres complètes*, vol. 1, 1431, n.1802.)

15 Montesquieu, *De l'esprit des lois*, vol. 3, 3.

16 J. Locke, *Two Treatises of Civil Government*, II, § 79.

17 See L. L. Bongie, *David Hume Prophet of the Counter-Revolution*.

18 See A. Martelloni, "Introduzione," E. Burke, *Scritti politici*, 20.

19 A. L. G. Necker de Staël, *Considérations*, 304, 314.

20 B. Constant, "De l'esprit de conquête," 1094ff., "Le cahier rouge," *Oeuvres*, 157. It is not by chance that, with regard to "usurpation," Constant considers Cromwell as merely anticipating Napoleon. Hegel's judgment, on the other hand, is completely different.

21 E. Burke, "Speech on Moving His Resolution for Conciliation with the Colonies," *The Works*, vol. 3, 8.

22 The Terror was "the most horrible epoch" in the history of France (A. L. G. Necker de Staël, *Considérations*, 307). The portrayal that Constant gives of '93 emerges from the claim according to which Napoleon's "usurpation" "and all of its horrible memories, [a usurpation that was] the product of all criminal theories," began during the French Revolution (B. Constant, "De l'esprit de conquête," 1091).

23 A. de Tocqueville, "Souvenirs," 120, 143.

24 R. Haym, *Hegel und seine Zeit*, 32, 262.

25 A. L. G. Necker de Staël, *Considérations*, 207ff.

26 Such as A. Mathiez, G. Lefebvre, and J. Godechot. See Godechot's note to A. L. G. Necker de Staël, *Considérations*, 614, n. 59.

27 Ibid., 114.

28 A. de Tocqueville, "L'Ancien Régime et la Révolution: Fragments et notes inédites sur la Révolution," *Oeuvres complètes*, vol. 2, 69, 71.

29 This is the position of H. Arendt in *On Revolution*. J. Habermas fails to take into consideration the radical force with which Hegel justifies and celebrates the French Revolution, even when it is hostile to liberal thought. In his evaluation of Hegel's political writings, Habermas continues to fall prey to the liberal-conservative dichotomy. It is only in this light that one can understand Habermas' claim that Hegel is affected by "alienation from the Western Spirit." J. Habermas, "Hegels Kritik der französischen Revolution," *Theorie und Praxis: Sozialphilosophische Studien*, 128–47. Infra, ch. XII, 2.

30 B. Constant, "De l'esprit de conquête," 1050–51.

31 F. Schlegel, *Philosophie der Geschichte*, 403–4.

32 "A total revolution" in which a nation is torn apart is "an immoral operation." F. von Gentz, *Über die Moralität in den Staatsrevolutionen*, 58.

33 A classic example of this point of view is Hannah Arendt's *On Revolution*.

34 On Kant, see D. Losurdo, *Autocensura e compromesso*, 128–36.

35 *Ph. G.* 692; Montesquieu, "Considérations sur les causes de la grandeur des Romains et de leur décadence," *Oeuvres complètes*, vol. 2, 71.

36 Montesquieu, *De l'esprit des lois*, vol. 11, 12. See also Montesquieu, "Considérations sur les causes de la grandeur des Romains," 74.

37 Montesquieu, *De l'esprit des lois*, vol. 11, 15.

38 Montesquieu, "Considérations sur les causes de la grandeur des Romains," 74.

39 Ibid., 112.

40 Ibid., 112–13.

41 Montesquieu, "Dialogue de Sylle et d'Euchrate," *Oeuvres complètes*, vol. 1, 503–4.

42 Montesquieu, *De l'esprit des lois*, vol. 3, 3.

43 Montesquieu, "Dialogue de Sylle et d'Euchrate," 507. For Marx's judgment on the Jacobin Terror, see K. Marx, "Die Bourgeoisie und die Konterrevolution," *MEW*, 6, 107.

44 Montesquieu, "Discours sur Cicéron," *Oeuvres complètes*, vol. 1, 98. On this subject see also A. Postigliola's introduction to the Italian translation of "Dialogue de Sylle et d'Euchrate" ("Dialogo tra Silla e Eucrate") in Montesquieu, *Le leggi della politica*, ed. A. Postigliola, 28–29.

45 Montesquieu, "Considérations sur les causes de la grandeur des Romains," 71.

46 The democrat in question is F. C. Laukhard. The passage cited (which is excerpted from his autobiography) is reprinted in N. Merker, *Alle origini dell'ideologia tedesca*, 183.

47 J.-J. Rousseau, "Fragments politiques," *OC*, vol. 3, 540–41. The assessment made in *Du contrat social* (*OC*, vol. 3, 454) is different and more complex. Agis is killed by the ephors, who, after having an initially positive role, become excessively powerful and turn into "tyrants." Robespierre essentially holds this position. Agis tries to restore the "good morals" and laws of Lycurgus. In any case, monarchy always represents a phase of degeneration. See "Discourse of 5 February 1794," M. Robespierre, *Textes choisis*, ed. J. Poperen, vol. 3, 116.

48 J.-J. Rousseau, "Fragments politiques," *OC*, vol. 3, 539.

49 "Discourse of 3 December 1792," M. Robespierre, *Discours*, ed. M. Bouloiseau et al., vol. 4, 70.

50 J.-J. Rousseau, *Du contrat social*, II, 8 (*OC*, vol. 3, 385).

51 Montesquieu, "Considérations sur les causes de la grandeur des Romains," 124.

52 Montesquieu, "Discours sur Cicéron," 97.

53 B. Constant, "Aperçues sur la marche et les révolutions de la philosophie à Rome," *Mélanges*, vol. 1, 11.

54 "Discourse of 5 February 1794," M. Robespierre, *Discours*, vol. 5, 111.

55 "Discourse of 13 November 1792," L. A. L. de Saint-Just, *Oeuvres complètes*, 377.

56 J.-J. Rousseau, *Du contrat social*, IV, 6 and 8 (*OC*, vol. 3, 447, 468n).

57 "Discourse of 7 May 1794," M. Robespierre, *Textes choisis*, vol. 3, 169.

58 A. de Tocqueville, "Souvenirs," 120. See also A. de Tocqueville, *L'Ancien Régime et la Révolution*, 320.

59 A. L. G. Necker de Staël, *Considérations*, 64.

60 K. Marx, "Theorien über den Mehrwert," *MEW*, vol. 26, 274.

61 J.-J. Rousseau, "Écrits sur l'Abbé de Saint-Pierre: Jugement sur La Polysynodie," *OC*, vol. 3, 645.

62 E. Burke, *Reflections on the Revolution in France*, 77–78.

63 T. Paine, *Rights of Man*, ed. G. J. Holyoake, 191–92.

64 One thinks of Boulainvilliers and Montlosier. See A. Omodeo, *Studi sull'età della Restaurazione*, 2nd ed., 214. Consider also the historian J. C. Bailleul, who had taken part in the Convention and who, unlike de Staël, lauds Richelieu's progressive, antifeudal role. Yet, there was another figure (whom historians have credited with giving the first "materialist" account of revolutionary events in which he himself played a part) who praises the alliance between the Crown and the masses against the aristocracy. A. P. J. M. Barnave, *Introduction à la révolution française*, ed. F. Rude, 8, 13–14, 40, 51.

65 A. de Tocqueville, "État social et politique de la France avant et depuis 1789," *Mélanges, fragments historiques et notes sur l'Ancien Régime, la Révolution et l'Empire*, ed. G. de Beaumont, vol. 8, 35–36.

66 Popper does this even before Bobbio. See K. Popper, *The Open Society and its Enemies*, vol. 2, 57; N. Bobbio, *Studi hegeliani*, xviii, 121, 135.

67 J.-J. Rousseau, *Du contrat social*, III, 15 (*OC*, vol. 3, 430).

68 These were the years in which the enemies of revolutionary France were branded "as British or Austrians, hired by Pitt and Coburg." This claim is made in a pamphlet of the same period as *Philosophy of Right*. C. L. von Haller, *De quelques dénominations de partis*, 33. The issue of the German conservatives or reactionaries appeal to England has already been addressed in D. Losurdo, *Hegel und das deutsche Erbe*, ch. 5, 3–4. (=*Hegel questione nazionale, Restaurazione*, ch. 3, 3–4.)

69 F. Engels, "Die neueste Heldentat des Hauses Bourbon," *MEW*, vol. 5, 19.

70 See D. Losurdo, *Autocensura e compromeso*, 89–92.

71 C. von Rotteck, *Lehrbuch des Vernunftrechts und der Staatswissenschaften*, vol. 1, 64, vol. 2, 45.

72 A. L. G. Necker de Staël, *Considérations*, 69.

73 A. de Tocqueville, "De la démocratie en Amérique," *Oeuvres complètes*, vol. 1, 113–14.

74 Note from his trip to England in 1833 in A. de Tocqueville, "Voyages en Angleterre, Irlande, Suisse et Algérie," *Oeuvres complètes*, vol. 5, 42–43.

75 B. Constant, "De la puissance de l'Angleterre durant la guerre, et de sa détresse à la paix, jusqu'en 1818," *Mélanges de littérature et de politique*, vol. 1, 21ff. On resorting to special agents, see G. M. Trevelyan, *History of England*, vol. 3, 164. The reality of the situation in England at the time was quite different from even the liberal interpretation that emerges in Bobbio. Two of Malthus' students describe the situation as follows: "From 1770 to 1798, the average national income, with prices fixed, declined by twenty percent . . . If, as is probable, the disparity between individual incomes increased, too, certainly it was the masses who suffered the greatest reduction in their already meager earnings. Not until 1845 will the average individual income reach the 1770 level: this decline over the course of more than fifty years will be the cruel price paid for victory over Napoleon, and for the construction of a new England."

"Such sufferings cannot increase in both degree and duration without provoking reactions and, in fact, there are sudden, abrupt flare-ups here and there. Rage and social turmoil erupt everywhere: in 1795 riots in the countryside caused by unemployment and hunger; in 1794 and 1795 uprisings in London, Birmingham, and

Dundee caused by low salaries and again hunger; mutinies in the military; various social crises from 1799–1800 and, finally, Luddism—the destruction of machine technology—and the peasant revolts of 1816. *Habeas corpus* is suspended for eight years beginning in 1794, and troops occupy the major portions of industrial zones as if they were occupied territories ... Pitt, supported by a large part of public opinion, relentlessly persecuted anyone in favor of liberal ideas, or inclined to French ones. Uprisings, strikes, insurrections or mutinies, whether justified or not, were mercilessly put down." J. M. Poursin and G. Dupuy, *Malthus*, 61–64. It is a true policy of "terror" or "counter-revolutionary measures." G. Bianco and E. Grendi, *Introduzione a la tradizione socialista in Inghilterra: Antologia di testi politici, 1820–1852*, xiii. And this continues even after Napoleon's defeat, given that the revolutionary danger re-emerges in the rising workers' movement. 1819 is the year of what comes to be known in the history books as the Peterloo massacre, or, to use the words of an English magazine of the time, "the futile and unjustified slaughter of defenseless men, women and children" in a "premeditated attack [by government forces] with a thoroughly insatiable thirst for blood and destruction." This passage, dated 18 August 1819, is taken from *Sherwin's Weekly Political Register*. It is cited in P. Casana Testore and N. Nada, *L'età della restaurazione: Reazione e rivoluzione in Europa, 1814–1830*, 226–28. On the other hand, the massacre was hardly an isolated event; indeed, it represented the culmination of a wave of repression based upon a position which regarded unions and criminal organizations as identical before the law. G. Bianco and E. Grendi, *Introduzione a La tradizione socialista in Inghilterra*, lxvii. When we read in *Das Kapital* about the "bloody laws against vagabonds" from the fifteenth to the nineteenth centuries, the reference is above all to England, as one might expect since capitalism is most developed there. But there is another important point to be added. In England, forms of disguised slavery last "well into the nineteenth century." K. Marx, "Das Kapital," bk. 1, ch. 24, *MEW*, vol. 24, 762–63.

76 In this case too, Hegel's judgment is hardly baseless. A scholar of Burke paints the following portrait of England at the time: "corruption [had become] a normal part of public life. It was commonly accepted that the 'interests' of great landlords—that is, the political pressure they could freely exercise at will upon their tenants and dependents—influenced elections. Namier calculates that for every twenty voters, only one could vote freely, without interference or pressure. In the counties, large or small landowners were indisputably in charge: the proof lies in the fact that, of the eighty representatives of the House of Commons in 1761, sixteen were the sons of members of the House of Lords, and thus inevitably destined for Parliament; and forty-nine of the representatives had practically inherited their seats, since it had become customary for their county to send to Parliament a member of their family ... Of the cities, only in London, where those who voted were local taxpayers, was the electorate too large to be corrupted, and the bourgeoisie united ... Bristol, the second largest English city (with 60,000 inhabitants) was in the hands of an oligarchy, as were many of the large urban areas. (A. Martelloni, "Introduzione," E. Burke, *Scritti politici*, 10–11.)

77 B. Constant, "De la division des propriétés foncières," *Mélanges de littérature et de politique*, vol. 2, 124.

78 B. Constant, *De la puissance de l'Angleterre*, 28–29.

79 A. de Tocqueville, "De la démocratie en Amérique," vol. 1, 44.

80 F. Engels, "Die Lage Englands," *MEW*, vol. 1, 590, 585. On the diffusion of this judgment in proto-socialist writings, see D. Losurdo, *Tra Hegel e Bismarck*, 100–107. In this case too, contemporary historians hardly disagree with Hegel's (and Engels') harsh judgment. In England at that time "it was common in cases where the accusers were indigent to commit them to prison as material witnesses, while setting the defendants free on bail." M. Ignatieff, *A Just Measure of Pain: The Penitentiary in the Industrial Revolution 1750–1850*, 133.

81 A. L. G. Necker de Staël, *Considérations*, 516, 579.

82 B. Constant, *Le cahier rouge*, 150–51, 155.

83 D. Hume, "Treatise of Human Nature," *The Philosophical Works*, ed. T. H. Green and T. H. Grose, vol. 2, 149.

84 A. de Tocqueville, "De la démocratie en Amérique," vol. 2, 185.

85 Ibid., vol. 2, 21–22.

86 S. Veca, *La società giusta*, 58–59. Veca bases this theory on Rawls, for whom giving freedom priority over equality is valid only above "a minimum level of income." J. Rawls, *A Theory of Justice*, 542.

87 A. de Tocqueville, *L'Ancien Régime et la Révolution*, 334. Yet the contrary position—it is there that "the great purpose of justice" is most thoroughly realized—requires one to forget the earlier harsh criticism of England. Tocqueville supports this claim by citing the same Blackstone who in *Democracy in America* was used to exemplify the class character of English justice (*L'Ancien Régime et la Révolution*, 309). More generally, after 1848, England is no longer an "aristocratic society" where masters and servants seem to be part of two "different humanities." To the contrary, England is "the only country" where, already before the French Revolution, the caste system was not "altered, but truly broken" (*L'Ancien Régime et la Révolution*, 148). On his trip in 1833 Tocqueville noted that the isolated assimilation of some external element serves to reinforce the privileges and power of the aristocracy (A. de Tocqueville, "Voyages en Angleterre, Irlande, Suisse et Algérie," 29). Now, however, England is the place where "classes are blurred" and where "equality before the law" and "fiscal equality" are enforced (*L'Ancien Régime et la Révolution*, 34). In sum, England is the land of freedom to the extent that it is no longer the country with the greatest inequality.

88 A. de Tocqueville, *L'Ancien Régime et la Révolution*, 214. Already in the course of the French Revolution, the moderate Barnave cautions against extending political rights to those without property. "Another step in the direction of equality would mean the destruction of liberty." F. Furet and D. Richet, *La Révolution française*, vol. 1, 98.

89 A. de Tocqueville, *L'Ancien Régime et la Révolution*, 217. See also A. de Tocqueville, "Voyages en Angleterre, Irlande, Suisse et Algérie," 81.

90 Reported in E. Halévy, *La formation du radicalisme philosophique, I: La jeunesse de Bentham*, 91–92.

91 K. Rosenkranz, "Aphorismen zur Geschichte der modernen Ethik," *Neue Studien*, vol. 2, 152–53.

92 "Letter from F. Lassalle to Otto von Bismarck, 8 June 1863," in G. von Uexküll, *Ferdinand Lassalle*, 104.

93 See D. Losurdo, *Tra Hegel e Bismarck*, 316ff.

94 G. W. F. Hegel, "Jenaer Systementwürfe III," *Gesammelte Werke*, ed. R. P. Horstmann and J. H. Trede, vol. 8, 263. [=*Jenaer Realphilosophie*, ed. J. Hoffmeister, 251.]

95 K. Marx, "Kritik des Gothaer Programms," *MEW*, vol. 19, 23.

96 F. Lassalle, "Das System der erworbenen Rechte," *Gesammelte Reden und Schriften*, vol. 9, 397, n. 1.

VI. The Intellectual, Property, and the Social Question

1 See K.-H. Ilting's note number 293 on page 342 of his edition of Hegel's 1817–18 and 1818–19 lecture courses on the philosophy of right.

2 K. Marx, *Kritik des Hegelschen Staatsrechts*, 259.

3 V. I. Lenin, *Philosophical Notebooks*, 117–18.

4 Engels vacillates, however. By "system" he at times means the "modest political conclusion" of the "method," that is, the immediate political option; at other times he means the "philosophical system" with its "traditional need" to "conclude with some sort of absolute truth" (F. Engels, *Ludwig Feuerbach*, 268–69). In the latter case, Bloch is right when he criticizes Engels for seeing, in the system, a sort of "will to bad faith" that is almost Nietzschean. (E. Bloch, "Problem der Engelschen Trennung von 'Methode' und 'System' bei Hegel," *Philosophische Aufsätze*.) Written in 1956, the essay was first published in Italian as E. Bloch, "Sulla distinzione del 'metodo' di Hegel dal 'sistema,' e alcune conseguenze," *Dialettica e speranza*, ed. L. Sichirollo, 43ff. In the sense we have given it, the distinction between 'method' and 'system' responds to the inescapable need to safeguard the primacy of theoretical categories over immediate political tactics. Thus, in its criticism of the Hegelian dialectic, Della Volpe's school, which is particularly passionate in its refutation of the distinction in question, ends up drawing on Trendelenburg's arguments and even "speculative texts" which are certainly "right" of Hegel in order to better dismiss Hegel's philosophy as inherently conservative. This is particularly true in N. Merker, *Le origini della logica hegeliana (Hegel a Jena)*.

5 See the already cited "Memorandum from F. A. L. von der Marwitz to Hardenberg," in *Adam Müllers Lebenszeugnisse*, vol. 1, 611.

6 F. K. von Savigny, *Vom Beruf unserer Zeit für Gesetzgebung und Rechtswissenschaft*, 2nd ed., 112–13.

7 F. X. von Baader, "Über den Evolutionismus und Revolutionismus," *Sämtliche Werke*, vol. 6, 73–108.

8 E. Burke, *Reflections on the Revolution in France*, 78.

9 R. Haym, *Hegen und seine Zeit*, 327.

10 Ibid., 404–5, 407.

11 Ibid., 400–401.

12 This claim is made in the context of the polemic against the first Strauss, who was accused of not having grasped the "force of the dark powers of sentiment" and religious beliefs. See the review of *Gespräche Huttens* by Strauss in *Preußische Jahrbücher*, 6, 1860, 309.

13 R. Haym, *Hegel und seine Zeit*, 400–402.

14 R. Haym, *Wilhelm von Humboldt: Lebensbild und Charakteristik*, 57.

15 W. von Humboldt, "Ideen zu einem Versuch die Gränzen der Wirksamkeit des Staats zu bestimmen," *Gesammelte Schriften*, vol. 1, 101.

16 F. Schiller, "Letter to Duke C. C. Augustenburg, 13 August 1793," H. E. Hass, ed., *Die deutsche Literatur: Texte und Zeugnisse*, vol. 5, 1539–41.

17 F. Gentz, "Einleitung," to the German translation of E. Burke, "Reflections on the Revolution in France," E. Burke, *Ausgewählte Schriften*, vol. 1, 9.

18 J.-J. Rousseau, *Discours sur l'économie politique*, 251.

19 I. Kant, "Handschriftlicher Nachlaß," *KGS*, vol. 15, 630.

20 I. Kant, *Zum ewigen Frieden*, 353n.

21 F. X. von Baader, *Über den Evolutionismus*, 78.

22 I. Kant, *Zum ewigen Frieden*, 366.

23 J.-J. Rousseau, "Narcisse ou l'Amant de lui-même, Préface," *OC*, vol. 2, 968.

24 K. Marx and F. Engels, "Die deutsche Ideologie," *MEW*, vol. 3, 20. The argument is directed against young Hegelians who had Fichteanized their teacher's system.

25 K. Marx, "Bemerkungen über die preußische Zensurinstruktion," *MEW*, vol. 1, 4.

26 K. Marx, "Rechtfertigung des ++-Korrespondenten von der Mosel," *MEW*, vol. 1, 177.

27 F. Engels, "Die Lage der arbeitenden Klasse in England," *MEW*, vol. 2, 505.

28 W. von Humboldt, *Ideen zu einem Versuch*, 117.

29 J. Locke, *Two Treatises of Civil Government*, II, §36.

30 This is the case with Bentham's disciple and collaborator, P. E. L. Arago, who faithfully synthesized his teacher's theory. See also J. Bentham, "Théorie des peines et des récompenses," *Oeuvres de Jérémie Bentham*, ed. E. Dumont, vol. 2, 201. See J. Bentham, "Principles of the Civil Code," *The Works*, vol. 1, 309.

31 A. de Tocqueville, "Souvenirs," 84. "There exists among men, in whatever society they live, and independent of the laws they have created, a certain quantity of resources, both real and ideal, which cannot of course be enjoyed except by a few." A. de Tocqueville, *État social et politique de la France*, 18.

32 F. A. Hayek, *Law, Legislation and Liberty*.

33 F. Nietzsche, "Nachgelassene Fragmente 1887–1889," *Sämtliche Werke*, ed. G. Colli and M. Montinari, vol. 13, 73–74.

34 F. A. Hayek, *Law, Legislation and Liberty*.

35 B. Constant, *Principes de politique*, 1147.

36 F. W. J. Schelling, *Philosophie der Mythologie*, 530, 530n.

37 B. Constant, *Principes de politique*, 1146.

38 E. Burke, *Reflections on the Revolution in France*, 105. See also E. Burke, "Thoughts and Details on Scarcity," *The Works*, vol. 7, 383.

39 Marcus Terentius Varro, *De re rustica*, 17.

40 A. Smith, *The Wealth of Nations*, bk. 1, ch. 1, part 3, art. 2, 782 , 784.

41 J. Locke, *Some Considerations of the Consequences of Lowering the Interest and Raising the Value of Money*, 23–24, 71.

42 J. Locke, "An Essay Concerning Human Understanding," IV, XX, 2 and IV, XX, 5. For Montaigne, see *Essais*, I, 42. For N. Bobbio's comparison of Locke and Hegel's views on the subject of labor, see N. Bobbio, *Studi hegeliani*, 181–82. Bobbio however abandons his principal theory about the difference between Hegel and the liberal tradition. Once again, Bobbio's theory is the same as K.-H. Ilting's, "The Structure of Hegel's *Philosophy of Right*," *Hegel's Political Philosophy*, ed. W. Kaufmann, 107, n. 45.

43 J. Locke, *An Essay Concerning Human Understanding*, IV, XVI, 12.

44 Ibid., IV, XX, 3.

45 Ibid., IV, XX, 6.

46 J. Locke, *Some Thoughts concerning Education*, §§ 204 , 206.

47 J. Locke, *Some Considerations of the Consequences of Lowering the Interest and Raising the Value of Money*, 20.

48 F. Guizot, *De la démocratie en France (Janvier 1849)*, 38–40. The "often hypocritical" nature of Guizot's "emphasis" on "productive activity" was already noted in F. M. de Sanctis, *Tempo di democrazia: Alexis de Tocqueville*, 215.

49 A. de Tocqueville, "Souvenirs," 131.

50 The centrality of this theme in Saint-Simon is brought to light in K. Marx and F. Engels, "Die deutsche Ideologie," *MEW*, vol. 3, 452. Yet, the condemnation of the unproductive and parasitical nature of "mere capitalists" is a theme that is also present to a certain extent in Hegel. See D. Losurdo, *Tra Hegel e Bismarck*, 116–20.

51 F. Guizot, *De la démocratie en France*, 39.

52 A. de Tocqueville, "Souvenirs," 120. See also A. de Tocqueville, *L'Ancien Régime et la Révolution*, 340. Not by chance, Tocqueville draws on Burke, the implacable debunker of the disastrous "abstractions" typical of revolutionary French intellectuals (infra, ch. XIII, 6).

53 B. Constant, *Cours de politique constitutionnelle*, 3rd ed., 106–7.

54 I. Kant, "Über den Gemeinspruch: Das mag in der Theorie richtig sein, taugt aber nicht für die Praxis," *KGS*, vol. 8, 277.

55 I. Kant, "Handschriftlicher Nachlaß," *KGS*, vol. 23, 155.

56 J. G. Fichte, "Einige Vorlesungen über die Bestimmung des Gelehrten," *FW*, vol. 6, 331–33.

57 I. Kant, "Handschriftlicher Nachlaß," *KGS*, vol. 23, 127.

58 I. Kant, "Von einem neuerdings erhobenen vornehmen Ton in der Philosophie," *KGS*, vol. 8, 390 , 395.

59 F. Nietzsche, *Jenseits von Gut und Böse*, § 211.

60 I. Kant, *Über den Gemeinspruch*, 295.

61 I. Kant, "Metaphysik der Sitten, Rechtslehre," § 46, *KGS*, vol. 6, 314.

62 B. Constant, *Principes de politique*, 1148.

63 For criticism of the idea of "German poverty," see C. Cesa, "G. W. F. Hegel: A centocinquant'anni dalla morte," *Studi senesi* 1 (1982): 11–12. The notion of German misery, however, is also present in a writer who is clearly hostile to Hegel. See "Letter 14," L. Börne, *Briefe aus Paris*, vol. 3, 67.

64 B. Constant, *Principes de politique*, 1132–45.

65 "Letter from Freiherr K. von Stein to H. von Gagern, 24 August 1821," in *Ausgewählte Schriften*, ed. K. Thiede, 281.

66 E. Burke, "Letters on a Regicide Peace," *The Works*, vol. 9, 49.

67 H. Arendt, *On Revolution*.

68 B. Constant, *Principes de politique*, 1151.

69 I. Kant, *Über den Gemeinspruch*, 295. See also I. Kant, "Metaphysik der Sitten, Rechtslehre," § 456, *KGS*, vol. 6, 313–15.

70 B. Constant, *Principes de politique*, 1148.

71 I. Kant, "Von der Unrechtmässigkeit des Büchernachdrucks," *KGS*, vol. 8, 77–87.

72 A. Schopenhauer, "Über die Universitäts Philosophie (Parerga und Paralipomena, I)," *Sämtliche Werke*, ed. W. Löhneysen, vol. 4, 238.

73 Ibid., vol. 4, 184.

74 Ibid., vol. 4, 237–38.

75 The author is J. M. R. Lenz. See R. Pascal, *The German Sturm und Drang*, 56–57.

76 "Letter from J. G. Fichte to I. Kant, 2 September 1791," J. G. Fichte, *Briefwechsel*, vol. 1, 200.

77 I. Kant, "Über Pädagogik," *KGS*, vol. 9, 452–53.

78 K. Rosenkranz, *Hegels Leben*, 42.

79 See M. Cranston, *John Locke: A Biography*, 2nd ed., 114–15, 377, 448. "Locke might therefore be considered a member of the investing class whose interests his economic writings signally upheld" (115, n.3).

80 J. Locke, *Some Thoughts Concerning Education*, §§ 89 , 94.

81 Ibid., § 70.

82 Ibid., § 90.

83 B. Constant, *Le cahier rouge*, 124.

84 J. Locke, *Some Thoughts Concerning Education*, § 91.

85 This is exactly how Hölderlin was considered by the banker Gontard and even the latter's distant descendents. See T. W. Adorno, "Stichworte, Kritische Modelle 2," *Gesammelte Schriften*, ed. R. Tiedemann, vol. 10, 659.

86 "Diary note from the summer of 1791," in J. G. Fichte, *Briefwechsel*, vol. 1, 200.

87 A. Schopenhauer, *Über die Universitäts-Philosophie*, 182.

88 A. de Tocqueville, *L'Ancien Régime et la Révolution*, 213.

89 A. Schopenhauer, *Über die Universitäts-Philosophie*, 213, 215. See infra, ch. IX, 7 as well as ch. XI, 3. Some decades earlier Caroline von Herder criticized the *rentiers'* intellectuals: "I recently read in the *Morgenblatt* that Humboldt refused to go to Paris because he holds that it is his sacred duty to remain where he is. I find such gestures repugnant. Prussia is his homeland: there, he has *possessions, resources, wealth;* not to abandon such fortunes requires no spirit of sacrifice, and thus enough with this exhibition of sacred duty!" "Letter from Caroline von Herder to Johannes von Müller, 28 August 1807," in J. von Müller, *Briefwechsel mit Gottfried Herder und Caroline von Herder geb. Flachsland*, ed. K. E. Hoffmann, 220. This rancorous comment is indicative of the social tensions among German intellectuals of the time.

90 J. G. Fichte, *Grundlage des Naturrechts*, § 18, *FW*, vol. 3, 214.

91 J. G. Fichte, "Zufällige Gedanken in einer schlaflosen Nacht," *Briefwechsel*, vol. 1, 10–13.

92 J.-J. Rousseau, *Discours sur l'économie politique*, 258–59 , 274.

93 J. G. Fichte, *Zufällige Gedanken*, 11.

94 The exchange of letters is with Theodor von Schön. See "Letter from T. von Schön, 5 September 1792," J. G. Fichte, *Briefwechsel*, vol. 1, 247, and "Letter from J. G. Fichte, 30 September 1792," Ibid., vol. 1, 257.

95 J. G. Fichte, *Beitrag zur Berichtigung der Urtheile des Publicums über die französische Revolution*, 182.

96 A. Smith, *The Wealth of Nations*, bk. 1, part 3, 794.

97 See Voltaire, "Le Mondain," and Voltaire, "Défense du 'Mondain' ou l'Apologie du luxe," *Oeuvres complètes de Voltaire*, vol. 14.

98 G. R. Havens, "Voltaire's Marginalia on the Pages of Rousseau," *Ohio State University Studies* 6 (1933): 15.

99 K. Marx, "Misère de la philosophie," German translation in *MEW*, vol. 4, 139.

VII. Right, Violence, and *Notrecht*

1   J. Locke, *Two Treatises of Government*, II, § 139.

2   T. Hobbes, *Leviathan*, ch. 21.

3   J. Locke, *Two Treatises of Government*, II, § 171.

4   I. Kant, "Metaphysik der Sitten: Rechtslehre, Einleitung," *KGS*, vol. 7, 235.

5   J. G. Fichte, *Grundlage des Naturrechts*, § 19 I, *FW*, vol. 3, 252–53.

6   J. Locke, *Two Treatises of Government*, II, § 41.

7   B. Mandeville, *The Fable of the Bees*, ed. F. B. Kaye, vol. 1, 26, 169ff.

8   A. Smith, *The Wealth of Nations*, bk. 1, ch. 1, 24.

9   A. Smith, "Early Draft of Part of The Wealth of Nations," *Adam Smith as Student and Professor*, ed. William Robert Scott, 325.

10 E. P. Sieyès, "Notes et fragments inédits," *Écrits politiques*, ed. R. Zapperi, 64. The fragment is "La division du travail, en faisant concourir une infinité de bras au bien-être le plus simple, n'ajoute pas à ce bien-être."

11 E. P. Sieyès, *Écrits politiques*, 73. The fragment is "Comparaison des différents âges de la société."

12 E. P. Sieyès, "Dire sur la question du veto royal," *Écrits politiques*, 236.

13 This category is, of course, dear to G. Lukács. See G. Lukács, *Die Zerstörung der Vernunft*.

14 A. de Tocqueville, *Mémoire sur le paupérisme*, 312.

15 Ibid., 308.

16 Ibid., 304, 307.

17 Ibid., 313.

18 Ibid.

19 Ibid., 306.

20 Ibid., 302.

21 A. de Tocqueville, "Le système pénitentiaire aux États-Unis et son application en France, suivi d'un appendice sur les colonies pénales et de notes statistiques," *Oeuvres complètes*, vol. 4, 321. In ch. 1, *Écrits sur le système pénitentiaire en France et à l'étranger*.

22 J. Locke, *Two Treatises of Government*, II, § 36.

23 On the spread of Malthus' ideas in Germany, see D. Losurdo, *Tra Hegel e Bismarck*, 157 60. We might add that Malthus is even cited repeatedly by Hugo (*Lehrbuch eines civilistischen Cursus*), a writer with whom Hegel explicitly disagrees.

24 C. von Rotteck, *Lehrbuch des Vernunftrechts und der Staatswissenschaften*, vol. 1, 155.

25 J. Locke, *Two Treatises of Government*, II, § 19.

26 Ibid., § 18.

27 Ibid., § 182.

28 J. G. Fichte, *Grundlage des Naturrechts*, § 18, *FW*, vol. 3, 214.

29 Ibid., § 18, *FW*, vol. 3, 213.

30 Ibid., § 19, *FW*, vol. 3, 250.

31 J. G. Fichte, *Rechtslehre*, ed. R. Schottky, 114.

32 J. G. Fichte, *Grundlage des Naturrechts*, § 19, *FW*, vol. 3, 250.

33 See R. Koselleck, *Preußen zwischen Reform und Revolution*, 3rd ed., 641–6.

34 J. Locke, *Two Treatises of Government*, II, §§ 85, 86.

35 D. Henrich, "Einleitung," *Rph.III* 20.

36 *Rph.*, §§ 88 , 95, *Enc.*, § 173 z, and *Wissenschaft der Logik, Das unendliche Urteil* (*W*, 6, 324–25).

37 The text edited by Henrich cites *des Verbrechens* (see G. W. F. Hegel, *Le filosofie del diritto*, ed. D. Losurdo, 378). However, the essential meaning does not change.

38 M.-J.-A.-N. de C. de Condorcet, "Lettre d'un laboureur de Picardie," *Oeuvres*, ed. A. Condorcet O'Connor and D. F. Arago, vol. 11, 10.

39 We are speaking of Aubert de Vitry, who affirms the "inviolable right of every man to existence" in R. Barny, *L'éclatement révolutionnaire du rousseauisme*, 22.

40 According to Robespierre, of the "indefeasible rights of man," the first is "the right to exist." "Discourse, 2 December 1792," *Textes choisis*, vol. 2, 85. For Marat, see his draft of the Declaration of the Rights of Man and Citizen, in *L'An 1 des droits de l'homme*, ed. A. de Baecque, W. Schmale and M. Vovelle, 293. On Babeuf, see in particular "Letter, 10 September 1791," F. N. Babeuf, *Écrits*, ed. C. Mazauric, 207.

41 G. Lefebvre, *La France sous le directoire 1795–1799*, 21, 27.

42 T. R. Malthus, *An Essay on the Principle of Population*, 6th ed, ed. John Murray, http://www.econlib.org/library/Malthus/malPlong31.html as of 5 January 2003.

43 See G. Himmelfarb, *The Idea of Poverty: England in the Early Industrial Age*, 212.

44 J. G. Fichte, *Rechtslehre*, 41.

45 His defense in 1832 is reported in A. Blanqui, *Textes choisis*, ed. V. P. Volguine, 71.

46 A. Laponneraye, "Draft of a 'Declaration des droits de l'homme et du citoyen,'" *Il socialismo prima di Marx*, 2nd ed., ed. G. M. Bravo, 153. On Laponneraye, see also A. Galante Garrone, *Filippo Buonarroti e i rivoluzionari dell'Ottocento 1828–1837*, 238–44.

47 See also D. Losurdo, *Tra Hegel e Bismarck*, 100–106, 204–6.

48 A. de Tocqueville, *L'Ancien Régime et la Révolution*, 271.

49 A. de Tocqueville, "Speech to the Legislative Assembly, 25 June 1849," A. de Tocqueville, *Études économiques, politiques et littéraires*, 570. This is vol. 9 of the edition edited by Tocqueville's widow and G. de Beaumont.

50 "Letter to L. de Kergorlay, 16 May 1858," A. de Tocqueville, *Oeuvres complètes*, vol. 13, 337.

51 Montesquieu, *De l'esprit des lois*, 23, 29.

52 See A. de Tocqueville, *Études économiques, politiques et littéraires*, 551–52.

53 "Letter to G. de Beaumont, 3 September 1848," A. de Tocqueville, *Oeuvres complètes*, vol. 8, 38.

54 "Letter to F. de Corcelle, 1 November 1856," A. de Tocqueville, *Oeuvres complètes*, vol. 15, 182.

55 A. de Tocqueville, "Souvenirs," 30, 91–92.

56 Ibid., 84.

57 "Letter to L. de Thun, 2 February 1835," *Oeuvres complètes*, vol. 7, 283.

58 T. H. Marshall, *Sociology at the Crossroads*, 83. On work-houses as total institutions, see also D. Losurdo, "Marx et l'histoire du totalitarisme," *Fin du communisme? Actualité du marxisme?*, ed. J. Bidet and J. Texier, 75–95.

59 A. de Tocqueville, *Le système pénitentiaire aux États-Unis*, 319.

60 G. Himmelfarb, *The Idea of Poverty: England in the Early Industrial Age*, 158–61. On the relations between Tocqueville and Nassau Senior, see the note by J. P. Mayer in A. de Tocqueville, in *Oeuvres complètes*, vol. 6, 72n; S. Drescher, *Tocqueville and England*; A. Jardin, *A. de Tocqueville 1805–1859*.

61 For Rousseau too, the slave "has no obligation to his owner." See J.-J. Rousseau, "Du contrat social," *OC*, vol. 3, 358.

62 E. Gans, *Rückblicke auf Personen und Zustände*, 100. This comparison is also made by other disciples of Hegel, even those on the "right." Rosenkranz calls modern workers "helots." K. Rosenkranz, "Pestalozzi," *Neue Studien*, vol. 1, 113–14.

63 K. Marx, *Das philosophische Manifest der historischen Rechtsschule*, 80–81.

64 G. Hugo, *Lehrbuch eines civilistischen Cursus: Zweyter Band welcher das Naturrecht, als eine Philosophie des positiven Rechts, besonders des Privatrechts enthält*, 4th ed., 251–52. In *Philosophy of Right*, Hegel expressly cites another work by Hugo, the *Lehrbuch der Geschichte des römischen Rechts*, 5th ed.

65 A. Smith, *The Wealth of Nations*, bk. 1, ch. 8, 84–85.

66 A. Müller, *Versuche einer neuen Theorie des Geldes mit besonderer Rücksicht auf Großbritannien*, 23–28. See also "Die innere Staatshaushaltung; systematisch dargestellt auf theologischer Grundlage," *Concordia*, ed. F. Schlegel, 110–11. The latter is explicitly criticized by Gans in his 1828–29 lecture course. See E. Gans, *Philosophische Schriften*, ed. H. Schröder, 68.

67 A. Müller, *Die innere Staatshaushaltung*, 111.

68 G. Hugo, *Lehrbuch eines civilistischen Cursus*, 120, 251.

69 K. Mannheim, *Das konservative Denken*, 429.

70 Marx also refers to "Shylock's law of the 10 Tables" (he speaks of ten instead of twelve) to denounce the extreme absolutization of the right to property which makes one regard "the flesh and blood of the debtor" as merely a fixed amount of "money" (and property) lent to the creditor. K. Marx, *Das Kapital*, bk. 1, ch. 8, *MEW*, vol. 23, 304. Marx also mentions Shylock in his early writings. K. Marx, "Debatten über das Holzdiebstahlsgesetz," *MEW*, vol. 1, 141. Hegel also refers to Shakespeare's *Merchant of Venice* (*Rph.*, § 3 A).

71 See D. Losurdo, "Le catene e i fiori: La critica dell'ideologia tra Marx e Nietzsche," *Hermeneutica* 6 (1986): 87–143.

72 G. Hugo, *Lehrbuch eines civilistischen Cursus*, 267.

73 I. Kant, "Metaphysik der Sitten, Rechtslehre, Einleitung," *KGS*, vol. 6, 234.

74 C. von Rotteck, *Lehrbuch des Vernunftrechts und der Staatswissenschaften*, vol. 1, 58.

VIII. "*Agora*" and "*Scholé*": Rousseau, Hegel, and the Liberal Tradition

1 A. de Tocqueville, *L'Ancien Régime et la Révolution*, 107.

2 B. Constant, "De la liberté des anciens comparée à celle des modernes," 504.

3 B. Constant, "De l'esprit de conquête," 1050–51nn.

4 K. Rosenkranz, *Hegels Leben*, 62.

5 J.-J. Rousseau, *Fragments politiques*, 539.

6 L. A. L. de Saint-Just, "Rapport, 11th Germinal year 11," in *Oeuvres complètes*, 778.

7 F. W. J. Schelling, *System des transzendentalen Idealismus*, 604.

8 F. W. J. Schelling, "Vorlesungen über die Methode des akademischen Studiums," *Sämmtliche Werke*, vol. 5, 225.

9 Ibid., vol. 5, 314.

10 W. von Humboldt, *Über das Studium des Altertums und des griechischen insbesondere*, § 26.

11 "Letter, 2 September 1758," *Voltaire's Correspondence*, ed. T. Besterman, vol. 34, 68.

12 See A. Aulard, *Histoire politique de la Révolution française*, 72.

13 G. W. F. Hegel, *Religionsphilosophie. Bd. 1: Die Vorlesung von 1821*, 619.

14 G. Hugo, *Lehrbuch des Naturrechts als einer Philosophie des positiven Rechts*, 4th ed., 28. Hugo, in turn, adds Diderot.

15 H. Taine, *Les origines de la France contemporaine*, vol. 2, 40.

16 "Letter to Franz Overbeck, 23 February 1887," F. Nietzsche, *Briefwechsel: Kritische Gesamtausgabe*, vol. 3, 28.

17 F. Nietzsche, "Nachgelassene Fragmente 1885–1887," *KSA*, vol. 12, 421.

18 F. Nietzsche, *Götzendämmerung, Streifzüge eines Unzeitgemäßen*, § 3.

19 F. Nietzsche, *Götzendämmerung, Streifzüge eines Unzeitgemäßen*, § 48.

20 F. Nietzsche, "Unzeitgemäße Betrachtungen, III," *KSA*, vol. 1, 369.

21 H. Taine, *Les origines de la France contemporaine*, vol. 4, 161–62.

22 Ibid., vol. 5, 21ff.

23 J. L. Talmon, *The Origins of Totalitarian Democracy*, 39. R. Dahrendorf in turn approvingly cites Talmon in his *Fragmente eines neuen Liberalismus* to denounce the "turbid influence" long exercised by Rousseau.

24 So says, with unique clarity, the first version of the *Social Contract* (1750–60). See J.-J. Rousseau, *Du contrat social*. First version, *OC*, vol. 3, 302. However, this theme is present throughout Rousseau's work.

25 G. Lukács, *Der junge Hegel und die Probleme der kapitalistischen Gesellschaft*, 37.

26 M.-J.-A.-N. de C. de Condorcet, "Lettre d'un laboureur de Picardie," and "Réflexions sur le commerce des blés," *Oeuvres*, vol. 11, p. 10, 167–68.

27 A. de Tocqueville, *L'Ancien Régime et la Révolution*.

28 J.-J. Rousseau, "*Discours sur l'origine et les fondements de l'inégalité parmi les hommes*," *OC*, vol. 3, 194.

29 J.-J. Rousseau, *Discours sur l'économie politique*, 255–56.

30 Ibid., 262.

31 J.-J. Rousseau, *Du contrat social*, I, 9, (*OC*, vol. 3, 367n).

32 J.-J. Rousseau, *Discours sur l'économie politique*, 271.

33 J.-J. Rousseau, *Du contrat social*, I, 9, (*OC*, vol. 3, 367).

34 J.-J. Rousseau, *Discours sur l'économie politique*, 276.

35 Ibid., 270, 273. Rather, we are dealing with a progressiveness that at times possesses a drastic character, to the extent that it even legitimizes the confiscation, in the case of necessity, of whatever is not "necessary." J.-J. Rousseau, *Discours sur l'économie politique* 271. On this, see A. Burgio, *Eguaglianza, interesse, unanimità: La politica di Rousseau*, 97–103.

36 See M.-J.-A.-N. de C. de Condorcet, "Sur l'impôt progressif," *Oeuvres*, vol. 12, 625.

37 G. W. F. Hegel, *Jenaer Systementwürfe* III, 252 (=*Jenaer Realphilosophie*, 238).

38 G. W. F. Hegel, *System der Sittlichkeit*, ed. G. Lasson, 84–85.

39 See R. Barny, *L'éclatement révolutionnaire du rousseauisme*, 26.

40 See G. Lefebvre, *La France sous le directoire 1795–1799*, 28–29, 35.

41 H. Guillemin, *Benjamin Constant muscadin 1795–1799*, 6th ed., 29 n. 2.

42 Ibid., 76–77.

43 A. L. G. Necker de Staël, *Considérations*, 347.

44 According to the testimony of Mallet Du Pan. H. Guillemin, *Benjamin Constant muscadin*, 37.

45 F. A. Hayek, *New Studies in Philosophy, Politics, Economics and the History of Ideas*.

46 G. W. F. Hegel, *Jenaer Systementwürfe* III, 252 (=*Jenaer Realphilosophie*, 238).

47 G. W. F. Hegel, *System der Sittlichkeit*, 84–85.

48 Montesquieu, *De l'esprit des lois*, XIII, 14.

49 J. Bentham, *Anarchical Fallacies*, 518.

50 A. de Tocqueville, *Mémoire sur le paupérisme*, 327. Infra, ch. x, § 5.

51 Ibid., 314.

52 A. de Tocqueville, *Le système pénitentiaire aux États-Unis*, 321.

53 A. de Tocqueville, "Voyages en Angleterre, Irlande, Suisse et Algérie," 42.

54 See C. B. Macpherson, *The Political Theory of Possessive Individualism*.

55 T. Hobbes, "De Cive," *Opera Philosophica*, vol. 2, 292.

56 T. Hobbes, *Leviathan*, part 2, ch. 30. Its difference from the liberal tradition is therefore not over the nature and function of taxation, but rather over which authority may levy taxes (sovereign and parliament). On this, see T. Hobbes, "Behemoth," *The English Works*, vol. 6, 169, 320.

57 J.-J. Rousseau, *Discours sur l'économie politique*, 271.

58 In *Du contrat social*, III, 15 (*OC*, vol. 3, 429) one reads: "I hold enforced labour to be less opposed to liberty than taxation." But here, of course, the reference is clearly to taxes which allow the rich, and only the rich, to avoid obligations (military service public service, etc.) that are typical of the community of *citoyens*. See J.-J. Rousseau, *Discours sur l'économie politique*, 272, and "Projet de constitution pour la Corse," *OC*, vol. 3, 931–32.

59 J.-J. Rousseau, *Discourse sur l'économie politique*, 270. Rousseau's criticism of Montesquieu has already been examined in A. Burgio, *Eguaglianza, interesse, unanimità*, 99.

60 See D. Losurdo, *Tra Hegel e Bismarck*, 153–64.

61 F. Engels, "Zwei Reden in Elberfeld," *MEW*, vol. 2, 548.

62 See R. Barny, *L'éclatement révolutionnaire du rousseauisme*, 177, 182ff. 271.

63 M.-J.-A.-N. de C. de Condorcet, "Sur la révolution de 1688, et sur celle du 10 Août 1792," *Oeuvres*, vol. 12, 203–4.

64 F. von Gentz, *Über die Moralität in den Staatsrevolutionen*, 58.

65 Ibid., 46.

66 "Memorandum from F. A. L. von der Marwitz to Hardenberg, 11 February 1811," *Adam Müllers Lebenszeugnisse*, ed. J. Baxa, vol. 1, 616.

67 J. Möser, "Vorrede" to the second part of the "Osnabrückische Geschichten," and "Über das Recht der Menschheit als den Grund der neuen französichen Konstitution," in J. Möser, *Patriotische Phantasien: Ausgewählte Schriften*, ed. W. Zieger, 253, 261–62.

68 J. Möser, "Der Bauerhof als eine Aktie betrachtet," 292–94.

69 J. Möser, "Der jetzige Hang zu allgemeinen Gesetzen und Verodnungen ist der gemeinen Freiheit gefährlich," in *Sämmtliche Werke*, vol. 2, 23.

70 J. Möser, "Der Bauerhof als eine Aktie betrachtet," 292–93.

71 E. J. Sieyès, "Préliminaire de la Constitution," *Écrits politiques*, 199.

72 See C. von Rotteck, "Census," H. Brandt ed. *Restauration und Frühliberalismus*, 390–91. See also C. von Rotteck, "Historisches Recht," *Staats-Lexikon*, vol. 8, 13.

73 Even John Stuart Mill compares the State to a "joint concern." The ideological

context is considerably different, but it is significant that, even in this case, the comparison has an explicit anti-egalitarian meaning: it aims at justifying a plural vote that benefits the most intelligent and virtuous, that is, for the most part, the bourgeoisie, given that "an employer of labour is on the average more intelligent than a labourer; for he must labour with his head, and not solely with his hands." J. S. Mill, "Considerations on Representative Government," *Utilitarianism, Liberty, Representative Government*, 284–85.

74 J.-J. Rousseau, *Du contrat social*, IV, 8, (*OC*, vol. 3, 466).

75 Ibid., IV, 8, (*OC*, vol. 3, 466).

76 Ibid., IV, 8, (*OC*, vol. 3, 467).

77 On this point, see D. Losurdo, *Hegel und das deutsche Erbe*, ch. 1, § 4, p. 37. One must include in this debate Kant's vigorous condemnation of slavery in "Perpetual Peace." See D. Losurdo, *Autocensura e compromesso*, ch. 3, § 4.

78 J.-J. Rousseau, *Du contrat social*, Première version, 287.

79 "Letter to Usteri, 30 April 1763," in J.-J. Rousseau, *The Political Writings*, ed. C. E. Vaughan, vol. 2, 166.

80 One is reminded of the following words used to condemn slavery: "Jurists, who have gravely determined that the child of a slave comes into the world a slave, have decided, in other words, that the child of a man shall come into the world not a man." J.-J. Rousseau, *Discours sur l'origine et les fundaments de l'inégalité parmi les hommes,"* 184.

81 J.-J. Rousseau, *Du contrat social*, IV, 8, (*OC*, vol. 3, 464).

82 Ibid., IV, 8, (*OC*, vol. 3, 467–68).

83 G. W. F. Hegel, *Vorlesungen über die Philosophie der Religion*, ed. G. Lasson, vol. 1, 306–7.

84 R. Haym, *Hegel und seine Zeit*, 413.

85 Ibid., 164. This observation is made particularly with the *System of Ethics* in mind. Haym, however, attributes a more general significance to it. On the debate about the relationship between religion and politics in Idealism and in nineteenth century Germany, see D. Losurdo, "Religione e ideologia nella filosofia classica tedesca," *Studi Urbinati*/B2 57 (1984): 9–60.

86 R. Haym, *Hegel und seine Zeit*, 25–26. The only significant difference between Constant and Haym is that for the latter this motive has nationalistic undertones. The pathos of ethicality in Hegel's system represents "the victory . . . of the ancient principle over the modern one, the Graeco-Roman principle over the German one" (377). For Haym and German national-liberals the category of ethicality is considered anti-German and typical of the French revolutionary and statist tradition. See D. Losurdo, *Hegel und das deutsche Erbe*, ch. 14, §§ 1–2, 14 (=*La catastrofe della Germania e l'immagine di Hegel*, ch. 1, §§ 1–2; and ch. 2, § 9).

87 B. Constant, "De l'esprit de conquête," 1015, 1057.

88 Ibid., 1050n.

89 See K. H. Scheidler, "Hegel'sche Philosophie und Schule," *Staats-Lexikon*, vol. 7, 619.

90 C. von Rotteck, *Historisches Recht*, 4. For the *Staats-Lexikon's* position on Hegel, see D. Losurdo, *Tra Hegel e Bismarck*, 44–51.

91 R. Haym, *Hegel und seine Zeit*, 32.

92 Ibid., 32.

93 B. Constant, *Principes de politique*, 1146–47.

94 Ibid., 1146.

95 J.-J. Rousseau, *Discours sur l'économie politique*, 255.

96 Ibid., 256. 97. Ibid., 258.

98 J.-J. Rousseau, "Notes sur 'De l'esprit' d'Helvétius," *OC*, vol. 14, 1126.

99 Such as G. de Ruggiero, *Storia del liberalismo europeo*, 361.

100 See in particular J. L. Talmon, *The Origins of Totalitarian Democracy*.

101 Such as C. E. Vaughan, "Introduction," J.-J. Rousseau, *The Political Writings*, 22. Even more peculiar is the case of Lecky (a Victorian English liberal). On the one hand, he seems to share Vaughan's position: see W. E. H. Lecky, *A History of England in the Eighteenth Century*, 2nd ed., vol. 5, 361–62. On the other hand, he accuses Rousseau of having "greatly exaggerated the power the State has over its members," thereby paving the way for "the worst tyrannies." W. E. H. Lecky, *Democracy and Liberty*, vol. 2, 204.

102 Saint-Just, "Rapport, 13 Ventôse Year II," *Oeuvres complètes*, 715.

103 Saint-Just, "Rapport, 8 Ventôse Year II," *Oeuvres complètes*, 707. We are dealing not by chance with the Saint-Just later called by Babeuf to appear before the court that will condemn him to death. F.-N. Babeuf, *Écrits*, 316. It is within this same tradition that one should probably place Fichte's theory that there should not be "any poor people" "in a rational State." J. G. Fichte, *Grundlage des Naturrechts*, § 18; *FW*, vol. 3, 214.

104 "Letter, 27 September 1766," J.-J. Rousseau, *Correspondance complète*, ed. R. A. Leigh, vol. 30, 385.

105 J.-J. Rousseau, *Du contrat social*, IV, 6 (*OC*, vol. 3, 455–56).

106 Montesquieu, *De l'Esprit des lois*, XII, 19.

107 See H. Guillemin, *Benjamin Constant muscadin*, 13, 275–79. See also H. Guillemin, *Madame de Staël, Benjamin Constant et Napoléon*, 4–24.

108 J. S. Mill, *Considerations on Representative Government*, 207.

109 J.-J. Rousseau, *Discours sur l'économie politique*, 258.

110 Ibid., 241.

111 Ibid., 256.

112 Ibid., 256.

113 A. Smith, *The Theory of Moral Sentiments*, 369.

114 B. de Mandeville, "An Essay on Charity and Charity-Schools," *The Fable of the Bees*, vol. 1, 287–88.

115 K. Marx, "Inauguraladresse der Internationalen Arbeiter-Assotiation," *MEW*, vol. 16, 11.

IX. School, Division of Labor, and Modern Man's Freedom

1 W. von Humboldt, *Ideen zu einem Versuch*, 143.

2 Ibid., 101.

3 Ibid., 101.

4 L. von Haller, *Über die Constitution der Spanischen Cortès*.

5 See H. Brunschwig, *Société et romantisme en Prusse au xviiie siècle*, 2nd ed., 28.

6 It is noteworthy that this passage does not appear in the text published in the *Preußische Staatszeitung*.

7   K. Rosenkranz, *Königsberger Skizzen*, vol. 1, p. xxxii n.

8   See J. Hoffmeister, "Einleitung," to G. W. F. Hegel, *Nürnberger Schriften,*, xii. Hoff-meister calls Hegel a "Protestant philosopher," but we must remember that the Protestantism celebrated here is more political than religious. It is this political Protestantism which is discussed both by Hegel's contemporaries and his disciples. Not by chance, after the July Revolution, Hegel excludes France from the circle of Catholic countries. See D. Losurdo, *Hegel und das deutsche Erbe*, ch. 2, §§ 2–3.

9   L. von Haller, *Über die Constitution der Spanischen Cortès.*

10 The reference is to the situation and struggle taking place in the Belgian provinces that were part of Holland at the time. See D. Losurdo, *Hegel und das deutsche Erbe*, ch. 11, § 5 (=*Hegel, questione nazionale, Restaurazione*, ch. 9, § 5).

11 Hoffmeister has drawn attention to this aspect in his "Einleitung," p. xxiv–xxv. In Berlin too, according to Rosenkranz, Hegel "scorns the fact that in some schools they speak too much about Christ or even about the devil." K. Rosenkranz, *Hegels Leben*, 329.

12 The expression is found in "Letter to Niethammer, 9 June 1821" (B, II, 270), and earlier, with a more clearly negative meaning (*verdächtige Liberalitäten*), in "Letter from Niethammer, 9 January 1819" (B, II, 209). It is worth noting that during these years even the feudal reactionaries employ liberal terminology, which therefore has no unequivocal meaning and is used to express different political positions and contents. See D. Losurdo, *Hegel und das deutsche Erbe*, ch. 2, § 9.

13 J. G. Fichte, *Grundlage des Naturrechts*, § 52, FW, vol. 3, 363.

14 J. G. Fichte, *Grundlage des Naturrechts*, § 43, FW, vol. 3, 358.

15 See U. Krautkrämer, *Staat und Erziehung. Begründung öffentlicher Erziehung bei Humboldt, Kant, Fichte, Hegel und Schleiermacher*, 293, 301.

16 J. G. Fichte, *Grundlage des Naturrechts*, § 57, FW, vol. 3, 366.

17 F. Mehring, *Geschichte der deutschen Sozialdemokratie.*

18 See D. Losurdo, *Tra Hegel e Bismarck*, 178–89.

19 F. A. L. von der Marwitz, "Von der Schrankenlosigkeit," *Die Eigentumslosen*, ed. C. Jantke and D. Hilger, 141–43.

20 B. de Mandeville, *An Essay on Charity and Charity-Schools*, 288.

21 Ibid., 322.

22 Ibid., 288.

23 Ibid., 302.

24 Ibid., 288.

25 Ibid., 269.

26 Ibid., 288.

27 Ibid., 290.

28 Ibid., 287.

29 L. Stone, *Literacy and Education in England, 1640–1900.*

30 Ibid.

31 A. Smith, *The Wealth of Nations*, bk. 5, ch. 1, part 3, art. 2, 785–86.

32 Ibid., 775–76.

33 Ibid., 782.

34 Ibid., 787–88.

35 Ibid., 785.

36 W. von Humboldt, *Ideen zu einem Versuch*, 125–26, 145–46.

37 See D. Losurdo, *Hegel und das deutsche Erbe*, ch. 8 (=*Hegel, questione nazionale, Restaurazione*, ch. 6).

38 F. W. J. Schelling, "Philosophie der Offenbarung," *Sämmtliche Werke*, vol. 13, 24–25, 28.

39 A. Schopenhauer, *Über die Universitäts-Philosophie*, 184, 237, 238.

40 Ibid., 205, 213.

41 Ibid., 182–83, 190.

42 F. Nietzsche, "Nachgelassene Fragmente 1870–1872," *KSA*, vol. 7, 243.

43 See D. Losurdo, *Hegel und das deutsche Erbe*, ch. 8 (=*Hegel, questione nazionale, Restaurazione*, ch. 6).

X. Moral Tension and the Primacy of Politics

1 S. Kierkegaard, "Postilla conclusiva non scientifica alle briciole di filosofia," *Opere*, 441.

2 On the death of art as the end of the aesthetic period, see D. Losurdo, "Intellettuali e impegno politico in Germania: 1789–1848," *Studi storici* 4 (1982): 783–819.

3 G. W. F. Hegel, *Die Religionsphilosophie. Band I: Die Vorlesung von 1821*, 617.

4 K. Fischer, *Geschichte der neueren Philosophie*, vol. 8, 1: *Hegel's Leben, Werke und Lehre*, 2nd ed., 278. Nicolao Merker has already drawn attention to this comment in G. W. F. Hegel, *Il dominio della politica*, N. Merker, ed., 197 n. 1.

5 See D. Losurdo, *Hegel und das deutsche Erbe*, ch. 10, § 3 (=*Hegel, questione nazionale, Restaurazione*, ch. 8, § 3).

6 See D. Losurdo, *Tra Hegel e Bismarck*, 111–16.

7 I. Kant, "Der Streit der Fakultäten," *KGS*, vol. 7, 91–92.

8 I. Kant, "Metaphysik der Sitten, Tugendlehre," § 31, *KGS*, vol. 6, 453.

9 I. Kant, § 31, *Kasuistische Fragen*, *KGS*, vol. 6, 454.

10 Ibid., § 30, *KGS*, vol. 6, 453.

11 Ibid., § 35, *KGS*, vol. 6, 458.

12 F. Schleiermacher, "Predigten über den christlichen Hausstand," *Werke*, ed. O. Braun and J. Bauer, vol. 3, 395–96. We have translated "bürgerlich" with "civic" because here the reference is to the "Bürger" member of the political community.

13 Ibid., 397.

14 C. von Rotteck, "Armenwesen," in *Staats-Lexikon*, C. von Rotteck and C. Welcker, vol. 2, 11–12.

15 F. J. Stahl, *Die Philosophie des Rechts*, vol. 1, 41.

16 Passages from David Hansemann, as well as from his "unofficial organ," the *Stadt Aachener Zeitung*, are printed in J. Droz, *Le libéralisme rhénan 1815–1848*, 241–43.

17 A. de Tocqueville, *Mémoire sur le paupérisme*, 313–14, 326–27.

18 Ibid., 326–27. See also supra, ch. VIII, § 5.

19 A. de Tocqueville, "'Notes,' presumably from 1847," *Oeuvres complètes*, vol. III, 2; A. de Tocqueville, *Écrit et discours politiques*, 727.

20 Ibid.

21 "Address to the Constituent Assembly, 12 September 1848," A. de Tocqueville, *Études économiques, politiques et littéraires*, 537, 551. It is notable that, when presenting his legal plan for insurance against accidents at work a few decades later, Bismarck rejects the right's accusation of "state socialism" and "communism" by

declaring that he intends to limit himself to "practical Christianity." See "Speech, 2 April 1881," and the parliamentary interventions which it addresses in H. Fenske ed., *Im Bismarckschen Reich 1871–1890*, 273–82.

22 A. de Tocqueville, *Mémoire sur le paupérisme*, 340.

23 Ibid., 340.

24 H. Spencer, "The Proper Sphere of Government," in *Man versus the State*, 197–99.

25 See in particular K. O. Apel, "Kann der postkantische Standpunkt der Moralität noch einmal in substantieller Sittlichkeit 'aufgehoben' werden?," W. Kuhlmann ed., *Moralität und Sittlichkeit*, 217–64; J. Habermas, "Legitimationsprobleme im modernen Staat," *Praktische Philosophie/Ethik*, ed. K. O. Apel et al., vol. 1, 392–401. On neo-Aristotelianism as neo-conservatism, see H. Schnädelbach, "Was ist Neoaristotelismus?" in W. Kuhlmann ed., *Moralität und Sittlichkeit*, 38–63.

26 J. Ritter, "'Politik' und 'Ethik' in der praktischen Philosophie des Aristoteles," *Metaphysik und Politik*, 114. Ritter quotes from Aristotle's *Politics*. 1287b 5–7.

27 F. W. J. Schelling, *Schlußwort zur öffentlichen Sitzung der Akademie*, 424. On Hegel's celebration of the *Charte* and of the invention of the press, both of which were scorned by the Romantics in the name of "living" tradition, see D. Losurdo, *Hegel und das deutsche Erbe*, ch. 7, § 19; ch. 9, § 4; ch. 11, § 3. As for Schelling's position on the *Charte*, see D. Losurdo, "Von Louis Philippe zu Louis Bonaparte. Schellings späte politische Entwicklung," *Die praktische Philosophie Schellings und die gegenwärtige Rechtsphilosophie*, ed. H. M. Pawlowski, S. Smid and R. Specht, 227–54.

28 E. Burke, "Letters on a Regicide Peace, III," *The Works*, vol. 8, 400.

29 E. Burke, *Letters to the Right Honourable Henry Dundas*, 281; *Letters on a Regicide Peace*, IV, 110. Even Burke's praise for the "cardinal virtue of *Temperance*" so dear to the "ancients," as a necessary foundation of "our physical well-being, our moral worth, our social happiness, our political tranquility" has a strong anti-Aristotelian tone (*Letters on a Regicide Peace*, III, 376). Burke's Aristotelianism has already been noted by J. Habermas, "Die klassische Lehre von der Politik in ihrem Verhältnis zur Sozialphilosophie," *Theorie und Praxis*, 48–49.

30 E. Burke, *Reflections on the Revolution in France*, 76.

31 Ibid., 76.

32 *Eudämonia oder deutsches Volksglück: Ein Journal für Freunde von Weisheit und Recht*.

33 I. Kant, *Über den Gemeinspruch*, 298.

34 I. Kant, *Metaphysik der Sitten. Rechtslehre*, § 49, KGS, vol. 6, 318.

35 H. Arendt, *Vita activa oder vom tätigen Leben*, 32–33.

36 For a different reading of the theme of economy in Aristotle and Hegel, see K.-H. Ilting, "Hegels Auseinandersetzung mit der aristotelischen Politik," *Philosophisches Jahrbuch* 17 (1963–64): 47–48.

37 This construction is not limited to liberation from the type of work which, in classical antiquity, was restricted to a "class of slaves" (*Sklavenstand*) (*Rph.*, § 356). The upheaval of the ancient *familia* affects not only the *servants*, but all *familiares* because in pre-Christian antiquity, not even women and children were fully included within the universal category of 'man' (see *Rph.*, § 2 *AL*, in *v.Rph.*, II, 85 and *v.Rph.*, IV, 466). On the historical establishment of the universal concept of 'man,' see D. Losurdo, "Realismus und Nominalismus als politische Kategorien," *Philosophie als Verteidigung des Ganzen der Vernunft*, ed. D. Losurdo and H. J. Sandkühler,

170–96. See also D. Losurdo, "Marx, la tradition libérale et le concept universel d'homme," *Actuel Marx* 5 (1989) 17–33.

38 For Tocqueville, the category of universality also refers, in the final analysis, to the French Revolution and its ideological preparation (infra, ch. XII, § 8).

39 On the pathos of universality in Kant, see D. Losurdo, *Immanuel Kant: Freiheit, Recht und Revolution*, 27–28. These pages do not appear in the original Italian edition, *Autocensura e compromesso*.

40 F. W. J. Schelling, *Stuttgarter Privatvorlesungen*, 462. Later, in order to counter democratic demands, Schelling does not hesitate to refer to Aristotle, the theorist of slavery ("that which can foresee by the exercise of the mind is by nature intended to be lord and master, and that which can with its body give effect to such foresight is a subject, and by nature a slave" (*Politics*, I, 2). Compare to *Philosophie der Mythologie*, 530 n. 2. Schelling's "Aristotelianism" may be compared to Hegel's "anti-Aristotelianism." According to Hegel, where there is slavery there is no real State: slavery "occurs *in a condition prior to right*" (*Rph.*, § 57 AL, in *V.Rph.*, II, 241).

41 "Letter to A. Ruge, May 1843," *MEW*, vol. 1, 339.

42 J.-J. Rousseau, *Confessions*, *OC*, vol. 1, 404; J.-J. Rousseau, *Narcisse ou l'Amant de lui-même*, *Préface*, 969.

43 C.-A. Helvétius, "De l'esprit," *Oeuvres complètes*, vol. 2, 237, 244, 249–50.

44 J.-J. Rousseau, "Émile," *OC*, vol. 4, 524.

45 P. H. T. d'Holbach, *Ethocratie ou le Gouvernement fondé sur la morale*, "Avertissement," 55.

46 Reported in B. Baczko, *Lumières de l'utopie*, 182.

47 I. Kant, "Grundlegung der Metaphysik der Sitten," *KGS*, vol. 4, 393–94.

48 I. Kant, *Zum ewigen Frieden*, 366.

49 I. Kant, "Handschriftlicher Nachlaß," *KGS*, vol. 23, 135.

50 I. Kant, *Grundlegung der Metaphysik der Sitten*, 394.

51 I. Kant, "Handschriftlicher Nachlaß," *KGS*, vol. 20, 151.

52 Ibid., *KGS*, vol. 23, 135.

53 I. Kant, *Zum ewigen Frieden*, 366. On the counter-argument made by Kant, see D. Losurdo, *Autocensura e compromesso*, ch. 3, § 6.

54 K. Rosenkranz, *Geschichte der Kantschen Philosophie*, 495.

55 I. Kant, *Zum ewigen Frieden*, 353n.

56 G. W. F. Hegel, *Religionsphilosophie. Band I: Die Vorlesung von 1821*, 641.

57 B. Brecht, "Flüchtlingsgespräche," *Prosa*, vol. 2, 277.

58 K. R. Popper, "Coscienza dell'occidente," *Criterio* 1 (1986): 77–79.

59 K. O. Apel, "Die Konflikte unserer Zeit und das Erfordernis einer ethisch-politischen Grundorientierung," *Praktische Philosophie/Ethik*, vol. 1, 272.

60 See D. Losurdo, *Realismus und Nominalismus als politische Kategorien*.

61 K. O. Apel, *Die Konflikte unserer Zeit*, 277, 283.

XI. Legitimacy of the Modern and Rationality of the Actual

1 I. Kant, *Metaphysik der Sitten, Tugendlehre*, § 33, *KGS*, vol. 6, 455–56.

2 I. Kant, "Logik," *KGS*, vol. 9, 79–80.

3 See D. Losurdo, *Hegel und das deutsche Erbe*, ch. 9 (=*Hegel, questione nazionale, Restaurazione*, ch. 7).

4   H. Heine, "Die romantische Schule," *Sämtliche Schriften*, vol. 3, 413–14.

5   A. Schopenhauer, *Über die Universitäts-Philosophie*, 190, 213.

6   F. Nietzsche, "Unzeitgemäße Betrachtungen, II," *KSA*, vol. 1, 309.

7   Ibid., 303–4.

8   Ibid., 309.

9   F. Nietzsche, "Götzendämmerung," "Streifzüge eines Unzeitgemäßen," § 40;
    F. Nietzsche, "Nachgelassene Fragmente 1887–1889," *KSA*, vol. 13, 30.

10 F. Nietzsche, "Über die Zukunft unserer Bildungsanstalten," *KSA*, vol. 1, 690–91.

11 F. Nietzsche, "Unzeitgemäße Betrachtungen, II," 310.

12 F. Nietzsche, "Über die Zukunft unserer Bildungsanstalten," 666, 700.

13 F. von Gentz, *Über die Moralität in den Staatsrevolutionen*, 34.

14 F. Engels, "Review of Carlyle," *Neue Rheinische Zeitung: Politisch-ökonomische
    Revue*, April 1850, *MEW*, vol. 7, 264–65.

15 See D. Losurdo, *Hegel und das deutsche Erbe*, ch. 10, § 3 (=*Hegel, questione na-
    zionale, Restaurazione*, ch. 7, § 3).

16 F. Nietzsche, "Unzeitgemäße Betrachtungen, I," *KSA*, vol. 1, 172.

17 T. Carlyle, *On Heroes, Hero-Worship, and the Heroic in History*, lecture 5. It is
    worth noting that Carlyle refers not to the text of 1794, cited by us, but to the *Über
    das Wesen des Gelehrten und seine Erscheinungen im Gebiete der Freiheit* of 1806.
    However, this does not change our argument's essential premise given that Fichte's
    work is characterized throughout by the pathos of the intellectual.

18 F. Nietzsche, "Unzeitgemäße Betrachtungen, II," 310–11.

19 Ibid., 310–11.

20 "Letter to W. von Zenge, 22 March 1801," H. von Kleist, *Sämtliche Werke und
    Briefe*, ed. H. Sembdner, 2nd ed., vol. 2, 634.

21 "Letter to U. von Kleist, 23 March 1801," H. von Kleist, *Sämtliche Werke und Briefe*,
    vol. 2, 636.

22 F. Nietzsche, "Unzeitgemäße Betrachtungen, III," *KSA*, vol. 1, 354.

23 Ibid., 339.

24 Ibid., 362.

25 Ibid., 362.

26 A. Schopenhauer, "Die Welt als Wille und Vorstellung: Ergänzungen," *Sämtliche
    Werke*, vol. 2, 567.

27 Ibid., 569.

28 A. Schopenhauer, *Über die Universitäts-Philosophie*, 213.

29 Ibid., 205.

30 Ibid., 194, 215.

31 E. Burke, *Reflections on the Revolution in France*, 149–50.

32 "Letter to an unknown recipient, January 1790," *The Correspondence of Edmund
    Burke*, eds. A. Cobban and R. A. Smith, vol. 6, 80.

33 W. von Humboldt, *Ideen zu einem Versuch*, 74, 85.

34 J. S. Mill, *On Liberty*, 123.

35 Ibid., 130.

36 F. A. Hayek, *The Counter-Revolution of Science*, 195.

37 See J. S. Mill, "Carlyle's French Revolution," *Collected Works*, ed. J. M. Robinson,
    vol. 20, 133–166, in particular 133; J. S. Mill, "Autobiography," *Collected Works*, ed.
    J. M. Robinson, vol. 1, 225.

38 F. Nietzsche, "Morgenröte," IV, 298. See also F. Nietzsche, "Nachgelassene Fragmente 1885–1887," *KSA,* vol. 12, 358.

39 See, for example, F. Nietzsche, *Morgenröte,* II, 132.

40 F. Nietzsche, "Nachgelassene Fragmente 1885–1887," *KSA,* vol. 12, 558.

41 J. S. Mill, *On Liberty,* 124.

42 Ibid., 130.

43 A. de Tocqueville, "De la démocratie en Amérique," vol. 1, 7.

44 Ibid., vol. 2, 43.

45 A. de Tocqueville, "Diary Note, 6 November 1831," "Voyage en Sicile et aux États-Unis," *Oeuvres complètes,* vol. 5, 1, 188.

46 "Letter to G. de Beaumont, 29 January 1851," A. de Tocqueville, *Oeuvres complètes,* vol. 8, 2, 369.

47 "Letter to G. de Beaumont, 21 February 1855," A. de Tocqueville, *Oeuvres complètes,* vol. 8, 3, 273.

48 "Letter to F. de Corcelle, 19 March 1838," A. de Tocqueville, *Oeuvres complètes,* vol. 15, 1, 97.

49 A. de Tocqueville, "Souvenirs," 37.

50 "Letter to G. de Beaumont, 9 August 1840," A. de Tocqueville, *Oeuvres complètes,* vol. 8, 1, 421. It is in this sense that Tocqueville celebrates the Opium War as "a great event . . . It is good not to be too judgmental about our century and ourselves; men are small, but events are great." "Letter to Henry Reeve, 12 April 1840," A. de Tocqueville, *Oeuvres complètes,* vol. 4, 1, 58.

51 F. Nietzsche, *Götzendämmerung; Moral als Widernatur,* § 3.

52 A. de Tocqueville, "Souvenirs," 31–32.

53 A. de Tocqueville, "Lettres sur la situation intérieure de la France," *Oeuvres complètes,* vol. 3, 2, 101.

54 A. de Tocqueville, "Commémoration des journées de juillet," *Oeuvres complètes,* vol. 3, 2, 134.

55 See K. Löwith, *Von Hegel zu Nietzsche.*

56 F. Nietzsche, *Götzendämmerung; Was den Deutschen abgeht,* § 5.

57 And at Taine's school too. supra, ch. VIII, § 3.

58 A. de Tocqueville, "Address to the Constituent Assembly, 12 September 1848," A. de Tocqueville, *Études économiques, politiques et littéraires,* 539.

59 Ibid., 542.

60 Ibid., 544.

61 A. Schopenhauer, *Über die Universitäts-Philosophie,* 190.

62 F. Nietzsche, *Also sprach Zarathustra; Vom höheren Menschen,* 3.

63 F. Nietzsche, *Zarathustras Vorrede,* 5.

64 F. Nietzsche, *Vom neuen Götzen.*

65 Ibid.

66 A. Schopenhauer, *Über die Universitäts-Philosophie,* 180, 182, 190.

67 "Letter to F. de Corcelle, 22 July 1854," A. de Tocqueville, *Oeuvres complètes,* vol. 15, 2, 107–8.

68 A. de Tocqueville, "Souvenirs," 31–32.

69 K. H. Scheidler, *Hegel'sche Philosophie und Schule,* 636–37.

70 Ibid., 619. For Schelling, see "Vorrede zu einer politischen Schrift des Herrn Victor Cousin," *Sämmtliche Werke,* vol. 10, 223.

71 See S. Drescher, *Tocqueville and England*, 59.

72 C. de Cavour, "Des idées communistes et des moyens d'en combattre le développe-ment," in *Il socialismo nella storia d'Italia*, ed. G. Manacorda, vol. 1, 12–3.

73 "Letter to F. de Corcelle, 22 July 1854," A. de Tocqueville, *Oeuvres complètes*, vol. 15, 2, 107–8. For the remarks of the editor, P. Gilbert, see Ibid., 108 n.6.

74 A. Schopenhauer, *Über die Universitäts-Philosophie*, 215.

75 A. Schopenhauer, "Über die Freiheit des menschlichen Willens," *Sämtliche Werke*, vol. 3, 610.

76 "Letter to D. Asher, 13 April 1858," *Der Briefwechsel Arthur Schopenhauers*, ed. A. Hübscher, vol. 2, 643.

77 F. Nietzsche, "Unzeitgemäße Betrachtungen, II," 309.

78 F. Nietzsche, "Nachgelassene Fragmente 1870–1872," *KSA*, vol. 7, 243.

79 A. Schopenhauer, *Über die Universitäts-Philosophie*, 183, 190, 213.

80 Ibid., 182–83, 190.

81 F. Nietzsche, *Menschliches, Allzumenschliches*, I, § 235.

82 F. Nietzsche, *Also sprach Zarathustra, Vom neuen Götzen*.

83 A. Jung, *Vorlesungen über die moderne Literatur*, 26, 50.

84 See D. Losurdo, *Hegel e la Germania*, ch. 8, § 3.

85 B. Spaventa, "Pensieri sull'insegnamento della filosofia," *Il primo hegelismo ital-iano*, ed. G. Oldrini, 333.

86 "Letter to his mother, January 1849," in G. von Uexküll, *Ferdinand Lassalle*, 70.

87 This appears in a fragment reprinted in S. Spaventa, *Dal 1848 al 1861: Lettere, scritti, documenti*, ed. B. Croce, 2nd ed., 194–95.

88 A. Herzen, "La jeune Moscou," from "Mémoires et pensées," in A. Herzen, *Textes philosophiques choisis*, 579.

89 K. Marx, "Die großen Männer des Exils," *MEW*, vol. 8, 275–76.

90 K. Marx, "Der Ritter vom edelmütigen Bewußtsein," *MEW*, vol. 9, 493, 496–97. See also K. Marx, *Die großen Männer des Exils*, 245.

91 F. Engels, "Antwort an Herrn Paul Ernst," *MEW*, vol. 22, 83–84.

92 M. Horkheimer, "Hegel und das Problem der Metaphysik," in M. Horkheimer, *Anfänge des bürgerlichen Geschichtsphilosophie*, 84–5, 95.

93 M. Horkheimer, "Appendix" to "Traditionelle und kritische Theorie," *Zeitschrift für Sozialforschung* 6 (1937): 631.

94 T. W. Adorno, *Drei Studien zu Hegel*, 102.

XII. The Second Thirty Years War and the "Philosophical Crusade" against Germany

1 L. T. Hobhouse, *The Metaphysical Theory of the State: A Criticism*, 6–7. Ironically, the term *gothas* calls to mind barbarians as well as Germany's attempt to be a sort of aristocracy among nations.

2 F. A. Hayek, *The Road to Serfdom*, 16.

3 É. Boutroux, "L'Allemagne et la guerre: Lettre à M. le Directeur de la 'Revue des Deux-Mondes,' 15 October 1914," *Études d'histoire de la philosophie allemande*, 118.

4 W. Sombart, *Händler und Helden: Patriotische Besinnungen*, 3.

5 É. Boutroux, "L'Allemagne et la guerre: Lettre à M. le Directeur de la 'Revue des Deux-Mondes,' 15 May 1916," *Études d'histoire de la philosophie allemande*, 231.

6   L. T. Hobhouse, *The Metaphysical Theory of the State*, 135.

7   Ibid., 134.

8   F. A. Hayek, *The Road to Serfdom*, 17.

9   K. R. Popper, *The Open Society*, vol. 1, 175.

10 J. Habermas, "Zu Hegels politischen Schriften," *Theorie und Praxis*, 170.

11 H. Mandt, "Tyrannislehre und Widerstandsrecht: Studien zur deutschen politischen Theorie des 19. Jahrhunderts," in *Materialien zu Kants Rechtsphilosophie*, ed. Z. Batscha.

12 K. R. Popper, *The Open Society*, vol. 1, 102.

13 É. Boutroux, "L'Allemagne et la guerre," 234.

14 E. Quinet, *Le Christianisme et la Révolution française*, 148.

15 F. Lieber, *Civil Liberty and Self-Government*, 2nd ed., 22n. For the relationship between Lieber and Tocqueville, see their correspondence in A. de Tocqueville, *Oeuvres complètes*, vol. 7. See also A. Jardin, *A. de Tocqueville 1805–1859*, esp. p. 373. For F. A. Hayek, see *The Constitution of Liberty*.

16 H. Arendt, *On Revolution*, 108.

17 C. Schmitt, *Der Nomos der Erde im Völkerrecht des Jus Publicum Europaeum*, 256. For a selection of some of the more significant passages from the Monroe Doctrine, see R. Romeo and G. Talamo, eds., *Documenti storici*, vol. 3, 23–5.

18 F. A. Hayek, *The Constitution of Liberty*, 56.

19 F. von Hayek, *The Road of Serfdom*, 16.

20 K. R. Popper, *The Open Society*, vol. 2, 336 n. 15.

21 F. A. Hayek, *Law, Legislation and Liberty*, 22.

22 K. R. Popper, *The Open Society*, vol. 2, 60, 226.

23 Ibid., vol. 2, 407 n. 41.

24 F. A. Hayek, *Law, Legislation and Liberty*.

25 K. R. Popper, *The Open Society*, vol. 2, 30.

26 F. A. Hayek, *Law, Legislation and Liberty*, vol. 2, 66–67.

27 Ibid., vol. 2, 66–67.

28 K. R. Popper, *The Open Society*, vol. 2, 30.

29 F. A. Hayek, *The Fatal Conceit: The Errors of Socialism*, 110.

30 Ibid., 64.

31 É. Boutroux, "L'Allemagne et la guerre," 234, 246.

32 R. Dahrendorf, *Fragmente eines neuen Liberalismus*.

33 J. Schumpeter, "Zur Soziologie der Imperialismen," *Archiv für Sozialwissenschaft und Sozialpolitik* 46 (1918–1919): 287–88nn.

34 I. Kant, "Handschriftlicher Nachlaß," *KGS*, vol. 19, 605.

35 R. Dahrendorf, *Reflections on the Revolution in Europe*, 124.

36 See the testimony printed in J. F. Abegg, *Reisetagebuch von 1798*, ed. W. and J. Abegg in collaboration with Z. Batscha, 186.

37 J. Locke, *Two Treatises of Civil Government*, I, § 130.

38 J. Locke, "The Fundamental Constitutions of Carolina," art. CX, in *Works*, vol. 10, 196.

39 J. Locke, *Two Treatises of Civil Government*, I, § 85.

40 J. Locke, "The Whole History of Navigation from the Original to This Time," *Works*, vol. 10, 414.

41 See M. Cranston, *John Locke: A Biography*, 115.

42 E. J. Sieyès, *Dire sur la question du veto royal*, 236; *Notes et fragments inédits*, 75 (the "Esclaves" fragment), and 81 (the *"Grèce: Citoyen-homme"* fragment).

43 The 1697 text, written by Locke in his capacity as a member of the Commission on Trade, is reprinted in H. R. F. Bourne, *The Life of John Locke*, vol. 2, 377–90.

44 F. Engels, *Die Lage der arbeitenden Klasse in England*, 496–98.

45 F. A. Hayek, *New Studies in Philosophy, Politics, Economics and the History of Ideas*, 259.

46 B. de Mandeville, *An Essay on Charity and Charity-Schools*, 307–8.

47 J. L. Talmon, *The Origins of Totalitarian Democracy*, 70.

48 E. J. Sieyès, *Notes et fragments inédits*, 76 (the "Esclaves" fragment).

49 See M. W. Jernegan, *Laboring and Dependent Classes in Colonial America: 1607–1783*, 45–46.

50 E. J. Sieyès, *Notes et fragments inédits*, 77 (the "Salaires: moyen de niveler leur prix dans les différents lieux" fragment).

51 J. L. Talmon, *The Origins of Totalitarian Democracy*, 5.

52 N. Bobbio, *L'età dei diritti*.

53 R. Dahrendorf, *Fragmente eines neuen Liberalismus*.

54 R. H. Tawney, *Religion and the Rise of Capitalism*, 269.

55 R. Dahrendorf, *Reflections on the Revolution in Europe*, 31, n. 35.

56 E. Burke, *Reflections on the Revolution in France*, 105–6, 154.

57 J. Bentham, *Anarchical Fallacies*, 498–99.

58 On the persistence of forms of compulsory labor in the Southern United States, see W. Kloosterboer, *Involuntary Labour since the Abolition of Slavery*, ch. 5. For Hamilton's argument, see *The Federalist*, number. 84, and E. Merriam, *A History of American Political Theories*, 96–142. For the influence of Burke on Hamilton and the American political tradition in general, see W. Gerhard, *Das politische System Alexander Hamiltons*, and H. J. Laski, *The American Democracy*, 10. For F. Gentz and J. Q. Adams, see D. Losurdo, "La révolution française a-t-elle échouée?," *La Pensée* 267 (Jan–Feb 1989): 85ff.

59 D. Losurdo, *Hegel und das deutsche Erbe*, ch. 14 (=*La catastrofe della Germania e l'immagine di Hegel*).

60 F. Meinecke, "Germanischer und romanischer Geist im Wandel der deutschen Geschichtsauffassung," *Berichte der Preußischen Akademie der Wissenschaften* 6 (1916): 116, 125.

61 J. G. Fichte, "Reden an die deutsche Nation," *FW*, vol. 7, 363–64.

62 G. Simmel, *Der Krieg und die geistigen Entscheidungen*, 39.

63 M. Scheler, "Die Ursachen des Deutschenhasses," *Gesammelte Werke*, vol. 4: *Politisch-pädagogische Schriften*, ed. M.S. Frings, 357.

64 C. Petersen, "Der Seher deutscher Volkheit Friedrich Hölderlin," cited by H. O. Burger, "Die Entwicklung des Hölderlinbildes seit 1933," *Deutsche Vierteljahresschrift für Literatur und Geisteswissenschaft* 18 (1940): Referateheft, 122.

65 A. Rosenberg, *Der Mythus des 20. Jahrhunderts*, 336–37.

66 A. Baeumler, "Nietzsche," *Studien zur deutschen Geistesgeschichte*, 244.

67 F. Böhm, *Anti-Cartesianismus: Deutsche Philosophie im Widerstand*, 27.

68 A. Rosenberg, *Der Mythus des 20. Jahrhunderts*, 237.

69 J. Evola, *Il fascismo*, 14.

70 See D. Losurdo, *Hegel und das deutsche Erbe*, ch. 14, §§ 16, 22 (=*La catastrofe della Germania e l'immagine di Hegel*, ch. 2, § 11 and ch. 3, § 5).

71 "Dinner Conversation, 18 May 1944," in M. Bormann, *Bormann-Vermerke* (these are the transcriptions, edited by Martin Bormann, of dinner conversations with Adolf Hitler).

72 H. Picker, ed., *Hitlers Tischgespräche* (Dinner Conversation, 7 March 1942), 122.

73 F. A. Hayek, *The Constitution of Liberty*.

74 See D. Losurdo, *Heidegger and the Ideology of War*.

75 H. Mandt, *Tyrannislehre und Widerstandsrecht*, 293.

76 F. A. Hayek, *The Road to Serfdom*, 16.

77 See E. Bernstein's note written after the October Revolution in "Die Voraussetzungen des Sozialismus und die Aufgaben der Sozialdemokratie." For M. Weber, see D. Beetham, *Max Weber and the Theory of Modern Politics*. For R. Mondolfo, see "Forza e violenza nella storia," in *Umanismo di Marx: Studi filosofici 1908–1966*, 210–11, 215. After World War II, Hans Kelsen's position becomes similar to Mondolfo's. See H. Kelsen, *The Political Theory of Bolshevism: A Critical Analysis*.

78 J. Bentham, "Nomography or the Art of Inditing Laws," *Works*, vol. 3, 240.

79 J. Bentham, "Essay on the Promulgation of Laws," *Works*, vol. 1, 157.

80 J. S. Mill, "Obituary of Bentham," *Collected Works*, vol. 10, 496.

81 J. Bentham, "A Fragment on Government: Historical Preface to the Second Edition," *Works*, vol. 1, 242.

82 J. Bentham, "Jeremy Bentham to his Fellow-Citizens of France on Houses of Peers and Senates," *Works*, vol. 4, 447.

83 J. Bentham, *A Fragment on Government*, 242–43.

84 A. de Tocqueville, "De la démocratie en Amérique," vol. I, 207–8.

85 "Letter to F. de Corcelle, (probably after) 15 October 1835," A de Tocqueville, *Oeuvres complètes*, vol. 15, 1, 57.

86 A. F. Pollard, "The Evolution of Parliament," in T. H. Marshall, *Sociology at the Crossroads*, 98.

87 K.-H. Ilting, *Hegel diverso*, 119–20. Paulus already expressed himself negatively in Hegel's time (*mat.*, 1, 63).

88 A. Smith, *Lectures on Jurisprudence*, ed. R. L. Meek, D. D. Raphael, and P. G. Stein, vol. 5, 455. This is from the 1766 lecture course.

89 K.-H. Ilting, *Hegel diverso*, 22.

90 See D. Losurdo, *Hegel und das deutsche Erbe*, especially ch. 2, § 8.

91 K.-H. Ilting, *Hegel diverso*, 24.

92 Ibid., 8.

93 Ibid., 45.

94 Ibid., 22–23.

95 K.-H. Ilting, *Hegel diverso*, 23.

96 See G. Lukács, *Gelebtes Denken*, ed. I. Eörsi. Arguing against Stalin is Mao Zedong, who, though he places Hegel among the "negative materials" of "bourgeois doctrines," contrasts Lenin's (and Engels's) theory that classic German philosophy was one of the "three integral parts of Marxism" to Stalin's theory that German idealism was the "reaction of the German aristocracy to the French Revolution." See Mao Zedong, "Discorso alla conferenza dei segretari dei comitati di partito delle prov-

ince, municipalità e regioni autonome," *Rivoluzione e costruzione: Scritti e discorsi 1949–1957*, 488. For Lenin, see "Tre fonti e tre parti integranti del marxismo," in V. I. Lenin, *Opere scelte*, 475–80. For Engels, see *Ludwig Feuerbach*, 307.

97 K. R. Popper, *The Open Society*, vol. 2, 30.
98 K. Kautsky, "Arthur Schopenhauer," *Die neue Zeit* vi (1888): 76.
99 G. Lukács, *Karl Marx und Friedrich Engels als Literaturhistoriker.*
100 G. Lukács, *Goethe und seine Zeit.*
101 N. Elias, *Über den Prozeß der Zivilisation: I. Wandlungen des Verhaltens in den weltlichen Oberschichten des Abendlandes*, 2nd ed.
102 K. Marx, "Die Lage in Preußen," *MEW*, vol. 12, 684.
103 F. Engels, *Ludwig Feuerbach*, 269, 271.
104 G. Lukács, *Die Zerstörung der Vernunft.*
105 F. Engels, *Ludwig Feuerbach*, 269.
106 "Letter to A. Seghers, 2 March 1939," in *Essays über Liberalismus* (Berlin, 1948), 210.
107 M.-J.-A.-N. de C. de Condorcet, "Aux Gérmains," *Oeuvres*, vol. 12, 162–63.
108 H. Heine, "Englische Fragmente," *Sämtliche Schriften*, vol. 2, 596.
109 F. Engels, "Die Polendebatte in Frankfurt," *MEW*, vol. 5, 359.

XIII. Liberalism, Conservatism, the French Revolution, and Classic German Philosophy

1 I. Kant, *Grundlegung der Metaphysik der Sitten*, 436–37.
2 I. Kant, "Kritik der reinen Vernunft: Einleitung," *KGS*, vol. 3, 28–29.
3 J. Möser, "Der jetzige Hang zu allgemeinen Gesetzen und Verordnungen ist der gemeinen Freiheit gefährlich," *Sämmtliche Werke*, vol. 2, 22–23.
4 K. Mannheim, *Das konservative Denken*, 477–78.
5 A. de Tocqueville, note from his trip to England in 1833, in "Voyages en Angleterre, Irlande, Suisse et Algérie," 39.
6 K. Marx and F. Engels, "Die heilige Familie," *MEW*, vol. 2, 41.
7 I. Kant, "Handschriftlicher Nachlaß," *KGS*, vol. 15, 610.
8 Ibid., *KGS*, vol. 19, 547.
9 Ibid., *KGS*, vol. 19, 545.
10 J. Möser, "Der jetzige Hang zu allgemeinen Gesetzen und Verordnungen ist der gemeinen Freiheit gefährlich," 21.
11 A. Müller, "Elemente der Staatskunst," in P. Kluckhohn, ed., *Deutsche Vergangenheit und deutscher Staat*, vol. x, 232–33.
12 K. Marx and F. Engels, "Die deutsche Ideologie," *MEW*, vol. 3,, 296.
13 K. Marx, "Das philosophische Manifest der historischen Rechtsschule," 80.
14 Novalis, "Blüthenstaub," *Werke, Tagebücher und Briefe*, ed. H. J. Mähl, vol. 2, 279.
15 See L. Marino, *I maestri della Germania: Göttingen 1770–1820*, especially 365–66. See also K. Epstein, *The Genesis of German Conservatism.* For a thorough examination of Burke's influence in Germany, see F. Braune, *Edmund Burke in Deutschland.*
16 F. Schlegel, "Signatur des Zeitalters," *Concordia*, ed. E. Behler, 354.
17 A. Müller, "Deutsche Wissenschaft und Literatur," *Kritische, ästhetische und philosophische Schriften*, eds. W. Schroeder and W. Siebert, vol. 1, 101–2.
18 E. Burke, *Letters on a Regicide Peace*, iv, 110. See also, E. Burke, *An Appeal from the New to the Old Whigs*, 118.

19 See D. Losurdo, *Hegel und das deutsche Erbe*, ch. 5, § 4 (=*Hegel, questione nazionale, Restaurazione*, ch. 3, § 4).

20 A. Müller, *Elemente der Staatskunst*, 231–32.

21 A. Müller, *Versuche einer neuen Theorie des Geldes, mit besonderer Rücksicht auf Großbritannien*, ed. H. Lieser, 110.

22 F. Schlegel, *Signatur des Zeitalters*, 64, 180, 354.

23 See D. Losurdo, *Von Louis Philippe bis Louis Bonaparte*, 227–30.

24 Burke is cited in a review attributed to Schelling. See L. Pareyson, ed., *Schellingiana rariora*, 263. In Jena, an Englishman compares the German philosopher to Burke, though only with regard to aesthetics and art theory. See Xavier Tilliette, ed., *Schelling im Spiegel seiner Zeitgenossen*, 100.

25 See F. J. Stahl, *Die Philosophie des Rechts*, vol. 1, 554ff.

26 See "Thronrede, 11 April 1840," in R. Buchner and W. Baumgart eds. *Quellen zum politischen Denken der Deutschen im 19 und 20 Jahrhundert*. vol. 4, ed. H. Feske, 199, 201.

27 F. Schlegel, "Zur österreichischen Geschichte," *Schriften und Fragmente*, ed. E. Behler, 321.

28 E. Burke, *Reflections on the Revolution in France*, 152.

29 Ibid., 184. For Gentz's German translation, see E. Burke, *Betrachtungen über die französische Revolution*, 160. Later, in 1852, Gentz also uses the term *Gemeinschaft* in his critical history of reactionism when paraphrasing this passage by Burke. See M. Stirner, *Geschichte der Reaktion*, vol. 1, 216.

30 A. Müller, "Elemente der Staatskunst," *Deutsche Vergangenheit und deutscher Staat*, vol. x, ed. P. Kluckhohn, 228–29.

31 Ibid., 221–22.

32 E. Burke, *Reflections on the Revolution in France*, 79–80.

33 E. Burke, "Speech on Moving His Resolution for Conciliation with the Colonies," *The Works*, vol. 3, 81.

34 E. Burke, *Reflections on the Revolution in France*, 183–84.

35 A. Müller, *Elemente der Staatskunst*, 213.

36 J. Görres, "Was zu verkaufen," *Gesellschaft und Staat im Spiegel deutscher Romantik*, ed. J. Baxa, 267.

37 J. Görres, "Politische und merkantilistische Bemerkungen," *Rheinischer Merkur* 97 (4 August 1814)

38 J. Görres, "Der deutsche Reichstag," *Gesellschaft und Staat im Spiegel deutscher Romantik*, 418–22.

39 H. Heine, "Französische Zustände," *Sämtliche Schriften*, vol. 3, 136.

40 Novalis, "Die Christenheit oder Europa," *Werke, Tagebücher und Briefe*, vol. 2, 748.

41 "Letter to Jacob Grimm, 24 December 1821," A. Stoll, ed., *F. K. von Savigny: Ein Bild seines Lebens mit einer Sammlung seiner Briefe*, vol. 2, 279.

42 F. K. von Savigny, *Vom Beruf unserer Zeit für Gesetzgebung und Rechtswissenschaft*, 115–17.

43 F. Schlegel, *Signatur des Zeitalters*, 66.

44 A. Müller, "Die innere Staatshaushaltung, Systematisch dargestellt auf theologischer Grundlage," *Concordia*, 99.

45 A. Müller, *Elemente der Staatskunst*, 235.

46 See L. von Haller, *Restauration der Staats-Wissenschaft, oder Theorie des natürlich*

geselligen Zustands der Chimäre des künstlich-bürgerlichen entgegengesetzt. See also supra, ch. III, § 4.

47   E. Burke, *Reflections on the Revolution in France*, 79, 104.

48   E. Burke, *Betrachtungen über die französische Revolution*, 70.

49   J. Möser, "Also sollte man die Einimpfung der Blattern ganz verbieten," *Sämmtliche Werke*, vol. 4, 63–67.

50   Similarities between the two authors are examined in F. Meinecke, *Die Entstehung des Historismus*, 323, 342, 347.

51   J. Möser, "Über die Art und Weise, wie unsre Vorfahren die Prozesse abgekürzt haben," *Sämmtliche Werke*, vol. 1, 384.

52   See L. Gumplowicz, *Der Rassenkampf*, cited in G. Lukács, *Die Zerstörung der Vernunft*, 545.

53   W. Sombart, *Händler und Helden*, 18.

54   A. Müller, *Versuche einer neuen Theorie des Geldes*, 161.

55   See D. Losurdo, *Heidegger and the Ideology of War*, ch. 3, § 1, ch. 7, § 6.

56   E. Lerch, " 'Gesellschaft' und 'Gemeinschaft,' " *Vierteljahresschrift für Literaturwissenschaft und Geistesgeschichte* 22 (1944): 114ff. See also O. Brunner, *Neue Wege der Verfassungs und Sozialgeschichte.*

57   J. Le Goff, *Storia e memoria*, 206.

58   Z. Sternhell, *Ni droite, ni gauche: L'idéologie fasciste en France*, 2nd ed., 357, 362. Burke even influences Italian nationalism via Barrès. Thus, we see Corradini condemn "democracy" because it is "guilty of concerning itself exclusively with present generations and their needs," while overlooking future generations, and ignoring the "divine law of life's continuity through the centuries" and the "life of nations . . . made up of countless individuals' deaths." See E. Corradini, *Scritti e discorsi 1901– 1904*, ed. L. Strappini, 67, 66–67nn.

59   Z. Sternhell, *Maurice Barrès et le nationalisme français*, 271.

60   Z. Sternhell, *La Droite révolutionnaire: Les origines français du fascisme 1885– 1914.*

61   See D. Losurdo, "Hannah Arendt e l'analisi delle rivoluzioni," *La pluralità irrappresentabile: Il pensiero politico di Hannah Arendt*, ed. R. Esposito. Also D. Losurdo, *Hegel und das deutsche Erbe*, ch. 14, §§ 24, 28 (=*La catastrofe della Germania e l'immagine di Hegel*, ch. 3, § 7, and ch. 4, § 3). Also D. Losurdo, "Vincenzo Cuoco, la rivoluzione napoletana del 1799 e la comparatistica delle rivoluzioni," *Società e storia* 46 (1990): 907–8.

62   R. Dahrendorf, *Reflections on the Revolution in Europe*, 39.

63   H. Marcuse, "Der Kampf gegen den Liberalismus in der totalitären Staatsauffassung," *Zeitschrift für Sozialforschung* (1934): 165.

64   Hayek calls Burke "great and far-sighted." F. A. Hayek, *Law, Legislation and Liberty*, vol. 1, 22.

65   A. L. G. Necker de Staël, *Considérations*, 268ff.

66   B. Constant, *Écrits et discours politiques*, ch. 1.

67   H. Guillemin, *Benjamin Constant muscadin.*

68   See in particular B. Constant, "Des réactions politiques," *Écrits et discours politiques*, 73.

69   B. Constant, "Journaux intimes," *Oeuvres*, 720, 722.

70   B. Constant, "De l'esprit de conquête," 1015.

71 A. W. Rehberg, *Untersuchungen über die französische Revolution*, vol. 1, 81–82, 162.

72 B. Constant, "De l'esprit de conquête," 1015.

73 A. L. G. Necker de Staël, *Considérations*, 268.

74 H. Guillemin, *Benjamin Constant muscadin*, 13–14.

75 E. Burke, *Remarks on the Policy of the Allies with Respect to France*, 123–24.

76 E. Burke, *Reflections on the Revolution in France*, 146. In his text, Burke quotes Lally-Tollendal's judgment approvingly.

77 See H. Guillemin, *Benjamin Constant muscadin*, 13.

78 "Letter to L. de Kergorlay, 16 May 1858," A. de Tocqueville, *Oeuvres complètes*, vol. 13, 2, pp. 337–38.

79 A. de Tocqueville, *L'Ancien régime et la Révolution*, 340–41.

80 Ibid., 152.

81 Ibid., 246.

82 Ibid., 340.

83 E. Burke, *Remarks on the Policy of the Allies with Respect to France*, 135.

84 A. de Tocqueville, *L'Ancien régime et la Révolution*, 342.

85 This is according to Welcker in the second edition of the *Staats-Lexicon*. C. Antoni, *La lotta contro la ragione*, 128.

86 R. Haym, *Hegel und seine Zeit*, 32.

87 See D. Losurdo, "Storia e tradizione: L'ideologia tedesca dalla Rivoluzione francese agli 'Annali Prussiani,'" *Studi Urbinati/B2* 55 (1981–82): 90–91.

88 F. Guizot, *Histoire de la révolution d'Angleterre*, 106–9. On the persistent vitality and inconsistency of a topos that contrasts the Glorious (or the American) Revolution to the French Revolution—always to the discredit of the latter—and which presents the "Glorious Revolution" as peaceful and painless, casually overlooking the long, bloody struggles and massacres in Ireland and Scotland, see D. Losurdo, *Hannah Arendt e l'analisi delle rivoluzioni* 139–53; D. Losurdo, "La révolution française a-t-elle échouée?", *La Pensée* 267 (Jan–Feb 1989): 85ff.

89 E. Burke, *Reflections on the Revolution in France*, 120. The line from Virgil (*Aeneid*, I, 140) is slightly changed by Burke.

90 I. Kant, *Über den Gemeinspruch*, 277.

91 R. Dahrendorf, *Reflections on the Revolution in Europe*, 124.

92 I. Kant, *Zum ewigen Frieden*, 353n.

93 J. Mallet du Pan, *Über die französische Revolution und die Ursachen ihrer Dauer*.

94 E. Burke, "Preface to the Address of M. Brissot to His Constituents," *The Works*, vol. 7, 324.

95 I. Kant, "Über die Buchmacherei," *KGS*, vol. 8, 433ff. On this see K. Vorländer, *I. Kant, Der Mann und das Werk*, 2nd ed., vol. 2, 278.

96 J. G. Fichte, *Beitrag zur Berichtigung der Urteile des Publikums über die Französische Revolution*.

97 See J. Hoffmeister, ed., *Dokumente zu Hegels Entwicklung*, 217–19.

98 G. Forster, "Geschichte der englischen Literatur vom Jahre 1790," *Werke in vier Bänden*, vol. 3, 326.

99 G. Forster, "Über das Verhältnis der Mainzer gegen die Franken," *Werke in vier Bänden*, vol. 3, 602.

100 On this, see D. Losurdo, *Hegel und das deutsche Erbe*, chs. 7–10 (=*Hegel, questione nazionale, Restaurazione*, chs. 5–8).

101   Cited in G. Lukács, *Der junge Hegel*, 588.

102   M.-J.-A.-N. de C. de Condorcet, "Sur l'admission des femmes au droit de cité," *Oeuvres*, vol. 10, 123.

103   H. Heine, "Einleitung zu: Kahldorf über den Adel," *Sämtliche Schriften*, vol. 2, 662.

104   See D. Losurdo, "Der Begriff 'bürgerliche Revolution' bei Marx und Engels," *Marxistische Studien* 14 (1988): 273–84.

105   F. A. Hayek, *The Constitution of Liberty*.

106   Ibid.

107   R. Rosenberg, *Literaturverhältnisse im deutschen Vormärz*, 144.

108   H. Laube, *Das deutsche Parlament*, vol. 1, 24–25.

109   The short story (*L'Hegélien*) is cited in J. D'Hondt, "Hegel et les socialistes," *De Hegel à Marx*, 188.

110   See D. Losurdo, "La rivoluzione del '48 e l'immagine di Hegel in Italia e in Germania," *Gli hegeliani di Napoli e la costruzione dello Stato unitario*, 188.

111   Ibid., 50.

112   F. A. Hayek, *The Constitution of Liberty*, 425.

113   T. H. Green, "Lecture on Liberal Legislation and Freedom of Contract," *Works*, ed. R. L. Nettleship, 3rd ed., vol. 3, 372.

114   Ibid., 367.

115   Ibid., 372–73.

116   F. Lassalle, *Das Arbeiterprogramm*, 221.

117   See J. Droz, *Le Libéralisme rhénan 1815–1848*, 265–69.

118   A. Smith, *Lectures on Jurisprudence*, 186.

119   Ibid., 452.

BIBLIOGRAPHY

Abegg, Johann Friedrich. *Reisetagebuch von 1798.* Ed. Walter and Jolanda Abegg in collaboration with Zwi Batscha. Frankfurt, 1976.

Adorno, Theodor Wiesengrund. *Drei Studien zu Hegel.* Frankfurt, 1963.

——. "Stichworte, Kritische Modelle 2." *Gesammelte Schriften.* Ed. Rolf Tiedemann. Vol. 10. Frankfurt, 1957.

Antoni, Carlo. *La lotta contro la ragione.* 1942. Florence, 1968.

Apel, Karl Otto, et al., eds. *Die Konflikte unserer Zeit und das Erfordernis einer ethisch-politischen Grundorientierung. Praktische Philosophie/Ethik I. Reader zum Funkkolleg.* Frankfurt am Main: Fischer, 1980.

——. "Kann der postkantische Standpunkt der Moralität noch einmal in substantieller Sittlichkeit 'aufgehoben' werden?" In *Moralität und Sittlichkeit.* Ed. Wolfgang Kuhlmann, n. p., 1986. 217–64.

Arendt, Hannah. *On Revolution.* New York: Penguin, 1990.

——. *Vita activa oder vom tätigen Leben.* Stuttgart, 1960.

Aulard, Alphonse. *Histoire politique de la Révolution française.* Paris, 1926.

Avineri, Shlomo. *Hegel's Theory of the Modern State.* Cambridge: Cambridge University Press, 1972.

Baader, Franz Xavier Benedict von. "Über das Revolutionieren des positiven Rechtsbestandes." 1831. *Sämtliche Werke.* Ed. Franz Hoffman, Julius Hamberger, et al. Vol. 6. Leipzig, 1851–60. Reprinted, Aalen, 1963.

Babeuf, François-Noël. *Écrits.* Ed. Claude Mazauric. Paris, 1988.

Baczko, Bronisław. *Lumières de l'utopie.* Paris, 1978.

Baeuler, Alfred. "Nietzsche." 1930. *Studien zur deutschen Geistesgeschichte.* Berlin, 1937.

Barnave, Antoine-Pierre-Joseph-Marie. *Introduction à la révolution française.* Ed. Fernand Rude. Paris, 1960.

Barny, Roger. *L'éclatement révolutionnaire du rousseauisme.* Besançon, 1988.

Bauer, Bruno. "Russland und das Germanenthum." 1853. In *La sinistra hegeliana.* Ed. Karl Löwith. Trans. Claudio Cesa. Bari, 1966.

Baxa, Jakob, ed. *Adam Müllers Lebenszeugnisse.* Vol. 1. Munich-Paderborn-Vienna, 1966.

Becchi, Paolo. *Contributi ad uno studio della filosofia del diritto di Hegel.* Genoa, 1984.

—. "Hegelsche Vorlesungsnachschriften und noch kein Ende?" *Materiali per una storia della cultura giuridica* 16. 1 (1986): 251–61.

—. "Im Schatten der Entscheidung: Hegels unterschiedliche Ansätze in seiner Lehre zur fürstlichen Gewalt." *Archiv für Rechts- und Sozialphilosophie* 72. 2 (1986): 231–45.

Beetham, David. *Max Weber and the Theory of Modern Politics.* Cambridge: Polity Press, 1985.

Bentham, Jeremy. "Anarchical Fallacies: A Critical Examination of the Declaration of Rights." 1838. *The Works.* Ed. John Bowring. Vol. 2. Edinburgh, 1838–43.

—. "Théorie des peines et des récompenses." 1811. *Oeuvres de Jerémie Bentham.* Ed. E. Dumont. Vol. 2. Brussels, 1840.

Blanqui, Louis-Auguste. *Textes choisis.* Ed. Vyacheslav Petrovich Volguine. Paris, 1955.

Bloch, Ernst. "Problem der Engelschen Trennung von 'Methode' und 'System' bei Hegel." *Philosophische Aufsätze.* Frankfurt, 1969.

—. "Sulla distinzione del 'metodo' di Hegel dal 'sistema,' e alcune conseguenze." In *Dialettica e speranza.* Ed. Livio Sichirollo. Florence, 1967.

Bianco, Gino, and Edoardo Grendi. *Introduzione a la tradizione socialista in Inghilterra: Antologia di testi politici, 1820–1852.* Turin, 1970.

Bobbio, Norberto. *Il contratto sociale oggi.* Naples, 1980.

—. *Il futuro della democrazia.* Turin, 1984.

—. *L'età dei diritti.* Turin, 1990.

—. *Studi hegeliani.* Turin, 1981.

Böhm, Franz. *Anti-Cartesianismus: Deutsche Philosophie im Widerstand.* Leipzig, 1938.

Bonchez, B. J., and P.-C. Roux. *Histoire parlementaire de la Révolution française.* Vol. 26. Paris, 1836.

Börne, Ludwig. "Briefe aus Paris (1832–34), Letters 24 and 35." *Sämtliche Schriften.* Ed. Inge and Peter Rippmann. Vol. 3. Dreieich, 1977.

Bourne, Henry Richard Fox. *The Life of John Locke.* Vol. 2. London: Henry S. King, 1876.

Boutroux, Émile. "L'Allemagne et la guerre: Lettre à M. le Directeur de la 'Revue des Deux-Mondes.'" 15 October 1914. In *Études d'histoire de la philosophie allemande.* Paris, 1926.

Brandt, Hartwig, ed. *Restauration und Frühliberalismus.* Darmstadt, 1979.

Braune, Frieda. *Edmund Burke in Deutschland.* Heidelberg, 1917.

Brecht, Bertolt. "Flüchtlingsgespräche." 1939. *Prosa.* Vol. 2. Frankfurt, 1965.

Brunschwig, Henri. *Société et romantisme en Prusse au XVIII siècle: La crise de l'État prussien à la fin du XVIII siècle et la genèse de la mentalité romantique.* 2nd ed. Paris, 1973.

Brunner, Otto. *Neue Wege der Verfassungs und Sozialgeschichte.* Göttingen, 1968.

Buchner, Rudolf, and Winfried Baumgart, eds. *Quellen zum politischen Denken der Deutschen im 19 und 20 Jahrhundert.* Freiherr vom Stein-Edächtnisausgabe. Vol. 4. Darmstadt, 1976.

Burger, Heinz Otto. "Die Entwicklung des Hölderlinbildes seit 1933." *Deutsche Vierteljahresschrift für Literatur und Geisteswissenschaft* 18 (1940): Referateheft, 122.

Burgio, Alberto. *Eguaglianza, interesse, unanimità: La politica di Rousseau.* Naples, 1989.

Burke, Edmund. *The Correspondence of Edmund Burke.* Ed. Alfred Cobban and Robert Arthur Smith. Vol. 6. Chicago: University of Chicago Press, 1967.

—. *The Works of the Right Honourable Edmund Burke.* London, 1826.

Carové, Friedrich Wilhelm. *Entwurf einer Burschenschafts-Ordnung und Versuch einer Begründung derselben.* Eisenach, 1818.

Caramella, Santino. "Introduzione." In Johann Gottlieb Fichte. *Filosofia della massoneria.* Genoa, 1924.

Carlyle, Thomas. *On Heroes, Hero-Worship, and the Heroic in History.* 1841. London: H. R. Allenson, 1905.

Casana Testore, P. and Narciso Nada. *L'età della restaurazione: Reazione e rivoluzione in Europa 1814–1830.* Turin, 1981.

Cavour, Camillo Benso di. "Des idées communistes et des moyens d'en combattre le Développement." 1845. In *Il socialismo nella storia d'Italia.* Ed. Gastone Manacorda. Vol. 1. Bari, 1970.

Cesa, Claudio. *Gli hegeliani liberali.* Rome, 1974.

——. "G. W. F. Hegel: A centocinquant'anni dalla morte." *Studi senesi* 1 (1982): 11–12.

——. *Hegel filosofo politico.* Naples, 1976.

——, ed. *Il pensiero politico di Hegel: Guida storica e critica.* Rome, 1979.

——, ed. *Scritti politici* di Hegel. Turin, 1974.

——. *Studi sulla sinistra hegeliana.* Urbino, 1972.

Ceserani, Remo, and Lidia de Federicis. *Il materiale e l'immaginario.* Vol. 6. Turin, 1981.

Chateaubriand, François-René. "De la monarchie selon la Charte." 1816. *Mélanges Politiques et Littéraires.* Paris, 1850.

——. *Itinéraire de Paris à Jérusalem.* Part 1. n. p., 1811.

——. *Mémoires d'outre-tombe.* Ed. Pierre Clarac. Vol. 2. Paris, 1973.

Colletti, Lucio. "L'equivoco di Lukács." *Mondo Operaio* (Jan. 1986): 99–103.

Condorcet, Marie-Jean-Antoine-Nicolas de Caritat de. "Lettre d'un laboureur de Picardie." 1775. *Oeuvres.* Ed. A. Condorcet O'Connor and Dominique-François Arago. Vol. 11. Paris, 1847. Reprinted, Stuttgart-Bad Cannstatt, 1968.

Constant, Benjamin. *Cours de politique constitutionnelle.* 3rd ed. Brussels, 1837.

——. *De la liberté chez les modernes: Écrits politiques.* Ed. Marcel Gauchet. Paris, 1980.

——. *Mélanges de littérature et de politique.* Vol. 1. Louvain, 1830.

——. *Oeuvres.* Ed. Alfred Roulin. Paris, 1957.

Corradini, Enrico. *Scritti e discorsi 1901–1904.* Ed. Lucia Strappini. Turin, 1980.

Cranston, Maurice. *John Locke: A Biography.* 2nd ed. London, 1959.

Cuoco, Vincenzo. *Saggio storico sulla rivoluzione napoletana del 1799.* 1806. 2nd ed. Rome-Bari, 1980.

Dahrendorf, Ralf. *Gesellschaft und Demokratie in Deutschland.* Munich, 1965.

——. *Reflections on the Revolution in Europe.* Toronto: Random House, 1990.

De Ruggiero, Guido. *Storia del liberalismo europeo.* 1925. Milan, 1971.

De Sanctis, Francesco M. *Tempo di democrazia: Alexis de Tocqueville.* Naples, 1986.

D'Hondt, Jacques. *Hegel en son temps (Berlin 1818–1831).* Paris, 1968.

——. "Hegel et les socialistes." *De Hegel à Marx.* Paris, 1972.

——. *Hegel secret. Recherches sur les sources cachées de la pensée de Hegel.* Paris, 1968.

——. "Théorie et pratique politique chez Hegel: le problème de la censure." In *Hegels Philosophie des Rechts.* Ed. Dieter Heinrich and Rolf Peter Horstmann. Stuttgart, 1982.

Drescher, Seymour. *Tocqueville and England.* Cambridge, Mass.: Harvard University Press, 1964.

Droz, Jacques. *Le libéralisme rhénan, 1815–1848.* Paris, 1940.

Epstein, Klaus. *The Genesis of German Conservatism*. Princeton, 1966.

Erdmann, Johann Eduard. *Grundriss der Geschichte der Philosophie. Anhang: Die deutsche Philosophie seit Hegels Tode*. Berlin, 1878.

———. *Eudämonia oder deutsches Volksglück: Ein Journal für Freunde von Weisheit und Recht*. Frankfurt, 1796.

Evola, Giulio (Julius). *Il Fascismo*. Rome, 1964.

Fenske, Hans, ed. *Im Bismarckschen Reich 1871–1890*. Darmstadt, 1978.

Fichte, Johann Gottlieb. *Ausgewählte politische Schriften*. Ed. Zwi Batscha and Richard Saage. Frankfurt, 1977.

———. *Briefwechsel*. Ed. Hans Schulz. Leipzig, 1930. Reprinted, Hildesheim, 1967.

———. *Eleusinen des 19. Jahrhunderts oder Resultate vereinigter Denker über Philosophie und Geschichte der Freimaurerei*. Berlin, 1802–3.

———. *Fichte in vertraulichen Briefen seiner Zeitgenossen*. Ed. Hans Schulz. Leipzig, 1923.

———. *Fichtes Werke*. Ed. Immanuel Hermann Fichte. Berlin, 1971. Cited as FW.

———. *Rechtslehre*. 1812. Ed. Richard Schottky. Hamburg, 1980.

Fischer, Kuno. *Geschichte der neueren Philosophie*. Vol. 8, 1: *Hegels Leben, Werke und Lehre*. 2nd ed. Heidelberg, 1911.

Forster, Georg. "Geschichte der englischen Literatur vom Jahre 1790." 1790. *Werke in vier Bänden*. Vol. 3. Frankfurt, 1967.

Furet, François, and Denis Richet. *La Révolution française*. Paris, 1965.

Gadamer, Hans Georg. *Wahrheit und Methode*. 3rd ed. Tübingen, 1972.

Galante Garrone, A. *Filippo Buonarroti e i rivoluzionari dell'Ottocento 1828–1837*. 1951. Turin, 1972.

Gans, Eduard. *Philosophische Schriften*. Ed. Horst Schröder. Glashütten Taunus, 1971.

———. *Rückblicke auf Personen und Zustände*. Berlin, 1836.

Gebhardt, Carl, ed. *Der Briefwechsel Arthur Schopenhauers*. Vol. 1. Munich, 1929.

Gentz, Friedrich von. "Über die National-Erziehung in Frankreich." 1793. *Ausgewählte Schriften*. Ed. Wilderich Weick. Vol. 2. Stuttgart and Leipzig, 1836–38.

Gerhard, Walter. *Das politische System Alexander Hamiltons*. Hamburg, 1929.

Görres, Joseph. "Kotzebue und was ihn gemordet." 1819. *Gesammelte Schriften*. Ed. Wilhelm Schellberg. Vol. 13. Cologne, 1926.

———. "Politische und merkantilistische Bemerkungen." *Rheinischer Merkur* 97 (4 August 1814): n.p.

———. "Was zu verkaufen." 1798. *Gesellschaft und Staat im Spiegel deutscher Romantik*. Ed. Jakob Baxa. Jena, 1924.

Guizot, François. *De la démocratie en France (Janvier 1849)*. Naples: n.p., 1849.

Gramsci, Antonio. *Quaderni del carcere*. Ed. Valentino Gerratana. Turin: n.p., 1975.

Green, Thomas Hill. "Lecture on Liberal Legislation and Freedom of Contract." 1881. *Works*. Ed. Richard Lewis Nettleship. 3rd ed. Vol. 3. London, 1891. Reprinted, London, 1973.

Guillemin, Henri. *Benjamin Constant muscadin 1795–1799*. 6th ed. Paris, 1958.

———. *Madame de Staël, Benjamin Constant et Napoléon*. Paris, 1959.

Guizot, François. "Discours sur l'histoire de la révolution d'Angleterre." *Histoire de la révolution d'Angleterre*. Brussels, 1850.

Gumplowicz, Ludwig. *Der Rassenkampf*. 1883. Innsbruck, 1928.

Habermas, Jürgen. "Hegels Kritik der französischen Revolution." 1962. *Theorie und Praxis: Sozialphilosophische Studien*. Frankfurt, 1988.

—. "Legitimationsprobleme im modernen Staat." In *Praktische Philosophie/Ethik*. Ed. Karl Otto Apel et al. Vol. 1. Frankfurt, 1980.

—. *Zur Logik der Sozialwissenschaften: Materialien*. Frankfurt, 1970.

Halévy, Elie. *La formation du radicalisme philosophique, I: La jeunesse de Bentham*. Paris, 1901.

Haller, Carl Ludwig von. *Analisi della costituzione delle Cortès di Spagna, opera del Signor Carlo Luigi di Haller*. Modena, 1821.

—. *De quelques dénominations de partis*. Geneva, 1822.

—. *Restauration der Staats-Wissenschaft, oder Theorie des natürlich gesellligen Zustands der Chimäre des künstlich-bürgerlichen entgegengesetzt*. Winterthur, 1820–34.

Hass, Hans-Egon, ed. *Die deutsche Literatur: Texte und Zeugnisse*. Vol. 5. Munich, 1966.

Havens, George Remington. "Voltaire's Marginalia on the Pages of Rousseau." *Ohio State University Studies* 6 (1933): 15.

Hayek, Friedrich August von. *Law, Legislation and Liberty*. 3 vols. Chicago: University of Chicago Press, 1973–79.

—. *New Studies in Philosophy, Politics, Economics and the History of Ideas*. London: Routledge, 1978.

—. *The Counter-Revolution of Science: Studies on the Abuse of Science*. Glencoe: Free Press, 1952.

—. *The Fatal Conceit: The Errors of Socialism*. 1989. London, 1990.

—. *The Road to Serfdom*. 1944. London, 1986.

Haym, Rudolf. *Die deutsche Nationalversammlung bis zu den Septemberereignissen: Ein Bericht aus der Partei des rechten Zentrums*. Frankfurt, 1848.

—. *Hegel und seine Zeit*. Berlin, 1857.

—. *Wilhelm von Humboldt: Lebensbild und Charakteristik*. 1856. Osnabrück, 1965.

Hegel, Georg Wilhelm Friedrich. *Berliner Schriften*. Ed. J. Hoffmeister. Hamburg, 1956. Cited as b.schr.

—. *Briefe von und an Hegel*. Ed. J. Hoffmeister and F. Nicolin. Hamburg, 1969–81. Cited as B.

—. *Die Philosophie des Rechts: Die Mitschriften Wannenmann (Heidelberg 1817–18) und Homeyer (Berlin 1818–19)*. Ed. K.-H. Ilting. Stuttgart, 1983. Cited as Rph. I.

—. *Die Vernunft in der Geschichte*. Ed. J. Hoffmeister. Hamburg, 1955. Cited as v.G.

—. *Hegel in Berichten seiner Zeitgenossen*. Ed. G. Nicolin. Hamburg, 1970. Cited as H.B.

—. *Il dominio della politica*. Ed. Nicolao Merker. Rome, 1980.

—. *Materialen zu Hegels Rechtsphilosophie*. Ed. M. Riedel. Frankfurt, 1975. Cited as Mat.

—. *Philosophie des Rechts: Die Vorlesung von 1819–20 in einer Nachschrift*. Ed. D. Henrich. Frankfurt, 1983. Cited as Rph.III.

—. *Religionsphilosophie: Die Vorlesung von 1821*. Ed. Karl-Heinz Ilting. Vol. 1. Naples, 1978.

—. *System der Sittlichkeit*. 1802. Ed. Georg Lasson. Hamburg, 1967.

—. *Vorlesungen über die Philosophie der Religion*. Ed. Georg Lasson. Vol. 1. Hamburg, 1966.

—. *Vorlesungen über die Philosophie der Weltgeschichte*. Ed. Georg Lasson. Leipzig, 1930. Cited as Ph G.

—. *Vorlesungen über Naturrecht und Staatswissenschaft*. Ed. C. Becker et al. Hamburg: Hegel-Archiv, 1983. Cited as Rph. I.

——. *Vorlesungen über Rechtsphilosophie.* Ed. Karl-Heinz Ilting. Stuttgart-Bad Cannstatt, 1973–74. Cited as *v.rph.*

——. *Werke in zwanzig Bänden.* Ed. E. Moldenhauer and K. M. Michel. Frankfurt, 1969–79. Cited as W.

Heine, Heinrich. *Sämtliche Schriften.* Ed. Klaus Briegleb, Günter Häntzschel, and Karl Pörnbacher. Vol. 4. Munich, 1969–78.

Helvétius, Claude-Adrien. "De l'esprit." 1758. Vol. 2. *Oeuvres complètes.* Paris, 1795. Reprinted, Hildesheim, 1969.

Herzen, Alexander Ivanovich. "La jeune Moscou" from "Mémoires et pensées." 1855–62. *Textes philosophiques choisis.* Moscow, 1950.

Himmelfarb, Gertrude. *The Idea of Poverty: England in the Early Industrial Age.* New York, 1985.

Hitler, Adolf. *Hitlers Tischgespräche.* Ed. Henry Picker. Frankfurt and Berlin, 1989.

Hobbes, Thomas. "Behemoth." 1679. *The English Works 1840.* Vol. 6. Aalen, 1962.

——. "De Cive." 1651. *Opera Philosophica 1839–45.* Vol. 2. Aalen, 1961.

Hobhouse, Leonard Trelawney. *The Metaphysical Theory of the State: A Criticism.* 1918. London: Routledge, 1993.

Hoffmeister, Johannes, ed. *Dokumente zu Hegels Entwicklung.* Vol. xi, Stuttgart, 1936.

d'Holbach, Paul Heinrich Dietrich. *Ethocratie ou le Gouvernement fondé sur la morale.* Amsterdam, 1776. Reprinted, Hildesheim, 1973.

Hook, Sidney. "Hegel Rehabilitated." In *Hegel's Political Philosophy.* Ed. Walter Kaufmann. New York, 1970.

Horkheimer, Max. "Appendix to 'Traditionelle und kritische Theorie.'" *Zeitschrift für Sozialforschung* 6 (1937): 631.

——. "Hegel und das Problem der Metaphysik," *Anfänge des bürgerlichen Geschichtsphilosophie.* Frankfurt, 1971.

Howald, Ernst, ed. *Zur deutschen Philosophie und Literatur.* Zürich, 1963.

Hugo, Gustav. *Lehrbuch des Naturrechts als einer Philosophie des positiven Rechts, besonders des Privatrechts.* 4th ed. Berlin, 1819.

——. *Lehrbuch eines civilistischen Cursus: Zweyter Band welcher das Naturrecht, als eine Philosophie des positiven Rechts, besonders des Privatrechts enthält.* 4th ed. Berlin, 1819.

Hume, David. "Treatise of Human Nature." 1739–40. *The Philosophical Works.* Ed. Thomas Hill Green, and Thomas Hodge Grose. Vol. 2. London, 1886. Reprinted, Aalen, 1964.

Ignatieff, Michael. *A Just Measure of Pain: The Penitentiary in the Industrial Revolution 1750–1850.* London: Pantheon, 1978.

Ilting, Karl-Heinz. "Die 'Rechtsphilosophie' von 1829 und Hegels Vorlesungen über Rechtsphilosophie." In G. W. F. Hegel, *Vorlesungen über Rechtsphilosophie.* Ed. Karl-Heinz Ilting. Stuttgart-Bad Cannstatt, 1973–74.

——. *Hegel diverso.* Rome-Bari, 1977.

——. "Hegels Auseinandersetzung mit der aristotelischen Politik." *Philosophisches Jahrbuch* 17 (1963–64): 47–48.

——. *Zur Genese der hegelschen "Rechtsphilosophie," "Philosophie Rundschau."* n. p., 1983.

Jardin, André. *A. de Tocqueville 1805–1859.* Paris, 1984.

Jaurès, Jean. *Storia socialista della rivoluzione francese.* Vol. 2. Milan, 1953.

Jernegan, Marcus Wilson. *Laboring and Dependent Classes in Colonial America: 1607–1783*. Chicago: University of Chicago Press, 1931.

Jung, Alexander. *Vorlesungen über die moderne Literatur*. Danzig, 1842.

Kant, Immanuel. *Gesammelte Schriften*. Ed. Academy of Science. n.p. Walter de Gruyter, Inc., 1983. Cited as *KGS*.

Kautsky, Karl. "Arthur Schopenhauer." *Die neue Zeit* 6 (1888): 76.

Kelsen, Hans. *The Political Theory of Bolshevism: A Critical Analysis*. Berkeley and Los Angeles, 1948.

Kierkegaard, Søren. "Postilla conclusiva non scientifica alle briciole di filosofia." 1846. *Opere*. Florence, 1972.

Kleist, Ulrike von. *Sämtliche Werke und Briefe*. Ed. H. Sembdner. 2nd ed. Vol. 2. Munich, 1961.

Kloosterboer, Willemins. *Involuntary Labour since the Abolition of Slavery*. Leiden, 1962.

Koselleck, Reinhart. *Preußen zwischen Reform und Revolution*. 3rd ed. Stuttgart, 1975.

Krautkrämer, Ursula. *Staat und Erziehung: Begründung öffentlicher Erziehung bei Humboldt, Kant, Fichte, Hegel und Schleiermacher*. Munich, 1979.

Kroneberg, Lutz, and Rolf Schloesser. *Weber-Revolte 1844*. Cologne, 1979.

Kuczynski, Jürgen. *Die Geschichte der Lage der Arbeiter unter dem Kapitalismus*. Vol. 1. Berlin, 1960.

Kuhlmann, Wolfgang, ed. *Moralität und Sittlichkeit*. Frankfurt, 1986.

Laponneraye, Albert. "Déclaration des droits de l'homme et du citoyen." 1832. In *Il socialismo prima di Marx*. Ed. Gian Mario Bravo. 2nd ed. Rome, 1973.

Laski, Harold Joseph. *The American Democracy*. 1948. Fairfield, 1977.

——. *The Rise of European Liberalism*. London: G. Allen and Unwin, 1936.

Lassalle, Ferdinand. "Das Arbeiterprogramm." 1862–63. *Gesammelte Reden und Schriften*. Ed. Eduard Bernstein. Vol. 2. Berlin, 1919.

Laube, Heinrich. *Das deutsche Parlament*. Vol. 1. Leipzig, 1849.

Lefebvre, Georges. *La France sous le directoire 1795–1799*. Paris, 1984.

Le Goff, Jacques. *Storia e memoria*. 1977. Turin, 1982.

Lenin, Vladimir I. *Collected Works*. Trans. Clemens Dutt. Vol. 38. Moscow: Foreign Languages Publishing House, 1961.

——. *Opere scelte*. Rome, 1968.

Lerch, Eugen. "'Gesellschaft' und 'Gemeinschaft,'" *Vierteljahresschrift für Literaturwissenschaft und Geistesgeschichte* 22 (1944): 114ff.

Locke, John. "Some Considerations of the Consequences of Lowering the Interest and Raising the Value of Money." 1691. *The Works*. Vol. 5. London, 1823. Anastatic reprint by Aalen, 1963.

——. *Two Treatises of Government*. 1690. London: Dent; New York: Dutton, 1953.

Losurdo, Domenico. *Autocensura e compromesso nel pensiero politico di Kant*. Naples: Istituto Italiano per gli Studi Filosofici, 1983.

——. "Der Begriff 'bürgerliche Revolution' bei Marx und Engels." *Marxistische Studien* 14 (1988): 273–84.

——. "Fichte, la resistenza antinapoleonica e la filosofia classica tedesca." *Studi Storici* 1–2 (1983): 189–216.

——. "Hannah Arendt e l'analisi delle rivoluzioni." In *La pluralità irrappresentabile: Il pensiero politico di Hannah Arendt*. Ed. Roberto Esposito. Urbino: Istituto Italiano per gli Studi Filosofici, 1987.

——. *Hegel, questione nazionale, restaurazione. Presupposti e sviluppi di una battaglia politica.* Urbino, 1983.

——. *Hegel und das deutsche Erbe: Philosophie und nationale Frage zwischen Revolution und Restauration.* Cologne: Istituto Italiano per gli Studi Filosofici, 1989.

——. *Heidegger and the Ideology of War.* Amherst: Humanity Books, 2001.

——. *Immanuel Kant: Freiheit, Recht und Revolution.* Cologne, 1987.

——. "Introduzione." In G. W. F. Hegel. *Le filosofie del diritto. Diritto, proprietà, questione sociale.* Milan: Istituto Italiano per gli Studi Filosofici, 1989.

——. *La catastrofe della Germania e l'immagine di Hegel.* Milan, 1987.

——. *La politica culturale di Hegel a Berlino. Illuminismo, rivoluzione e tradizione nazionale.* Urbino, 1981.

——. "La rivoluzione del '48 e l'immagine di Hegel in Italia e in Germania." *Gli hegeliani di Napoli e la costruzione dello Stato unitario.* Rome, 1972.

——. "Marx, la tradition libérale et le concept universel d'homme." *Actuel Marx* 5 (1989): 17–33.

——. "Realismus und Nominalismus als politische Kategorien." In *Philosophie als Verteidigung des Ganzen der Vernunft.* Ed. Domenico Losurdo and Hans J. Sandkühler. Cologne, 1988.

——. "Religione e ideologia nella filosofia classica tedesca." *Studi Urbinati/B2* 57 (1984): 9–60.

——. "La révolution française a-t-elle échouée?" *La Pensée* 267 (Jan–Feb 1989): 85ff.

——. "Marx et l'histoire du totalitarisme." In *Fin du communisme? Actualité du marxisme?* Ed. Jacques Bidet and Jacques Texier. Paris, 1991.

——. "Storia e tradizione: L'ideologia tedesca dalla Rivoluzione francese agli 'Annali Prussiani.'" *Studi Urbinati/B2* 55 (1981–82): 90–91.

——. *Tra Hegel e Bismarck.* Rome, 1983.

——. "Vincenzo Cuoco, la rivoluzione napoletana del 1799 e la comparatistica delle rivoluzioni." *Società e storia* 46 (1990): 907–8.

——. "Von Louis Philippe zu Louis Bonaparte: Schellings späte politische Entwicklung." In *Die praktische Philosophie Schellings und die gegenwärtige Rechtsphilosophie.* Ed. Hans-Martin Pawlowski, Stefan Smid, and Rainer Specht. Stuttgart-Bad Cannstatt, 1990.

Lübbe, Hermann, ed. *Die Hegelsche Rechte.* Stuttgart, 1962.

——. *Politische Philosophie in Deutschland.* Basel: Benno Schwab Verlag, 1963.

Lukács, György. *Der junge Hegel und die Probleme der kapitalistischen Gesellschaft.* Zürich, 1948.

——. *Die Zerstörung der Vernunft.* Berlin, 1954.

——. *Goethe und seine Zeit.* Berne, Francke Verlag, 1947

——. *Karl Marx und Friedrich Engels als Literaturhistoriker.* Berlin, Aufbau-Verlag, 1948.

——. *Schicksalswende: Beiträge zu einer neuen deutschen Ideologie.* Berlin, 1948.

Macpherson, C. B. *The Political Theory of Possessive Individualism: Hobbes to Locke.* London: Oxford University Press, 1962.

de Maistre, Joseph-Marie. "Considérations sur la France." *Oeuvres complètes.* Vol. 1. Lyons, 1884.

Mallet du Pan, Jacques. *Über die französische Revolution und die Ursachen ihrer Dauer.* Berlin, 1794.

Malthus, Thomas R. *An Essay on the Principle of Population*. 1798. 6th ed. Library of Economics and Liberty. London: John Murray, 2003.

Mandeville, Bernard. *An Essay on Charity and Charity-Schools*. New York: Frederick A. Praeger, 1960.

———. *The Fable of the Bees*. 1705, 1714. Ed. Frederick Benjamin Kaye. Oxford, 1924. Reprinted, Indianapolis, 1988.

Mandt, Hella. *Tyrannislehre und Widerstandsrecht: Studien zur deutschen politischen Theorie des 19. Jahrhunderts*. Darmstadt, 1974. Reprinted in *Materialien zu Kants Rechtsphilosophie*. Ed. Zwi Batscha. Frankfurt, 1976.

Mannheim, Karl. "Das Konservative Denken." 1927. *Wissenssoziologie: Auswahl aus dem Werk*. Ed. Kurt H. Wolff. Berlin and Neuwied, 1964.

Marat, Jean-Paul. *L'An 1 des droits de l'homme*. Ed. A. de Baecque, W. Schmale and M. Vovelle. Paris, 1988.

Marcuse, Herbert. "Der Kampf gegen den Liberalismus in der totalitären Staatsauffassung." *Zeitschrift für Sozialforschung* (1934): 165.

Marino, Luigi. "Hegel e le origini del diritto borghese." *Rivista di filosofia* 1 (1985): 167.

———. *I maestri della Germania: Göttingen 1770–1820*. Turin, 1975.

Martelloni, Anna. "Introduzione." In Edmund Burke, *Scritti politici*. Ed. Anna Martelloni. Turin, 1963.

Marwitz, Friedrich August Ludwig von der. "Von der Schrankenlosigkeit." 1836. In *Die Eigentumslosen*. Ed. Carl Jantke and Dietrich Hilger. Munich, 1963.

Marx, Karl. *Scritti politici giovanili*. Trans. Luigi Firpo. Turin, n. p., 1950.

Marx, Karl, and Friedrich Engels. *Werke*. Berlin, 1955. Cited as MEW.

Mehring, Franz. *Geschichte der deutschen Sozialdemokratie*. n. p., 1897–98.

Meinecke, Friedrich. *Die Entstehung des Historismus*. 1936. Munich, 1965.

———. "Germanischer und romanischer Geist im Wandel der deutschen Geschichtsauffassung." *Berichte der Preußischen Akademie der Wissenschaften* 6 (1916).

Merker, Nicolao. *Alle origini dell'ideologia tedesca*. Rome, 1977.

———. *Le origini della logica hegeliana (Hegel a Jena)*. Milan, 1961.

Merriam, Charles Edward. *A History of American Political Theories*. 1903. New York, 1969.

Mill, John Stuart. *Collected Works*. Ed. John Mercel Robson. Vol. 20. Toronto: University of Toronto Press, 1965.

———. "On Liberty." 1858. *Utilitarianism, Liberty, Representative Government*. Ed. H. B. Acton. London, 1972.

Mondolfo, Rodolfo. "Forza e violenza nella storia." 1921. *Umanismo di Marx: Studi filosofici 1908–1966*. Turin, 1968.

Montesquieu, Charles-Louis de Secondat, Baron de. "De la politique." 1725. *Oeuvres complètes*. Ed. Roger Caillois. Vol. 1. Paris, 1949–51.

———. *Oeuvres complètes*. Ed. André Masson. Vol. 3. Paris, 1950–55.

Mornet, Daniel. *Les origines intellectuelles de la révolution française, 1715–1787*. Paris, 1947.

Möser, Justus. *Patriotische Phantasien: Ausgewählte Schriften*. Ed. W. Zieger. Leipzig, 1986.

———. *Sämmtliche Werke*. Ed. Bernard Rudolph Abeken and Johanne Wilhelmina Juliane von Voigt. Vol. 3. Berlin, 1842.

Müller, Adam Heinrich. "Deutsche Wissenschaft und Literatur." 1806. In *Kritische, äs-thetische und philosophische Schriften*. Ed. Walter Schroeder and Werner Siebert. Vol. 1. Neuwied and Berlin, 1967.

——. "Die innere Staatshaushaltung; systematisch dargestellt auf theologischer Grund-lage." *Concordia*. Ed. Friedrich Schlegel. Vienna, 1820–23.

——. "Elemente der Staatskunst." 1809–10. *Deutsche Vergangenheit und deutscher Staat*. (Deutsche Literatur, Reihe Romantik). Ed. Paul Kluckhohn. Vol. X. Leipzig, 1935.

——. *Versuche einer neuen Theorie des Geldes mit besonderer Rücksicht auf Großbri-tannien*. Leipzig and Altenburg, 1816. Reprinted, Jena, 1922.

Nicolai, Christian Friedrich. *Neun Gespräche zwischen Christian Wolff und einem Kan-tianer über Kants metaphysische Anfangsgründe der Rechtslehre und Tugendlehre*. Berlin, 1798.

Nietzsche, Friedrich. *Briefwechsel: Kritische Gesamtausgabe*. Ed. Giorgio Colli and Mazzino Montinari. Vol. 2. Berlin and New York, 1975.

——. *Menschliches, Allzumenschliches* (1878–79). Ed. Mazzino Montinari. Berlin and New York: W. de Gruyter, 1969.

——. "Nachgelassene Fragmente 1887–1889." *Sämtliche Werke: Kritische Studienaus-gabe*. Ed. Giorgio Colli and Mazzino Montinari. Vol. 13. Munich, 1980.

Noack, Ludwig. "Hegel." In *Philosophie-geschichtliches Lexicon*. Leipzig, 1879.

Nozick, Robert. *Anarchy, State and Utopia*. London, 1974.

Novalis, Friedrich von Hardenberg. "Blüthenstaub." 1798. *Werke, Tagebücher und Briefe*. Ed. Hans-Joachim Mähl. Vol. 2. Munich-Vienna, 1978.

Omodeo, Adolfo. *Studi sull'età della Restaurazione*. 2nd ed. Turin, 1974.

Ottmann, Horst Henning. "Hegels Rechtsphilosophie und das Problem der Akkomoda-tion." *Zeitschrift für philosophische Forschung* 33 (1979): 242–243.

——. *Individuum und Gemeinschaft bei Hegel*. Vol. 1. Berlin, 1977.

Paine, Thomas. *Rights of Man*. Ed. George Jacob Holyoake. London, 1954.

Pareyson, Luigi, ed. *Schellingiana rariora*. Turin, 1977.

Pascal, Roy. *The German Sturm und Drang*. Manchester, 1953.

Popper, Karl Raimund. "Coscienza dell'occidente." *Criterio* 1 (1986): 77–79.

——. *The Open Society and its Enemies*. 1943. Vol. 1. London, 1973.

Postigliola, Alberto, ed. *Le leggi della politica*. Rome, 1979.

Poursin, Jean-Marie, and Gabriel Dupuy. *Malthus*. Rome, 1972.

Proudhon, Pierre-Joseph. *De la justice dans la révolution et dans l'église*. 1858. Vol. 1. Paris, 1985.

Quinet, Edgar. *Le Christianisme et la Révolution française*. 1845. Paris, 1984.

Rawls, John. *A Theory of Justice*. Cambridge: Harvard University Press, 1971.

Rehberg, August Wilhelm. *Untersuchungen über die französische Revolution*. Vol. 1. Hanover and Osnabrück, 1793.

Ritter, J. " 'Politik' und 'Ethik' in der praktischen Philosophie des Aristoteles." 1967. *Metaphysik und Politik*. Frankfurt, 1977.

Robespierre, Maximilien Marie Isidore de. *Textes choisis*. Ed. Jean Poperen. Vol. 3. Paris, 1958.

Rogalla von Biberstein, Johannes. *Die These von der Verschwörung 1776–1945*. Berne, 1976.

Romeo, Rosario, and Giuseppe Talamo, eds. *Documenti storici*. Vol. 3. Turin, 1974.

Rosenberg, Alfred. *Der Mythus des 20. Jahrhunderts*. 1930. Munich, 1937.

Rosenberg, Rainer. *Literaturverhältnisse im deutschen Vormärz*. Berlin, 1976.

Rosenkranz, Johanna Karl Friedrich. *Geschichte der Kantschen Philosophie*. Leipzig, 1840.

———. *Hegel als deutscher national Philosoph*. Leipzig, 1870.

———. *Hegels Leben*. Berlin, 1844. Reprinted, Darmstadt, 1963.

———. *Königsberger Skizzen*. Vol. 2. Danzig, 1842.

———. *Kritische Erläuterungen des Hegelschen Systems*. Königsberg, n. p., 1840. Reprinted, Hildesheim, 1963.

———. "Über Schelling und Hegel: Ein Sendschreiben an Pierre Leroux." 1843. *Neue Studien*. Vol. 4. Leipzig, 1875–78.

———. *Vita di Hegel*. Ed. Remo Bodei. Florence, 1966.

———. *Von Magdeburg bis Königsberg*. Leipzig, 1878.

Rotta, Salvatore. "Il pensiero francese da Bayle a Montesquieu." *Storia delle idee politiche, economiche e sociali*. Ed. Luigi Firpo. Vol. 4. Turin, 1975.

Rotteck, Carl von. "Census." In *Restauration und Frühliberalismus*. Ed. Hartwig Brandt. Darmstadt, 1979.

———. *Lehrbuch des Vernunftrechts und der Staatswissenschaften*. Vol. 1. Stuttgart, 1840. 2nd ed. reprinted, Aalen, 1964.

Rousseau, Jean-Jacques. *Correspondance complète*. Ed. Ralph Alexander Leigh. Vol. 30. Oxford, 1977.

———. *Oeuvres complètes*. Ed. Bernard Gagnebin and Marcel Raymond. Paris, 1964. Cited as OC.

———. *The Political Writings*. Ed. Charles Edwin Vaughan. Vol. 2. Oxford, 1962.

Ruge, Arnold. "Über das Verhältnis von Philosophie, Politik und Religion (Kants und Hegels Accomodation)." 1841. *Sämmtliche Werke*. Vol. 4. Mannheim, 1847–48.

Sainte-Beuve, Charles Augustin. *Causeries du lundi*. Vol. 15. Paris, n.d.

Saint-Just, Louis Antoine Léon de. *Oeuvres complètes*. Ed. Michèle Duval. Paris, 1984.

Saint-Simon, Claude Henri de Rouvroy de. "Catéchisme des industriels." 1823–25. *Oeuvres*. Ed. Enfantin. Vol. 8. Paris: E. Dentu, 1875.

Sandkühler, Hans Jörg. *Praxis und Geschichtsbewußtsein*. Frankfurt, 1973.

Savigny, Friedrich Karl von. *Vom Beruf unserer Zeit für Gesetzgebung und Rechtswissenschaft*. 1840. 2nd ed. Hildesheim, 1967.

Scheel, Wolfgang. *Das 'Berliner Politisches Wochenblatt' und die politische und soziale Revolution in Frankreich und England*. Göttingen, 1964.

Scheler, Max. "Die Ursachen des Deutschenhasses." 1916. *Gesammelte Werke*. Vol. 4. Ed. Manfred S. Frings. Berne and Munich, 1982.

Schelling, Friedrich Wilhelm Joseph. "Philosophische Briefe über Dogmatismus und Kriticismus." 1795. *Sämmtliche Werke*. Vol. 1. Stuttgart, 1856–61.

Schiller, Friedrich. *Voyage en Syrie et en Egypte pendant les années 1782–85*. Paris, 1787.

Schlegel, Friedrich. "Philosophie der Geschichte." 1828. *Kritische Friedrich-Schlegel-Ausgabe*. Ed. Ernst Behler. Vol. 1. Munich, n.d.

———. "Signatur des Zeitalters." *Concordia*. 1823. Ed. Ernst Behler. Darmstadt, 1967.

———. "Zur österreichischen Geschichte." 1807. *Schriften und Fragmente*. Ed. Ernst Behler. Stuttgart, 1956.

Schleiermacher, Friedrich Ernst Daniel. "Grundlinien einer Kritik der bisherigen Sittenlehre." 1803. *Werke: Auswahl in vier Bänden*. Ed. Otto Braun and Johannes Bauer. Leipzig: Aalen, 1967.

Bibliography 365

Schmitt, Carl. *Der Nomos der Erde im Völkerrecht des Jus Publicum Europaeum*. Cologne, 1950.

Schnädelbach, Herbert. "Was ist Neoaristotelismus?" In *Moralität und Sittlichkeit*. Ed. Wolfgang Kuhlmann, n. p., 1986, 38–63.

Schopenhauer, Arthur. *Der Briefwechsel Arthur Schopenhauers*. Ed. Carl Gebhardt. Vol. 1. Munich, 1929.

——. "Über die Universitäts-Philosophie (Parerga und Paralipomena, I)." 1851. *Sämtliche Werke*. Ed. Wolfgang Löhneysen. Vol. 4. Darmstadt, 1976–82.

Schrader, Wilhelm, ed. *Gesammelte Aufsätze*. Berlin, 1903.

Schumpeter, Joseph. "Zur Soziologie der Imperialismen." *Archiv für Sozialwissenschaft und Sozialpolitik* 46 (1918–1919): 287–88.

Schulz, Hans, ed. *Fichte in vertraulichen Briefen seiner Zeitgenossen*. Leipzig, 1923.

Sieyès, Emmanuel-Joseph. *Écrits politiques*. Ed. Roberto Zapperi. Paris, 1985.

Simmel, Georg. *Der Krieg und die geistigen Entscheidungen*. Munich and Leipzig, 1917.

Smith, Adam. *An Inquiry into the Nature and Causes of the Wealth of Nations*. 1776–1783. 3rd ed. Indianapolis, 1981. (Reprint of the Glasgow edition.)

——. "Early Draft of Part of The Wealth of Nations." *Adam Smith as Student and Professor*. Ed. William Robert Scott. Glasgow: Jackson, Sons, 1937.

——. *Lectures on Jurisprudence*. 1762–66. Ed. R. L. Meek, D. D. Raphael and P. G. Stein. Vol. 5. Oxford: Clarendon Press, 1978.

Sombart, Werner. *Händler und Helden: Patriotische Besinnungen*. Leipzig, 1915.

Spaventa, Bertrando. "Pensieri sull'insegnamento della filosofia." 1850. *Il primo hegelismo italiano*. Ed. Guido Oldrini. Florence, 1969.

Spaventa, Silvio. *Dal 1848 al 1861: Lettere, scritti, documenti*. Ed. Benedetto Croce. 2nd ed. Bari, 1923.

Spencer, Herbert. "The Proper Sphere of Government." 1842. *The Man versus the State*. Indianapolis, 1981.

Staël, A. L. G. Necker de. *Considérations sur la Révolution française*. Ed. J. Godechot. Paris, 1983.

Stahl, Friedrich Julius. *Die Philosophie des Rechts*. 5th ed. Vol. 2. No. 1. Hildesheim, 1963.

Staiger, Emil, ed. *Der Briefwechsel zwischen Schiller und Goethe*. Frankfurt, 1977.

Stein, Freiherr K. von. "Letter to H. von Gagern, 24 August 1821." *Ausgewählte Schriften*. Ed. Klaus Thiede. Jena, 1929.

Sternhell, Zeev. *La Droite révolutionnaire: Les origines français du fascisme 1885–1914*. Paris, 1978.

——. *Maurice Barrès et le nationalisme français*. 1972. Paris, 1985.

Stirner, Max. *Geschichte der Reaktion*. Vol. 1. Berlin, 1852. Reprinted, Aalen, 1967.

Stoll, Adolf, ed. *F. K. von Savigny: Ein Bild seines Lebens mit einer Sammlung seiner Briefe*. Vol. 2. Berlin, 1929.

Stone, Lawrence. "Literacy and Education in England, 1640–1900." *Past and Present* 42 (1969): 69–139.

Strauss, Leo. *Persecution and the Art of Writing*. Glencoe, 1952.

Taine, Hippolyte-Adolphe. *Les origines de la France contemporaine 1876–94*. Vol. 2. Paris, 1899.

Talmon, Jacob Leib. *The Origins of Totalitarian Democracy*. New York: Frederick A. Praeger, 1960.

Tawney, Richard Henry. *Religion and the Rise of Capitalism.* New York: Harcourt, Brace, 1929.

Tilliette, Xavier, ed. *Schelling im Spiegel seiner Zeitgenossen.* Turin, 1974–81.

Tocqueville, Alexis Charles Henri Maurice Clérel de. *Études Économiques, Politiques et Littéraires.* Paris, 1866.

——. "Mémoire sur le paupérisme." *Mémoires de la Société Royale Académique de Cherbourg.* Cherbourg, 1835.

——. *Oeuvres complètes.* Ed. Jacob Peter Mayer. Paris: Gallimard, 1952.

Trendelenburg, Friedrich Adolf. *Die logische Frage: Zwei Streitschriften.* Leipzig, 1843.

Uexküll, Gösta von. *Ferdinand Lassalle.* Hamburg, 1974.

Veca, Salvatore. *La società giusta.* Milan, 1982.

Verucci, Guido. "La Restaurazione." *Storia delle idee politiche, economiche e sociali.* Ed. Luigi Firpo. Vol. 4.2. Turin, 1975.

——, ed. *L'Avenir 1830–31.* Rome, 1967.

Voltaire, François-Marie Arouet. *Oeuvres complètes de Voltaire.* Vol. 7. Paris, 1879.

——. *Voltaire's Correspondence.* Ed. Théodore Besterman. Vol. 34. Geneva, 1952.

Vorländer, Karl. *I. Kant: Der Mann und das Werk.* 1924. 2nd ed. Vol. 2. Hamburg, 1977.

Zedong, Mao. "Discorso alla conferenza dei segretari dei comitati di partito delle province, municipalità e regioni autonome." 1957. *Rivoluzione e costruzione: Scritti e discorsi 1949–1957.* Turin, 1979.

INDEX

Burke, Edmund (*cont.*)
104, 107, 114, 117, 125–26, 134, 139–
40, 142, 193, 195, 234, 236, 238, 253,
270, 273, 275–76, 284, 289, 291, 297–
98, 299, 306, 313 n.45, 331 n.52, 342
n.29, 351 n.24; influence on European
liberalism, 300–302; influence on German conservatism, 292–96; *Reflections
on the Revolution in France*, 292, 298,
301, 303; *Remarks on the Policy of the
Allies with respect to France*, 301
Burke, Richard, 292
Burschenschaften, 16, 24, 50

Caesar, Gaius Julius, 110, 112–13
Carlyle, Thomas, 249–50, 254, 344 n.17
Carové, Friedrich Wilhelm, 16, 28, 312
n.34
Catiline, Lucius Sergius, 113
Cato, Marcus Porcius, 113
Cavour, Camillo Benso di, 258, 259
censorship, 4, 5, 7, 8, 9; adjustment to, 9–
15, 32, 39, 42, 46–50, 259–60, 284; and
double-dealing, 7–14; pragmatic compromise with, 10–11, 38; self-
censorship, 4, 7–8, 11, 13, 42; theoret-
ical compromise with 9–11
Cesa, Claudio, 4, 7–8, 15–16, 315 n.78
chambre introuvable, 40–41, 43–44
Charles I (king of England), 104–5, 112
Charles X, 24, 44
Charte, 40–41, 235, 293
Chateaubriand, François–René, 22–23,
43–45, 95, 323 n.57; *Le Conservateur*,
92
China, 248
Cicero, Marcus Tullius, 22, 113
Cinna, Lucius Cornelius, 110
citoyens and bourgeois, 182–83, 198, 220,
223–24
city vs. country, 149–50
"class war," 185, 233
Cleomenes III (king of Sparta), 112
Commodus, Lucius Aelius Aurelius (Ro-
man emperor), 240
Condorcet, Marie–Jean–Antoine–Nicolas

de Caritat de, 166, 185, 189–90, 193–94,
304
Constant, Benjamin, 59–60, 66, 74–75,
80, 85–86, 93–94, 103–5, 107, 112, 118–
21, 134, 136–44, 146, 180, 182–83, 185,
188, 190, 192, 199–202, 300–303, 324
n.20, 324 n.22; *Principles of Politics*,
143
constitutional monarchy, 16, 25, 40, 46,
48
contractualism, 53–70; conservative or reactionary meaning of, 53–58, 69–70,
193–95, 280–81, 294, 307–8; and defense of slavery, 63, 65, 272–73; and
doctrine of Natural Law, 59, 63
contradictions, 31, 35–36, 87–88, 115,
126, 172–75, 178–79, 184–85, 188–89,
203, 249, 260, 308
Corneille, Pierre, 182
Corradini, Enrico, 352 n.58
coup d'état, 45, 48, 201
Cousin, Victor, 24, 46, 95, 247
Cranston, Maurice, 332 n.79
Crispin, Saint, 173–75, 225
Cromwell, Oliver, 97, 104–5, 324 n.20

Dahlmann, Friedrich Christoph, 85–86
Dahrendorf, Ralf, 93, 272, 275, 279, 285,
299, 303
Della Volpe, Galvano, 329 n.4
Desmoulins, Camille, 182
despotism, positive connotation of, 101–
2, 309–10, 323 n.6
D'Hondt, Jacques, 13–14, 16–24, 49–50,
312 n.30
Diogenes, 150, 181
Dupuy, Gabriel, 326–7 n.75

education: private vs. public, 145–46,
204–13, 220; subject to control of the
clergy, 44
Elias, Norbert, 287
Engels, Friedrich, 3, 8, 25–28, 30–31, 36–
37, 91, 103, 117, 121, 125–26, 131, 249,
261, 263, 274, 287–88, 305, 308
England: and child–labor, 214; and com-

pulsory education, 217–18; as example of constitutional monarchy, 42; as example of owners' monopoly of political power, 79, 118–20, 139–40, 179; home of aristocratic privilege, 6, 91–92, 114–15, 116–17, 118–23, 288, 296, 327 n.76, 328 n.87; home of the cult of peculiarity, 293; home of customary right, 6, 118, 236–37, 280, 300–301; home of formal freedom, 90–92; and social question, 118–20, 122, 168, 273–74, 326–27 n.75; and taxation, 192; 327 n.76, 328 n.80

Enlightenment, 8, 18, 36, 60, 63, 73, 93, 101, 127–28, 239, 246, 291; French, 3–4, 122, 127, 194, 243, 296; German, 8

Epstein, Klaus, 18

equality: abstract, 103; of conditions, 37–38, 165, 188–89; and difference, 292; formal, 186–87; legal, 61, 165, 189, 307; against nature, 297; and safety of property, 122; and universality, 251, 290–91, 295–96

esotericism (and exotericism), 20–23, 31

ethicality, notion of, 29

Eudämonia, 236

Evola, Giulio (known as Julius), 278

Fascism, 15–16, 298–99

Ferdinand VII (king of Spain), 208

Feuerbach, Ludwig Andreas, 198

Fichte, Johann Gottlieb, 17–21, 85, 139, 140–41, 145–49, 156–57, 160, 166, 176, 213–14, 249–50, 277, 302–3, 305, 312 n.36, 313 n.50, 313 n.52, 314 n.66, 339 n.103; *Address to the German People*, 277; *Doctrine of Right*, 161; *Foundations of Natural Right*, 161; *Vorlesungen über die Freimaurerei*, 21–22

Filmer, Robert, 104

Fontenelle, Bernard le Bovier de, 246

Forster, Georg, 303–4

Frankfurt school, 263

freedom: ancient, 199; of barons, 115–16, 282; civil, 181; conflicts of, 73–76, 115, 309–10; English, 92, 114, 116, 119–20, 236–37, 292–93, 297, 304; vs. equality, 73, 90–94, 106, 122–23, 291–92, 303, 307, 328 n.86; formal vs. actual (substantive objective), 45, 48, 72–75, 90–92, 110–12, 116, 119–20, 122–23, 129–30, 162–63, 272, 307–9; and French liberty, 293, 295, 304; German, 293, 302, 304; German-Protestant, 29–30; historical English, 295; modern, 30, 65–66, 73, 123, 148–50, 153, 180–81, 187–88, 196–97, 212, 241–43, 285, 305; negative, 272–74, 306–7, 310; Polish, 91, 101, 116, 282; positive, 284, 306–7, 309–10; public, 308

Freemasonry, 16–22

Friedrich II the Great (king of Prussia), 3, 102, 167, 206

Friedrich Wilhelm III (king of Prussia), 19, 25, 41, 69, 91

Friedrich Wilhelm IV (king of Prussia), 6, 9, 49, 287, 293, 299

Fries, Jakob Friedrich, 17, 24, 28–29, 49–50

Furet, François, 306

Gadamer, Hans Georg, 31, 235, 316 n.97

Galiani, Ferdinando, 170

Gans, Eduard, 7, 13, 30, 170

Gemeinschaft and partnership, 294–95, 298, 351 n.29

Gentile, Giovanni, 15–16

Gentz, Friedrich von, 55, 74, 83, 107, 128, 194, 276, 292, 294, 297, 323 n.2, 351 n.29

"German misery," 31, 48, 141–42, 286–88, 331 n.63

Godwin, William, 270

Goethe, Johann Wolfgang, 17, 19, 22, 136, 221, 240, 313 n.51

Görres, Joseph, 102, 295

Gracchus family, 98, 109, 164

Gramsci, Antonio, 35

Green, Thomas Hill, 307–8

Gregory VII, 78

Grundkonzeption, 12

Guizot, François, 44–45, 137–38, 302, 306, 331 n.48
Gumplowicz, Ludwig, 297

Habermas, Jürgen, 234–35, 268, 271–72, 324 n.29
Habsburg dynasty, 98
Haller, Carl Ludwig von, 61–62, 83, 100, 102, 206–7, 216, 319 n.14; *Restauration der Wissenschaft*, 297
Hamann, Johann Georg, 4
Hamilton, Alexander, 276
Hansemann, David, 74–75, 199, 232–33, 244
Hayek, Friedrich August von, 30, 77, 82, 133, 267–71, 274, 279, 284–85, 292, 300, 306–8
Haym, Rudolf, 14, 24–31, 34, 50, 93–94, 127–30, 198–99, 259, 278, 289, 302, 338 n.85, 338 n.86; *Hegel and His Time*, 130; *Prussian Annals*, 105
Hegel, Georg Wilhelm Friedrich: actuality vs. appearance, 35–36, 252; actuality vs. existence, 33–34, 36; actual vs. ideal, 34, 36–37, 227, 260; and Catholicism, 127, 197–98, 206–10; and Christianity, 98, 182–83, 195–99, 237, 243; and civil society, 30, 62; and classic political economy, 117, 237; and communism, 224, 257–60, 279–80; "conservative," 53, 58, 71–95; critic of absolute monarchy, 39–48; critic of alienation, 136, 162–63; critic of a capital and private conception of the State, 55, 64, 102; critic of child labor, 69, 73–74, 214; critic of contractualism, 12, 46, 53–70, 193, 195, 280, 282; critic of customary right, 6, 235, 280; critic of despotism, 39–40, 102, 198, 209, 212; critic of elective monarchy, 48, 101, 282; critic of Luddism, 171; critic of morality, 37, 172–77, 212, 221–22, 225–45, 249–53, 260–63; critic of owners' monopoly of political representation, 141–43, 281; critic of reification, 65, 74–75, 162–63, 213; critic of the right to resistance, 83–

87; critic of slavery and serfdom, 57, 62–63, 65, 98–99, 115, 162–63, 169–70, 175–79, 235, 237, 342 n.37, 347 n.40; critic of Teutonic movement, 41–42, 47, 49, 50; critic of the venality of public offices, 55, 65, 101, 206; "despotic," 279; "different," 8, 13, 49; enemy of the Restoration, 15–16, 23–24, 27, 39–46, 50, 55, 96; and England, 5, 41, 79, 114, 119–23, 179, 187, 214, 236, 280–82, 327 n.76, 328 n.80; historical necessity, 36–38; individualist, 81–82, 123, 131–32, 148–50, 153, 175, 180, 186, 247–48, 202–3, 241–43, 285, 306; and Jacobinism, 63, 105, 185, 304–7, 309; "liberal," 27–29, 31, 40, 43–46, 50, 53; Mason, 16–20; master and servant, 134, 136–37, 169–70; "materialist," 257–58, 278; method vs. system, 15, 31, 125, 128, 133, 287–88, 329 n.4; and natural law, 56–61, 63–64, 70, 123, 235–36; on negative judgment and negatively infinite judgment, 5, 155, 161–66, 169, 179; "organicist," 64, 70, 80; "philosopher of the Restoration," 7, 12, 14, 17, 24–25, 27–29, 34, 39–48, 50, 105, 199, 282, 287–88, 319 n.47; "pragmatist," 278; and primacy of politics, 39–41, 42, 46–47, 128–31, 172–77, 198–99, 225–45, 260–61; and private property, 4, 76, 87–90, 141–45, 153–79, 185–87, 190–91, 193; on reason and actuality, 32–38, 58–59, 247–52, 257–63, 276–78, 282, 316 n.2; and the Reformation, 98, 206–7, 210, 340 n.8; and religion as representation and myth, 11, 127–28; on revolutions and reforms, 124–26; "secret," 8, 13, 16–23, 312 n.30; "socialist," 199, 232–33, 257–58, 308; and the social question, 70, 75–77, 131–32, 148–50, 157–60, 171–72, 178–79, 184, 189–93, 215, 260; "statist" and "State idolater," 29, 70–72, 77, 80, 279, 282–83, 285; supporter of American, English, Dutch, and Spanish Revolutions, 96–100, 104, 117, 208–9, 291, 317 n.21; supporter of

State (*cont.*)
81, 131–32, 171, 186; and recognition of freedom, 178–79; theory of the limitations of intervention by, 66–68, 73–74, 76–77, 81–83, 86–87, 93–94, 167, 191–92, 204–6, 233–34, 273, 307–8
statism, 70, 72, 74–75, 78, 80–81
Stein, Freiherr Karl Heinrich Friedrich vom, 142
Stein-Hardenberg, reforms of, 56, 91
Strauss, Leo, 312 n.20, 329 n.12
Stuart dynasty, 193
Sulla, Lucius Cornelius, 109–10

Taine, Hippolyte-Adolphe, 183, 184, 298
Talmon, Jakob Leib, 184, 274–75, 283, 285
Tarquin the Proud, 108–9, 112
taxes, imposition of, 80, 101, 189–93, 336 n.35, 337 n.56
Thaden, Nikolaus von, 49
Theognis, 223
Tocqueville, Alexis Charles Henri Maurice Clérel de, 72–73, 83, 87, 92–94, 105–6, 113, 116, 118, 120–22, 132–33, 137, 142, 147, 159, 167–68, 180, 185, 191, 233–34, 255–59, 269, 281, 291, 301, 306–7, 317 n.14, 322 n.48, 328 n.87, 330 n.31, 343 n.38, 345 n.50; *L'Ancien Régime et la Révolution*, 301; *Democracy in America*, 37–38, 67–68
Topitsch, Ernst, 30
totalitarianism, 30, 200, 263, 270, 273, 298, 310; and totalitarian democracy, 274, 283–85, 306–7, 310
Toussaint, François-Dominique (known as Toussaint-Louverture), 309
trade unions, 70, 81
Treaty of Utrecht, 273

Treitschke, Heinrich von, 302–3
Trendelenburg, Friedrich Adolf, 26

universal concept of man, 291, 298, 309
universality and revolution, 290–92, 295–96
utilitarianism, 200–201; and criticism of contractualism, 280–81; and criticism of doctrine of Natural Law, 60, 90

Varnhagen von Ense, Karl August, 19, 30, 318
Varro, Marcus Terentius, 134
Vaughan, Charles Edwin, 339 n.101
Vendée, 100
Vitry, Aubert de, 334 n.39
Volney, Constantin-François de Chasseboeuf de, 22–23
Voltaire, François-Marie Arouet de, 30, 65, 72–73, 83, 96, 182–83, 322 n.37; *Le Mondain*, 150

wage labor, 134, 136–37, 170, 200
Weber, Max, 280
Welcker, Carl, 199, 303–4
Western world, 82, 268–72, 274, 276–83, 285, 299, 308–10, 324 n.29
Wilberforce, Samuel, 218
Windischmann, Karl J. H., 17
Wirklichkeit, 32–35
"work–houses," 76, 168, 273–75

Young, Edward, 23
Young Germany, 30

Zhdanov, Andrey Aleksandrovich, 286, 288

Domenico Losurdo is a professor of philosophy at the
University of Urbino and the director of the Institute for
Philosophical and Pedagogical Sciences; he is president of
the International Hegel-Marx Society for Dialectical
Thought. His recent books include *Nietzsche, il ribelle
aristocratico: Biografia intellettuale e bilancio critico*
(2002), *Ipocondria dell'impolitico: La critica di Hegel ieri e
oggi* (2001), and *Fuga dalla storia? Il movimento comunista
tra autocritica e autofobia* (1999).

Library of Congress Cataloging-in-Publication Data
Losurdo, Domenico.
[Hegel e la liberta dei moderni. English]
Hegel and the freedom of moderns / Domenico Losurdo;
translated from the Italian by Marella and Jon Morris.
p. cm. — (Post-contemporary interventions)
Includes bibliographical references and index.
ISBN 0-8223-3253-1 (cloth : alk. paper)
ISBN 0-8223-3291-4 (pbk. : alk. paper)
1. Hegel, Georg Wilhelm Friedrich, 1770–1831. 2. Political
science—Germany—History—19th century. 3. Liberalism.
I. Title. II. Series.
JC233.H46L57813 2004   320'.01—dc22   2004001302

www.ingramcontent.com/pod-product-compliance
Lightning Source LLC
Chambersburg PA
CBHW050329270326
41926CB00016B/3381